Simulation with Arena

McGraw-Hill Series in Industrial Engineering and Management Science

Consulting Editors

Kenneth E. Case, *Department of Industrial Engineering and Management, Oklahoma State University*

Philip M. Wolfe, *Department of Industrial and Management Systems Engineering, Arizona State University*

Barnes: *Statistical Analysis for Engineers and Scientists: A Computer-Based Approach*
Bedworth, Henderson, and Wolfe: *Computer-Integrated Design and Manufacturing*
Black: *The Design of the Factory with a Future*
Blank: *Engineering Economy*
Blank: *Statistical Procedures for Engineering, Management, and Science*
Bridger: *Introduction to Ergonomics*
Denton: *Safety Management: Improving Performance*
Ebeling: *An Introduction to Reliability and Maintainability Engineering*
Grant and Leavenworth: *Statistical Quality Control*
Hicks: *Industrial Engineering and Management: A New Perspective*
Hillier and Lieberman: *Introduction to Mathematical Programming*
Hillier and Lieberman: *Introduction to Operations Research*
Huchingson: *New Horizons for Human Factors in Design*
Juran and Gryna: *Quality Planning and Analysis: From Product Development through Use*
Kelton, Sadowski, and Sadowski: *Simulation with Arena*
Khoshnevis: *Discrete Systems Simulation*
Kolarik: *Creating Quality: Concepts, Systems, Strategies, and Tools*
Law and Kelton: *Simulation Modeling and Analysis*
Marshall and Oliver: *Decision Making and Forecasting*
Moen, Nolan, and Provost: *Improving Quality through Planned Experimentation*
Nash and Sofer: *Linear and Nonlinear Programming*
Nelson: *Stochastic Modeling: Analysis and Simulation*
Niebel, Draper, and Wysk: *Modern Manufacturing Process Engineering*
Pegden, Shannon, and Sadowski: *Introduction to Simulation Using SIMAN*
Riggs, Bedworth, and Randhawa: *Engineering Economics*
Steiner: *Engineering Economic Principles*
Taguchi, Elsayed, and Hsiang: *Quality Engineering in Production Systems*
Wu and Coppins: *Linear Programming and Extensions*

Simulation with Arena

W. David Kelton
Professor
Department of Quantitative Analysis and Operations Management
University of Cincinnati

Randall P. Sadowski
Chief Applications Officer and Director of Educational Services
Systems Modeling Corporation

Deborah A. Sadowski
Senior Product Engineer
Systems Modeling Corporation

Boston, Massachusetts   Burr Ridge, Illinois   Dubuque, Iowa
Madison, Wisconsin   New York, New York   San Francisco, California   St. Louis, Missouri

WCB/McGraw-Hill

*A Division of The **McGraw·Hill** Companies*

SIMULATION WITH ARENA

Copyright © 1998 by The McGraw-Hill Companies, Inc. All rights reserved. Printed in the United States of America. Except as permitted under the United States Copyright Act of 1976, no part of this publication may be reproduced or distributed in any form or by any means, or stored in a data base or retrieval system, without the prior written permission of the publisher.

This book is printed on acid-free paper.

4 5 6 7 8 9 0 DOC/DOC 9 0 9

ISBN 0-07-027509-2

Vice president and editorial director: *Kevin T. Kane*
Editorial director: *Tom Casson*
Executive editor: *Eric Munson*
Developmental editor: *Kelly Lee*
Marketing manager: *John Wannemacher*
Typeface: *10/12 Times New Roman*
Printer: *R. R. Donnelley & Sons Company*

Library of Congress Cataloging-in-Publication Data

Kelton, W. David
    Simulation with arena/W. David Kelton, Randall P. Sadowski, Deborah A. Sadowski.
       p. cm.
    ISBN   0-07-027509-2
    Includes bibliographical references and index.
    1. Computer simulation.   2. Arena (Computer file).   I. Sadowski, Randall P.   II. Sadowski, Deborah A.
QA76.9.C65 K45   1998
003'.35369 dc—21   97-26265

http://www.mhhe.com

About the Authors

W. DAVID KELTON is a professor in the Department of Quantitative Analysis and Operations Management, College of Business Administration, University of Cincinnati. He received a B.A. in mathematics from the University of Wisconsin-Madison, an M.S. in mathematics from Ohio University, and M.S. and Ph.D. degrees in industrial engineering from Wisconsin. He was formerly on the faculty at the University of Minnesota, The University of Michigan, and Kent State University.

His research and publications are in the probabilistic and statistical aspects of simulation, applications of simulation, and stochastic models. He is co-author, with Averill M. Law, of *Simulation Modeling and Analysis*, in its second edition with McGraw-Hill.

He serves as simulation area editor for the *INFORMS Journal on Computing* and simulation department co-editor for *IIE Transactions*, and is associate editor of *Operations Research*, the *Journal of Manufacturing Systems*, and *Simulation*; he was also guest co-editor for a special simulation issue of *IIE Transactions*. In 1994 he received the IIE Operations Research Division Award. He is a past president of the TIMS College on Simulation, and is the INFORMS College on Simulation co-representative to the Winter Simulation Conference board of directors. In 1987 he was program chair for the Winter Simulation Conference, and in 1991 was general chair. He has worked on grants and consulting contracts from a number of corporations, foundations, and agencies. He likes to think of himself as a reasonably competent bicycle mechanic and a neat barn painter.

RANDALL P. SADOWSKI is currently director of university relations and chief applications officer at Systems Modeling Corporation. He was previously vice president of consulting services and user education.

Before joining Systems Modeling, he was on the faculty at Purdue University in the School of Industrial Engineering, and at the University of Massachusetts. He received his bachelor's and master's degrees in industrial engineering from Ohio University, and his Ph.D. in industrial engineering from Purdue.

He has authored over 50 technical articles and papers, served as chair of the Third International Conference on Production Research, and was the general chair of the 1990 Winter Simulation Conference. He is on the visiting committee for the IE departments at Lehigh University and the University of Pittsburgh. He is co-author, with C. Dennis Pegden and Robert E. Shannon, of *Introduction to Simulation Using SIMAN*, now in its second edition with McGraw-Hill.

He is a senior member of the Institute of Industrial Engineers and served as editor of a two-year series on Computer Integrated Manufacturing Systems for *IE Magazine* that received the 1987 IIE Outstanding Publication award. He has served in several positions at IIE, including president at the chapter and division levels, and vice president of Systems Integration at the international level. He founded and continues to organize the annual IIE/SM Student Simulation Contest. Some people claim they actually like the beef jerky he makes and he's envied for his three chain saws, but he is a sloppy barn painter.

DEBORAH A. SADOWSKI is a senior member of Systems Modeling's Arena product team. At present, she works on numerous special projects related to product creation and application, as well as customer training and support. Previously, she served as vice president of development for SM, ushering in the age of Arena, and as a product manager and developer. Since joining the company, she has delivered simulation consulting projects and has trained hundreds of budding simulationists. She also has written product manuals and online help, aided customers via the help desk (see Chapter 8), marketed and sold SM products, and performed quality assurance on product releases.

She received her bachelor's and master's degrees in industrial engineering and operations research from The Pennsylvania State University. She continues affiliation with her alma mater through service on its Engineering Industrial and Professional Advisory Council, whose industrial engineering team she recently chaired.

Professionally, Deb currently represents the IEEE Computer Society on the Winter Simulation Conference board of directors. She was the general chair of WSC 1994, as well as serving as business and exhibits chairs for previous conferences. In addition to INFORMS, IIE, SCS, ACM, and IEEE, Deb is a member of BPA (Barn Painters Anonymous), a support group for families and friends of barn painters neat and sloppy alike.

To those in the truly important arena of our lives:

Albert, Anna, Anne, Charity, Christie, Jenny, Molly, Noah, Sammy, Sean, Shelley, Tierney, and yet unnamed. And may we not forget Mr. Munchkin.

Preface

This book provides an introduction to simulation using Arena. It is intended to be used as an entry-level simulation text, most likely in a first course on simulation at the undergraduate or beginning graduate level. However, material from the later chapters could be incorporated into a second, graduate-level course. The book can also be used to learn simulation independent of a formal course (more specifically, by Arena users). The primary objective is to present the concepts and methodology of simulation using Arena as a vehicle. While we'll cover most of the capabilities of Arena, the book is not meant to be an exhaustive reference on the software, which is fully documented in its reference materials and extensive online help system.

We've chosen an organization and writing style for this book to aid the beginner in fully and easily understanding the concepts presented. Nearly all of the modeling and analysis ideas are presented in the context of examples. Ideally, readers would build simulation models as they read through each of these chapters. Rather than confining the simulation process and statistical-analysis issues to their own chapters, we've incorporated most of this material into the modeling chapters. This allows readers to absorb basic project-planning and analysis ideas along with the modeling concepts, which mirror how actual simulation projects ought to proceed. We've also devoted chapters to each of these topics individually so that we can cover the more advanced issues not treated in our modeling chapters. We believe that this approach greatly enhances the learning process by placing it in a more realistic and (frankly) less boring setting.

We assume that the reader has no prior knowledge of simulation, and no computer-programming experience is required. We assume basic familiarity with computing in general (files, folders, basic editing operations, etc.), but nothing advanced. Some basic understanding of probability and statistics is needed, though we provide a self-contained refresher on what's required from these subjects in Appendices C and D.

The book starts in Chapter 1 with a general introduction and brief history of simulation and modeling concepts. Chapter 2 addresses the simulation process using a simple hand simulation. Chapter 3 acquaints readers with Arena by examining a completed simulation model of the problem simulated by hand in Chapter 2. Chapter 4 introduces the Arena user interface and provides an overview of its modeling capabilities, which will allow readers to begin to build small simulation models effectively.

The next five chapters are devoted to modeling concepts and methodologies for simulation of complex systems. Chapter 5 starts this journey by introducing sufficient high-level modeling constructs to allow readers to begin modeling more realistic systems. Included is a discussion of input data analysis and the Arena Input Analyzer tool as part of the modeling process. Chapter 6 expands on the basic modeling constructs presented in Chapter 5, discusses model verification, and shows readers how to enhance animations. Additionally, it illustrates how to conduct basic statistical analysis on the output from terminating systems using the Arena Output Analyzer tool. At this point, readers should have learned the techniques to allow them to model systems in considerable detail using the high-level constructs provided by Arena. They should also have an understanding of the issues and approaches for verification and statistical analysis of simulation models.

Chapter 7 covers the concepts associated with limiting entity travel in the simulation model. Specifically, it presents material handling modeling constructs that allow effective modeling of most material handling systems, including transportation devices and conveyors. This chapter also covers the basic statistical issues for setting up and analyzing the output from steady-state systems. Chapter 8 introduces readers to a rich selection of lower-level modeling constructs that facilitate building very detailed and complex models. Chapter 9 continues this theme by digging even deeper into the extensive modeling constructs provided by Arena. It uses a series of small, focused models to present a wide variety of special-purpose modeling capabilities, including selected constructs from the underlying SIMAN simulation language. This chapter is intended primarily for the more advanced simulation user and would probably not be covered in a beginning simulation course.

Chapter 10 combines a number of topics under the aegis of customizing Arena and integrating it with other applications like spreadsheets and word processors. Included in this chapter is a high-level exploration of the capabilities of Visual Basic® for Applications (VBA) and the Arena Professional Edition, as well as how to craft custom reports for Arena models.

Chapter 11 is devoted to some of the more advanced statistical concepts underlying and often applied to simulation analysis, including random-number generators, variate and process generation, variance-reduction techniques, sequential sampling, the more specialized capabilities of the Arena Output Analyzer, and designing simulation experiments. Chapter 12 provides a broad overview of the simulation process and discusses more specifically the issues of managing a large simulation project. It also has a brief discussion of the Arena Viewer, which allows Arena models to be disseminated to systems not having the full Arena software installed.

The Appendices provide background and reference material. Appendix A describes a complete modeling specification for an actual project carried out for *The Washington Post* newspaper. In Appendix B, we give three problem statements for the Arena modeling contest held annually by the Institute of Industrial Engineers (IIE) and Systems Modeling. Appendix C gives a complete but concise review of the basics of probability and statistics couched in the framework of their role in simulation modeling and analysis. The probability distributions supported by Arena are detailed in Appendix D. Installation instructions for the Arena Academic software can be found in Appendix E.

All references are collected in a single References section at the end of the book. The index is extensive, to aid readers in locating topics and seeing how they relate to each other. The index includes authors cited.

The writing and organization have been done in what might be called "tutorial style." This style is built around a sequence of carefully crafted examples to present the concepts and applications rather than adopting the more traditional style of describing concepts first and then citing examples as an afterthought. For this reason, it probably makes sense to read (or teach) this material essentially in the order presented. A one-semester or one-quarter first course in simulation could cover all the material in Chapters 1–8, including the statistical issues. Time permitting, selected modeling and computing topics from Chapters 9 and 10 could be included, or some of the more advanced statistical issues from Chapter 11, or the project-management material from Chapter 12, according to the instructor's tastes. A second course in simulation could assume most of the material in Chapters 1–6, then cover the more advanced modeling ideas in Chapters 7–10, followed by topics from Chapters 11 and 12 as desired. For self study, we'd suggest at a minimum going through Chapters 1–5 to understand the basics of simulation and modeling with Arena, getting at least familiar with Chapters 6 and 7, then regarding the rest of the book as a source for more advanced topics and reference as needed. Regardless of what topics are covered, and whether the book is used in a formal course or independently, it will be helpful to follow along in Arena on a computer while reading this book.

To that end, the book includes a CD containing the Academic version of Arena (see Appendix E for installation instructions), which has all the modeling and analysis capabilities of the complete commercial version (the Arena Standard Edition) but limits the model size. All the examples presented in the book, as well as all the exercises at the ends of the chapters, will run with this educational version of Arena. The CD also contains files for all the example models in the book, as well as other support materials. This software can be installed on any university computer as well as on students' computers. It is intended for use in conjunction with this book for the purpose of learning simulation and Arena. It is not authorized for use in commercial environments.

Furthermore, a Web site is maintained at http://www.sm.com/arena.book with a variety of materials to support instructors, students, and readers. There is a set of Microsoft® PowerPoint® lecture files that are ideal for use in the classroom with computer-projection equipment to allow for quick changing back and forth to Arena itself so students can see exactly how to work with the software and how it behaves (including dynamic animations). These files may be downloaded by instructors and used exactly as they are, as a starting point for minor or major editing, as inspiration for an individual teaching style, or ignored. The site also has an electronic "Suggestion Box" where we welcome input and comments on the book. For instructors, we have a password-protected area in the site (contact the publisher for permission to access this area) with complete solutions to all the exercises (model files or text as appropriate), and an area where instructors can contribute additional exercises and solutions for other instructors to see and use; contributed exercises incorporated into future editions of the book will acknowledge the contributor unless otherwise requested. Downloading the material we provide is possible via a standard Web browser or by anonymous ftp (see instructions on the Web site itself). The site will be maintained and updated as warranted to support the book's users, so its structure may evolve, but it will always contain descriptions and instructions.

As with any labor like this, there are a lot of people and institutions that supported us in a lot of different ways. First and foremost, Lynn Barrett at Systems Modeling really made this all happen by reading (and re-reading and re-re-reading and fixing) our semi-literate drafts, orchestrating the composing and production, reminding us of what month it was, and tolerating our tardiness and fussiness and quirky personal-hyphenation habits. Systems Modeling Corporation provided resources in the form of time, software, hardware, technical assistance, and moral encouragement; we'd particularly like to thank Sherri Blaszkiewicz, Nancy Markovitch, Tom Gurgiolo, Steve Frank, Scott Miller, Wendy Krah, Teri King, Nicoletta Bleiel, and Dennis Pegden. The Department of Quantitative Analysis and Operations Management at the University of Cincinnati was also quite supportive.

We are also grateful to Gary Lucke and Olivier Girod of *The Washington Post* for allowing us to include a simulation specification that was developed for them by Systems Modeling as part of a larger project. Special thanks go to Pete Kauffman for his cover design and production assistance, and to Jim McClure for his cartoon and illustration design. And we appreciate the skillful motivation and gentle nudging by our editor at McGraw-Hill, Eric Munson. The reviewers, Mansooreh Mollaghasemi (University of Central Florida); Barry Nelson (Northwestern University); Edward Watson (Louisiana State University); and Preston White, Jr. (University of Virginia), provided extremely valuable input and help, ranging from overall organization and content all the way to the downright subatomic. Thanks are also due to the many individuals who have used part or all of the early material in classes (with particular thanks to the students who were subjected to these early drafts). These include Michael Branson (Oklahoma State University); Chun-Hung Chen (University of Pennsylvania); John J. Clifford (The Ohio State University); Tom Crowe (University of Missouri); Patrick Delaney (United States Military Academy); Darrell Donahue (University of Maine); David Goldsman (Georgia Tech); Byron Gottfried (University of Pittsburgh); Frank Grange (Colorado School of Mines); Arthur Hsu (Carnegie Mellon University); Keebom Kang (Naval Postgraduate School); Michael Kwinn, Jr. (United States Military Academy); Mansooreth Mollaghasemi (University of Central Florida); Barry Nelson (Northwestern University); Mike Proctor (University of Central Florida); Thomas Rohleder (University of Calgary); Marvin Seppanen (University of St. Thomas); Julie Ann Stuart (The Ohio State University); Michael Taaffe (University of Minnesota); Wayne Wakeland (Portland State University); Edward Watson (Louisiana State University); Preston White, Jr. (University of Virginia); and Irving Winters (Morgan State University).

In addition, we appreciate the help, suggestions, and encouragement of a host of other people, including Christos Alexopoulos, Ken Bauer, Diane Bischak, Eberhard Blümel, Colin Campbell, John Charnes, Chun-Hung Chen, Hong Chen, Russell Cheng, Christopher Chung, Frank Ciarallo, Mary Court, Halim Damerdji, Ken Ebeling, Gerald Evans, Steve Fisk, Michael Fu, David Goldsman, John Gum, Jorge Haddock, Joe Heim, Michael Howard, Eric Johnson, Elena Joshi, Elena Katok, Gary Kochenberger, Patrick

Koelling, David Kohler, Bradley Kramer, Averill Law, Larry Leemis, Marty Levy, Gerald Mackulak, Deborah Mederios, Brian Melloy, Ed Mooney, Jack Morris, Charles Mosier, Marvin Nakayama, Richard Nance, James Patell, Cecil Peterson, Dave Pratt, Madhu Rao, James Reeve, Steve Roberts, Paul Rogers, Ralph Rogers, Jerzy Rozenblit, Salim Salloum, G. Sathyanarayanan, Bruce Schmeiser, Carl Schultz, Thomas Schulze, David Sieger, Robert Signorile, Darryl Starks, Jim Swain, Michael Taaffe, Laurel Travis, Reha Tutuncu, Michael Weng, Jim Wilson, Chih-Hang (John) Wu, James Wynne, Susan Xu, and Stefanos Zenios.

And, of course, we have to thank all those around us, both big and small (and in some cases, each other) who for some reason put up with us.

W. DAVID KELTON
University of Cincinnati
david.kelton@uc.edu

RANDALL P. SADOWSKI
Systems Modeling Corporation
rps@mail.sm.com

DEBORAH A. SADOWSKI
Systems Modeling Corporation
deb@mail.sm.com

SYSTEMS MODELING

The Park Building
504 Beaver Street
Sewickley, PA 15143 U.S.A.
phone: 412-741-3727
fax: 412-741-5635
e-mail: smcorp@mail.sm.com
internet: www.sm.com

Contents

Chapter 9 A Sampler of Further Modeling Issues and Techniques

Chapter 10 Arena Customization and Integration

Chapter 11   Further Statistical Issues

Chapter 12   Conducting Simulation Studies

Appendix A   A Functional Specification for *The Washington Post*

Appendix E   Academic Software Installation Instructions

References

Index

What is Simulation?

CHAPTER 1

What is Simulation?

Simulation refers to a broad collection of methods and applications to mimic the behavior of real systems, usually on a computer with appropriate software. In fact, "simulation" can be an extremely general term since the idea applies across many fields, industries, and applications. These days, simulation is more popular and powerful than ever since computers and software are better than ever.

This book gives you a comprehensive treatment of simulation in general and the Arena simulation software in particular. We cover the general idea of simulation and its logic in Chapters 1 and 2 and Arena in Chapters 3–9. We don't, however, intend for this book to be a complete reference on everything in Arena (that's what the software manuals and online help systems are for). In Chapter 10, we show you how to integrate Arena with external files and other applications and give an overview of some advanced Arena capabilities. Chapters 11–12 cover issues related to planning and interpreting the results of simulation experiments, as well as managing a simulation project. Appendix A is a detailed account of a simulation project carried out for *The Washington Post* newspaper. In Appendix B, we give statements of fairly complex problems from recent student competitions on Arena modeling held by the Institute of Industrial Engineers and Systems Modeling. Appendix C provides a quick review of probability and statistics necessary for simulation, and Appendix D describes Arena's probability distributions, and Appendix E provides software installation instructions. After reading this book, you should be able to model systems with Arena and carry out effective and successful simulation studies.

This chapter touches on the general notion of simulation. In Section 1.1, we describe some general ideas about how you might study models of systems and give some examples of where simulation has been useful. Section 1.2 contains more specific information about simulation and its popularity, mentions some good things (and one bad thing) about simulation, and attempts to classify the many different kinds of simulations that people do. In Section 1.3, we talk a little bit about software options. Finally, Section 1.4 traces changes over time in how and when simulation is used. After reading this chapter, you should have an appreciation for where simulation fits in, the kinds of things it can do, and how Arena might be able to help you do them.

1.1 Modeling

Simulation, like most analysis methods, involves systems and models of them. So in this section, we give you some examples of models and describe options for studying them to learn about the corresponding system.

1.1.1 What's Being Modeled?

Computer simulation deals with models of systems. A *system* is a facility or process, either actual or planned, such as:

- A manufacturing plant with machines, people, transport devices, conveyor belts, and storage space.
- A bank or other personal-service operation, with different kinds of customers, servers, and facilities like teller windows, automated teller machines (ATMs), loan desks, and safety deposit boxes.
- A distribution network of plants, warehouses, and transportation links.
- An emergency facility in a hospital, including personnel, rooms, equipment, supplies, and patient transport.
- A field service operation for appliances or office equipment, with potential customers scattered across a geographic area, service technicians with different qualifications, trucks with different parts and tools, and a central depot and dispatch center.
- A computer network with servers, clients, disk drives, tape drives, printers, networking capabilities, and operators.
- A freeway system of road segments, interchanges, controls, and traffic.
- A central insurance claims office where a lot of paperwork is received, reviewed, copied, filed, and mailed by people and machines.
- A criminal justice system of courts, judges, support staff, probation officers, parole agents, defendants, plaintiffs, convicted offenders, and schedules.
- A chemical products plant with storage tanks, pipelines, reactor vessels, and railway tanker cars in which to ship the finished product.
- A fast-food restaurant with workers of different types, customers, equipment, and supplies.
- A supermarket with inventory control, checkout, and customer service.
- A theme park with rides, stores, restaurants, workers, guests, and parking lots.
- The response of emergency personnel to the occurrence of a catastrophic event.

People often study a system to measure its performance, improve its operation, or design it if it doesn't exist. Managers or controllers of a system might also like to have a readily available aid for day-to-day operations, like help in deciding what to do in a factory if an important machine goes down.

We're even aware of managers who requested that simulations be constructed but didn't really care about the final results. Their primary goal was to focus attention on understanding how their system currently worked. Often simulation analysts find that the process of defining how the system works, which must be done before you can start developing the simulation model, provides great insight into what changes need to be made. Part of this is due to the fact that rarely is there one individual responsible for understanding how an entire system works. There are experts in machine design, material handling, processes, etc., but not in the day-to-day operation of the system. So as you read on, be aware that simulation is much more than just building a model and conducting a statistical experiment. There is much to be learned at each step of a simulation project, and the decisions you make along the way can greatly affect the significance of your findings.

1.1.2 How About Just Playing with the System?

It might be possible to experiment with the actual physical system. For instance:

- Some cities have installed entrance-ramp traffic lights on their freeway systems to experiment with different sequencing to find settings that make rush hour as smooth and safe as possible.
- A supermarket manager might try different policies for inventory control and checkout personnel assignment to see what combinations seem to be most profitable and provide the best service.
- A computer facility can experiment with different network layouts and job priorities to see how they affect machine utilization and turnaround.

This approach certainly has its advantages. If you can directly experiment with the system and know that nothing else about it will change significantly, then you're unquestionably looking at the right thing and needn't worry about whether a model or proxy for the system faithfully mimics it for your purposes.

1.1.3 Sometimes You Can't (or Shouldn't) Play with the System

In many cases, it's just too difficult, costly, or downright impossible to do physical studies on the system itself.

- Obviously, you can't experiment with alternative layouts of a factory if it's not yet built.
- Even in an existing factory, it might be very costly to change to an experimental layout that might not work out anyway.
- It would be hard to run twice as many customers through a bank to see what will happen when a nearby branch closes.
- Trying a new check-in procedure at an airport might initially cause a lot of people to miss their flights if there are unforeseen problems with the new procedure.
- Fiddling around with emergency room staffing in a hospital clearly won't do.

In these situations, you might build a *model* to serve as a stand-in for studying the system and ask pertinent questions about what *would* happen in the system *if* you did this or that, or *if* some situation beyond your control were to develop. *Nobody gets hurt, and your freedom to try wide-ranging ideas with the model could uncover attractive alternatives that you might not have been able to try with the real system.*

However, you have to build models carefully and with enough detail so that what you learn about the model will never[1] be different from what you would have learned about the system by playing with it directly. This is called model *validity*, and we'll have more to say about it later, in Chapter 12.

1.1.4 Physical Models

There are lots of different kinds of models. Maybe the first thing the word evokes is a physical replica or scale model of the system, sometimes called an *iconic* model. For instance:

[1] Well, hardly ever.

▪ People have built *tabletop* models of material handling systems that are miniature versions of the facility, not unlike electric train sets, to consider the effect on performance of alternative layouts, vehicle routes, and transport equipment.

▪ A full-scale version of a fast-food restaurant placed inside a warehouse to experiment with different service procedures was described by Swart and Donno (1981). In fact, most large fast-food chains now have full-scale restaurants in their corporate office buildings for experimentation with new products and services.

▪ Simulated control rooms have been developed to train operators for nuclear power plants.

▪ Physical flight simulators are widely used to train pilots. There are also flight-simulation computer programs, with which you may be familiar in game form, that represent purely logical models executing inside a computer. Further, physical flight simulators might have computer screens to simulate airport approaches, so they have elements of both physical and computer-simulation models.

Although iconic models have proven useful in many areas, we won't consider them.

1.1.5   Logical (or Mathematical) Models

Instead, we'll consider *logical* (or *mathematical*) models of systems. Such a model is just a set of approximations and assumptions, both structural and quantitative, about the way the system does or will work.

A logical model is usually represented in a computer program that's exercised to address questions about the model's behavior; if your model is a valid representation of your system, you hope to learn about the system's behavior too. And since you're dealing with a mere computer program rather than the actual system, it's usually easy, cheap, and fast to get answers to a lot of questions about the model and system by simply manipulating the program's inputs and form. Thus, you can make your mistakes on the computer where they don't count, rather than for real where they do. As in many other fields, recent dramatic increases in computing power (and decreases in computing costs) have impressively advanced your ability to carry out computer analyses of logical models.

1.1.6   What Do You Do with a Logical Model?

After making the approximations and stating the assumptions for a valid logical model of the target system, you need to find a way to deal with the model and analyze its behavior.

If the model is simple enough, you might be able to use traditional mathematical tools like queueing theory, differential-equation methods, or something like linear programming to get the answers you need. This is a nice situation since you might get fairly simple formulas to answer your questions, which can easily be evaluated numerically; working with the formula (for instance, taking partial derivatives of it with respect to controllable input parameters) might provide insight itself. Even if you don't get a simple closed-form formula, but rather an algorithm to generate numerical answers, you'll still have exact answers (up to roundoff, anyway) rather than estimates that are subject to uncertainty.

However, most systems that people model and study are pretty complicated, so that *valid* models[2] of them are pretty complicated too. For such models, there may not be exact mathematical solutions worked out, which is where simulation comes in.

1.2 Computer Simulation

Computer simulation refers to methods for studying a wide variety of models of real-world systems by numerical evaluation using software designed to imitate the system's operations or characteristics, often over time. From a practical viewpoint, simulation is the process of designing and creating a computerized model of a real or proposed system for the purpose of conducting numerical experiments to give us a better understanding of the behavior of that system for a given set of conditions. Although it can be used to study simple systems, the real power of this technique is fully realized when we use it to study complex systems.

While simulation may not be the only tool you could use to study the model, it's frequently the method of choice. The reason for this is that the simulation model can be allowed to become quite complex, if needed to represent the system faithfully, and you can still do a simulation analysis. Other methods may require stronger simplifying assumptions about the system to enable an analysis, which might bring the validity of the model into question.

1.2.1 Popularity and Advantages

Over the last two decades or so, simulation has been consistently reported as the most popular operations research tool:

- Rasmussen and George (1978) asked M.S. graduates from the Operations Research Department at Case Western Reserve University (of which there are many since that department has been around a long time) about the value of methods after graduation. The first four methods were *statistical analysis*, *forecasting*, *systems analysis*, and *information systems*, all of which are very broad and general categories. Simulation was next, and ranked higher than other more traditional operations research tools like linear programming and queueing theory.

- Thomas and DaCosta (1979) gave analysts in 137 large firms a list of tools and asked them to check off which ones they used. Statistical analysis came in first, with 93% of the firms reporting that they use it (it's hard to imagine a large firm that wouldn't), followed by simulation (84%). Again, simulation came in higher than tools like linear programming, PERT/CPM, inventory theory, and nonlinear programming.

- Shannon, Long, and Buckles (1980) surveyed members of the Operations Research Division of the American Institute of Industrial Engineers (now the Institute of Industrial Engineers) and found that among the tools listed, simulation ranked first in utility and interest. Simulation was second in familiarity, behind linear programming, which might suggest that simulation should be given a stronger emphasis in academic curricula.[3]

---

[2] You can always build a simple (maybe simplistic) model of a complicated system, but there's a good chance that it won't be valid. If you go ahead and analyze such a model, you may be getting nice, clean, simple answers to the wrong questions.

[3] It would be interesting to see the results of another such survey in the 1990s.

▪ Forgionne (1983); Harpell, Lane, and Mansour (1989); and Lane, Mansour, and Harpell (1993) all report that, in terms of utilization of methods by practitioners in large corporations, statistical analysis was first and simulation was second. Again, though, academic curricula seem to be behind since linear programming was more frequently *taught*, as opposed to being *used* by practitioners, than was simulation.

▪ Morgan (1989) reviewed many surveys of the above type, and reported that "heavy" use of simulation was consistently found. Even in an industry with the lowest reported use of operations research tools (motor carriers), simulation ranked first in usage.

The main reason for simulation's popularity is its ability to deal with very complicated models of correspondingly complicated systems. This makes it a versatile and powerful tool. Another reason for simulation's increasing popularity is the obvious improvement in performance/price ratios of computer hardware, making it ever more cost effective to do what was prohibitively expensive computing just a few years ago. Finally, advances in simulation software power, flexibility, and ease of use have moved the approach from the realm of tedious and error-prone low-level programming to the arena of quick and valid decision making.

Our guess is that simulation's popularity and effectiveness are now even greater than reported in the surveys described above, precisely due to these advances in computer hardware and software.

1.2.2   The Bad News

However, simulation isn't *quite* paradise, either.

Because many real systems are affected by uncontrollable and random inputs, many simulation models involve random, or *stochastic*, input components, causing their output to be random too. For example, a model of a distribution center would have arrivals, departures, and lot sizes arising randomly according to particular probability distributions, which will propagate through the model's logic to cause output performance measures like throughput and cycle times to be random as well. So running a stochastic simulation once is like performing a random physical experiment once, or watching the distribution center for one day—you'll probably see something different next time, even if you don't change anything yourself. In many simulations, as the time frame becomes longer (like months instead of a day), most results averaged over the run will tend to settle down and become less variable, but it can be hard to determine how long is "long enough" for this to happen. Moreover, the model or study might dictate that the simulation stop at a particular point (for instance, a bank is open from 9 to 5), so running it longer to calm the output is inappropriate.

Thus, you have to think carefully about designing and analyzing simulation experiments to take account of this uncertainty in the results, especially if the appropriate time frame for your model is relatively short. We'll return to this idea repeatedly in the book and illustrate proper statistical design and analysis tools, some of which are built into Arena, but others you have to worry about yourself.

Even though simulation output may be uncertain, we can deal with, quantify, and reduce this uncertainty. You might be able to get rid of the uncertainty completely by making a lot of over-simplifying assumptions about the system; this would get you a nice, simple model that will produce nice, non-random results. Unfortunately, though, such an over-simplified model will probably not be a *valid* representation of the system, and the error due to such model invalidity is impossible to measure or reduce. For our money, we'd prefer an approximate answer to the right problem rather than an exact answer to the wrong problem.

1.2.3 Different Kinds of Simulations

There are a lot of ways to classify simulation models, but one useful way is along these three dimensions:

- **Static vs. Dynamic:** Time doesn't play a natural role in static models but does in dynamic models. The Buffon Needle Problem, described at the beginning of Section 1.3.1, is a static simulation. The small manufacturing model described in Chapters 2 and 3 is a dynamic model. Most operational models are dynamic; Arena was designed with them in mind, so our primary focus will be on such models.

- **Continuous vs. Discrete:** In a continuous model, the state of the system can change continuously over time; an example would be the level of a reservoir as water flows in and is let out, and as precipitation and evaporation occur. In a discrete model, though, change can occur only at separated points in time, such as a manufacturing system with parts arriving and leaving at specific times, machines going down and coming back up at specific times, and breaks for workers. You can have elements of both continuous and discrete change in the same model, which are called *mixed continuous-discrete models*; an example might be a refinery with continuously changing pressure inside vessels and discretely occurring shutdowns. Arena can handle continuous, discrete, and mixed models, but our focus will be on the discrete.

- **Deterministic vs. Stochastic:** Models that have no random input are deterministic; a strict appointment-book operation with fixed service times would be an example. Stochastic models, on the other hand, operate with random input—like a bank with randomly arriving customers requiring varying service times. A model can have both deterministic and random inputs in different components; which elements are modeled as deterministic and which as random are issues of modeling realism. Arena easily handles deterministic and stochastic inputs to models and provides many different probability distributions that you can use to represent the random inputs. Since we feel that at least some element of uncertainty is usually present in reality, most of our illustrations will involve random inputs somewhere in the model. As noted earlier, though, stochastic models produce uncertain output, which is a fact you must consider carefully in designing and interpreting the runs in your project.

1.3 How Simulations Get Done

If you've determined that a simulation of some sort is appropriate, you next have to decide how to carry it out. In this section, we'll discuss options for running a simulation, including software.

1.3.1 By Hand

In the beginning, people really *did* do simulations by hand (we'll show you just one, which is painful enough, in Chapter 2).

For instance, around 1733 a fellow by the name of George Louis Leclerc (who later was invited into the nobility, due no doubt to his simulation prowess, as Le Compte de Buffon) described an experiment to estimate the value of π. If you toss a needle of length l onto a table painted with parallel lines spaced d apart (d must be $\geq l$), it turns out that the needle will cross a line with probability $p = 2l/(\pi d)$. So Figure 1-1 shows a simulation experiment to estimate the value of π. (Don't try this at home, or at least not with a big needle.)

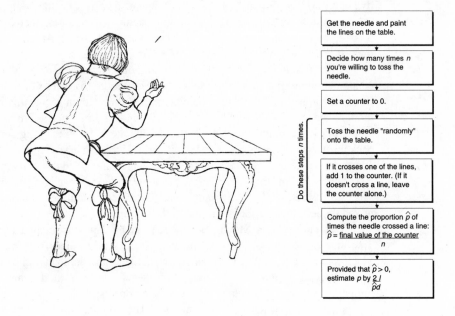

Figure 1-1. The Buffon Needle Problem

Though this experiment may seem pretty simple (probably even silly) to you, there are some aspects of it that are common to most simulations:

- The purpose is to estimate something (in this case, π) whose value would be hard to compute exactly (OK, maybe in 1733 that was true).

- The estimate we get at the end is not going to be exactly right; i.e., it has some error associated with it, and it might be nice to get an idea of how large that error is likely to be.

- It seems intuitive that the more tosses we make (i.e., the bigger n is), the smaller the error is likely to be and thus the better the estimate is likely to be.

- In fact, you could do a *sequential* experiment and just keep tossing until the probable error is small enough for you to live with instead of deciding on the number n of tosses beforehand.

We'll come back to these kinds of issues as we talk about more interesting and helpful simulations. (For more on the Buffon Needle Problem, as well as other such interesting historical curiosities, see Morgan, 1984.)

In the 1920s and 1930s, statisticians began using random-number machines and tables in numerical experiments to help them develop and understand statistical theory. For instance, Walter A. Shewhart (the quality control pioneer) did numerical experiments by drawing numbered chips from a bowl to study the first control charts. Guinness Brewery employee W. S. Gossett did similar numerical sampling experiments to help him gain insight into what was going on in mathematical statistics. (To protect his job at Guinness, he published his research under the pseudonym "Student" and later developed the t distribution used widely in statistical inference.) Engineers, physicists, and mathematicians have used various kinds of hand-simulation ideas for many years on a wide variety of problems.

1.3.2 Programming in General-Purpose Languages
As digital computers appeared in the 1950s and 1960s, people began writing computer programs in general-purpose procedural languages like FORTRAN to do simulations of more complicated systems. Support packages were written to help out with routine chores like list processing, keeping track of simulated events, and statistical bookkeeping.

This approach was highly customizable and flexible (in terms of the kinds of models and manipulations possible), but also painfully tedious and error-prone since models had to be coded pretty much from scratch every time. (Plus, if you dropped your cards, it could take quite a while to reconstruct your "model.") For a more detailed history of discrete-event simulation languages, see Nance (1996).

1.3.3 Simulation Languages
Special-purpose *simulation languages* like GPSS, SIMSCRIPT, SLAM, and SIMAN appeared on the scene some time later and provided a much better framework for the kinds of simulations many people do. Simulation languages have become very popular and are in wide use.

Nonetheless, you still have to invest quite a bit of time to learn about their features and how to use them effectively. And, depending on the user interface provided, there can be picky, apparently arbitrary, and certainly frustrating syntactical idiosyncrasies that bedevil even old hands.

1.3.4 High-Level Simulators
Thus, several high-level "simulator" products emerged that are indeed very easy to use. They typically operate by intuitive mouse-driven graphical user interfaces, menus, and dialogs. You select from available simulation-modeling constructs, connect them, and run the model along with a dynamic graphical animation of system components as they move around and change.

However, the domains of many simulators are also rather restricted (like manufacturing or communications) and are generally not as flexible as you might like to build valid models of your systems. Some people feel that these packages may have gone too far up the software-hierarchy food chain and have traded away too much flexibility to achieve the ease-of-use goal.

1.3.5   Where Arena Fits In

Arena combines the ease of use found in high-level simulators with the flexibility of simulation languages, and even all the way down to general-purpose procedural languages like the Microsoft® Visual Basic® programming system, FORTRAN, or C if you really want. It does this by providing alternative and interchangeable *templates* of graphical simulation modeling-and-analysis *modules* that you can combine to build a fairly wide variety of simulation models. For ease of display and organization, modules are typically grouped into *panels* to compose a template. By switching templates, you gain access to a whole different set of simulation modeling constructs and capabilities. In many cases, modules from different panels and templates can be mixed together in the same model.

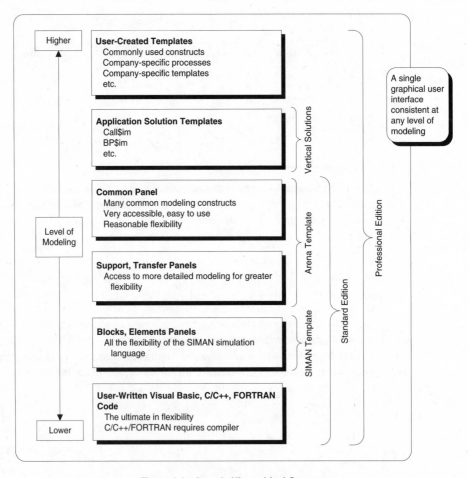

Figure 1-2. Arena's Hierarchical Structure

Arena maintains its modeling flexibility by being fully *hierarchical*, as depicted in Figure 1-2. At any time, you can pull in modules from the SIMAN template and gain access to simulation-language flexibility if you need to and mix in SIMAN constructs together with the higher-level modules from another template. For specialized needs, like complex decision algorithms or accessing data from an external application, you can write pieces of your model in a procedural language like Visual Basic, FORTRAN, or C/C++. All of this, regardless of how high or low you want to go in the hierarchy, takes place in the same consistent graphical user interface.

In fact, the modules in Arena templates are composed of SIMAN components and, using the Professional Edition of Arena, you can create your own modules and collect them into your own templates for various classes of systems. For instance, Systems Modeling has built templates for general modeling (the Arena template, which is the primary focus of this book), business-process re-engineering, call centers, and other industries. Other people have built templates for their company in industries as diverse as mining, auto manufacturing, fast-food, and forest-resource management. In this way, you don't have to compromise between modeling flexibility and ease of use. While this textbook focuses on modeling with the Arena template, you can get a taste of what the Professional Edition offers in Chapter 10.

Further, Arena includes dynamic animation in the same work environment. It also provides integrated support, including graphics, for some of the statistical design and analysis issues that are part and parcel of a good simulation study.

1.4 When Simulations Are Used

Just as the capabilities and sophistication of simulation languages and packages have increased dramatically over the last 40 years, the concept of how and when to use simulation has changed.

1.4.1 The Early Years

In the late 1950s and 1960s, simulation was a very expensive and specialized tool that was generally used only by large corporations that required large capital investments. Typical simulation users were found in steel and aerospace corporations. These organizations would form groups of six to 12 people, mostly Ph.D.s, who would develop large, complex simulation models using available languages, such as FORTRAN. These models would then be run on large mainframes charging from $600 to $1,000 per hour. Interestingly, the PCs that reside on most engineers' desks today are probably much more powerful and certainly much faster than the mainframes of the 1960s.

1.4.2 The Formative Years

The use of simulation as we know it today began during the 1970s and early 1980s. Computers were becoming faster and cheaper, and the value of simulation was being discovered by other industries, although most of the companies were still quite large. However, simulation was seldom considered until there was a disaster. It became the tool of choice for many companies, most notably the automotive and heavy industries, for determining why the disaster occurred and, sometimes, where to point the finger of blame.

We recall the startup of an automotive assembly line, an investment of over $100 million, that was not achieving its full, or even partial, potential. The line was producing a newly released vehicle that was in great demand—far greater than could be satisfied by the existing output of the line. Management appointed a S.W.A.T. team to analyze the problem, and that team quickly estimated the lost potential profit to be in excess of $500,000 per day. The team was told, "Find the problem and fix it." In about three weeks, a simulation was developed and used to identify the problem, which turned out not to have been on the initial suspect list. The line was ultimately modified and did produce according to specifications; unfortunately, by that time the competition was producing similar vehicles, and the additional output was no longer needed. Ironically, a simulation model had been used during the design of the assembly line to determine its feasibility. Unfortunately, many of the processes were new, and engineering had relied on equipment vendors to provide estimates of failures and throughputs. As is often the case, the vendors were extremely optimistic in their estimates. If the original design team had used the simulation to perform a good sensitivity analysis on these questionable data, the problem might have been uncovered and resolved well before implementation.

During this time, simulation also found a home in academia as a standard part of industrial engineering and operations research curricula. Its growing use in industry compelled universities to teach it more widely. At the same time, simulation began to reach into quantitative business programs, broadening the number and type of students and researchers exposed to its potential.

1.4.3 The Recent Past

During the late 1980s, simulation began to establish its real roots in business. A large part of this was due to the introduction of the personal computer and animation. Although simulation was still being used to analyze failed systems, many people were requesting simulations before production was to begin. (However, in most cases, it was really too late to affect the system design, but it did offer the plant manager and system designer the opportunity to spruce up their resumes.) By the end of the 1980s, the value of simulation was being recognized by many larger firms, several of which actually made simulation a requirement before approval of any major capital investment. However, simulation was still not in widespread use and was rarely used by smaller firms.

1.4.4 The Present

Simulation really began to mature during the early 1990s. Many smaller firms embraced the tool, and it began to see use at the very early stages of projects—where it could have the greatest impact. Better animation, ease of use, faster computers, easy integration with other packages, and the emergence of simulators have all helped simulation become a standard tool in many companies. Although most managers will readily admit that simulation can add value to their enterprise, it has yet to become a standard tool that resides on everyone's computers. The manner in which simulation is used is also changing; it is being employed earlier in the design phase and is often being updated as changes are made to operating systems. This provides a living simulation model that can be used for systems analysis on very short notice. Simulation has also invaded the service industry where it is being applied in many non-traditional areas.

The major impediments preventing simulation from becoming a universally accepted and well-utilized tool are model-development time and the modeling skills required for the development of a successful simulation. Those are probably the reasons why you're reading this book!

1.4.5 The Future

The rate of change in simulation has accelerated in recent years, and there is every reason to believe that it will continue its rapid growth and cross the bridges to mainstream acceptance. Simulation software has taken advantage of new operating systems to provide greater ease of use, particularly for the first-time user. This trend must continue if simulation is to become a state-of-the-art tool resident on every systems-analysis computer. These new operating systems have also allowed for greater integration of simulation with other packages (like spreadsheets, databases, and word processors). It is now becoming possible to foresee the complete integration of simulation with other software packages that collect, store, and analyze system data at the front end along with software that helps control the system at the back end.

In order to make simulation easier to use by more people, we will see more vertical products aimed at very narrow markets. This will allow analysts to construct simulations easily, using modeling constructs designed for their industry or company using terminology that directly relates to their environment. These may be very specialized tools designed for very specific environments, but they should still have the capability to model any system activities that are unique to each simulation project. The first generation of these types of products are on the market today in application areas such as communications, semiconductors, call centers, and business-process re-engineering.

Today's simulation projects concentrate on the design or redesign of complex systems. They often must deal with complex system-control issues, which can lead to the development of new system-control logic that is tested using the developed simulation. The next logical step is to use that same simulation to control the real system (Wysk, Smith, Sturrock, Ramaswamy, Smith, and Joshi, 1994). This approach requires that the simulation model be kept current, but it also allows for the easy testing of new system controls as the system or products change over time. As we progress to this next logical step, simulations will no longer be disposable or used only once, but will become a critical part of the operation of the ongoing system.

With the rapid advances being made in computers and software, it is very difficult to predict much about the simulations of the distant future, but one can easily imagine features such as automatic statistical analysis, software that recommends system changes, simulations totally integrated with system operating software, and yes, even virtual reality.

Fundamental Simulation Concepts

CHAPTER 2

Fundamental Simulation Concepts

In this chapter, we introduce some of the underlying ideas, methods, and issues in simulation before getting into the Arena software itself in Chapter 3 and beyond. These concepts are the same across any kind of simulation software, and some familiarity with them is essential to understanding how Arena simulates a model you've built.

We do this mostly by carrying through a simple example, which is described in Section 2.1. In Section 2.2, we explore some options for dealing with the example model. Section 2.3 describes the various pieces of a simulation model, and Section 2.4 carries out the simulation (by hand), describing the fundamental organization and action. After that, two different simulation-modeling approaches are contrasted in Section 2.5, and the issue of randomness in both input and output is introduced in Section 2.6. Finally, Section 2.7 steps back and looks at what's involved in a simulation project, although this is taken up more thoroughly as part of Chapter 12.

By the end of this chapter, you'll understand the fundamental logic, structure, components, and management of a simulation modeling project. All of this underlies Arena and the richer models you'll build with it after reading subsequent chapters.

2.1 An Example

In this section, we describe the example system and decide what we'd like to know about its behavior and performance.

2.1.1 The System

Since a lot of simulation models involve waiting lines or *queues* as building blocks, we'll start with a very simple case of such a model representing a portion of a manufacturing facility. "Blank" parts arrive, are processed by a single machine, and then leave; see Figure 2-1. If a part arrives and finds the machine idle, its processing by the machine starts right away; otherwise, it waits in a first-in, first-out (FIFO) queue. This is the *logical* structure of the model.

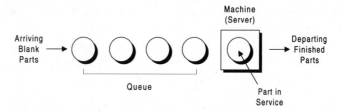

Figure 2-1. A Simple Processing System

You have to specify the *numerical* aspects as well, including how the simulation starts and stops. First, decide on and *be consistent about* the units with which time will be measured; we'll use minutes here. It doesn't logically matter what the time units are, so pick whatever is most appropriate, familiar, and convenient for your application[1]—just remember to *be consistent about it everywhere.*

The system starts at time 0 minutes with no parts present and the machine idle. This *empty-and-idle* assumption would be realistic if the system starts afresh each morning, but might not be so great as a model of the initial situation to simulate an ongoing operation.

The time durations that will make the simulation move are in Table 2-1. The (sequential) part number is in the first column, the second column has the time of arrival of each part, the third column gives the time *between* a part's arrival and that of the next part (called an *interarrival time*), and the service time (required to process on the machine, not counting any time spent waiting in the queue) is in the last column. Of course, all times are in minutes. You're probably wondering where all these numbers came from; don't worry about it right now, and just pretend that we observed them in the factory or that we brashly made them up.

Table 2-1. Arrival, Interarrival, and Service Times of Parts

Part Number	Arrival Time	Interarrival Time	Service Time
1	0.00	6.84	4.58
2	6.84	2.40	2.96
3	9.24	2.70	5.86
4	11.94	2.59	3.21
5	14.53	0.73	3.11

We've decided that the simulation will stop at exactly time 15 minutes. If there are any parts present at that time (in service at the machine or waiting in the queue), they never are finished.

2.1.2 Goals of the Study

Given a logical/numerical model like this, you next have to decide what output performance measures you want to collect. Here's what we decided to compute:

- The *total production* (number of parts that complete their service at the machine and leave) during the 15 minutes of operation. Presumably, more is better.
- The *average waiting time in queue* of parts that enter service at the machine during the simulation. This time in queue records only the time a part is waiting in the queue and

---

[1] Not only should you be sensible about choosing the time units (e.g., for a simulation of 20 years, don't choose milliseconds as your units, and for a simulation of two minutes, don't measure time in days), but you should also choose units that avoid both extremely big and extremely tiny time values in the same model since, even with Arena's double-precision values, the computer might have trouble with roundoff error.

not the time it spends being served at the machine. If D_i is the delay in queue of the ith part and it turns out that N parts complete their delays in queue during the 15-minute run, this average is

$$\frac{\sum_{i=1}^{N} D_i}{N}.$$

(Note that since Part 1 arrives at time 0 to find the machine idle, $D_1 = 0$ and $N \geq 1$ for sure so we don't have to worry about dividing by zero.) This is generally called a *discrete-time* (or *discrete-parameter*) statistic since it refers to data, in this case the delays $D_1, D_2, \ldots$, for which there is a natural first, second, ... observation; in Arena, these are called *tally* statistics since values of them are "tallied" when they are observed (using a feature of the underlying SIMAN simulation language called *Tally*). From a performance standpoint, small is good.

- The *maximum time waiting in queue* of parts that enter service at the machine during the simulation. This is a worst-case measure, which might be of interest in giving service-level guarantees to customers. Small is good.

- The *time-average number of parts waiting in the queue* (again, not counting any part in service at the machine). By "time average" we mean a weighted average of the possible queue lengths $(0, 1, 2, \ldots)$ weighted by the proportion of time during the run that the queue was at that length. Letting $Q(t)$ be the number of parts in the queue at any time instant t, this time-average queue length is the total area under the $Q(t)$ curve, divided by the length of the run, 15. In integral-calculus terms, this is

$$\frac{\int_{0}^{15} Q(t)\,dt}{15}.$$

Such *time-persistent* statistics are common in simulation. This one indicates how long the queue is (on average), which might be of interest for allocating floor space.

- The *maximum number of parts that were ever waiting in the queue*. Actually, this might be a better indication of how much floor space is needed than is the time average if you want to be reasonably sure to have room at all times. This is another worst-case measure, and smaller is presumably better.

- The *average* and *maximum flowtime* of parts that finish being processed on the machine and leave; *flowtime*, also called *cycle time*, for a part is the time that elapses between its arrival and its departure, so it's the sum of the part's delay in queue and its service time at the machine. This is a kind of turnaround time, so smaller is better.

- The *utilization* of the machine, defined as the proportion of time the machine is busy during the simulation. Think of this as another time-persistent statistic, but of the "busy" function

$$B(t) = \begin{cases} 1 \text{ if the machine is busy at time } t \\ 0 \text{ if the machine is idle at time } t \end{cases}.$$

The utilization is the area under $B(t)$, divided by the length of the run:

$$\frac{\displaystyle\int_{0}^{15} B(t)\,dt}{15}.$$

Resource utilizations are of obvious interest in many simulations, but it's hard to say whether you "want" them to be high (close to 1) or low (close to 0). High is good since it indicates little excess capacity, but can also be bad since it might mean a lot of congestion in the form of long queues and slow throughput.

There are usually a lot of possible output performance measures, and it's probably a good idea to observe a lot of things in a simulation since you can always ignore things you have but can never look at things you don't have, plus sometimes you might find a surprise. The only downside is that collecting extraneous data can slow execution somewhat.

2.2   Analysis Options

With the model, its inputs, and its outputs defined, you next have to figure out how to get the outputs by transforming the inputs according to the model's logic. In this section, we'll briefly explore a few options for doing this.

2.2.1   Educated Guessing

While we're not big fans of guessing, a crude "back-of-the-envelope" calculation can sometimes lend at least qualitative insight (and sometimes not). How this goes, of course, completely depends on the situation (and on how good you are at guessing).

A possible first cut in our example is to look at the average inflow and processing rates. From Table 2-1, it turns out that the average of the five interarrival times is 3.05 minutes, and the average of the five service requirements is 3.94 minutes. This looks pretty bad, since parts are arriving faster than they're being served, implying heavy congestion (at least after a while, probably longer than the 15-minute run we have planned). Indeed, if this situation persists, the queue will "explode"—not a happy thought.

Suppose, on the other hand, that the numbers had come out so that the average interarrival time was *more* than the average service time. As long as you're supposing, suppose further that these averages were *exactly* what happened for each part—no variation either way. Then there would never be a queue, and all delays in queue would be zero, which *is* a happy thought.

The truth, as usual, will probably be between the extremes. Clearly, guessing has its limits.

2.2.2   Queueing Theory

Since this is a queue, why not use queueing theory? It's been around for almost a century, and a lot of very bright people have worked very hard to develop it. In some situations, it can result in simple formulas from which you can get a lot of insight.

Probably the simplest and most popular object of queueing theory is the *M/M/1 queue*. The first "M" states that the arrival process is *Markovian*; i.e., the interarrival times are independent and identically distributed "draws" from an exponential probability distribution (see Appendices C and D for a brief refresher on probability and distributions). The second "M" stands for the service-time distribution, and here it's also exponential. The "1" indicates that there's just a single server. So at least on the surface this looks pretty good for our model.

Better yet, most of our output performance measures can be expressed as simple formulas. For instance, the average delay in queue (expected from a long run) is just

$$\frac{\mu_S^2}{\mu_A - \mu_S}$$

where μ_A is the expected value of the interarrival-time distribution and μ_S is the expected value of the service-time distribution (assuming that $\mu_A > \mu_S$ so the queue doesn't explode). So one immediate idea is to use the data to estimate μ_A and μ_S, then plug these estimates into the formula (although this won't work in our case since the average interarrival time is less than the average service time).

Such an approach can sometimes give a reasonable order-of-magnitude approximation that might facilitate crude comparisons. But there are problems too:

- The estimates of μ_A and μ_S aren't exact, so there will be error in the result as well.
- The assumptions of exponential interarrival-time and service-time distributions are essential to deriving the formula above, and we probably don't satisfy these assumptions. This calls into question the validity of the formula. While there are more sophisticated versions for more general queueing models, there will always be assumptions to worry about.
- The formula is for long-run performance, not the 15-minute period we want. This is typical of most (but not all) queueing theory.
- The formula doesn't capture the natural variability in the system. This is not only a difficulty in analysis but might also be of inherent interest itself, as in the variability of production. (It's sometimes possible, though, to find other formulas that measure variability.)

Many people feel that queueing theory can prove valuable as a first-cut approximation to get an idea of where things stand and to provide guidance about what kinds of simulations might be appropriate at the next step in the project. We agree, but urge you to keep in mind the problems listed above and temper your interpretations accordingly.

2.2.3 Mechanistic Simulation
So all of this brings us back to simulation. By "mechanistic" we mean that the individual operations (arrivals, service by the machine, etc.) will occur as they would in reality. The movements and changes of things in the simulation model occur at the right "time," in the right order, and have the right effects on each other and the statistical-accumulator variables.

In this way, simulation provides a completely concrete, "brute-force" way of dealing directly with the model. There's nothing mysterious about how it works—just a few basic ideas and then a whole lot of details and bookkeeping that software like Arena handles for you.

2.3 Pieces of a Simulation Model

We'll talk about the various parts of a simulation model in this section, all in reference to our example.

2.3.1 Entities

Most simulations involve "players" called *entities* that move around, change status, affect and are affected by other entities and the state of the system, and affect the output performance measures. Entities are the *dynamic* objects in the simulation—they usually are created, move around for a while, and then are disposed of as they leave. It's possible, though, to have entities that never leave but just keep circulating in the system. However, all entities have to be created, either by you or automatically by the software.

The entities for our example are the parts to be processed. They're created when they arrive, move through the queue (if necessary), are served by the machine, and are then disposed of as they leave. Even though there's only one kind of entity in our example, there can be many independent "copies," or *realizations* of it in existence at a time, just as there can be many different individual parts of this type in the real system at a time.

Most entities represent "real" things in a simulation. You can have lots of different kinds of entities and many realizations of each kind of entity existing in the model at a time. For instance, you could have several different *kinds* of parts, perhaps requiring different processing and routing and having different priority; moreover, there could be several realizations of each kind of part floating around in the model at a time.

There are situations, though, where "fake" entities not corresponding to anything tangible can be conjured up to take care of certain modeling operations. For instance, one way to model machine failures is to create a "breakdown demon" (see Figure 2-2) that lurks in the shadows during the machine's up time, runs out and kicks the machine when it's supposed to break down, stands triumphantly over it until it gets repaired, then scurries back to the shadows and begins another lurking period representing the machine's next up time. A similar example is a "break angel" that arrives periodically and takes a server off duty.

Figuring out what the entities are is probably the first thing you need to do in modeling a system.

Figure 2-2. A Victorious Breakdown Demon

2.3.2 Attributes

To individualize entities, you attach *attributes* to them. An attribute is a characteristic of all entities, but with a specific value that can differ from one entity to another. For instance, our part entities could have attributes called Arrival Time, Due Date, Priority, and Color to indicate these characteristics for each individual entity. It's up to you to figure out what attributes your entities need, name them, assign values to them, change them as appropriate, and then use them when it's time. (That's all part of modeling.)

The most important thing to remember about attributes is that their values are tied to specific entities. The same attribute will generally have different values for different entities, just as different parts have different arrival times, due dates, priorities, and color codes. Think of an attribute as a tag attached to each entity, but what's written on this tag can differ across entities to characterize them individually. An analogy to traditional computer programming is that attributes are *local* variables—in this case, local to an individual entity.

Arena keeps track of some attributes automatically, but you may need to define, assign values to, change, and use attributes of your own.

2.3.3 (Global) Variables

A *variable* (or a *global* variable) is a piece of information that reflects some characteristic of your system, regardless of how many or what kinds of entities might be around. You can have many different variables in a model, but each one is unique. There are two types of variables: Arena built-in variables (number in queue, number of busy resources, simulation time, etc.) and user-defined variables (number in system, current shift, etc.). In contrast to attributes, variables are not tied to any specific entity, but rather pertain to the system at large. They're accessible by all entities, and many can be changed by any entity. If you think of attributes as tags attached to the entities currently floating around in the room, then think of variables as writing on the wall.

Variables are used for lots of different purposes. For instance, you could create one called Number In System whose value is the total number of parts in the system, including those in queue and in service at the machine. When a part entity is created, it adds 1 to Number In System, and when a part is done it subtracts 1 from Number In System just before it leaves. Some built-in Arena variables for our model include the status of the machine, the time (simulation clock), and the current length of the queue in our model.

2.3.4 Resources

Entities often compete with each other for service from *resources* that represent things like personnel, equipment, or space in a storage area of limited size. An entity *seizes* (units of) a resource when available and *releases* it (or them) when finished. It's better to think of the resource as being given to the entity rather than the entity being assigned to the resource since an entity (like a part) could need simultaneous service from multiple resources (such as a machine and a person).

A resource can represent a group of several individual servers, each of which is called a *unit* of that resource. This is useful to model, for instance, several identical "parallel" agents at an airline ticketing counter. The number of units of a resource can be changed along the way to represent agents going on break or opening up their stations if things get busy. In our example, there is just a single machine, so this resource has only a single unit.

2.3.5 Queues

When an entity can't move on, perhaps because it needs to seize a unit of a resource that's tied up by another entity, it needs a place to wait, which is the purpose of a *queue*. In Arena, queues have names and can also have capacities to represent, for instance, limited floor space for a buffer. You'd have to decide as part of your modeling how to handle an entity arriving at a queue that's already full.

2.3.6 Statistical Accumulators

To get your output performance measures, you have to keep track of various intermediate *statistical-accumulator variables* as the simulation progresses. In our example, we'll watch:

- The number of parts produced so far
- The total of the time spent in queue so far
- The number of parts that have passed through the queue so far (since we'll need this as the denominator in the average-delay output measure)
- The longest time spent in queue we've seen so far
- The total of the flowtimes so far
- The longest flowtime we've seen so far
- The area so far under the queue-length curve $Q(t)$
- The highest level that $Q(t)$ has so far attained
- The area so far under the server-busy function $B(t)$

All of these accumulators should be initialized to 0. When something happens in the simulation, you have to update the affected accumulators in the appropriate way.

Arena takes care of most of the statistical accumulation you're likely to want, so most of this will be invisible to you except for asking for it in some situations. But in our hand simulation, we'll do it all manually so you can see how it goes.

2.3.7 Events

Now let's turn to how things work when we run our model. Basically, everything's centered around events. An *event* is something that happens at an instant of (simulated) time that might change attributes, variables, or statistical accumulators. In our example, there are three kinds of events:

- **Arrival:** A new part enters the system.
- **Departure:** A part finishes its service at the machine and leaves the system.
- **The End:** The simulation is stopped at time 15 minutes. (It might seem rather artificial to anoint this as an event, but it certainly changes things and this is one way to stop a simulation.)

In addition to the above events, there of course must be an initialization to set things up. We'll explain the logic of each event in more detail later.

Other things happen in our example model, but needn't be separate events. For instance, parts leave the queue and begin service at the machine, which changes the system, but this only happens because of some other entity's departure, which is already an event.

To execute, a simulation has to keep track of the events that are supposed to happen in the (simulated) future. In Arena, this information is stored in an *event calendar*. We won't get into the details of the event calendar's data structure, but here's the idea: When the logic of the simulation calls for it, a *record* of information for a future event is placed on the event calendar. This event record contains identification of the entity involved, the event time, and the kind of event it will be. Arena places each newly scheduled event on the calendar so that the next (soonest) event is always at the top of the calendar (i.e., the new event record is *sorted* onto the calendar in increasing order of event times). When it's time to execute the next event, the top record is removed from the calendar and the information in this record is used to execute the appropriate logic; it could be that part of this logic is to place one or more new event records onto the calendar. It's possible that, at a certain time, it doesn't make sense to have a certain event type scheduled (in our model, if the machine is idle, you don't want a departure event to be scheduled), in which case there's just no record for that kind of event on the calendar, so it obviously can't happen next. Though our model here doesn't require it, it's also possible to have several events of the same kind scheduled on the calendar at once, for different times and for different entities.

In a discrete-event model, the variables that describe the system don't change between successive events. Most of the work in event-driven simulation involves getting the logic right for what happens with each kind of event. As you'll see later, though, modeling with Arena usually gets you out of having to define this detailed event logic explicitly, although you can do so if you want in order to represent something very peculiar to your model that Arena isn't set up to do directly.

2.3.8 Simulation Clock

The current value of time in the simulation is simply held in a variable called the *simulation clock*. Unlike real time, the simulation clock does not take on all values and flow continuously; rather, it lurches from the time of one event to the time of the next event scheduled to happen. Since nothing changes between events, there is no need to waste (real) time looking at (simulated) times that don't matter.

The simulation clock interacts closely with the event calendar. At initialization of the simulation, and then after executing each event, the event calendar's top record (always the one for the next event) is taken off the calendar. The simulation clock lurches forward to the time of that event (one of the data fields in the event record), and the information in the removed event record (entity identification, event time, and event type) is used to execute the event at that instant of simulated time. How the event is executed clearly depends on what kind of event it is as well as on the model state at that time, but in general could include updating variables and statistical accumulators, altering entity attributes, and placing new event records onto the calendar.

While we'll keep track of the simulation clock and event calendar ourselves in the hand simulation, these are clearly important pieces of any dynamic simulation, so Arena keeps track of them. (The clock is a variable called TNOW.)

2.3.9 Starting and Stopping

Important, but sometimes overlooked, issues in a simulation are how it will start and stop. For our example, we've made specific assumptions about this, so it'll be easy to figure out how to translate them into values for attributes, variables, accumulators, the event calendar, and the clock.

Arena does a lot of things for you automatically, but it can't decide modeling issues like starting and stopping rules. You have to determine the appropriate starting conditions, how long a run should last, and whether it should stop at a particular time (as we'll do at time 15 minutes) or whether it should stop when something specific happens (like as soon as 20 parts are produced). It's important to think about this and make assumptions consistent with what you're modeling; these decisions can have just as great an effect on your results as can more obvious things like values of input parameters (such as interarrival-time means, service-time variances, and the number of machines).

You should do *something* specific (and conscious) to stop the simulation with Arena, since it turns out that, in many situations, taking all the defaults will cause your simulation to run forever (or until you get sick of waiting and kill it, whichever comes first).

2.4 Event-Driven Hand Simulation

We'll let you have the gory details of the hand simulation in this section, after outlining the action and defining how to keep track of things.

2.4.1 Outline of the Action

Here's roughly how things go for each event:

- **Arrival:** A new part shows up.
  - Update the time-persistent statistics (between the last event and now).
  - "Mark" the arriving part with an attribute giving its time of arrival (the current value of the clock), which will be needed later to compute its flowtime and possibly the time it spends in the queue.
  - If the machine is idle, the arriving part goes right into service (experiencing a time in queue of zero), so the machine is made busy and the end of this part's service is scheduled. Tally this part's time in queue (zero).
  - On the other hand, if the machine is already busy with another part, the arriving part is put at the end of the queue and the queue-length variable is incremented.
  - Finally, schedule a new entity to arrive at the next arrival time by placing a new event record for it onto the event calendar.
- **Departure:** The part being served by the machine is done and ready to leave.
  - Increment the number-produced statistical accumulator.
  - Compute and tally the flowtime of the departing part by taking the current value of the clock minus the entity's arrival time ("marked" in an attribute as part of the Arrival event).

- ⋆ Update the time-persistent statistics.
- ⋆ If there are any parts in queue, take the first one out, compute and tally its time in queue (which is now ending), and begin its service at the machine by scheduling its departure event (i.e., place it on the event calendar).
- ⋆ On the other hand, if the queue is empty, then make the machine idle. Note that in this case, there's no departure event scheduled on the event calendar.
- ▪ **The End:** The simulation is over.
  - ⋆ Update the time-persistent statistics to the end of the simulation.
  - ⋆ Compute the final summary output performance measures.

After each event (except the end event), the event calendar's top record is removed, indicating what event will happen next and at what time. The simulation clock is advanced to that time, and the appropriate logic is carried out.

2.4.2   Keeping Track

All the calculations for the hand simulation are detailed in Table 2-2. Traces of $Q(t)$ and $B(t)$ over the whole simulation are in Figure 2-3, with the dots indicating the events. Each row in Table 2-2 represents an event concerning a particular entity (in the first column) at time t (second column), and the situation *after* completion of the logic for that event (in the other columns). The other column groups are:

- ▪ **Event:** This describes what just happened; Arr and Dep refer respectively to an arrival and a departure.
- ▪ **Variables:** These are the values of the number $Q(t)$ of parts in queue and the server-busy function $B(t)$.
- ▪ **Attributes:** Each arriving entity is "marked" with its arrival time when it arrives and carries this attribute along with it throughout. If a part is in service at the machine, its arrival time is <u>underlined</u> at the right edge of the column. The arrival times of any parts in the queue, in right-to-left order (to agree with Figure 2-1), extend back toward the left. For instance, at the end of the run, the part in service arrived at time 9.24, the part that's first in the queue arrived at time 11.94, and the part that's second in queue arrived at time 14.53. We have to keep track of these to compute the time in queue of a part when it enters service at the machine after having waited in the queue as well as the flowtime of a part when it leaves.
- ▪ **Statistical Accumulators:** We have to initialize and then update these as we go along to watch what happens. They are:

P =   the total number of parts produced so far
N =   the number of entities that have passed through the queue so far
ΣD =   the sum of the queue times that have been observed so far
D^* =   the maximum time in queue observed so far
ΣF =   the sum of the flowtimes that have been observed so far
F^* =   the maximum flowtime observed so far
$\int Q$ =   the area under the $Q(t)$ curve so far
Q^* =   the maximum value of $Q(t)$ so far
$\int B$ =   the area under the $B(t)$ curve so far

Table 2-2. Record of the Hand Simulation

Just-Finished Event			Variables		Attributes Arrival Times:		Statistical Accumulators									Event Calendar
Entity No.	Time t	Event Type	$Q(t)$	$B(t)$	(In Queue)	In Service	P	N	ΣD	D^*	ΣF	F^*	$\int Q$	Q^*	$\int B$	[Entity No., Time, Type]
—	0.00	Init	0	0	( )	—	0	0	0.00	0.00	0.00	0.00	0.00	0	0.00	[1, 0.00, Arr] / [−, 15.00, End]
1	0.00	Arr	0	1	( )	0.00	0	1	0.00	0.00	0.00	0.00	0.00	0	0.00	[1, 4.58, Dep] / [2, 6.84, Arr] / [−, 15.00, End]
1	4.58	Dep	0	0	( )	—	1	1	0.00	0.00	4.58	4.58	0.00	0	4.58	[2, 6.84, Arr] / [−, 15.00, End]
2	6.84	Arr	0	1	( )	6.84	1	2	0.00	0.00	4.58	4.58	0.00	0	4.58	[3, 9.24, Arr] / [2, 9.80, Dep] / [−, 15.00, End]
3	9.24	Arr	1	1	(9.24)	6.84	1	2	0.00	0.00	4.58	4.58	0.00	1	6.98	[2, 9.80, Dep] / [4, 11.94, Arr] / [−, 15.00, End]
2	9.80	Dep	0	1	( )	9.24	2	3	0.56	0.56	7.54	4.58	0.56	1	7.54	[4, 11.94, Arr] / [−, 15.00, End] / [3, 15.66, Dep]
4	11.94	Arr	1	1	(11.94)	9.24	2	3	0.56	0.56	7.54	4.58	0.56	1	9.68	[5, 14.53, Arr] / [−, 15.00, End] / [3, 15.66, Dep]
5	14.53	Arr	2	1	(14.53, 11.94)	9.24	2	3	0.56	0.56	7.54	4.58	3.15	2	12.27	[−, 15.00, End] / [6, 15.26, Arr] / [3, 15.66, Dep]
—	15.00	End	2	1	(14.53, 11.94)	9.24	2	3	0.56	0.56	7.54	4.58	4.09	2	12.74	[6, 15.26, Arr] / [3, 15.66, Dep]

▪ **Event Calendar:** These are the event records as described earlier. Note that, at each event time, the top record on the event calendar is transferred to the first three entries in the next row, at the next event time.

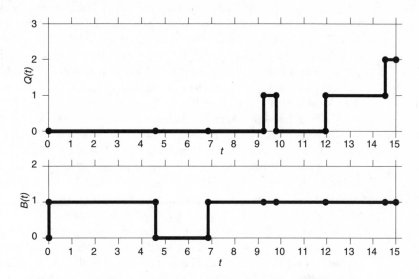

Figure 2-3. Time-Persistent Curves for the Hand Simulation

2.4.3 Carrying It Out

Here's a brief narrative of the action:

▪ $t = 0.00$, **Init:** The model is initialized, with all variables and accumulators set to 0, the queue empty, the server idle, and the event calendar primed with the first arrival happening at time 0.00 and the end of the simulation scheduled for time 15.00. To see what happens next, just take the first event record off the event calendar—the arrival of Entity 1 at time 0.00.

▪ *Entity 1, t = 0.00*, **Arr:** The first part arrives, makes the machine busy, and the arrival time of the part is marked as its attribute (underlined, <u>0.00</u>). The queue is still empty because this part finds the machine idle and begins service immediately. Since the entity passed through the queue (with time in queue of 0), N is incremented, ΣD is augmented by the time in queue (0), and we check to see if a new maximum time in queue has occurred (no). There has been no production yet, so P stays at 0. No flowtimes have yet been observed, so ΣF and F^* are unchanged. The time-persistent statistics $\int Q$, Q^*, and $\int B$ remain at 0 since no time has yet passed. Referring to Table 2-1, the service time for Part 1 is set to 4.58 minutes, and the Part 1 entity is returned to the event calendar. Finally, the next part arrival is scheduled by creating a Part 2 entity, setting its Arrival Time to the current time plus its interarrival time (from Table 2-1), and placing it on the event calendar. Taking the top record off the event calendar, the next event will be the departure of Entity 1 at time 4.58.

▪ *Entity 1, t = 4.58,* **Dep:** Part 1 is finished processing, so the system empties again, which the variables and attributes reflect. A part has been produced, so P is incremented by 1. No new queue times have been completed, so N, ΣD, and D^* are not updated. The part that was just produced had a flowtime of 4.58 (the current clock value minus the part's arrival time, read from the underlined entry in the preceding event's line), so ΣF and F^* are updated. Since time has elapsed, we must update the time-persistent statistics $\int Q$, Q^*, and $\int B$; refer to Figure 2-3. We're now at time 4.58, so we need to add in the rectangle area $0 \times (4.58 - 0) = 0$ to $\int Q$, and the rectangle area $1 \times (4.58 - 0) = 4.58$ to $\int B$. No new maximum of $Q(t)$ has occurred, so Q^* is unchanged. The next event will be the arrival of Entity 2 at time 6.84.

▪ *Entity 2, t = 6.84,* **Arr:** Part 2 arrives at an empty-and-idle system, as did Part 1, so the variables and attributes undergo the same changes as when Part 1 arrived at time 0, except that the arrival-time attribute of the part in service is 6.84. Another queue time, also of duration 0, has occurred, so N is incremented, ΣD is augmented by the queue time duration (0), and we check to see if a new maximum delay has occurred (no). No new production has happened, so P, ΣF, and F^* are unchanged. $\int Q$ is augmented by $0 \times (6.84 - 4.58) = 0$ and $\int B$ is augmented by the same amount. No new maximum of $Q(t)$ has occurred, so Q^* is unchanged. The next arrival is scheduled for 2.40 minutes from now, at time $6.84 + 2.40 = 9.24$, and the next departure (of the arriving Part 2) will happen at time $6.84 + 2.96 = 9.80$. The next event will be the arrival of Entity 3 at time 9.24.

▪ *Entity 3, t = 9.24,* **Arr:** Part 3 arrives but finds the machine busy already (with Part 2), so it must join the queue. The server is still busy, so $B(t)$ stays at 1, but $Q(t)$ is incremented. Now there is a queue, and the arrival time of the part in the queue is stored as an attribute of that part (Part 2, which arrived at time 6.84, is still in service). This event has resulted in no new production and no new time-in-queue observations, so P, N, ΣD, D^*, ΣF, and F^* are unchanged. $\int Q$ is augmented by $0 \times (9.24 - 6.84) = 0$ and $\int B$ is augmented by $1 \times (9.24 - 6.84) = 2.40$. Since the new value of $Q(t)$ is 1, which is greater than the former $Q^* = 0$, we set $Q^* = 1$ as the new maximum queue length observed. The next arrival will be at time $9.24 + 2.70 = 11.94$. The next event will be the departure of Entity 2 at time 9.80.

▪ *Entity 2, t = 9.80,* **Dep:** Part 2 now is done and ready to leave. Since there is a queue, the machine will stay busy so $B(t)$ remains at 1, but $Q(t)$ is decremented and the queue becomes empty (as Part 3, which arrived at time 9.24, leaves it to enter service). A time in queue of duration $9.80 - 9.24 = 0.56$ has now been completed, which is added into ΣD, and N is incremented; this is a new maximum queue time, so D^* is reset to 0.56. A new part has been produced so P is incremented and the flowtime of the part now leaving is computed as $9.80 - 6.84 = 2.96$, which is added into ΣF; this is not a new maximum flowtime, though, so F^* is unchanged. $\int Q$ is augmented by $1 \times (9.80 - 9.24) = 0.56$ and $\int B$ is augmented by the same amount. No new maximum for $Q(t)$ has been realized, so Q^* is unchanged. The next departure (of Part 3, which is now entering service) will be at time $9.80 + 5.86 = 15.66$ (after the simulation ends, so we won't see it). The next event is the arrival of Entity 4 at time 11.94.

▪ *Entity 4, t = 11.94,* **Arr:** Part 4 arrives, and the logic is just like the arrival of Part 3 at time 9.24, although the numbers are different for updating the queue, event calendar, and statistical accumulators (we'll skip the arithmetic). The next event is the arrival of Entity 5 at time 14.53.

- *Entity 5, t* = **14.53, Arr:** Part 5 arrives, and the logic is similar to the preceding event except that $Q(t)$ becomes 2. Also, $\int Q$ is augmented by $1 \times (14.53 - 11.94) = 2.59$ since the queue length during the preceding period was 1, and that's the height of the rectangle involved. The next event is the end of the simulation at time 15.00.
- *t* = **15.00, The End:** The only job is to update the areas $\int Q$ and $\int B$ to the end of the simulation.

The bottom row of Table 2-2 shows the ending situation, including the final value of the statistical accumulators.

2.4.4 Finishing Up
The only cleanup is to compute the final values of the output performance measures:

- The average time in queue is $\Sigma D/N = 0.56/3 = 0.19$ minute per part.
- The average flowtime is $\Sigma F/P = 7.54/2 = 3.77$ minutes per part.
- The time-average length of the queue is $\int Q/t = 4.09/15.00 = 0.27$ part (t here is the final value, 15.00, of the simulation clock).
- The utilization of the machine is $\int B/t = 12.74/15.00 = 0.85$.

Table 2-3 summarizes all the final output measures together with their units of measurement.

Table 2-3. Final Output Performance Measures from the Hand Simulation

Performance Measure	Value
Total production	2 parts
Average delay in queue	0.19 minute per part (3 parts)
Maximum delay in queue	0.56 minute
Average flowtime	3.77 minutes per part (2 parts)
Maximum flowtime	4.58 minutes
Time-average number of parts in queue	0.27 part
Maximum number of parts in queue	2 parts
Machine utilization	0.85 (dimensionless proportion)

During the 15 minutes, we produced two parts; the delays in queue, flowtimes, and queue lengths did not seem too bad; and the machine was busy 85% of the time. These values are considerably different from what we might have guessed or obtained via an oversimplified queueing model.

2.5 Event and Process-Oriented Simulation
The hand simulation we struggled through in Section 2.4 uses the *event orientation* since the modeling and computational work is centered around the events, when they occur, and what happens when they do. This allows you to control everything; have complete

flexibility with regard to attributes, variables, and logic flow; and to know the state of everything at any time. You easily see how this could be coded up in any programming language or maybe with macros in a spreadsheet, and people have done this a lot. For one thing, computation is pretty quick with a custom-written, event-oriented code. While the event orientation seems simple enough in principle (although not much fun by hand) and has some advantages, you can imagine that it becomes very complicated for large models with lots of different kinds of events, entities, and resources.

A more natural way to think about many simulations is to take the viewpoint of a "typical" entity as it works its way through the model, rather than the omniscient orientation of the master controller keeping track of all events, entities, attributes, variables, and statistical accumulators as we did in the event-oriented hand simulation. This alternative view centers on the *processes* that entities undergo, so is called the *process orientation*. As you'll see, this is strongly analogous to another common business modeling tool— namely, flowcharting. In this view, we might model the hand-simulated example in steps like this (put yourself in the position of a typical part entity):

- Create yourself (a new entity arrives).
- Mark what time it is now on one of your attributes so you'll know your arrival time later for the delay-in-queue and flowtime computations.
- Put yourself at the end of the queue.
- Wait in the queue until the machine becomes free (this wait could be of 0 duration, if you're lucky).
- Seize the machine (and take yourself out of the queue).
- Compute and tally your waiting time in queue.
- Stay put, or *delay*, for an amount of time equal to your service requirement.
- Release the machine (so other entities can seize it).
- Increment the production-counter accumulator on the wall and tally your flowtime.
- Dispose of yourself and go away.

This is the sort of "program" you write with a process-oriented simulation language like SIMAN, and is also the view of things normally taken by Arena. It's a much more natural way to think about modeling, and (importantly) big models can be built without the extreme complexity they'd require in an event-oriented program. It does, though, require more behind-the-scenes support for chores like time advance, keeping track of time-persistent statistics (which didn't show up in the process-oriented logic), and output-report generation. Simulation software like Arena provides this support as well as a rich variety of powerful modeling constructs to enable you to build complicated models relatively quickly and reliably.

Most discrete-event simulations are actually *executed* in the event orientation, even though you may never see it if you do your modeling in the process orientation. Arena's hierarchical nature allows you to get down into the event orientation if you need to in order to regain the control to model something peculiar, and in that case you have to think (and code) with event-oriented logic as we did in the hand simulation.

Because of its ease and power, process-oriented logic has become very popular and is the approach we'll take from now on. However, it's good to have some understanding of what's going on under the hood, so we first made you suffer through the laborious event simulation.

2.6 Randomness in Simulation

In this section, we'll discuss how (and why) you model randomness in a simulation model's input and the effect this can have on your output. We'll need some probability and statistics here, so this might be a good time to take a quick glance at Appendix C to review some basic ideas, terminology, and notation.

2.6.1 Random Input, Random Output

The simulation in Section 2.4 used the input data in Table 2-1 to drive the simulation recorded in Table 2-2, resulting in the numerical output performance measures reported in Table 2-3. This might be what happened from 8:00 to 8:15 on some particular Monday morning, and if that's all you're interested in, you're done.

But you're probably interested in more, like what you'd expect to see on a "typical" morning and how the results might differ from day to day. And since the arrival and service times of parts on other days would probably differ from those in Table 2-1, the numerical output performance measures will probably be different from what we got in Table 2-3. Therefore, the single run of the example just won't do since we really have no idea how "typical" our results are or how much variability might be associated with them. In statistical terms, what you get from a single run of a simulation is a *sample size of one*, which usually isn't worth much. It would be pretty unwise to put much faith in it, much less make important decisions based on it alone.

So random input looks like a curse. But you must often allow for it to make your model a valid representation of reality, where there may also be considerable uncertainty. The way people usually model this, instead of using a table of numerical input values, is to specify *probability distributions* from which observations are *generated* (or *drawn* or *sampled*) and drive the simulation with them. We'll talk in Section 5.4 about how you can determine these input probability distributions using the Arena Input Analyzer. Arena internally handles generation of observations from distributions you specify. Not only does this make your model more realistic, but it also sets you free to do more simulation than you might have observed data for and to explore situations that you didn't actually observe. As for the tedium of generating the input observations and doing the simulation logic, that's exactly what Arena (and computers) like to do for you.

But random input induces randomness in the output too. We'll explore this a little bit in the remainder of this chapter, but will take it up more fully in Section 6.5, Section 7.5, and Chapter 11 and show you how to use the Arena Output Analyzer to help interpret and appropriately cope with randomness in the output.

2.6.2 Replicating the Example

It's time to confess: We generated the input values in Table 2-1 from probability distributions in Arena. The interarrival times came from an exponential distribution with a mean of 5 minutes, and the service times came from a triangular distribution with a minimum of 1 minute, mode of 4 minutes, and maximum of 8 minutes. (You'll see in Chapters 3 and 4 how all this works in Arena.) See Appendix D for a description of Arena's probability distributions.

So instead of just the single 15-minute run, we could make several (we'll do five, one for each workday) independent, identical 15-minute runs and investigate how the results change from run to run, indicating how things in reality might change from morning to morning. Each run starts and stops the same way and uses the same input-parameter settings (that's the "identical" part), but uses separate input random numbers (that's the "independent" part) to generate the interarrival and service times. These are called *replications* of the simulation, and Arena makes it very easy for you to make them—just enter the number of replications you want into a dialog on your screen. You can think of this as having five replications of Table 2-1 for the input values, each one generating a replication of the simulation record in Table 2-2, resulting in five replications of Table 2-3 for all the results.

We wish you'd admire (or pity) us for slugging all this out by hand, but we really just asked Arena to do it for us; the results are in Table 2-4. The column for Replication 1 is the same as what's in Table 2-3, but you can see that there can be substantial variation across replications, just as things vary across days in the factory. It looks like Wednesday (Replication 3) was very busy, but not much work got done on Thursday or Friday (we did *not* rig this—honest!).

The last two columns in Table 2-4 give the sample mean and sample standard deviation (see Appendix C) across the individual-replication results for the output performance measure in each row. The sample mean provides a more stable indication of what to expect from each performance measure than what happens on an individual replication, and the sample standard deviation indicates cross-replication variation.

Table 2-4. Final Output Performance Measures from Five Replications of the Hand Simulation

Performance Measure	Replication					Sample	
	1	2	3	4	5	Mean	Std. Dev.
Total production	2	3	3	1	1	2.00	1.00
Average delay in queue	0.19	1.12	3.72	0.00	0.00	1.01	1.59
Maximum delay in queue	0.56	2.73	7.43	0.00	0.00	2.14*	3.16*
Average flowtime	3.77	4.90	6.82	4.77	3.31	4.71	1.35
Maximum flowtime	4.58	5.84	8.43	4.77	3.31	5.39*	1.92*
Time-average number of parts in queue	0.27	0.30	0.99	0.00	0.00	0.31	0.41
Maximum number of parts in queue	2	1	2	0	0	1.00*	1.00*
Machine utilization	0.85	0.91	1.00	0.32	0.37	0.69	0.32

*Taking means and standard deviations of the "maximum" measures is probably not meaningful—what is the "mean maximum" supposed to, well, mean? It might be better in these cases to take the *maximum* of the individual-replication maxima if you really want to know about the extremes.

Since the individual replication results are independent and identically distributed, you could form a confidence interval for the true expected performance measure μ (think of μ as the sample mean across an infinite number of replications) as

$$\overline{X} \pm t_{n-1,1-\alpha/2} \frac{s}{\sqrt{n}}$$

where $\overline{X}$ is the sample mean, s is the sample standard deviation, n is the number of replications, and $t_{n-1,1-\alpha/2}$ is the upper $1 - \alpha/2$ critical point from Student's t distribution with $n - 1$ degrees of freedom. Using the total-production measure, for example, this works out for a 95% confidence interval ($\alpha = 0.05$) to

$$2.00 \pm 2.776 \frac{1.00}{\sqrt{5}}$$

or 2.00 ± 1.24. The correct interpretation here is that in about 95% of the cases of making five simulation replications as we did, the interval formed like this will contain or "cover" the true expected value of total production. You might notice that the half-width of this interval (1.24) is pretty big compared to the value at its center (2.00); i.e., the *precision* is not too good. This could be remedied by simply making more than the five replications we made, which looks like it was not enough to learn anything precise about the expected value of this output performance measure. The great thing about collecting your data by simulation is that you can always[2] go get more by simply calling for more replications.

2.6.3 Comparing Alternatives

Most simulation studies involve more than just a single setup or configuration of the system. People often want to see how changes in design, parameters (controllable in reality or not), or operation might affect performance. To see how randomness in simulation plays a role in these comparisons, we made a simple change to the example model and re-simulated (five replications).

The change we made was just to double the arrival rate—in other words, the mean interarrival time is now 2.5 minutes instead of 5 minutes. The exponential distribution is still used to generate interarrival times, and everything else in the simulation stays the same. This could represent, for instance, acquiring another customer for the facility, whose part-processing demands would be intermingled with the existing customer base.

Figure 2-4 indicates what happened to the five "non-extreme" performance measures; the upper row of each plot indicates the original configuration (and are taken right out of Table 2-4), and the lower row is for the new configuration. For each performance measure, the results of the five replications of each model are indicated, and the result from the first replication in each case is numbered.

It's not clear that total production really increases with the double-time arrivals, due to limited processing capacity. It does appear, though, that the queue length and machine utilization tend to increase, although not in every case (due to variability). While formal statistical analyses would be possible here, simple plots like these can often pretty much tell the tale.

Moreover, note that relying on just one replication (the first, indicated by the numbered symbols) could be misleading. For instance, the average time in queue in the first

---

[2] Well, almost always.

replications of each model variant would have suggested that it is far greater for the double-time arrivals, but looking at the spread across replications indicates that the difference isn't so clear-cut. This is exactly the danger in relying on only a single run to make important decisions.

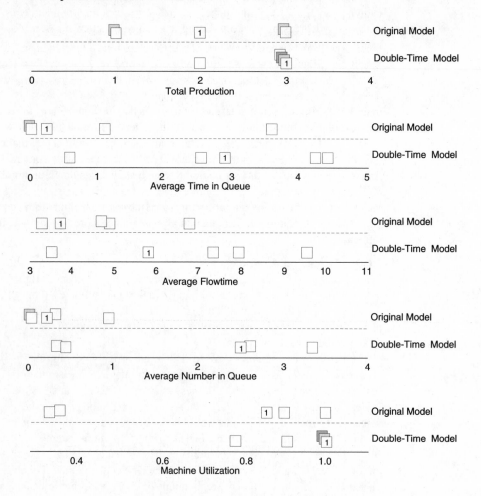

Figure 2-4. *Comparing the Original and Double-Time Arrival Systems*

2.7   Overview of a Simulation Study

In deciding how to model the system, you'll find that issues related to design and analysis and representing the model in the software certainly are essential to a successful simulation study, but they're not the only ingredients. We'll take all this up in Chapter 12 in some detail, but we want to mention briefly at this early point what's involved.

Presentation Evaluation Form

Group Members: _____

Scale: 5- outstanding, 4 – very good, 3 – average or good, 2 – below average, 1 – poor

Appearance of slides (easy to read, clear, visible colors)	5	4	3	2	1
Presentation style (good volume, well organized)	5	4	3	2	1
System description (includes objectives, boundary, outputs, modeling approach)	5	4	3	2	1
Analysis plan (includes data inputs, validation, experimentation)	5	4	3	2	1
Overall evaluation	5	4	3	2	1

Comments regarding part of the presentation that worked well:

Comments for improvement:

No simulation study will follow a cut-and-dried "formula," but there are several aspects that do tend to come up frequently:

- *Understand the system.* Whether it exists or not, you must have an intuitive, down-to-earth feel for what's going on. This will entail site visits and involvement of people who work in the system on a day-to-day basis.
- *Be clear about your goals.* Realism is the watchword here; don't promise the sun, moon, and stars. Understand what can be learned from the study, and expect no more. Specificity about what is to be observed, manipulated, changed, and delivered is essential.
- *Formulate the model representation.* What level of detail is appropriate? What needs to be modeled carefully and what can be dealt with in a fairly crude, high-level manner? Get buy-ins to the modeling assumptions from management and those in decision-making positions.
- *Translate into modeling software.* Once the modeling assumptions are agreed upon, represent them faithfully in the simulation software. If there are difficulties, be sure to iron them out in an open and honest way rather than bury them. Involve those who really know what's going on (animation can be a big help here).
- *Verify that your computer representation represents the conceptual model faithfully.* Probe the extreme regions, verify that the right things happen with "obvious" input, and walk through the logic with those familiar with the system.
- *Validate the model.* Do the input distributions match what you've observed in the field? Do the output performance measures from the model match up with those from reality? While statistical tests can be carried out here, a good dose of common sense is also valuable.
- *Design the experiments.* Plan out what it is you want to know and how your simulation experiments will get you to the answers in a precise and efficient way. Often, principles of classical statistical experimental design can be of great help here.
- *Run the experiments.* This is where you go to lunch while the computer is grinding merrily away, or maybe go home for the night or the weekend, or go on vacation. The need for careful experimental design here is clear. But don't panic—your computer probably spends most of its time doing nothing, so carrying out your erroneous instructions doesn't constitute the end of the world (remember, you're going to make your mistakes on the computer where they don't count rather than for real where they do).
- *Analyze your results.* Carry out the right kinds of statistical analyses to be able to make accurate and precise statements. This is clearly tied up intimately with the design of the simulation experiments.
- *Get insight.* This is far more easily said than done. What do the results mean at the gut level? Does it all make sense? What are the implications? What further questions (and maybe simulations) are suggested by the results? Are you looking at all the right performance measures?
- *Document what you've done.* You're not going to be around forever, so make it easier on the next person to understand what you've done and to carry things further. Documentation is also critical for getting management buy-in and implementation of the recommendations you've worked so hard to be able to make with precision and confidence.

By paying attention to these and similar issues, your shot at a successful simulation project will be greatly improved.

2.8 Exercises

2.1   For the hand simulation of the simple processing system, define another time-persistent statistic as the total number of parts in the system, including any parts in queue and in service. Augment Table 2-2 to track this as a new global variable, add new statistical accumulators to get its time average and maximum, and compute these values at the end.

2.2   In the preceding exercise, did you really need to add state variables and keep track of new accumulators to get the *time-average* number of parts in the system? If not, why not? How about the *maximum* number of parts in the system?

2.3   In the hand simulation of the simple processing system, suppose that the *queue discipline* were changed so that when the machine becomes idle and finds parts waiting in queue, instead of taking the first one, it instead takes the one that will require the *shortest processing time* (this is sometimes called an *SPT* queue discipline). To make this work, you'll need to assign a second attribute to parts in the system when they arrive, representing what their service time at the machine will be. Re-do the hand simulation. Is this a better rule? From what perspective?

2.4   Suppose that, in the hand simulation of the simple processing system, a constant setup time of 2 minutes was required once a part entered the machine but before its service could actually begin. When a setup is going on, regard the machine as being busy. Re-do the hand simulation and discuss the results.

2.5   Suppose the machine can work on two parts simultaneously (and they enter, are processed, and leave the machine independently). There's no difference in processing speed if there are two parts in the machine instead of one. Redefine $B(t)$ to be the number of parts in service at the machine at time (so $0 \le B(t) \le 2$), and the machine utilization is redefined as

$$\frac{\int_0^T B(t)dt}{2T}.$$

Re-run the original simulation to measure the effect of this change.

A Quick Peek at Arena

CHAPTER 3

A Quick Peek at Arena

As we were honest enough to admit in Chapter 2, we really carried out the "hand" simulation in Section 2.4 with Arena, as well as the replications and the modified model with the double-time arrivals in Section 2.6. In this chapter, we'll lead you through a little bit of Arena by having you load the ready-made model we built for the hand simulation, run it, make a few modifications, and exercise it to address some different kinds of questions.

Section 3.1 gets you to start Arena on your computer. Then you'll go through the model in Section 3.2, browsing the dialogs and animation, running the model, and taking a look at the results. Finally, Section 3.3 explains how the fundamental simulation concepts of Chapter 2 tie into the Arena model. By the end of this chapter, you'll have a good feel for how Arena works and have an idea of the things you can do with it. More information on how you work with Arena is in Chapter 4, and building your own models with Arena is discussed in Chapter 5 and beyond.

Arena is a true Microsoft® Windows® 95 and Windows NT® operating systems application, so all the usual features are there and all the usual operations work. We're assuming you know the basics of Windows 95 or Windows NT such as disks; files and folders; using the mouse and keyboard; moving around; the Taskbar and Start button; and window operations like moving, resizing, maximizing, minimizing, and closing. If not, it would probably be a good idea for you to go through a tutorial on these things before going on.

3.1 Starting Up

The first thing to note: there is a lot of mouse action in Arena, and when we say "click" or "double-click" something, we'll mean for you to use the left mouse button (for right-handers, at least) unless we say otherwise. If you have a track ball or pad or stick or some other pointing device, we mean the "first" or "primary" button.

Go to your computer, on which Arena is already installed per the instructions that came with it. Approach the computer cautiously but with confidence—if it senses you're afraid, it could attack. Locate the Arena icon (or a shortcut to it) and double-click on it. In a moment, the Arena copyright window will come up; if you're running an evaluation or educational edition, you'll get a message box to this effect, which you should read and then click the "OK" button (or just hit the Enter key on your keyboard since the OK button is already selected by default).

Next, you see a Welcome window as in Figure 3-1, with the Tip of the Day, which is part of Arena's extensive online Help system (it might be a good idea to click the blue Next Tip hyperlink or button and cycle through a few tips each time you start Arena). From here, you can also click on the Introduction tab at the bottom and explore some information, examples, and vendor-contact information, or click on the About tab to check your version. You can also click check boxes at the bottom left to request "expert" tips on the next startup, or no tips at all next time (a lousy attitude). When you're done with the Welcome window, click the Close button at the bottom right.

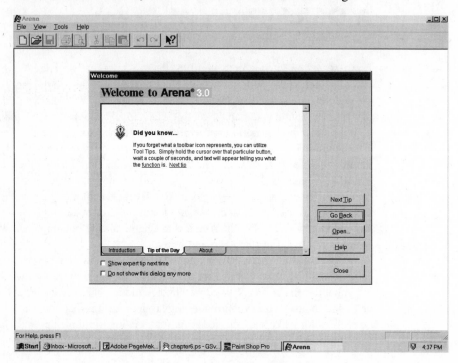

Figure 3-1. Arena Welcome Window

After closing the Welcome window, you'll see the main Arena menu items at the top of your screen: File, View, Tools, and Help. You'll also see a toolbar with various buttons, only three of which are active: these buttons will bring up a New model window ( ), display a dialog to open a previously saved model ( ), or provide help on a menu or toolbar item ( ). The first two of these are also available from the File menu.

Pulling down and selecting things from menus works just like other software with which you're probably familiar. A click on the name of the menu you want pulls it down; then a click on a menu item activates it. Alternatively, you can click on the menu item but leave the mouse button depressed, drag the mouse cursor down the menu until you get to what you want, and finally let go of the mouse button. When you're done with your Arena session and want to get back out to the operating system, select Exit from the File menu (or click the × button at the upper right).

3.2   Browsing an Existing Model

To load the ready-made model for the hand simulation, pull down the File menu and select Open (or just click the button from the toolbar) to bring up the Open dialog.

File names appear in the scrolling box, and you can also navigate to other folders or drives; find Mod_03_1.doe. Click on this file name (highlighting it), and then click the Open button (alternatively, double-click on the file name). Your screen should now look something like Figure 3-2. We'll call this Model 3.1.

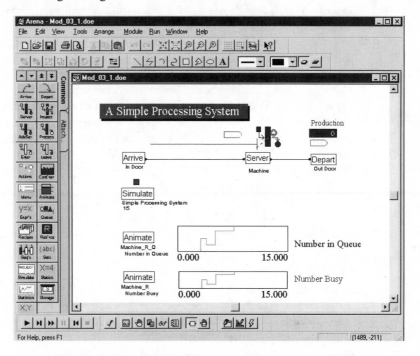

Figure 3-2. Arena Model Window for the Simple Processing System

The new window (inside the main Arena window you already had displayed) is the *model window* for this model, and most of it is occupied with the model itself; the name of the file is displayed at the top of the model window. Along the left side of the window are file-folder tabs labeled Common and Attach. These tabs are connected to alternative modeling *panels* that can be displayed, one at a time, along the left side of the model window. Right now the Common panel is the only occupied tab, and it is selected for display (i.e., it appears to be "on top"). It contains a collection of modeling constructs used most commonly in the form of *modules* like Arrive, Depart, Server, Animate, and Simulate. If you click on the Attach tab, a dialog comes up that allows you to attach other modeling panels (file names with extension *.tpo*), which we'll discuss in later chapters; for now, just click the Cancel button, then bring the Common panel to the front again by clicking on its tab.

3.2.1 Viewing the Model Window
The model window you see is just one of many possible *views* of the model and the big *world space* in which a model lives. To make the model window itself as big as possible,

click the □ button. To see different parts of the model, you can pan around in a model window using the scroll bars on the lower and right edges or the arrow keys (try it). You can also zoom in (with the ⌗ button or the + key or Zoom In on the View menu) or out (with the ⌗ button or the − key or Zoom Out on the View menu) to see parts of the model from different "altitudes." To pan/zoom automatically so that the window "sees" all the model at the closest possible zoom, click the ℘ button (or on the View menu, select Views, then All, or just hit the * key). If you want to go back to the preceding view, just click the ℘ button.

If you find a view you like, you can "save" it to a *named view* and assign a "hot" key to it by selecting Named Views from the View menu (or just hitting the **?** key) and then the Add button. To snap back to this view at any time, select Named Views from the View menu (or hit the **?** key) and Show the view you want; you can also hit the hot key assigned to the view at any time. Hot keys for named views are one of the few places in Arena where characters are case-sensitive. We've set up three named views for this model, `all` (hot key a), `logic` (hot key l), and `plots` (hot key p); try them out.

To get your visual bearings on where things are physically, you can display a background grid of little dots by checking (selecting) Grid from the View menu (or clicking the ⠿ button). If you further want to cause everything to snap to attention on this grid, check Snap from the View menu (or click the ⊞ button). Both of these actions are toggles; i.e., repeat the action to undo it. To customize the spacing of the grid dots, select Grid Settings from the View menu.

3.2.2 *The Arrive Module*

To see how the model is set up, we'll walk you through the modules and how they're related, starting with the Arrive module. To open each module in the displayed model window—Arrive, Server, Depart, the two Animate modules, and Simulate—double-click on each *module handle* (the white module name inside the blue outlined box).

The Arrive module is the "birth" node for arrival of entities, representing parts here, into the model from outside. Double-click on it to open a dialog like the one in Figure 3-3.

Note that the Arrive main dialog is divided into three areas: Enter Data, which describes the nature of the entry point for entities; Arrival Data, which describes the nature of the arrivals themselves; and Leave Data, which describes what happens to entities once they've arrived at the model.

In the Enter Data area is the "Station" name, which we decided to call `In Door`. A station in Arena is a physical location in the model, with a name, for reference in transferring entities. You *must* fill in something here (or accept the default name that Arena might supply) as you do with all dark gray entry fields in dialogs in Arena.

In the Arrival Data area, you'll see the Batch Size of 1 (the default), meaning that parts arrive one at a time. We entered `EXPO(5.0)` into the Time Between box, representing the interarrival time distribution's being exponential with a mean of 5. (The units throughout are minutes, which you must keep track of yourself.) Though we entered `5.0`, we could have entered `5.` or just `5` since Arena is generally quite forgiving about mixing up integers and real numbers. The ▾ at the right of the Time Between box pulls down a menu of Arena's probability distributions from which you can choose and then type in just your parameters, instead of typing in the name as well (which would require that you remember it, or look it up). In the Mark Time Attribute box, note that we filled in `Time of Arrival`, which is the name we gave to the attribute that's "marked" with the time of each part's arrival in this module, for use in computing flowtimes of parts when they are later finished and depart.

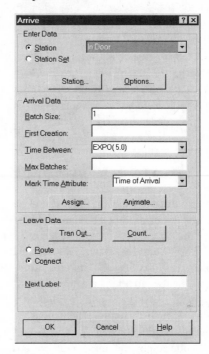

Figure 3-3. The Arrive Main Dialog for the Simple Processing System

In the Leave Data area, the Connect button is selected (rather than the default Route button); this indicates that we want arriving parts to go immediately to the machine (or its queue) without any "travel" time or waiting to get picked up and moved. Generally, groups of round buttons like this indicate that exactly one of them must be pushed, so are sometimes called *radio buttons*, reminiscent of old car radios with station push buttons.

Everything else is at its default value. To close the Arrive main dialog, click the Cancel button at the bottom or the **X** button at the upper right; if you'd made any changes that you wanted to retain, you'd click the OK button instead.

3.2.3 *The Server Module*
The Server module represents the machine, including the resource, its queue, and the processing time required there for parts. Open it by double-clicking on its name, and you should see the dialog in Figure 3-4.

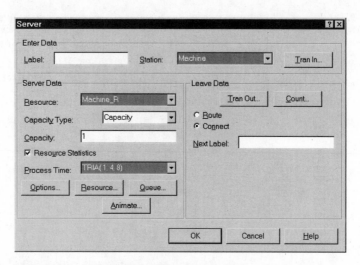

Figure 3-4. *The Server Main Dialog for the Simple Processing System*

There are three areas here: Enter Data, Server Data, and Leave Data. Enter Data, in this case, gives this module its required station name; Server Data describes what happens to entities at the server; and Leave Data controls how entities leave this module.

In the Enter Data area, all we did was name this Station `Machine` (we didn't like the default name). In the Server Data area, we accepted the Resource name `Machine_R` (which was the default after we'd named the Station `Machine`) and filled in the Process Time box with the service-time distribution we want, again picking its name from the pull-down list via the ▼ button. The Resource Statistics box is checked to get us the utilization figures on the machine (this is the default). The queue length and the times in queue are collected by default; to confirm this, click on the Queue button to bring up a secondary dialog called Resource Queue, and note that the boxes for # in Queue Statistics and Time in Queue Statistics are both already checked (if you didn't want these statistics reported, you'd just uncheck these boxes). Click OK to return to the Server main dialog.

As with the Arrive module, we want parts to proceed immediately to the next station rather than after a travel time away from the machine or a wait to get transported, so we pushed the Connect radio button in the Leave Data area rather than accept the default. If we'd wanted to Route to the next station, possibly with a delay, then we'd be required to enter a Station name in the Station entry field that appears when the Route radio button is selected (try it). In that case, the ▼ button of the Station box pulls down a list showing all the existing stations in the model at that point; for this reason, it might be easier to place and name all the stations in a new model first, then go through and open them up to fill in things like next stations.

Close the Server main dialog with the Cancel button; again, if you had made changes that you wanted to retain, you'd click OK.

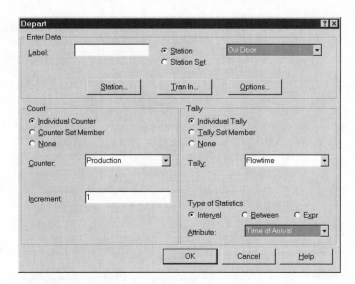

Figure 3-5. The Depart Main Dialog for the Simple Processing System

3.2.4   The Depart Module

The Depart module represents entities leaving the system; double-click on its name to bring up the dialog in Figure 3-5.

The three areas of the Depart module are Enter Data (for how entities begin the departure process), the Count area (if we want to get counts of departing entities), and the Tally area (if we want to make note of things about entities as they depart).

In the Enter Data area, we named this Station `Out Door` and accepted the defaults on everything else, indicating that this is just a single departure point.

In the Count area, we pushed the Individual Counter radio button to get the production counts, naming this counter `Production`. This is what creates the number above the icon for the Depart module (initially at 0), which will tick itself up as parts depart through this module.

To compute and record the flowtimes of departing parts, in the Tally area, we selected the Individual Tally radio button, named it `Flowtime`, and selected Interval on the Attribute `Time of Arrival` (the attribute we marked in the Arrive module on each arriving entity with its time of arrival and which shows up on the pull-down list from the ▾button). Selecting Interval means that we want to record (as a flowtime) the interval of time that elapsed from when the indicated Attribute (`Time of Arrival`) was marked until now (which is when the part is leaving, so its flowtime is ending).

Close the Depart main dialog with its Cancel button.

3.2.5   The Simulate Module

Things like run length and number of replications are set in the Simulate module; open its main dialog by double-clicking on its name to see something like Figure 3-6.

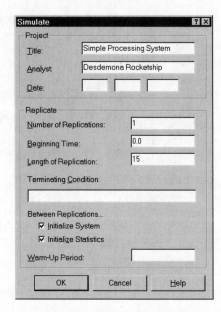

Figure 3-6. The Simulate Main Dialog for the Simple Processing System

In the Project area, you can give your project a title, list the name of the analyst (that's you), and record the date (which defaults to your system's date).

In the Replicate area, the default Number of Replications is 1 (which we'll accept for now, although you know better), the default Beginning Time is 0.0, and we'll specify the Length of Replication to be 15 (minutes). You can also specify other things here, like a Warm-Up Period at the beginning of each replication, after which the statistical accumulators are all cleared to allow the effect of possibly atypical initial conditions to wear off.

Close the Simulate main dialog with its Cancel button.

3.2.6 Module Connections

Note that the Arrive, Server, and Depart modules are connected (in that order) by lines. These establish the sequence that all parts will follow as they progress from one module to another. Recall that in the Leave Data areas of both the Arrive and Server modules we selected Connect (rather than taking the default of Route), indicating instant transfer of entities between modules, which is why these black connection lines are appropriate. To make the connections, you can click the ⇄ button or select Connect from the Module menu, which changes the mouse cursor to cross hairs, then click on the exit point (black triangle) from the source module and finally on the entry point (black square) on the destination module (you can make intermediate clicks if you want this connection to be just a series of line segments). If the Auto Connect feature is turned on (Module menu), you can also connect a newly placed module to whichever other connect-out module is selected when you place the new module.

If we had wanted to model non-zero travel times instead, we would have accepted the Route default and these black connection lines wouldn't be there (the exit points would disappear too). In this case, we could establish visual routes from module to module, along which icons for the entities would move in the animation during (or after) the simulation, by using the Route button (⌞ᴿ) in the Animate toolbar.

The Simulate module isn't connected to anything. This is because it's a *data module* through which entities don't "flow," and is there only to establish some values or conditions or displays for the whole run (in our case, its length and some labeling). The other kind of modules in Arena are *logic modules*, like Arrive, Server, and Depart, that control the logic of how entities move. In general, these need to be connected in some way either by connection lines or by routes or by other more advanced options to control entity flow.

3.2.7 Dynamic Plots

The two plots were created with Animate modules from the Common panel. Open up the top one, for the Number in Queue. To see how we set up the plot for Queue Length, double-click inside its plot area to get the dialog in Figure 3-7. In the Data Object area, we've selected Queue and then picked which queue from the pull-down list in the Queue Name box. (There's only one here, but in big models there could be many and having this pull-down menu eliminates the need for you to remember all their names.) In the Information area, we selected Number in Queue; in the Display As area, we left only the Plot box checked (they're all checked by default). Click the Cancel button to close this dialog.

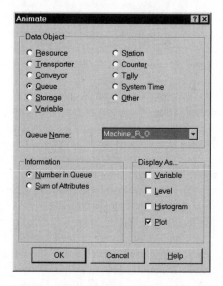

Figure 3-7. The Animate Module for the Queue Length Plot

The size of the plot is determined by dragging the handles on its borders; click (once) on the plot and try this (don't worry, there's an Undo option on the Edit menu). Other physical properties of the plot can be modified by double-clicking on the plot itself to bring up the dialog in Figure 3-8. The Expressions area lists what's being plotted, as specified earlier in the Animate module. You could, however, add other curves to this same plot like lengths of other queues (if there were any). We specified the Time Range to be the length of our simulation. We like to see a Bounding Box around the plot, so we pushed that radio button. We also asked for the *x* axis to be labeled with the end points. We specified no Refresh since the Time Range covers the whole simulation. Though we didn't do it, the Fill Area box fills in the area under the curve. The Area, Border, and Fill Area buttons on the right allow you to change colors.

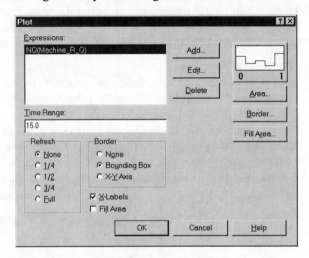

Figure 3-8. The Plot Dialog

Arena is clueless about what kind of numbers you might be asking it to plot (you may be too, initially) so you can't expect it to do a uniformly good job of scaling the *y* axis. To specify the Minimum and Maximum for the *y* axis, select (click once on) the expression being plotted under Expressions, then click the Edit button to bring up the Plot Expressions box and fill in your best guesses. If your guess on the Maximum is too big, you'll squish your plot toward the bottom, and if you underguess the Maximum, you'll decapitate it. After the run, you can look at the summary output (discussed in Section 3.2.9) to see what the realized maximum during the run was for this quantity, then adjust your Maximum. The # History Points specifies the maximum number of points that are saved for display on your plot during the run. If you notice that the points on the first part of your plot are disappearing, increase the number of points. Cancel yourself out of this dialog, then Cancel again to get out of the Plot window.

The Animate and Plot dialogs for the Number Busy plot are similar, so we won't go through them in detail (but go ahead and open them up to look at them if you want). The only really different thing is that in the Animate dialog we chose Resource for `Machine_R` as the Data Object and Number Busy as the Information to plot.

3.2.8   Dressing Things Up

The various labels in the model window, like the title at the upper left, the production counter, and the plot titles, were done with the Text tool on the Draw toolbar. You can control the usual things like font, size, and style from there. To change color, select the text (click on it once), select Text from the color palette on the right side of the screen, then click on your favorite text color (maybe even one that'll show up). You can also resize or rotate text by selecting it and dragging the underline bar.

The Draw toolbar also has boxes, shapes, lines, etc., that you can use to decorate your model window, depending on your artistic creativity and talent (as you can see, ours is severely limited). This is how we made the simple shadow box behind the model title in the upper left of the model window. The Arrange toolbar has buttons that allow you to manipulate objects such as sending a draw object to the back or front of a stack of objects, grouping, flipping, etc.

3.2.9 Running It

To run the model, click on the ▶ button in the Run toolbar (the collection of VCR-like controls at the bottom left of the screen), or select Go from the Run menu. The first time you run a model (and after you make changes to it) Arena checks your model for errors and compiles it (you can do this step by itself with the ✓ button on the Run Interaction toolbar or Check Model on the Run menu or the F4 key); if you have errors, you'll be gently scolded about them now, together with receiving some help on finding and correcting them. Then you can watch the model run (you'll have to look fast for a run this short unless your computer is pretty laid back), noting the entities arriving and departing, the digital clock at the bottom of the screen advancing, the production counter going up (although only to 2 here), and the plots being drawn.

The final state of things should look like Figure 3-9, with the plots being similar to Figure 2-3 and the clock and production counter frozen at their final values.

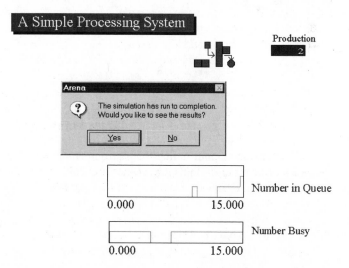

Figure 3-9. Ending State of the Simple Processing System

If you'd like to see the numerical summary results now, click Yes in answer to this question; this brings up a text window (using Microsoft® Notepad™) as in Figure 3-10 (after resizing the window and scrolling to see as much of it as possible). Browse through this report and note that the output performance measures in Table 2-3 are all here, as well as a lot of other stuff too that Arena collected automatically (we'll talk more about these things later). Close the summary report (and quit Notepad) by hitting the **X** button in the upper right. To view the summary report later, select View Results on the Run menu.

```
Mod_03_1.out - Notepad                                              _ □ X
File  Edit  Search  Help
Project:  Simple Processin
Analyst:  Desdemona Rocket

Replication ended at time      : 15.0

                     TALLY VARIABLES

Identifier           Average   Half Width  Minimum   Maximum   Observations
-------------------------------------------------------------------------------

Machine_R_Q Queue Time  .18608   (Insuf)    .00000    .55824        3
Flowtime                3.7669   (Insuf)   2.9552    4.5786         2

                  DISCRETE-CHANGE VARIABLES

Identifier           Average   Half Width  Minimum   Maximum   Final Value
-------------------------------------------------------------------------------

Machine_R Busy         .84926   (Insuf)    .00000   1.0000     1.0000
# in Machine_R_Q       .27271   (Insuf)    .00000   2.0000     2.0000
Machine_R Available   1.0000    (Insuf)   1.0000    1.0000     1.0000

                        COUNTERS

           Identifier            Count    Limit
           ----------------------------------------

           Production              2    Infinite
```

Figure 3-10. Summary Output Report for the Simple Processing System

Note that the module names in your model are hidden and that your mouse doesn't work on things in the model (try double-clicking on the server, for instance). To get things back to editable conditions in the model window, click the ■ button in the Run toolbar or select End from the Run menu.

3.3 Understanding What Just Happened

At this point, you're probably in one of two states: anxious to play around with the model or totally confused—or perhaps some combination of both. If your fingers are aching to point, click, drag, and drop, please go right ahead and do so. That's exactly what simulation should encourage—toying around with a model of a system in a safe computerized "laboratory." We've provided exercises at the end of the chapter to give some reasonable targets for your experimentation; give them a try, then return to this section when you've satiated your need to explore the great unknown territories of the Simple Processing System model. When you're typing changes in dialog fields, the usual text-editing features work. For instance, to change a whole word, you can double-click on it to highlight it, then just type the replacement. If you do something to your model that you want to save, pull down the File menu, select Save As, and pick a *different* name or place (so we can ask you later to come back to this model in its original form).

If, on the other hand, you're a bit confused about how all of these concepts fit together and would like a better base for your future simulation excursions, read on. . .we'll fill you in!

3.3.1   Arena's Modeling Orientation

As we mentioned in Chapter 2, the hand simulation that we carried out there used an *event orientation*. Our bookkeeping recorded each event that could change the state of the system, tracking the pertinent characteristics of the system (statistical accumulators, event calendar entries, etc.) for use by the logic behind each subsequent event. We also introduced the concept of a *process orientation*, in which the system is represented by combining a flowchart of processes that entities undergo with the data required to characterize the system completely. And as it turns out, Arena uses a combination of these approaches. You define the model using a process orientation, laying out the sequence of activities required to move the entity through the system, supplying the data required to support these entity actions, etc. Arena uses an event orientation to perform the actual simulation, keeping track of the state of the system, accumulating statistics, and moving the entities around through the model's logic at the appropriate times. This is the "best of both worlds." *You* get to think in natural terms, fundamentally asking "What's the entity going to do next?" at each step of its life in the system. *Arena* executes your experiment using an approach that's optimized for fast simulations, which you'll appreciate when you reach the point of using your model to analyze dozens or potentially hundreds of scenarios to help you hone in on the right decisions.

So how does the novice modeler put these two together? Well, fortunately, you don't really have to, at least not yet. Arena is designed so that you can think—and model—with an entity-based, process orientation. In our Simple Processing System, we used three logic modules (Arrive, Server, and Depart) to depict the process sequence for producing parts, a data module (Simulate) to supplement the processes with additional information required to perform our study, and two Animate modules to display two key performance measures dynamically. In the remainder of this section, we'll explain what functions the Arrive, Server, Depart, and Simulate modules perform in the context of the Simple Processing System model, and we'll contrast it with the event-oriented hand simulation from Chapter 2.

3.3.2   Launching Entities Into the Model—The Arrive Module Revisited

Let's start by viewing the Simple Processing System from the part's perspective (i.e., the entity-based, or process orientation). We gave you a sneak preview of this in Section 2.5 and are returning to it now that you're wiser about how an Arena model looks and behaves.

The starting point of activities in an Arena model is an entity-creation process. Looking at things from the entity's viewpoint, its creation in the model represents the point at which the model first cares about it. The entity could exist outside the boundaries of the modeled system, but won't appear in the model until this creation process brings it to life. To characterize an entity's birth, you'll need to define at least its time of arrival. This might be generated from a time-based sequence of entity arrivals to the modeled system, with the time between arrivals often represented by a probability distribution, as in the case of our Simple Processing System with its exponential interarrival times. When the part is created, you'll also want to think about what information will be needed to characterize the part as it moves through the modeled system. This will translate into assignments of values to entity attributes, such as storing the arrival time of each part entity in an attribute.

The Arrive module takes care of everything required to create the new entities and launch them into the system at the appropriate intervals. All you need to do as the modeler is to provide the data that characterizes the interarrival times, such as EXPO(5.0) for exponentially distributed interarrival times with a mean of 5. (Remember, it's up to you to decide on and be consistent about time units.) The Arrive module also will mark each entity's creation time in an entity attribute if you ask it to by specifying a Mark Time Attribute (in our case, Time of Arrival). The Assign button in the Arrive module allows you to establish values for other entity attributes, though this wasn't necessary in our model.

During the simulation run, Arena will use this information to do the work necessary to drive the appropriate simulation *events*, such as creating a new entity record, scheduling the next entity arrival on the event calendar, etc., as we did manually in the hand simulation. At the beginning of the simulation run, Arena schedules on the event calendar the initial entity arrival to each of the model's Arrive modules at a time dictated by the First Creation value from its particular Arrive module, which we defaulted to be at the beginning of the run (time 0). Thereafter, the Arena logic behind an entity's arrival takes care of scheduling the next entity's creation at the Arrive module (using the Time Between value), until the maximum number of arrivals has been reached (the Max Batches value) or the simulation run has been terminated in some other way. Each arriving entity is given the appropriate attribute assignments (according to the options selected in its Arrive module).

The Arrive module provides a number of additional options such as seizing resources on arrival to the system, counting the number of created entities, and establishing an animation picture for the entity. We suggest that as you become more comfortable with the basic goings-on in an Arena module, you explore these other capabilities. You might start by browsing Arena's *What's This?* help, which is accessed by clicking on the question-mark button (**?**) in a module's dialog then clicking on the dialog item that's aroused your curiosity. This will provide a quick overview of what an option does. We'll leave the remainder of the Arrive module options as a mystery for now (though don't let that hinder you from exploring on your own).

That said, there is one additional item of (brief) note regarding the Arrive module. We saw that it requires a station name, which had been defined to be In Door in the Simple

Processing System model. The concept of stations is an important part of Arena's modeling framework, which we will introduce in Chapter 5. While we'll be giving names to stations in the model we're building here, we won't exploit these names until later.

3.3.3 *Processing the Entity—The Server Module Revisited*

Returning to the part entity, once it has arrived at the boundary of our modeled system via the Arrive module, it next moves into a series of activities that center around processing the part on the machine. From the part's point of view, one of two things is going to happen—either it will have to wait its turn or it'll be loaded on the machine immediately. If it has to wait, it will do so by entering a queue, where it will reside until its turn to be processed on the machine. (If you have children or were once a child yourself, you know how hard it is to wait your turn, but our parts are well-disciplined and very patient.) Eventually, the part's desire to be processed on the machine will be fulfilled when it is loaded onto the machine. The part then undergoes a processing delay, after which it vacates its spot on the machine.

As it turns out, even for this very simple process, there's quite a lot going on. First, let's identify the components at work in governing this process. Naturally, there's the entity (the part), which will trigger each of the events. There's also the queue, which stores entities that are waiting to be loaded onto the machine. Characteristics of the queue include its *capacity* (how many entities can fit before it's full) and its *ranking discipline* (the rule dictating the position in the queue of newly arriving entities). At the heart of the process is the machine itself, modeled in Arena as a *resource*, which has properties such as its capacity, whether this capacity changes over time, and whether it ever breaks down. We also need to supply some data to characterize the process. At a minimum, we need to dictate how long a part will spend in process on the machine so that it knows when it's finished.

Arena's Server module combines these components—a resource, a queue for waiting parts, and a service process—inside a station, as well as providing a number of additional capabilities that we won't explore quite yet. In our Simple Processing System, we gave the name Machine to the station in the Server module, which also contains a resource and a queue; in our module, the resource is named Machine_R (Arena automatically appended the "_R" to the station name to distinguish between the station and the resource), and, as you saw if you explored the Queue dialog, a queue named Machine_R_Q. We also entered the processing time (it would be a stretch to expect Arena to provide that automatically) as TRIA(1,4,8). The last section of the Server module dialog determined what the entity should do when it completes the service process; namely, transfer to the module connected to the exit point of the Server module.

During the simulation run, the Server module's events center around changes in the resource state that are triggered by two events: a new entity arriving to the Server module and an entity completing its processing on the Machine_R resource. For the first event type, when an entity enters the Server module, Arena will perform the logic described earlier. Namely, if the resource is idle, then the entity will seize it (changing the resource state to busy) and be placed on the event calendar, to return to the model at the completion of its process time as sampled from the triangular distribution. If the resource is busy when the entity arrives, then Arena will place the entity in the queue. The process-completion event is handled by Arena much as we saw in our hand simulation in Chapter 2. The entity that activates the event releases the resource, causing Arena to allow the first waiting entity (if any) to seize the resource, or setting the resource state to idle if none are in its queue. The active entity then proceeds out of the Server module; in our Simple Processing System model, it is transferred to the Depart module.

You might notice that the Server module also is accompanied by a number of animation objects representing the fundamental Arena elements that it defines. There are two *station symbols*, a *queue line*, and a *resource picture*. During the simulation run, you might notice that the resource picture changes colors, representing its idle and busy states. Also, at the end of the run, it was readily apparent that there were two entities waiting in the queue to seize the resource.

You may have noticed that in this discussion of the Server module, there was no mention of characteristics of the server, animation of the server, or anything else related to the server itself. Instead, we describe what's contained in the *Server module*—the station, resource and queue; its animation; the data to be entered; etc. In fact, Arena's Server module is just like any other module, including a dialog in which you enter data to help define the process represented by the module, underlying logic that will be performed during the simulation run, statistics to be collected, and (in many cases) graphical animation. From an entity's perspective during the run, it simply enters a station, moves through a queue, is processed on a resource, and continues to the next module dictated by the Server module's transfer out options. While this may seem obvious, it's important to understand the distinction between the fundamental components of Arena models—such as an entity, station, resource, or queue—and a module that's been designed to help you model your system effectively using prepackaged combinations of these components and the logic to control them. While the Server module may seem like something whose characteristics you could define directly, which you could animate, and on which you could collect statistics, it's actually the *components* contained in the Server module that will be part of your running simulation model and that the entities will encounter when it's their turn to move into the logic created by the Server module.

3.3.4   Leaving the Modeled System—The Depart Module Revisited

By now, you should have the hang of how things work, and the Depart module should be pretty straightforward. The part entities in the Simple Processing System enter the Depart module when they've finished processing on the Machine_R resource in the Server module. The Depart module defines a station (the Out Door), which we'll disregard for the moment. We did request that two statistics be collected as parts leave the system—a count of the number of parts produced (the Production counter) and a tally statistic on the Flowtime of each part, which was defined as an interval between the departure time of the part and the value stored in its Time of Arrival attribute. When an entity encounters this section of the process during the run, Arena will simply record the two statistics and dispose of the entity, since the Depart module represents the end of the road for entity processing.

3.3.5 Controlling the Run—The Simulate Module Revisited

The Arrive, Server, and Depart modules completely characterize the logic and data required to represent the Simple Processing System from an entity's perspective. The part is born at the Arrive module, undergoes some form of machining process at the Server module, and perishes at the Depart module, leaving behind traces of its existence via its effect on the state of the system during its lifetime and the statistics collected on its way out the door.

The Simulate module provides one additional and important part of a model by characterizing the type of simulation run to be performed. By defining that a single replication of duration 15 is to be performed, our Simulate module causes Arena to terminate the run and generate a summary report at time 15. It also establishes a default animation picture for the model's entities (the red box). There's really only a need for one Simulate module in a model, and you'll usually have one, but as mentioned earlier, if you don't, Arena will still go ahead and process your logic until some other mechanism terminates the run—either via model logic or by human intervention.

3.4   Exercises

(Note: All these exercises refer to the ready-made model, Mod_03_1.doe, of this chapter, which you can open and modify.)

3.1   Make multiple replications by just asking for them in the Simulate module's main dialog. Look at the summary report and note how the performance measures vary across replications, confirming Table 2-4.

3.2   Implement the double-time arrival modification discussed in Section 2.6.3 by opening the Arrive module and changing the 5.0 to 2.5 in the argument of the EXPO function in the Time Between box (don't forget to click OK, rather than Cancel, if you want this change to happen). Rerun the model and compare it with what we got in the hand simulation (see Figure 2-3).

3.3   Lengthen the run beyond 15 minutes to 12 hours (= 720 minutes), for example, for a more interesting show. If you want the plots to be complete, you'll have to open them and extend the Time Range, as well as possibly the Maximum value for the y axis in the Number in Queue plot. You should also increase # History Points in the Number in Queue Plot.

3.4   Implement the change in Exercise 2.4 from Chapter 2. Double-click on the Server module, click in the Process Time box, and append a "+2" to the expression appearing there (then click OK). Run the model and check your hand-simulation results. Try running this for 24 hours (= 1,440 minutes—double-click on the Simulate module and put in 1440 for Length of Replication) and watch the queue-length plot (double-click inside the plot and change the Time Range to 1440; also click the Edit button to the right of the Expressions area and change the Maximum to 60). To allow more room in the queue animation, click on the line for the queue and drag its left end to the left; reduce the size of the entity picture by double-clicking on it above the Simulate module and reducing its Size Factor. What's happening? Why?

3.5   Modify the Simple Processing model of this chapter with all of the following changes:

- Add a second machine to which all parts go immediately after exiting the first machine for a separate kind of processing (e.g., the first machine is cutting and the second machine is cleaning). Processing times at the second machine are the same as for the first machine. Gather all the statistics as before, plus the time in queue, queue length, and utilization at the second machine.

- Immediately after the second machine, there's a pass/fail inspection that takes a constant 5 minutes to determine and has a 20% chance of failure. All parts exit the system regardless of whether they pass the test. Count the number that fail and the number that pass, and gather statistics on the time in queue, queue length, and utilization at the inspection station. (Hint: Try the Inspect module.)

- Add plots to track the queue length and number busy at all three stations.

- Run the simulation for 480 minutes instead of 15 minutes.

Working with Arena

CHAPTER 4

Working with Arena

This chapter covers the basics of interacting with and using Arena. In Chapter 3, we took you through some of the mechanics of getting into Arena, loading a ready-made model, running it, viewing the results, making a few modifications, and getting out. If you haven't read Chapter 3, please do so before reading on since we assume in this chapter that you're familiar with these mechanics.

Arena is a true Microsoft® Windows® 95 and Windows NT® application, so the basic look and feel, as well as a lot of the way things work, will already be familiar to you. (We assume you know your way around the Windows® operating system; if you don't, this would be a good time for you to take a break and go through a tutorial on it.) In addition, Arena is fully compatible with other Windows software, like word processors, spread-sheets, and CAD packages, so you can easily move things back and forth.

We'll start out in Section 4.1 with the fundamentals of Arena's user interface. Sections 4.2 and 4.3 introduce most of the pieces and capabilities of Arena, and Section 4.4 gets you into the extensive online help system. The model window, where you'll do the bulk of your work, is described in Section 4.5. Though Arena isn't intended to be a comprehensive drawing or CAD package, it does have most of the usual graphics tools, discussed in Section 4.6. If you want to print directly from Arena, Section 4.7 tells you how (even though you can use the standard Windows functions to copy all or pieces of the screen into other applications, like word processors, for later printing as part of a complete polished report). When it comes to running simulations, Section 4.8 discusses a lot of options and ways to control things. Finally, we'll walk you through the building of Model 3.1 (the simple processing system) in Section 4.9.

By the end of this chapter, you'll be able to work effectively with Arena to build simple models and maybe take a stab at doing some not-so-simple things as well by cruising the menus and dialogs on your own, with the help of the online help system. There are, however, some aspects of the interface that we won't cover here; refer to the help system for more complete details. While you can probably make some sense out of things by just reading this chapter, you'll be a lot better off if you follow along in Arena on your computer.

4.1 Basic Interaction

Since Arena is a true Microsoft Windows 95 and Windows NT application, you'll already know a lot about working with it. This includes working with toolbars, menus, and windows; entering and changing data in dialogs; clicking and double-clicking the mouse buttons to select, move, and resize objects; and a variety of other standard interactions involving mouse and keyboard use. Because many of Arena's operations can be launched via menu items, we'll use notation like "*M/S/C*" to mean "pull down the menu (*M*), select (*S*) from it, then select from the cascading (*C*) menu (if any)," etc. And by "Ctrl+whatever," we'll mean to hold down the Ctrl key and hit the "whatever" key (this will also apply for Alt+whatever and Shift+whatever). You will notice that we follow Windows 95 convention by presenting the "whatever" as a capital letter, but this is actually not a case-sensitive entry. It is acceptable to enter either a lowercase letter or a letter with Caps Lock on.

File operations work as usual. You can open a new model via *File/New* (or Ctrl+N or click the ⃞ button), and an existing model can be opened by *File/Open* (or Ctrl+O or 📂). If necessary, you can get to the right directory and disk with the customary disk/directory navigation dialog. Save your models via *File/Save* (or Ctrl+S or 💾) or *File/Save As* (to change the name or location). You can print directly from Arena via *File/Print* or Ctrl+P or 🖨. Preview your print job with *File/Print Preview* or 🔍.

The familiar cut, copy, and paste operations work within Arena as well as between Arena and other applications. For instance, you might have several Arena model windows open at once, and you might want to copy some objects from one to another. Just select the objects with the mouse (Ctrl+click to extend the selection set, or drag a box across them if they're positioned close together), copy them to the Clipboard (*Edit/Copy* or Ctrl+C or 📋), switch to the other window, and paste them in (*Edit/Paste* or Ctrl+V or 📋). After selecting the paste operation, the mouse cursor changes to cross hairs that you click where you want the northwest corner of the selection. Or, you might have Arena running simultaneously with a spreadsheet in which there's a long number you want to put in an Arena dialog entry. Copy the number from the spreadsheet cell, switch to Arena (either via the Windows® Taskbar or by using Alt+Tab to cycle through the open applications), position the insertion cursor in the Arena dialog where you want the number, and Paste it in. If you're writing a report in a word processor and want to Paste in a "snapshot" of an Arena screen, go to Arena, press the PrtSc (Print Screen) key, switch over to your word-processing document, and Paste the shot where you want it; if you want just the active window (like a dialog you want to document), press Alt+PrtSc instead, then Paste it into the word-processing document.

A few miscellaneous points:

- In Arena's object-based drawing system, you first select an object (like a modeling module or some graphic element) and then operate on it (like double-clicking a module to get into a dialog or changing the color of the graphic).
- There are Undo (*Edit/Undo* or Ctrl+Z or ↶) and Redo (*Edit/Redo* or Ctrl+Y or ↷) operations for changing object characteristics.
- One handy operation in Arena involves the right (secondary) mouse button—clicking it repeats the most recent mouse operation (like placing a module in your model, of which you may need multiple instances), bails you out of the current function, or terminates some functions like drawing polylines.
- When drawing, holding down the Shift key while moving the mouse constrains the action depending on the object—lines are forced to lie on horizontal, vertical, or 45° angles; rectangles must be boxes; and ellipses must be circles.

- If you have several Arena windows open and are unable to view them all at the same time, you can cycle among them via Ctrl+Tab.
- Ctrl+D or hitting the Ins key duplicates whatever is selected into the same model window. You'll then probably want to drag it somewhere else and do something to it.

4.2 Menus

In this section, we'll give you a quick tour of the main menus. We won't get into much detail here, but will use a lot of these menus and entries in later chapters (complete information is available in the online help system).

When you start Arena, the File, View, Tools, and Help menus are available. With a model window open, the Edit, Arrange, Module, Run and Window menus are added. Each menu item has under it various actions and capabilities grouped together in a logical way. As usual, a menu entry can be selected by clicking (once) on the menu name, then again on the entry you want; alternatively, you can hold down the left mouse button on the menu name, drag down to the entry you want, then let go of the mouse button.

A lot of the menu items are standard functions for Windows. Therefore, we'll concentrate on the Arena-specific things below, and will go into them in more detail as we describe how to build and work with models. We're also showing the menus as they appear with a model window open; some of them are shorter if you don't have a model open. Some menu entries have a keyboard shortcut that you can invoke at any time (even if the menu isn't pulled down), which appears on the right edge of each menu. Also, many menu entries can be invoked alternatively when the menu is pulled down by typing the underlined character in the menu entry.

File menu. This is where you create new Arena model files, open existing ones, close windows, save your models or create a view-only model. You can also import CAD drawings from AutoCAD® (and from other CAD programs in standard DXF format) for use as Arena "backdrops" and, in some cases, active elements (like paths for wire-guided vehicles) to allow you to use existing detailed drawings of facilities. If you change the colors Arena uses (see Section 4.3), you can save them as a color palette (you can do some of this with the Windows® operating system as well); you can also open previously saved color palettes. The Arena printing functions are accessible from this menu. The Send command allows you to send mail from within Arena and attaches any active model to your message. Like many Windows applications, Arena remembers the most recent documents, and you can open them quickly. The Exit command is one of the ways to quit Arena.

Edit menu. Here you'll find the usual options as applied to objects in Arena models. You can Undo previous actions or Redo your Undos. You can Cut or Copy a selected object (or group of objects) to the clipboard for placement elsewhere in the current model, to other models, or in some cases, to other applications.

Paste allows you to insert the clipboard contents into a model, and Paste Link creates an OLE link to the source document that's currently in the clipboard. Duplicate makes a copy of what's selected and places it nearby in the current model, and Delete permanently removes whatever you selected. You can Select All objects in a model as well as Deselect All. Arena's Find function searches all modules and animation objects in the active model for a text string with the usual control over whole-word searches and case sensitivity. You can display additional object Properties, such as its unique object tag. If you have links in your model to other files, such as a spreadsheet or sound file, Links tells you about them and allows you to modify them. Insert New Object lets you make placements from other applications, like graphics and multimedia. Object lets you edit something you've brought into the model from another application.

View menu. From this menu, you can control how your model appears on the screen, as well as which toolbars you want to display. Zooming lets you view the model from different "altitudes" so you can see the big picture or smaller sections in more detail. The Zoom Factor allows you to set how much you zoom in or out each time. Views (whose cascading menu is shown) offers certain "canned" views of your model; and Named Views lets you define, change, and use your own views. Grid and Snap are useful if you want to line things up geographically. Layers lets you control what kinds of objects show up during the edit or runtime mode. Toolbars is one way you can designate which sets of buttons are displayed on your screen (see Section 4.3), and the Status Bar entry lets you decide whether you want to see the horizontal bar at the very bottom of the screen that tells you what's going on and indicates the "world coordinates" of the mouse cursor in the Arena workspace.

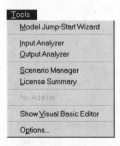

Tools menu. Arena comes not only with the modeling capability, but also a suite of related tools. The Model Jump-Start Wizard constructs a basic Arena model based on a few inputs; it helps you launch a new project quickly. The Input Analyzer fits probability distributions to observed data for specifying model inputs, and the Output Analyzer helps you with a proper statistical analysis of your simulation's results. The Scenario Manager lets you run a batch of simulations, which might represent different model configurations you want to compare so you may analyze them later. The License Summary item gives you information about commercial Arena product options that have been installed. The next item, shown here as

"No Add-Ins," lists executable programs that have been installed in your Add-Ins folder. These are utility programs, such as ones to automate performing a task in Arena. (Your menu may have one or more entries in this region, listing the add-ins that have been installed on your machine.) Show Visual Basic Editor opens a window in which you can write Visual Basic code to accompany your model; see Chapter 10 for more information about this option. Finally, the Options item lets you change and customize a lot of how Arena works and looks to suit your needs (or tastes).

Arrange menu. The items here pertain to the position of modeling modules and graphics; only the first two and last two items can be applied to modeling modules. Bring to Front and Send to Back position the selected object(s) on the top and bottom, respectively, of a "stack" of objects that may overlap. Group and Ungroup, respectively, put together and subsequently take apart objects logically, without affecting their physical appearance; Grouping is useful if you want to move or copy a complex picture built from a lot of individual objects. The Flip entries invert the selected object(s) around a line in the indicated direction, and Rotate spins the selection clockwise 90°. Snap to Grid forces the selection to align to the underlying grid of points, and Change Snap Point lets you alter the exact point on the selected object that gets snapped.

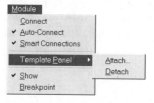

Module menu. These items relate to the model's logic modules and the templates from which they come. Connect changes the cursor to cross hairs and lets you establish graphically a connection between modules for entities to follow. Auto-Connect is a toggle that allows you automatically to connect a newly placed module to one that's already selected. Smart Connections causes newly added connections to be drawn in three horizontal/vertical segments instead of one (possibly diagonal) line. Template Panel lets you Attach a collection of modeling constructs to the Template toolbar and to Detach such a collection that's no longer needed. The Show toggle determines whether the module's name appears on the screen or just its animation. A module can be Breakpointed to interrupt the simulation when an entity reaches it—useful for debugging purposes.

Run menu. This contains entries for running the simulation, checking it, and pausing or stepping through it slowly for debugging or illustration. It also provides several alternative ways to watch the execution, to view its results (or errors), and to set up and control how the run goes and is displayed on your screen. We'll describe these capabilities further in Section 4.8.

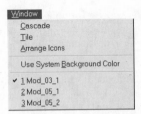

Window menu. If you have several models open at once, you can arrange them physically in an overlapping Cascade, or in a non-overlapping Tile arrangement. If you have several models minimized (via the ▬ button in each window), select Arrange Icons to organize them. The Use System Background Color entry causes this model to use whatever background color is selected at the Windows® operating system level rather than what is set internal to Arena; to return your model to Arena's internal color, select this item again. (This menu item changes/toggles between "System" and "Custom" each time you select it.) Finally, you can activate an open model by selecting it at the bottom of the menu.

Help menu. This is one of several ways to access Arena's online Help system (see Section 4.4 for more help on Help). If you select Arena Help Topics, you'll get to the Table of Contents, an Index, and a Find utility for getting to the topic you want. Using Help describes how to use the Windows® operating systems help in general. The modeling panels you have attached to the Template toolbar are then listed, and selecting one of them gets you directly into Help for that panel. Introduction, Tip of the Day, and About Arena each bring up the original Welcome screen (the only difference between them is which tab is selected for display), from which you can get to various help and information, such as the Quick Preview on getting started, the SMARTs library of little models that illustrate particular modeling capabilities, full-scale Example Models, vendor contact information, the "Tip of the Day," and the version number for your software.

4.3 Toolbars

Arena has several *Toolbars* with groups of buttons and pull-down menus to facilitate quick access to common activities. Some of these buttons are just faster ways to get at menu items (discussed above), and some represent the only way to do something.

You don't have to display all the toolbars if you don't need some of them for particular stages of model building or execution. *View/Toolbars* (or clicking the right mouse button in a toolbar area) gives you a list of check boxes to decide; note that the Standard and View toolbars can be combined into a merged "Standard View" toolbar. You can also decide where on your screen you want a displayed toolbar to show up by "tearing it off" and putting it someplace else—drag the toolbar around by clicking on an area in it that's not part of a button. If you drop it in the interior of your screen, its title shows up and it's technically called a "palette." If you drop it near an edge of the screen, it automatically "docks" to that edge and loses its title. There's a handy feature to docking/undocking that you might occasionally find useful. You can float toolbars near the window's edge (without having them dock) if you hold the Ctrl key while undocking the toolbars. In addition, you can customize how toolbars are displayed, etc., by choosing *Tools/Options* and selecting the Toolbars tab. You won't have to set your toolbar configuration every time you use Arena as it will remember your last configuration. You can also have different configurations for when you're editing your model, when the simulation is running, and when various other Arena window types are active (such as the Picture Editor), and again, Arena will remember what each was.

We'll mention each toolbar in turn.

- Here's the *Standard* toolbar:

It starts with buttons to create a New model, Open an existing one, and Save the active model, as on the File menu; also from that menu are buttons to Print and do a Print Preview. From the Edit menu are Cut, Copy, and Paste, as well as Undo and Redo. The Standard toolbar ends with the context-sensitive Help button ▶?; to see how it works, click on it (note the **?** that gets added to the mouse cursor), then click on a toolbar button somewhere else on the screen or select something from a menu to learn about it.

- The *View* toolbar has buttons that are identical to selections from the View menu:

From here you can Zoom In and Out or choose views for All the model, the Previous view, or Select a specific region for viewing. To select a region, click on ⋒. The mouse cursor changes to cross hairs that you position, click, and then drag to define a box for the screen-size view. There are also buttons to reveal the Grid and to Snap new objects to it and for deciding what Layers (different kinds of objects) you want to display.

- The *Arrange* toolbar has most of the Arrange menu and one item from the Module menu:

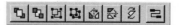

You can Bring a selected object to the Front or Send it to the Back. A selection of multiple drawing objects (but not modeling modules—Ctrl+click to do so) can be made into a logical Group or be Ungrouped later. Drawing objects can also be Flipped around a Vertical or Horizontal line on their midpoint or Rotated clockwise 90°. Finally, the Connect button from the Module menu lets you establish connections between modeling modules for entities to follow.

- Buttons on the *Draw* toolbar have no corresponding menu options, so drawing can be done only by toolbar access:

This is how you can draw static Lines, Polylines, Arcs of ellipse boundaries, Bézier curves, Boxes, Polygons, and Ellipses to dress up your model, as well as add Text to annotate it. You've probably used draw features in other applications, so Arena's capabilities will be familiar. By far, the best way to familiarize yourself with these things is to open up a "test" model window and just try them out; see Section 4.6 for more on drawing.

■ The *Color* toolbar (shown at the left) lets you control the color of parts of drawing and animation objects, text, and the model window background. Use the pull-down menu at the top to select what it is whose color is to be controlled—a Line (or edge of a solid), the Fill of a solid, the Text, or the background Window of the active model. To change the color, select the object, select the appropriate entry from this pull-down menu, then click on the color you want from among the 16 shown. You can change the set of colors available by *File/Open Color Palette* and selecting from one of several available palettes. You can alter any of the 16 colors on a palette by double-clicking on it on the Color toolbar, which brings up a *color cube* allowing you to fine-tune the color (click In and Out to navigate through the 3-D cube) or change it altogether. If you develop a palette of colors you'd like to save for other models, you can do so by *File/Save Color Palette*. You can also increase or decrease the number of available colors using the toolbars section of *Tools/Options*.

■ The *Animate* toolbar (shown at the left) contains capabilities to allow you to animate your model or enhance the animation that is inherent in some Arena modules. Typically, click on one of these buttons, enter a dialog to describe exactly what you want, then place the animation in your model. There are a lot of different capabilities here, and we'll illustrate most of them as we progress through building models in later chapters.

■ The *Template* toolbar (not shown) contains the modeling constructs for Arena, organized into *panels* (like Common, Support, etc.). To use a construct, called a *module*, select the tab of the panel you want, choose and click on a module, then place an instance of it in your model window using the cross hairs for positioning. These activities are really the basics of modeling with Arena, so we'll be showing you a lot of this as we go along.

■ The *Run* toolbar contains buttons in the style of tape players that correspond to the Go, Step, Fast-Forward, Pause, Start Over, and End entries from the Run menu:

We'll describe these capabilities in Section 4.8.

■ The *Run Interaction* toolbar has buttons corresponding to the Check Model, Command, Break, Trace, Watch, and Report entries from the Run menu (see Section 4.8 for more):

The last two buttons correspond to Show and Breakpoint from the Module menu.

■ The *Integration* toolbar contains buttons related to Arena's Module Data Transfer wizard and VBA (the Visual Basic Editor and VBA Design Mode button).

4.4 Help

Arena has an extensive and comprehensive online Help system to serve as a reference, guide you through various operations, and supply examples of modeling facets as well as complete projects. The Help system is carefully integrated and provides extensive hyperlinks to other areas to aid you in getting the information you need quickly and easily. There are several different ways to access the Help system, which we'll describe briefly in this section. However, you may find that the best way to learn about Help is just to get in and start exploring.

When you first start Arena, you see a *Welcome* screen that itself shows some Help items; this screen is also available at any time via *Help/Introduction*. The Welcome screen is divided into three different "tabs" along the bottom: Introduction, Tip of the Day, and About.

- The *Introduction* tab provides hyperlinks to a Quick Preview tutorial of how to get started with modeling. There's also a link to the aforementioned Model Jump-Start Wizard. It also links to the *SMARTs Library*, an extensive, indexed collection of small models illustrating particular modeling capabilities, tools, and even a few shortcuts. The Example Models hyperlink points to a collection of larger, complete Arena models. Both the SMARTs library and the Example Models are actual models that you can load, run, and copy. (If you are using the Arena Academic version, you may find that you won't be able to run some of the larger examples, although you can load and copy from them.) To find out how to get in touch with Systems Modeling, click on the Contact Information link.

- The *Tip of the Day* tab shows one of a cycling collection of modeling and usage tips, which will show up every time you start Arena (until you turn it off). At some point, you may promote yourself to "expert tips." Some tips contain hyperlinks to additional information.

- The *About* tab gives you information about your version of the software.

At any time, you can pull down the *Help menu* for access to the full Help system. The Arena Help Topics item gets you into a complete set of Contents, Index, and Find functions where you can quickly get the information you need. You can also get help directly on whatever modeling templates you have attached to your model, as well as the elements of the Welcome screen described above.

The ▶? button invokes Arena's *context-sensitive help*. To use it, just click on the button, then move the mouse and click on whatever you're curious about—it could be a toolbar button, an entry from a menu, or a module on a panel. In this way, you can get to the information you need via a visual path.

Most Arena dialogs have a *Help button* that you can push. This is a good way to get direct information on what that part of the software is about, what your options are, how relevant things are defined, related concepts (via hyperlinks to other parts of the Help system), and examples. You can also use the **?** button at the top of the dialog to access *What's This?* help information on individual items in a dialog. Simply click on the **?** and then click on the selected item.

In case you forget what a particular button does, you can let your mouse cursor stay motionless on it for a second or two; a little boxed *Tool tip* will appear to remind you what it is.

4.5 Model Windows

A model is built, edited, and run in a *model window*.

You can have several models open at once, just as you can have several documents open at once in a word processing program. Switch between them by just clicking in them (if the one you want is visible), or use the window menu to select from the entire list. If you have a lot of models open, you can cycle among them via Ctrl+Tab, or you might want to minimize some of them to icons on your screen with the - button in each one. The Window menu also has options (Cascade, Tile, etc.) for how you'd like to arrange the open models or their minimized icons.

Create a new (blank) model window via *File/New* (or Ctrl+N or ▭), save the active model window via *File/Save* (or Ctrl+S or 🖫) or *File/Save As,* and open a previously saved model window via *File/Open* (or Ctrl+O or 🖝). Resizing and repositioning a model window works just like any Windows® operating system application.

A model window typically shows just a portion of the (large) available underlying *world*, which has (x, y) coordinates called *world units* (the coordinates of the mouse cursor show up on the Status Bar along the bottom of your screen). To see different parts of the world, you can pan around using the arrow keys or scroll bars; the "altitude" from which you view the model can be altered with the zoom capabilities (+ or – keys, View menu selection, or View toolbar buttons). There are also some "canned" views (particular pan/zoom settings) available on the View menu and toolbar, and you can define your own (and name them) via *View/Named Views* (or the **?** key).

To add a modeling construct to a model window, select the panel containing the construct you want with the appropriate tab on the Template toolbar, click on the module you want, then place it where you want it in the model window by clicking once (the mouse cursor turns to cross hairs for this placement). You'll then probably want to double-click on this module to open its dialog(s) to configure it to this instance of its use. To add drawing objects, just click on what you want from the Draw toolbar and place the item. Similarly, animation objects are selected from the Animate panel and placed in the model window.

4.6 Drawing

The Draw toolbar, mentioned in Section 4.3, has a variety of shapes, text tools, and control features to allow you to enhance the model by placing static (no participation in the simulation or animation) objects in the model window to help document things or to make the animation seem more "real" by adding walls, aisles, potted plants, etc. This isn't intended to be a complete, full-featured CAD or artwork capability, but it usually proves adequate; of course, you can always paste in graphics from other packages. Arena's drawing tools work a lot like other drawing packages, so we'll just point out what's there and let you play with things to get used to them:

- *Line*, \ : Click once on this button, changing the mouse cursor to cross hairs, then click where you want the line to start and again where you want it to end. To constrain the line to be vertical or horizontal or on a 45° angle, hold down the Shift key while moving to the end of the line.

- *Polyline*, ⤸: This lets you draw a jagged line with an unlimited number of points. After selecting this button, click where you want to start and then again for each new point. Click the right mouse button after you've placed the endpoint. Hold down the Shift key during a segment to constrain it to vertical, horizontal, or 45°.

- *Arc*, ⌒: You can draw part of the border of an ellipse with this tool. Click first for the center of the ellipse, then move the mouse and follow the wire frame, clicking again when it's the size and shape you want. At this point, the mouse cursor becomes the end of a line emanating from the ellipse's center; click to define one end of the arc, then again for the other end. To edit the arc later, select it and use the lines to change what part of the arc is shown and use the disconnected handle to change the ellipse size or shape.

- *Bézier curve*, ∂: These have become popular due to their ability to assume a lot of different shapes yet maintain their smoothness and inherent beauty. Click for one endpoint, then make intermediate clicks (up to 30) for the interior "attractor" points; click the right mouse button after placing what you want to be the other endpoint. Holding down the Shift key while moving to the next point causes the (invisible) lines connecting them to be horizontal, vertical, or at 45°. To change the curvature, select the curve and drag the interior attractor points around; dragging the endpoints anchors the curve to different places.

- *Box*, ☐: Click first for one corner, then again for the opposite corner. Hold down the shift key to constrain it to a square. This object, like the next two, has a border regarded as a "line" for width and color, as well as a "fill" for color or pattern choices.

- *Polygon*, ⊿: Click for the first point, then for the others; after clicking the point you want to connect back to the first one, click the right mouse button. Hold down the Shift key to force line segments to be horizontal, vertical, or at 45°. This object has line and fill like a box.

- *Ellipse*, ◔: First click for the center, move the mouse and follow the wire frame to the size and shape you want, and finally click again. Hold the Shift key to force it to a circle. This object has line and fill like a box.

- *Text*, A: This is how you add annotation to your model to label things or provide documentation. Clicking the button brings up a dialog where you type in your text; use Ctrl+Enter to go to a new line and Ctrl+Tab for a tab. The Font button lets you change the font, style, and size. Closing this dialog changes the mouse cursor to cross hairs, which you click where you want to position the northwest corner of your text. Use the underline to move, resize, or reorient the text to a different angle (hold the Shift key to constrain the angle to horizontal, vertical, or 45°).

- *Visible* and *Hidden Object Settings*, ⬛ ▨: This pair of buttons toggles between whether a drawing object is *Visible* or *Hidden* when in run mode. If the Visible button is selected, whatever you draw will be visible while in run mode. You can change an object from Visible to Hidden by selecting it and pushing the Hidden button (and the reverse). *View/Layers* allows you to hide even Visible objects during a run.

After placing an object, you can change its position, size, orientation, etc., by selecting it and dragging borders, corners, control points, or handles. You can also alter effects like the width or dash pattern of lines or borders, fill patterns of solids, and colors by selecting the object(s) and then choosing what you want from the pull-down menus for Line Widths/Styles ([— ▾]), Fill Patterns ([■ ▾]), and the Color toolbar. To set these things for all future objects, select them without having any draw objects selected; Arena will remember these settings not only for future drawing objects in this window, but also for new windows and future Arena sessions as well.

4.7 Printing

All or parts of a model window can be printed directly from Arena (in color, if you have it). The three print-related entries on the File menu let you Preview (or 🔍) what's coming, Print it (or 🖨 or Ctrl+P), or do a Setup of your printer. If your model is big, the print will extend across several pages. And if you have Named Views, you'll get a print of the current view, followed by a separate print of each named view. If you don't want all this, use Print Preview to see what's on which page, then selectively print only the pages you want.

4.8 Running

Usually you'll just want to run your model to completion as you have it set up, but there are times when you might like to control how the run is done. Entries from the Run menu, as well as corresponding buttons from the Run and Run Interaction toolbars, let you do this. (See Section 8.11 for details and examples of using many of these capabilities.)

- *Go* from the Run menu (or ▶ from the Run toolbar or the F5 function key) just does it (or resumes it after a Pause). If you've made changes to the model since the last Check (see below), it gets Checked before it's run.

- *Step* (or ▶I or F10) executes the model one action at a time so you can see in detail what's going on. This gets really boring so is useful primarily as a debugging or demonstration tool. As with the *Go* button, use of *Step* causes the model to be Checked if Arena detects changes since the last Check was performed.

- *Fast-Forward* (or ▶▶) disables the animation and executes the run at a much faster rate. You can pause at any time during the run to view the animation. As with the *Go* button, use of *Fast-Forward* causes the model to be Checked if Arena detects changes since the last Check was performed.

- *Pause* (or ❚❚ or Esc) interrupts the run so you can look at something. Hit ▶, ▶I , or ▶▶ to resume it.

- *Start Over* (or I◀ or Shift+F5) goes back to the beginning and reruns the model. As with the *Go* button, use of *Start Over* causes the model to be Checked if Arena detects changes since the last Check was performed.

- While Arena is running your model, it's in what's called *run mode*, and most of the model-building tools are disabled. So when the run is over, you need to select *End* (or ■ or Alt+F5) to get out of run mode and enable the modeling tools again.

▪ Use *Check Model* (or ✔ or F4) to "compile" your model without running it. If Arena detects errors at this stage, you're told about them (gently, of course) in an Errors/ Warnings window; the buttons at the bottom of this window help you Find the problem (e.g., by getting the offending module selected in the Model window).

▪ *Review Errors* recalls the most recent Errors/Warning window containing whatever Arena found wrong during the check.

▪ *View Results* shows the summary output of the current or most recent run. If you want, you can generate, View, and Write to files exactly how Arena translated your model into the underlying SIMAN simulation language with the *SIMAN* cascading menu.

▪ *Command* (or ▣) gets you to an interactive command line window that allows control over a lot of how the run is done—like interrupts and altering values. Use of *Command* also Checks the model, if required, and starts the run if it's not yet started.

▪ *Break* (or ✋) lets you set times or conditions to interrupt the model in order to check on or illustrate something.

▪ *Trace* (or ▤) generates a detailed history of many things going on in the simulation; this is used primarily for debugging. (It's no mistake that the icon on the button warns of a tall stack of output accumulating.)

▪ *Watch* (or ∞) establishes a window in which you can observe the value of a variable or expression as the run progresses. The *Run/Setup/Miscellaneous* tab lets you determine whether this is concurrent with the run or only when the Watch window is active.

▪ *Report* (or ▤) allows you to see the numerical status of something during the simulation, after you Pause it.

▪ *Setup* gives you access to several options for how runs are made for the current active models, like deciding whether to see the animation and perhaps running in full-screen mode. This overrides any global preferences specified in *Tools/Options*.

▪ *Speed* (shown in Section 4.2 with its menu cascaded) lets you control how fast the animation goes. (The keyboard equivalents > and < are probably more useful during the run than getting at this via the menu or toolbar.)

4.9 Building the Simple Processing Model

In this section, we'll lead you through the construction of Model 3.1.

Open a new model window by *File/New* (or 🗋 or Ctrl+N), which will automatically be given the default name Model1 (with the default extension .doe when you save it). You can change this name when you decide to save the contents of the window. Subsequent new model windows will get the default names Model2, Model3, etc. You might want to maximize your new model window by clicking ▣ near its northeast corner.

Next, attach the panel(s) required to build your model if they're not already there (you can tell Arena to attach certain panels automatically to the Template toolbar via the Toolbars tab in *Tools/Options*). For this model, we only need the Common panel, which you can attach by clicking on the Attach panel tab in the Templates toolbar. This opens the Attach Template Panel dialog in Figure 4-1, where you open the Common panel (click on it, then hit the Open button, or just double-click on it).

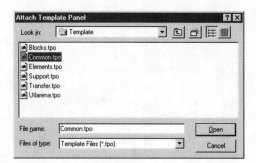

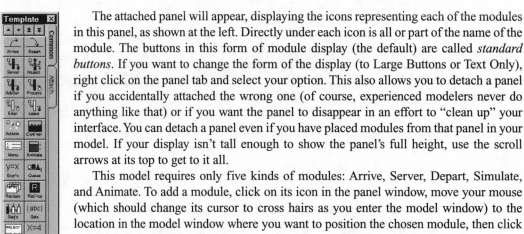

Figure 4-1. The Attach Template Panel Dialog

The attached panel will appear, displaying the icons representing each of the modules in this panel, as shown at the left. Directly under each icon is all or part of the name of the module. The buttons in this form of module display (the default) are called *standard buttons*. If you want to change the form of the display (to Large Buttons or Text Only), right click on the panel tab and select your option. This also allows you to detach a panel if you accidentally attached the wrong one (of course, experienced modelers never do anything like that) or if you want the panel to disappear in an effort to "clean up" your interface. You can detach a panel even if you have placed modules from that panel in your model. If your display isn't tall enough to show the panel's full height, use the scroll arrows at its top to get to it all.

This model requires only five kinds of modules: Arrive, Server, Depart, Simulate, and Animate. To add a module, click on its icon in the panel window, move your mouse (which should change its cursor to cross hairs as you enter the model window) to the location in the model window where you want to position the chosen module, then click to "drop" it there. This places an instance of the module in the workspace.

The placed module will always consist of at least a *module handle*, the box that contains the module name. In many cases, the module will also include animation features or a default name. The animation features will normally appear above the module handle, and default names will normally be below. For example, when you place the Arrive module, it includes an animation feature called a *station marker* (the rectangle with the rounded end) and a default name, as is shown below at the left.

When you add your own data to a module, you can change both the animation features as well as the name. Add data to a module by double-clicking on its handle to "open it up." This causes the dialog for that module to open, as in Figure 4-2.

For the Arrive module of our simple processing system, we specified several pieces of data. We first changed the Station name in the Enter Data area from the default, Arrive 1, to `In Door`, and we entered `EXPO(5.0)` in the Arrival Data area for the Time Between arrivals. You could click the cursor on the correct field and type in the entry, or you could click on the down arrow and select "EXPO(Mean)" from the list and then re-place the text string "Mean" with 5. When entering something that takes the form of a distribution, always enter the first four letters of the distribution followed by an open parenthesis "(", the parameters of the distribution separated by commas, and finally a close parenthesis ")". When in doubt, click on the down arrow, select the proper distribution, and then replace the text string(s) with the parameter value(s) you want. In the Arrival Data area, Mark Time Attribute portion of the dialog, we also entered an attribute called `Time of Arrival`. Finally, we clicked on the Connect button in the Leave Data area. After accepting the entered data by clicking OK, notice that the module view changed as shown. The handle remained the same, but the default name changed to In Door, and the station marker disappeared. Hopefully, the reasons for these changes will become apparent as you learn more about Arena.

Arrive
Arrive 1

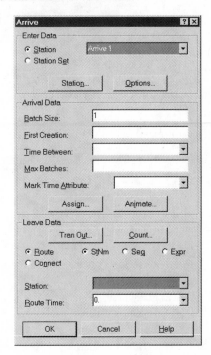

Figure 4-2. The Arrive Dialog

As we introduce new modules and new concepts, we'll try to lead you through each dialog. Even though the Arrive module is fairly simple and we only used a few of its options, the above description was fairly lengthy. To convey this in a more efficient and orderly fashion, we'll use a set of visuals, called *Displays*, as shown in Display 4-1. Note that there are three parts to this display. The top right portion has the filled-in dialog. In some cases, it may show several related dialogs. The top left shows the module with which the dialog is associated. Later, this portion may also show buttons we clicked to get the dialog(s) shown. The bottom portion of the display is a table showing the actions required to complete the dialog(s). The left column of the table defines the dialog prompts, and the right column contains the entered data or action (italics). In general, we'll try to provide the complete display when we introduce a new module or a new secondary dialog of a module we've already covered. For modules we've already covered, we'll normally give you only the table at the bottom of the display, which should allow you to create easily all of the models we develop.

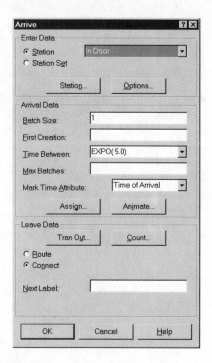

Enter Data	
Station	In Door
Arrival Data	
Time Between	EXPO(5.0)
Mark Time Attribute	Time of Arrival
Leave Data	
Connect	*select*

Display 4-1. Completed Arrive Module

This might be a good time to save your model; choose a name different from ours (which was Mod_03_1.doe), or put it in a different folder.

Next, place a Server module in your model and edit it according to Display 4-2. Connect the Arrive module to it, either by explicit use of the Connect tool or select the Arrive module before clicking on the Server button in the Common panel and placing the module in the model window. You also might want to make the area for the queue animation longer; click on the queue (the ⊣), then drag its left end back to the left (hold down the Shift key to constrain its angle, just like drawing a line).

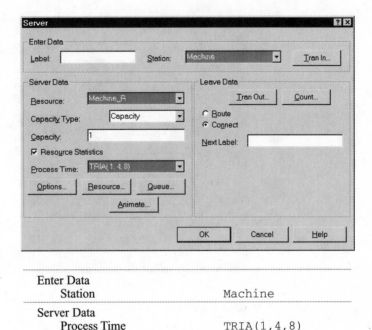

Enter Data	
Station	Machine
Server Data	
Process Time	TRIA(1,4,8)
Leave Data	
Connect	*select*

Display 4-2. Completed Server Module

The final logic module is the Depart; drop one in your window, and get the incoming connection from the Server you just finished. Display 4-3 shows how to edit your Depart module. Note that, in the Tally area, you can't see the Tally name, Type of Statistics, or Attribute fields until you select the Individual Tally button (since they wouldn't make sense otherwise). Also, the Attribute Time of Arrival is available in the pull-down menu for this field since it was defined earlier (in the Arrive module); in this way, you don't have remember all the Attribute names or take a chance on mistyping them when you need them.

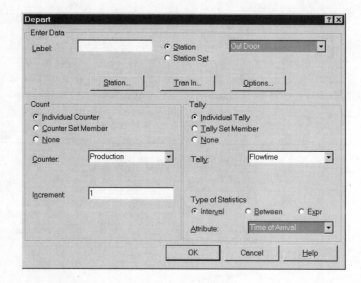

Enter Data	
Station	Out Door
Count	
Individual Counter	*select*
Counter	Production
Tally	
Individual Tally	*select*
Tally	Flowtime
Attribute	Time of Arrival

Display 4-3. Completed Depart Module

Now, drop in a Simulate model. Fill it in as indicated in Display 4-4. Note that there are a lot of other options here, which you can explore with the Help system or by trying them. Leaving the Date field blank defaults the date to whatever your computer thinks the date is.

To add the plots, place two separate instances of the Animate module. You could also get these plots via the Plot button (📈) on the Animate toolbar, but this way is a bit easier since you get a menu of things you're likely to want to plot, and the dialog knows about names that Arena uses as well as those you've defined. We won't bore you (further) with the complete Displays for these since they're really quite straightforward. Look back at Figure 3-7 for how to fill out the Animate dialog and Figure 3-8 for the resulting Plot dialog, both for the queue-length plot; doing the number-busy plot is similar except that you choose Resource for Machine_R as the Data Object and Number Busy as the Information to plot. Note that the Animate dialog defaults to displaying the information as *all* of Variable, Level, Histogram, and Plot so you need to clear boxes for whatever you *don't* want to see (all we wanted was the Plot).

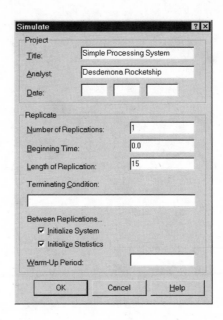

Project	
Title	Simple Processing System
Analyst	Desdemona Rocketship
Replicate	
Length of Replication	15

Display 4-4. Completed Simulate Module

To set up a Named View for your model, first pan and zoom to the scene you want to remember, then *View/Named Views* (or type **?**), hit the Add button, then pick a name and hot key (case-sensitive). If you want to change this view's definition later, hit the Edit button instead; to delete it from the list, hit the Delete button. Like panning and zooming, you can invoke a Named View anytime, even during a run. At first blush, setting up Named Views might seem like a frill, but trust us—you'll want some of these when your models grow.

Finally, there are four text annotations on the model, which you make with the Text tool (**A**) from the Draw toolbar. As for the tasteful backdrops for the model title in the upper left, draw a couple of boxes, color them, drag them around, and get them layered properly vis-à-vis the text and each other with 🔲 and 🔲 from the Arrange toolbar.

Modeling Basic Operations and Inputs

CHAPTER 5

Modeling Basic Operations and Inputs

In Chapters 2 and 3, we introduced you to a simple processing system (Model 3.1), conducted a hand simulation (Chapter 2), and examined an Arena model (Chapter 3). In this chapter, we'll embellish this simple system to represent a more realistic environment and develop a complete model of that system, including specification of the input probability distributions.

Section 5.1 describes this more complicated system—a sealed electronic assembly and test system. We then discuss how to develop a modeling approach, introduce several new Arena concepts, build the model, and show you how to run it and view the results. By this time, you should start to become dangerous in your modeling skills. In Section 5.2, we'll enhance the model by introducing new concepts and give you alternate methods for studying the results. Section 5.3 shows you how to dress up the animation a little bit. In Section 5.4, we'll take up the issue of how you specify quantitative inputs, including probability distributions from which observations on random variables are "generated," to drive your simulation. When you finish this chapter, you should be able to build some reasonably elaborate models of your own, as well as specify appropriate and realistic distributions as input to your models.

5.1 Model 5.1: An Electronic Assembly and Test System

This system represents the final operations of the production of two different sealed electronic units, Figure 5-1. The arriving parts are cast metal cases for the units that have already been machined to accept the electronic parts.

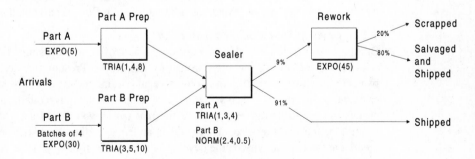

Figure 5-1. Electronic Assembly and Test System

The first units, named Part A, are produced in an adjacent department, outside the bounds of this model, with interarrival times to our model being exponentially distributed with a mean of 5 minutes. Upon arrival, they're transferred to the Part A Prep area, with a transit time of 2 minutes. At the Part A Prep area, the mating faces of the cases are machined to assure a good seal, and the part is then deburred and cleaned; the process time for the combined operation follows a triangular (1, 4, 8) distribution. The part is then transferred to the sealer, with a transit time of 2 minutes.

The second units, named Part B, are produced in a different building, outside this model's bounds, where they are held until a batch of four units is available; the batch is then sent to the final production area we are modeling. The time between the arrivals of successive batches of Part B to our model is exponential with a mean of 30 minutes. Upon arrival at the Part B Prep area, the batch is separated into the four units, which are processed individually. The processing at the Part B Prep area has the same three steps as at the Part A Prep area, except that the process time for the combined operation follows a triangular (3, 5, 10) distribution. The part is then sent to the sealer, with a transit time of 2 minutes.

At the sealer operation, the electronic components are inserted, the case is assembled and sealed, and the sealed unit is tested. The total process time for these operations depends on the part type: triangular (1, 3, 4) for Part A and normal (2.4, 0.5) for Part B (2.4 is the mean and 0.5 is the standard deviation). Ninety-one percent of the parts pass the inspection and are transferred directly to the shipping department. The remaining parts are transferred to the rework area where the parts are disassembled, repaired, cleaned, assembled, and re-tested. Eighty percent of the parts here are salvaged and transferred to the shipping department as reworked parts. The remaining parts are transferred to the scrap area. The time to rework a part follows an exponential distribution with mean of 45 minutes and is independent of part type or part status, salvaged or scrapped. Assume all transfer times are 2 minutes.

We want to collect statistics in each area on resource utilization, number in queue, time in queue, and the cycle time (or flowtime) by shipped parts, salvaged parts, or scrapped parts. We will initially run the simulation for 2,000 minutes. Since we have part transfers between areas, we would also like to see that flow of parts on the animation.

5.1.1 Developing a Modeling Approach

Building a simulation model is only one component of a complete simulation project. We will discuss the entire simulation project in Chapter 12. Presume for now that the first two activities are to state the study objective and define the system to be studied. In this case, our objective is to teach you how to develop a simulation model using Arena. The system definition was given above. In the real world, you would have to develop that definition, and you may also have to collect and analyze the data to be used. We recommend that the next activity be the development of a modeling approach. For a real problem, this may require the definition of a data structure, the segmentation of the system into submodels, or the development of control logic. For this problem, it only requires that we decide which Arena modules will provide the capabilities we need to capture the operation of the system at an appropriate level of detail. In addition, we must decide how we're going to model the different processing times at the sealer operation. To simplify this task, let's separate the model into the following components: part arrival, prep areas, sealer operation, rework, part departure, part transfers, and part animation. Also, we'll assume that all entities in the system represent parts that are being processed.

Because we have two distinct streams of arriving entities to our model, each with its own timing pattern, we will use two separate Arrive modules (one for each part type) to generate the arriving parts. Each of the two prep areas will be modeled with its own Server module, very much like the Server module used in the simple processing system of Model 3.1. The sealer operation includes a process and an inspection that results in parts going to different places based on a "coin flip" (with just the right bias in the coin). The Inspect module provides this capability; it is basically a Server module with the pass or fail output being based on the coin flip. The rework area will be modeled with another Inspect module, as it also has a pass or fail option. The part departures will be modeled with three separate Depart modules (shipped, salvaged, and scrapped) so we can keep corresponding individual flowtime statistics.

To model the transit times between stations, we'll use the Route option in the Arrive, Server, and Inspect modules with a route time of 2 minutes in each case. We'll add a Simulate module to define the run length and the part animation picture. All of these modules can be found on the Common panel. Finally, we'll use the Route object from the Animate toolbar to show part movement within the system.

Because we have different processing times by part type at the sealer operation, we'll define an attribute called `Sealer Time` that will be assigned the appropriate sealer processing time when the parts are generated at the Arrive modules. This is easy to do for this problem since we are using a different Arrive module for each part. When the parts are processed at the sealer operation, we'll use the time contained in the `Sealer Time` attribute for the processing delay rather than generating them within the Server module itself.

5.1.2   Some New Arena Concepts: Stations, Transfers, and Pictures

In the first model, the flow of entities through the system was accomplished using the direct Connect option in the Leave Data portion of the Arrive and Server modules. When you select this option, it results in an entity's being sent immediately to the next module, according to the connection, with no time advance in the simulation. If we used the Connect option in this new model, it would result in the correct flow of parts; however, it wouldn't allow for the 2-minute transfer delay, and it wouldn't allow us to animate the part flow. In order to model the 2-minute transfer time and show the part movement, we need to understand three new Arena concepts: *Stations, Station Transfers*, and *Pictures*.

Arena approaches the modeling of systems by dividing them into locations called *Stations*. Stations may be thought of as a location at which some process occurs. In our example, stations will represent the locations for each of the part arrivals, operations, and part departures. Each station is assigned a unique name or identifier. These stations provide a means to model entity flow. Later we'll show you how stations can be used as a framework for control of the modeling effort and to make it more manageable.

Station Transfers allow us to send an entity from one station location to another without a direct connect. Arena provides several different types of station transfers that allow for positive transfer times, constrained movement using material handling devices, and flexible routings that depend on the entity type. The station transfer we'll use is called a *Route*, which allows the movement of entities from one station to another. Routes assume that time may be required for the movement between stations, but that no additional delay is incurred because of other constraints, such as blocked passageways or unavailable material handling equipment. The route time can be expressed as a constant, a sample from a distribution, or for that matter, any valid expression.

We often think of stations as representing a physical location in a system; however, there's no strict requirement that this is so, and in fact they can be used effectively to serve many other modeling objectives. Stepping back for a moment from their intended use in representing a system, let's examine what happens in Arena when an entity is transferred (e.g., routed) to a station. First, we'll look at the model logic—moving entities from module to module during the run. Underneath the hood, as we discovered (in painstaking detail) in Chapter 2, a simulation run is driven by the entities—creating them, moving them through logic, placing them on the event calendar when a time delay is to be incurred, and eventually destroying them. From this perspective, a station transfer (route) is simply another means of incurring a time delay. So when an entity leaves a module that specifies a Route as the transfer mechanism, Arena places the entity on the event calendar with an event time dictated by the route duration. Later, when it's the entity's turn to be removed from the event calendar, Arena returns the entity to the flow of model logic by finding the module that defines its destination station, such as a Server or Depart module. This is in slight contrast to the direct module connections we saw in Model 3.1, where the transfer of an entity from module to module occurred without placing the entity on the event calendar and was represented graphically in the model window. While the direct connections provide a flowchart-like look to a model, making it obvious how entities will move between modules, station transfers provide a great deal of power and flexibility in dispatching entities through a model, as we'll see when we study Sequences in Chapter 6.

Stations and station transfers also provide the driving force behind an important part of the model's animation—displaying the movement of entities among stations as the model run progresses. The stations themselves are represented in the model using station marker symbols, as we saw in the Arrive module from Section 4.9, which was accompanied by a station marker. These stations establish locations on the model's drawing where station transfers can be initiated or terminated. The movement of entities between the stations is defined by route path objects, which connect the stations to each other and establish the path of movement for entities that are routed between the stations. You'll soon see that the station markers accompany Arena modules that either define a station (for the ending station of a route path) or that allow transfer out of the module via a station transfer (for a route's beginning station). You can add more stations via the Station object from the Animate toolbar. Routes, on the other hand, don't accompany Arena modules; you add these by using the Route object from the Animate toolbar and drawing a polyline that establishes the graphical path entities should follow during their routes. When the simulation is running, what you'll see is entity pictures moving smoothly along these route paths. This begs the question: How does this relate to the underlying logic where we just learned that an entity resides on the event calendar during its route time delay? The answer is that Arena's animation "engine" coordinates with the underlying logic "engine"; in this case, the event calendar. When an entity encounters a route in the model logic and is placed on the event calendar, the animation shows the entity's picture moving between the stations on the route path. The two engines coordinate so that the timing of the entity finishing its animation movement on the route and being removed from the event calendar to continue through model logic coincide resulting in an animation display that is representative of the model logic at any snapshot in time.

While we're on the topic of animation, there's also the issue of how to establish the graphical picture that's to be used to represent the entity. Back in Chapter 3, you may have noticed that small, red boxes appeared next to the resource picture throughout the run. These were entity pictures, used to display the model's entities as they move among animation components. A default picture accompanies the Simulate module (the red box); you can change this and/or add new pictures to depict different types of entities or changes in a particular entity as it progresses through the model. You also can design your own graphics for the resource pictures on the animation. We'll discuss later in this chapter how these pictures can be changed.

5.1.3 Building the Model

To build the model, you need to open a new model window, attach the Common panel, and place the required modules on the screen: two Arrive, two Server, two Inspect, three Depart, and a Simulate module. In placing more than one module of the same type, you might want to use the right mouse button to activate the "repeat-last-function" operation. For example, select the Arrive module from the Common panel and place it on the screen. Now click the right mouse button to repeat the last function—in this case, placing an Arrive module. Your model window should now look something like Figure 5-2. At this point, you might want to use the *File/Save* function to save your model under a name of your choosing.

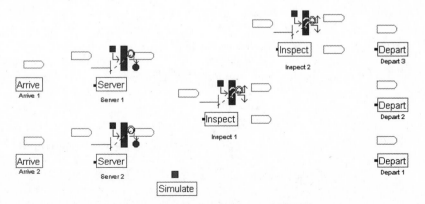

Figure 5-2. Model Window of Placed Modules

Now let's open each module and enter the information required to complete the model. Start with the Arrive 1 module that will create the arriving Part A's. Display 5-1 (the "Display" device was described in Section 4.9) provides the information required to complete this module. Note that this is very similar to the Arrive module used in Model 3.1. We've given the station a different name and accepted the default options for the Leave Data section, Route–StNm. This implies that created entities will be routed to the station named `Part A Prep` and that transfer will take 2 minutes.

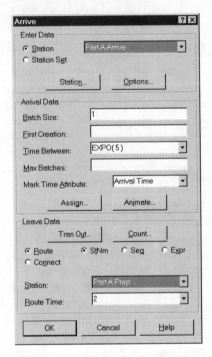

Enter Data	
Station	`Part A Arrive`
Arrival Data	
Time Between	`EXPO(5)`
Mark Time Attribute	`Arrival Time`
Leave Data	
Station	`Part A Prep`
Route Time	`2`

Display 5-1. The Completed Part A Arrive Dialog

Before we accept this information, we must define the attribute `Sealer Time` and assign it a value from a triangular (1, 3, 4) distribution. To do this, click on the Assign button, then on the Add button in the new dialog, and fill in the required information; see Display 5-2. We can now accept the module. Note that the completed module icon retains the station marker, which is now named `Part A Arrive`.

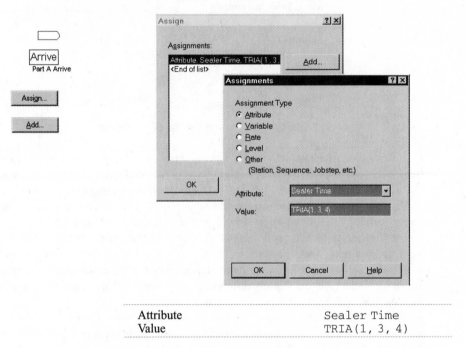

Attribute	Sealer Time
Value	TRIA(1, 3, 4)

Display 5-2. Assigning the Sealer Time

The Arrive module for the Part B arrivals is very similar to that for Part A, as shown in Display 5-3 (we'll skip the graphics since they're almost the same as what you just saw), except we have filled in one additional field in the Arrive data section, a batch size of 4. Recall that the Part B's arrive in batches of four. Thus, this entry will cause each arrival to consist of four separate entities rather than one. The assignment to the `Sealer Time` attribute is also shown. Since four entities are created for each arrival, they'll each be assigned a different value from the sealer time distribution.

Enter Data	
Station	Part B Arrive
Arrival Data	
Batch Size	4
Time Between	EXPO(30)
Mark Time Attribute	Arrival Time
Leave Data	
Station	Part B Prep
Route Time	2
Assignments	
Attribute	Sealer Time
Value	NORM(2.4, 0.5)

Display 5-3. The Part B Arrive Dialog Entries

Having completed the two part-arrival modules, we can now move to the two prep areas that are to be modeled using the two Servers previously placed. The completed dialog for the Part A Prep area is given in Display 5-4. In entering data, we strongly urge you to make use of the pull-down list whenever possible. Remember that we entered the station name Part A Prep in the Part A Arrive module, so we can pick it directly from the list. The reason for this caution is that if you retype the name, it must match what you typed the first time. Arena names are not case-sensitive, but the spelling and any embedded blanks must be identical. Picking the name from the list assures that the names are the same. If you type in a slightly different name, Arena will give you an error message the first time you check or attempt to run the model.

Also note that after you enter the station name in the Enter Data section and you hit the Tab key or move the cursor, Arena automatically renames the default resource name in the Server Data area. That name becomes the station name with an appended "_R" notation. There are two reason for this. The first is a matter of convenience—you don't have to enter a resource name, but you can change it if you want (though the default name makes it clear which station contains which resource). The second reason is that all names for any objects in Arena must be unique. This is true even if the object type is different. Otherwise, Arena would have a difficult time determining which object to associate with a name that had been used more than once.

To help you out, Arena does a lot of automatic naming, most of which you won't even notice. For example, if you click on the Queue button, a Resource Queue dialog appears, and you'll see that Arena also assigned the name Part A Prep_R_Q to the queue at this prep area. By now, you have probably figured out that the appended "_R" implies a resource name and the "_Q" implies a queue name. Of course, you can always assign your own names rather than accepting the default names.

Remember that as part of the simulation output we wanted to collect statistics on resource utilization, number in queue, and time in queue at each of the operations. Note that in the Server Data area of this module there is a check box called Resource Statistics that, by default, is checked. This will give us the required resource utilization. If you do not want this information, simply click on the check box and Arena will neither collect nor report it. Likewise, when you clicked on the Queue button, the queue characteristics section of the Resource Queue dialog is automatically checked for the # in Queue Statistics and Time in Queue Statistics. These three statistics are automatically collected whenever you use a Server or Inspect module.

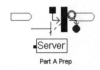

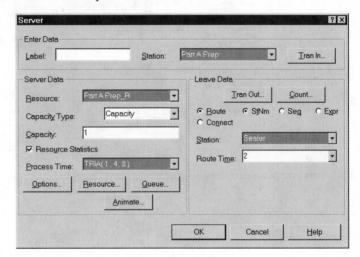

Enter Data	
Station	Part A Prep
Server Data	
Process Time	TRIA(1, 4, 8)
Leave Data	
Station	Sealer
Route Time	2

Display 5-4. Part A Prep Area Dialog

The second server is filled out in an almost-identical fashion, with the exception of the station name, Part B Prep, and the parameters for the process time, TRIA(3, 5,10). We have not bothered to include a display for this module.

The next step is to enter data for the sealer operation, which is the first Inspect module we placed. The Inspect dialog has several features in addition to those in a Server module. It requires that we enter a failure probability, and it provides two ways to leave the module—Pass or Fail. The completed dialog is shown in Display 5-5. Note that in the Server Data section we have entered the attribute Sealer Time to which we assigned values when the arriving parts were created. When an entity gains control of, or *seizes*, the resource, it will undergo a process delay equal to the value contained in the Sealer Time attribute. The Failure Probability (*not* the pass probability) is entered as 0.09.

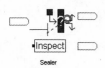

Sealer

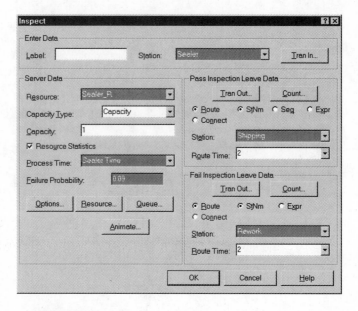

Enter Data	
Station	Sealer
Server Data	
Process Time	Sealer Time
Failure Probability	0.09
Pass Inspection Leave Data	
Station	Shipping
Route Time	2
Fail Inspection Leave Data	
Station	Rework
Route Time	2

Display 5-5. The Sealer Dialog

The Leave Data section of this dialog is separated into two areas, one for the parts that pass the inspection and one for those that fail. Parts that pass are routed to Shipping, and parts that fail are routed to Rework. The data for the second Inspect module, the rework operation, is shown in Display 5-6. By the way, if you've been building this model as we've moved through the material, now would be a good time to click on the Save button—you never know when somebody might bump the power switch!

Having completed all the operations, we now need to fill in the three Depart modules. The completed dialog for the Shipping area is shown in Display 5-7. We picked the station name from the pull-down list and checked the Individual Counter and Individual Tally buttons. The only additional entry was to enter, or select from the pull-down list, the attribute name Arrival Time that we marked back in the arrival modules; we accepted the defaults on the Counter and Tally names.

Enter Data	
Station	Rework
Server Data	
Process Time	EXPO(45)
Failure Probability	0.2
Pass Inspection Leave Data	
Station	Salvaged Parts
Route Time	2
Fail Inspection Leave Data	
Station	Scrap
Route Time	2

Display 5-6. The Rework Dialog

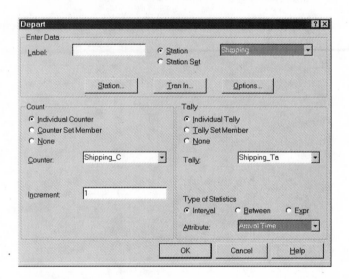

Enter Data	
Station	Shipping
Count	
Individual Counter	*select*
Tally	
Individual Tally	*select*
Attribute	Arrival Time

Display 5-7. The Shipping Dialog

When you accept this dialog, you'll see a blue rectangle with a white number above the module. This animation variable will display the current count for the total number of entities that have passed through this module during the run. This count also will be listed on the summary report.

The two other Depart modules, Salvaged Parts and Scrap, are filled out in a similar fashion. Entities sent to each of these Depart modules are disposed of, and part count and flowtime statistics are collected.

We're finally ready to fill in the last module, Simulate. It may have taken you some time to get this far, but once you get accustomed to working with Arena, you'll find that you could have completed this in only a few minutes. You could actually run the model at this point without filling in the Simulate module, although Arena would not know when to stop the simulation, so it would just continue running forever. The completed dialog is shown in Display 5-8. We've entered the project and analyst name so they will appear on the output report. We've defaulted on the date, thus allowing Arena to use dates from the computer. Finally, we've entered the run length. You might notice, after you've closed the dialog, that directly above the Simulate handle is a small red box. This is the default entity picture—we'll show you how to change it later.

Simulate
Electronic Assembly and Test
2000

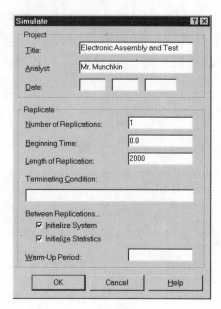

Project	
Title	Electronic Assembly and Test
Analyst	Mr. Munchkin
Replicate	
Length of Replication	2000

Display 5-8. The Simulate Dialog

The last step in building this model is to add the route paths that the entities will follow as they are transferred from one station location to another. We'll add these paths using the Route object from the Animate toolbar. If you click on this object, the Route dialog shown in Display 5-9 will appear. Normally, you'll simply accept the defaults, although you can change the characteristics of the path by selectively clicking different buttons. To explore what the other Route options are, click on the What's This? help button, then click on the item of interest to display a brief description.

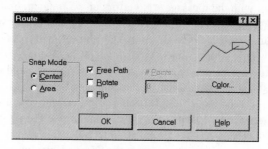

Display 5-9. The Route Dialog

After you accept the Route dialog, the cursor changes to cross hairs. Place the cross hairs inside a station marker at the start of a path and click; this will start the route path. Move the cursor and build the remainder of the path by clicking where you want "corners," much like drawing a polyline. The route path will automatically end when you click inside the end station marker.

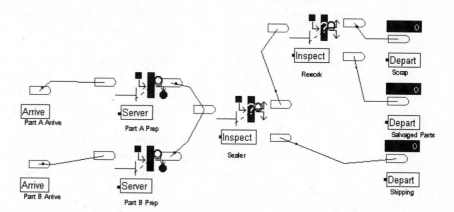

Figure 5-3. The Final Model 5.1

You can choose which routes to animate. If an entity is transferred between two locations that are not connected by a route path, the time to transfer will be incurred as the model runs, but the transfer will not show in the animation. After adding the first route, you can use the repeat function (right click) to start placing the next route path. For this model, you need to have route paths from arrivals to prep to sealer to rework and depart. Your final model should look something like Figure 5-3. Don't worry about the station markers and route paths because they will disappear when you run the model.

5.1.4 Running the Model

Before running your model, you might want to check it for errors. You can do this by clicking the Check button (✓) on the Run Interaction toolbar, the *Run/Check Model* option, or the F4 key on the keyboard. With a little luck, the response will be a small window with the message, "No errors or warnings in model." If you have no luck at all, an error window will open with a message describing the error. If this occurs, you might want to select the Find option, if the button is enabled. This feature attempts to point you to where Arena thinks the error might be. We suggest you intentionally insert an error into your model and try these features. As you build more complex models, you might just find yourself using these features quite often.

If your model check results in no errors, you're now ready to run the simulation. There are four ways to run a simulation; we'll only talk about three of them here. The first way is to run the simulation with the animation. Use the Go button (▶) on the Run toolbar, the *Run/Go* option, or the F5 key. If you've not already Checked your model or if you've made a change since the last check, Arena will first Check your model, then initialize the model with your data, and finally run it. You'll notice that during the run, Arena hides some of the graphics so that your attention can be drawn to the animation—the module handles, station markers, queue lines, seize areas, and route lines in this model all disappear. Don't worry, though. They'll return when you end the run (or you can check to see that they're still there by using the *Edit/Layers* option).

You can tell what Arena is doing if you leave the status bar active (at the bottom of the screen). Toward the right of this bar will be listed three pieces of information: the replication number, the current simulation time, and the simulation status.

After the simulation starts to run, you may want to speed up or slow down the animation. You can do this while the model is running by pressing the "<" key to slow it down or the ">" key to speed it up. If you press one of these keys, the current Animation Speed Factor is displayed at the far left of the status bar. You can also increase or decrease the animation speed factor using the *Run/Speed* option. This option can also be used to enter an exact speed factor.

During the simulation run, you can also pause the simulation using the Pause button (❚❚) on the Run toolbar, the *Run/Pause* option, or the Esc key. This temporarily suspends the simulation and the message User Interrupted will appear on the status bar.

While you're in Pause mode, you might want to double-click on one of the entities that is visible in the animation. An Entity Summary dialog lists the values of each of the entity's attributes. This can be a very useful feature when trying to debug a model. You can also use the Step button (▶❚) on the Run toolbar to move entities through the system one step at a time. You can continue the simulation run at any time with the Go button.

This method of running a simulation provides the greatest amount of information, but it can take a long time to complete a simulation run. In this case, the time required to complete the run depends on the speed factor. You can skip ahead in time by selecting the Fast-Forward button (▶▶) on the Run toolbar, or *Run/Fast-Forward*. This will cause the simulation to run at a much faster speed by not updating the animation. At any time during the run, you can pause and return to the animation mode, or you can Zoom In (+), Zoom Out (–), or move about the simulation window (arrow keys or scroll bars).

Using Fast-Forward will run the simulation in much less time, but if you're only interested in the numerical simulation results, you might want to disable the animation altogether. You do this with the *Run/Setup* option. The Run Setup window allows you to configure a number of runtime options. For now, select the Mode tab and click on Batch Run (No Animation) under the Settings section. Accept this option and click the Run button. Note how much faster the simulation runs. The only disadvantage is that you must terminate the run and reset the settings in order to get the animation back. If you have large models or long runs and you're only interested in the numerical results, this is the option to choose.

While you're building a model, you should probably have most of the toolbars visible and accessible. However, when you're running a model, many of the toolbars simply consume space because they are not active during runtime. Arena recognizes this and will save your toolbar settings for each mode. To take advantage of this, pause during runtime and remove the toolbars that you don't want to have active during runtime. When you end the run, these toolbars will reappear.

5.1.5 *Viewing the Results*

If you run the model to completion, Arena will ask if you want to see the results. If you select Yes, you should get a window of the summary report that resembles Figure 5-4.

The summary report is separated into three sets of information. The first set, Tally Variables, contains the cycle-time and queue-time statistics. The Discrete-Change Variables set contains the resource utilizations (denoted by "busy"), resource availability, and number in queue statistics. The last set, Counters, contains the counts by part status. You might note that these counts are also recorded in the number of observations for our flowtime tallies.

The Tally and Discrete-Change statistics provide the average, 95% confidence-interval half width, and the minimum and maximum observed values. As mentioned, you also get the number of observations for each Tally and the final or ending value for each Discrete-Change statistic. With the exception of the half-width column, these entries should be self-explanatory.

At the end of each replication, Arena attempts to calculate a 95% confidence-interval half width for the steady-state (long run) expected value of each observed statistic. Arena first checks to see if sufficient data have been collected to justify the normality assumption. This requires a minimum of 320 observations for tallies and 5 time units for Discrete-Change statistics. If this is not the case, Arena will report insufficient (Insuf) data, as can be seen for several of the results. If a statistic passes this test, Arena will then check to see if the data are correlated, in violation of the independence assumption. If it fails this test, which is the case for the remainder of the statistics, it will report that the data are correlated (Corr). If a statistic passes this test, Arena will calculate and report the half width. The details and importance of these tests will be further discussed in Section 7.5.3. For now, it's clear that we haven't run our model long enough to collect statistically meaningful results (for steady-state analysis).

```
Project:  Electronic Assembly
Analyst:  Mr. Munchkin

Replication ended at time     : 2000.0
```

TALLY VARIABLES

Identifier	Average	Half Width	Minimum	Maximum	Observations
Salvaged Parts_Ta	540.48	(Insuf)	101.91	874.90	31
Rework_R_Q Queue Time	429.95	(Insuf)	.00000	782.19	36
Sealer_R_Q Queue Time	1.9247	(Corr)	.00000	12.850	603
Scrap_Ta	334.79	(Insuf)	76.343	821.27	4
Part B Prep_R_Q Queue	42.308	(Insuf)	.00000	105.34	240
Shipping_Ta	35.911	(Corr)	9.7800	117.85	548
Part A Prep_R_Q Queue	6.0259	(Corr)	.00000	28.804	365

DISCRETE-CHANGE VARIABLES

Identifier	Average	Half Width	Minimum	Maximum	Final Value
# in Rework_R_Q	11.615	(Insuf)	.00000	22.000	19.000
Part A Prep_R Busy	.79647	(Corr)	.00000	1.0000	1.0000
# in Sealer_R_Q	.58031	(Corr)	.00000	4.0000	.00000
Part B Prep_R Availabl	1.0000	(Insuf)	1.0000	1.0000	1.0000
# in Part A Prep_R_Q	1.0999	(Corr)	.00000	6.0000	2.0000
Sealer_R Available	1.0000	(Insuf)	1.0000	1.0000	1.0000
Part A Prep_R Availabl	1.0000	(Insuf)	1.0000	1.0000	1.0000
Rework_R Available	1.0000	(Insuf)	1.0000	1.0000	1.0000
Sealer_R Busy	.77139	(Corr)	.00000	1.0000	.00000
Rework_R Busy	.99029	(Insuf)	.00000	1.0000	1.0000
Part B Prep_R Busy	.72774	(Insuf)	.00000	1.0000	.00000
# in Part B Prep_R_Q	5.0770	(Insuf)	.00000	19.000	.00000

COUNTERS

Identifier	Count	Limit
Salvaged Parts_C	31	Infinite
Scrap_C	4	Infinite
Shipping_C	548	Infinite

Figure 5-4. The Arena Summary Report: Model 5.1

Trying to draw conclusions from this single short run would be dangerous as we haven't addressed issues like steady state or sample size. However, if you look closely at the results, you should note that the Rework resource is busy more than 99% of the time, and the rework queue has 19 parts in it at the end of the simulation. This implies that the rework area doesn't have enough capacity to handle its work or that there is a great deal of variability at this station. We'll address this issue in the next section.

5.2   Model 5.2: The Enhanced Electronic Assembly and Test System

Having constructed and run our model, the next activity would be to verify and validate that the model really represents the system being studied. For this example, that's fairly easy. We can examine the logic constructs we selected from the modules we used and compare this to the problem definition. With much larger and more complex systems, this can become a challenging task. An animation is often very useful during the verification and validation phases because it allows you to view the entire system being modeled as it operates. If you ran the model we developed and viewed the animation, you should have noted that it appeared to operate quite similarly to the way we described the system. Although verification can be very difficult, complete validation (the next activity) can sometimes be almost impossible. That's because validation implies that the simulation is behaving just like the real-world system, which may not even exist. And even if the system does exist, you have to convince yourself and other nonbelievers that your model can really capture and predict the events of the real system. We'll discuss both of these activities in much more detail in Chapter 12.

For now, let's assume that as part of this effort you showed the animation and accompanying results to the production manager. His first observation was that you didn't have a complete definition of how the system works. Whoever developed the problem definition looked only at the operation of the first shift. This system actually operates two shifts a day, and on the second shift, there are two operators assigned to the rework operation. This would explain our earlier observation where we thought the rework operation might not have enough capacity. The production manager also noted that they have a failure problem at the sealer operation. Periodically, the sealer machine breaks down. Engineering looked at the problem some time ago and collected data to determine the effect on the sealer operation. They felt that these failures did not merit any significant effort to correct the problem because they didn't feel that the sealer operation was a bottleneck. They did, however, log their observations, which are still available. Let's assume that the mean uptime between failures was found to be 120 minutes and that the distribution is exponential (which, by the way, is often used as a realistic model for uptimes). The time to repair also follows an exponential distribution with a mean of 4 minutes. Our next step is to modify the model to include these two new aspects, which will allow us to employ some additional Arena features.

In order to incorporate these changes into our model, we will need to introduce several new concepts. Changing from a one- to a two-shift operation is fairly easy. In Model 5.1, we set our run length to 2,000 minutes and made no attempt to keep track of the day/shift during the run. We just assumed that the system conditions at the end of a shift were the same at the start of the next shift and ignored the intervening time. As a result, our run of 2,000 minutes resulted in just over four simulated shifts (2000/480, or 4.1667, to be more exact). Now we need to model the change in shifts explicitly, because we have only one operator in the first shift and two in the second shift. We'll add this to our model by including a Resource Schedule for the rework resource, which will automatically change the number of rework resources throughout the run by adjusting the resource capacity. While we're making this change, we'll also increase the run length so that we simulate more than two days of a two-shift operation. Finally, we'll model the sealer failures using a Resource Failure or Downtime, which allows us to change the available capacity of the resource (much like the Resource Schedule), but has additional features specifically designed for representing equipment failures.

Before we show you how to expand the way you can keep track of resources, we want to mention one thing about getting and displaying your results. If you remember Model 3.1, you'll recall that we included several data plots on the animation. We'll show you how to do this at the end of this section, but these plots are generally limited in terms of the time frame; once you've ended the run, you've lost the plots. You might also want to display the plot information in other ways, perform statistical analysis on the output data, or possibly export the output data to another application (like a spreadsheet or statistical package). Unfortunately, the animation plots don't save the data for later use. However, the Statistics module, found on the Common panel, provides the capability to save these data and also to define other system statistics that you might want to include in your summary report. Saving some of the data from one of our simulation runs will allow us to show you how to use the Arena Output Analyzer.

5.2.1 *Expanding Resource Representation: Schedules and States*

So far we have modeled our resources (prep area, sealer, and rework) as a single resource with a capacity of 1. You might recall that we defaulted all of this information in the Server and Inspect modules. To model the additional rework operator, we could simply change the capacity of the rework resource to 2, but this would mean that we would always have two operators available. What we need to do is to schedule one rework operator for the first shift (assume each shift is 480 minutes) and two rework operators for the second shift. Arena has a built-in construct to model this, called a *Schedule*, which allows you to vary the capacity of a resource over time. A resource Schedule is defined by a sequence of time-dependent resource capacity changes. As we'll show you shortly, this capability is readily available in the modules we have already used.

We also need to capture in our model the periodic breakdowns (or failures) of the sealer machine. This could be modeled using a Schedule, which would define an available resource capacity of 1 for the uptimes and a capacity of 0 for the time to repair. However, the Server and Inspect modules have two built-in constructs designed specifically to model failures: *Failures* and *Downtimes*. In this case, we could use either of these constructs to model our sealer failure, but there's a difference in how Arena causes the failure to occur. First, let's introduce the concept of *Resource States*.

Arena automatically has four Resource States: *Idle, Busy, Inactive,* and *Failed*. So far you've been aware of only the first two. When you were running the animation, you might have noticed that the resource symbol changed color when the resource state changed from idle to busy and back. You can see this by highlighting the sealer resource symbol and double-clicking on it. This will cause the Resource Picture Placement window to appear. Notice the four resource states and the default pictures associated with each. The Inactive state has the symbol with no filled-in color, and the Failure state has no symbol associated with it. Go ahead and close this window; we'll come back to it later in this chapter.

Arena not only changes the resource picture based on the status of the resource, but it also keeps track of the time the resource was in each of the four states for statistical reporting. The resource is said to be Idle if no entity has seized it. As soon as an entity enters the Server and seizes the resource, the state and picture are changed to Busy. (If the resource capacity is greater than 1, the picture will show busy whenever one or more units of the resource are busy. It will only show Idle if all units of the resource are idle.) The picture will show Inactive if Arena has made the resource unavailable for allocation; this could be accomplished with a Schedule changing the capacity to 0. It will show Failed if Arena has placed the resource in the Failed state, which also implies it's unavailable for allocation. More on this later; for now, let's go back to the concepts of Failures and Downtimes.

When the capacity of a resource is 1, a Failure and a Downtime will yield essentially the same statistical results, though the results will be reported differently since Arena places the resource in a different state during the repair time. If the capacity of the resource is greater than 1, the results will be different. This is due to the way that the two constructs are implemented. When a failure occurs, Arena basically causes the entire resource to become unavailable. If the capacity is 2, for example, both units of the resource will be placed in the Failed state during the repair time. On the other hand, a Downtime will cause only one unit of the resource to become unavailable during the repair time. Also, during this time, the resource unit is placed in the Inactive state. You should also note that you can implement multiple Failures, Downtimes, or both for the same resource.

Recall from the previous summary output report that Arena reported two Time-Persistent Statistics for each of the resources we defined (for example, the sealer resource). We really only look at the Sealer_R Busy statistic, which indicates the fraction of time the resource was busy. The other statistic, Sealer_R Available, told us the fraction of time that resource was available; in this case, 1.0. If we had specified the sealer resource capacity as 2, this statistic would have been reported as a 2.0. If we had caused the resource to be placed in an Inactive state during the run by specifying a Downtime or with a Schedule with 0 capacity, the Sealer_R Available statistic value would have been reduced by the fraction of time that it had been placed in the Inactive state. If we specify a Failure, the resource will be placed in the Failed state, and an additional statistic will be included in the output report. You'll see this new statistic shortly.

5.2.2 Resource Schedules

You start the definition of a resource Schedule in the main dialog of either the Server or Inspect module. In this case, we're interested in defining a Schedule for the rework area that's being modeled with an Inspect module. Open the module dialog and go to the Server Data section. Display 5-10 shows that section of the dialog completed. If you're modifying your own model, go to the Capacity Type prompt, activate the pull-down list, and select Schedule. When you do this, you might watch the Capacity prompt (just below) and the blank area to the left of the Animate button. As soon as you select the Schedule option for the Capacity Type, the Capacity prompt is changed to Schedule with two required fields. The first requires a schedule name, and the second allows you to choose the timing of how the schedule is implemented.

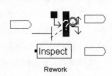

Rework

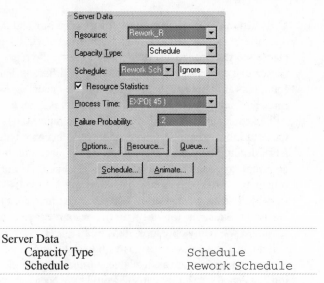

Server Data
    Capacity Type   Schedule
    Schedule   Rework Schedule

Display 5-10. Selecting a Resource Schedule

There are three options for the schedule timing: Ignore (the default), Preempt, and Wait. If a capacity decrease is scheduled to occur and the resource is idle, all three options immediately cause the resource to become Inactive. If the resource is currently allocated to an entity, each responds differently.

The Ignore option decreases the resource capacity immediately, ignoring the fact that the resource is currently allocated to an entity. When the resource is released by the entity, it is placed in the Inactive state. However, if the resource capacity is increased again (i.e., the scheduled time at the lower capacity expires) before the entity releases the resource, it's as if the schedule change never occurred. The net effect is that the time the capacity is scheduled to be reduced may be shortened with this option.

The Wait option, as its name implies, will wait until the entity releases the resource before starting the actual capacity decrease. Thus the reduced capacity time will always be modeled correctly, but the time between these reductions may increase.

The Preempt option actually preempts the resource by taking it away from the controlling entity and starts the capacity reduction. The preempted entity is held internally by Arena until the resource becomes available, at which time the entity will be reallocated the resource and continue with its processing time. This provides an accurate way to model schedules and failures because, in many cases, the work or processing of a part is terminated at the end of a shift and certainly when the resource fails. However, there are several special rules that govern the way entities can be preempted.

This brings us to the question of when to use each of the rules. While there are no strict guidelines, a few rules of thumb may be of help. First, if the duration of the scheduled decrease in capacity is very large compared to the processing time, the Ignore option may be an adequate representation. If the time between capacity decreases is large compared to the duration of the decrease, the Wait option could be considered.

Generally, we recommend that you closely examine the actual process and select the option that best describes what actually occurs at the time of a schedule change or resource failure. If the resource under consideration is the bottleneck for the system, your choice could significantly affect the results obtained. For this model, we've selected the Ignore option because, in most cases, an operator will finish his task before leaving, and that additional work time is seldom considered.

Having named the schedule and indicated the Schedule option, you must now define the schedule the resource should follow. You do this by clicking on the Schedule button and opening the Schedule dialog. Then click on the Add button to open the Capacity Duration window. Here you define the (Capacity, Duration) pairs that will make up the schedule. In this case, our two pairs are 1, 480 and 2, 480. This implies that the capacity will be set to 1 for the first 480 minutes, then 2 for the next 480 minutes. This schedule will then repeat for the duration of the simulation run. You may have as many (Capacity, Duration) pairs as are required to model your system accurately. For example, you might want to include operator breaks and the lunch period in your schedule. There is one caution, or feature,[1] of which you should be aware. If, for any pair, no entry is made for the Duration, it will default to infinity. This will cause the resource to have that capacity for the duration of the simulation run. As long as there are positive entries for all durations, the schedule will repeat for the entire simulation run. See Display 5-11 for the steps required to complete this schedule.

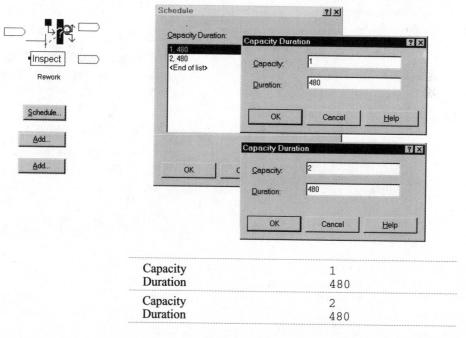

Capacity	1
Duration	480
Capacity	2
Duration	480

Display 5-11. The Resource Schedule

[1] This is called a feature if you do it intentionally and an error if you do it accidentally.

5.2.3 Resource Failures

Schedules are intended to model the planned variation in the availability of resources due to shift changes, breaks, meetings, etc. Failures are primarily intended to model random events that cause the resource to become unavailable. Failure constructs are part of the resource definition in both the Server and Inspect modules. When you open the Resource Information dialog, you see three sections: StateSets, Failures, and Downtimes. The StateSets section allows you to define your own States; for now we require only the four standard States provided by Arena. The Downtimes section allows the definition of Arena downtimes as discussed earlier. The Failure section is where we will implement the Sealer failures.

Clicking on the Failure Add button opens the Failures dialog as shown in Display 5-12. After entering the Failure name, `Sealer Failure`, you select whether the failure is count-based or time-based. A count-based failure causes the resource to become failed after the specified number of entities have used the resource. This count may be a fixed number or generated from any expression. Count-based activities are fairly common in industrial models. For example, tooling replacement, cleaning, and machine adjustment are typically based on the number of parts that have been processed rather than elapsed time. Although these may not normally be viewed as "failures," they do occur on a periodic basis and prevent the resource from producing parts.

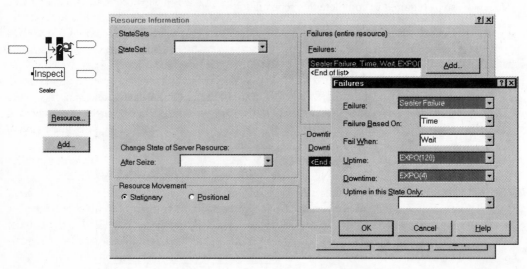

Failure	Sealer Failure
Failure Based On	Time
Fail When	Wait
Uptime	EXPO(120)
Downtime	EXPO(4)

Display 5-12. The Resource Failures Dialog

On the other hand, we frequently model failures as time-based because that's the way we have collected the failure data. In our model, the problem calls for a time-based failure. We must also select the Fail When option—Ignore, Wait, or Preempt. These options are the same as for schedules, and you respond in an identical manner. Returning to our rules of thumb for choosing the Fail When option, because our expected uptime (120 minutes) is large compared to our failure duration (4 minutes), we'll use the Wait option.

Our Uptime and Downtime entries are exponential distributions with means of 120 and 4, respectively. The last field, Uptime in this State Only, allows us to define the state that should be used to determine the uptimes. If this field is defaulted, then all states are considered. Use of this feature is very dependent on how your data were collected and the calendar timing of your model. Most failure data are simply logged data; e.g., only the time of the failure is logged. If this is the case, then holidays, lunch breaks, and idle time are included in the time between failures, and you should default this field. Only if your time between failures can be directly linked to a specific state should this option be chosen. Many times equipment vendors will supply you with failure data based on actual operating hours; in this case, you would want to select this option and specify the Busy state.

5.2.4 Saving Statistical Data

As discussed earlier, we can easily animate our model with time-dependent plots, histograms, and variables, but we lose these displays as soon as we end our simulation run. Sometimes it's desirable to save and post-process these data. For example, our Discrete-Change statistical output gives us the mean, half width, minimum, maximum, and final value for the number in queue at the rework area. If we suspect that storage may be a problem in this area, we would really like to know the percent of time that the queue exceeded certain values. We might also want to plot different data together in an attempt to identify relationships, such as how the number in queue relates to flowtime. If we save these data to files during the simulation run, we can post-analyze them or export them to other applications. An easy way to accomplish this is with the Statistics module found in the Common panel.

The Statistics module defines additional statistics to be collected, as well as specifying which data we would like to save to files. If you place and open the Statistics dialog, you'll see five sections: Time-Persistent (or Discrete-Change), Tallies, Counters, Outputs, and Frequencies. For now, we'll only work with the first two—which, by the way, were discussed in Chapter 2. Let's assume that we're primarily interested in the number of parts in the queues at the Prep B area, the Sealer area, and the Rework area. In addition, we'd like to save the cycle times for all parts that do not go through rework.

Let's first request data files for our Time-Persistent statistics. Clicking on the Time-Persistent Add button opens the Time-Persistent Statistics dialog. The statistics of concern are queue statistics, so select the Queue option and pick the statistic from the pull-down list. Most of the remaining fields will be filled in automatically. We need to check Save Observations to a File and then enter a file name (inside double quotes), which can contain disk drive and path information. The completed dialog for the Part B Prep queue is shown in Display 5-13.

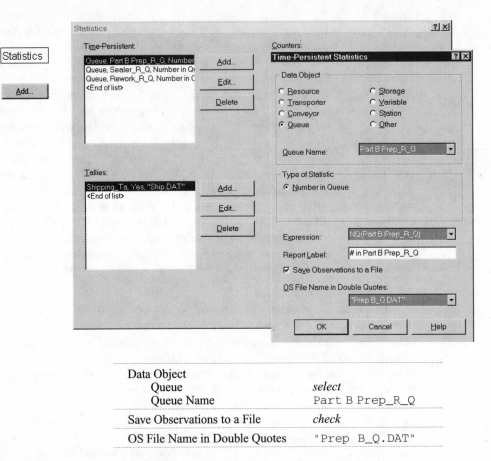

Data Object	
Queue	*select*
Queue Name	Part B Prep_R_Q
Save Observations to a File	*check*
OS File Name in Double Quotes	"Prep B_Q.DAT"

Display 5-13. Saving Part B Prep Queue Statistical Data

Repeat the process for the Sealer and Rework queues, entering the data shown in Display 5-14.

Follow similar steps to request the data file for the shipping tally, as shown in Display 5-15. Now when you run the simulation, Arena will open the four different specified files and write each data point or system status change to that file. In the case of the Tally file, the information written to the file will consist of pairs of data—tally value and the time this value was observed and recorded. The queue data will also be written in pairs of data—queue status after the change and time of change. Although these data files are binary (to conserve disk space), they can easily be read by the Arena Output Analyzer.

Data Object	
Queue	*select*
Queue Name	`Sealer_R_Q`
Save Observations to a File	*check*
OS File Name in Double Quotes	`"Sealer_Q.DAT"`

Data Object	
Queue	*select*
Queue Name	`Rework_R_Q`
Save Observations to a File	*check*
OS File Name in Double Quotes	`"Rework_Q.DAT"`

Display 5-14. Saving Sealer and Rework Queue Statistical Data

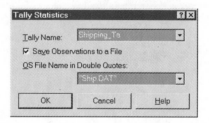

Tally Name	`Shipping_Ta`
Save Observations to a File	*check*
OS File Name in Double Quotes	`"Ship.DAT"`

Display 5-15. Saving Tally Observation Data

Before we leave the Statistics module, let's address the issue of the part storage at the Rework area. Since we're already saving the data for this queue, we could post-process these data to determine the necessary storage requirements. For now, let's assume that we store the parts at the Rework area in special racks, which can hold 10 assemblies per rack, and we would like to know how many racks to buy. We can use the *Frequencies* statistic type to obtain this information. Frequencies are used to record the time-persistent occurrence frequency of an Arena variable, expression, or resource state. You'll notice when the model runs that Arena elected to show the Sealer resource statistics as a Frequency statistic for the Sealer failure we had defined. We're interested in the status of the rework queue—specifically, how many racks of 10 should we buy to assure that we have sufficient storage almost all of the time. To request this information, we need to know the Arena variable for the number in queue, NQ. You might recall that when we requested that this information be written to a file, the Time-Persistent dialog automatically gave us the proper notation, NQ(Rework_R_Q). In this case, we're interested in the amount of time the number in queue was 0, greater than 0 and less than or equal to 10, greater than 10 and less than or equal to 20, etc.

We start by entering the expression and then building the categories. Display 5-16 shows the entries for the first three categories. The first entry is for a queue size of a constant 0; the next entry is for one rack, two racks, etc. For now, we will only request this information for up to five racks. If the queue exceeds 50 parts, Arena will create an out-of-range category on the output report.

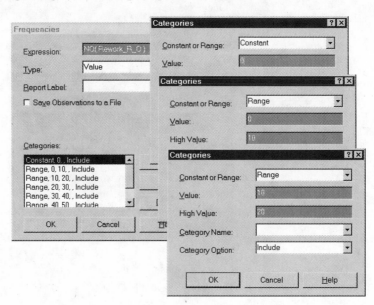

Expression	NQ(Rework_R_Q)
Constant or Range	Constant
Value	0
Constant or Range	Range
Value	0
High Value	10
Constant or Range	Range
Value	10
High Value	20
. . .	

Display 5-16. Requesting Frequency Statistics

Before we run our model, let's change our Length of Replication, in the Simulate module, to 50,000 time units (minutes). (Note: When typing large numbers in Arena, don't type the commas. We'll include them in our narrative only for readability.) This should give us a reasonable amount of data from a single "long" run on which to base our observations. Before you run this model, we strongly recommend that you use the *Run/Setup* option to select the Batch Run (No Animation) option, which will greatly reduce the amount of time required to run the model. This would be a good time to save your work too. Note that you can still pause the run at any time to determine how far you have progressed. Of course, the actual run time will depend on the hardware you are using.

5.2.5   Results of Model 5.2

The Arena Summary Report for this extended run is given in Figure 5-5. Note specifically the statistics for the rework area. The maximum number in queue was 28, and the queue was empty at the end of the run. The Rework availability was 1.4992 and Rework busy was 1.3732. The rework availability reflects the additional capacity added to the second shift. The actual rework utilization is 91.60% (100 × 1.3732 / 1.4992).

```
Project:  Electronic Assembly
Analyst:  Mr. Munchkin

Replication ended at time      : 50000.0
```

TALLY VARIABLES

Identifier	Average	Half Width	Minimum	Maximum	Observations
Salvaged Parts_Ta	302.17	(Corr)	19.439	1229.2	1199
Rework_R_Q Queue Time	193.93	48.888	.00000	674.58	1467
Sealer_R_Q Queue Time	6.2386	1.5828	.00000	50.795	16499
Scrap_Ta	285.39	(Insuf)	25.366	1159.2	267
Part B Prep_R_Q Queue	70.972	(Corr)	.00000	541.65	6624
Shipping_Ta	57.472	(Corr)	9.0197	564.91	15031
Part A Prep_R_Q Queue	15.183	2.5646	.00000	99.536	9876

DISCRETE-CHANGE VARIABLES

Identifier	Average	Half Width	Minimum	Maximum	Final Value
# in Rework_R_Q	5.6899	1.6284	.00000	28.000	.00000
Part A Prep_R Busy	.85391	.02036	.00000	1.0000	1.0000
# in Sealer_R_Q	2.0586	.59611	.00000	21.000	.00000
Part B Prep_R Availabl	1.0000	(Insuf)	1.0000	1.0000	1.0000
# in Part A Prep_R_Q	2.9990	.61504	.00000	24.000	1.0000
Sealer_R Available	1.0000	(Insuf)	1.0000	1.0000	1.0000
Part A Prep_R Availabl	1.0000	(Insuf)	1.0000	1.0000	1.0000
Rework_R Available	1.4992	(Insuf)	1.0000	2.0000	1.0000
Sealer_R Busy	.84177	.02003	.00000	1.0000	.00000
Rework_R Busy	1.3732	.06088	.00000	2.0000	1.0000
Part B Prep_R Busy	.79305	.04708	.00000	1.0000	.00000
# in Part B Prep_R_Q	9.4023	(Corr)	.00000	88.000	.00000

COUNTERS

Identifier	Count	Limit
Salvaged Parts_C	1199	Infinite
Scrap_C	267	Infinite
Shipping_C	15031	Infinite

```
                                        FREQUENCIES

                                    —Occurrences—      Standard     Restricted
Identifier                  Category    Number  AvgTime   Percent      Percent
Value(NQ(REWORK_R_Q))       Constant(0,)   112   81.559    18.27        18.27
                            Range(0,10)    163  197.97     64.54        64.54
                            Range(10,20)    63  120.45     15.18        15.18
                            Range(20,30)    11   91.559     2.01         2.01

STATE(Sealer_R)             BUSY          3635   11.578    84.18        84.18
                            IDLE          3339    1.9188   12.81        12.81
                            FAILED         387    3.8871    3.01         3.01
```

Figure 5-5. The Arena Summary Report: Model 5.2

The Sealer available and busy statistics are still included in the Discrete-Change section, but a more complete form can be found in the new section, Frequencies. Recall that this form is automatically included if failures or downtimes are attached to a resource. In this case, it provides the results in percentages for the states Busy, Idle, and Failed. Finally, we should note the frequency statistics we requested for the number in the rework queue. There were never more than 30 in that queue and there were more than 20 only 2.01% of the time. This would imply that you might only need two racks, or at most three.

One last note is worth mentioning about frequency statistics. For our results, the last two columns, Standard and Restricted Percent, have the same values. It is possible to exclude selective data from the last column. For example, if you exclude the Failed data for the sealer Frequency, the Standard Percents would remain the same, but the Restricted Percent column would only have values for Busy and Idle, which would sum to 100. We'll show you how to do this in Section 9.5.2.

5.2.6   The Output Analyzer

The Arena Output Analyzer provides the capability to perform a post-run analysis of simulation data that were saved to an output file during a simulation run. It provides the ability to display these data, as well as to analyze and draw statistical conclusions about the data without having to rerun the simulation. For now, we'll deal only with the features that allow you to display the data. The Output Analyzer is a separate program that can be started the same way you would start any other program, or it can be started using the *Tools/Output Analyzer* menu option from within Arena.

Normally, you interact with the Output Analyzer by first defining a *data group*. A data group is a collection of Arena output files that are usually all from the same simulation model, although you can define a data group to contain any files you want. It's not absolutely necessary to define a data group, but it does make it easier to use the Output Analyzer. You define a data group by using the *File/New* menu option or the New button on the toolbar. This opens a data group window named *Output1*. Much like the model window in Arena, this name will change when you save the data group definition under a name of your choice. We'll add the four files we generated with our simulation (Prep B_Q.DAT, Rework_Q.DAT, Sealer_Q.DAT, and Ship.DAT), by clicking the Add button and selecting the file from the Open dialog, as shown in Display 5-17.

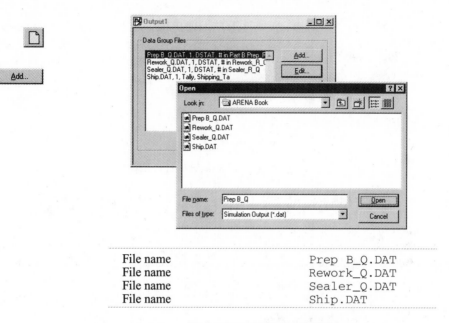

File name	Prep B_Q.DAT
File name	Rework_Q.DAT
File name	Sealer_Q.DAT
File name	Ship.DAT

Display 5-17. Defining a Data Group

Now we can generate plots of the data using the *Graph/Plot* menu option or the Plot button ( ) on the toolbar. Display 5-18 shows the Plot dialog. As before, we suggest you use the pull-down list to enter the file name. If you add just one file and click OK on the main Plot dialog, a single curve will be plotted, as in Figure 5-6. Or, if you'd like to plot a number of curves together, add each of them to the Plot list before clicking OK, in which case Arena will draw each curve in a different color.

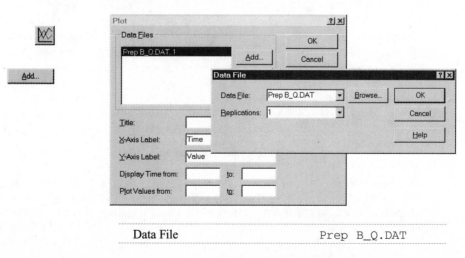

| Data File | Prep B_Q.DAT |

Display 5-18. The Plot Dialog

You can also title the plot and control the time span. The plot for the number in queue at the Prep B area over the entire simulation run (50,000 time units or 50×10^3) is shown in Figure 5-6.

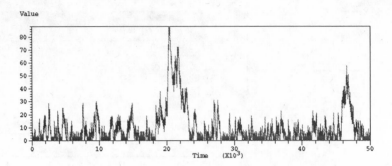

Figure 5-6. Plot of Number in Queue at Prep B Area

If you were also to plot the Shipping tally values, you would note that the peaks in that plot follow very closely the peaks for the Prep B area plot, which is not unexpected. Now let's use the *Graph/Barchart* menu option or the Barchart button () to create a barchart of a portion of the rework data to illustrate another type of graph. For this example, we'll just plot the data between time 20,000 and 21,000, as shown in Display 5-19.

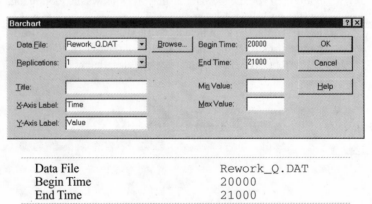

Data File	Rework_Q.DAT
Begin Time	20000
End Time	21000

Display 5-19. The Barchart Dialog

The results for this barchart are shown in Figure 5-7. Note that over this period of time, the queue size built from 0 to 24. In analyzing simulation results, it's always a good idea to notice trends like these and then to try to understand why they occurred.

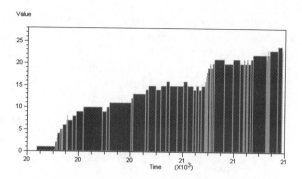

Figure 5-7. Barchart of Rework Queue Data

Finally, let's turn our attention to the limited storage at the rework area. We could have used the histogram feature to determine the percent of time the number in queue exceeded various limits. The *Graph/Histogram* option or the Histogram button () on the Output Analyzer toolbar will allow us to display the queue data and generate this same information. Display 5-20 shows the Histogram dialog. For this case, we've entered the number of interior cells and lower limit so we would duplicate the results obtained from the Frequencies output.

Data File	Rework_Q.DAT
Histogram Cells	
Number (Interior)	3
Lower Limit	0.5

Display 5-20. The Histogram Dialog

Note that the lower limit is 0.5. This is actually the lower limit for the second cell; the first cell includes all observations from $-\infty$ to 0.5. Since the number in queue is always an integer, any number greater than 0 but less than 1 would provide the same results. The results are given in Figure 5-8. In addition to the histogram plot, there is a summary of the histogram data. You might also observe that the cell values in the Relative Frequency column are the same as those we obtained in our Frequencies shown in the summary report, Figure 5-5.

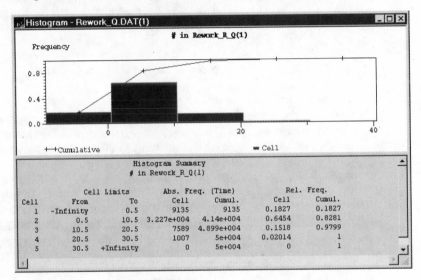

Figure 5-8. Histogram of the Rework Queue Data

We'll revisit the Output Analyzer in Chapters 6, 7, and 11 to show you several of its statistical features.

5.3   Enhancing the Animation

So far in this chapter we've simply accepted the default animation provided with the modules we used. Although this base animation is almost always sufficient for determining whether your model is working correctly, you might want the animation to look more like the real system before allowing decision makers to view the model. Making the animation more realistic is really very easy and seldom requires a lot of time. To a large extent, the amount of time you decide to invest depends on the level of detail you decide to add and the nature of the audience for your efforts. A general observation is that, for presentation purposes, the higher you go in an organization, the more time you should probably spend on the animation. You will also find that making the animation beautiful can be a lot of fun and can even become an obsession. So with that thought in mind, let's explore some of what can be done.

We'll start by looking at the existing animation. Notice that the Server and Inspect modules actually consist of several different Arena constructs. There is a module handle, two (or three) station markers, a resource picture, and a queue, as seen in Figure 5-9. The last three items are animation constructs that came with the modules. You can delete or move any of these items. For example, if you click on the station marker to the left of the Sealer, the name of the station (`Sealer`) will appear below the marker. You can drag the station marker anywhere you want (well, almost anywhere, as long as you stay in the model window). Note that if you move the station marker, the routes stay attached. You can do the same thing for the resource symbol and the queue.

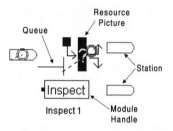

Figure 5-9. Components of the Station Marker

As suggested by how they came to exist in the model—namely, they were added when you placed the module—the animation constructs are "attached" to the module in two respects. First, their names, or *Identifiers*, come from values in the module dialog; you can't change them directly in the animation construct's dialog. Second, if you move the module handle, its animation objects move with it. If you want the animation to stay where it is, though, just hold the Shift key when you move the module handle.

Sometimes it's helpful to "pull apart" the animation to a completely different area in the model window, away from the logic. If you do so, you might consider setting up some Named Views (see Section 4.9) to facilitate going back and forth. If you want to completely disconnect an animation construct from the module it originally accompanied, Cut it to the Clipboard and Paste it back into the model. It will retain all of its characteristics, but no longer will have any association with the module.

5.3.1 Changing Animation Queues

If you watched the animation closely, you might have noticed that there were never more than three entities showing in any of the queues, even though our summary report indicated otherwise. This is because Arena restricts the number of animated entities that show in any queue to the number that will fit in the drawn space for the animation queue. The simulation may have 10 entities in the queue, but if only three will fit on the animation, only the first three will show. Then as any entity is removed from the queue, the next undisplayed entity in the queue will be shown. This can be rather deceptive to the novice user and may lead you to assume that the system is working fine when in fact the queues are quite large. There are three obvious ways (at least to us) to avoid this problem: one is to add an animation variable for the number in queue, the second is to increase the size of the animation queue, and the third is to decrease the size of the entity picture (if visually accurate).

Let's first increase the size of the queue. Figure 5-10 shows the steps we'll go through as we modify our queue. We first select the queue (View 1) by single-clicking on the queue in front of the sealer. Notice that two handles appear, one at each end. You can now place your cursor over the handle at the left end, and it will change to cross hairs. Drag the handle to stretch the queue to any length and direction you want (View 2). In fact, you can place the end of the queue anywhere you like. If you now run the simulation, you should occasionally see a lot more parts waiting at the sealer.

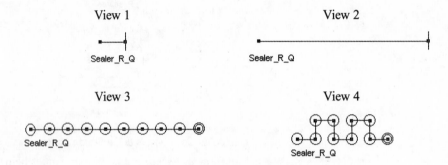

Figure 5-10. Alternate Ways to Display a Queue

We can also change the form of the queue to represent the physical location *point* of each entity in it. Double-click on the selected queue and the Queue dialog will appear as in Display 5-21.

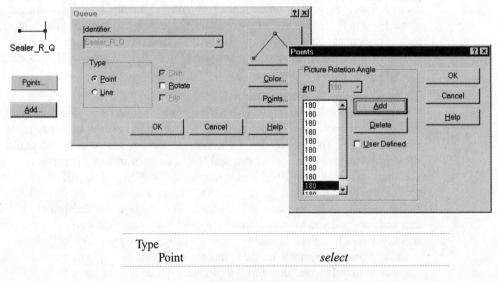

Type	
Point	*select*

Display 5-21. The Queue Dialog

Select the Point Type of queue and click on the Points button. Then Add points by successively clicking on the Add button. We could change the rotation of the entity at each point, but for now we'll accept the default of these values. When you accept these changes, the resulting queue should look something like the one shown in View 3 of Figure 5-10. Note that the front of the queue is denoted by a point surrounded by two circles. You can then click-hold on any of these points and drag them to any formation you like (View 4). If you want all these points to line up neatly, you may want to use the Snap option discussed in Chapter 4. Arena will now place entities on the points during an animation run and move them forward, much like a real-life waiting line functions. For now, we'll simply stretch the queue as shown in View 2 of Figure 5-10. You can repeat this operation for all the queues in the model.

5.3.2 Changing Entity Pictures

Now let's focus our attention on our animation entities. For one thing, we might want to distinguish between Part A and B. There's also one other subtle point that you may not have noticed. Run your animation and watch the Part B entities as they travel from the arrival to the Part B Prep area. Remember that we're creating four entities at a time, but we see only one moving. Now note what happens as they arrive at the queue—suddenly there are four entities. As it turns out, there are really four entities being transferred, it's just that they're all on top of one another. You can check this out by opening the Part B Arrive module and changing the route time from a constant 2 to EXPO(2), causing the entities' individual travel times to differ. Now when you run the animation, you should see all four entities start out on top of one another and then separate as they move toward the queue. You can exaggerate this by clicking on the route path and making the physical length much longer. Although this will show four entities moving, it may not represent reality (although your boss will probably never know). If we show the B parts arriving, each animated as a "big batch" picture, we'll get the desired visual results. There will still be four moving across, but only the top one will show. We need only convert the picture back to a single entity when they enter the queue at the prep area.

You define the entity Picture names in the Animate dialog of the Arrive, Server, or Inspect modules. Open the Part A Arrive dialog and click on the Animate button as in Display 5-22. We'll define this as Picture Part A (now wasn't that obvious?). You should do the same thing for the Part B Arrive, except let's call it Batch B.

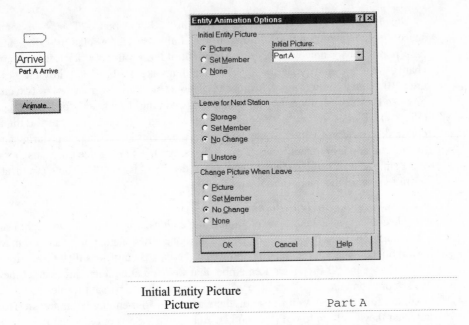

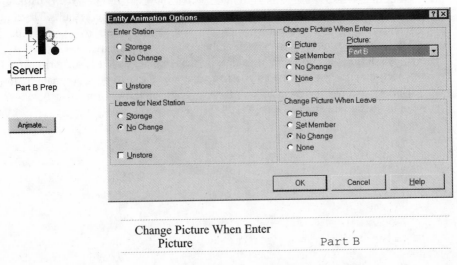

Display 5-22. The Arrive Animate Dialog

Now open the Animate dialog in the Part B Prep area, a Server module. Here we want to change the Picture when the entity enters the module before it enters the queue. We'll call this entity Picture Part B, shown in Display 5-23.

Display 5-23. The Server Animate Dialog

Having defined the picture names, we must associate a drawing with each name. We do this by double-clicking on the current default entity, the red square directly above the Simulate module. This opens the Entity Picture Placement window, as shown in Figure 5-11. This window contains one or more entity pictures, displayed as a list of buttons with the graphical picture and its associated name. The right half of this window is used for accessing *picture libraries*, which are simply saved collections of pictures stored in a file.

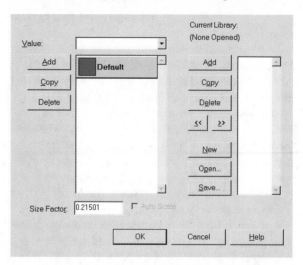

Figure 5-11. The Entity Picture Placement Window

For this example, as for most of our examples, we'll keep our pictures fairly simple, but you can make your entity and resource pictures as fancy as you want. We'll use the default entity picture, the red square, for Part A. Click on that picture and the name Default appears in the Value field that's directly above the picture. Use the pull-down list to select the picture name Part A. (This name was created when you typed it in the Arrive module.) Now click the copy button and rename the new picture to be Part B (a copy of Part A). To change the picture, double-click on the picture icon. This opens the Picture Editor window that will allow you to modify the drawing of Part B. Before you change this picture, notice the small gray circle in the center of the square; this is the *entity reference point*, which determines the entity's relation with the other animation objects. Basically, this point will follow the route paths when the entity is moving, will reside on the seize point when the entity has control of a resource, etc. We'll change this picture by drawing a blue circle of approximately the same size directly on top of the square, and then delete the square.

When you close this window, the new drawing will be displayed beside the Part B name. Now make a copy of this picture and rename it Batch B. Edit this new picture's drawing by double-clicking on its button in the list. In the Picture Editor, duplicate to get four circles as shown in Figure 5-12. Accept these pictures and run the simulation with the animation turned on.

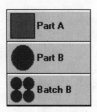

Figure 5-12. The Final Entity Pictures

Adding the different entity pictures allows you to see the different types of parts move through the system. Note the batch of four B parts when they enter the system. Although there are still four of these pictures, each on top of the other, the new Batch B picture gives the illusion of a single batch of four parts entering.

For this model, we used the Picture Editor to draw our own pictures. There are also several other ways to add different pictures. When we opened the Entity Picture Placement window (see Figure 5-11), we mentioned that the picture library area on the right contains the current library of pictures. Arena provides several of these libraries with a starting selection of icons; you might want to open and examine several of them before you animate your next model (their file names end with *.plb*). To add a picture from a library to your entity picture list, highlight the picture you want to replace, highlight the new selection from a library, and click on the left arrow button (≤<) to copy the picture to your picture list. You can also build and maintain your own picture libraries by choosing the New button, creating your own pictures, and saving the file for future use. Or you can use clip art by using the standard copy and paste commands.

5.3.3 Changing Resource Pictures

There's very little difference between an entity picture and a resource picture other than the way we refer to them. Entities acquire pictures by assigning a *picture name* somewhere in the model. Resources acquire pictures depending on their state. Early in this chapter, we discussed the four automatic resource states (Idle, Busy, Failed, and Inactive) and the default pictures associated with them. When you open a Resource Picture Placement window (e.g., by double-clicking on the Sealer resource picture), you might notice that the Identifier for the resource is given, but you are not allowed to change it (Figure 5-13). This is because you have already defined the resource name in the Server or Inspect modules. You can, however, change the drawings used to depict the resource in its various states.

Let's replace these pictures as we did for the entity pictures. Double-click on the Idle picture and replace it with a single box. Use the background color for the fill, change the line size to 7 points (from the Draw toolbar), and change the line color. The small circle with the cross is the *reference point* for the resource, indicating how other objects align to its picture; drag this into the middle of your box. Accept this icon (by closing the Picture Editor window) and return to the Resource Picture Placement window. Now let's develop our own picture library. Choosing the New button from the Resource Picture Placement window opens a new, empty library file. Now select your newly created icon, click Add under the current library area, and then click on the right arrow button. Choose the Save button to name and save your new library file (e.g., `Book.plb`).

Figure 5-13. The Default Resource Pictures

We'll now use this picture to create the rest of our resource pictures. Highlight the busy picture and the new library picture and use the left arrow button to make your busy picture look just like your idle picture. When the animation is running, the entity picture will sit in the center of this box, so we'll know it's busy. Now copy the same library picture to the inactive and failed states. Open each of these pictures and fill the box with a color that will denote whether the resource is in the failed or inactive state; e.g., red for failed. Now copy these two new pictures to your library and save the library. Your final resource pictures should look something like those shown in Figure 5-14.

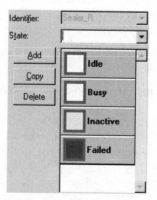

Figure 5-14. The Final Resource Pictures

Accept the resource pictures and return to the main model window. (By the way, have you remembered to save your model recently?) Your new resource icon may be larger than you want, so adjust it appropriately. The resource picture also contains an object that appears as a double circle with a dashed line connected to the lower left portion of the resource picture—the *Seize Area*. This Seize Area is where your entity will sit when it has control of the resource; drag it to the center of your resource picture. Now run your animation to see if your entity and resource pictures are the sizes you want. If not, you can adjust the position of the seize area by pausing the run, displaying seize areas (using the *Edit/Layers* menu option), and dragging it to the desired location. After you've fine-tuned its position, you'll probably want to turn off the display of the seize area layer before ending the run.

Once you're satisfied with your animation of the sealer resource, double-click on the sealer resource to open the Resource Picture Placement window and note the size factor in the lower left portion of the window. You might want to round this number up or down to a value that you can easily remember (in our animation, we used a size factor of 0.4). Now exit this window and use your new library to copy the appropriate pictures for the Part A Prep and Part B Prep resource pictures.

The picture of the rework resource will have to be modified because it has a capacity of 2 during the second shift. Open the resource picture placement window for the rework resource and copy the idle symbol from your library. Edit the picture and add another square (Edit/Duplicate) beside or under the first picture. This will allow room for two entities to reside during the second shift. Copy this new picture to the library and use it to create the remaining rework pictures. Set your size factor and close the window.

The original resource animation had only one seize area, so double-click on the seize area, click on the Points button, and add a second seize area. Seize areas are much like queues and can have any number of points, although the number of points used depends on the resource capacity. Like a queue, seize areas can also be shown as a line. Close this window and position the two seize area points inside the two boxes representing the resource.

You should now have an animation that's starting to look more like your perceived system. You may want to reposition the resources, queues, stations, etc., until you're happy with the way the animation looks. You also could add text to label things, lines to indicate queues or walls, and maybe a few potted plants.

5.3.4 Adding Plots and Variables

The last thing we'll do is add some plots and variables to our animation. We could use the plot and variable objects from the Animate toolbar for this, but it's much easier to use the Animate module from the Common panel. Let's add a plot for the number in queue and a variable for the number of available resources at the rework area. First let's place and fill out an Animate module for the number in queue, shown in Display 5-24. Once you've selected the data object, Queue, we suggest that you use the pull-down list to make sure you get the correct name. Also, you might note that each animate module allows you to animate only one type of information, but you can animate it with any or all of the available displays. If you want an additional information type or another data object, use another Animate module.

Animate

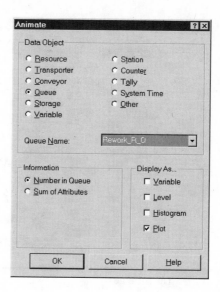

Data Object		
Queue		*select*
Queue Name		Rework_R_Q
Display As		
Variable		*uncheck*
Level		*uncheck*
Histogram		*uncheck*

Display 5-24. The Animate Module: Number in Queue

Before you run your model, we suggest that you edit the plot. Double-click on the plot to open its dialog, as shown in Display 5-25. The time range is the range you want to see on your plot. We've also requested labels for the X axis and that the area under the plot be filled. You might also want to click on the Area button and change the color of the filled region.

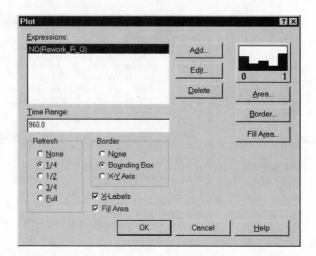

Time Range	960.0
Bounding Box	*select*
X-Labels	*check*
Fill Area	*check*

Display 5-25. The Plot Window

Before exiting this window, let's edit the plot data, Display 5-26. For this example, we've only increased the Maximum value of the Y axis and requested a Stepped plot. The # of History Points tells Arena the maximum number of possible points it will have on the plot at any time. If this number is too small, the left portion of your plot will not show any data. If this happens, simply increase this number until it's large enough.

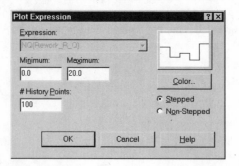

Maximum	20.0
Stepped	*select*

Display 5-26. The Plot Data

After you've accepted these data, you may want to increase the size of the plot in the model window and move it somewhere else on the animation. Next, let's place a second Animate module for the number of available resources for the rework area and edit the window as shown in Display 5-27.

Data Object	
Resource	*select*
Resource Name	`Rework_R`
Display As	
Level	*uncheck*
Histogram	*uncheck*
Plot	*uncheck*

Display 5-27. The Animate Module: Number of Available Resources

Now double-click on the variable and change the format as in Display 5-28. Resize the variable and move it near the rework station.

Finally, we used the Text tool from the Animate toolbar to label the stations, counters, and the plot to identify them while the simulation runs. We also added some polylines to indicate the Routes during the animation.

Your model and animation should now be complete and look something like the snapshot shown in Figure 5-15, which was taken at about simulation time 1367.

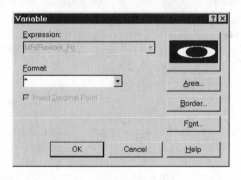

Format	*

Display 5-28. The Variable Data

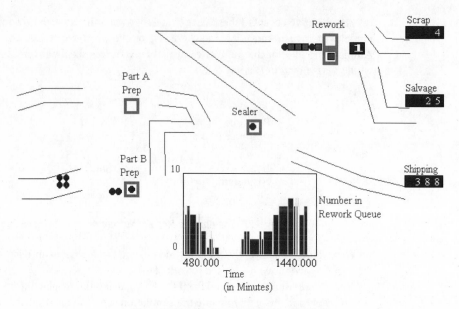

Figure 5-15. The Final Animation: Model 5.3

5.4   Input Analysis: Specifying Model Parameters and Distributions

As you've no doubt noticed, there are a lot of details that you have to specify completely in order to define a working simulation model. Probably you think first of the logical aspects of the model, like what the entities and resources are, how entities enter and maybe leave the model, the resources they need, the paths they follow, and so on. These kinds of activities might be called *structural* modeling since they lay out the fundamental logic of what you want your model to look like and do.

You've also noticed that there are other things in specifying a model that are more numerical or mathematical in nature (and maybe therefore more mundane). For example, in specifying Model 5.2, we declared that interarrival times for Part A were exponentially distributed with a mean of 5 minutes, total processing times for Part B Prep followed a triangular (3, 5, 10) distribution, the "up" times for the sealer were draws from an exponential (120) distribution, and we set up a Schedule for the number of rework operators at different times. You also have to make these kinds of specifications, which might be called *quantitative* modeling, and are potentially just as important to what happens as are the structural-modeling assumptions.

So where did we get all these numbers and distributions for Model 5.2 (as well as for practically all the other models in this book)? OK, we admit that we just made them up, after playing around for a while, to get the kinds of results we wanted in order to illustrate various points. We get to do this since we're just writing a book rather than doing any real work, but unfortunately, you won't have this luxury. Rather, you need to observe the real system (if it exists) or use specifications for it (if it doesn't exist), collect data on what corresponds to your input quantitative modeling, and analyze these data to come up with reasonable "models," or representations of how they'll be specified or generated in the simulation. For Model 5.2, this would entail collecting data on actual interarrival times for Part A, processing times for Part B Prep, up times for the sealer, and actual staffing at the rework station (as well as all the other quantitative inputs required to specify the model). You'd then need to take a look at these data and do some kind of analysis on them to specify the corresponding inputs to your model in an accurate, realistic, and valid way.

In this section, we'll describe this process and show you how to use the Arena Input Analyzer (which, like the Output Analyzer introduced in Section 5.2.6, is a separate application that accompanies and works with Arena) to help you fit probability distributions to data observed on quantities subject to variation.

5.4.1 Deterministic vs. Random Inputs

One fundamental issue in quantitative modeling is whether you're going to model an input quantity as a deterministic (i.e., non-random) quantity, or whether you're going to model it as a *random variable* following some probability distribution. Sometimes it's clear that something should be deterministic, like the number of rework operators, though you might want to vary the values from run to run to see what effect they have on performance.

But sometimes it's not so clear, and we can only offer the (obvious) advice that you should do what appears most realistic and valid so far as possible. In Section 5.4.2, we'll talk a little about using your model for what's called *sensitivity analysis* to measure how important a particular input is to your output, which might indicate how much you need to worry about whether it should be modeled as deterministic or random.

You might be tempted to assume away your input's randomness, since this seems simpler and has the advantage that the model's outputs will be non-random. This can be pretty dangerous, though, from the model-validity viewpoint because it's often the randomness itself that leads to important system behavior that you'd certainly want to capture in your simulation model. For instance, in a simple single-server queue, we might assume that all interarrival times are *exactly* 1 minute and that all processing times are *exactly* 59 seconds; both of these figures might agree with *average* values from observed data on arrivals and service. If the model starts empty with the server idle and the first arrival is at time 0, then there will never be a queue since each customer will finish service and leave 1 second before the next customer arrives. However, if the reality is that the interarrival and service times are exponential random variables with respective means of 1 minute and 59 seconds (rather than constant at these values), you get a very different story in terms of queue length (go ahead and build a little Arena model for this, and run it for a long time); in fact, in the long run, it turns out that the average number of customers in the queue is 58.0167, a far cry from 0. Intuitively, what's going on here is that, with the (correct) random model, it sometimes happens that some obnoxious customer has a long service demand, or that several customers arrive at almost the same time; it's precisely these kinds of random occurrences that cause the queue to build up, which never happen in the (incorrect) deterministic model.

5.4.2 Collecting Data

One of the very early steps in planning your simulation project should be to identify what data you'll need to support the model. Finding the data and preparing them for use in your model can be time consuming, expensive, and often frustrating; and the availability and quality of data can influence the modeling approach you take and the level of detail you capture in the model.

There are many types of data that you might need to collect. Most models require a good bit of information involving time delays: interarrival times, processing times, travel times, operator work schedules, etc. In many cases, you'll also need to estimate probabilities, such as the percentage yield from an operation, the proportions of each type of customer, or the probability that a caller has a touch-tone phone. If you're modeling a system where the physical movement of entities among stations will be represented in the model, the operating parameters and physical layout of the material handling system will also be needed.

You can go to many sources for data, ranging from electronic databases to interviews of people working in the system to be studied. It seems that when it comes to finding data for a simulation study, it's either "feast or famine," with each presenting its own unique challenges.

If the system you're modeling exists (or is similar to an actual system somewhere else), you may think that your job's easier, since there should be a lot of data available. However, what you're likely to find is that the data you get are not the data you need. For example, it's common to collect processing-time data on machines (i.e., a part's time span from arriving at the machine to completing the process), which at first glance might look like a good source for processing times in the simulation model. But, if the observed processing-time data included the queue time or included machine failure times, they might not fit into the model's logic, which explicitly models the queueing logic and the machine failures separately from the machining time.

On the other hand, if you're about to model a brand new system or a significant modification to an existing one, you may find yourself at the other end of the spectrum, with little or no data. In this case, your model is at the mercy of rough approximations from designers, equipment vendors, etc. We'll have a few suggestions (as opposed to solutions) for you in Section 5.4.5.

In either case, as you decide what and how much data to collect, it's important to keep the following helpful hints in mind:

▪ **Sensitivity analysis:** One often-ignored aspect of performing simulation studies is developing an understanding of what's important and what's not. Sensitivity analysis can be used even very early in a project to assess the impact of changes in data on the model results. If you can't easily obtain good data about some aspect of your system, run the model with a range of values to see if the system's performance changes significantly. If it doesn't, you may not need to invest in collecting data and still can have good confidence in your conclusions. If it does, then you'll either need to find a way to obtain reliable data or your results and recommendations will be coarser.

- **Match model detail with quality of data:** A benefit of developing an early understanding of the quality of your input data is that it can help you to decide how much detail to incorporate in the model logic. Typically, it doesn't make any sense to model carefully the detailed logic of a part of your system for which you have unreliable values of the associated data, unless you think that, at a later time, you'll be able to obtain better data.

- **Cost:** Because it can be expensive to collect and prepare data for use in a model, you may decide to use looser estimates for some data. In making this assessment, sensitivity analysis can be helpful so that you have an idea of the value of the data in affecting your recommendations.

- **"Garbage in, garbage out":** Remember that the results and recommendations you present from your simulation study are only as reliable as the model and its inputs. If you can't locate accurate data concerning critical elements of the model, you can't place a great deal of confidence in the accuracy of your conclusions. This doesn't mean that there's no value in performing a simulation study if you can't obtain "good" data. You still can develop tremendous insight into the operation of a complex system, the interactions among its elements, and some level of prediction regarding how it will perform. But take care to articulate the reliability of your predictions based on the quality of the input data.

A final hint that we might offer is that data collection (and some of their analysis) is often identified as the most difficult, costly, time-consuming, and tedious part of a simulation study. This is due in part to various difficulties you might encounter in collecting and analyzing data, and in part due to the undeniable fact that it's just not as much fun as building the logical model and playing around with it. So, be of good cheer in this activity, and keep reminding yourself that it's an important if not pleasant or exciting part of why you're using simulation.

5.4.3 Using Data

If you have historical data (e.g., a record of breakdowns and repair times for a machine), or if you know how part of a system will work (e.g., planned operator schedules), you still face decisions concerning how to incorporate the data into your model. The fundamental choice is whether to use the data directly or whether to fit a probability distribution to the existing data. Which approach you decide to use can be chosen based on both theoretical issues and practical considerations.

From a theoretical standpoint, your collected data represent what's happened in the past, which may or may not be an unbiased prediction of what will happen in the future. If the conditions surrounding the generation of these historical data no longer apply (or if they changed during the time span in which the data were recorded), then the historical data may be biased or may simply be missing some important aspects of the process. For example, if the historical data are from a database of product orders placed over the last 12 months, but 4 months ago a new product option was introduced, then the order data stored in the preceding 8 months are no longer directly useful since they don't contain the new option. The tradeoffs are that if you use the historical data directly, no values other than those recorded can be experienced; but if you sample from a fitted probability distribution, it's possible to get values that aren't possible (e.g., from the tails of un-bounded distributions) or to lose important characteristics (e.g., bimodal data, sequential patterns).

Practical considerations can come into play too. You may not have enough historical data to drive a simulation run that's long enough to support your analysis. You may need to consider the effect of file access on the speed of your simulation runs, as well. Reading a lot of data from a file is typically slower than sampling from a probability distribution, so driving the model with the historical data during a run can slow you down.

Regardless of your choice, Arena supplies built-in tools to take care of the mechanics of using the historical data in your model. If you decide to fit a probability distribution to the data, the Input Analyzer automates this process, providing an expression that you can use directly in your model; we'll go into this in the next subsection. If you want to drive the model directly from the historical data, you can bring the values in once to become part of the model's data structure, or you can read the data dynamically during the simulation run, which will be discussed in Section 10.1.

5.4.4 *Fitting Input Distributions via the Input Analyzer*

If you decide to incorporate your existing data values by fitting a probability distribution to them, you can either select the distribution yourself and use the Input Analyzer to provide numerical estimates of the appropriate parameters, or you can fit a number of distributions to the data and select the most appropriate one. In either case, the Input Analyzer provides you with estimates of the parameter values (based on the data you supply) and a ready-made expression that you can just copy and paste into your model.

When the Input Analyzer fits a distribution to your data, it estimates the distribution's parameters (including any shift or offset that's required to formulate a valid expression) and calculates a number of measures of how good the distribution fits your data. You can use this information to select which distribution you want to use in your model, which we discuss below.

Probability distributions can be thought of as falling into two main types: *theoretical* and *empirical*. The theoretical distributions, such as the exponential and normal, generate samples based on a mathematical formulation. The empirical distributions simply divide the actual data into groupings and calculate the proportion of values in each group.

Each type of distribution is further broken into *continuous* and *discrete* types. The continuous theoretical distributions that Arena supports for use in your model are the exponential, triangular, normal, and uniform distributions mentioned previously, as well as the beta, Erlang, gamma, lognormal, and Weibull distributions. These distributions are referred to as continuous distributions because they can return any real-valued quantity (within a range for the bounded types). They're usually used to represent time durations in a simulation model. The Poisson distribution is a discrete distribution; it can return only integer-valued quantities. It's often used to describe the number of events that occur in an interval of time or the distribution of randomly varying batch sizes.

You also can use one of two empirical distributions: the discrete and continuous probability distributions. Each is defined using a series of probability/value pairs representing a histogram of the data values that can be returned. The *discrete empirical distribution* returns only the data values themselves, using the probabilities to choose from among the individual values. It's often used for probabilistically assigning entity types. The *continuous empirical distribution* uses the probabilities and values to return a real-valued quantity. It can be used in place of a theoretical distribution in cases where the data have unusual characteristics or where none of the theoretical distributions provide a good fit.

The Input Analyzer can fit any of the above distributions to your data. However, you must decide whether to use a theoretical or empirical distribution, and unfortunately, there aren't any standard rules for making this choice. Generally, if a histogram of your data (displayed automatically by the Input Analyzer) appears to be fairly uniform or has a single "hump," and if it doesn't have any large gaps where there aren't any values, then you're likely to obtain a good fit from one of the theoretical distributions. However, if there are a number of value groupings that have many observations (multimodal) or there are a number of data points that have a value that's significantly different from the main set of observations, an empirical distribution may provide a better representation of the data; an alternative to an empirical distribution is to divide the data somehow, which we'll describe at the end of this subsection.

The Input Analyzer is a standard tool that accompanies Arena and is designed specifically to fit distributions to observed data, provide estimates of their parameters, and measure how well they fit the data. There are four steps required to use the Input Analyzer to fit a probability distribution to your data for use in your model:

- Create a text file containing the data values.
- Fit one or more distributions to the data in the Input Analyzer.
- Select which distribution you'd like to use.
- Copy the expression generated by the Input Analyzer into the appropriate field in your Arena model.

To prepare the data file, simply create an ordinary ASCII text file containing the data in free format. Any text editor, word processor, or spreadsheet program can be used. The individual data values must be separated by one or more "white space characters" (blank spaces, tabs, or linefeeds). There are no other formatting requirements; in particular, you can have as many data values on a line as you want, and the number of values per line can vary from line to line. When using a word processor or spreadsheet program, be sure to save the file in a "text only" format. This eliminates any character or paragraph formatting that otherwise would be included. For example, Figure 5-16 shows the contents of an ASCII file called `partbprp.dst` (the default file extension for data files for the Input Analyzer is .dst) containing observations on 187 Part B Prep times; note that the values are separated by blanks or linefeeds, there are different numbers of observations per line, and there is no particular order or layout to the data.

```
6.1   9.4   8.1   3.2   6.5   7.2   7.8   4.9   3.5   6.6   6.1   5.1   4.9   4.2
6.4   8.1   6.0   8.2   6.8   5.9   5.2
6.5   5.4   5.9   9.3   5.4   6.5   7.4
6.0  12.6   6.8   5.6   5.8   6.2   5.6   6.4   9.5   7.2   5.6   4.7   4.5   7.0
7.7   6.9   5.4   6.3   8.1   4.9   5.3   5.0   4.7   5.7   4.9   5.3   6.4   7.5
4.4   4.9   7.6   3.6   8.3   5.6   6.2   5.0
7.4   5.2   5.0   6.5   8.0   6.2   5.0   4.8   6.2   4.9
7.0   7.7   4.7   5.0   6.0   9.0   5.7   7.1   5.0   5.6
4.9   7.8   7.1   7.1  11.5   5.4   5.2
6.1   6.8   5.4   3.5   7.1   5.7   5.4
5.7   6.1   4.2   8.8   7.4   5.5
5.3   5.9   5.2   6.4   4.5   5.1   5.6   6.1
8.1   8.1   5.1   8.3   7.5   7.6  10.9   6.5   9.0   5.9   6.8   9.0   6.5   6.0
5.8   5.0   6.4   4.7   4.5   6.2   5.2   7.9   5.5   4.9   7.2   4.9   4.5   6.0
6.3   8.3   5.5   7.8   5.4   5.3   6.6   3.6   7.3   5.3   8.9   6.8   7.1   8.7
6.4   3.3   7.0   7.7   6.7   7.6   7.6   7.1   5.6   5.9   4.1   7.5   7.7   5.4
4.8   5.5   8.8   7.2   6.3  10.0   4.3   4.9   5.7   5.1   6.7   6.0   5.6   7.2
7.0   7.8   6.3   6.1   8.4
```

Figure 5-16. Listing of the ASCII File partbprp.dst

To fit a distribution to these data, run the Input Analyzer (e.g., select the *Tools/Input Analyzer* menu option from Arena). In the Input Analyzer, load the data file into a data fit window by creating a new window (*File/New* or the 🗋 button) and then attaching your data file using either the *File/Data File/Use Existing* menu option or the 📂 button. The Input Analyzer displays a histogram of the data in the top half of the window and a summary of the data characteristics in the bottom half, as shown in Figure 5-17.

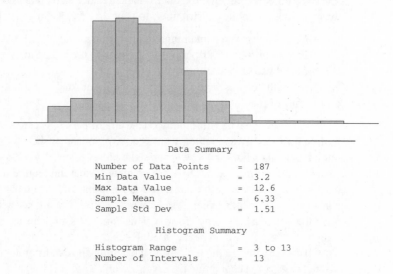

```
                        Data Summary

        Number of Data Points    =    187
        Min Data Value           =    3.2
        Max Data Value           =    12.6
        Sample Mean              =    6.33
        Sample Std Dev           =    1.51

                     Histogram Summary

        Histogram Range          =    3 to 13
        Number of Intervals      =    13
```

Figure 5-17. Histogram and Summary of partbprp.dst

You can adjust the relative size of the windows by dragging the splitter bar in the center of the window. Or, to see more of the data summary, you can scroll down through the text. Other options, such as changing the characteristics of the histogram, are described in online help.

The Input Analyzer's *Fit* menu provides options for fitting individual probability distributions to the data (i.e., estimating the required parameters for a given distribution). After you fit a distribution, its density function is drawn on top of the histogram display and a summary of the characteristics of the fit is displayed in the text section of the window. (This information also is written to a file named *distribution.out*, where *distribution* indicates the distribution you chose to fit, such as *triangle* for triangular.) The exact expression required to represent the data in Arena is also given in the text window. You can transfer this to Arena by selecting the *Edit/Copy Expression* menu option in the Input Analyzer, opening the appropriate dialog in Arena, and pasting the expression (Ctrl + V) in the desired field. Figure 5-18 shows this for fitting a triangular distribution to the data in `partbprp.dst`. Though we'll go into the goodness-of-fit issue below, it's apparent from the plot in Figure 5-18 that the triangular distribution doesn't fit these data particularly well.

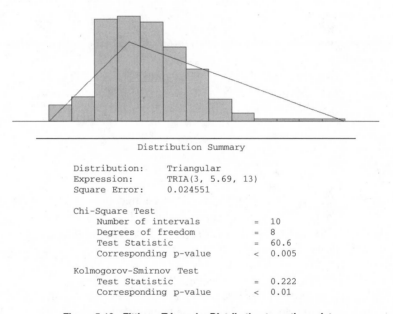

```
                          Distribution Summary

          Distribution:    Triangular
          Expression:      TRIA(3, 5.69, 13)
          Square Error:    0.024551

      Chi-Square Test
           Number of intervals          =   10
           Degrees of freedom           =   8
           Test Statistic               =   60.6
           Corresponding p-value        <   0.005

      Kolmogorov-Smirnov Test
           Test Statistic               =   0.222
           Corresponding p-value        <   0.01
```

Figure 5-18. Fitting a Triangular Distribution to partbprp.dst

If you plan to use a theoretical distribution in your model, you may want to start by selecting the *Fit/Fit All* menu option. This automatically fits all of the applicable distributions to the data, calculates test statistics for each (discussed below), and displays the distribution that has the minimum square error value (a measure of the quality of the distribution's match to the data). Figure 5-19 shows the results of the Fit All option for our Part B Prep times and indicates that a gamma distribution with $\beta = 0.775$ and $\alpha = 4.29$, shifted to the right by 3, provides the "best" fit in the sense of minimum square error. Comparing the plot with that in Figure 5-18 indicates that this fitted gamma distribution certainly appears to be a better representation of the data than the fitted triangular distribution. Other considerations for selecting which theoretical distribution to use in your model are discussed below.

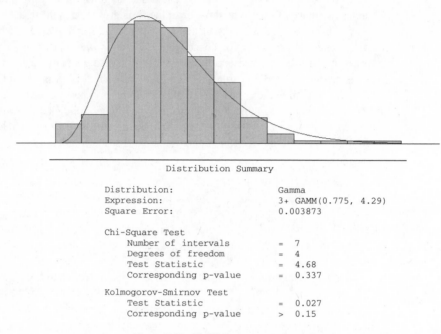

```
                          Distribution Summary

        Distribution:                 Gamma
        Expression:                   3+ GAMM(0.775, 4.29)
        Square Error:                 0.003873

    Chi-Square Test
        Number of intervals      =    7
        Degrees of freedom       =    4
        Test Statistic           =    4.68
        Corresponding p-value    =    0.337

    Kolmogorov-Smirnov Test
        Test Statistic           =    0.027
        Corresponding p-value    >    0.15
```

Figure 5-19. Fit All Option to partbprp.dst

If you want to use a discrete or continuous empirical distribution, use the *Empirical* option from the *Fit* menu. You may first want to adjust the number of histogram cells, which determines how many probability/value pairs will be calculated for the empirical distribution. To do so, select the *Options/Parameters/Histogram* menu option and change the number of intervals.

In addition to "eyeballing" the fitted densities on top of the histograms, the Input Analyzer provides three numerical measures of the quality of fit of a distribution to the data to help you decide. The first, and simplest to understand, is the *mean square error*. This is the average of the square error terms for each histogram cell, which are the squares of the differences between the relative frequencies of the observations in a cell and the relative frequency for the fitted probability distribution function over that cell's data range. The larger this square error value, the further away the distribution is from the actual data. If you fit all applicable distributions to the data, the Fit All Summary table orders the distributions from smallest to largest square error (select the *Window/Fit All Summary* menu option), shown in Figure 5-20 for partbprp.dst. While we see that gamma won the square-error contest, it was followed closely by Weibull, beta, and Erlang, any of which would probably be just as accurate as gamma to use as input to the model.

Function	Sq Error
Gamma	0.00387
Weibull	0.00443
Beta	0.00444
Erlang	0.00487
Normal	0.00633
Lognormal	0.00871
Triangular	0.0246
Uniform	0.0773
Exponential	0.0806

Figure 5-20. Fit All Summary for partbprp.dst

The other two measures of a distribution's fit to the data are the chi-square and Kolmogorov-Smirnov (K-S) goodness-of-fit hypothesis tests. These are standard statistical hypothesis tests that can be used to assess whether a fitted theoretical distribution is a good fit to the data. The Input Analyzer reports information about the tests in the text window (see the bottoms of Figures 5-18 and 5-19). Of particular interest is the *Corresponding p-value*, which will always fall between 0 and 1.[2] To interpret this, larger *p*-values indicate better fits. Corresponding *p*-values less than about 0.05 indicate that the distribution's not a very good fit. Of course, as with any statistical hypothesis test, a high *p*-value doesn't constitute "proof" of a good fit—just a lack of evidence against the fit.

When it comes down to fitting or choosing a distribution to use, there's no rigorous, universally agreed-upon approach that you can employ to pick the "best" distribution. Different statistical tests (such as the K-S and chi-square) might rank distributions differently, or changes in the preparation of the data (e.g., the number of histogram cells) might reorder the distributions.

Your first critical decision is whether to use a theoretical distribution or an empirical one. Examining the results of the K-S and chi-square tests can be helpful. If the *p*-values for one or more distributions are fairly high (e.g., 0.10 or greater), then you can use a theoretical distribution and have a fair degree of confidence that you're getting a good representation of the data (unless your sample is quite small, in which case the discriminatory power of goodness-of-fit tests is quite weak). If the *p*-values are low, you may want to use an empirical distribution to better capture the characteristics of the data.

If you've decided to use a theoretical distribution, there often will be a number of them with very close goodness-of-fit statistics. In this case, other issues may be worth considering for selecting among them.

First of all, you may want to limit yourself to considering only bounded or unbounded distributions, based on your understanding of how the data will be used in your model. For instance, often the triangular (bounded) and normal (unbounded) distributions will be good fits to data such as process times. Over a long simulation run, they each might provide similar results, but during the run, the normal distribution might periodically return fairly large values that might not practically occur in the real system.

---

[2] More precisely, the *p*-value is the probability of getting a data set that's more inconsistent with the fitted distribution than the data set you actually got, if the fitted distribution is truly "the truth."

A normal distribution with a mean that's close to zero may return an artificially large number of zero-valued samples if the distribution's being used for something that can't be negative, such as a time. On the other hand, bounding the triangular to obtain a faithful overall representation of the data might exclude a few outlying values that should be captured in the simulation model.

Another consideration is of a more practical nature; namely, that it's easier to adjust parameters of some distributions than of others. If you're planning to make any changes to your model that include adjusting the parameters of the distribution (e.g., for sensitivity analysis or to analyze different scenarios), you might favor those with more easily understood parameters. For example, in representing interarrival times, Weibull and exponential distributions might provide fits of similar quality, but it's much easier to change an interarrival time by adjusting an exponential mean than by changing the parameters of a Weibull distribution.

If you're concerned about whether you're making the correct choice, run the model with each of your options to see if there's a significant difference in the results (you may have to wait until the model's nearly complete to be able to draw a good conclusion). You can further investigate the factors affecting distribution fits (such as the goodness-of-fit tests) by consulting Arena's online help or other sources, such as Pegden, Shannon, and Sadowski (1995) or Law and Kelton (1991). Otherwise, select a distribution based on the qualitative and practical issues discussed above.

Before leaving our discussion of the Input Analyzer, we'd like to revisit an issue we mentioned earlier in the subsection, namely what to do if your data appear to have multiple peaks or perhaps a few extreme values, sometimes called *outliers*. Either of these situations usually makes it impossible to get a decent fit from any standard theoretical distribution. As we mentioned before, one option is to use an empirical distribution, which is probably the best route unless your sample size is quite small. In the case of outliers, you should certainly go back to your data set and make sure that they're actually correct rather than just being some kind of error, perhaps a simple clerical mistake; if data values appear to be in error and you can't backtrack to confirm or correct them, you should probably just remove them.

In the case of either multiple peaks or (correct) outliers, you might want to consider dividing your data set into two (maybe more) subsets before reading them into the Input Analyzer. For example, suppose you have data on machine downtimes and notice from the histogram that there are two distinct peaks; i.e., the data are *bimodal*. Reviewing the original records, you discover that these downtimes resulted from two different situations—breakdowns and scheduled maintenance. Separating the data into two subsets reveals that downtimes resulting from breakdowns tend to be longer than downtimes due to scheduled maintenance, explaining the two peaks. You could then separate the data (before going into the Input Analyzer), fit separate distributions to these data sets, and then modify your model logic to account for both kinds of downtimes.

You can also do a different kind of separation of the data directly in the Input Analyzer, based purely on their range. After loading the data file, select *Options/Parameters/ Histogram* to specify cutoffs for the Low Value and High Value you want to define the bounds of a *subset* of your entire data set. For bimodal data, you'd focus on the left peak by leaving the Low Value alone and specifying the High Value as the point where the histogram bottoms out between the two peaks, and later focus on the right peak by using this cutpoint as the Low Value and using the original High Value for the entire data set; getting the right cutpoint could require some trial and error. Then fit whatever distribution seems promising to each subset (or use the Fit All option) to represent that range of the data. If you've already fit a distribution (or used Fit All) before making Low/High Value cut, the Input Analyzer will immediately re-do the fit(s) and give you the new results for the data subset included in your cut; if you've done Fit All, a different distribution form altogether might come up as "the best." You'd need to repeat this process for each subset of the data. As a practical matter, you probably should limit the number of subsets to two or three since this process can become cumbersome, and it's probably not obvious where the best cutpoints are. To generate draws in your simulation model representing the original entire data set, the idea is to select one of your data subsets randomly, with probabilities corresponding to the relative sizes of the subsets, then generate a value from the distribution you decided on for that subset. For instance, if you started out with a bimodal data set of size 200 and set your cutpoint so that the smallest 120 points represented the left peak and the largest 80 points represented the right peak, you'd generate from the distribution fitted to the left part of the data with probability 0.6 and generate from the distribution fitted to the right part of the data with probability 0.4. This kind of operation isn't exactly provided automatically in a single Arena module, so you'd have to put something together yourself. If the value involved is an activity time like a time delay an entity incurs, one possibility would be to use the Inspect module if you have just two subsets (or the Chance module from the Support panel if you have more than two subsets) to do a "coin flip" to decide from which subset to generate, then Connect to one of several Actions or Assign modules to Assign a value to an entity attribute as a draw from the appropriate distribution, and use this attribute downstream for whatever it's supposed to do. A different approach would be to set up an Arena Expression for the entire thing; Expressions are covered in Section 6.2.2.

5.4.5 No Data?

Whether you like it or not, there are times when you just can't get reliable data on what you need for input modeling. This can arise from several situations, like (obviously) the system doesn't exist, data collection is too expensive or disruptive, or maybe you don't have the cooperation or clearance you need. In this case, you'll have to rely on some fairly arbitrary assumptions or guesses, which we dignify as "*ad hoc data*." We don't pretend to have any great solutions for you here, but have a few suggestions that people have found useful. No matter what you do, though, you really should carry out some kind of sensitivity analysis of the output to these *ad hoc* inputs to have a realistic idea of how much faith to put in your results. You'll either need to pick some deterministic value that you'll use in your study (or run the model a number of times with different values), or you'll want to represent the system characteristic using a probability distribution.

If the values are for something other than a time delay, such as probabilities, operating parameters, or physical layout characteristics, you can either select a value or, in some cases, use a probability distribution. If you use a deterministic value by entering a constant in the model (e.g., 0.15 probability of failing inspection), it's a good idea to perform some sensitivity analysis to assess what effect the parameter has on the model's results. If small changes to the value influence the performance of the system, you may want to analyze the system explicitly for a range of values (maybe small, medium, and large) rather than just for your best guess.

If the data represent a time delay, you'll almost certainly want to use a probability distribution to capture both the activity's inherent variability as well as your uncertainty about the value itself. Which distribution you'll use will be based on both the nature of the activity and the type of data you have. When you've selected the distribution, then you'll need to supply the proper parameters based on your estimates and your assessment of the variability in the process.

For selecting the distribution in the absence of empirical data, you might first look at the exponential, triangular, normal, and uniform distributions. The parameters for these distributions are fairly easy to understand, and they provide a good range of characteristics for a range of modeling applications, as indicated in Table 5-1.

Table 5-1. Possible No-Data Distributions

Distribution	Parameters	Characteristics	Example Use
Exponential	Mean	High variance Bounded on left Unbounded on right	Interarrival times Time to machine failure (constant failure rate)
Triangular	Min, Mode, Max	Symmetric or non-symmetric Bounded on both sides	Activity times
Normal	Mean, Std. Dev.	Symmetric Unbounded on both sides Can generate negative values	Activity times
Uniform	Min, Max	All values equally likely Bounded on both sides	Little known about process

If the times you're estimating vary independently (i.e., one value doesn't influence the next one), your estimate of the mean isn't too large, and there's a large amount of variability in the times, the exponential distribution might be a good choice. It's most often used for interarrival times where there's no common process generating the arriving entities; examples would be customers coming to a restaurant or pick requests from a warehouse.

If the times represent an activity where there's a "most likely" time with some variation around it, the triangular and normal distributions are often used because they can capture processes with small or large degrees of variability and their parameters are fairly easy to understand. The triangular distribution is defined by minimum, most likely, and maximum values, which is a natural way to estimate the time required for some activity. It has the advantage of allowing a non-symmetric distribution of values around the most likely, which is commonly encountered in real processes. It's also a bounded distribution—no value will be less than the minimum or greater than the maximum—which may or may not be a good representation of the real process.

The normal distribution is the classical "bell curve," defined by a mean and standard deviation. It returns values that are symmetrically distributed around the mean and is an unbounded distribution, meaning that you could get a very large or very small value once in a while. In cases where negative values can't be used in a model (e.g., the delay time in a process), negative samples from a normal distribution are set to a value of 0; if the mean of your distribution is close to 0 (e.g., no more than about three or four times the standard deviation from 0), the normal distribution may be inappropriate. Because the standard deviation directly defines the variability, it's easy to change the amount of variability in the values simply by changing the standard deviation.

Finally, if you really don't know much about the process but can guess what the minimum and maximum values will be, you might use the uniform distribution. It returns all values between a minimum and maximum with equal likelihood.

5.4.6   Nonstationary Arrival Processes

This somewhat specialized topic deserves mention on its own since it seems to come up often and can be very important in terms of representing system behavior validly. Many systems subject to external arrivals, like service systems for people, telephone call centers, and manufacturing systems with outside customer demands, experience arrival loads that can vary dramatically over the time frame of the simulation. Examples include a noon rush for burgers, heavy calls to a technical support line in the middle of the afternoon, and strong demand on a manufacturing system during certain seasons. A specific probabilistic model for this, the *nonstationary Poisson process*, is very useful and often provides an accurate way to reflect time-varying arrival patterns. You need to deal with two issues: how to estimate or specify the rate function, and then how to generate the arrival pattern in the simulation.

There are a lot of ways to estimate or specify a rate function from the data, some of which can be pretty complicated. We'll stick to one fairly simple method, which seems to work well in many applications, called the *piecewise-constant* rate function. First, identify lengths of time within which the arrival rate appears to be fairly flat; for instance, a call center's arrivals might be fairly constant over half-hour periods but could be quite different in different periods. Count up the numbers of arrivals in each period, and then compute a different rate for each period. For instance, suppose the call center experiences the following numbers of calls for the four half-hour periods between 8:00 AM and 10:00 AM: 20, 35, 45, and 50. Then the rates, *in units of calls per minute*, for the first four 30-minute periods would be 0.67, 1.17, 1.5, and 1.67 (note that you must use the same time units for these rate calculations as you do in the rest of your model).

Once you've estimated a rate function in this way, you next need to coax your Arena model into generating arrivals in accordance with this pattern. We do this in some detail in Section 8.2 (for a call center model with the above rate function for its first 2 hours), so we refer you there for the complete picture. The basic idea is that we generate "candidate" arrivals at the peak rate, but accept a candidate arrival only with probability given by the current rate divided by the peak rate, which "thins out" the arrivals during low-rate periods. We'd caution you that this is pretty tricky business and that other generation methods that *seem* correct can in fact give seriously wrong results; this too is taken up in Section 8.2 as well as Section 11.3.

5.4.7 Multivariate and Correlated Input Data

Most of the time we assume that all random variables driving a simulation are generated independently of each other from whatever distribution we decide on to represent them. Sometimes, though, this may not be the best assumption, for purely physical reasons. For instance, in Model 5.2 you could imagine that certain parts are "difficult"; maybe you'd detect this by noticing that a large prep time for a specific part tends to be followed by a large sealer time for that part; i.e., these two times are positively correlated. Ignoring this correlation could lead to an invalid model.

There are a number of ways to model situations like this, to estimate the required parameters (including the strength of the correlations), and to generate the required observations on the random variables during the simulation. Some of these methods entail viewing the associated random variables as coordinates of a random *vector* having some joint *multivariate* distribution to be fitted and generated from. You might also be able to specify some kind of formula-based association between related input quantities. Frankly, though, this is a pretty difficult issue in terms of both estimating the behavior and generating it during the simulation. For more on these and related issues, see Law and Kelton (1991) or Devroye (1986).

5.5 Summary and Forecast

If you've read and understood the material in this chapter, you should be getting dangerous in the use of Arena. We encourage you to press other buttons in the modules we've used and even try modules that we've not used. If you get stuck, try the online help feature, which may not answer your question, but will answer the questions you should be asking. You might also want to try other animation features or provide nicer pictures. At this point, the best advice we can give you is to *use* Arena. Chapters 6-11 will cover most of the modeling capabilities (and some of the statistical-analysis capabilities) of Arena in more depth.

5.6 Exercises

5.1 Travelers arrive at the main entrance door of an airline terminal according to an exponential interarrival-time distribution with mean 1.6 minutes. The travel time from the entrance to the check-in is distributed uniformly between 2 and 3 minutes. At the check-in counter, travelers wait in a single line until one of five agents is available to serve them. The check-in time follows a normal distribution with mean of 7 minutes and standard deviation of 2 minutes. Upon completion of their check-in, they are free to travel to their gates. Create a simulation model, with animation, of this system. Run the simulation for 16 hours to determine the average time in system, number of passengers completing check-in, and the average length of the check-in queue.

5.2 Develop a model of a simple serial two-process system. Items arrive at the system with a mean time between arrivals of 10 minutes. They are immediately sent to Process 1, which has an unlimited queue and a single resource with a mean service time of 9 minutes. Upon completion, they are sent to Process 2, which is identical to Process 1. Items depart the system upon completion of Process 2. Performance measures of interest are the average numbers in queue at each process and the system cycle time. Using a replication length of 10,000 minutes, make the following four runs and compare the results:

Run 1: exponential interarrival times and exponential service times
Run 2: constant interarrival times and exponential service times
Run 3: exponential interarrival times and constant service times
Run 4: constant interarrival times and constant service times

5.3   Modify the Exercise 5.1 check-in problem by adding agent breaks. The 16 hours are divided into two 8-hour shifts. Agent breaks are staggered, starting at 90 minutes into each shift. Each agent is given one 15-minute break. Agent lunch breaks (30 minutes) are also staggered, starting 3 ½ hours into each shift. Compare the result of this model to the result without agent breaks.

5.4   Two different part types arrive at the same system for processing. Part Type 1 arrives according to a lognormal distribution with a log mean of 11.5 hours and log standard deviation of 2.0 hours. These arriving parts wait in a queue designated for Part Type 1's only until an operator is available to process them. The processing time follows a triangular distribution with parameters 5, 6, and 8 hours. Part Type 2 arrives according to an exponential distribution with mean of 15 hours. These parts wait in a second queue until the same operator is available to process them. The processing time follows a triangular distribution with parameters 3, 7, and 8 hours. After being processed by the operator, all parts are sent for processing to a second operation that does not require an operator, triangular with parameters of 4, 6, and 8 hours. Completed parts exit the system. Assume that the times for all part transfers are negligible. Run the simulation for 5,000 hours to determine the average cycle time for all parts and the average number of items in the queues designated for the arriving parts.

5.5   During the verification process of the airline check-in system from Exercise 5.3, it was discovered that there were really two types of passengers. The first passenger type arrives according to an exponential interarrival distribution with mean 2.4 minutes and has a service time following a normal distribution with mean of 6 minutes and standard deviation of 1.5 minutes. The second type of passenger arrives according to an exponential distribution with mean 4.4 minutes and has a service time following a normal distribution with mean of 11 minutes and standard deviation of 2 minutes. Modify the model from Exercise 5.3 to include this new information. Compare the results.

5.6   Parts arrive at a single workstation system according to an exponential interarrival distribution with mean 20 seconds. After being transferred to the workstation, the parts are processed. The processing time distribution is TRIA(16, 19, 22) seconds. There are several easily identifiable visual characteristics that determine if a part has a potential quality problem. These parts, about 10%, are transferred to a station where they undergo an extensive inspection. The remaining parts are considered good and are transferred out of the system. The inspection time distribution is NORM(120, 12) seconds. About 14% of these parts fail the inspection and are transferred to scrap. The parts that pass the inspection are classified as good and are transferred out of the system. Assume all transfer times are 2 minutes. Run the simulation for 10,000 seconds to determine the number of good parts that exit the system, the number of scrapped parts, and the number of parts that are inspected.

5.7   A proposed production system consists of five serial automatic workstations. The processing times at each workstation are constant: 11, 10, 11, 11, and 12 (all times given in this problem are in minutes). The part interarrival times are UNIF(13, 15). There is an unlimited buffer in front of all workstations, and we will assume that the downstream transfer time is negligible or zero. The unique aspect of this system is that at workstations 2 through 5 there is a chance that the part will need to be reprocessed by the workstation that precedes it. For example, after completion at Workstation 2, the part can be sent back to the queue in front of Workstation 1. When this occurs, the transfer requires 3 minutes. The probability of revisiting a workstation is independent in that the same part could be sent back many times with no change in the probability. At the present time, it is estimated that this probability, the same for all four workstations, will be between 5% and 10%. Develop the simulation model and make six runs of 10,000 minutes each for probabilities of 5, 6, 7, 8, 9, and 10%. Using the results, construct a plot of the average cycle time (system time) against the probability of a revisit. Also include the maximum cycle time for each run on your plot.

5.8   A production system consists of four serial automatic workstations. All transfer times are assumed to be zero and all processing times are constant. There are two types of failures: major and jams. The data for this system are given in the table below (all times are in minutes). Use exponential distributions for the uptimes and uniform distributions for repair times (for instance, repairing jams at Workstation 3 is UNIF(2.8, 4.2)). Model the major failures using the Failure constructs (Time with Wait option) and the jams using the Downtimes constructs. Run your simulation for 10,000 minutes to determine the percent of time each resource spends in the failure states and the ending status of each workstation queue.

Number	Mean Process Time	Major Failures		Jams	
		MTBF	Repair	MTBF	Repair
1	8.5	475	20, 30	47.5	2, 3
2	8.3	570	24, 36	57	2.4, 3.6
3	8.6	665	28, 42	66.5	2.8, 4.2
4	8.6	475	20, 30	47.5	2, 3

5.9   An office that dispenses automotive license plates has divided its customers into categories to level the office workload. Customers arrive and enter one of three lines based on their residence location. Model this arrival activity as three independent arrival streams using an exponential interarrival distribution with mean of 10 minutes for each stream. Each customer type is assigned a single clerk that processes the application forms and accepts payment. The service time is UNIF(8, 10) minutes for all three customer types. After completion of this step, all customers are sent to a second clerk who checks the forms and issues the plates. The service time for this activity is UNIF(2.66, 3.33) minutes for all customer types. Develop a model of this system and run the simulation for 5,000 minutes.

A consultant has recommended that the office eliminate the step of differentiating between customers and use a single line with three clerks who can process any customer type. Develop a model of this system, run it for 5,000 minutes, and compare the results with the first system.

5.10 Customers arrive at an order counter with exponential interarrivals with a mean of 10 minutes. A single clerk accepts and checks their orders and processes payments, UNIF(8, 10) minutes. Upon completion of this activity, orders are randomly assigned to one of two available stock persons who retrieve the orders for the customers, UNIF(16, 20) minutes. These stock persons only retrieve orders for customers who have been assigned specifically to them. Upon receiving their orders, the customers depart the system. Develop a model of this system and run the simulation for 5,000 minutes.

A bright, young engineer has recommend that they eliminate the assignment of an order to a specific stock person and allow both stock persons to select their next activity from a single order queue. Develop a model of this system, run it for 5,000 minutes, and compare the results to the first system.

5.11 Using the model from Exercise 5.2, set the interarrival-time distribution to exponential and the process-time distribution for each Process to normal with a mean of 9 minutes. Setting the standard deviation of the normal distribution to values of 1, 2, and 3, make three different runs of 10,000 minutes each and compare the results.

5.12 Using the model from Exercise 5.11, assume the process time has a mean of 9 and a *variance* of 4. Calculate the parameters for the gamma, uniform, and normal distributions that will give these values. Make three runs (one for each distribution) and compare the results.

5.13 Using the Input Analyzer, open a new window and generate a new data file (use the *File/Data File/Generate New* option) containing 50 points for an Erlang distribution with parameters: ExpMean equal to 12, k equal to 3, and Offset equal to 5. Once you have the data file, perform a best fit. Repeat this process for 500, 5,000, and 25,000 data points, using the same Erlang parameters. Compare the results of the best fit for the four different sample sizes.

5.14 Hungry's Fine Fast Foods is interested in looking at their staffing for the lunch rush, running from 10 AM to 2 PM. People arrive as walk-ins, by car, or on a (roughly) scheduled bus, as follows:

- Walk-ins—one at a time, interarrivals are exponential with mean 3 minutes; the first walk-in occurs EXPO(3) minutes past 10 AM.
- By car—with 1, 2, 3, or 4 people to a car with respective probabilities 0.2, 0.3, 0.3, and 0.2; interarrivals distributed as exponential with mean 5 minutes; the first car arrives EXPO(5) minutes past 10 AM.

- A single bus arrives every day sometime between 11 AM and 1 PM (arrival time distributed uniformly over this period). The number of people on the bus varies from day to day, but it appears to follow a Poisson distribution with a mean of 30 people.

Once people arrive, either alone or in a group from any source, they operate independently regardless of their source. The first stop is with one of the servers at the order/payment counter, where ordering takes triangular (1, 2, 4) minutes and payment then takes triangular (1, 2, 3) minutes; these two operations are sequential, first order-taking then payment, by the same server for a given customer. The next stop is to pick up the food ordered, which takes an amount of time distributed uniformly between 30 seconds and 2 minutes. Then each customer goes to the dining room, which has 30 seats (people are willing to sit anywhere, not necessarily with their group), and partakes of the sublime victuals, taking an enjoyable triangular (10, 20, 30) minutes. After that, the customer walks fulfilled to the door and leaves. Queueing at each of the three "service" stations (order/pay, pickup food, and dining room) is allowed, with FIFO discipline. There is a travel time of EXPO(30) seconds from each station to all but the exit door—entry to order/pay, order/pay to pickup food, and pickup food to dining. After dining, people move somewhat more slowly, so the travel time from the dining room to the exit is EXPO(1) minute.

The servers at both order/pay and pickup food have a single break that they "share" on a rotating basis. More specifically, at 10:50, 11:50, 12:50, and 1:50 one server from each station goes on a 10-minute break; if the person due to go on break at a station is busy at break time, he or she finishes serving the customer but still has to be back at the top of the hour (so the break could be a little shorter than 10 minutes).

The main issue Hungry's faces is staffing. Currently, there are six servers at the order/pay station and two at the pickup food station throughout the four-hour period. Since they know that the bus arrives sometime during the middle two hours, they're considering a variable staffing plan that, for the first and last hour would have three at order/pay and one at pickup food, and for the middle two hours would have nine at order/pay and three at pickup food (note that the total number of person-hours on the payroll is the same, 32, under either the current staffing plan or the alternate plan, so they cost the same). What's your advice?

In terms of output, observe the average and maximum length of each queue, the average and maximum time in each queue, and the total number of customers completely served and out the door. Make animation plots of the order/pay and dining room queues to see that things are making sense. Animate all movements between stations. Pick from a .plb picture library a humanoid picture for the entities, and make an appropriate change to their appearance after they've finished eating and leave the dining room. Also, while you won't be able to animate the individual servers or seats in the dining room, pick reasonable pictures for them as well.

Intermediate Modeling and Terminating Statistical Analysis

CHAPTER 6

Intermediate Modeling and Terminating Statistical Analysis

Many of the essential elements of modeling with Arena were covered in Chapter 5, including the basic use of some of the Common panel modules, controlling the flow of entities, Stations and Transfers, Resource Schedules and States, saving output data, and enhancing the animation. In this chapter, we'll expand on several concepts that allow you to do more detailed modeling. As before, we'll illustrate things concretely by means of a fairly elaborate example.

The example is described in Section 6.1; expressing it in Arena requires the new ideas of entity-dependent Sequences, Variables, Expressions, and Sets, discussed in Section 6.2. Then in Section 6.3, we take up the general issue of how to go about modeling a system, the level of detail appropriate for a project, and the need to pay attention to data requirements and availability. The model is built in Section 6.4, including discussion of importing existing CAD drawings for the layout and verifying that the representation of a model in Arena really does what you want. Section 6.5 goes on to exercise the model and, with the help of the Output Analyzer, carry out some statistical analysis of the output data.

By the time you read and digest the material in this chapter, you'll have a pretty good idea of how to model things in considerable detail with the Common panel tools. You'll also have an understanding of the issues and approaches for verification and statistical analysis in simulation.

6.1 Model 6.1: A Small Manufacturing System

A layout for our small manufacturing system is shown in Figure 6-1.

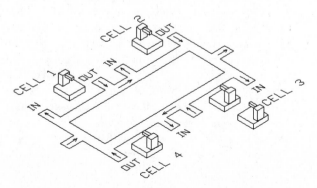

Figure 6-1. The Small Manufacturing System Layout

The system to be modeled consists of part arrivals, four manufacturing cells, and part departures. Cells 1, 2, and 4 each have a single machine; Cell 3 has two machines. The two machines at Cell 3 are not identical; one of these machines is a newer model that can process parts in 80% of the time required by the older machine. The system produces three parts types, each visiting a different sequence of stations. The part steps and process times (in minutes) are given in Table 6-1. All process times are triangularly distributed; the process times given in Table 6-1 at Cell 3 are for the older machine.

Table 6-1. Part Routings and Process Times

Part Type	Cell/Time	Cell/Time	Cell/Time	Cell/Time	Cell/Time
1	1	2	3	4	
	6, 8, 10	5, 8, 10	15, 20, 25	8, 12, 16	
2	1	2	4	2	3
	11, 13, 15	4, 6, 8	15, 18, 21	6, 9, 12	27, 33, 39
3	2	1	3		
	7, 9, 11	7, 10, 13	18, 23, 28		

The interarrival times between successive part arrivals (all types combined) are exponentially distributed with a mean of 13 minutes. The distribution by type is 26%, Part 1; 48%, Part 2; and 26%, Part 3. Parts enter from the left, exit at the right, and move only in a clockwise direction through the system. For now, we'll also assume that the time to move between any cells is 2 minutes.

We want to collect statistics on resource utilization, time and number in queue, as well as cycle time (time in system, from entry to exit) by part type. Initially, we'll run our simulation for 2,000 minutes.

6.2 New Arena Concepts

There are several characteristics of this problem that require new Arena concepts. The first characteristic is that there are three part types that follow different process plans or steps through the system. In our previous models, we simply routed all entities to the same next station. For this type of system, we need a process plan with an automatic routing capability. The second characteristic is that the two machines in Cell 3 are not identical—the newer machine can process parts in 80% of the time required by the old machine. Here we need to be able to distinguish between these two machines. We also need to collect cycle time by part type, and it would be nice if we could easily associate a different picture with each part type. The following new Arena concepts will allow us to implement these modeling requirements easily, as well as a few we have yet to mention. (There is really no sense in confusing you any more than necessary.)

6.2.1 Sequences

Many systems are characterized by entities that follow predefined, but different paths through the system. Most manufacturing systems have part or process plans that define the operations or steps each part type must complete before exiting the system. Many service systems have similar types of requirements. For example, a model of passenger traffic in an airport may require different paths through the airport depending on whether the passengers check baggage or have only carry-on pieces, or whether the passengers have domestic or international flights.

Arena can send entities through a system automatically according to a predefined *sequence* of station visitations. In Chapter 5, when we placed an Arrive, Server, Inspect, or Depart module, we associated a station name with these modules. The Sequences module, found on the Common panel, allows us to define a sequence of station visitations consisting of a list of destination stations and optional assignments of attributes or variables at each station. To direct an entity to follow this pattern of station visitations, we assign the sequence to the entity (using a built-in sequence attribute, described below) and use the Seq (sequence) option when we transfer the entity to its next destination (rather than Connect or Route).

As the entity makes its way along its sequence, Arena will do all the necessary book-keeping to keep track of where the entity is and where it will go next. This is accomplished through the use of three special, automatically defined Arena attributes: Station (M), Sequence (NS), and Jobstep (IS). Each entity has these three attributes, with the default values for newly created entities being 0 for all attributes. The *Station* attribute contains the name of the current station location of the entity or the station to which the entity is being transferred. The *Sequence* attribute is user-defined and contains the name of the sequence the entity will follow, if any. The *Jobstep* attribute specifies the entity's position within the sequence.

We first define and name the paths through the system for each type of entity (by part type, in our example) using the Sequences module. Then, when we cause a new part to arrive in the system, we associate a specific Sequence with that entity by assigning the name of the sequence to the entity's sequence attribute, NS.[1] When the entity is ready to transfer to the next station in its sequence, we select the Seq option in the Leave Data section of the module. At this point during the run, Arena first increments the Jobstep attribute (IS) by 1. Then it retrieves the destination station from the Sequence based on the current values for the Sequence and Jobstep attributes. Any optional assignments are made (as defined in the Sequence) and the entity's Station attribute (M) is set to the destination station. Finally, Arena transfers the entity to that station.

Typically, an entity will follow a sequence through to completion and will then exit the model. However, this is not a requirement. The Jobstep attribute is incremented only when the entity is transferred using the Seq option. You can temporarily suspend transfer via the sequence, transfer the entity "manually" to another station using Connect or Route, and then re-enter the sequence later. This might be useful if some of parts are required to be reworked at some point in the process. Upon completion of the rework, they might re-enter the normal sequence.

---

[1] Arena uses M, NS, and IS internally as names for these attributes, but provides the aliases *Station*, *Sequence*, and *Jobstep* in most dialogs.

You can also reassign the sequence attributes at any time. For example, you might handle a part failure by assigning a new Sequence attribute and resetting the Jobstep attribute to 0. This new Sequence could transfer the part through a series of stations in a rework area. You can also back up or jump forward in the sequence by decreasing or increasing the Jobstep attribute. However, caution is advised as you must be sure to reset the Jobstep attribute correctly, remembering that Arena will first increment it, then look up the destination station in the sequence.

As indicated earlier, attribute and variable assignments can also be made at each jobstep in a sequence. For example, you could change the entity picture or assign a process time to a user-defined attribute. For the model of our small manufacturing system, we'll use this option to define some of our processing times that are part- and station-specific.

6.2.2 Variables and Expressions

In many models, we might want to reuse data in several different places. For example, in our small manufacturing system, we have assumed a route time of 2 minutes for all part transfers. If we decide to change this value during our experimentation, we'd have to open each dialog that included a route time and change the value. There are other situations where we might want to keep track of the total number of entities in a system or in a portion of the system. In other cases, we may want to use complex expressions throughout the model. For example, we might want the route times to follow a distribution or base a processing time on the part type. Arena *Variables* and *Expressions* allow us to fulfill these kinds of needs easily.

The Variables module allows you to define your own global variables and their initial values. Variables can then be referenced in the model by their names. They can also be specified as one- or two-dimensional arrays. The Expressions module allows you to define expressions and their associated values. Similar to variables, expressions are referenced in the model by their names and can also be specified as one- or two-dimensional arrays. Although variables and expressions may appear to be quite similar, they serve distinctly different functions.

User-defined Variables store some real-valued quantity that can be reassigned during the simulation run. For example, we could define a variable called `Transfer Time` with an initial value of 2 and enter the variable name wherever a route time was required. We could also define a variable called `Number In System` with an initial value of 0, add 1 to this variable every time a new part entered the system, and subtract 1 every time a part exited the system. For our small manufacturing system, we'll use a one-dimensional arrayed variable called `Factor` to allow us to obtain the correct processing time at Cell 3 depending on which machine, new or old, we're using.

User-defined Expressions, on the other hand, don't store a value. Instead, they provide a way of associating a name with some mathematical expression. Whenever the name is referenced in the model, the associated expression is evaluated, and its value is returned. Typically, they are used to compute values from a distribution or from a complex equation based on the entity's attribute values or even current system and system variable values. If the mathematical expression is used in only one place in the model, it might be easier to enter it directly where it is required. However, if the expression is used in several places or the form of the expression to be used depends on an entity attribute, a user-defined expression is often better. For our small manufacturing system, we'll use the Expressions module to define a one-dimensional arrayed expression to generate the part processing time at Cell 1, which depends on the part type.

Variables and Expressions have many other uses that we hope will become obvious as you become more familiar with Arena.

6.2.3 Sets

As your models become more complex, you'll often find the need to model an entity arriving at a location or station and selecting from one of several similar (but not quite identical) objects. The most common situation is the selection of an available resource from a pool of resources. Let's assume you have three operators: Paul, Lynn, and Ann. Any one of these operators can perform the required task, and you would like to select any of the three, as long as one is currently available. The Sets module provides the basis for this functionality. Arena *sets* are groups of similar objects that can be referenced by a common name (the *set name*) and a *set index*. The objects that make up the set are re-ferred to as *members* of the set. Members of a particular set must all be the same type of object, such as resources, queues, pictures, etc. You can collect almost any type of Arena objects into a set, depending on your modeling requirements. An object can also reside in more than one set. Let's assume in our Operators set that Lynn is also qualified as a setup person. Therefore, we might define a second resource set called Setup as Lynn and Doug (Doug's not an operator). Now, if an operator is required, we'd select from the set called Operators; if a setup person is required, we would select from the set called Setup. Lynn might be chosen via either case because she's a member of both sets. You can have as many sets as you want with as much overlap as required.

For our small manufacturing system, we'll use sets for four different types of objects: resources, sequences, pictures, and tallies. The resource set will contain the two ma-chines, Old and New, at Cell 3. The use of the Sequences, Pictures and Tally sets will allow us to assign the correct sequence and picture easily and to collect statistics by part type as parts exit the system.

6.3 The Modeling Approach

The modeling approach to use for a specific simulation model will often depend on the system's complexity and the nature of the available data. In simple models, it's usually ob-vious what modules you'll require and the order in which you'll place them. But in more complex models, you will often need to take a considerable amount of care developing the proper approach. As you learn more about Arena, you'll find that there are often a number of ways to model a system or a portion of a system. You will often hear experienced model-ers say that there's not just a single, correct way to model a system. There are, however, wrong ways if they fail to capture the required system detail correctly.

The design of complex models is often driven by the data requirements of the model and what real data are available. Experienced modelers will often spend a great deal of time determining how they'll enter, store, and use their data, and then let this design determine which modeling constructs are required. As the data requirements become more demanding, this approach is often the only one that will allow the development of an accurate model in a short period of time. This is particularly true of simulation models of supply-chain systems, warehousing, distribution networks, and service networks. For example, a typical warehouse can have hundreds of thousands of uniquely different items, called SKUs (Stock-Keeping Units). Each SKU may require data characterizing its location in the warehouse, its size, and its weight, as well as reorder or restocking data for this SKU. In addition to specifying data for the contents of the warehouse, you also have customer order data and information on the types of storage devices or equipment that hold the SKUs. If your model requires the ability to change SKU locations, storage devices, restocking options, etc., during your experimentation, the data structure you use is critical. Although the models we'll develop in this book are not that complicated, it's always advisable to consider your data requirements before you start your modeling.

For our small manufacturing system, the data structure will, to a limited extent, affect our model design. We will use Sequences to control the flow of parts through the system, and the optional assignment feature to enter part process times for all but Cell 1. We'll use an Expression to define part process times for Cell 1. The part transfer time and the 80% factor for the time required by the new machine in Cell 3 will exploit the Variables concept. Although we don't normally think of Sets as part of our data design, their use can affect the modeling method. In this model, we'll use Sets, combined with a user-defined index, to ensure that we associate the correct sequence and picture with each part type, as well as to collect statistics by part type.

6.4   Building the Model

First, we'll enter the data modules as discussed earlier. We'll then enter the main model portion, which will require several new constructs or modules. Next, we'll animate the model using a CAD or other drawing as a starting point. Finally, we'll discuss briefly the concept of model verification. By this time, you should be fairly familiar with opening and filling Arena dialogs, so we will not dwell on the mundane details of how to enter the information in Arena. In the case of modules and concepts that were introduced in Chapter 5, we'll only indicate the data that must be entered. To see the "big picture" of where we're heading, you may want to peek ahead at Figure 6-4, which shows the complete model.

6.4.1   The Data Modules

We start by placing the Sequences module from the Common panel. When you add a sequence name (e.g., `Part 1 Process Plan` for the first sequence), note that there are no further options available until you press the Tab key to accept that name. (This will happen in other dialogs as well; when in doubt, press the Tab key.) Having entered the sequence name, you next need to enter the process steps, which are Arena stations. For example, the `Part 1 Process Plan` requires you to enter the following steps: `Cell 1`, `Cell 2`, `Cell 3`, `Cell 4`, and `Exit System`. The most common error in entering sequences is to forget to enter the last step, which is typically where the entity exits the system. If you forget this step, you'll get an Arena run-time error when the first entity completes its process route and Arena is not told where to send it next. As you define the Sequences, remember that after you've entered a station name once, you can subsequently pick it from a pull-down list. You'll also need to assign attribute values for the part process times for Cells 2, 3, and 4. Recall that we'll define an Expression for the part process times at Cell 1, so we won't need to make an attribute assignment.

Display 6-1 shows the procedure for Sequence `Part 1 Process Plan`, Step `Cell 2`, and Assignment of `Process Time`. Using the data in Table 6-1, it should be fairly straightforward to enter the remaining sequence steps. Shortly, we'll show you how to reference these sequences in the model logic.

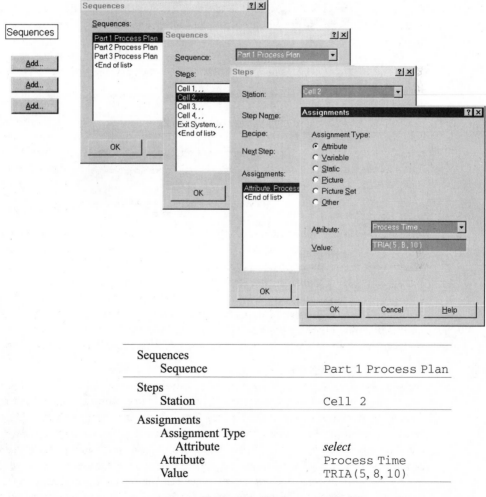

Sequences	
Sequence	Part 1 Process Plan
Steps	
Station	Cell 2
Assignments	
Assignment Type	
Attribute	*select*
Attribute	Process Time
Value	TRIA(5, 8, 10)

Display 6-1. The Sequences Module

Next, we'll define the expression for the part process times at Cell 1. The Expressions module is on the Common panel and is filled out similarly to the Sequences module. The expression we want will be called `Cell 1 Times`, and it will contain the part-process-time distributions for the three parts at Cell 1. We could just as easily have entered these in the previous Sequences module, but we used an expression so you can see a new Arena concept. We have three different parts that use Cell 1, so we need an arrayed expression with three rows, one for each part type. Display 6-2 shows the dialogs for this module. As with the sequences, we'll show you how to use this later.

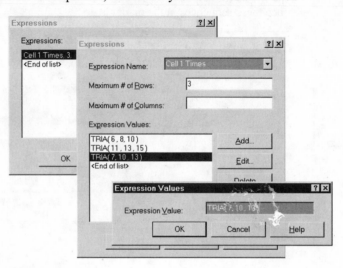

Expressions		
Expression Name	Cell 1 Times	
Maximum # of Rows	3	
Expression Values		
Expression Values	TRIA(6, 8, 10)	
Expression Values	TRIA(11, 13, 15)	
Expression Values	TRIA(7, 10, 13)	

Display 6-2. The Expression for Cell 1 Part Process Times

Next, we'll use the Variables module found on the Common panel to define the machine factor for Cell 3 and the transfer time. These dialogs are similar to those for expressions, except we can enter only a constant for the initial value. Prior to defining our `Factor` variable, we made the following observation and assumption. The part process times for Cell 3, entered in the Sequences module, are for the old machine. We'll assume that the new machine will be referenced as 1 and the old machine will be referenced as 2. Thus, the first factor value is 0.8 (for the new machine), and the second factor is 1.0 (for the old machine). The transfer-time value (which doesn't need to be an array) is simply entered as 2. This allows us to change this value in a single place at a later time. If we thought we might have wanted to change this to a distribution, we would have entered it as an Expression instead of a Variable. Display 6-3 shows the required entries.

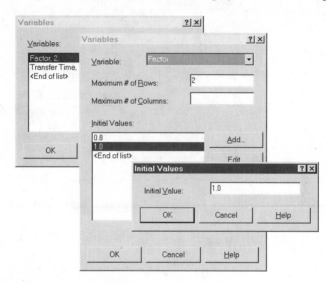

Variables	
Variable	Factor
Maximum # of Rows	2

Initial Values	
Initial Value	0.8
Initial Value	1.0

Variables	
Variable	Transfer Time

Initial Values	
Initial Value	2

Display 6-3. The Factor and Transfer Time Variables

The Sets module allows us to form sets of resources, queues, storages, stations, pictures, counters, and tallies. There is also a catch-all option called Other that allows you to form sets of almost any similar Arena objects. First, let's form the set of resources for Cell 3. Recall that we assumed the new machine was to be referenced as 1, so it must be entered as the first member of the set, as indicated in Display 6-4.

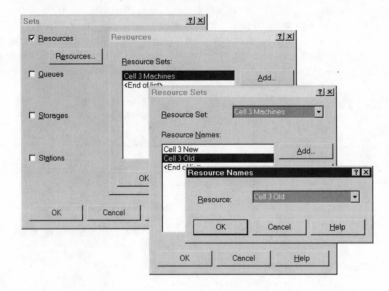

Resources	*check*
Resources Sets	
Resource Set	Cell 3 Machines
Resources Sets	
Resource	Cell 3 New
Resource	Cell 3 Old

Display 6-4. The Resource Set for Cell 3 Machines

Displays 6-5, 6-6, and 6-7 show the data for the Sequence, Picture and Tally sets. Be sure to enter these names in the same order as given. As soon as we have defined the pictures, we'll show you how to reference these sets in the model.

Other	*check*
Other Sets	
Set Name	Part Sequences
Members	
Object	Part 1 Process Plan
Object	Part 2 Process Plan
Object	Part 3 Process Plan

Display 6-5. The Sequence Set

Pictures	*check*
Picture Sets	
Pictures Set	Parts
Picture Names	
Picture	Part 1
Picture	Part 2
Picture	Part 3

Display 6-6. The Picture Set

Tallies	*check*
Tally Sets	
Tally Set	Part Cycle Times
Tally Names	
Tally	Part 1 Cycle Time
Tally	Part 2 Cycle Time
Tally	Part 3 Cycle Time

Display 6-7. The Tally Set

Display 6-8 shows the entries for the Simulate module. We also double-clicked on its entity symbol to open the Entity Picture Placement window, where we created three different pictures—Part 1, Part 2, and Part 3. In our example, we retained the simple red box and placed a text object with 1, 2, and 3, respectively, to denote the three different part types.

Project	
Title	Small Manufacturing System
Analyst	Pippi
Replicate	
Length of Replication	2000

Display 6-8. The Simulate Module

Having defined all of the data modules, we're now ready to place and fill out the modules for the main model to define the system's logical characteristics.

6.4.2 The Logic Modules

The main portion will consist of logic modules to represent part arrivals, cells, and part departures. The part arrivals will be modeled using an Arrive module as shown in Display 6-9. With the exception of the names and the Leave Data section's entries, this is identical to the Arrive modules we used in Chapter 5. In the Leave Data section, we selected the Seq option. This causes the Station Name field to disappear, and when we run the model, Arena will route the arriving entities according to the sequences we defined. Also note that we have entered the previously defined variable `Transfer Time` as the route time.

Enter Data	
Station	`Order Release`
Arrival Data	
Time Between	`EXPO(13)`
Mark Time Attribute	`Enter Time`
Leave Data	
Seq	*select*
Route Time	`Transfer Time`

Display 6-9. Generating Part Arrivals

At this point, we have not yet associated a sequence with each arriving entity. We make this association in the Assign portion of the module as shown in Display 6-10.

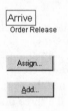
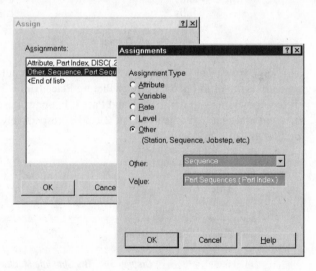

Assignment Type	
Attribute	*select*
Attribute	`Part Index`
Value	`DISC(.26, 1, .74, 2, 1.0, 3)`
Assignment Type	
Other	*select*
Other	`Sequence`
Value	`Part Sequences(Part Index)`

Display 6-10. Assigning the Part Type and Sequence

These assignments serve two purposes: they determine which part type has arrived, and they define an index, `Part Index`, for our sets that will allow us to associate the proper sequence with each arrival. We first determine the part index, or part type, with a discrete distribution. The distribution allows us to generate certain values with given probabilities. In our example, these values are the integers 1, 2, and 3 with probabilities 26%, 48%, and 26%, respectively. You enter these values in pairs—*cumulative* probability and value. The cumulative probability for the last value (in our case, 3) should be 1.0. In general, the values need not be integers, but can take on any values, including negative numbers. The part index values of 1, 2, and 3 allow us not only to refer to the part type, but in this case, they also allow us to index into the previously defined set `Part Sequences` so that the proper sequence will be associated with the part. To do so, we assign the proper sequence to the Arena Sequence attribute (NS), which can be found under the Other assignment type, by using the `Part Index` attribute as an index into the `Part Sequences`.

Before we finish with the Arrive module, we need to associate the proper picture type with the newly arrived part. We do this in the Animate dialog, Display 6-11, by selecting the Set Member option. Recall that we defined three pictures (`Part 1`, `Part 2`, and `Part 3`) and grouped them into a set called `Parts`, Display 6-6. You can think of this set as an arrayed variable (one-dimensional) with the index being the `Part Index` attribute we just assigned. This is true in this case because we have a one-to-one relationship among the `Part Index`, part type, and the sequence that a part follows. An index of 1 implies `Part 1` follows the first sequence, etc. (Be careful in future models because this may not always be true. It is only true in this case because we defined our data structure so we would have this one-to-one relationship.)

Initial Entity Picture	
Set Member	*select*
Picture Set	Parts
Set Index	Part Index

Display 6-11. *Assigning the Entity Picture from a Set*

In this case, the completed Arrive module creates the parts, determines the part type, assigns the proper sequence, assigns the proper picture, and automatically routes the part to the next station in its sequence.

With the exception of Cell 3, the cells can be modeled easily using the Server module presented in Chapter 5. The data entries for Cell 1 are given in Display 6-12. As was the case for the Arrive module, we have selected the Route according to the Sequence option in the Leave Data section. Again, Arena will automatically route the part to its next station as defined in our sequences.

For the Process Time, we have entered the previously defined expression `Cell 1 Times` using the `Part Index` attribute to reference the appropriate part-processing time. This expression will generate a sample from the triangular distribution with the parameters we defined earlier.

Enter Data	
Station	Cell 1
Server Data	
Process Time	Cell 1 Times(Part Index)
Leave Data	
Route	*select*
Seq	*select*
Route Time	Transfer Time

Display 6-12. Cell 1 Server Module Data

Display 6-13 shows the data entries for the Cell 2 Server module. With the exception of the cell name and process-time entries, the remaining data are identical to Cell 1. Recall that in the Sequences module we defined the part processing times for Cells 2, 3, and 4 by assigning them to the entity attribute Process Time. When the part was routed to Cell 2 from its last station, Arena automatically would have assigned this value so it could be used in this module. The Data entries for Cell 4 are identical to Cell 2, except for the cell name, and are not shown.

Enter Data	
Station	Cell 2
Server Data	
Process Time	Process Time
Leave Data	
Route	*select*
Seq	*select*
Route Time	Transfer Time

Display 6-13. Cell 2 Server Module Data

At this point, you should be aware that we've somewhat arbitrarily used an Expression for the Cell 1 part processing times and attribute assignments in the sequences for the remaining cells. We actually used this approach to illustrate a point (and to introduce you to Expressions). There are often several different ways to structure data and access them in a simulation model. We could just as easily have incorporated the part processing times at Cell 1 into the sequences, along with the rest of the times. We also could have used Expressions for these times at Cells 3 and 4. However, it would have been difficult to use an Expression for these times at Cell 2, because Part 2 visits that cell twice and the processing times are different, as shown in Table 6-1. Thus, we would have had to somehow include in our model the ability to know whether the part was on its first or second visit to Cell 2 and define our expression to recognize that. It might be an interesting exercise, but from the modeler's point of view, why not just define these values in the sequences? You should also recognize that this sample model is relatively small in terms of the number of cells and parts. In practice, it would not be uncommon to have 30 to 50 machines with hundreds of different part types. If you undertake a problem of that size, we strongly recommend that you take great care in designing the data structure as it may make the difference between a success or failure of the simulation project.

We couldn't use a Server module for Cell 3 since our only option in the Process Data section of the module was a single resource. Recall that we have two different machines at Cell 3, a new one and an old one, that process parts at different rates. If the machines were identical, we could have used the Server module and entered a capacity of 2. We made note of this earlier and grouped these two machines into a Set called Cell 3 Machines. Now we need the ability to use this set at Cell 3. We could use the Advanced Server module or the Enter, Process, and Leave modules to incorporate the sets concept. In this case, the two methods are identical.

As the name implies, the Advanced Server has all the capabilities of a regular server, plus several advanced features. The Enter, Process, and Leave modules contain the features we would find in the Enter Data, Server Data, and Leave Data sections, respectively, of the Advanced Server module. So using these three modules is equivalent to using an Advanced Server module. However, breaking the Advanced Server into these three components allows us to model other types of more complex servers. For example, we could use the sequence combination, Enter–Process–Process–Leave to model a cell that had two resources in series. So our intent is to expose you to additional capabilities, even though we won't fully exploit these capabilities.

Let's first place all three modules as shown in Figure 6-2. If you place the Enter module and then place the Process module while the Enter module is still highlighted, you'll note that a line connects the two. This is the Arena Auto-Connect feature. You can turn this feature off in the Module menu. For now, highlight and delete this line.

Figure 6-2. The Enter, Process, and Leave Modules

Display 6-14 shows the data entries required to complete the Enter module. You might note that this dialog looks very similar to the Enter Data section of the Server module except that you can enter either a Station or a Station Set. In our case, we only need to enter the station name, Cell 3, which defines the location of Cell 3. You might notice that there appears to be a free queue that is included as part of the animation objects for the Enter module. If you highlight this object, you will note that it has a name that is the station name followed by the extension _S1. If you double-click on this object, you will discover that it is an Arena *storage*. This is included in case you specify a positive unload time; the entity will reside in this storage during the unload delay time. We won't use it in our model; you can turn its display off be selecting the No Change option and unchecking the Unstore option in the Animate dialog.

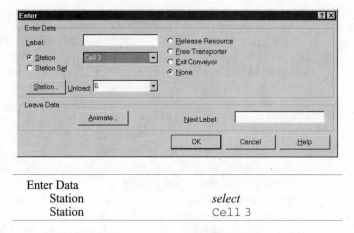

Enter Data
    Station   *select*
    Station   Cell 3

Display 6-14. Cell 3 Enter Module Data

Display 6-15 shows the data entries required to complete the Process module. This is where you'll find most of the additional features, as compared to the regular server.

Process Data
    Resource Set   *select*
    Resource Set   Cell 3 Machines
    Store Index in Att   Index
    Process Time   Process Time * Factor(Index)

Display 6-15. Cell 3 Process Module Data

In the Process Data section of the dialog, we can make one of three selections: Seize, Request, or None. You might note that most of the remaining dialog entries will change depending on your choice. At this point, we need to acquaint you with some Arena key words. The term *Seize* is used whenever you are allocating an Arena resource to an entity. Upon completion of the required task, Arena will *Release* the resource so it can be allocated to the next entity. The key word *Request* is used whenever we want to allocate a transporter to an entity. (We'll discuss transporters in Section 7.3.) The Process module also allows for no action, the None option. Recall that in the Server module we were required to seize a resource. For this model, we select the Seize option because we want to allocate a resource from a set of resources.

Having selected the Seize option, we now must select the form: Resource, Resource Set, Specific Member, or Expression. The Resource option would be equivalent to selecting a single resource. Our selection, Resource Set, allows us to select from our specified `Cell 3 Machines` set. You can also Seize a Specific Member of a set; that member can be specified as an entity attribute. Finally, you could use an Expression to determine which resource was required. For our selection of Resource Set, we've accepted the default selection rule, Cyclical, which causes the entity to select the first available resource beginning with the successor of the last resource selected. In our case, Arena will attempt to select our two resources alternately; however, if only one resource is currently available, it will be selected. Obviously, these rules are only used if more than one resource is available for selection. The Random rule would cause a random selection, and the Preferred Order rule would allocate the first available resource in the set. Had we selected this option, Arena would have always used the new machine, if available, because it's the first resource in the set. The remaining rules would only apply if one or more of our resources had a capacity greater than 1.

The Store Index in Att option allows us to save the index, which is a reference to the selected set member, in a user-specified attribute. In our case, we will save this value in Attribute `Index`. If the new machine is selected, this attribute will be assigned a value of 1, and if the old machine is selected, the attribute will be assigned a value of 2. This numbering is based on the order in which we entered our resources when we defined the set. The Process Time entry is an expression of our attribute `Process Time`, assigned by the sequence, multiplied by our variable `Factor`. Recall that our process times are for the old machine and that the new machine can process parts in 80% of that time. Although it's probably obvious by now how this expression works, we'll illustrate it. If the first resource in the set (the new machine) is selected, `Index` will be assigned a value of 1 and the variable `Factor` will use this attribute to take on a value of 0.8. If the second machine (the old machine) is selected, the `Factor` variable will take on a value of 1, and the original process time will be used. Although this method may seem overly complicated for this example, it is used to illustrate the tremendous flexibility that Arena provides. An alternate method, which would not require the variable, would have used the following logical expression:

```
Process Time * (((Index == 1)*0.8) + (Index == 2))
```
   or
```
Process Time * (1 - ((Index == 1)*0.2)).
```

We leave it to the reader to figure out how these expressions work (Hint: "a==b" evaluates to 1 if a equals b and to 0 otherwise).

You might have noticed that when we initially placed this module, Figure 6-2, it included a resource animation symbol. When we accepted the dialog entries, this symbol was automatically deleted, Display 6-15. This symbol was deleted because we selected the Resource Set option that could consist of any number of resources. Thus, Arena deletes the default symbol that was intended to represent a *single* resource.

Having completed the processing, we need only send the entities on their way. We use the Leave module, the last of our three new modules, for this purpose. Display 6-16 shows the data entries for this module.

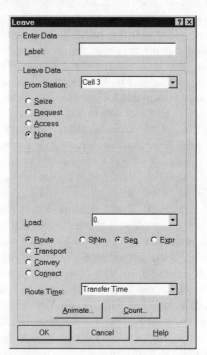

Leave Data
From Station	Cell 3
Seq	*select*
Route Time	Transfer Time

Display 6-16. Cell 3 Leave Module Data

The major difference between this dialog and the Leave Data section of a Server module is that the entity might not currently know where it is. In our model, all entities are routed to the Enter, passed to the Process, and routed out by the Leave. However, there is nothing to prevent entities from arriving at the Leave from other model logic. Thus, Arena forces us to enter the current location, or From Station, so it knows what route to use. Before we move on, we have two details to resolve. The first is that we have not specifically told Arena that the entities that arrive at Cell 3, the Enter module, should be sent directly to the Process and then to the Leave. We have assumed that this would happen, but so far, that's a bad assumption. There are several ways to cause or control the flow of entities from module to module. We'll briefly discuss three: Transfer, Connect, and Labels.

So far we've used only the Transfer method, such as a Route. A Transfer involves directing the departing entity to a station or location. In this case, we're remaining at the same station, Cell 3, so we should probably use a direct Connection or Labels.

You might have noticed that in almost every logic module we've used so far, there's an optional field in the Enter Data section. There is also an equivalent optional Label field in the Leave Data section that requests the Next label (it may not always be obvious, but it is almost always there). Thus, we could have entered a Label name (Process 3, for example) for the Next Label in the Enter module and the same Label name for the Queue Label field of the Process module, and Arena would now know where to direct the entity. Remember that in Arena all names must be unique, even if they are for different types of objects. Thus, we could not have specified the Label as "Cell 3 Machines" because that is the Resource Set name. Although this method works, it can cause confusion because the entity flow is not at all obvious when looking at a model. Therefore, we generally recommend against this method. However, if your models become very complicated, it can occasionally be useful for directing an entity to other distant parts of a model.

The more straightforward method is to Connect the modules to control the entity flow. If you look closely at the Process module, Figure 6-2, you will notice that at the left side of the handle (the box with the module name) is a small square, and on the right side is a small triangle. We normally refer to these as "do-dads," "whatchamacallits," or "thingamajigs." However, for the sake of clarity, we'll refer to them as Entry (the box) and Exit (the triangle) points. We make these connections by selecting the Arena Connect feature (*Module/Connect* option or ⊒ button, Arrange toolbar). This works very much like drawing a polyline, but we start at an Exit point and end at an Entry point. The result is a visible line that graphically shows the entity flow. Before you do this, you might notice that due to the way we placed our three modules, the flow is from right to left, but our entry and exit points are obviously positioned for a left to right flow. No problem. You can select these points to move them anywhere you want, and use the Vertical Flip (Arrange toolbar) option to change the direction of the Exit point. The connected modules should look something like Figure 6-3.

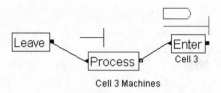

Figure 6-3. The Connected Enter, Process, and Leave Modules

The second remaining detail is that we haven't yet defined the two Resources, or machines, at Cell 3. We made reference to them when we developed our resource sets, but we haven't explicitly defined them. The Resources for Cells 1, 2, and 4 were defined by the Server modules we used in our model. In our Process module, we only referenced the Set that includes these two machines. We'll define these resources using the Resource module on the Common panel. (Actually, this is a data module, but we waited until we needed it to introduce it.) Display 6-17 shows the entries for this module. We also need to place a second Resource module to define the Cell 3 Old machine.

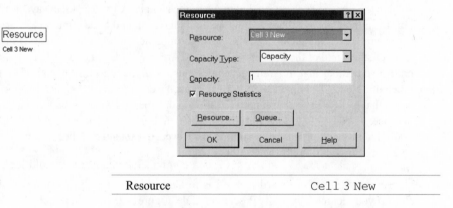

Resource	Cell 3 New

Display 6-17. Defining the Cell 3 New Resources

Having completely defined all our data, the part arrival process, and the four cells, we're left only with defining the parts' exit from the system. As before, we'll use the Depart module from the Common panel to represent this activity and to collect cycle-time statistics. Display 6-18 shows the data entries for this module. Even though we've used this module type before, we've given the complete display because we've elected to collect cycle times by part type. Recall that we defined a Set of Tallies containing our three part types. In the Tally section of the module, we selected the Tally Set Member option and entered the Tally Set name Part Cycle Time. The index into this set is the attribute Part Index that we defined and assigned in our Arrive module. When we defined the Sequence, Picture, and Tally sets, we were careful to ensure that the first member of each set was for Part 1, the second for Part 2, and the third for Part 3. Using a Tally set in this fashion will result in three different Tallies, one for each part type. The remaining data entries are essentially the same as for our previous models.

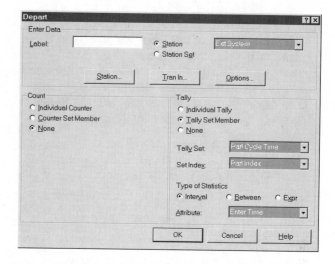

Enter Data	
Station	Exit System
Tally	
Tally Set Member	*select*
Tally Set	Part Cycle Time
Set Index	Part Index
Type of Statistics	
Interval	Enter Time

Display 6-18. The Exit System Module

Our completed model (although it is not completely animated) should look something like Figure 6-4.

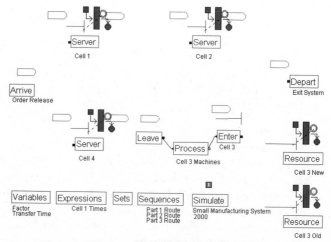

Figure 6-4. The Completed Model

For the models we developed in Chapter 5, we defined the flow of entities in the Leave Data section of the Server and Inspect modules. We placed routes in the layout before we ran our model so we could see the flow of entities in our animation. For this model, we defined the flow of entities in our Sequences (with the exception of the connects in Cell 3). If we run our model at this stage, we won't see any movement of entities in the animation, but we will see entities in the queues and at the machines. The summary results for this model are shown in Figure 6-5.

```
Project:  Small Manufacturing System
Analyst:  Pippi

Replication ended at time      : 2000.0
```

TALLY VARIABLES

Identifier	Average	Half Width	Minimum	Maximum	Observations
Cell 1_R_Q Queue Time	18.339	(Insuf)	.00000	85.057	152
Part 3 Cycle Time	97.596	(Insuf)	46.333	196.32	35
Cell 2_R_Q Queue Time	15.013	(Insuf)	.00000	49.152	223
Cell 3 Machines_Q Queu	14.781	(Insuf)	.00000	56.120	142
Part 1 Cycle time	133.16	(Insuf)	55.626	244.72	37
Cell 4_R_Q Queue Time	29.963	(Insuf)	.00000	71.920	110
Part 2 Cycle Time	173.23	(Insuf)	91.773	306.74	68

DISCRETE-CHANGE VARIABLES

Identifier	Average	Half Width	Minimum	Maximum	Final Value
Cell 2_R Busy	.85679	(Insuf)	.00000	1.0000	1.0000
# in Cell 3 Machines_Q	1.0604	(Insuf)	.00000	5.0000	2.0000
Cell 1_R Busy	.84052	(Insuf)	.00000	1.0000	1.0000
# in Cell 4_R_Q	1.6872	(Insuf)	.00000	6.0000	3.0000
Cell 3 New Available	1.0000	(Insuf)	1.0000	1.0000	1.0000
Cell 3 New Busy	.83712	(Insuf)	.00000	1.0000	1.0000
# in Cell 2_R_Q	1.6845	(Corr)	.00000	7.0000	2.0000
# in Cell 1_R_Q	1.4721	(Insuf)	.00000	10.000	4.0000
Cell 4_R Available	1.0000	(Insuf)	1.0000	1.0000	1.0000
Cell 2_R Available	1.0000	(Insuf)	1.0000	1.0000	1.0000
Cell 1_R Available	1.0000	(Insuf)	1.0000	1.0000	1.0000
Cell 4_R Busy	.87733	(Insuf)	.00000	1.0000	1.0000
Cell 3 Old Available	1.0000	(Insuf)	1.0000	1.0000	1.0000
Cell 3 Old Busy	.87330	(Insuf)	.00000	1.0000	1.0000

Figure 6-5. The Small Manufacturing System Summary Report

At this point, we could simply place the necessary routes in the layout and rearrange our resources to get a complete animation, but let's assume that we'll have to present this model to higher-level management, so we want to develop a fancier animation.

6.4.3 Animation

We could develop our animation in the same manner as we did in Chapter 5—create our own entity pictures, resource symbols, and background based on the picture that was presented in Figure 6-1. However, a picture might exist that someone already developed that reflects an accurate representation of the system. In fact, it might even exist as a CAD file somewhere in your organization. For instance, the drawing presented in Figure 6-1 was developed using the AutoCAD® package from AutoDesk. Arena supports integration of files from CAD programs into its workspaces. Files saved in the DXF format defined by AutoCAD can be imported directly into Arena. Files generated from other CAD or drawing programs (e.g., Visio®) should transfer into Arena as long as they adhere to the AutoCAD standard DXF format.

If the original CAD drawing is 2-D, you only need to save it in the DXF format and then import that file directly into Arena. Most CAD objects (polygons, etc.) will be represented as the same or similar objects in Arena. If the drawing is 3-D, you must first convert the file to 2-D. Colors are lost during this conversion to 2-D, but they may be added again in AutoCAD or in Arena. This conversion also transforms all objects to lines, so the imported drawing can only be manipulated in Arena as individual lines, or the lines may be grouped as objects. We'll assume that you have a DXF file and refer you to online help (the DXF File Importation topic) for details on creating the DXF file or converting a 3-D drawing. One word of advice: a converted file is imported into Arena as white lines so if your current background is white, it may appear that the file was not imported. Simply change the background color!

For our small manufacturing system, we started with a 3-D drawing and converted it to 2-D. We then saved the 2-D file in the DXF format. A DXF file is imported into your current model file by selecting the *File/DXF Import* option. Select the file, and when you move your cursor to the model window, it will appear as cross hairs. Using the cursor, draw a box to contain the entire drawing to be imported. If the imported drawing is not the correct size, you can select the entire drawing and resize it as required. You can now use this drawing as the start of your animation.

For our animation, we first want to delete all the lettering and arrows. Then we'll move the Cell 1 resource and queue to their approximate positions on the drawing. The next step is to copy one of the machines on the drawing to the clipboard. Now we'll open the Resource Picture Placement window, by double-clicking on the resource, and replace the current Idle resource picture with a copy of the contents of the clipboard. Delete the base of the machine and draw two boxes on top of the representation for the top part of the machine. This is necessary as our drawing consists of all lines, and we want to add a fill color to the machine. Now delete all the lines from the original copy and fill the boxes with your favorite color. Copy this new symbol to your library and then copy that symbol to the Busy picture. Save your library and exit the resource window. You now have a resource picture that will not change, but we could go back later and add more animation effects.

For the next step, draw a box the same size as the base of the machine and then delete the entire drawing of the machine. Fill this new box with a different color and then place the resource symbol on top of this box (we may have to resize the resource symbol to be the correct size). Now move the seize point so that it is positioned at about the center of our new machine. We could repeat this for the remaining four machines, but an easier method is to delete all the remaining resource symbols that came with the Server and Resource modules and make successive copies of our new resource and the machine base, then change the names. If you follow this procedure, note that you will need to flip the resources for Cells 3 and 4.

To complete this phase of the animation, we need to move and resize the remaining queues. Once this is complete, you can run your animation and see your handiwork. You won't see parts moving about the system (there are no routes yet), but you will see the parts in the queues and at the machines. If you look closely at one of the machines while the animation is running, you'll notice that the parts sit right on top of the entire machine. This display is not what we want. Ideally, the part should sit on top of the base, but under the top part of our machine (the resource). Representing this is not a problem. Select a resource (you can do this in edit mode or by temporarily stopping the animation) and use the Bring to Front feature with the *Arrange/Bring to Front* menu option or the ⬚ button on the Arrange toolbar. Now when you run the animation, you'll get the desired effect. We're now ready to animate our part movement.

In our previous animations, we basically had only one path through the system so adding the routes was fairly straightforward. In our small manufacturing system, there are multiple paths through the system, so you must be careful to add routes for each travel possibility. For example, a part leaving Cell 2 can go to Cell 1, 3, or 4. The stations need to be positioned first; you can move the existing stations or just add new ones using the Station feature on the Animate toolbar. Next, place the routes. If you somehow neglect to place a route, the simulation will still send the entity to the correct station with a transfer time of 2; however, that entity movement will not appear in your animation. Also be aware that routes can be used in both directions. For example, let's assume that you added the route from Cell 1 to Cell 2, but missed the route from 2 to 1. When a Part 2 completes its processing at Cell 2, Arena looks to route that part to Cell 1, routing from 2 to 1. If the route was missing, it would look for the route from 1 to 2 and use that. Thus, you would see that part moving from the entrance of Cell 2 to the Exit of Cell 1 in a counterclockwise direction (an animation mistake for this model).

If you run and watch your newly animated model, you should notice that occasionally parts will run over or pass each other. This is due to a combination of the data supplied and the manner in which we animated the model. Remember that all part transfers were assumed to be 2 minutes. Arena sets the speed of a routed entity based on the transfer time and the length of the route on the animation. In our model, some of these routes are very short (from Cell 1 to Cell 2) and some are very long (from Cell 2 to Cell 1). Thus, the entities being transferred will be moving at quite different speeds relative to each other. If this was important, we could request or collect better transfer times and incorporate these into our model. The easiest way would be to delete the variable Transfer Time and define an attribute with the same name and then assign these new transfer times to this new attribute in the Sequences module. If your Transfer times and drawing are accurate, the entities should now all move at the same speed. The only potential problem is that a part may enter the main aisle at the same time another part is passing by, resulting in one of the parts overlapping the other until their paths diverge. This is a more difficult problem to resolve, and it may not be worth the bother. If the only concern is for purposes of presentation, watch the animation and find a long period of time when this does not occur. Then show only this period of time during your presentation. The alternative is to use material handling constructs, which we'll do in Chapter 7.

After adding a little annotation, the final animation should look something like Figure 6-6 (view of the system at time 1822.2765). At this point in your animation, you might want to check to see if your model is running correctly or at least the way you intended it.

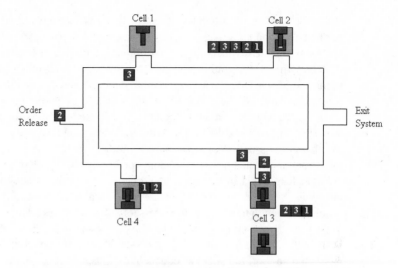

Figure 6-6. The Animated Small Manufacturing System: Model 6.1

6.4.4   Verification

Verification is the process of ensuring that the Arena model behaves in the way it was intended according to the modeling assumptions made. This is actually very easy compared to model *validation*, which is the process of ensuring that the model behaves the same as the real system. We'll discuss both of these aspects in more detail in Chapter 12. Here we'll only briefly introduce the topic of model verification.

Verification deals with both the obvious problems as well as the not-so-obvious. For example, if you had tried to run your model and Arena returned an error message that indicated that you had neglected to define one of the machine resources at Cell 3, the model is obviously not working the way you intended. Actually, we would normally call this the process of debugging! However, since we assume that you'll not make these kinds of errors, we'll deal with the not-so-obvious problems.

Verification is fairly easy when you're developing small classroom-size problems like the ones in this book. When you start developing more realistically-sized models, you'll find that it's a much more difficult process, and you may never be 100% sure on very, very large models.

One easy verification method is to allow only a single entity to enter the system and follow that entity to be sure that the model logic and data are correct. You could use the Step feature found on the Run toolbar to control the model execution and step the entity through the system. For this model, you could set the Max Batches field in the Arrive module to 1. To control the entity type, you could replace the discrete distribution that determines the part type with the specific part type you want to observe. This would allow you to check each of the part sequences. Another common method is to replace some or all model data with constants. Using deterministic data allows you to predict the system behavior exactly.

If you're going to use your model to make real decisions, you should also check to see how the model behaves under extreme conditions. For example, introduce only one part type or increase/decrease the part interarrival times. If your model is going to have problems, they will most likely show up during these kinds of stressed-out runs. Also, try to make effective use of your animation—it can often reveal problems when viewed by a person familiar with the operation of the system being modeled.

It's often a good idea, and a good test, to make long runs for different data and observe the summary results for potential problems. One skill that can be of great use during this process is that of *performance estimation*. A long, long time ago, before the invention of calculators and certainly before personal computers, engineers carried around sticks called *slide rules* (often protected by leather cases and proudly attached to engineers' belts). Basically, these were used to calculate the answers to the complicated problems given to them by their professors or bosses. These devices achieved this magic feat by adding or subtracting logs (not tree logs, but logarithms). Although they worked rather well (but not as well, as easily, or as fast as a calculator), they only returned (actually you read it off the stick) a sequence of digits, say 3642. It was up to the engineer to figure out where to put the decimal point. Therefore, engineers had to become very good at developing rough estimates of the answers to problems before they used the sticks. For example, if the engineer estimated the answer to be about 400, then the answer was 364.2. However, if the estimate was about 900, there was a problem. At that point, it was necessary to determine if the problem was in the estimation process or the slide-rule process. We suspect that at this point you're asking two questions: 1) why the long irrelevant story, and 2) did we really ever use such sticks? Well, the answers are: 1) to illustrate a point, and 2) just one of the authors!

So how do you use this great performance-estimation skill? Basically, you define a set of conditions for the simulation, estimate what will result, make a run, and look at the summary data to see if you were correct. If you were, feel good and try it for a different set of conditions. If you weren't correct, find out why not. It may be due to bad estimation, a lack of understanding of the system, or a faulty model. Sometimes not-so-obvious (but real) results are created by not-so-obvious interactions in the model. In general, you should thoroughly exercise your simulation models and be comfortable with the results before you use them to make decisions.

Back in Chapter 2 when we mentioned verification, we suggested that you verify your code. Your response could have been, "What code?" Well, there *is* code, so the last verification technique to be discussed in this chapter requires a little bit of background (yes, another history lesson). The formation of Systems Modeling and the initial release of the simulation language SIMAN® (on which Arena is based and to which you can gain access through Arena) occurred in 1982. Personal computers were just starting to hit the market, and SIMAN was designed to run on these new types of machines. In fact, SIMAN only required 64 Kbytes of memory, which was a lot in those days. There was no animation capability (Cinema®, the accompanying animation tool, was released in 1985), and you created models using a text editor, just like using a programming language. A complete model required the development of two files, a *model file* and an *experiment file.* The model file, often referred to as the MOD file, contained the model logic. The experiment file, referred to as the EXP file, defined the experimental conditions. It required the user to list all stations, attributes, resources, etc., that were used in the model. The creation of these files required that the user follow a rather exacting syntax for each type of model or experiment construct. In other words, you had to start certain statements only in column 10; you had to follow certain entries with the required comma, semicolon, or colon; all resources and attributes were referenced only by number; and only a limited set of key words could be used. (Many of your professors learned simulation this way.)

Since 1982, SIMAN has been enhanced continually and still provides the basis for an Arena simulation model. When you run an Arena simulation, Arena examines each option you selected in your modules and the data that you supplied and then creates SIMAN MOD and EXP files. These are the files that are used to run your simulations. The implication is that all the modules found in the Common panel are based on the constructs found in the SIMAN simulation language. The idea is to provide a simulation tool (Arena) that is easy to use, yet one that is still based on the powerful and flexible SIMAN language. So you see, it is still possible, and sometimes desirable, to look at the SIMAN code. In fact, you can even write out and edit these files. However, it is only possible to go down (from Arena to SIMAN code), and not possible to go back up (from SIMAN code to Arena). As you become more proficient with Arena, occasionally you might want to look at this code to be assured that the model is doing exactly what you want it to— verification.

You can view the SIMAN code for our small manufacturing model by using the *Run/ SIMAN/View* menu option. Selecting this option will generate both files, each in a separate window. Figure 6-7 shows a small portion of the MOD file, the code written out for the Process module used at Cell 3. The SIMAN language is rather descriptive, so it is possible to follow the general logic. An entity that arrives at this module enters a queue, `Cell 3 Machines_Q`, waits to seize a resource from the set `Cell 3 Machines`, tallies the queue time, delays for the process time (adjusted by our factor), releases the resource, and exits the module. A trace and two zero time delays are also included, but the reason for their existence is too lengthy to explain here.

```
;
;     Model statements for module:  Process 1
;
8$          QUEUE,      Cell 3 Machines_Q:MARK(QueueTime);
442$        SEIZE,      1:SELECT(Cell 3 Machines,CYC,Index),1;
487$        TALLY:      Cell 3 Machines_Q Queue Time,INT(QueueTime),1;
            TRACE,      -1,"-Delay for processing time Process Time *
                        Factor(Index)\n";
454$        DELAY:      Process Time * Factor(Index);
462$        RELEASE:    SELECT(Cell 3 Machines,,Index),1;
505$        DELAY:      0.000;
515$        DELAY:      0.0:NEXT(10$);
```

Figure 6-7. SIMAN Model File for the Process Module

Figure 6-8 shows a portion of the EXP file that defines our two variables and the queues and resources used in our model.

```
VARIABLES:     Transfer Time,2:
               Factor(2),0.8,1.0;

QUEUES:        Cell 3 Machines_Q,FIFO:
               Cell 1_R_Q,FIFO:
               Cell 2_R_Q,FIFO:
               Cell 4_R_Q,FIFO;

RESOURCES:     Cell 1_R,Capacity(1,),:
               Cell 2_R,Capacity(1,),:
               Cell 4_R,Capacity(1,),:
               Cell 3 Old,Capacity(1,),:
               Cell 3 New,Capacity(1,),;
```

Figure 6-8. SIMAN Experiment File for the Process Module

We won't go into a detailed explanation of the statements in these files; the purpose of this exercise is merely to make you aware of their existence. For a more comprehensive explanation, refer to Pegden, Shannon, and Sadowski (1995).

If you're familiar with SIMAN or you would just like to learn more about how this process works, we might suggest that you place a few modules, enter some data, and write out the MOD and EXP files. Then edit the modules by selecting different options and write out the new files. Look for the differences between the two MOD files. Doing so should give you a fair amount of insight as to how this process works.

6.5 Confidence Intervals for Terminating Simulations via the Output Analyzer

As we warned you back in Section 2.6 with the hand simulation, there's an issue of randomness and thus statistical analysis when you build a model with any random (i.e., distribution- or probability-driven) inputs, as has been the case with all our models. In this section, we'll show you how to collect the appropriate data and then analyze them after the run with the help of Arena's Output Analyzer.

6.5.1 Time Frame of Simulations

Most (not all) simulations can be classified as either terminating or steady state. This is primarily an issue of intent or the goal of the study, rather than having much to do with internal model logic or construction.

A *terminating* simulation is one in which the model dictates specific starting and stopping conditions as a natural reflection of how the target system actually operates. As the name suggests, the simulation will terminate according to some model-specified rule or condition. For instance, a store opens at 9 AM with no customers present, closes its doors at 9 PM, and then continues operation until all customers are "flushed" out. Another example is a job shop that operates for as long as it takes to produce a "run" of 500 completed assemblies specified by the order. The key notion is that the time frame of the simulation has a well-defined (though possibly unknown at the outset) and natural end, as well as a clearly defined way to start up.

A *steady-state* simulation, on the other hand, is one in which the quantities to be estimated are defined in the long run; i.e., over a theoretically infinite time frame. In principle (though usually not in practice), the initial conditions for the simulation don't matter. Of course, a steady-state simulation has to stop at some point, and as you might guess, these runs can get pretty long; you need to do something to make sure that you're running it long enough, an issue we'll take up in Section 7.5. For example, a pediatric emergency room never really stops or restarts, so a steady-state simulation might be appropriate. Sometimes people do a steady-state simulation of a system that actually terminates in order to design for some kind of worst-case or peak-load situation.

In this chapter, we'll stick to a terminating analysis of the model just constructed, since steady-state analyses have to be done differently. (We'll do this in Section 7.5.)

6.5.2   Model 6.2: Modifying Model 6.1 for a Terminating Analysis

As it stands, the small manufacturing system (Model 6.1) simply stops at time 2,000 minutes, which doesn't seem like a particularly natural termination rule as part of the model. It also doesn't have a single overall measure of performance on which we might easily make comparisons across different configurations. We'll make a couple of modifications here to Model 6.1 to remedy these issues (as well as to point out some more modeling tools and techniques).

First, let's change the termination rule. Instead of stopping cold at a fixed time, suppose the system is to process an incoming order of 100 parts (of all types combined), whatever amount of simulated time that might take. Parts arrive according to the same time patterns as before, but only 100 will show up and the system stops when the last of these parts exits the system. This certainly qualifies as a model-defined termination rule, setting things up for a terminating analysis. To model this, we first opened the Simulate module and removed the 2,000 (minutes) from the Length of Replication field, leaving it blank; this defaults it to infinity, removing this as a stopping method. Then we opened up the Arrive module and filled in the Max Batches field to be 100 (since the Batch Size is still 1, this is the same as 100 individual parts). Specifying a value for Max Batches in this way means that this Arrive module is "shut off" as soon as it creates the specified number of batches. As the last few parts make their way through the model, the event calendar will get shorter and eventually become empty; this is one of the conditions under which Arena terminates the run (when there's nothing left to do). Note that since there's only a single Arrive module in this model, there are no other kinds of entities floating around to cause events to be on the event calendar; in a more complex model, this approach to stopping the simulation may not work properly if there are other things going on that cause other kinds of events to be on the calendar. This underscores the need to be familiar with the model's logic and how it operates. One additional modeling subtlety is that we "choked off" the *input* here, rather than counting the *output* and terminating when 100 parts exit but letting the input continue to flow in; this makes a difference toward the end of the simulation and affects the output (see Exercise 6.13).

Secondly, let's think about a single overall performance measure that we might use to compare alternative configurations, as we will in Section 6.5.5. There are many possibilities for this, depending on what's important in the project. We decided to track the total number of parts in the system at a time, sometimes called the *work in process* (WIP). To keep track of WIP, we defined a new (global) Variable called WIP and incremented and decremented it as parts arrived and departed. Incrementing WIP as a new part arrives is easy; just push the Assign button in the Arrive module, push Add, select Variable as the Assignment Type, and define WIP as the Variable and WIP + 1 as the Value.

Decrementing WIP as a finished part leaves, though, is not as simple since the Depart module does not offer the Assign option like the Arrive module does. Therefore, we need to insert something to decrement WIP just before an entity departs. This capability (among many others) is present in the Actions module from the Common panel. We placed an Actions module just to the left of the existing Depart module and gave this new Actions module the Station Name Decrement WIP; Display 6-19 indicates the data for this module.

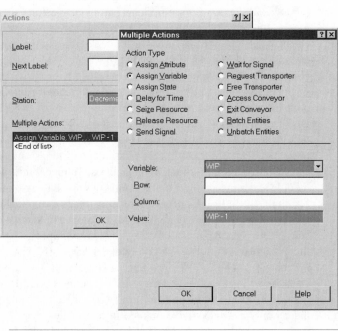

Station	Decrement WIP
Multiple Actions	
Assign Variable	*select*
Variable	WIP
Value	WIP - 1

Display 6-19. The Actions Module to Decrement WIP Just Before Entity Departure

To get the entities to this Actions module before the Depart, we changed the last jobstep for each part-type sequence in the Sequences module to `Decrement WIP` instead of `Exit System`. We then connected the output from the Actions module directly to the Depart module. Finally, in the animation, we moved the Routes out of `Cell 3` and `Cell 4` (the only ones serving as the end of a sequence for part types) to connect with the Station for `Decrement WIP`, which we placed where the Station for `Exit System` had been. (The Station for `Exit System` could have been deleted, but we just moved it back near its module handle.) This establishes the correct bookkeeping for `WIP`, which we regard as a time-persistent variable. An alternative method to keeping the correct bookkeeping would be to rename our Depart module station and give the old Station name, `Exit System`, to our new Actions module. We still need to request that summary statistics on the WIP variable (average, maximum, etc.) be produced at the end of a run. To do this, we placed a Statistics module, shown in Display 6-20.

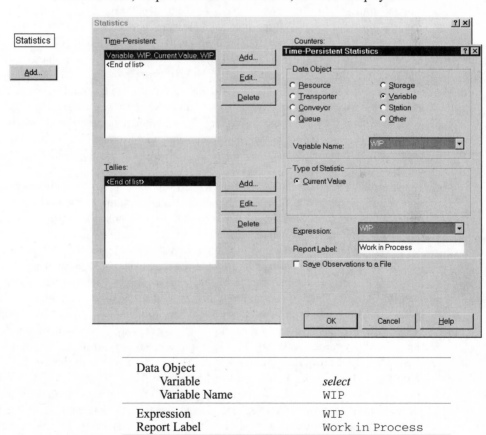

Data Object		
Variable	*select*	
Variable Name	WIP	
Expression	WIP	
Report Label	Work in Process	

Display 6-20. *The Statistics Module to Track and Summarize the WIP Variable*

6.5.3 Strategy for Data Collection and Analysis

With a terminating simulation, it's conceptually simple to collect the appropriate data for statistical analysis—just make some number n of independent replications.[2]

To do this, open the Simulate module and enter the value of n you want for the Number of Replications. Also be sure that the boxes under Between Replications are both checked (the default) to cause both the system-state variables and the statistical accumulators to be cleared at the end of each replication. There are reasons to leave one or both of these boxes unchecked, but to get true, statistically independent and identically distributed (IID) replications for terminating analysis, you need to make sure that both boxes are checked. These changes will cause the simulation to be replicated n times, with each replication starting afresh (fresh system state and fresh statistical accumulators) and using separate basic random numbers[3] to drive the simulation. For each replication, a separate summary report is generated in the output file containing the values for all of the outputs on that replication. For instance, we made $n = 20$ replications of the model and obtained for the average WIP performance measure the values 7.7828, 9.3190, 8.3350, 12.064, 6.3666, 13.813, 10.916, 15.748, 18.704, 14.761, 8.0204, 16.741, 7.8765, 8.3537, 9.0029, 17.983, 6.9032, 10.714, 12.598, and 10.551. It's important to remember that each of these values is the average of the WIP variable over an entire simulation run and that each is an "observation" (or "realization") of a random variable representing the average WIP over a "random" replication with these starting and stopping conditions. The above list is for the average WIP values, but we could make a similar list of 20 values for any of the other output performance measures, like average Part 2 cycle times, the proportion of time the old machine in Cell 3 was busy, or the average number of parts in queue for Cell 1.

How did we know ahead of time that $n = 20$ was the appropriate number of replications to make? We didn't. In fact, we're mature enough to admit to you that the first time we tried this we made 10 replications but were frankly surprised at the amount of variation across replications of measures like average WIP. (Just eyeball the above list if you haven't noticed already that the values range from about 6.4 to about 18.7.) When we did the confidence-interval construction from these 10 replications, we were disappointed at how wide (imprecise) the intervals were, so we decided to go back and rerun the experiment for $n = 20$. This is typical of how things go when you don't know up front how much variation you have in your output. We'll have more to say below about picking (or guessing) a reasonable value for the sample size. By the way, when cranking out replications like this for statistical analysis, you might want to turn off the animation to move things along: pull down *Run/Setup,* select the Mode tab, and check the box for Batch Run (No Animation). To get the animation back later, you'll need to uncheck this same box.

You're probably not going to want to copy out all the values for all the performance measures of interest over all the replications and then type or paste them into some statistical package or spreadsheet or (gasp!) calculator for analysis. You can have Arena save

---

[2] While *conceptually* simple, this could still imply a lot of run time for big or highly variable models.

[3] Actually, each replication just keeps marching through the random-number "streams" being used; see Chapter 11 for more on how random-number generators work and can be controlled.

to binary ".dat" files (to be fed into the Arena Output Analyzer) whatever you want from the summary of each replication. Arena will also display them at the end of the Summary report for each replication. Just Add entries in the Outputs area of the Statistics module we placed earlier to produce the WIP statistics here. Display 6-21 illustrates how this is done for three output measures, although only the entries for the average Work in Process are included in the table. For each measure added, we had to select the Type of Statistic, its Name (matching the label in the Summary reports), what Information was desired (Average, Maximum, etc.), the Expression for the value desired, and then check the box to Save Observations to a File and name the file (inside double quotes). This seems like a lot of information to specify, but Arena helps you along the way by supplying pull-down lists and suggesting defaults for later things as you decide on earlier things. We saved the "average" data on eight output values: cycle times for the three types of parts, queue lengths at the four cells, and WIP (Display 6-21 illustrates only three of these). You can select any file names you want in which to save the observations, but ".dat" extensions are customary and what the Output Analyzer will expect by default.

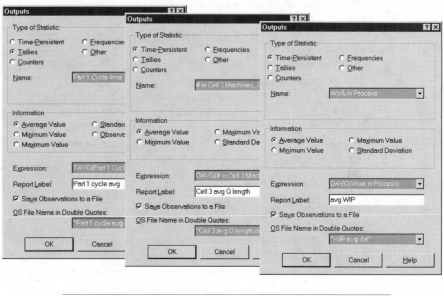

Type of Statistic	
Time-Persistent	*select*
Name	Work in Process
Save Observations to a File	*check*
OS File Name in Double Quotes	"WIP avg.dat"

Display 6-21. Statistics Module to Save Summary Measures Across Replications

6.5.4   Confidence Intervals for Terminating Systems

We introduced the Arena Output Analyzer in Section 5.2.6 and described the notion of a Data Group there; if you haven't read Section 5.2.6, you probably should do so before going on here. Our earlier use of the Output Analyzer was just to make some plots and output data displays of the simulation after it had run. Here, we'll use the Output Analyzer to do some statistical inference from the output saved over the 20 replications of Model 6.2.

After starting the Output Analyzer, we created a new data group by Adding the eight ".dat" files we saved via the Outputs area of the Statistics module, described in Section 6.5.3, and then saved it under the name Mod_06_2.dgr. We then asked for 95% confidence intervals on the expected average cycle times for each of the three part types, as illustrated in Display 6-22.

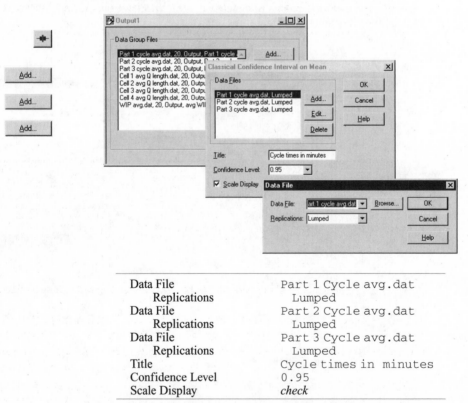

Data File	Part 1 Cycle avg.dat
Replications	Lumped
Data File	Part 2 Cycle avg.dat
Replications	Lumped
Data File	Part 3 Cycle avg.dat
Replications	Lumped
Title	Cycle times in minutes
Confidence Level	0.95
Scale Display	*check*

Display 6-22. Output Analyzer's Classical Confidence Interval on Mean for Cycle Times by Part Type

Note that for the Replications entry on each data file, we entered Lumped; this tells the Output Analyzer that we want to "lump" all 20 replications together and view them as a single data set for purposes of computing the confidence interval. We accepted the default 95% confidence level for each of the three intervals, but we could have filled in something different. In order to facilitate visual comparison, checking the Scale Display box forces the graphical display for all the intervals to be on the same scale.

Figure 6-9 shows the results in a split window arranged so that everything shows up. (You can drag the horizontal splitter bar up and down to resize the sub-windows and scroll within them.) The top sub-window gives the graphical display, annotated with the values of the mean, confidence limits, and extreme values; and the bottom sub-window gives the corresponding numerical information. The method for constructing each interval is exactly as described in Section 2.6.2, except that the Output Analyzer reads the ".dat" files saved from the runs, does the arithmetic (including the t-table lookup), and displays the results in useful formats.

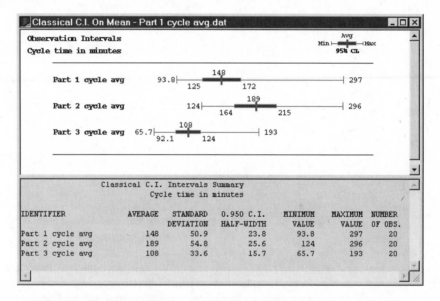

Figure 6-9. Confidence Intervals on the Expected Average Cycle Times by Part Type

The Confidence Interval display shows that while Part Type 2 tends to have the longest cycle times, they cannot really be said to be significantly longer (statistically) than those for Part Type 1 since their confidence intervals overlap. However, it does seem safe to say that the mean Cycle Time for Part Type 3 is less than those for the other two part types. We don't want to make too much of the notion of looking for whether confidence intervals do or don't overlap (these aren't formal hypothesis tests), but we certainly have a better idea now about what kind of variability we have in our output and what differences appear to be real and what differences could be explained by "noise."

Figure 6-10 gives a similar display, except for the time-persistent output statistics. From this it appears that there is really no discernible difference in the average lengths of the four queues. We also see that the expected average WIP, which includes the processing times as well as the queue times, is not very precisely estimated even from these 20 replications (maybe we should have done even more); it is more variable than the queue-length statistics since it contains all the variability in them as well as the variability in the processing times at the machines.

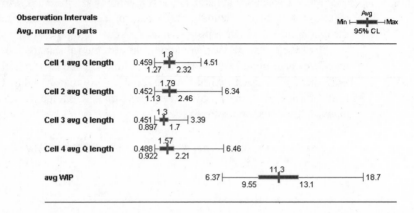

IDENTIFIER	AVERAGE	STANDARD DEVIATION	0.950 C.I. HALF WIDTH	MINIMUM VALUE	MAXIMUM VALUE	NUMBER OF OBS.
Cell 1 avg Q length	1.8	1.12	0.525	0.459	4.51	20
Cell 2 avg Q length	1.79	1.42	0.666	0.452	6.34	20
Cell 3 avg Q length	1.3	0.856	0.401	0.451	3.39	20
Cell 4 avg Q length	1.57	1.38	0.644	0.488	6.46	20
avg WIP	11.3	3.81	1.78	6.37	18.7	20

Figure 6-10. Confidence Intervals on the Expected Average Numbers of Parts in Queue and in Process

Arena will automatically give you confidence-interval information if you call for more than a single replication in your Simulate module and if you have a Statistics module with entries in the Outputs area. An "Output Summary" section will be appended at the bottom of your summary output report, following the results from your final replication, giving you the over-replications mean, half width of a 95% confidence interval, minimum and maximum over the replications, and the number of replications you made. This information will be produced only for those output measures you've listed in the Outputs area of a Statistics module, rather than for all the statistics your model is collecting and reporting for each individual replication. (If you don't have a Statistics module with something in the Outputs area, you won't get this extra section.) If you run Model 6.2 and look at the end of the summary report, you'll see this section, labeled "Output Summary for 20 Replications." For example, on the expected average WIP, the 95% confidence interval is 11.327 ± 1.7801 with a minimum single-replication average of 6.3666 and a maximum of 18.704, consistent with the results in Figure 6-10; on the expected average cycle times for Part Type 3, the 95% confidence interval is 107.80 ± 15.704, with a minimum of 65.692 and maximum of 193.10, the same as in Figure 6-9. Though these results agree with what we got above via doing it ourselves with the Output Analyzer, and were produced automatically, you may still want to go through the process with the Output Analyzer if you want to control the conditions and reporting in some way, such as specifying the confidence level to something other than 95%, producing the results in particular groupings or orderings, or if you want to get the graphical displays of the confidence intervals, minima, and maxima.

It's probably obvious that the way to reduce the half width of the confidence interval on expected average WIP (or on anything, for that matter) is to increase the sample size n. But by how much? If you have a certain "smallness" in mind that you'd like (or could tolerate) for the half width, you can easily get an idea, but not an exact answer, of how big n will have to be to achieve this goal. Suppose you have an initial set of replications from which you compute a sample average and standard deviation, and then a confidence interval whose half width is disappointingly large. For instance, for our initial 20 replications above in the case of WIP, we got $\overline{X} = 11.3$, $s = 3.81$, and the half width of the 95% confidence interval turned out to be

$$t_{n-1,1-\alpha/2}\,\frac{s}{\sqrt{n}} = 2.09\,\frac{3.81}{\sqrt{20}} = 1.78\,,$$

which represents some 16% error in the point estimate 11.3. If you want to achieve a specific half-width h, presumably smaller than the one you got from your initial set of replications, try setting h equal to the half-width formula above and solve for n:

$$n = t_{n-1,1-\alpha/2}^2\,\frac{s^2}{h^2}\,.$$

The difficulty with this is that it isn't really solved for n since the right-hand side still depends on n (via the degrees of freedom in the t distribution critical value and, though the notation doesn't show it, via the sample standard deviation s, which depends not only on n but also on the data obtained from the initial set of replications). However, to get at least a rough approximation to the sample size required, you could replace the t distribution critical value in the formula above with the standard normal critical value $z_{1-\alpha/2}$ (they're close for n more than about 30), and pretend that the current estimate s will be about the same when you compute it from the larger sample. This leads to the following as an approximate required sample size to achieve a confidence interval with half width equal to a prespecified desired value h:

$$n \cong z_{1-\alpha/2}^2\,\frac{s^2}{h^2}$$

where s is the sample standard deviation from an initial set of replications (which you'd have to make before doing this). An easier but slightly different approximation is (we'll leave the algebra to you)

$$n \cong n_0\,\frac{h_0^2}{h^2}$$

where n_0 is the number of initial replications you have and h_0 is the half width you got from them. In the WIP example above, to reduce the half width from $h_0 = 1.78$ to, say, $h = 0.5$, we'd thus need a total of something like

$$n \cong 1.96^2 \frac{3.81^2}{0.5^2} = 223.1 \ \text{(first approximation)} \ \text{or} \ \ n \cong 20\frac{1.78^2}{0.5^2} = 253.5 \ \text{(second approximation)}$$

(round up) replications instead of the 20 we originally made. The second approximation will always be bigger since it uses $t_{n_0-1,1-\alpha/2}$ rather than $z_{1-\alpha/2}$. Note the depressing quadratic growth of sample size as h shrinks (i.e., we demand more precision)—to reduce the half width to half its initial value, you need about *four* times as much data. While this might seem unfair (to do twice as well you have to work four times as hard), the intuition is that as you add more and more replications, each additional replication carries less and less percentage increase in your accumulating storehouse of knowledge.

It's important to understand just what a confidence interval is (and what it isn't). Take the average WIP output measure as an example. Each replication produces an average WIP value (earlier we showed you our 20 values) over that replication, and due to random inputs, these values vary across replications. The average of the 20 values, you'll agree, is a "better" indicator of what to expect from a "typical" run than any of the individual values. Also, it's intuitive that the more replications you make, the "better" this average will be. The *expected* average, which is usually denoted by some kind of notation like μ, can be thought of as the average WIP taken over an *infinite* number of replications; as such, μ will have no uncertainty associated with it.

Unfortunately, mere mortals like us can't wait for an infinite number of replications, so we have to make do with a finite-sample estimate like the 11.3 from our 20 replications. The confidence interval centered around 11.3 can be thought of as a "random" interval (the next set of 20 replications will give you a different interval) that has approximately a 95% (in this case) chance of containing or "covering" μ in the sense that if we made a lot of sets of 20 replications and made such an interval from each set, about 95% of these intervals would cover μ. Thus, a confidence interval gives you both a "point" estimate (11.3) of μ, as well as an idea of how precise this estimate is.

A confidence interval is *not* an interval in which, for example, 95% of the average-WIP measures from replications will fall. Such an interval, called a *prediction interval*, is useful as well, and can basically be derived from the same data. One clear difference between these two types of intervals is that a confidence interval will shrink to a point as n increases, but a prediction interval won't since it needs to allow for the variation in (future) replications.

A final word about confidence intervals concerns our hedging the confidence-level statement ("approximately" 95%, etc.). The standard methods for doing this, which the Output Analyzer uses, assumes that the basic data, such as the 20 observations on average WIP across the replications, are IID (that's satisfied for us) and normally distributed (that's not satisfied). Basically, use of the t distribution in the confidence-interval formula requires normality of the data. So what's the effect on the actual (as opposed to stated) confidence level of violation of this normality assumption? We can firmly and absolutely state that it depends on several things, including the "true" distribution as well as the number, n, of replications. The *central limit theorem*, one of the fundamental cornerstones of statistics, reassures us that we'll be pretty much OK (in terms of actual confidence being close to stated confidence) if n is "large." But how large? The answer to this is fairly imponderable and depends on how closely the distribution of the data resembles a normal distribution, particularly in terms of symmetry. This can be at least qualitatively checked out by making a histogram of the data values, as we do in Figure 6-11 for $n = 1000$ replications rather than the original 20 (the histogram with 20 didn't illustrate much); we made this plot with the Output Analyzer's Histogram (*Graph/Histogram* or) facility.

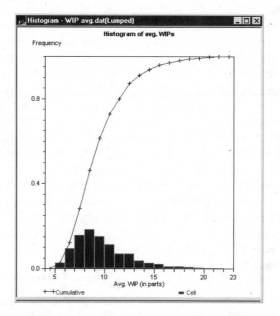

Figure 6-11. Histogram of 1000 Average WIP Values

Though admittedly just eyeballing the data, we see that the shape of the histogram (the solid bars in the "Cell" plot) is a little skewed to the right, but overall it's not too far from the familiar "bell" curve of the normal density function, suggesting that we're probably OK in terms of using the standard confidence-interval method even for a small value of n. For this model, which took only about a second per replication on a low-end Pentium machine, we had the luxury of doing these 1000 replications to check for normality; with a bigger model, you won't be able to do anything of the sort. So how do you check this out in practice? Or is it just an article of faith? Though far from being a statement of general truth, a lot of simulation experience indicates that if the value you're getting out of each individual replication is an average of something (either observational or over a time-persistent curve like WIP), as opposed to an extreme value, using standard normal-theory statistical-inference methods is fairly safe.

6.5.5 Comparing Alternatives

In most simulation studies, people eventually become interested in comparing different versions, or *alternatives*, of some general model. What makes the alternatives differ from each other could be anything from a simple parameter change to fundamentally different logic. In any case, you need to take care to apply the appropriate statistical methods to the output from the alternatives to ensure that valid conclusions are drawn.

Let's take up Model 6.2 again and focus on the Transfer Time that parts need to move between stations. As it stands, the value is set in the Variables module to be 2 minutes in every case throughout the model. This smells suspiciously like some rough guess, perhaps because good information was not available on what's really going on. Or, perhaps consideration is being given to changing it either up (slower and presumably cheaper) or down (faster and presumably more expensive). Whatever the situation, let's compare two different alternatives of this model—one with Transfer Time = 1 and another with Transfer Time = 3. Just open the Variables module, double-click on the Transfer Time entry in the Variables list, double-click on the 2 to edit it, make the change, then OK your way back out. While we could examine the effect of varying Transfer Time on any of the output performance measures, let's use the average WIP as a reasonable overall single figure of merit to simplify our comparisons. Since we'll want to save the average WIP over our 20 replications, and since we'll have two such files, we either need to change the name of it in the Outputs area of the Statistics module (to something like WIP avg 1.dat and WIP avg 3.dat for the two alternatives) before running, or rename this file in the operating system after each run.

The Output Analyzer can make the comparison we want via the *Analyze/Compare Means* menu. Display 6-23 fills in the information for the Compare Means function.

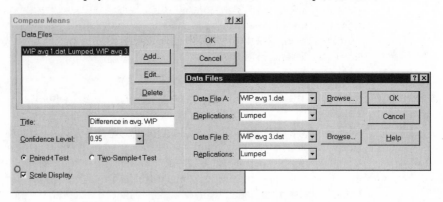

Title	Difference in avg. WIP
Data File A Replication	WIP avg 1.dat Lumped
Data File B Replication	WIP avg 3.dat Lumped

Display 6-23. Using the Output Analyzer's Compare Means Facility

We first Add the data files, requiring specification of those from both alternatives (called A and B in the dialog, both Lumped as before), then maybe fill in a Title and accept or change the Confidence Level. The radio button group for Paired-t Test (the default) vs. Two-Sample-t Test refers to an issue of random number allocation and statistical independence, which we'll take up in Section 11.4.1; the Paired-t approach is somewhat more general and will be the one to use if we try to improve precision by allocating the random numbers carefully (which we haven't done here).

The results are in Figure 6-12. Since we ordered this comparison as subtracting the slow-transfer-time (3) model from the fast-transfer-time (1) model, and since faster transfer times tend to reduce WIP, the average difference in the average WIPs is negative, –2.5. To see whether this is a statistically significant difference (i.e., whether this difference is too far away from zero to be reasonably explained by random noise), the Output Analyzer gives you a 95% confidence interval on the expected difference; since this interval misses zero, we conclude that there is indeed a statistically significant difference in evidence here (the results of the equivalent two-sided hypothesis test for zero-expected difference is also shown in the lower part of the window), and in fact, that average WIP is lower for transfer times of 1 instead of 3. The confidence interval is really a better way to express all this since it contains the "reject" conclusion from the test (the interval misses zero), but also quantifies the magnitude of the difference. If you did this comparison because you're considering implementing one of these alternatives, you now have an idea of what the reduction in average WIP will be if you have faster transfer times; you'd then have to trade off this benefit against the cost of speeding up the transfers. If you did this comparison as a sensitivity analysis of average WIP to your uncertainty about what the transfer times really are (as part of model building), this is bad news. It means that this parameter *does* matter, so you need to try to nail it down as best you can—perhaps by collecting more (or at least some) data on it. More likely in this case, you'd want to model the fact that the distances between the cells are different and allow for different travel times; we'll take up this issue for this model in Chapter 7.

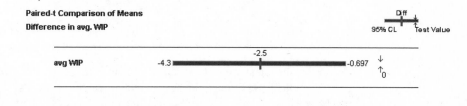

IDENTIFIER	ESTD. MEAN DIFFERENCE	STANDARD DEVIATION	0.950 C.I. HALF WIDTH	MINIMUM VALUE	MAXIMUM VALUE	NUMBER OF OBS.
avg WIP	-2.5	3.84	1.8	5.36	21	20
				7.54	18.4	20

REJECT HO => MEANS ARE NOT EQUAL AT 0.05 LEVEL

Figure 6-12. Confidence Interval and Hypothesis Test on the Expected Difference Between Average WIPs

6.6 Summary and Forecast

Now you should have a very good set of skills for carrying out fairly detailed modeling with the tools from the Common panel and have an understanding of (and know what to do about) issues like verification and statistical analysis of simulation output data. In the following chapter, we'll expand on this to show you how to model complicated and realistic material-handling operations. In the chapters beyond, you'll drill down deeper into Arena's modeling and analysis capabilities to exploit its powerful and flexible hierarchical structure.

6.7 Exercises

6.1 Modify Model 6.2 from the text to merge all three part cycle times into a single performance measure rather than sorting them by part type. Make 20 replications of the terminating simulation with the same starting and stopping rules as for Model 6.2, and use the Output Analyzer to compute a 95% confidence interval for the expected average overall part cycle time.

6.2 A part arrives every 10 minutes to a three-workstation system. There are four part types, each with equal probability of arriving. The process plans for the four part types are given below. The entries for the process times are the mean and standard-deviation parameters for a normal distribution (in minutes).

Part Type	Workstation/ Process Time	Workstation/ Process Time	Workstation/ Process Time
Part 1	A 9.5, 2	C 14.1, 2.8	
Part 2	A 13.5, 2.3	B 15, 3	C 8.5, 2.1
Part 3	A 12, 1.8	B 9.5, 2.1	
Part 4	B 12.6, 1.7	C 11.4, 1.4	

Assume that the transfer time between all stations is three minutes. Use the Sequence feature to direct the parts through the system and to assign the processing times at each station. Use the Sets feature to collect cycle times for each of the part types separately. Run the simulation for 5,000 minutes.

6.3 Modify your solution for Exercise 6.2 to use the Expressions feature for determining the processing times. Run for 5,000 minutes and compare the results to those from exercise 6.2 Are the results different? If so, why?

6.4 Modify your solution Exercise 6.2 or 6.3 so that all parts follow the same path through the system: Workstation A–Workstation B–Workstation C. If a part does not require processing at a workstation, it must still wait in queue, but incurs a zero processing-time delay. Compare the results to those obtained from 6.2 and 6.3.

6.5   Modify the models from Exercises 6.2, 6.3, and 6.4 to make 25 replications of length 5,000 minutes each, and save the average cycle time for Part 2 as a statistic to compare the different models. Use the Output Analyzer to compute a 95% confidence limit on the expected cycle times from each of the three models. Also use the Output Analyzer to estimate the expected difference between each of the systems.

6.6   An office of a state license bureau has two types of arrivals. Individuals interested in purchasing new plates are characterized have interarrival times distributed as EXPO(6.8) and service times as TRIA(8.7, 13.7, 15.2). Individuals who want to renew or apply for a new driver's license have interarrival times distributed as EXPO(8.7) and service times as TRIA(16.7, 20.5, 29.2). The office has two lines, one for each customer type. The office has five clerks: two devoted to plates (Tom and Patty), two devoted to licenses (Nancy and Loretta), and the team leader (Sherri) who can serve both customer types. Sherri will serve the customer who has been waiting the longest. Assume that all clerks are available all the time for the 8-hour day. Make 30 replications and compute a 95% confidence interval on the expected system or cycle time for both customer types.

6.7   The office described in Exercise 6.6 is considering cross-training Patty so she can serve both customer types. Modify the model, make 30 replications, and use the Output Analyzer to estimate the expected difference between each of the systems (based on system time by customer).

6.8   Modify the model from Exercise 6.7 to include 30-minute lunch breaks for each clerk. Start the first lunch break 180 minutes into the day. Lunch breaks should follow one after the other covering a 150-minute time span during the middle of the day. The breaks should be given in the following order: Tom, Nancy, Sherri, Patty, and Loretta. Make 30 replications and use the Output Analyzer to estimate the expected difference between each of the systems (based on system by customer).

6.9   Three types of customers arrive at a small airport: check baggage (30%), purchase tickets (15%), and carry-on (55%). The interarrival-time distribution for all customers combined is EXPO(1.3). The bag checkers go directly to the check-bag counter to check their bags—the time for which is distributed TRIA(2, 4, 5)—proceed to X-ray, and then go to the gate. The ticket buyers go directly to the ticket counter to purchase their tickets—the time for which is distributed EXPO(7)—proceed to X-ray, and then go to the gate. The carry-ons go directly to the X-ray, then to the gate counter to a get boarding pass—the time for which is distributed TRIA(1, 1.5, 3). All three counters are staffed all the time with one agent each. The X-ray time is EXPO(1). All travel times are EXPO(2), except for the carry time to the X-ray, which is EXPO(3). Run your model for 920 minutes, and collect statistics on resource utilization, queues, and system time from entrance to gate for all customers combined.

6.10   The airport, described in Exercise 6.9, is considering consolidating the ticket and check-bag counters into a single counter with two agents. Make the modification and run this, as well as the original model, for 20 replications, and compare the results based on combined system time. Be sure to use an appropriate statistical technique.

6.11 A unique product requires two days to produce. The operations during the first day require that the base product be created, which must sit overnight before the finishing operations can be performed on the second day. The first day's operations have no capacity problem. On the second day, two finishing operations are performed by one of three teams, with no preference for any particular team. Each team has two operators, one for each operation. You might think of each team as a workstation that performs both operations. Because the finishing operations require great skill, the operation times for each operation are different. The times (in minutes) for each operator are given below as parameters of a triangular distribution. The finished parts are then sent to a single packer who packs the products, requiring a time distributed as TRIA(2.2, 2.9, 4.1). All parts delivered to the finishing department must be finished that same day or they are scrapped. Develop a model of this system that releases 130 products/day. If there are 460 minutes in a day, what percent of the time will the parts be complete before the end of the day, based on 50 replications? (Hint: Request an output statistic on TNOW and save it to a data file. This will be the amount of time required to produce all parts for that day.)

Team	Operation 1 Time	Operation 2 Time
1	6.1, 8.2, 11.4	5.1, 7.3, 13.6
2	6.9, 9.1, 12.7	5.7, 8.6, 14.2
3	8.2, 10.3, 14.1	7.1, 9.2, 15.9

6.12 Modify your model from Exercise 6.1 to account for acquiring a new customer, in addition to the one supplying the existing three part types. This new customer will supply two new types of parts—call them Type 4 and Type 5. The arrival process is in addition to and independent of that for the original three part types and has exponential interarrival times with mean 15 minutes. When the parts arrive, assign 40% of the new parts to be Type 4 and the rest to be Type 5. Here are the process plans and mean processing times (in minutes) for the new part types:

Part Type	Cell/ Mean Proc. Time	Cell/ Mean Proc. Time	Cell/ Mean Proc. Time	Cell/ Mean Proc. Time
4	1 6.1	3 5.2	2 1.3	4 2.4
5	2 3.5	3 4.1	4 3.2	1 2.0

While people feel comfortable with these mean processing times, there's not very good information on their distributions, so you're asked just to assume that the distributions are uniform with the indicated mean but plus or minus 0.2 minute in each case; for example, if a mean of 6.1 is shown, assume that the distribution is uniform between 5.9 and 6.3. As with the original three parts, allow a total of 100 parts (Type 4 plus Type 5) from this new customer to enter the system. Make all necessary changes to the model, including the modules, animation pictures (create new entity pictures for the new part types), and anything else required. Be sure that the animation works properly, including the clockwise-only movement of all entities and the new part types.

(a) Clearly, adding this new customer is going to clog the system compared to what it was. Using the overall average part cycle time (now with all five types of parts merged), how bad does it get compared to the original system? Make 20 replications and carry out the proper statistical comparison using the Output Analyzer between this system and the original one.

(b) In an effort to alleviate the added congestion introduced by the new customer, you've been given a budget to buy one new machine to be placed either in Cell 1, 2, or 4 (not in Cell 3). Where would you recommend placing it? Assume that it will work at the same rate as the machine it joins in whatever cell. Make 20 replications and compute a 95% confidence interval for the expected average overall part cycle time using the Output Analyzer.

6.13 Reconsider the terminating-simulation stopping rule discussed in Section 6.5.2. As it stands, Model 6.2 "chokes off" the input after 100 unprocessed parts arrive, which is what we wanted to model. A different modeling assumption would be to terminate the simulation after 100 parts exit the system, but leave the input running to the bitter end; unlike Model 6.2, there will be parts "stranded" in the system at termination. Modify Model 6.2 first to plot the WIP variable over time, but keep the existing termination rule; note that WIP drops to 0 as the simulation ends. Then, modify Model 6.2 to implement this alternate stopping rule. To do this, set up a counter in the Depart module to count parts as they exit, then use the Terminating Condition field in the Simulate module to stop the run when this counter hits 100. (NC(CounterID) is the internal Arena variable tracking the current value of the indicated counter.) Compare the end of the WIP plots from these two models.

Entity Transfer and Steady-State Statistical Analysis

CHAPTER 7

Entity Transfer and Steady-State Statistical Analysis

Up to now, we've considered two different ways to direct an entity's flow through a model. We've had them move from module to module with no travel time via Connections. In other models, we've moved them by Routing between stations with some transit-time delay and an optional animation. In both cases, the entities proceed uninhibited, as though they all had their own feet and there was enough room in the transitways for as many of them at a time as wanted to be moving.

Of course, things aren't always so nice. There could be a limit on the number of entities in transit at a time, such as a communications system where the entities are packets of information and the bandwidth is limited to a certain number of packets in transit at a time. There could also be situations in which something like a forklift or a person needs to come pick up an entity and then transport it. There are also different kinds of conveyors where entities can be viewed as competing for space on the belt or line. We'll explore some of these modeling ideas and capabilities in this chapter. This often is an important practical problem to model accurately since studies have shown that delays and inefficiencies in operations might be caused more by the need just to move things around rather than in actually doing the work.

Section 7.1 discusses in more detail the different kinds of entity movement and transfers and how they can be modeled. In Section 7.2, we'll indicate how you can use the Arena modeling tools you already have to represent a constraint on the number of entities that can be in motion at a time (though all entities still have their own feet). Transport devices like forklifts, pushcarts, and (of course) people are taken up in Section 7.3. Modeling conveyors of different kinds is described in Section 7.4. Continuing our theme of viewing all aspects of simulation projects throughout a study, we resume the topic of using the Output Analyzer for statistical analysis of the output data in Section 7.5, but this time it's for steady-state simulations.

After reading this chapter and considering the examples, you'll be able to model a rich variety of entity movement and transfer that can add validity to your model and realism to your animations. You'll also be in a position to draw statistically valid conclusions about the performance of systems as they operate in the long run.

7.1 Types of Entity Transfers

To transfer entities between modules, we initially used the Connect option (Chapter 3) to transfer entities directly between modules with no time delay. In Section 6.4.2, we discussed another option using Labels. These two options are essentially the same in how they function; they differ only in that the Connect allows you to see the flow, whereas the

Label does not. In Chapter 5, we introduced the concept of a Route that allows you to transfer entities between stations allowing a time delay in the transfer. We first showed how to use Routes for entity transfer to a specific station; then in Chapter 6, we generalized this concept by using Sequences.

Although this gives us the ability to model most situations, we sometimes find it necessary to limit or constrain the number of transfers occurring at any point in time. For example, in modeling a communications network, the links have a limited capacity. Thus, we must have a method to limit the number of simultaneous messages that are being transferred by each network link or for the entire network. The solution is rather simple; we think of the network links as resources with a capacity equal to the number of simultaneous messages allowed. If the capacity is dependent upon the size of the messages, then we define the resource capacity in terms of this size and require each message to seize the required number of resources, determined by its size, before it can be transferred. Let's call this type of entity transfer *resource constrained*, and we'll discuss it in more detail in Section 7.2.

Using a resource to constrain the number of simultaneous transfers may work fine for a communications network, but it doesn't allow us to model accurately an entire class or category of entity transfers generally referred to as *material handling*. The modeling requirements for different material handling systems can vary greatly, and the number of different types of material handling devices is enormous. In fact, there is an entire handbook devoted to this subject (see Kulwiec, 1985). However, it's possible to divide these devices into two general categories based on their modeling requirements.

- The first category constrains the number of simultaneous transfers based on the number of material handling devices available. Material handing devices that fall into this category are carts, hand trucks, fork trucks, AGVs, people, etc. However, there is an additional requirement in that each of these devices has a physical location. If a transfer is required, we may first have to move the device to the location where the requesting entity resides before we can perform the actual transfer. From a modeling standpoint, you might think of these as *moveable resources*, referred to in Arena as *Transporters*.

- The second category constrains the ability to start a transfer based on space availability. It also requires that we limit the total number of simultaneous transfers between two locations, but this limit is typically based on the space requirement. Material handing devices that fall into this category include conveyors, overhead trolleys, power-and-free systems, tow lines, etc. An escalator is a more common example of this type of material handling device. If a transfer is required, we first have to obtain the required amount of available or unoccupied space on the device, at the location where we are waiting, before we can initiate our transfer. These devices require a quite different modeling capability, referred to in Arena as *Conveyors*.

The Arena Transporter and Conveyor constructs allow us to model almost any type of material handling system easily. However, there are a few material handling devices that have very unique requirements that can create a modeling challenge. Gantry or bridge cranes are classic examples of such devices. A single crane is easily modeled with the transporter constructs. If you have more than one crane on a single track, the method used to control how the cranes move is critical to modeling these devices accurately. Unfortunately, almost all systems that have multiple cranes are controlled by the crane operators who generally reside in the cabs located on the cranes. These operators can see and talk to one another, and their decisions are not necessarily predictable. In this case, it is easy to model the cranes; the difficult part is how to incorporate the human logic that prevents the cranes from colliding or gridlocking.

Thus, we've defined three types of constrained entity transfers: resource constrained, transporters, and conveyors. We'll first briefly discuss resource-constrained transfers in Section 7.2, then introduce transporters and conveyors by using them in our small manufacturing system from Chapter 6 (Model 6.1) in Sections 7.3 and 7.4.

7.2 Resource-Constrained Transfers

Using a resource to constrain the number of simultaneous entity transfers is a relatively easy addition to a model. We'll describe the steps to implement this logic and encourage the interested modeler to add it to Model 6.1 (but we won't do it here). We need to define what we think of as a new kind of transferring resource, seize one unit of that resource before we initiate our route to leave a location, and release the resource when we arrive at the next station or location. This is an ordinary Arena resource, but we're thinking of it differently to model the transfers.

You might first look back at the dialogs for the Enter and Leave modules for Cell 3, Displays 6-14 and 6-16. The Leave module dialog gave us four options for controlling the departure of the entities: Seize, Request, Access, and None. The Enter module provided the corresponding four options for the arrival of the entity to the station. The same features can be found in the Arrive, Server, and Depart modules through the Tran Out and Tran In buttons. Selecting these options results in the Transfer Out and Transfer In dialogs shown in Figure 7-1. These dialogs are the same, regardless of which module activates them.

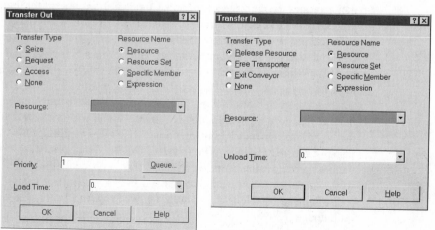

Figure 7-1. *The Transfer Out and Transfer In Dialogs*

The Transfer Out allows you to seize a transferring resource before leaving the station. Which resource to seize can be defined as a particular resource, a resource set, a specific member of a set, or a resource based on the evaluation of an expression. For our system, you would only have to select the Seize and Resource options and enter a transferring resource name. When you arrive at the destination module, you'll release the transferring resource through the Transfer In dialog. These dialogs also give you the option of including Load and Unload Times to account for such activities. You can also specify a Priority in the Transfer Out dialog that would allow you to control which entity would be given the transferring resource if more than one entity was waiting. The smaller the number, the higher the priority.

In summary, if you want to limit the number of simultaneous part transfers for our model by using a constraining resource, you would only need to select these options and enter the resource name in the Arrive, Depart, Enter, Leave, and the three Server modules. You should be aware that we have not yet defined the capacity of our constraining resource, which determines the maximum number of parts that could be transferring at one time. Although we have defined the existence of this resource, Arena defaults to a capacity of 1 for it. To increase this capacity, we need to place a Resource module from the Common panel that will allow us to define a larger capacity. Recall that some animation features accompany this module; simply delete them as they are not required.

7.3   Model 7.1: The Small Manufacturing System with Transporters

In our initial model of the small manufacturing system, we assumed that all transfer times were 2 minutes. If these transfer times depend on the availability of material handling devices, the actual times may be quite different. Because of this, the earlier model would give us good estimates of the system capacity; however, it would most likely not provide very accurate estimates on the part cycle times. If the material transfer became a constraint, it might even *overestimate* the system capacity. Let's assume that all material transfers are accomplished with some type of Transporter; for example, carts, hand trucks, or fork trucks. Let's further assume that there are two of these carts, each moving at 50 feet per minute, whether loaded or empty. Each cart can transport only one part at a time and there are 0.25 minute load and unload times at the start and end of each transport. We'll provide the distances between stations after we've added the carts to our model.

There are two types of Arena Transporters: Free-Path and Guided. *Free-Path Transporters* can move freely through the system without encountering delays due to congestion. The time to travel from one point to another depends only on the Transporter velocity and the distance to be traveled. *Guided Transporters* are restricted to moving within a predefined network. Their travel times depend on the vehicles' speeds, the network paths they follow, and potential congestion along those paths. The most common type of guided vehicle is an *automated guided vehicle* (AGV). The carts for our system fall into the free-path category.

The transfer of a part with a Transporter requires three activities: Request a transporter, Transport the part, and Free the transporter. The key words are Request, Transport, and

Free. The *Request* activity, which is analogous to seizing a resource, allocates an available transporter to the requesting entity and moves the allocated transporter to the location of the entity, if it's not already there. The *Transport* activity causes the transporter to move the entity to the destination station. This is analogous to a route, but in the case of a Transport, the transporter and entity move together. The *Free* activity frees the transporter for the next request, much like the action of releasing a resource.

If there are multiple transporters in the system, we face two issues regarding their assignment to entities. First, we might have the situation during the run where an entity requests a transporter and more than one is available. In this case, a *Transporter Selection Rule* dictates which one of the transporter units will fulfill the request. In most modeled systems, the *Smallest Distance* rule makes sense—allocate the transporter unit that's closest to the requesting entity. Other rules are available, including Largest Distance, though it takes a creative mind to imagine a case where it would be sensible. The second issue concerning transporter allocation arises when a transporter is freed and there are multiple entities waiting to request it. In this case, Arena applies a priority (specified in the Transfer Out dialog, as mentioned earlier), allocating the transporter to the waiting entity that has the highest priority (lowest priority number). If there's a tie among entities, the transporter will be allocated to the closest one.

To represent the carts in our small manufacturing system model, let's start by first defining the carts. We do this with the Transporter module found on the Transfer panel (you might have to attach the Transfer panel if it's not already there). In this case, we need only enter the Transporter name, Number of Units, and Velocity (Display 7-1). We'll accept the default Free Path option, Distance Set name (we'll return to this concept later), and Initial Position of the carts. We need to take care when defining the Velocity that we enter a quantity that's appropriate for the time and distance units we're using in the model. When we built the basic model, our times (e.g., interarrival and processing times) were in minutes. We haven't yet defined any distances, so we can select a distance unit now. We'll use feet, so that a value of 50 for the Velocity will correspond to 50 feet per minute.

Additional capabilities are available for defining Schedules or Failures; we'll assume our carts are always available. The Options feature allows you to select what happens when a transporter is freed—Go To a Home Station, Follow a Looping Pattern, or Remain Where Freed (the default). You can also push the Stats button to request statistics on the Idle, Busy, or Inactive states of the individual carts (we selected the first two). You'll automatically be given statistics on the busy and available carts as a group.

Having defined the transporter, we can alter the picture that represents the cart (just above the *Transporter* module handle). This is done in almost the same way as it was for an entity or resource. For our carts, let's replace the default picture with a box (we used a 5-point line width) that's green when the cart is idle and blue when it's busy. When the cart is carrying a part, Arena also needs to know where on the cart's busy picture to position the part. This placement is somewhat similar to a seize point for a resource. In this case, it's called a *ride point* and can be found under the Object menu of the Arena Picture Editor window when you're editing the busy picture. The default Busy Transporter picture already has a ride point (directly above the cart or wagon picture), so this option is initially grayed out. It will become available if you delete the existing ride point. The placement of the ride point, which appears as ⊗, on the busy cart will result in the entities being positioned so their reference points are aligned with this ride point.

Transporter
Cart

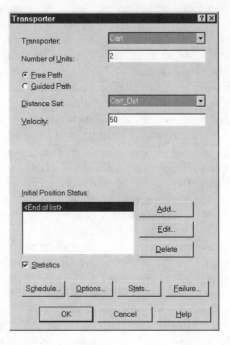

Transporter	Cart
Number of Units	2
Velocity	50

Display 7-1. The Transporter Module

To request the cart in the model logic, we use the same dialogs that we did for seizing a resource—the Transfer Out dialog in the Arrive and Server modules and in the main dialog of the Leave module. Display 7-2 shows the entries for the Arrive module; the other Transfer Out dialog entries are identical.

The Rule entry determines which transporter will be allocated if more than one is currently free: Cyclic, Random, Preferred Order, Largest Distance, or Smallest Distance. The Cyclic rule attempts to cycle through the transporters, thus leveling their utilizations. The Preferred Order rule attempts always to select the available transporter with the lowest number. We've chosen the Smallest Distance rule, which results in an allocation of the cart closest to the requesting entity. Accepting this dialog automatically changes the route selection on the Leave Data portion of the main Arrive module to Transport.

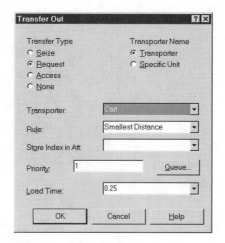

Transfer Type	
Request	*select*

Transporter	Cart
Rule	Smallest Distance
Load Time	0.25

Display 7-2. The Transfer Out Dialog

Before leaving the Arrive module, let's consider the animation of this request process. When the entity completes its processing at a cell, it enters a queue to wait its turn to request a cart. Once a cart is allocated, the entity is no longer in the request queue during the cart's travel to the entity location. (We really don't need to go into detail about where the entity really is at this time.) The simplest way to animate this activity is with the Storage feature found in the Animate dialog. An Arena storage is a place for the entity to reside while its waiting for the transporter to move to its location so that it will show on the animation. Each time an entity enters a storage, an internal storage variable is incremented by 1, and when the entity exits the storage, this variable is decremented by 1. This allows us to obtain statistics on the number in the storage (more about this later).

The required additional entries for this storage feature are shown in Display 7-3. We simply select the Storage option, which automatically provides a default storage name. Neglecting to check Unstore will not have an effect on the animation, but it will affect any statistics based on this value as the storage variable would continue to increase over time. Accepting these changes to the Arrive module will result in an animated storage feature appearing next to the module handle. It will look exactly like a queue, except that it's typically a different color. From an animation standpoint, it's exactly like a queue in the way it functions and the ways it can be edited. You'll need to make identical entries for the Leave and the three Server modules.

Arrive
Order Release

Animate...

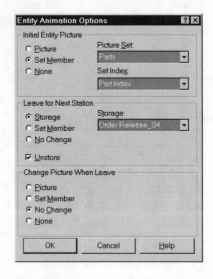

Leave for Next Station	
Storage	*select*
Unstore	*check*

Display 7-3. The Modified Animate Dialog

When we arrive at our next location, we need to free the cart so it can be used by other parts. This is done in the main dialog of the Enter module and in the Transfer In dialog of the three Servers and the Depart modules, as shown in Display 7-4. Unlike the Release Resource option shown in Section 7.2, we need only check to Free the Transporter and enter the Unload Time. Arena keeps track of which cart was allocated to the entity and frees that cart. We need to make these entries for the Depart, Enter, and the three Server modules.

So far we've defined the carts, and we've changed the model logic to Request, Transport, and Free the carts to model the logic required to transfer the parts through the system. The actual travel time depends on the transporter velocity, which is defined with the carts, and the distance of the transfer. When we defined the carts, Display 7-1, we accepted a default reference to a Distance Set, Cart_Dst. We must now provide these distances so that Arena can reference them whenever a request or transport occurs. Essentially, we must define the contents of the Cart_Dst distance set. Let's start by considering only the moves from one station to the next station made by the parts as they make their way through the system (Table 6-1). This information is provided in Table 7-1. These table entries include a pair of stations, or locations, and the distance (in feet) between those stations. For example, the first entry is for the move from Order Release to Cell 1, which is a distance of 37 feet. Blank entries in Table 7-1 are for from-to pairs that don't occur (see Table 6-1).

Server

Cell 1

Tran In...

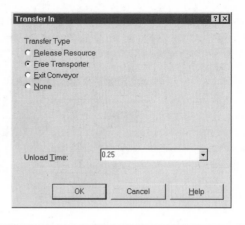

Transfer Type	
Free Transporter	*select*
Unload Time	0.25

Display 7-4. The Transfer In Dialog

Table 7-1. The Part Transfer Distances

		To				
		Cell 1	Cell 2	Cell 3	Cell 4	Exit System
From	Order Release	37	74			
	Cell 1		45	92		
	Cell 2	139		55	147	
	Cell 3				45	155
	Cell 4		92			118

We enter our distances using the Distance module found on the Transfer panel. We need to place a module for the distance between each pair of stations or locations; in this case, 11 separate modules. The entries for the first pair of distances are shown in Display 7-5. You really only need to type the Distance since the first three entries can be selected from the pull-down lists. You should also note that a direction is implied, *from* Order Release *to* Cell 1 in the case of Display 7-5. As was the case with the Routes module, we can place another module to define the distance from Cell 1 to Order Release if the distance or path is different (but no entity ever takes this route in this model, so it's unnecessary).

Now let's take a look at the animation component of this module, which consists of two stations connected by a distance and a *Parking Area*. If you click on the stations, the names will appear—Order Release on the left and Cell 1 on the right. Click on the line and the Distance Set Name Cart_Dst will appear. When you transport a part from the

Order Release to Cell 1, the cart (and the part) will follow this line (or distance) on the animation. At some point, we'll need to place these animation objects at an appropriate location in the model window.

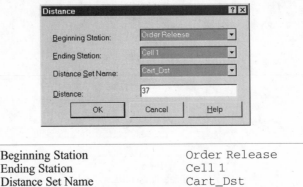

Beginning Station	Order Release
Ending Station	Cell 1
Distance Set Name	Cart_Dst
Distance	37

Display 7-5. The Distance Module

Before you start to move these animation objects, you might want to give some thought to the arrangement of the Distance module handles so that later you can easily find a specific distance. We might suggest that you place them off to the side of the animation layout, grouped by a common starting station. Remember that the animation objects are positioned relative to the module handle; thus, it is easy to group the module handles now. If you decide to move them later, hold the Shift key down while dragging the handle to a new location, which moves the handle only, leaving the stations and distances where you've placed them.

To incorporate these animation objects in the model window, we move the stations to their correct locations and position the line so it follows the layout path. Before we do this, let's take a look at the line characteristics by double-clicking on the line. The resulting dialog allows us to modify these characteristics, Display 7-6. In this case, we requested that neither the cart nor the part riding on the cart be rotated or flipped as they move along the path. These features are not necessary as our pictures are all squares and, for easy identification, we placed numbers on the parts. We also increased the number of points on the line to five.

The next step is to increase the number of Parking Areas from one to two. This is desirable because it's possible to have more than one cart at the same location at the same time. We do this by following the procedure given in Display 7-7. Note that no data need to be entered. The Parking Areas position the points where a transporter will reside when it is at that station. Just like queues and storages, they can take the form of points or a line.

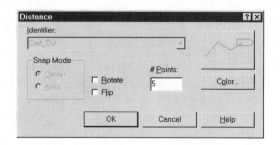

Rotate	*uncheck*
Flip	*uncheck*
# Points	5

Display 7-6. The Distance Line Dialog

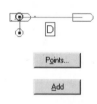

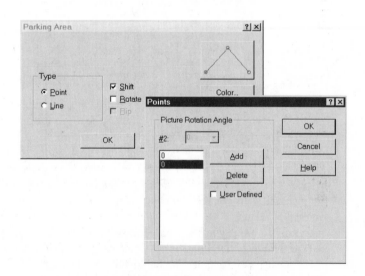

Display 7-7. The Parking Area Dialog

Before you place the animation objects in the model window, we might suggest that you copy the Distance module to the clipboard; we'll explain why shortly. You might also want to consider activating the Grid and Snap options from the View toolbar. You can now place the animation objects. We suggest that you start with the beginning station, Order Release, and move it to the beginning location, see Figure 7-2. Next, select the second point on the line—the first point is at the Order Release station—and position it where you want it. Continue moving the points until you've matched the line to the layout. Pay close attention to the shape of the cursor during this process. When you highlight the line, the five handles (points) will appear on the line. When you move your cursor directly over a point, it will change to cross hairs; click and hold to drag the point. If the cursor is still an arrow and you click and hold, all the interior points on the line will be moved. If you accidentally do this, don't forget that you can use the Undo button. If you find you need additional points, or you have too many, simply open the dialog to change the number. When you add or subtract line points, they're always added or subtracted at the destination-station end of the line. Finally, move the ending station, Cell 1, to its position. The final positioning should look something like Figure 7-2.

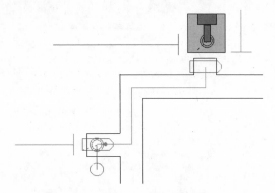

Figure 7-2. Place the Distance Animation Objects

Now you're ready to place the second distance, from the Order Release station to Cell 2. If you use the copy from the clipboard as a starting point, you'll reduce the number of changes required. When you position this on the layout, you'll have two Order Release Stations. This is not a problem as far as the stations are concerned (as you proceed, you'll have even more), but we want only one set of parking areas. Otherwise, Arena will always position the cart on the parking area associated with the distance set just used. This could result in one cart's sitting directly on top of another—not a good animation feature. So just delete the parking area before you move the station. As you proceed, make sure you allow only one set of parking areas at each location. You can now define and position the remaining Distances given in Table 7-1.

You can run your model and animation at this point, but if you do, very quickly the execution will pause and the Arena Error/Warning window will appear. A warning will be displayed telling you that a distance between a pair of stations has not been specified, forcing Arena to assume a distance of 0, and it will recommend that you fix the problem (Arena makes the rash assumption that you forgot to enter the value). You can close this window and continue the run, but the message will reappear. The problem is most likely caused by a cart being freed at the Exit System, Cell 3, or Cell 4 locations when the cart is being requested at the Order Release location. Arena attempts to transfer the cart to the Order Release and fails to find a distance; thus, we have a problem. In fact, there are more problems. If a cart is freed at Cell 1 or Cell 2 and is requested at the Order Release location, it will travel backward rather than clockwise as we desire. To avoid this, we'll add distances for all possible loaded and empty transfers that might occur.

In general, if you have *n* locations, there are $n(n–1)$ possible distances. You can roughly think of this as an *n* by *n* matrix with a 0 diagonal. This assumes that all moves are possible and that the distance between any two locations depends on the direction of travel. For our example, we have six locations, or 30 possible distances (distance *does* depend on direction of travel). If the distances are not travel-dependent, you only have half this number of distances. Also, there are often many moves that will never occur. In our example, the empty cart may be required to move from the `Exit System` location to the `Order Release` location, but never in the opposite direction (think about it!). The data contained in Table 7-1 were for *loaded* cart moves only. If we enumerate all possible *empty* cart moves and eliminate any duplicates from the first set, we have the additional distances given in Table 7-2. The shaded entries are from the earlier distances, Table 7-1. Altogether, there are 25 possible moves.

Table 7-2. Possible Cart Moves Including Empty Moves

		To					
		Order Release	Cell 1	Cell 2	Cell 3	Cell 4	Exit System
From	Order Release		37	74			
	Cell 1	155		45	92	129	
	Cell 2	118	139		55	147	
	Cell 3	71	92	129		45	155
	Cell 4	34	55	92	139		118
	Exit System	100	121	158	37	74	

If the number of distances becomes excessive, we suggest that you consider switching to guided transporters, which use a network rather than individual pairs of distances. For a review of the concepts of guided transporters, we refer you to Chapter 9, "Advanced Manufacturing Features," of Pegden, Shannon, and Sadowski (1995).

The final animation will look very similar to our first animation, but when you run the model, you'll see the carts moving around and the parts waiting for the carts. It's still possible for one cart to appear on top of another—we're using free-path transporters. However, with only two carts in the system, it should occur much less frequently than in the previous model that used unconstrained routes. A view of the running animation at time 795 is shown in Figure 7-3.

The summary report for this new model is shown in Figure 7-4. If you watch the animation, you'd rarely see a queue of parts waiting for the carts, so you would not expect any major differences between this run and the original run, Figure 6-5. The carts are in use only about 68% of the time. Again, we caution you against assuming there are no differences between these two systems. The run time is relatively short, and we may still be in a transient startup state, not to mention the effects of statistical variation that can cloud the comparison.

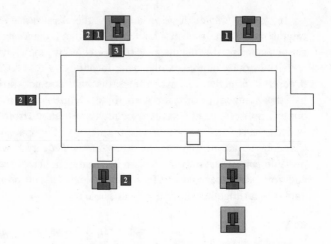

Figure 7-3. The Small Manufacturing System with Transporters

Project: Small Manufacturing System
Analyst: Pippi

Replication ended at time   : 2000.0

TALLY VARIABLES

Identifier	Average	Half Width	Minimum	Maximum	Observations
Cell 1_R_Q Queue Time	14.754	(Insuf)	.00000	59.390	153
Part 3 Cycle Time	86.288	(Insuf)	63.842	154.69	38
Cell 2_R_Q Queue Time	8.3235	(Insuf)	.00000	37.301	216
Cell 3 Machines_Q Queu	10.586	(Insuf)	.00000	43.229	144
Part 1 Cycle time	114.99	(Insuf)	54.158	170.45	40
Cell 4_R_Q Queue Time	13.603	(Insuf)	.00000	43.559	108
Part 2 Cycle Time	150.09	(Insuf)	95.256	221.21	62

DISCRETE-CHANGE VARIABLES

Identifier	Average	Half Width	Minimum	Maximum	Final Value
Cell 2_R Busy	.83682	(Insuf)	.00000	1.0000	1.0000
# in Cell 3 Machines_Q	.76225	(Insuf)	.00000	5.0000	.00000
Cell 1_R Busy	2.0000	(Insuf)	2.0000	2.0000	2.0000
Cart 1 Idle	.30286	(Corr)	.00000	1.0000	.00000
Cart 1 Busy	.69714	(Corr)	.00000	1.0000	1.0000
Cart 2 Idle	.33899	(Corr)	.00000	1.0000	.00000
Cart 2 Busy	.66101	(Corr)	.00000	1.0000	1.0000
# in Cell 4_R_Q	.74005	(Insuf)	.00000	3.0000	2.0000
Cell 3 New Available	1.0000	(Insuf)	1.0000	1.0000	1.0000
Cart Busy	1.3581	(Corr)	.00000	2.0000	2.0000
Cell 3 New Busy	.85374	(Insuf)	.00000	1.0000	1.0000
# in Cell 2_R_Q	.94266	(Corr)	.00000	6.0000	5.0000
# in Cell 1_R_Q	1.3340	(Insuf)	.00000	11.000	9.0000
Cell 4_R Available	1.0000	(Insuf)	1.0000	1.0000	1.0000
Cell 2_R Available	1.0000	(Insuf)	1.0000	1.0000	1.0000
Cell 1_R Available	1.0000	(Insuf)	1.0000	1.0000	1.0000
Cell 4_R Busy	.84757	(Insuf)	.00000	1.0000	1.0000
Cell 3 Old Available	1.0000	(Insuf)	1.0000	1.0000	1.0000
Cell 3 Old Busy	.83340	(Insuf)	.00000	1.0000	.00000

Figure 7-4. Summary Report for the Small Manufacturing System with Transporters

If we change the cart velocity to 25 (half the original speed) and run the model, we'll see that there is only a little difference in the results between the runs. If you think about this, it actually makes sense. The average distance traveled per cart movement is less than 100 feet, and when the carts become busier, they're less likely to travel empty (sometimes called *deadheading*). Remember that if a cart is freed and there are several requests, the cart will take the closest part. So the average part movement time is only about 2 minutes. Also, there was a load and unload time of 0.25 minute, which remains unchanged (remember the slide rule?). We might suggest that you experiment with this model by changing the cart Velocity, the Load and Unload times, the Transporter Selection Rule, and the number of carts to see how the system performs. Of course, you ought to make an appropriate number of replications and perform the correct statistical comparisons, as described in Section 6.5.5.

7.4 Conveyors

Having incorporated carts into our system for material movement, let's now replace the carts with a conveyor system. We'll keep the system fairly simple and concentrate on the modeling techniques. Let's assume we want a loop conveyor that will follow the main path of the aisle in the same clockwise direction we required for the transporters. There will be entrance and exit points for parts at each of the six locations in the system. The conveyor will move at a speed of 20 feet per minute. The travel distances, in feet, are given in Figure 7-5. We will also assume that there is still a requirement for the 0.25-minute load and unload activity. Let's further assume that each part is 4 feet per side, and we want 6 feet of conveyor space during transit to provide clearance on the corners and to avoid any possible damage.

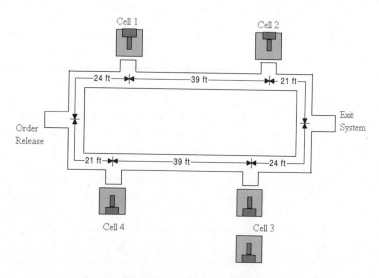

Figure 7-5. Conveyor Lengths

Arena conveyors operate on the concept that each entity to be conveyed must wait until sufficient space on the conveyor is available at its location before it can gain access to the conveyor. Arena assumes that a conveyor consists of cells of equal length that are constantly moving. When an entity tries to get on the conveyor, it must wait until a defined number of unoccupied consecutive cells are available at that point. Again, it may help to think in terms of a narrow escalator in an airport, with each step corresponding to a cell and different people requiring different numbers of steps. For example, a traveler with several bags may require two or three steps, whereas a person with no bags may require only one step. When you look at an escalator, the cell size is rather obvious. However, if you consider a belt or roller conveyor, the cell size is not at all obvious.

In order to make the Conveyor features as flexible as possible, Arena allows you to define the *cell size*; i.e., to divide the conveyor length into a series of consecutive, equal cells. This creates a rather interesting dilemma because you would like the cells to be as small as possible to obtain the greatest accuracy, yet you would also like the cells to be as large as possible to obtain the greatest computational efficiency. Let's use a simple example to illustrate this dilemma. You have a conveyor that is 100 feet long and you want to convey parts that are 2 feet long. Because we've expressed our lengths in feet, your first response might be to set your cell size to 1 foot. This means that your conveyor has 100 cells and each part requires two cells for conveyance. We could have just as easily set the cell size at 2 feet (50 cells), or 1 inch (1200 cells). With today's computers, why should we worry about whether we have 50 or 1200 cells? There should be a negligible impact on the computation speed of the model, right? However, we've seen models that have included over 5 *miles* of conveyors, and there is certainly a concern about the speed of the model. The difference between a cell size of 1 inch or 100 feet would have a significant impact on the time to run the model.

So why not always make your cells as large as possible? Well, when an entity attempts to gain access to a conveyor, it's only allowed on the conveyor when the end of the previous cell, or the start of the next cell, is lined up with the entity location. In our escalator analogy, this corresponds to waiting for the next step to appear at the *load* area. Consider the situation where an entity has just arrived at an empty conveyor and tries to get on. You have specified a cell size of 100 feet, and the end of the last cell has just passed that location, say by ½ inch. That entity would have to wait for the end of the current cell to arrive, in 99 feet 11½ inches. If you had specified the cell size at 1 inch, the wait would only have been for ½ inch of conveyor to pass by.

The basic message is that you need to consider the impact of cell size with respect to the specific application you're modeling. If the conveyor is not highly utilized, or the potential slight delay in timing has no impact on the system's performance, use a large cell size. If any of these are critical to the system performance, use a very small cell size. There are two constraints to consider when making this decision. The entity size, expressed in number of cells, must be an integer. So you cannot have an entity requiring 1.5 cells; you would have to use one or two cells as the entity size. Also, the conveyor segments (the length of a conveyor section from one location to another) must consist of an integral number of cells. So, if your conveyor was 100 feet long, you could not use a cell size of three.

Before we start adding Conveyors to our model, let's go over a few more concepts that we hope will be helpful when you try to build your own models with conveyors. As with Resources and Transporters, Conveyors have several key words: Access, Convey, and Exit. To transfer an entity with Arena conveyors, you must first *Access* space on the Conveyor, then *Convey* the entity to its destination, and finally *Exit* the conveyor (to free up the space). For representing the physical layout, an Arena Conveyor consists of a series of Segments that are linked together to form the entire Conveyor. Each Segment starts and ends at an Arena station. You can only link these Segments to form a line or loop conveyor. Thus, a single Conveyor cannot have a diverge point that results in a Conveyor splitting into two or more lines or a converge point where two or more Conveyors join. However, you can define multiple Conveyors for these types of systems. For example, in a diverging system, you would Convey the entity to the diverge point, Access space on the appropriate Conveyor leg, Exit the current Conveyor, and Convey the entity to its next destination. For our small manufacturing system, we'll use a single loop Conveyor.

Arena has two types of Conveyors: *Nonaccumulating* and *Accumulating*. Both types of Conveyors travel only in a single direction, and you can't reverse them. These Conveyors function very much as their name would imply. Examples of a Nonaccumulating Conveyor would be a bucket or belt conveyor or our escalator. The spacing between entities traveling on these types of conveyors never changes, unless one entity exits and re-accesses space. Because of this constraint, Nonaccumulating Conveyors operate in a unique manner. When an entity accesses space on this type of conveyor, the conveyor actually stops moving, or is disengaged. When the entity is conveyed, the conveyor is re-engaged while the entity travels to its destination. The conveyor is stopped when the entity reaches its destination, the entity exits, and the conveyor is then restarted. If there is no elapsed time between the Access and Convey, or when the entity reaches its destination and the exit, then it's as if the conveyor was never stopped. However, if there is a delay, such as for a Load or Unload activity of positive duration (which is the case in our system), you'll see the Conveyor temporarily stop while the load or unload occurs.

Accumulating Conveyors differ in that they never stop moving. If an entity is stopped on an Accumulating Conveyor, all other entities on that Conveyor will continue on their way. However, the stopped entity blocks any other entities from arriving at that location so that the arriving entities accumulate behind the blocking entity. When the blocking entity exits the conveyor or conveys on its way, the accumulated entities are also free to move on to their destinations. However, depending on the spacing requirements specified in the model, they may not all start moving at the same time. You might think of cars accumulated or backed up on a freeway. When the cars are stopped, they tend to be fairly close together (mostly to prevent some inconsiderate driver from sneaking in ahead of them). When the blockage is removed, the cars start moving one at a time in order to allow for more space between them. We'll describe these data requirements later in this chapter.

7.4.1   Model 7.2: The Small Manufacturing System with Nonaccumulating Conveyors

We're now ready to incorporate Nonaccumulating conveyors into our system. If you're building this model along with us (after all, that was the idea), you might want to consider making another change. After including conveyors and running our model, we're likely to find that the Load and Unload times are so small relative to the other times that it's hard to see if the conveyor is working properly. (Actually, we've already run the model and know that this will happen.) Also, you may want to do some experimentation to see what impact these activities have on system performance. So we suggest that you define two new Variables, `Load Time` and `Unload Time`. You can set the initial values equal to 0.25 minute. Then replace the current constant times with the proper variable name; this will allow you to make global changes for these times in one place. You should know how to do this by now (if not, reread Sections 6.1-6.4), so we'll not bore you with the details.

Let's start by taking our transporter model, Model 7.1, and deleting the Transporter module and all the Distance modules. You might want to use the Save As feature to save this new model under a different name and preserve the transporter model (or, before exiting, copy Model 7.1 to a new file and rename it in Windows®). Define the conveyor using the Conveyor module from the Transfer panel as in Display 7-8.

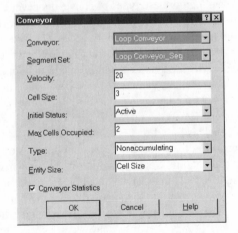

Conveyor	Loop Conveyor
Velocity	20
Cell Size	3
Max Cells Occupied	2
Type	Nonaccumulating

Display 7-8. The Conveyor Module Dialog

Two of these entries, Cell Size and Max Cells Occupied, require some discussion. Based on the results from the previous model, it's fairly clear that there is not a lot of traffic in our system. Also, if there's a slight delay before a part can Access space on the conveyor, the only impact would be to increase the part cycle time slightly. So we decided to make the conveyor cells as large as possible. We chose a cell size of 3 feet, because this will result in an integer number of cells for each of the conveyor lengths (actually, we cheated a little bit on these lengths to make this work). Since we require 6 feet of space for each part, there is a maximum of two cells occupied by any part. This information is required by Arena to assure that it has sufficient storage space to keep track of an entity when it arrives at the end of the conveyor. Since our conveyor is a loop and has no end, it really has no impact for this model. But, in general, you need to enter the largest number of cells that any entity can occupy during transit. As before, we've defaulted on the Segment Set name.

Incorporating conveyors into the model is very similar to the earlier discussion for including transporters, so we won't go into a lot of detail. We need to change every dialog where we Request a cart to Access the Loop conveyor, in the Transfer Out dialogs. This will automatically change the option in the main dialog from Transport to Convey. Conversely, we need to change every dialog where we used Free Transporter to be Exit Conveyor, in the Transfer In dialogs. These basic dialogs are shown in Display 7-9. You might also note that each part requires two cells (with a size of 3 feet each) to access the conveyor, and that we've replaced the constant Load Time with the variables we suggested earlier that you define.

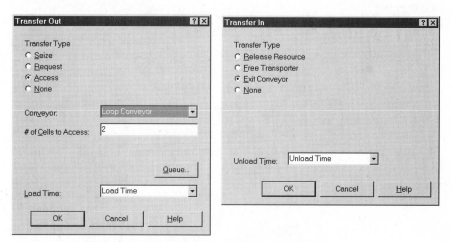

Display 7-9. The Transfer Out and Transfer In Dialogs, Conveyors

We're now ready to place the conveyor segments on our animation. As was the case with the Distances used in our last model, these segments provide data required for both the model and animation.

We define these segments using the Segment module found on the Transfer panel. Display 7-10 shows the data entries for the first segment. Notice that the Length is expressed in terms of the actual length, not the number of cells (eight), for that segment.

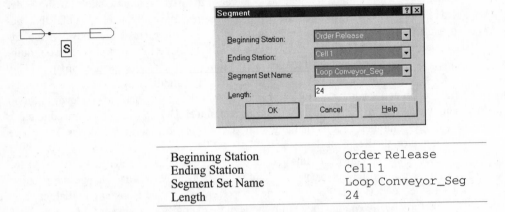

Beginning Station	Order Release
Ending Station	Cell 1
Segment Set Name	Loop Conveyor_Seg
Length	24

Display 7-10. The Segment Module Dialog

You'll also need to edit the segments and stations, just like we did for Transporters. For this model, you only need to place six segments, as shown in Figure 7-6.

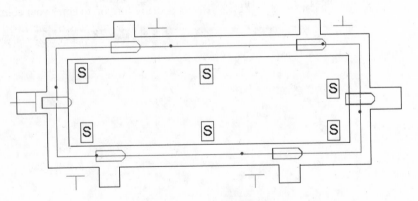

Figure 7-6. The Conveyor Segments

You're now ready to run your animated model. If you run the model to completion, you'll notice two new statistics for the conveyor, shown in Figure 7-7. These two statistics tell us that there was an average of a little fewer than two parts on the conveyor at a time, with a maximum of seven. It also gives us information on the length of the conveyor occupied by these parts. This information can be calculated from the first statistic only because all of the parts are the same size. If each part required a different amount of space on the conveyor, this statistic would be quite different.

Identifier	Average	Half Width	Minimum	Maximum	Final Value
# Conveying on Loop Co	1.9212	(Corr)	.00000	7.0000	.00000
Length Conveying on Lo	11.527	(Corr)	.00000	42.000	.00000

Figure 7-7. The Nonaccumulating Conveyor Statistics

If you can't see the conveyor stop during the load and unload activity (even if you set the animation speed factor at its lowest setting), edit your model by changing these variables to a constant 2 or 3 minutes. The stopping should be quite obvious with these new values.

There are also several alternate ways to change variable values during a simulation. If you want to make such changes frequently during a simulation run, you might want to consider using the Menu module found on the Common panel (covered in Section 9.4.2) or the Arena interface for Visual Basic® for Applications (VBA) (see Chapter 10). The second method is to use the Arena command-driven Run Controller. Although this is a very powerful tool, you really need to know how SIMAN works in order to use it effectively. As you progress in your Arena skills, you might want to experiment with this feature. For now, we'll only show you how to view and change the variables of interest.

Begin running your model, and after it has run for a while (we waited until about time 301), use the *Run/Pause* menu option or the Pause button (**II**) on the Run toolbar to suspend the execution of the model temporarily. Then use the *Run/Command* menu option or the Command button (⊡) on the Run Interaction toolbar to open the command window. This text window will have the current simulation time displayed, followed by the ">" character as a prompt. Arena is ready for you to enter your commands. We used the SHOW command to view the current value of the variable Load Time and then the ASSIGN command to change that value—see Figure 7-8. We then repeated these two steps for the Unload Time. Now close this window and use the *Run/Go* menu option or the Go button (▶) on the Run toolbar to run the simulation with the new variable values from the current time.

```
SIMAN Run Controller.
301.885>SHOW Load Time
   LOAD TIME =          0.25

301.885>ASSIGN Load Time = 2

301.885>SHOW Unload Time
   UNLOAD TIME =          0.25

301.885>ASSIGN Unload Time = 2

301.885>
```

Figure 7-8. Changing Variables with the Run Controller

You can stop the simulation run at any time to change these values. It's worth noting that the changes you make in the Run Controller are temporary changes. They aren't saved in the model, and the next time you run your model, it will use the original values for these variables. You can do a lot more with the Run Controller, and we refer you to the Arena help system for a complete listing of all the commands available.

Although viewing the animation and making these types of changes as the model is running are excellent ways to verify your model, when you finally are using the model for the purposes of evaluation, you should not change the model conditions during a run. This can give you very misleading performance values on your summary report.

7.4.2   Model 7.3: The Small Manufacturing System with Accumulating Conveyors

Changing our conveyor model so the conveyor is accumulating is very easy. We need to make only two minor changes in a single dialog. Open the Conveyor dialog, change the conveyor Type to `Accumulating`, and enter an Entity Size of 4, Display 7-11. Adding the entity size allows the accumulated parts to require only 4 feet of space on the conveyor. Note that this entity size, which applies only when an entity is stopped on the conveyor, does not need to be an integral number of cells. When the blockage is removed, the parts will automatically re-space to the 6 feet, or two cells, required for transit on the conveyor.

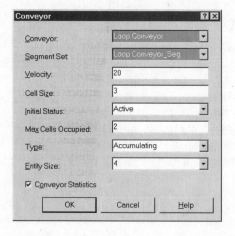

| Type | Accumulating |
| Entity Size | 4 |

Display 7-11. The Accumulating Conveyor Module Dialog

Having made these changes, run your model and you should note that very little accumulation occurs. You can confirm this by looking at the conveyor statistics on the summary report (Figure 7-9).

Identifier	Average	Half Width	Minimum	Maximum	Final Value
# Conveying on Loop Co	1.4445	(Corr)	.00000	6.0000	4.0000
Length Accumulated on	.92771	(Corr)	.00000	16.000	.00000
# Accumulated on Loop	.23193	(Corr)	.00000	4.0000	.00000
Length Conveying on Lo	8.6675	(Corr)	.00000	36.000	24.000

Figure 7-9. The Accumulating Conveyor Statistics

Note that there are two additional statistics reported for accumulating conveyors: the number of accumulated entities and the length of occupied space by the accumulated entities. You can see that these results are very similar to the results for the nonaccumulating system.

To increase the amount of accumulation, which is a good idea for verification, simply change the load and unload times to 4 or 5 minutes. The effect should be quite visible.

7.5   Statistical Analysis of Steady-State Simulations

In Section 6.5, we described the difference between terminating and steady-state simulations and indicated how you can use the Arena Output Analyzer to do statistical analyses in the terminating case. In this section, we'll show you how to use the Output Analyzer to do statistical inference on steady-state simulations.

Before proceeding, we should encourage you to be *sure* that a steady-state simulation is appropriate for what you want to do. Often people simply *assume* that a long-run, steady-state simulation is the thing to do, which might in fact be true. But if the starting and stopping conditions are part of the essence of your model, a terminating analysis is probably more appropriate; if so, you should just proceed as in Section 6.5. The reason for avoiding steady-state simulation is that, as you're about to see, it's a *lot* harder to carry out anything approaching a valid statistical analysis than in the terminating case if you want anything beyond Arena's standard 95% confidence intervals on mean performance measures; so if you don't need to get into this, you shouldn't.

One more caution before we wade into this material: As you can imagine, the run lengths for steady-state simulations need to be pretty long. Because of this, there are more opportunities for Arena to sequence its internal operations a little differently, causing the random-number stream (see Section 11.1) to be used differently. This doesn't make your model in any sense "wrong" or inaccurate, but it can affect the numerical results, especially for models that have a lot of statistical variability inherent in them. So if you follow along on your computer and run our models, there's a chance that you're going to get numerical answers that differ from what we report here. Don't panic over this since it is, in a sense, to be expected. If anything, this just amplifies the need for some kind of statistical analysis of simulation output data since variability can come not only from "nature" in the model's properties, but also from internal computational issues.

In Section 7.5.1, we'll discuss determination of model warm-up and run length. Section 7.5.2 describes the truncated-replication strategy for analysis, which is by far the simplest approach (and, in some ways, the best). Batching is described in Section 7.5.3, and Arena's automatic batching process is detailed in Section 7.5.4. A brief summary is given in Section 7.5.5, and Section 7.5.6 mentions some other issues in steady-state analysis.

7.5.1   Warm Up and Run Length

As you might have noticed, our examples have all been characterized by a model that's initially in an *empty-and-idle* state. This means that the model starts out empty of entities and all resources are idle. In a terminating system, this might be the way things actually start out, so everything is fine. But in a steady-state simulation, initial conditions aren't supposed to matter, and the run goes forever.

Actually, though, even in a steady-state simulation, you have to initialize and stop the run somehow. And since you're doing a simulation in the first place, it's a pretty safe bet that you don't know much about the "typical" system state in steady state or how "long" a run is long enough. So you're probably going to wind up initializing in a state that's pretty weird from the viewpoint of steady state and just trying some (long) run lengths. If you're initializing empty and idle in a simulation where things eventually become congested, your output data for some period of time after initialization will tend to understate the eventual congestion; i.e., will be *biased* toward low values of typical performance measures.

To remedy this, you might try to initialize in a state that's "better" than empty and idle. This would mean placing, at time 0, some number of entities around the model and starting things out that way. While it's possible to do this in your model, it's pretty inconvenient. More problematic is that you'd generally have no idea how many entities to place around at time 0; this is, after all, one of the questions the simulation is supposed to answer.

Another way of dealing with initialization bias is just to run the model for so long that whatever bias may have been there at the beginning is overwhelmed by the amount of later data. This can work in some models if the biasing effects of the initial conditions wear off quickly.

However, what people usually do is to initialize empty and idle, realizing that this is unrepresentative of steady state, but then let the model *warm up* for a while until it appears that the effect of the artificial initial conditions have worn off. At that time, you can clear the statistical accumulators and start afresh, gathering statistics for analysis from then on. In effect, this *is* initializing in a state other than empty and idle, but you let the model decide how many entities to have around when you start to watch your performance measures. The run length should still be long, but maybe not as long as you'd need to overwhelm the initial bias by sheer arithmetic.

It's very easy to specify an initial Warm-Up Period in Arena. Just open the Simulate module and fill in a value (in whatever time units you're using) for the warm-up period. Your model (every replication of it) still runs starting initially as it did before, but after the Warm-Up Period, all statistics are cleared and your summary report and any saved data from the Outputs area in the Statistics module of results across the replications reflect only what happened after the Warm-Up Period ends. (However, if you saved data files for the Time-Persistent or Tallies areas of the Statistics module, the data from the Warm-Up Period are not thrown out; as we'll indicate later, you can throw these data out later when doing statistical analysis in the Output Analyzer.) In this way, you can "decontaminate" your data from the biasing initial conditions.

The hard part is knowing how long the Warm-Up Period should be. Probably the most practical idea is just to make some plots of key outputs from within a run, as described in Sections 5.2.4 and 5.2.6, and eyeball when they appear to stabilize. To illustrate this, we took Model 7.1 (the one using Transporters) from Section 7.3, extended its run length from 2,000 minutes to 100,000 minutes, made 10 replications (each starting empty and idle), added the WIP performance measure (described in Section 6.5.2 for

Model 6.2), and saved the within-run WIP values to a file in the Time-Persistent area of a Statistics module we dropped in, as well as the cycle times of the three part types in the Tallies area of this Statistics module. We'll call the result Model 7.4, and for the record, it took about 15 minutes to run all this on a humble 75 MHz Pentium machine (with the animation turned off, of course). Figure 7-10 shows plots, made with the Output Analyzer, of the WIP and Cycle Times by Part Type across the simulations, with the curves for all 10 replications superimposed. From these plots, it seems that the run length of 100,000 minutes is certainly enough for the model to have settled out, and also it seems pretty clear that the model isn't "exploding" with entities, as would be the case if processing couldn't keep up with the arrival rate.

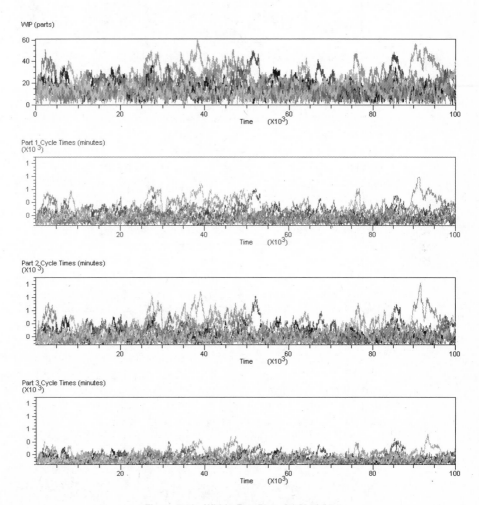

Figure 7-10. Within-Run Plots for Model 7.4

It's pretty hard to identify from Figure 7-10 what an appropriate warm-up period might be, though. Figure 7-11 shows the same plots, except we "zoomed in" on just the first 5,000 minutes of each replication. (We specified this time range in the "Display Time from . . . to . . ." area in the Plot dialog.) While this information is contained in the plots in Figure 7-10, the reason for doing the new plots was to get a better look at the warm-up phase.

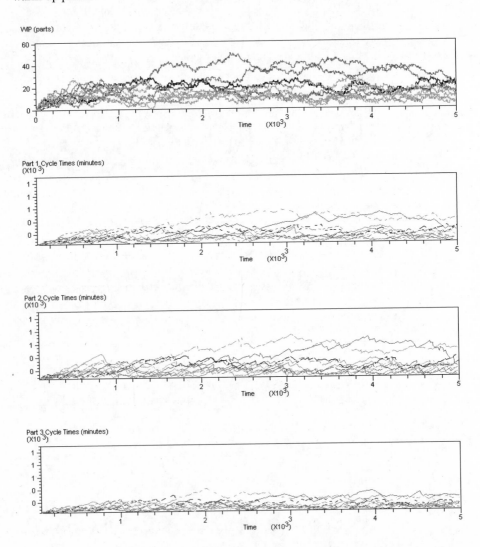

Figure 7-11. Warm-Up Determination for Model 7.4

The effect of the empty-and-idle initial conditions for the first few hundred minutes on each of these performance measures is evident. The three measures appear to agree on a Warm-Up Period of, to be conservative, about 2,000 minutes. However, in some models, there could be disagreement, in which case the safe move is to take the maximum of the individual warm-ups as the one to use overall.

7.5.2 Truncated Replications

If you can identify a Warm-Up Period, and if this period is reasonably short relative to the run lengths you plan to make, then life is fairly simple for steady-state statistical analysis: just make IID (that's independent and identically distributed, in case you've forgotten) replications, as was done for terminating simulations in Section 6.5.3, except that you also specify a Warm-Up Period for each replication in your Simulate module. With these appropriate warm-up and run-length values specified, you simply proceed to make independent replications. This idea applies to comparing alternatives (Section 6.5.5) as well as to single-system analysis, although there could be different warm-up and run-length periods needed for different alternatives.

We did this for the 10 replications of the 100,000-minute run length and 2,000-minute Warm-Up Period we determined for Model 7.4. In order to save the summary results (for the final 98,000 minutes) from each replication, we added entries to the Outputs area of the Statistics module already present, as described in Section 6.5.3; we called the resulting model Model 7.5. (Note our practice of saving successive changes to models under different names so we don't cover up our tracks in case we need to backtrack at some point.) Invoking the classical confidence intervals across replications, exactly as in Section 6.5.4, for the average WIP performance measure yielded the interval in Figure 7-12, and for the average cycle times by part type yielded those in Figure 7-13. (We didn't combine these figures on a common scale since their units of measurement are different, so plotting them together wouldn't have made sense.)

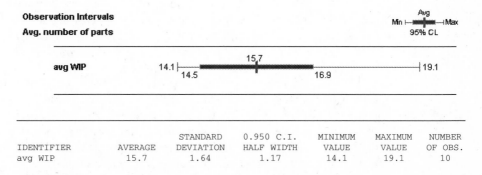

Figure 7-12. *Truncated Replication Confidence Interval for Steady-State Average WIP*

These intervals should be interpreted as in Section 6.5, except that now they are for steady-state expected performance measures rather than for measures defined relative to specific initialization and termination conditions.

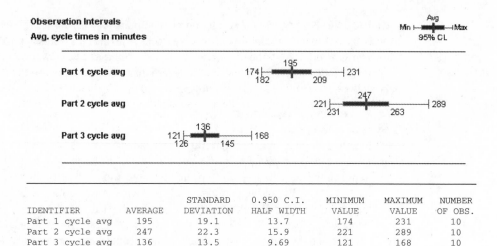

Figure 7-13. Truncated Replication Confidence Intervals for Steady-State
Average Cycle Times by Part Type

The confidence intervals in Figures 7-12 and 7-13 appear to be reasonably precise relative to the magnitudes of their midpoints, but if more precision is desired, you could get it by simulating some more. Now, however, you have a choice as to whether to make more replications with this run length and warm-up or keep the same number of replications and extend the run length. (Presumably the original warm-up would still be adequate.) It's probably simplest to stick with the same run length and just make more replications, which is the same thing as increasing the statistical sample size. There is something to be said, though, for extending the run lengths and keeping the same number of replications (though you'd have to rerun all the replications from the beginning); the increased precision with this strategy comes not from increasing the "sample size" (statistically, degrees of freedom) but rather from decreasing the variability of each within-run average since it's being taken over a longer run. Furthermore, by making the runs longer, you're even more sure that you're running long enough to "get to" steady state.

If you can identify an appropriate run length and Warm-Up Period for your model, and if the Warm-Up Period is not too long, then the truncated-replication strategy is quite appealing. It's fairly simple, relative to other steady-state analysis strategies, and gives you truly independent observations (the results from each truncated replication), which is a big advantage in doing statistical analysis. This goes not only for simply making confidence intervals as we've done here, but also for comparing alternatives as well as other statistical goals that we'll get to in Chapter 11.

7.5.3   Batching in a Single Run

Some models take a long time to warm up to steady state, and since each replication would have to pass through this long warm-up phase, the truncated-replication strategy of Section 7.5.2 can become inefficient. In this case, it might be better to make just one *really* long run and thus have to "pay" the warm-up only once. We modified Model 7.4 to make a single replication of length 1,000,000 minutes[1] including a warm-up of 2,000 minutes (we call this Model 7.6); this is the same simulation "effort" as making the 10 replications of length 100,000, and it took about the same amount of computer time. Figure 7-14 plots WIP and the Cycle Times by Part across this run, with time of observation as the horizontal axis in each case. (For now, ignore the thick vertical bars we drew in the WIP plot.)

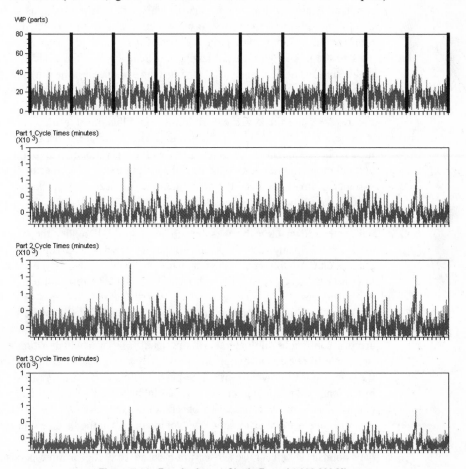

Figure 7-14. Results from a Single Run of 1,000,000 Minutes

The difficulty now is that we have only one "replication" on each performance measure from which to do our analysis, and it's not clear how we're going to compute a variance estimate, which is the basic quantity needed to do statistical inference. Viewing each individual observation or time-persistent value within a run as a separate "data point" would allow us to do the arithmetic to compute a within-run sample variance, but

---

[1] That's about 1.9 years of non-stop operation, in case you're counting.

doing so is extremely dangerous since the possibly heavy correlation (see Section C.2.4 in Appendix C) of points within a run will cause this estimate to be severely biased with respect to the true variance of an observation. Somehow, we need to take this correlation into account or else "manufacture" some more "independent observations" from this single long run in order to get a decent estimate of the variance.

There are several different ways to proceed with statistical analysis from a single long run. One relatively simple idea (that also appears to work about as well as other more complicated methods) is to try to manufacture almost-uncorrelated "observations" by breaking the run into a few large *batches* of many individual points, compute the averages of the points within each batch, and treat them as the basic IID observations on which to do statistical analysis (starting with variance estimation). These *batch means* then take the place of the means from within the multiple replications in the truncated-replication approach—we've replaced the replications by batches. In the WIP plot of Figure 7-14, the thick vertical dividing lines illustrate the idea; we'd take the time-average WIP level between the lines as the basic "data" for statistical analysis. (The same idea applies to the three cycle-time plots with observational data, but we didn't draw the vertical dividing lines for reasons we'll mention below.) In order to obtain an unbiased variance estimate, we need the batch means to be nearly uncorrelated, which is why we need to make the batches big; there will still be some heavy correlation of individual points near either side of a batch boundary, but these points will be a small minority within their own large batches, which we hope will render the batch means nearly uncorrelated. In any case, the Arena Output Analyzer will let you know if it appears that your batches are too small for your batch means to "look" (in the sense of a statistical test) nearly uncorrelated, in which case, you'd have to re-batch using larger (and thus fewer) batches.

When batching, a question arises as to the basis on which the batches should be formed—based on Time or based on Observations. Batches in the Time-based approach are just contiguous subintervals of simulated time over which a time-persistent curve, like our WIP or a queue length, is continuously averaged. (Recall from Section 2.1.2 that the continuous time average of a time-persistent curve is the integral of the curve divided by the length of the time interval.) Batches in the Observation-based approach are simply counts of how many consecutive observational data points, like our Cycle Times, are grouped together and arithmetically averaged to form the batch mean. While it's operationally possible with the Output Analyzer to use Time-based batching on observational data points, as well as use Observation-based batching on time-persistent curves, we strongly advise against doing so since it's not clear what the results really mean. The moral: do Time-based batching on time-persistent curves and Observation-based batching on observational data points. (All morals have exemptions, and in this case, the exemption pertains to time-based truncation of initial observational points to correspond to the Arena run Warm-Up Period, which we'll illustrate shortly.) This is why we refrained from drawing vertical batch-dividing lines for the cycle-time plots in Figure 7-14 since the horizontal axis was time, so dividing lines would have implied Time-based batching on these observational data.

The next thing you have to decide is how big a batch should be, whether Time-based or Observation-based. There's no foolproof recipe for doing this, so you primarily just have to try (and maybe try again). For observational data points, you might be able to get a hint by computing a *Correlogram* of the output series, which is a plot or table of the correlation between points at various *lags*, or distances apart from each other. The Output Analyzer will make a Correlogram (*Analyze/Correlogram* or the ⊡ button); the dialog filled out for the Cycle Times for Part 1 is in Figure 7-15, and the result is in Figure 7-16. (The results for the other two Part Types were similar, so we'll omit them.)

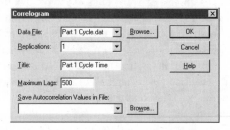

Figure 7-15. Dialog for Correlogram Construction

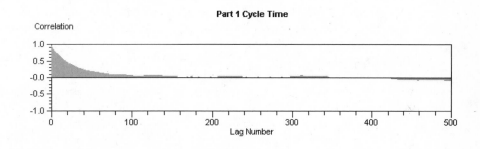

Figure 7-16. Correlogram to Lag 500 of Cycle Times for Part 1

Correlogram Summary
Part 1 Cycle Time

Sample Mean:	189.6
Sample Variance:	9128
Sample Size:	19871
Weighted Sum of Cov.:	5.8263+005

Correlation/Covariance Values

Lag	Covariance	Correlation
1	8617.7	0.94406
2	8240.7	0.90277
3	7898.2	0.86524
4	7605.7	0.8332
5	7316.4	0.80151

The Correlogram indicates that at Lag 1 (i.e., neighboring observations) the correlation is extremely heavy, and as the lag increases (the points in the series are farther apart), the correlation diminishes, albeit slowly. It appears that at about Lag 200 it's pretty much gone, meaning that observations spaced 200 apart are essentially uncorrelated.

Does this mean that a batch size of 200 is big enough? Not really. What it means is that a point on the very edge of a batch will be uncorrelated with points that are deeper than 200 into the neighboring batch. Looking at it the other way, the first and last 200 points in a batch probably have some correlation with the edge points on the preceding and next batch, respectively. Thus, we know that the batch size needs to be at least several hundred in this case to wash away the correlation. This isn't an answer, but it's a start.[2]

To see what the batch size *can* be, we need to know how many points we're working with; the summary report from this run indicated that there were 19,837 Part 1 Cycle Times observed during the non-truncated part of the simulation (for Part 2 there were 36,620, and for Part 3 there were 20,015). In view of the previous paragraph, let's try batches of size 1,000 points each (we'll just waste a few at the end of the run, though it's sad to waste nearly a whole batch for the Part 1 Cycle Times). Batching is done in the Output Analyzer with the Batch/Truncate Obs'ns option on the *Analyze* menu (or ▦); Figure 7-17 shows the dialog.

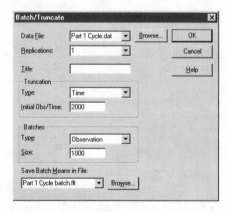

Figure 7-17. The Batch/Truncate Dialog

In the Truncation, we said to delete however many observations occur in the first 2,000 minutes (Time-based truncation on observational data, invoking the exemption to the moral above), which we determined earlier was our Warm-Up Period. Specifying a Warm-Up Period in the Arena run affects the summary report from the simulation and any values saved in files in the Outputs area of the Statistics module, but the within-run files saved from the Statistics module's Time-Persistent and Tallies areas contain *all* the data, including those observed during warm-up, so we need to Truncate them here again. It's important to Save Batch Means in a File (the bottom entry) since this is where the results will go to be fed into other procedures like classical confidence-interval

[2] You can't always get what you want.

formation. Note that the file name here is *not* enclosed in quotes, unlike file names in the Statistics module in Arena. The customary (and default) extension for files containing batch means is .flt.[3]

In addition to putting the batch means in the file `Part 1 Cycle Batches.flt`, the Batch/Truncate command gives you a brief summary of what it did, as shown in Figure 7-18.

```
                    Batch/Truncate Summary
                       Part 1 Cycle time

    Batched observations stored in file:      Part 1 Cycle batch.flt
                  Initial Time Truncated:           2000
                       Number of Batches:             19
          Number of Observations Per Batch:         1000
        Number of Trailing Obs'ns Truncated:         836
      Estimate of Covariance Between Batches:    -0.03946
```

Figure 7-18. Batch/Truncate Summary for Batch Size of 1,000

In this case, there's really nothing to do with this information, but if your batches had been too small to "look" uncorrelated, you'd get a warning message indicating rejection of a statistical hypothesis test for no correlation (or, equivalently, no covariance) between batches, as shown in Figure 7-19 when we (foolishly) made batches of size 200 instead of 1,000. This test is due to Fishman (1978).

```
                    Batch/Truncate Summary
                       Part 1 Cycle time

    Batched observations stored in file:      Part 1 Cycle batch.flt
                  Initial Time Truncated:           2000
                       Number of Batches:             99
          Number of Observations Per Batch:          200
        Number of Trailing Obs'ns Truncated:          36
      Estimate of Covariance Between Batches:     0.1713

  Covariance equal to 0 rejected in favor of Covariance > 0 at 0.05 level.
```

Figure 7-19. Batch/Truncate Summary for Batch Size of 200

We repeated the batching, with batch sizes of 1,000 observations, for the Cycle Times of Parts 2 and 3; the summaries indicated that this batch size was large enough in each case.

Now let's batch up the WIP time-persistent data, which must be done by Time-based batching. First, we'll try to get an idea about an appropriate time period for batching, but you can't make a Correlogram from the WIP data directly since Correlograms must be fed observational data. What you can do, though, is use Time-based Batching to make a whole bunch of little continuous-time batch means, save them in a .flt file, and make a Correlogram of *them*; this is referred to as *discretizing* the time-persistent WIP curve and is sometimes a useful trick. Recall that our run length was 1,000,000 minutes minus the 2,000 warm-up, for a retained period of 998,000 minutes. So we tried batching average WIP over intervals of 100 minutes each, of which there will be 9,980, done with Batch/Truncate as shown in Figure 7-20.

---

[3] This is an abbreviation of "filter," which is what batching was called in older versions of the Output Analyzer.

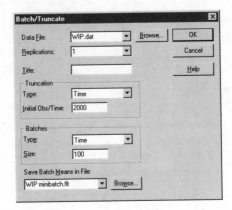

Figure 7-20. Batch/Truncate Dialog to Discretize WIP for a Correlogram

A Correlogram from all these little batch means is in Figure 7-21 and indicates that the correlation pretty much disappears by about Lag 100, which represents 100 batches × 100 minutes/batch = 10,000 minutes.

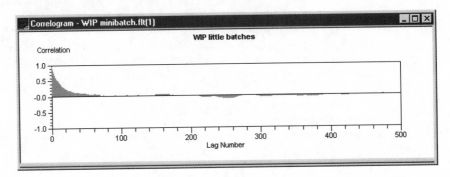

Figure 7-21. Correlogram for Discretized WIP (Batches of 100 Minutes)

So as a start, we might try batches of, say, about 100,000 minutes; since we have 1,000,000 − 2,000 = 998,000 minutes, let's adjust the batch sizes down a bit to 99,800 minutes so that we can get exactly 10 of them in our truncated run without wasting anything at the end. So we finally executed a Batch/Truncate as in Figure 7-20 except that the Size in the Batches area was 99800 and the File name was WIP batch.flt; as expected we got 10 batch means with no leftover time at the end.

Well, after all that, we're finally ready to do some statistical analysis. What we have are four files (Part 1 Cycle batch.flt, Part 2 Cycle batch.flt, Part 3 Cycle batch.flt, and WIP batch.flt) with (big) batch means in them, which we expect to be nearly uncorrelated. We fed these files into the Classical Confidence Intervals procedure as before (with the Lumped option), resulting in Figures 7-22 and 7-23.

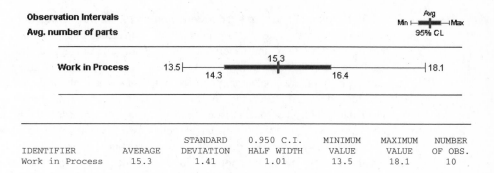

IDENTIFIER	AVERAGE	STANDARD DEVIATION	0.950 C.I. HALF WIDTH	MINIMUM VALUE	MAXIMUM VALUE	NUMBER OF OBS.
Work in Process	15.3	1.41	1.01	13.5	18.1	10

Figure 7-22. *Batch Means Confidence Interval for Steady-State Average WIP*

These batch-means intervals are directly comparable to those via truncated replications in Figures 7-12 and 7-13 and are quite consistent with them. The only consistent difference is that the batch-means intervals are slightly narrower than are those from truncated replications; we're just guessing (and we don't know that the differences are statistically significant), but one possible explanation for this is that with batch means we threw out only a single warm-up period of 2,000 minutes, but in truncated replications, we threw out 10 of these so that batch means had a bit more data with which to work. But all things considered, the truncated-replication and batch-means strategies appear to be telling us consistent stories about what's going on in steady state with these processes in this model.

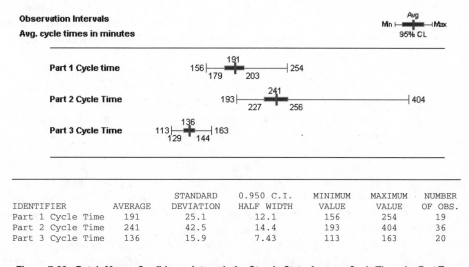

IDENTIFIER	AVERAGE	STANDARD DEVIATION	0.950 C.I. HALF WIDTH	MINIMUM VALUE	MAXIMUM VALUE	NUMBER OF OBS.
Part 1 Cycle Time	191	25.1	12.1	156	254	19
Part 2 Cycle Time	241	42.5	14.4	193	404	36
Part 3 Cycle Time	136	15.9	7.43	113	163	20

Figure 7-23. *Batch Means Confidence Intervals for Steady-State Average Cycle Times by Part Type*

7.5.4   Automatic Run-Time Confidence Intervals via Batch Means

Arena automatically attempts to compute 95% confidence intervals via batch means for the means of all Tally and Discrete-Change (Dstat) output statistics and gives you the results in the Half Width column next to the Average column in the summary report for each replication. We say "attempts to compute" since internal checks are done to see if your replication is long enough to produce enough data for a valid batch-means confidence interval on an output statistic; if not, you get only a message to this effect, without a half-width value (on the theory that a wrong answer is worse than no answer at all) for this statistic. If you've specified a Warm-Up Period in your Simulate module, data collected during this period are not used in the confidence-interval calculation. To understand how this procedure works, think of Arena as batching "on the fly" (i.e., observing the output data during your run and throwing them into batches as your simulation goes along).

So what does "enough data" mean? There are two levels of checks to be passed, the first of which is just to get started. For a Tally statistic, Arena demands a minimum of 320 observations. For a Dstat statistic, you must have had at least five units of simulated time during which there were at least 320 changes in the level of the discrete-change variable. Admittedly, these are somewhat arbitrary values and conditions, but we need to get started somehow, and the more definitive statistical test, which must also be passed, is done at the end of this procedure. If your run is not long enough to meet this first check, Arena reports "(Insuf)" in the Half-Width column for this variable. Just making your run longer should eventually produce enough data to meet these getting-started requirements.

If you have enough data to get started, Arena then begins batching by forming 20 batch means for each Tally and Dstat statistic. For Tally statistics, each batch mean will be the average of 16 consecutive observations; for Dstat statistics each will be the time average over 0.25 time unit. As your run progresses, you will eventually accumulate enough data for another batch of these same "sizes," which is then formed as batch number 21. If you continue your simulation, you'll get batches 22, 23, and so on, until you reach 40 batches. At this point, Arena will re-batch these 40 batches by averaging batches one and two into a new (and bigger) batch one, batches three and four into a new (bigger) batch two, etc., so that you'll then be back to 20 batches, but each twice as "big." As your simulation proceeds, Arena will continue to form new batches (21, 22, and so on), each of this larger size, until again 40 batches are formed, when re-batching back down to 20 is once again performed. Thus, when you're done, you'll have between 20 and 39 complete batches of some size. Unless you're really lucky, you'll also have some data left over at the end in a partial batch that won't be used in the confidence-interval computation. The reason for this re-batching into larger batches stems from an analysis by Schmeiser (1982), which demonstrated that there's no advantage to the other option, of continuing to gather more and more batches of a fixed size to reduce the half width, since the larger batches will have inherently lower variance, compensating for having fewer of them. On the other hand, having batches that are too small, even if you have a lot of them, is dangerous since they're more likely to produce correlated batch means, and thus an invalid confidence interval.

The final check is to see if the batches are big enough to support the assumption of independence between the batch means. Arena runs the same statistical hypothesis test as in the Batch/Truncate module (see Section 7.5.3). If this test is passed, you'll get the Half Width for this output variable in your summary report. If not, you'll get "(Corr)" indicating that your process is evidently too heavily autocorrelated for your run length to produce nearly-uncorrelated batches; again, lengthening your run should resolve this problem, though depending on the situation you may have to lengthen it a lot.

As an example, consider the 1,000,000-minute run of Model 7.6 in Section 7.5.3, with the 2,000-minute Warm-Up Period. Figure 7-24 shows a portion of the summary report, edited down to just the Cycle Times by part type, and WIP. Comparing to the "hand-made" batch-means confidence intervals of Figures 7-22 and 7-23, you see that things here are a little different but really pretty consistent (all these intervals are at the 95% confidence level). The difference is due to the fact that here the batching was automatically determined by Arena, resulting generally in different numbers of batches of different sizes, with different amounts of data left over at the ends, than what we decided to do by hand in Section 7.5.3.

```
Replication ended at time      : 1e+006.0
Statistics were cleared at time: 2000.0
Statistics accumulated for time: 998000.0
```

TALLY VARIABLES

Identifier	Average	Half Width	Minimum	Maximum	Observations
Part 1 Cycle Time	189.72	10.851	49.946	797.84	19837
Part 2 Cycle Time	241.27	12.764	81.769	956.47	36620
Part 3 Cycle Time	136.36	6.8694	47.691	579.01	20015

DISCRETE-CHANGE VARIABLES

Identifier	Average	Half Width	Minimum	Maximum	Final Value
Work in Process	15.338	.82146	.00000	63.000	16.000

Figure 7-24. Run-Time Batch Means Confidence Intervals from Model 7.6

In many cases, these automatic run-time confidence intervals will be enough for you to understand how precise your averages are, and they're certainly easy (requiring no work at all on your part). But there are a few considerations to bear in mind. First, don't forget that these are relevant only for steady-state simulations; if you have a terminating simulation (Section 6.5), you should be making independent replications and doing your analysis on them, so you should ignore these automatic run-time intervals. Secondly, you still ought to take a look at the Warm-Up Period for your model, as in Section 7.5.1, since the automatic run-time intervals don't do anything to correct for initialization bias if you don't specify a Warm-Up Period in your Simulate module. Third, if you want something other than a 95% confidence level, or if you want to make the most efficient use of your data and minimize waste at the end, you should use the methods described in Section 7.5.3 to exert more control. Finally, you can check the value of the automatic run-time half width as it is computed during your run, via the Arena variables THALF(Tally ID) for Tally statistics and DHALF(Dstat ID) for Dstat statistics; one reason to be interested in this is that you could use one of these for a critical output measure in the Terminating Condition field of your Simulate module to run your model long enough for it to become small enough to suit you; see Section 11.5 for more on this and related ideas.

7.5.5   What To Do?

We've shown you how to attack the same problem by a couple of different methods and hinted that there are a lot more methods out there. So which one should you use? As usual, the answer isn't obvious (we warned you that steady-state output analysis is difficult). Sometimes there are tradeoffs between scientific results and conceptual (and practical) simplicity, and that's certainly the case here.

In our opinion (and we don't want to peddle this as anything more than opinion), we might suggest the following list, in decreasing order of appeal:

1.   Try to get out of doing a steady-state simulation altogether by convincing yourself (or your patron) that the appropriate modeling assumptions really entail specific starting and stopping conditions. Go to Section 6.5.

2.   If your model is such that the warm-up is relatively short, probably the simplest and most direct approach is truncated replication. This has obvious intuitive appeal, is easy to do (once you've made some plots and identified a reasonable Warm-Up Period), and basically winds up proceeding just like statistical analysis for terminating simulations, except for the warm-up.

3.   If you find that your model warms up slowly, then you might consider batch means, with a single warm-up at the beginning of your single really long run. You could either accept Arena's automatic run-time batch-means confidence intervals (Section 7.5.4) or handcraft your own (Section 7.5.3).

7.5.6 Other Methods and Goals for Steady-State Statistical Analysis

We've described two different strategies (truncated replications and batch means) for doing steady-state statistical analysis; both of these methods are available in the Output Analyzer. This has been an area that's received a lot of attention among researchers, so there are a number of other strategies for this difficult problem: econometric time-series modeling, spectral analysis from electrical engineering, regenerative models from stochastic processes, standardized time series, as well as variations on batch means like separating or weighting the batches. If you're interested in exploring these ideas, you might consult Chapter 9 of Law and Kelton (1991), a survey paper like Sargent, Kang, and Goldsman (1992), or peruse a recent volume of the annual *Proceedings of the Winter Simulation Conference*, where there are usually tutorials, surveys, and papers covering the latest developments on these subjects.

There are statistical goals in steady-state analysis other than just forming confidence intervals for output processes from a single simulated system. Comparing alternatives on the basis of steady-state performance is commonly done, and the methods for this described in Section 6.5.5 for terminating simulations basically carry over to steady state by replacing the replication results there with either truncated replications or (big) batch means as described in Sections 7.5.2 and 7.5.3. In addition, there are other goals like variance estimation, ranking and selection of alternatives, gradient estimation, and optimization; we'll describe some of these in Chapter 11, and you can also look in the references cited in the preceding paragraph.

7.6 Summary and Forecast

Entity movement is an important part of most simulation models. This chapter has illustrated several of Arena's facilities for modeling such movement under different circumstances to allow for valid modeling. It has also indicated how you can approach the thorny issue of statistical analysis of steady-state simulations.

In the following chapter, we'll "drill down" to the next lower level of Arena modeling (the Support panel) and indicate how you can exploit its powerful modeling capabilities to capture a great amount of operational detail that might not be easily represented using only the high-level constructs we've covered so far.

7.7 Exercises

7.1 Implement the simple resource-constrained movement of entities in Model 6.1, as described in Section 7.2. Drop in a new Resource module, call the resource something like `Traffic Capacity`, and then edit the existing Server modules' Tran Out and Tran In dialogs, as well as the Enter and Leave modules for Cell 3, as described in Section 7.2. Explore the effect of the number of units of `Traffic Capacity` by running the simulation for values of 1, 2, 3, and 100. Compare with the results of Model 6.1 (with no limit on the number of entities en route at a time). Explain.

7.2 Change your model for Exercise 6.2 to include fork trucks to transport the parts between stations. Assume that there are two fork trucks that each travel at 85 feet per minute. It requires 0.25 minute to either load or unload a part by the fork truck. The distance between stations is given (in feet) in the following table; note that the distances are in general directional:

		To				
		Arrive	WS A	WS B	WS C	Exit System
	Arrive	0	100	100	200	300
	WS A	100	0	150	100	225
From	WS B	100	150	0	100	200
	WS C	250	100	100	0	100
	Exit	350	250	225	100	0

Instead of running the simulation for 5,000 minutes as in Exercise 6.2, run it for 100,000 minutes (you may want to turn off the animation via the *Run/Setup/Mode* option after confirming that things are working properly).

(*a*) Assume that fork trucks remain at the station where they unloaded the last part, if no other request is pending.

(*b*) Assume that fork trucks follow a looping pattern (Arrive, WS A, WS B, WS C, Exit).

7.3 For modeling option (*a*) in Exercise 7.2, confirm that the run length of 100,000 appears to be adequate for steady-state analysis by looking at time-based plots of the cycle times by part type, as in Section 7.5.1. Identify an appropriate Warm-Up Period from your plots. Rerun option (*a*) from Exercise 7.2 with the Warm-Up Period in effect; does the warm-up make much difference in this case?

7.4 In Exercise 7.2, consider the following comparisons based on run lengths of 100,000 minutes with no warm-up period. In each case, use batching within the run to form nearly-uncorrelated batch means on which the basic statistical analysis will be done.

(*a*) Compare modeling options (*a*) and (*b*) based on cycle times for part type 2 (the only one of the four part types that visits all workstations during its process plan).

(*b*) If you reduce the number of trucks to 1, is there a difference? Use modeling option (*a*) from Exercise 7.2, and base your results on cycle times for part type 2.

7.5 Change your model for Exercise 6.2 to use nonaccumulating conveyors to transfer the parts between stations. Assume there is a single conveyor that starts at the arrive area and continues to the exit area: Arrive–WS A–WS B–WS C–Exit. Assume the distances between all adjacent stations on the conveyor are 100 feet. Further assume the cells of the conveyor are 2 feet and that each part requires 4 feet of conveyor space. Load and unload times are each 0.25 minute. The conveyor speed is 20 feet per minute.

7.6 A prototype of a new airport bag screening system is currently being designed, as in the figure below. Bags arrive to the system with interarrival times of EXPO(0.25) (all times are in minutes), and are loaded on a Load conveyor (75 feet long) and conveyed to an initial scan area. At the initial scan area the bags are dropped into a chute to wait for the initial scan, which is of duration TRIA(0.1, 0.25, 0.35). Based on the results of the scan, accepted bags (79%) are loaded on an Out conveyor (40 feet long) and conveyed to exit the system, whereas rejected bags are loaded on a Secondary conveyor (20 feet long) and conveyed to a secondary scan area. At the secondary scan area the bags are dropped into a chute to wait for a visual inspection, which takes TRIA(0.6,1.2,1.4). After the inspection they are sent through a secondary scanner that is about 10 feet long. This scan takes 1.2 minutes and only one bag can be in the scanner at a time. At the end of the secondary scanner the bags are examined by another inspector, EXPO(0.4). Based on the results of this secondary inspection, 10% of the bags are sent to a reject area for further inspection, accepted bags are loaded on an Out 2 conveyor (20 feet long) and conveyed to exit the system. All conveyors are nonaccumulating with a velocity of 40 feet per minute. Develop a model of this system and run for 2,000 minutes. Use a resource-constrained route to model the second scanner.

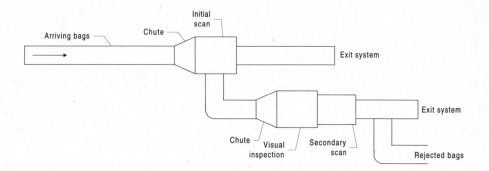

The current design calls for a chute capacity of 20 at the initial scan area and a total capacity of 25 at the secondary scan area, not including the bag undergoing the visual inspection. What percent of the time would you expect this capacity be exceeded? Hint: Add two time-persistent statistics to collect this information using logical expressions that evaluate to zero if the number of bags is less than the capacity, and to one if the capacity is exceeded.

7.7   Modify Model 5.3 to include the use of a single truck to transfer parts from the two prep areas to the sealer. Assume that the distance between any pair of the three stations is 100 feet and that the truck travels at a rate of 75 feet per minute. Animate your solution.

7.8   Modify Model 5.3 to include the use of two conveyors to transfer parts from the two prep areas to the sealer. Both conveyors are 100 feet long and are made up of 20 cells of 5 feet each. The conveyor velocity is 30 feet per minute. Animate your solution.

7.9   Develop a model of a cross-dock system that groups and transfers material for further shipment. This facility has five incoming docks and three outgoing docks. Trucks arrive to each of the incoming docks with loads of material on pallets. The interarrival time is UNIF(30, 60) between truck arrivals on each incoming dock (all times are in minutes). Each truck will have a number of pallets drawn from a UNIF(10, 25) distribution (round to the nearest integer) that need to be transferred to one of the outgoing docks. Assume an equal probability of any pallet going to any of the three outgoing docks. When trucks arrive, an automatic unloading device unloads the pallets at the incoming dock. Assume that this requires no time, so the pallets are immediately ready for transfer. The pallets are transferred by five fork trucks to the outgoing docks, which are located on the other side of the building. The distance between any incoming dock and any outgoing dock is 75 feet and the fork trucks travel at 75 feet per minute. The time for a fork truck to load a pallet is UNIF(0.3, 0.4) and to unload a pallet is UNIF(0.2, 0.4). The performance measure of interest is the time the pallet spends in the system. (Hint: If you place all fork trucks at the outgoing docks for their initial position, you don't have to add distances between the incoming docks.) Develop a model for each of the following three cases, and animate your models:

(*a*) Assume the priority is such that you want to transfer the pallets that have been waiting the longest. (Hint: Enter the name of the attribute with the arrival time in the priority field of the Transfer Out dialog.)

(*b*) Because of potential congestion, devote a single fork truck to each dock. Modify your model to include this option. (Hint: Select Specific Unit in the Transfer Out dialog.)

(*c*) Because we want to be assured that an incoming truck can always unload, modify your model from part (*a*) above such that the pick-up priority is placed on the incoming dock with the most pallets. (Hint: Develop an expression using NQ for the priority field.)

Which of the above three options would appear to be "best"? Choose your own criterion and be sure to justify your conclusions with a valid statistical analysis. Furthermore, for each of options (*a*) and (*c*), study the effect of having one fewer fork truck (down to 4) or one more (up to 6); again, mind the gap in credibility that results from an inadequate statistical analysis.

Detailed Modeling

CHAPTER 8

Detailed Modeling

In Chapters 5, 6, and 7, we showed you a lot of the kind of modeling you can do with modules from the Common and Transfer panels. These are relatively high-level and easy-to-use modules that will usually take you a long way toward building a model at a level of detail you need. Sometimes it's *all* you'll need.

But sometimes it isn't. As you gain experience in modeling, and as your models become bigger, more complex, and more detailed, you might find that you'd like to be able to control or model things at a lower level, in more detail, or just differently from what the high-level modules of the Common panel have to offer. Arena doesn't strand you at the high level, forcing you to accept a limited number of "canned" modeling constructs. Nor does it force you to learn a programming language or some pseudo-programming syntax to capture complicated system aspects. Rather, it offers a rich and deep hierarchy of levels that you can fathom to get the flexibility you might need to model some peculiar logic just right. It's probably a good idea to start with the high-level modules, take them as far as they'll go (maybe that's all the way), and when you need greater flexibility than they provide, go to a lower and more detailed level. This structure allows you to exploit the easy high-level modeling to the extent possible, yet allows you to drill down lower when you need to. And because all of this modeling power is provided by standard Arena modules, you'll already be familiar with how to use them; to put them to work, you simply need to become familiar with what they do.

This chapter explores some (certainly not all) of the detailed, lower-level modeling constructs available in the Support and Blocks panels; the latter panel provides the lowest-level model logic as modules corresponding to the blocks in the SIMAN language. The example we'll use for this is a fairly complex telephone call center, including technical support, sales, and order-status checking. We'll also touch on the important topics of nonstationary (time-dependent) arrival processes, model debugging, and a greater level of customization in animation.

Section 8.1 describes the system and Section 8.2 talks about how to model it (including the nonstationary arrival process). In Section 8.3, we debate whether to take a terminating or steady-state time frame of the system and discuss related modeling issues. Section 8.4 describes our basic modeling strategy, and Section 8.5 sets up the data needed. The model logic is developed in Sections 8.6-8.10. The unhappy (but inevitable) issue of debugging is taken up in Section 8.11. Corresponding to the more detailed modeling in this chapter, Section 8.12 indicates some ways you can fine-tune your animations to create some nonstandard effects.

After reading this chapter, you should be able to build very detailed and complex models and be able to exploit Arena's rich and deep hierarchy of modeling levels.

8.1   Model 8.1: A Generic Call Center System

Our generic call center system provides a central number in an organization that customers call for technical support, sales information, and order status. This central number feeds 26 trunk lines. If all 26 lines are in use, a caller gets a busy signal; hopefully, the caller will try again later. An answered caller hears a recording describing three caller options: transfer to technical support, sales information, or order-status inquiry (76%, 16%, and 8%, respectively). The estimated time for this activity is uniform (0.1, 0.6); all times are in minutes.

If the caller chooses technical support, a second recording requests which of three product types the caller is using, which requires uniform (0.1, 0.5) minutes. The percentage of requests for product types 1, 2, and 3 are 25%, 34%, and 41%, respectively. If a qualified technical support person is available for the selected product type, the call is automatically routed to that person. If none are currently available, the customer is placed in an electronic queue where he listens to annoying rock music until a support person is available. The time for all technical support calls is estimated to be triangular (3, 6, 18) minutes. Upon completion of the call, the customer exits the system. Four percent of these technical calls require further investigation after completion of the phone call. The questions raised by these callers are forwarded to another technical group that prepares a response. The time to prepare these responses is highly variable, but is estimated to be exponential (60) minutes. The resulting response is sent back to the technical support person who answered the original call. This person then calls the customer, which takes triangular (2, 4, 9) minutes. These returned calls require the use of one of the 26 trunk lines and receive priority over incoming technical calls. If a returned call is not completed on the same day the original call was received, it's carried over to the next day.

Sales calls are automatically routed to the sales staff. If a sales person is not available, the caller is treated to soothing new-age space music (after all, we're hoping for a sale). Sales calls are estimated to be triangular (4, 15, 45)—sales people tend to talk a lot more! Upon completion of the call, the happy customer exits the system.

Callers requesting order-status information are automatically handled by the phone system, and there is no limit on the number the system can handle (of course, there are only 26 trunk lines, which is itself a limit). The estimated time for these transactions is triangular (2, 3, 4) minutes, with 15% of these callers wanting to speak to a real person after they have received their order status, and they are given this option. These calls are routed back to the sales staff where they wait with the same priority as other sales calls. These follow-up order-status calls are estimated to be triangular (3, 5, 10) minutes. These callers then exit the system.

The call system hours are from 8 AM until 6 PM, with a small proportion of the staff on duty until 7 PM. Although the system closes to new calls after 6 PM, all calls that enter the system by that time are answered.

The call arrival rate to this system is highly variable over the course of the day, which is typical of these types of systems, and is expressed in calls per hour for each 30-minute period during which the system is open. These call arrival rates are given in Table 8-1.

Table 8-1. Call Arrival Rates (Calls Per Hour)

Time	Rate	Time	Rate	Time	Rate	Time	Rate
8:00 - 8:30	20	10:30 - 11:00	75	1:00 - 1:30	110	3:30 - 4:00	90
8:30 - 9:00	35	11:00 - 11:30	75	1:30 - 2:00	95	4:00 - 4:30	70
9:00 - 9:30	45	11:30 - 12:00	90	2:00 - 2:30	105	4:30 - 5:00	65
9:30 - 10:00	50	12:00 - 12:30	95	2:30 - 3:00	90	5:00 - 5:30	45
10:00 - 10:30	70	12:30 - 1:00	105	3:00 - 3:30	85	5:30 - 6:00	30

All employees work an eight-hour day with 30 minutes off for lunch. There are seven sales people with the staggered daily schedules summarized as (number of people @ time period): 3@90, 7@90, 6@90, 7@60, 6@120, 7@120, and 4@90.

There are 11 technical support people whose work schedules are shown in Table 8-2. Charity and Noah are qualified to handle calls for Product Type 1; Tierney, Sean, and Deb are qualified to handle calls for Product Type 2; Shelley, Jenny, and Christie are qualified to handle calls for Product Type 3. Molly is qualified to handle Product Types 1 and 3, and Anna and Sammy are qualified to handle all three product type calls.

Table 8-2. Technical Support Schedules

Name	Product Lines	Time Period (30 minutes)																					
		1	2	3	4	5	6	7	8	9	10	11	12	13	14	15	16	17	18	19	20	21	22
Charity	1	•	•	•	•	•	•	•		•	•	•	•	•	•	•	•	•					
Noah	1						•	•	•	•	•	•		•	•	•	•	•	•	•	•	•	•
Molly	1, 3			•	•	•	•	•	•	•		•	•	•	•	•	•	•	•	•	•		
Anna	1, 2, 3				•	•	•	•	•		•	•	•	•	•	•	•	•	•	•	•	•	
Sammy	1, 2, 3				•	•	•	•	•	•	•		•	•	•	•	•	•	•	•	•		
Tierney	2	•	•	•	•	•	•	•		•	•	•	•	•	•	•	•	•					
Sean	2						•	•	•	•		•	•	•	•	•	•	•	•	•	•	•	•
Deb	2				•	•	•	•	•		•	•	•	•	•	•	•	•	•	•	•		
Shelley	3	•	•	•	•	•	•	•		•	•	•	•	•	•	•	•	•					
Jenny	3						•	•	•	•		•	•	•	•	•	•	•	•	•	•	•	•
Christie	3			•	•	•	•	•	•		•	•	•	•	•	•	•	•	•	•	•		

As a point of interest, we'll consider balking in this system by counting customer calls that are not able to get a trunk line. However, we won't consider *reneging*—customers who hang up the phone before reaching a real person (see Section 9.3 for a discussion of how to model reneging).

Some statistics of interest for these types of systems are: number of customer balks (busy signals), total time on the line by customer type, time waiting for a real person by customer type, contact time by customer type, number of calls waiting for service by customer type, and personnel utilization.

8.2 New Modeling Issues

From a simulation viewpoint, this problem is quite different from those we covered in previous chapters. The most obvious difference is that the previous systems were all manufacturing oriented, and this system is of a service nature. Although the original version of SIMAN was developed for manufacturing applications, the current Arena capabilities also allow for accurate modeling of service systems. Applications include fast-food restaurants, banks, insurance companies, service centers, and many others. Although these systems have some special characteristics, the basic modeling requirements are the same as for manufacturing systems. Now let's take a look at our call center and explore the new requirements. As we proceed, it should become clear that the modeling constructs that we've covered up to this point are insufficient to model this system at the level of detail requested.

The differences start with the arrival process, which has a rate that varies over time. This type of arrival process is fairly typical of service systems and requires a different approach. Arrivals at many systems are modeled as a *stationary* Poisson process in which arrivals occur one at a time, are independent of one another, and the average rate is constant over time. For those of you who are not big fans of probability, this means that we have exponential interarrival times with a fixed mean. You may not have realized it, but this is the process we used to model arrivals in all of our previous models. There was a slight variation of this used for the Part B arrivals in our Electronic and Test System modeled in Chapter 5. In that case, we assumed that an arrival was a batch of four; therefore, our arrivals still occurred one batch at a time.

For this model, the mean arrival rate is a function of time. These types of arrivals are modeled as a *nonstationary* Poisson process. An obvious, but incorrect, modeling approach would be to enter an exponential distribution with a user-defined variable as a mean for the time between arrivals, then change the value of the mean variable based on the rate for the current time period. For our example, we'd change this value every 30 minutes. This would provide an approximate solution if the rate change between the periods was rather small. But if the rate change is large, this method can give very misleading (and wrong) results. The easiest way to illustrate the potential problem is to consider an extreme example. Let's say we have only two periods, each 30 minutes long. The rate for the first period is 3 (average arrivals per hour), or an interarrival-time mean of 20 minutes, and the rate for the second period is 60, or an interarrival-time mean of 1 minute. Let's suppose that the last arrival in the first time period occurred at time 29 minutes. We'd generate the next arrival using an interarrival time of 20 minutes. Using an exponential distribution with a mean of 20 could easily[1] return a value more than 31 for the time to the next arrival. This would result in no arrivals during the second period, when in

---

[1] With probability $e^{-31/20} = 0.21$, to be (almost) exact. Actually this figure is the *conditional* probability of no arrivals in the second period, *given* that there were arrivals in the first period and that the last of these was at time 29. This is not quite what we want, though; we want the *unconditional* probability of seeing no arrivals in the second period. It's possible to work this out, but it's complicated. However, it's easy to see that a lower bound on this probability is given by the probability that the first arrival after time 0, generated as exponential with mean 20 minutes, occurs after time 60—this is one way (not the only way) to have no arrivals in the second period, and has probability $e^{-60/20} = e^{-3} = 0.0498$. Thus, the incorrect method would give us at least a 5% chance of having no arrivals in the second period. Now, go back to the text, read the next sentence, and see the next footnote.

fact there should be an expected value of 30.[2] In general, using this simplistic method causes a decrease in the number of arrivals when going from one period to the next with an increase in the rate, or a decrease in the interarrival time. Going from one period to the next with a decrease in the rate will increase the number of arrivals in the second period.

The simplest way to avoid these problems is to use a method called *thinning* (Lewis and Shedler, 1979) to generate the arrivals for a nonstationary Poisson process. To implement this method, first determine the maximum arrival rate over all time periods. For our call center, the maximum arrival rate is 110 calls per hour (mean interarrival time of 60/110 minutes), which occurs for the time period from 1:00 to 1:30. We then use a *stationary* Poisson process (exponential distribution) to generate arrivals using this rate for all time periods. However, each arrival is subject to being "thinned" or "rejected," in which case, we discard that arrival. The probability that an arrival generated using the maximum rate will be allowed to enter the system is the current arrival rate divided by the maximum rate. For our call center, we'd use a mean interarrival time of 60/110. During the first period, the probability that an arrival generated by this stationary Poisson process will enter the system is 20/110 (8:00 to 8:30). We still need to define our arrival rates in a user-defined variable, but we use them as part of the thinning process rather than as the mean of our arrival process. We'll show you how to do this in Section 8.7.

A call generated by our nonstationary Poisson process is really a customer *trying* to access one of the 26 trunk lines. If all 26 lines are currently in use, a busy signal is received and the customer departs the system. The term for this is *balking*. This is easy to implement in Arena, but let's first talk about this concept more generally. Consider a drive-through at a fast-food restaurant that has a single window with room for only five cars to wait for service. The arriving entities would be cars entering a queue to wait to seize a resource called "Window Service." We'd simply enter a queue capacity of 5 (you generally find this entry by pressing the Queue button in, for instance, a Server module). This would allow one car to be in service and a maximum of five cars to be waiting. If a sixth car would attempt to enter the queue, it would balk. You determine what happens to these balked cars or entities. They might be disposed of or we might assume that they would drive around the block and try to re-enter the queue a little later. Our call center balking works the same way, except that the queue capacity is 0. An arriving entity (call) enters the zero-capacity queue and attempts to seize one unit of a resource called "Trunk Line." If a unit is available, it's allocated to the call and the call enters the system. If a unit of the resource is not available, the entity attempts to stay in the queue. But since the queue has a capacity of 0, the call would be balked from the queue and disposed of.

Once a call is allocated a trunk line and enters the system, we must then determine the call type so we can direct it to the proper part of the system for service. To do this, we need the ability to send entities or calls to *three* different parts of the system based on the given probabilities. The same requirement is true for technical calls since there are three different product types. We could get out our calculator and dust off our probability concepts and compute the probability of each call type—there are a total five if we don't

---

[2] The probability of no arrivals in the second period should be $e^{-60(1/2)} = 0.000000000000093576$.

count returned technical calls or order-status calls that require a follow-up. We could then define Sequences (see Section 6.2.1) for each of these call types and route them through the system. Although this might work, you would have to re-compute the probabilities each time you change the distribution of call types, which you might want to do to test the flexibility or robustness of the system. Also, unlike our previous models, a call can be allocated and can control two different resources at the same time: a trunk line and a technical support person. Clearly, we'll need some new Arena modeling capabilities to simulate this system as described.

Finally, we need to consider how to model the returned technical support calls. These are unique in that they must be returned by the same person who handled the original call, so we must have a way to track who handled the original call. Although these new issues have created the need for a number of new modeling constructs, we'll soon show you how to create an Arena model of this system easily.

Before we do that, let's talk about the statistical and animation requirements for our call center system. The statistics requested are not unusual or greatly different from what we've collected in previous models. However, the type of system and the analysis needs are quite different. Let's deal with the analysis needs first. When analyzing service systems, one is generally trying to maximize customer satisfaction while minimizing costs. (In the extreme, of course, these are incompatible goals.) The key customer satisfaction measurements for our call center would be the number of busy signals and the customer wait time. We'd like to minimize the number of customers receiving busy signals and reduce the waiting time until the caller reaches a real person. The key factors affecting these measurements are the number of trunk lines and the staffing schedule. Once we've created a model, we could easily increase or decrease the number of trunk lines and determine the impact. This requires that we give more thought to how long we run our simulation and what type of system we have. We'll deal with this in the next section.

Analyzing and improving the staff schedule is a more difficult problem. Because our staffing varies over the day and our arrival process is nonstationary, the system performance could vary significantly from one time period to the next. Thus, if we're going to manipulate our staffing schedule in an attempt to improve performance, we'd like information that would tell us what time periods are under- or over-staffed. Our normal summary report won't give us this information. One method would be to view the animation over several days, much like you might watch the real system. Unfortunately, and unlike our previous models, there's really nothing to animate that will show the movement through the system. We could animate the call waiting queues and the resources, but the resulting animation would be very jumpy and wouldn't provide the time perspective that we need. Although we often see these types of systems animated, the animation is typically used for "show and tell" rather than for analysis.

What we need is the ability to draw a relationship between staffing and performance. Plots probably provide the best mechanism for getting this type of information. The key variables of interest are the number of customer balks, the number of customers waiting in queue, and the number of idle staff. Plots will allow us to view this information over a day or more and assess where we need more or fewer staff. We can then attempt to alter our staffing schedule to improve performance. Thus, for this model, our animation will consist solely of plots. We could also write this information to output files and perform post-run analysis as in Chapter 5. The last issue we need to deal with is the system type and the impact it has on the type of statistical analysis we might perform.

8.3   Terminating or Steady-State

In Section 6.5.1, we briefly described terminating versus steady-state time frames for simulations. We now have to decide which to do for this call center model. Systems are normally classified as terminating or non-terminating. Although we'll lead you to believe it's a very clear distinction, that's seldom the case. Some systems appear at first to be one type, but on closer examination, they turn out to be the other. This issue is further complicated by the fact that some systems have elements of both types, and system classification may depend on the types of questions that the analyst needs to address.

The classification of a system may depend on what type of analysis we want to perform. For example, consider a fast-food restaurant that opens at 11 AM and closes at 11 PM. If we're interested in the daily operational issues of this restaurant, we'd use a nonstationary arrival process and analyze the system as a terminating system. If we were interested only in the operation during the rush that occurs for two hours over lunch, we might assume a stationary arrival process at the peak arrival rate and analyze the system as a steady-state system.

At first glance, our call center definitely appears to be a terminating system. The system would appear to start and end empty and idle. However, there are technical staff return calls that might remain in the system overnight. Approximately 3% of all calls (you can do the arithmetic yourself) are returned by the technical staff. If the calls that are held overnight significantly affected the starting conditions for the next day, we might want to consider the system to be steady-state. We're going to assume that this is not the case and will proceed to analyze our call center system as a terminating system later in this chapter.

8.4   Modeling Approach

In Chapter 1, Figure 1-2, we briefly discussed the Arena hierarchical structure. This structure freely allows you to combine the modeling constructs from any level into a single simulation model. In Chapters 5-7, we were able to develop our models using the high-level constructs found in the Common panel (yes, we planned it that way), although we did require the use of several constructs found in the Transfer panel for our material handling examples in Chapter 7.

The general modeling approach that we recommend is that you stay at the highest level possible when creating your models. However, as soon as you find that these high-level constructs don't allow you to capture the necessary detail, we suggest that you drop down to the next level rather than sacrifice the accuracy of the simulation model. As you become more familiar with the various panels (and modeling levels), you should find that you'll do this naturally. Before we proceed, let's briefly discuss the available panels.

The Common panel provides the highest level of modeling. It is designed to allow you to create high-level models of most systems quickly and easily. Using a combination of the Arrive, Server, Inspect, Depart, Advanced Server, Enter, Process, and Leave modules allows a great deal of flexibility. In fact, if you look around in these modules, you'll find many additional features that we've yet to touch upon. In many cases, the use of these modules alone will provide all the detail required for a simulation project.

The Support panel provides the next lower (more detailed) level of modeling. For example, the sequence of modules Station–Seize–Delay–Release–Route provides basically the same fundamental modeling logic as a Server module. The handy feature of the Support panel modules is that you can put them together in almost any combination required for your model. In fact, many experienced modelers start at this level because they feel that the resulting model is more transparent to the user, who may or may not be the modeler. The Support panel modules also give you additional capabilities not found in the Common panel modules.

The Transfer panel provides the lower-level modeling constructs for material handling activities (transporters and conveyors). Similar to the general modeling capabilities provided by the Support panel, the Transfer panel modules give you more flexibility in modeling material handling systems.

The Blocks panel (the SIMAN template) provides an even lower level of modeling capability. In fact, it provides the basic functionality that was used to create all of the modules found in the three panels of the Arena template (Common, Transfer, and Support). In addition, it provides many other special-purpose modeling constructs not available in the higher-level modules. Examples would include "while" loops, combined probabilistic and logic branching, and automatic search features. You might note that several of the modules have the same names as those found in the three Arena template panels. Although the names are the same, the modules are not. You can distinguish between the two by the color and capitalization. The Arena template module names are spelled with an initial capital with the remaining letters in lowercase. The Blocks modules are shown in all capital letters. The difference between the two is easy to explain if you've used SIMAN previously, where you define the model and experiment frames separately, even though you may do this all in Arena. It is best illustrated with the difference between the Assign modules on the two panels. When you use the Support panel module, you're given the option of the type of assignment you want to make. If you make an assignment to a new attribute, Arena will automatically define that new attribute and add it to the pull-down lists for attributes everywhere in your model. One reason for staying at the highest level possible is that the Blocks module only allows you to make the assignment—it doesn't define the new attribute. Even with this shortcoming, there are numerous powerful and useful features available only in the Blocks panel.

In addition, the Elements panel (the SIMAN template) is where you find the experiment frame modules. This is where, for example, you find the ATTRIBUTES module to define your new attribute. You'll rarely need these features since they're combined with the modules of the Arena template, but if you need this lowest level for a special modeling feature (you can go to C or FORTRAN if you're a real glutton for punishment), it's available via the same Arena interface as everything else.

Now let's return to our call center system, which *does* require features not found in the Common panel modules. Although we could use selected modules (e.g., Arrive) from the Common panel, we'll use modules from the Support panel where possible, mostly to illustrate their capabilities. When you model with lower-level constructs, you need to approach the model development in a slightly different fashion. With the higher-level constructs, we tend to group activities into servers or inspect stations and then use the appropriate modules. With the lower-level constructs, we need to concentrate on the actual activities. In a sense, your model becomes a detailed *flowchart* of these activities. Unfortunately, until you're familiar with the logic in the available modules, it's difficult to develop that flowchart.

So at this point, let's divide our model into sections and go directly to that development where we can simultaneously show you the capabilities available. The six sections, in the order they'll be presented, are as follows:

Section 8.5:   Data section (resources, variables, expressions, sets, simulate),
Section 8.6:   Determine the maximum arrival rate and increment the time period,
Section 8.7:   Create the arrivals and direct them to the proper service,
Section 8.8:   Technical support calls,
Section 8.9:   Sales calls, and
Section 8.10: Order-status calls.

Since we're not animating our model (other than plots), we'll delete all animation objects that are included with the modules we place.

8.5 Defining the Data

The data modules we need to place for this model are shown in Figure 8-1. We've already covered almost all of the needed concepts contained in these modules in previous chapters, so we won't bore you with the details of each module. We'll only comment on each and discuss any issues of which you should be aware.

Let's start with the Variables module, which contains a user-defined variable `Arrive Rate`. We've defined this variable as a single array with a maximum of 22 rows, to correspond to the 30-minute periods of the working day. We initialized the first 20 values using the data provided in Table 8-1. The values for rows 21 and 22 are for the two time periods from 6 PM to 7 PM, which have no arrivals because the phone lines are shut down. You might initially want to enter a 0 for each of these values. However, as we'll be using these values to calculate the probability of an arrival with the expression `60/Arrive Rate`, we could cause an error because we attempt to divide by 0. Therefore, we've arbitrarily entered a very small value, 0.001, for these time periods. Although this will not guarantee that no arrivals occur, the probability will be very, very small. We'll briefly discuss how to clean up this problem in the next section.

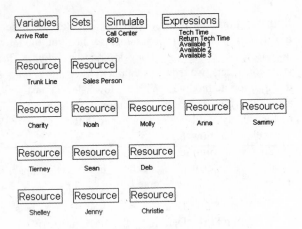

Figure 8-1. The Data Modules

We've placed a total of 13 Resource modules (one for the 26 trunk lines, one for the sales staff, and the remaining 11 for the individual technical support staff). All but the trunk lines follow a schedule. Resource schedules were defined in Section 5.2. The dialogs provided by the Resource module are identical and therefore won't be covered here. We defined a separate schedule for each resource; however, as several of the technical support staff follow the same schedule (e.g., Charity, Tierney, and Shelley), you could simply reuse a single schedule. If you're building this model along with us, be sure that each schedule covers the entire 660 minutes of each day, from 8 AM to 7 PM. For example, Molly's schedule would be: 0@60, 1@180, 0@30, 1@300, 0@90. This is important because we'll run our simulation model for more than one day, and if a schedule is not exactly 660 minutes, it would provide an invalid schedule after the first day.

Having defined our resources, we can now define our sets using the Sets module. We first define three resource sets. They are:

```
Product 1: Charity, Noah, Molly, Anna, Sammy
Product 2: Tierney, Sean, Deb, Anna, Sammy
Product 3: Shelley, Jenny, Christie, Molly, Anna, Sammy
```

The contents of these sets correspond to the technical staff qualified to handle the calls for each product type. Note that Molly, Anna, and Sammy are included in more than one set. Also note that we've consistently placed these three staff members at the end of each set; the reason will become clear when we cover the technical support calls portion of the model.

We also defined two Tally sets. They are:

```
Tech Calls: Product 1 Call, Product 2 Call, Product 3 Call
Return Time: Return 1 Call, Return 2 Call, Return 3 Call
```

These sets are required because we're interested in these statistics by product type. Note that the first item in each set references Product 1, etc. If the reason is not apparent, it will be when we cover that section of the model.

The Simulate module would be straightforward if it were not for the fact that we have a terminating system that we want to replicate. In the Replicate section, we've somewhat arbitrarily requested 10 replications, each of 660 minutes. Because we've requested multiple replications, we need to tell Arena what to do between replications. There are four possible options.

Option 1: Initialize System (yes), Initialize Statistics (yes)

This will result in 10 statistically independent and identical replications and summary reports, each starting with an empty system at time 0 and each running for 660 minutes. The random-number stream (see Section 11.1) just keeps on going between replications, making them IID.

Option 2: Initialize System (yes), Initialize Statistics (no)

This will result in 10 independent replications, each starting with an empty system at time 0 and each running for 660 minutes, with the summary reports being cumulative. Thus, Report 2 would include the statistics for the first two replications, Report 3 would contain the statistics for the first three replications, etc. The random-number stream behaves as in Option 1.

Option 3: Initialize System (no), Initialize Statistics (yes)

This will result in 10 runs, the first starting at time 0, the second at time 660, the third at 1320, etc. Since the system is not initialized between replications, the time continues to advance, and any technical calls that were not returned will be carried over to the next day. The summary reports will contain only the statistics for a single replication or day.

Option 4: Initialize System (no), Initialize Statistics (no)

This will result in 10 runs, the first starting at time 0, the second at time 660, the third at 1320, etc. Since the system is not initialized between replications, the time continues to advance, and any technical calls that were not returned will be carried over to the next day. The summary reports will be cumulative. The tenth summary report will be the same as if we'd made a single replication of length 6600 minutes.

Since we'd like to carry all non-returned technical calls into the next day, we need to select either Option 3 or 4. We select Option 3, which will easily allow us to see the amount of variation day to day.

Our last two data items are contained in the Expressions module. We've chosen to define the time for a technical support call and the time for a returned technical support call as expressions although we could just as easily have entered these distributions directly into the model as needed. Having completed our data requirements, we're now ready to move on to our logic development.

8.6 Determine Maximum Arrival Rate and Increment Time Period

This section of logic will determine the maximum arrival rate and increment a time-period indicator that will be used to determine the thinning probability of potential arrivals.

In essence, we're setting up a structure or procedure that will initialize our model each time we run it. We could take the easy way out and require the user, or modeler, to identify and enter the maximum rate as a user-defined variable directly into the arrival process. Although this is tempting, we'd really like to develop a more generic model that doesn't require the user to remember to check this value each time a rate change is made during the analysis.

Let's start with the logic that sets the time-period indicator, Figure 8-2. These five modules are for setting and incrementing the time-period indicator and assigning variables that we'll use later in our model. All these modules are new and can be found in the Support panel. The general idea is to create an entity at the start of each day that will be assigned the current time period. Then delay that entity for 30 minutes (one time period) and increment the time period by 1. When the time period equals 22 (the end of the day), dispose of the entity. Up to now, we've always considered an entity to have a physical counterpart. In this case, however, these entities have no physical meaning and are normally referred to as *logical entities* as they are included in the model for purposes of implementing logic or changing system conditions.

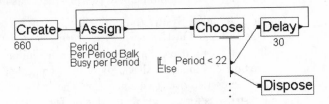

Figure 8-2. Incrementing the Time Period Indicator

The first module is the Create module, Display 8-1, which is very similar to the Arrive module without the Enter and Leave Data sections. We enter a constant 660 for the time between arrivals—the length of each day. Thus, at the start of each new day, we create an arrival and set the user-defined variable `Period` equal to 0. We've also checked the None option for animation as this is a logic entity.

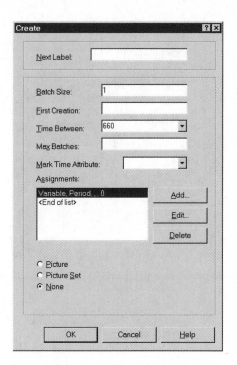

Time Between	660
Assignments	
Assignment Type	
Variable	*select*
Variable	Period
Value	0
None	*select*

Display 8-1. The Create Module

    The entity is then sent to the Assign module where three assignments are made, Display 8-2. The variable Period is incremented by 1 to reflect the start of the current 30-minute time period. The two additional user-defined variables, Per Period Balk and Busy per Period, are for keeping track of the number of balked phone calls during the 30-minute time period. In the next section of our model, we'll increment the variable Busy per Period by 1 each time a call balks from the system. Thus, the first assignment sets the variable Per Period Balk equal to the number of calls balked during the last time period—0 for the start of the day. The next assignment sets the variable Busy per Period equal to 0, as we want to start over at the start of each time period.

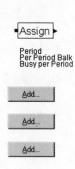

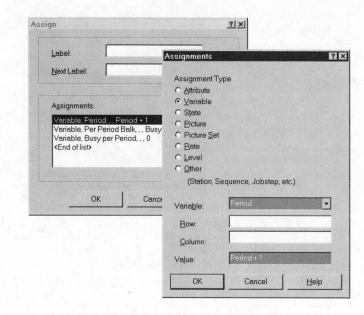

Assignment Type	
Variable	*select*
Variable	Period
Value	Period + 1

Assignment Type	
Variable	*select*
Variable	Per Period Balk
Value	Busy per Period

Assignment Type	
Variable	*select*
Variable	Busy per Period
Value	0

Display 8-2. The Assign Module

The entity is then sent to the Choose module. The Choose module provides entity branching based on user-defined logic. Branch destinations are defined by graphical connections or by specifying a Label destination. An arriving entity examines each of the user-defined branch options and sends the original arriving entity (called the *primary* entity) to the destination of the first branch whose condition is satisfied. This process continues, creating duplicates (called *secondary* entities) of the original entity for each "true" branch encountered until all defined branches are exhausted or until Maximum Branches Taken copies of the arriving entity have been generated. All secondary entities are duplicates (i.e., same attribute values and animation picture) of the original arriving entity. If no branches are taken, the arriving entity is disposed.

In our example, we've selected the default option, Take First True Condition, and defined our branches so there will always be a condition satisfied, Display 8-3. Thus, there will never be duplicate entities created or entities disposed. If you select the last option, Specify Max To Take, be aware that the default is infinity.

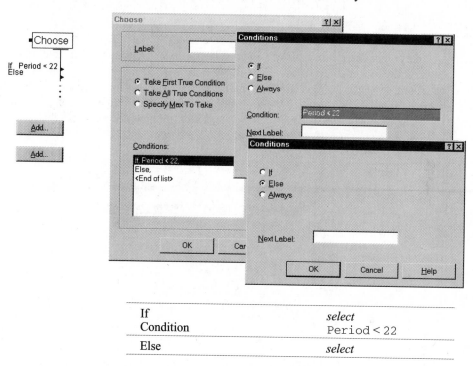

If	*select*
Condition	`Period < 22`
Else	*select*

Display 8-3. The Choose Module

An If condition can be any valid expression but typically contains some type of comparison. Such conditions may include any of the notations shown in Table 8-3. Logical expressions can also be used.

Table 8-3. The Choose Module Condition Notation

Description	Syntax Options		Description	Syntax Options	
And	`.AND.`		Or	`.OR.`	
Greater than	`.GT.`	`>`	Greater than or equal to	`.GE.`	`>=`
Less than	`.LT.`	`<`	Less than or equal to	`.LE.`	`<=`
Equal to	`.EQ.`	`==`	Not equal to	`.NE.`	`<>`

Only one Else branch should be used, and it should appear as the last statement specified since it's taken only when Maximum Branches Taken has not been satisfied. If the Maximum Branches Taken has been satisfied and there is a remaining Always branch, an error will occur.

Our Choose module has two possible branches. The first branch is taken if the current value of the variable Period is less than 22. In this case, the logical entity is sent back to the Delay module where it will be delayed for one time period before updating the assignments. If the value of the variable Period is equal to 22 (the end of the day), the entity is sent to the Dispose module where it is destroyed. We could have omitted the second branch and Arena would have disposed of the entity automatically. However, we recommend that you explicitly define all possible branches in the event that you, or your colleague, decide later to change the logic. By defining this second branch, we've made it very obvious that the entity is disposed, hopefully eliminating the possibility of missing this important step if the logic is changed.

If the entity is sent to the Delay module, Display 8-4, it is delayed for 30 minutes. It then returns to the first Assign module to update our assignments for the next time period.

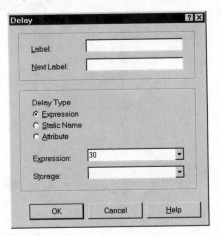

Delay Type	
Expression	*select*
Expression	30

Display 8-4. The Delay Module

The Dispose module, Display 8-5, has only one optional entry, a Label. This module destroys entities, thus there is no exit (which would have pleased Jean-Paul Sartre). It serves the same function as the Depart module, removing an entity from the system, without the statistical and transfer options.

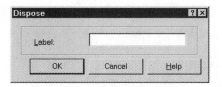

Display 8-5. The Dispose Module

The next part of the model initialization requires us to find and save the maximum arrival rate, Figure 8-3. The one new module, FINDJ, can be found in the Blocks panel. As we said earlier, we could require the analyst to perform this task by hand, but it's fairly easy to incorporate a FINDJ module into the model, and it allows us to use one of the many specialized modules from the SIMAN template. The Create model at the start of the logic, Figure 8-2, creates only one entity at the very start of the simulation. We could simply default on all the entries or enter a value of 1 for the Max Batches field. Since we default the Time Between arrivals to no entry, Arena assumes an infinite interarrival time. Thus only one entity is created at the beginning of the simulation run.

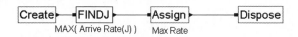

Figure 8-3. Finding the Maximum Arrival Rate

This entity is then sent to the FINDJ module. The FINDJ module searches over an index from the Start of Range to the End of Range to find the value of the global variable J that satisfies the specified Search Condition. The global variable J is a predefined Arena variable, much like the M, NS, and IS attributes. J is set to the value of the first index value that satisfies the Search Condition, or to 0 if no value of J in the specified range satisfies the Search Condition. There are many predefined Arena variables, as well as module names, that fall into a category called *reserved words*. If you inadvertently define your own variable or expression using one of these reserved words, Arena will give you a warning message.

When an entity arrives at a FINDJ module, Arena sets the index J equal to Start of Range and checks the Search Condition. If the Search Condition is satisfied, the current value of the index is assigned to J and the entity exits the module. Otherwise, the index J is incremented and the condition is checked. This process repeats until the condition is satisfied or until the End of Range value is reached, whichever comes first.

The Search Condition must always contain the variable J, and can contain any of the notations given in Table 8-3, including logical expressions. In addition, two special key words, MIN and MAX, can also be used. If Search Condition contains the MIN or MAX key word, Arena checks the complete range for the value of J that minimizes or maximizes the expression, respectively. If a tie exists, the first tested index is selected. If the starting index is larger than the ending index, the search goes backward. Runtime errors can result if FINDJ attempts to search over an undefined range.

The FINDJ module is very useful when you want to search a range of system status variables. In our example, we use it to search over the user-defined variable array that contains the arrival rates per period, `Arrive Rate`. Our search condition is over the range from 1 to 20, which corresponds to the 20 half-hour time periods from 8 AM to 5 PM, for the maximum arrival rate, Display 8-6. Note that we have intentionally excluded periods 21 and 22 because they are assumed to have zero arrivals. In our example, the maximum arrival rate would be found in period 11, from 1 to 1:30 PM, which has an arrival rate of 110. Thus, our FINDJ module will set the global variable J to a value of 11, and the entity will exit the module.

Start of Range	1
End of Range	20
Search Condition	MAX(Arrive Rate(J))

Display 8-6. The FINDJ Module

We need to caution you on your use of the global variable J. You should not assume that you are the only one using this variable, as some of the Arena modules use it without your knowledge. As long as your logic uses the value of the variable J immediately, you should have no problems. However, if the entity undergoes a time delay before your logic uses the value, it may have been changed by some other entity's logic. In this case, you should think of a time delay as anything that will cause the simulation time to be advanced. Examples would be a Delay module, waiting in a queue, a Route activity, etc.

Having found the maximum arrival rate, and being aware of the above caution, we now need to save it for later use. This is accomplished by sending the entity to the following Assign module, Display 8-7, which assigns this value, using the index J, to the user-defined variable `Max Rate`. The entity is then sent to a Dispose module. (The poor little guy has a very short life, but he serves a very useful purpose.) This completes the model logic for determining the maximum arrival rate and incrementing the time period.

Assignment Type	
Variable	*select*
Variable	Max Rate
Value	Arrive Rate(J)

Display 8-7. Assigning the Maximum Arrival Rate

8.7 Create Arrivals and Direct to Service

As you learn more about the capabilities of Arena and develop more complex models, you'll find it necessary to plan your logic in advance of building the model. Otherwise, you may find yourself constantly moving modules around or deleting modules that were erroneously selected. Whatever method you adopt for planning your models will normally come about naturally, but you might want to give it some thought before your models become really complicated—and they will! A lot of modelers use pencil (a pen for the overconfident) and paper to sketch out their logic using familiar terminology. Others use a more formal approach and create a logic diagram of sorts using standard flowcharting symbols. Still another approach is to develop a sequential list of activities that need to occur. We've developed such a list for the logic that's required for the next section of our model (which happens to look a lot like the model, see Figure 8-4):

Create arriving calls (at maximum rate)
Thin out arrivals
If a trunk line is available - seize
    Delay for recording
    Determine call type
    Direct call
Else (all trunk lines are busy)
    Count balked call
    Increment Busy per Period variable
    Dispose of call

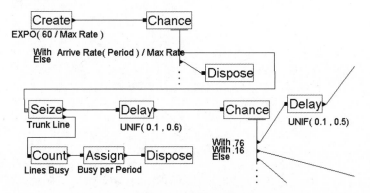

Figure 8-4. Arrival and Service Selection Process Logic

These types of approaches will help you formalize the modeling steps and reduce the number of errors and model changes. As you become more proficient, you may even progress to the point where you'll start by laying out your basic logic using Arena modules. However, even then we recommend that you lay out your complete logic before you start filling in the details.

Although you have already seen the Create module, we've chosen to show the entire module again because it has two rather unique entries, Display 8-8. The first is that we've offset after time 0 the first creation by a very small, and somewhat arbitrary, value. This is because we want to be sure that the logic that defines the value of the variable Max Rate has occurred first. Otherwise, the value of this variable would be equal to 0, and a runtime error would occur because we'd be trying to divide by 0 when Arena attempted to schedule the next arrival. The second point to note is that we've used an expression, $60/\text{Max Rate}$, to define the mean of our time between arrivals. We could just as easily have defined a variable Min Time equal to $60/\text{Arrive Rate(J)}$ and simply entered this variable for our mean.

Create ▶
EXPO(60 / Max Rate)

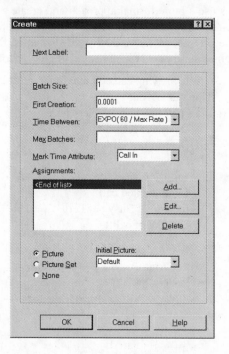

First Creation	0.0001
Time Between	EXPO(60/Max Rate)
Mark Time Attribute	Call In

Display 8-8. Creating the Call Arrivals

This Create module will cause call entities to arrive at the maximum rate. We now need to thin these calls so they reflect the rate of calls that should arrive during each 30-minute period of the day. This thinning process is accomplished with the Chance module, Display 8-9.

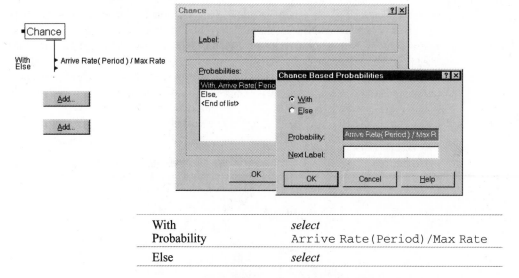

With	*select*
Probability	`Arrive Rate(Period)/Max Rate`
Else	*select*

Display 8-9. The Chance Module: Thinning the Calls

The Chance module provides entity branching based on probabilities that you specify. As with the Choose module, branch destinations are defined by graphical connections or by specifying a Label destination. When an entity arrives at a Chance module, it determines which branch to take based on a random number (continuously and uniformly distributed between 0 and 1). Multiple branches may be defined; however, the sum of all branch probabilities should not exceed 1. An Else branch can be used, only as the last branch, if the sum of the probabilities of all the "With" branches is less than 1. If this condition occurs and an Else branch has not been defined, the arriving entity is disposed. Probabilities may be expressed as constants or expressions, but if probabilities sum to a value greater than 1, an error will be reported. Duplicate entities are not created from this module.

The probability of allowing our created entity to enter the system is based on an expression of the current arrival rate, `Arrive Rate(Period)`, and the maximum arrival rate, `Max Rate`. Recall that all the arrival rates are stored in the variable array `Arrive Rate`, and the variable or index `Period` is being changed every 30 minutes by the logic described earlier. Those entities that are thinned are condemned to the attached Dispose module.

The entities that are allowed to enter the system are sent to a Seize module, Display 8-10, where they attempt to seize control of an available trunk line. The trunk lines are represented as a single resource, `Trunk Line`, with a capacity of 26, which was defined in our data section. If a unit of the resource `Trunk Line` is available, it's allocated to the arriving call, and the entity is immediately sent out of the upper connection point on the right side of the Seize module to the following Delay module (see Figure 8-4) where it incurs a UNIF(0.1, 0.6) delay representing the recording and option-selection time. After the delay, it's sent to the Chance module (see Figure 8-4) where the call type is determined according to the probabilities originally stated. The first branch represents a technical support call that is sent to a UNIF(0.1, 0.5) delay for the recording and selecting of product type. This entity is then sent to the technical support section of our model, discussed in the next section. The second and third branches send the call to the sales-information or order-status sections, respectively. The entries for these two Delay modules and the Chance module are not given here, but all the information can be seen in Figure 8-4.

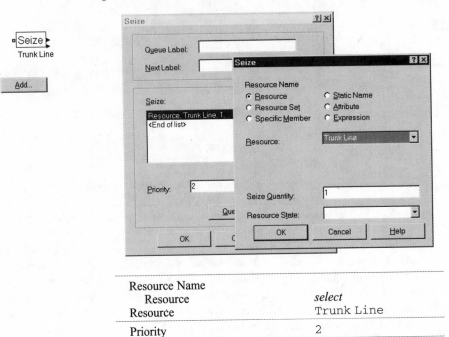

Resource Name	
Resource	*select*
Resource	Trunk Line
Priority	2

Display 8-10. The Seize Module: Allocation of Trunk Line

Having dealt with the arriving calls that are allocated a trunk line, we must now deal with those calls that receive a busy signal. In most environments where we use a Seize module, we want to represent an allocation of a resource and a queue where entities can wait if the resource is currently not available. However in this case, if a resource is not available, we don't want the entities (calls) to wait in a queue, but rather to be balked from the system. In effect, we want a zero-length queue.

To understand this concept, it might help if we spend a little time explaining how this process works in Arena. When an entity arrives at a Queue–Seize combination, it first checks the status of the resource. If the resource is available, then there are clearly no entities waiting in the queue—obviously, they would have already been allocated the available resource. If the resource is not available, the entity tries to enter the queue. If no space is available, the entity is balked from the queue. We specify the queue capacity in the Resource Queue dialog, Display 8-11.

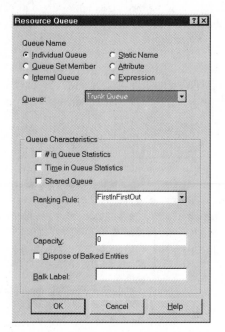

Queue Name	
Individual Queue	*select*
Queue	Trunk Queue

Queue Characteristics	
# in Queue Statistics	*uncheck*
Time in Queue Statistics	*uncheck*
Capacity	0

Display 8-11. The Trunk Allocation Seize Queue

When you initially open this dialog, you might note that the default is for an Internal Queue. Whenever an entity is potentially required to wait, as in the case of a Seize module, there must be a place for that entity to reside during that wait. In most cases, that place where entities wait is referred to as a *queue*. Arena is fully aware that a queue must precede each seize operation in the event that the resource is not available. Therefore, it automatically provides what is called an *Internal Queue* where waiting entities will reside. A user has no access to an internal queue; it has no name, cannot be animated, and statistics cannot be collected on the queue activities. However, if none of these features are required, an internal queue works just fine (and is certainly simple). In our example, we've requested an Individual Queue, instead of going with the Internal Queue, so we can assign a capacity of 0. We also turned off the statistics as there will never be any entities in the queue. When you assign a capacity to a queue, Arena needs to know what to do with any entities that might be balked from that queue. You have three options: dispose, send them to a module label, or use a direct connect (which we selected).

Note that when you accept the dialog, a second triangular exit point appears at the lower right side of the Seize module, Figure 8-4. This is the exit point for our balked entities.

Before we continue with the balked entities, we should clear up one rather minor point. You might have noticed (we bet you didn't) that we entered a priority of 2 when we filled in the main Seize dialog, Display 8-10. At the time, we thought we were being rather clever since we were going to show you how to set different priorities for seizing resources at different points in our model. As you'll see shortly when we develop the model section for the technical support activities, a returned call takes priority over an incoming call. Thus, our intent was for someone returning a call to request the same trunk-line resource with a priority of 1—the smaller the number, the higher the priority. At the time, it made sense. However, in retrospect, it wasn't really required. This is because there will never be any incoming calls in this Trunk Queue since it has a 0 capacity. So although we included it in our final model (mostly to give us an excuse to discuss Seize priorities, but partially to show you that even we don't always get our models right the first time), it really has no impact; we'd get the same result for any priority.

Lines Busy

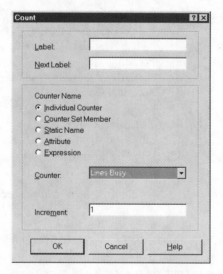

Counter Name	
Individual Counter	Lines Busy

Display 8-12. The Count Module: Counting the Balked Calls

The balked entities are sent to a Count module where the counter Lines Busy is incremented by 1, Display 8-12. This will give us a total count of all calls that receive a busy signal during the simulation run.

They're then directed to an Assign module where the variable Busy per Period is incremented by 1, Display 8-13. Recall that in the previous section we reset this variable to 0 at the start of each 30-minute period. Thus, at the end of each period, this variable will be equal to the total number of balked calls during *that* period. Later we'll show you how to plot this variable as part of our animation. These entities are finally sent to a Dispose module where they exit the system.

Assignment Type	
Variable	*select*
Variable	Busy per Period
Value	Busy per Period + 1

Display 8-13. Incrementing the Per Period Balks

8.8 Technical Support Calls

We've developed the basic logic steps for the technical support calls section of our model just as we did for the call arrivals section. The logic steps are as follows:

Determine product type
    Seize technical support person
    Save product type and call start time
    Delay for call
    Release technical support person and trunk line
    Tally call and line time
    If return call not required
        Dispose
    Else (return call required)
        Delay for investigation
        Seize trunk line and technical support person
        Delay for return call
        Release technical support person and trunk line
        Tally return call time
        Dispose

The Arena modules for this defined logic are shown in Figure 8-5. At first glance, this looks like a lot of modules, and it is; notice that many of these are duplicates because there are three product types. What you do is develop the model for the first product type and then use the copy and paste features. Of course, you'll have to edit the copied modules.

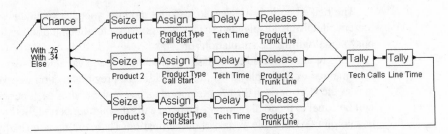

Figure 8-5. The Technical Support Calls Process Logic

Incoming calls first enter a Chance module where the product type is determined according to the specified probabilities. The calls are then sent to one of the three sets of Seize, Assign, Delay, and Release modules that represent the three product types. We'll lead you through only the Product Type 1 set of modules because the other two products are essentially the same.

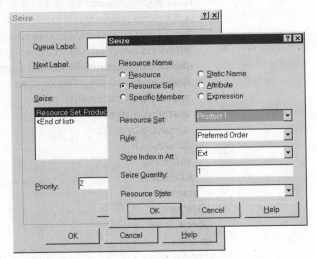

Resource Name	
Resource Set	*select*
Resource Set	Product 1
Store Index in Att	Ext
Priority	2
Queue Name	
Individual Queue	*select*
Queue	Product 1_Q

Display 8-14. Allocation of Technical Support Person

Product Type 1 calls are sent to a Seize module, Display 8-14, where they request a technical support person from the resource set `Product 1`. We've defaulted on the resource selection rule, Preferred Order, but that was done intentionally. Recall that technical support staff Molly, Anna, and Sammy were placed as the last resources in the set. Thus, if possible, we'd like to allocate Charity or Noah to a call as they can only handle Product Type 1 calls. This selection rule attempts to keep Molly, Anna, and Sammy available; remember that they can handle other call types as well. We've also stored the index of the resource allocated in the attribute `Ext` because we'll need to know which person took the call if further investigation and a return call are required. Finally, we've set the seize Priority to 2 and requested an Individual Queue (with a name) so we can obtain statistics on the number in queue and the waiting time of calls that are not immediately allocated a technical support person.

Once allocated a technical support resource, the entities are sent to an Assign module where two assignments are made, Display 8-15. The first is to save the value of the product type, both for later collection of statistics and in the event a return call is required. The second assignment is to record (or Mark) the time, for later statistical collection, that the call acquired the technical support resource. The value of the second assignment is entered as TNOW, which is an Arena variable that gives the current simulation clock time. This variable, like many Arena variables, can be accessed at any time, but it's not a user-assignable variable.

Assignment Type	
Attribute	*select*
Attribute	`Product Type`
Value	`1`
Assignment Type	
Attribute	*select*
Attribute	`Call Start`
Value	`TNOW`

Display 8-15. Assigning the Product Type and Call Start Time

The entity is then sent to the following Delay module where it is delayed by a value from the expression `Tech Time`, defined in our data section. Upon completion of the delay, the entity is sent to the Release module (Display 8-16) where both the technical support and `Trunk Line` resources are released. Note that in order to release the correct technical support resource, we need to reference both the resource set and the specific member of the set, stored in attribute `Ext` when we originally seized the resource. You might note that even though the two resources were seized at different places in our model (and at different times when we run our model), they're being released simultaneously.

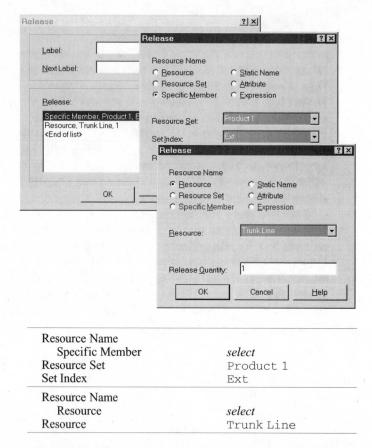

Resource Name	
Specific Member	*select*
Resource Set	Product 1
Set Index	Ext

Resource Name	
Resource	*select*
Resource	Trunk Line

Display 8-16. Releasing the Technical Support Person and Trunk Line

The entity that represents a completed call is then directed to the following Tally module (Display 8-17) where the technical support time is tallied. Note that entities from all three products enter this module. Therefore, we are using the Tally Set defined earlier and the Product Type attribute value that we saved in the earlier Assign module.

The next Tally module records the total line time for all three product types (Display 8-18). This time represents the entire time the customer was on the line; remember that we assigned (Marked) the attribute Call In when we created the original call.

Tech Calls

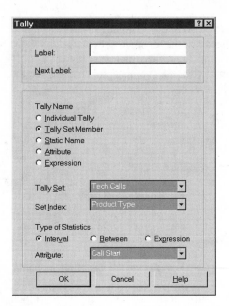

Tally Name	
Tally Set Member	*select*
Tally Set	Tech Calls
Set Index	Product Type
Type of Statistics	
Interval	*select*
Attribute	Call Start

Display 8-17. Tallying the Technical Support Time

Tally	Line Time
Attribute	Call In

Display 8-18. Tallying the Customer Line Time

   Although the call is completed, we now need to check to see if further investigation and a return call are required. We won't show the details of these modules, but all the information is provided in the following text or in Figure 8-6. The entity is first sent to a Chance module where 96% of the calls are considered complete and are directed to a Dispose module where they leave the system. The remaining 4% are sent to a Delay module where they are delayed by the time required for further investigation, which is conducted by undefined resources. If a call enters this delay at the end of a day, or replication, the call will be carried over into the next day as we do not reinitialize the system at the end of each run. After the delay, we determine the product type with a Choose module and direct the call to a Seize module, where we request the specific technical support person who originally serviced the call. We assure this by seizing a specific member from the resource set for the given product type using the attribute `Ext` as our index. You should note that this Seize module is given a Priority of 1, whereas all the other Seize modules requesting a trunk line or technical support person were given a Priority of 2. Thus, a returned call will be given priority over incoming calls.

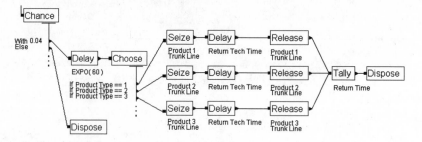

Figure 8-6. Technical Support Return Call Process Logic

The call is then delayed in the Delay module by the expression `Returned Tech Time` defined in our data section. Upon completion of the delay, the trunk line and technical support person are released and the call duration is tallied. The call is now complete and the entity is disposed.

8.9 Sales Calls

The logic for the sales calls is very similar to that described for the technical support calls. The number of modules required is much smaller as we do not have the complexities of dealing with multiple product types, different resources, and returned calls. The required logic steps for the sales calls are as follows (the modules representing these logic steps are given in Figure 8-7):

> Seize sales person
> Assign call start time
> Delay for call
> Release sales person
> Tally call time
> Release trunk line
> Tally line time
> Dispose

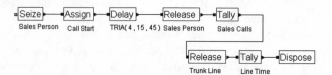

Figure 8-7. The Sales Calls Process Logic

We've used all of these modules in previous sections of this chapter; however, there is one difference that requires some explanation. We must acquaint you with how Arena allocates resources to waiting entities. We hope by now that this allocation process is fairly clear if all entities requesting a resource are resident in the same queue. However, if there are several places within a model (different Queue–Seize combinations) where the same resource could be allocated, some special rules apply. Let's first consider the various circumstances under which a resource could be allocated to an entity: an entity requests a resource and the resource is available, a resource becomes available and there are only entities in one of the queues, or a resource becomes available and there are entities in more than one queue requesting the resource. It should be rather obvious what occurs under the first two scenarios, but we'll cover them anyway.

If an entity requests a resource and the resource is available, you guessed it, the resource is allocated to the entity. If a resource becomes available and there are only entities in one of the queues, then the resource is allocated to the first entity in that queue. In this second case, the determining factor is the queue ranking rule used to order the entities. Arena automatically provides four queue ranking rules: First In, First Out (FIFO); Last In, First Out (LIFO); Low Value First; and High Value First. The default, FIFO, essentially ranks the entities in the order that they entered the queue. LIFO puts the most recent arrival at the front of the queue. The last two rules rank the queue based on an expression you define, which would usually be based on an attribute value. For example, as each entity arrives in the system, you might assign a due date to an attribute of that entity. Then if you selected Low Value First based on the due-date attribute, you'd have the equivalent of an earliest-due-date queue ranking rule. As each successive entity arrives in the queue, it would be placed in the queue based on increasing due dates.

The last case, where entities in more than one queue request the resource, is a bit more complicated. Arena first checks the seize priorities; if one of the seize priorities is a smaller number (higher priority) than the rest, the resource is allocated to the first entity in the queue preceding that seize. If all priorities are equal, Arena applies a default tie-breaking rule, and the resource is allocated based on the entity that has waited the longest. Thus, it's essentially a FIFO tie-breaking rule. This means that if your queues were ranked according to earliest due date, the entity that met that criterion might not always be allocated the resource. For example, a late job might have just entered a queue, whereas an early job may be at the front of another queue and have been waiting for a longer time.

As you would expect, Arena provides a solution to this potential problem in the form of a *shared queue*. A shared queue is just what its name implies—a single queue that can be shared by two or more seize activities. This allows you to define a single, shared queue where all entities requesting the resource will be placed. Although the seize activities may occur at many different places within your model, Arena will perform the bookkeeping to ensure that an entity in a shared queue continues in the proper place in the model logic when it's allocated a resource.

In our model, each sales call, and a small percentage of the order-status calls, will require a `Sales Person` resource. Since these activities are modeled separately, we'll use a shared queue when we attempt to seize a `Sales Person` resource. As both types of calls are allocated a `Sales Person` resource based on FIFO, or the longest waiting time, a shared queue is not required to assure that the proper call is allocated the resource. However, a shared queue also allows us to collect composite statistics easily on the number of calls waiting for a `Sales Person` and provides the ability to show all of these waiting calls in the same queue—if we decide to animate that queue. Also, it allows us to introduce this concept without presenting a different model!

In our model, we'll first seize a `Sales Person` resource, using a shared queue as shown in Display 8-19.

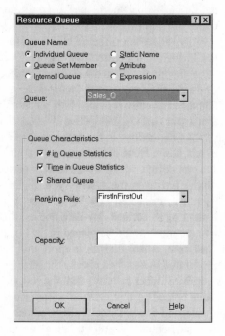

Queue Name		
Individual Queue	*select*	
Queue	`Sales_Q`	
Queue Characteristics		
Shared Queue	*check*	

Display 8-19. The Shared Sales Queue

We then save the start time of the call, delay for service, release the resource, tally the call time, release the line, tally the line time, and dispose of the entity. We've not shown the details, but you should be able to figure them out easily by referring to Figure 8-7. Note that we could have released both resources in the same Release module, as we did in our technical support section, but we chose to release them separately since we'll reuse the last three modules in the next section.

8.10 Order-Status Calls

The order-status calls are handled automatically, so at least initially they don't require a resource, other than the Trunk Line. The logic steps for order-status calls are:

> Assign call start time
> Delay for call
> If customer wants to speak to a real person
> > Seize sales person
> > Delay for call
> > Release sales person
> Tally call time
> Release trunk line
> Tally line time
> Dispose

The Arena logic is shown in Figure 8-8. We won't provide any details for this section as you have seen all the modules, and the information given in Figure 8-7 should be sufficient if you are building the model yourself. (If you have difficulties, we refer you to the file Mod_08_1.doe, which is our completed model.) One note: You should request a shared queue, Sales_Q, when entering the data for the Seize module. Also note that the three modules at the top right, Release–Tally–Dispose, are the same modules used for the sales call logic.

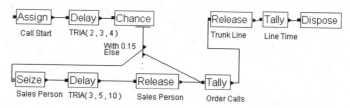

Figure 8-8. The Order-Status Calls Process Logic

By now you should have a fairly good understanding of how to use the modules from the Support panel, and hopefully, a better grasp of what comprises the major modules found in the Common panel; e.g., Server and Inspect. You might have noticed that the logic for the last two sections, sales and order-status calls, have several common components. By defining and assigning a call type and expressions for the time delays, we could have developed one general section of logic that would have handled both call types (we did consider this approach). However, this approach can sometimes become quite complicated, and this type of logic is seldom obvious to another modeler (or the client) if someone else has to use or modify your model. Unless you can combine significant amounts of model logic and make it relatively transparent, we recommend that you lay out each section of logic separately, even if doing so might be technically a bit redundant at times.

This completes the development of our model logic, and we're afraid that it's now the time to address a rather delicate issue—errors!

8.11 Finding and Fixing Model Errors

If you develop enough models, particularly large models, sooner or later you'll find that your model either will not run or will run incorrectly. It happens to all of us. If you're building a model and you've committed an error that Arena can detect and it prevents the model from running, Arena will attempt to help you quickly and easily find that error. We suspect that this has probably already happened to you by this time, so consider yourself lucky if that's not the case.

Typical errors that prevent a model from running include: undefined variables, attributes, stations or resources; unconnected modules; duplicate use of module names; misspelling of names; etc. Although Arena tries to prevent you from committing these types of errors, it can't give you maximum modeling flexibility without the possibility of an occasional error occurring. Arena will find most of these errors when you attempt to check or run your newly created model. To illustrate this feature or capability, let's intentionally insert some errors into the model we've been developing. Unless you're really good, we suggest that you save your model under a different name before you start putting in intentional errors.

Now let's put in two errors. First, select the connector between the Chance module and the Seize module for the sales call logic and delete this connector. Next, open the dialog for the first Assign module in the sales call logic and change the value of the assignment from TNOW to TNO. These two errors are typical of the types of errors that new (and sometimes experienced) modelers make. After making these two changes, use the *Run/Check* option or the Check button (✓) on the Run Interaction toolbar to check your model. An Arena Errors/Warnings window should open with the following message:

```
ERROR:

With,.76,65$,Yes:
With,.16,,Yes:
     ^
Block label is required, it cannot be defaulted.
11477:GGTLAB
```

Readers who are familiar with SIMAN might recognize this as an error because the connection from the second branch is missing. Note the module listing that represents the branch where the error was found, the up arrow (^) that points to the source of the error, and the message about the missing block label. If this doesn't help you find the source of the error, look for the Find and Edit buttons at the bottom of the window. If you puh the Find button, Arena will take you to and highlight the offending module. If you push the Edit button, Arena will take you directly to the dialog of that offending module. Thus, Arena attempts to help you find and fix the discovered error. So, push the Find button and add the connector that we deleted.

Having fixed this problem, a new check of the model will expose the second error:

```
ERROR:

A linker error was detected at the following block:

  *  102 167$              ASSIGN:Call Start=TNO:NEXT(46$);

Undefined symbol : TNO
11514:EELINK
```

This message tells you that the symbol TNO (the misspelled Arena variable TNOW) is undefined. Push the Edit button and Arena will take you directly to the dialog of the Assign module where we planted the error. Go ahead and fix the error. During checking, if you find that you've misused a name or just want to know where a variable is used, use the *Edit/Find* option to locate all occurrences of a string of characters. You might try this option using the string TNOW. If for some reason you forgot what the error was, use the *Run/Review Errors* option to reopen the error window with the last error message.

In Section 7.4.1, we briefly introduced you to the Arena command-driven Run Controller and used it to show and change the value of a variable while the simulation was running. We're now going to cover this feature in somewhat greater detail before we discuss the other options on the Run Interaction toolbar, which allows you to perform easily many of the functions provided by the Run Controller. The Run Controller can be used to find and eradicate bad logic or runtime errors. Before we go into the Run Controller, let's define three Arena variables that we'll use: NQ, MR, and NR. You have already seen two of these variables. There are many Arena variables that can be used in developing model logic or be viewed during runtime. The three of interest are:

NQ(Queue ID)	–	Number in queue
MR(Resource ID)	–	Resource capacity
NR(Resource ID)	–	Number of busy resource units

Note that these will generally change during the simulation.

You can think of Arena variables as magic words in that they provide information about the current simulation status. However, they're also reserved words in that you can't redefine their meanings or use them as names. We recommend that you look over the extensive list of Arena variables, which can be found in online help. You might start by looking at the variables summary and then look at the detailed definition if you need more information on a specific variable.

We're now going to use the Run Controller to illustrate just a few of the many commands available. We're not going to explain these commands in any detail; we leave it up to you to explore this capability further, and we recommend starting with online help.

Enter the Run Controller by the *Run/Command* option or the Command button (⊞) on the Run Interaction toolbar. This opens the command window. At this point, the model is ready to run, but it has not started yet. Notice that the current time is 0.0. Now let's use the VIEW command to look at the first eight lines of the model. Enter the command

```
0.0>view source 1-8
```

The response will be

```
Model name: MOD_08_1
1 69$      CREATE,1,0:,1;
2 76$      TRACE,-1,"-Entity Created\n":;
3 75$      ASSIGN:Picture=0:NEXT(0$);
4 0$       FINDJ,1,20:MAX( Arrive Rate(J) ):NEXT(63$);
5 63$      TRACE,-1,"-Making assignments\n":;
6 77$      ASSIGN:Max Rate=Arrive Rate(J):NEXT(62$);
7 62$      TRACE,-1,"-Disposing entity\n":;
8 78$      DISPOSE;
```

The Run Controller has listed the first eight lines of SIMAN code generated by our Arena model. This code corresponds to the sequence of the four modules, Create–FINDJ–Assign–Dispose, that we used to find and keep the maximum Arrive Rate. Note that Arena has included three extra Trace blocks and an Assign block that are part of the modules we placed. Now that we know what the first eight lines of code are, let's watch what happens when we run that code. First, we need to change the Run Controller settings so it will display what happens. We do this with the SET TRACE command, so enter

```
0.0>SET TRACE *
```

This will activate a trace of all actions performed by Arena/SIMAN when we run our model. Let's only let it run for these eight lines of code. Use the STEP command to do this by requesting that Arena step through the first, or next, nine blocks of the model. We enter the command as

```
0.0>step 9
```

Arena/SIMAN responds with

```
SIMAN System Trace Beginning at Time: 0.0
Seq#  Label            Block       System Status Change
Time: 0.0  Entity: 14
    1 70$             CREATE
                                  Arrival stream terminated
    2 77$             TRACE
    3 76$             ASSIGN
                                  Entity 14 picture changed to 0
    4 0$              FINDJ
                                  J set to 11
    5 63$             TRACE
    6 77$             ASSIGN
                                  MAX RATE set to 110.0
    7 69$             TRACE
    8 79$             DISPOSE
                                  Disposed entity 14
Time: 0.0  Entity: 16
SIMAN Run Controller.
*  139 285$             CREATE,1:660;
```

A single entity is created at time 0.0, and the create stream is terminated, as planned. It enters the FINDJ module and finds that Arrive Rate(11) has the maximum value. Thus, it sets J equal to 11. The entity is then sent to the Assign module where Max Rate is assigned, and the entity is directed to the Dispose module where it's disposed. Note that the next step would be to create the entity that will set the time period variable.

Now let's turn off the trace, using the CANCEL command, and advance the simulation time to 77 using the GO UNTIL command.

```
0.0>cancel trace *
***   All trace options canceled.
0.0>go until 77
Break at time: 77.0
```

We are now at simulation time 77.0, so let's see what we have in the queue waiting for a salesperson. We'll use the SHOW command to find the number in queue, the queue number, and the status of all other queues in the model, as follows,

```
77.0>show NQ(Sales_Q)
    NQ(SALES_Q) =   3
77.0>show Sales_Q
    SALES_Q =        2
77.0>show NQ(*)
    NQ(    1) =      0
    NQ(    2) =      3
    NQ(    3) =      3
    NQ(    4) =      1
    NQ(    5) =      0
```

As shown, there are three entities currently in the Sales_Q, and the number assigned by Arena to that queue is also 2. When Arena checks a model, it assigns every resource, queue, station, etc., a number that it uses internally to reference these items during the run. The number that it assigns to each item depends on how it writes out the experiment frame. A word of caution—if you edit and save your model, Arena may write it out slightly differently; thus the next time you run the model, the Sales_Q may not be number 2. There are ways to force the Sales_Q always to be number 2, and we'll discuss them later in this chapter. Now let's look at the entities in the queue by using the VIEW QUEUE command as follows

```
77.0>view queue Sales_Q
***   Queue contains 3 Entities   ***

***   Rank 1: Entity number 29
Station attribute (M)   = 0
Sequence attribute (NS) = 0
Sequence index attribute (IS) = 0
PRODUCT TYPE = 0.0
CALL IN = 74.8588
QUEUETIME = 75.3399
CALL START = 0.0
EXT = 0.0

***   Rank 2: Entity number 25
Station attribute (M)   = 0
Sequence attribute (NS) = 0
Sequence index attribute (IS) = 0
PRODUCT TYPE = 0.0
CALL IN = 74.8588
QUEUETIME = 75.3399
CALL START = 0.0
EXT = 0.0
```

```
***   Rank 3: Entity number 19
Station attribute (M)  = 0
Sequence attribute (NS) = 0
Sequence index attribute (IS) = 0
PRODUCT = 0.0
CALL IN = 75.4231
QUEUETIME = 75.5908
CALL START = 0.0
EXT = 0.0
```

This displays the internal entity number and all of the attribute values for each entity. You might note that the attribute QUEUETIME is an attribute defined by one of the modules we placed.

Since there are calls waiting in the queue for a Sales Person, all units of the resource currently available must be allocated. We can check this by using the SHOW command as follows

```
77.0>show NR(Sales Person), MR(Sales Person)
    NR(SALES PERSON) =   3
    MR(SALES PERSON) =   3
```

Just for fun, let's add some resources to the pool using the ASSIGN command

```
77.0>assign MR(Sales Person) =   6
```

This increases the number available to six. If we step forward, Arena should allocate the extra resources to the waiting calls. Let's do this with the STEP command and then check the status of the queue and resource.

```
77.0>step
SIMAN Run Controller.
*99 166$   ASSIGN:j=j;
77.0>show NQ(2),NR(Sales Person)
    NQ(2) =        0
    NR(SALES PERSON) =   6
```

As expected, the additional resources were allocated and the queue is now empty. It may surprise you that we can change the value for the number of resources on the fly, but that's actually what a schedule does. Just be aware that there are some Arena variables you can't change; e.g., NQ and NR. Now close out the command window and terminate the simulation.

This should give you a good idea how the Run Controller works. It really allows you to get at the SIMAN model that's running underneath; however, it's not for the timid, and you really need to spend some time with it and also have at least a cursory understanding of the SIMAN language.

There are easier, or at least less frightening, ways to check the model accuracy or find logic errors. The most obvious is through the use of an animation that shows what the model logic is doing. However, there are times when you must dig a little deeper in order to resolve a problem. The Run Interaction toolbar provides some of the tools you may need. We've already looked at the Check and Command options, so now let's look at the

Trace option. Selecting the *Run/Trace* option or pushing the Trace button opens the Trace dialog shown in Display 8-20. Recall the Trace blocks that were added by Arena when we viewed the model source in the Run Controller; selecting any of the Module trace options on the left side of the dialog will cause those trace messages to be written to the command window or to the Arena output file. These options don't display the detailed block trace, but only those messages. The detailed block trace we observed earlier can be obtained by checking the Enable Block Trace option on the right side of the dialog. The Save Trace to File option (the default) will write all trace statements both to the command window and to the Arena output file.

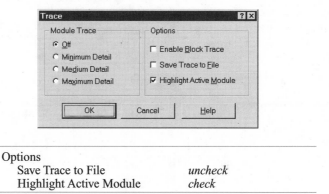

Options
Save Trace to File		*uncheck*
Highlight Active Module		*check*

Display 8-20. The Trace Option

We've checked the Highlight Active Module option. Save these settings (click OK) and return to the main model window. Now use the *View/Views/All* option or the View All button to make your entire model visible in the model window. Now use the *View/Views/Region* option or the View Region button to select only that portion of the model that contains the logic modules. In other words, you don't need to include any data modules or any animation that you (or we, if you're using our model) have added.

Now push the Start Over button (◄) to start the model run. Next push the Show Modules button (⬚), and you'll see all the modules you placed visible in the window during the run. Arena assumes that normally you don't want to see the modules during the run, so it doesn't show them unless you specifically request that they be visible. If you want to see the connections, use the *View/Layers* option or the Layers button (≋) to bring up the dialog shown in Display 8-21. You should do this while you're still in run mode. Check the Layers option to cause the connections, connection points, and the operand values to show during the run as well.

Logic   *check*

Display 8-21. The Layers Option

Pushing the Go button (▶), you should now see various modules being highlighted as the model runs. Arena is highlighting each module that an entity passes through. However, on most computers, this is happening so fast you'll typically only see the modules highlighted where the entity stops; e.g., Delay and Dispose modules. If you don't believe us, use the Region option to zoom in so that only one or two modules fill the entire screen. Now press the Go or Step button and you'll see that Arena jumps around and tries to show you only the active modules. Again, it's generally working so fast that not all the modules are highlighted, but it does at least try to show them. If you've selected these settings and your starting window doesn't contain all the logic modules, Arena will change the window view each time it needs to show a module that isn't currently visible. It basically puts that module in the center of your window, and that view remains until it encounters another module that's not in the current view. Although this allows you to see more of the active modules, you may get dizzy watching the screen jump around. So let's pause your run and go back to the view showing all the logic modules. Hit the Trace button and uncheck the box to Highlight Active Module. For now, leave these settings active.

Now let's assume that you have a problem with your model and you're suspicious of the Release module in the sales order logic. It would be nice if the simulation would stop when it reaches this module; there are three ways to cause this to happen. You could enter the command window and figure out the right setting or take the easy way out and use the *Run/Break* option or the Break button (✋). Before you activate this option, we need to know the *module ID* of the selected Release module. Highlight that module (make sure you're in run mode) and double-click. The module dialog will appear with the module ID at the top. Note that you can view the module entries but you can't make changes during the run; those entries are grayed out. In our model, the module ID is Release 13 (if you constructed your own model, it could be a different number). Close the Release dialog and open the Break dialog (push the Add button). The Break dialog provides four options. The first three are Break on Time, which causes the model run to pause at the entered time much like the Go Until command in the Run Controller; Break on Condition, which allows you to enter a condition (such as NQ(Sales_Q)>3) that would cause the run to pause whenever this condition is satisfied; and Break on Entity, which would cause the run to pause whenever the selected entity is about to become active. For the third option, you need to know the entity ID number, which can be found using the Run Controller or by double-clicking on the entity picture during a simulation run. The final option (the one we want) is Break on Module, which will cause the run to pause whenever an entity enters the selected module. For our example, enter Release 14 as shown in Display 8-22.

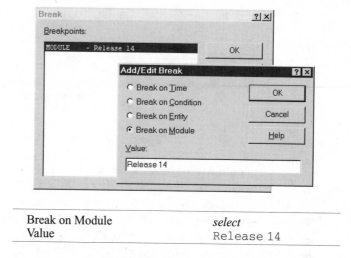

| Break on Module | *select* |
| Value | Release 14 |

Display 8-22. The Break Option

Accept this entry and push the Go button. Your model will run until an entity arrives at the selected Release module—it may take a while! Note that an exclamation mark (!) is added to the name in the module handle. Once you pause the run, you can push the Go button, and the run will continue until the next entity arrives at this module. When you no longer want this break, re-enter the dialog and delete the selection.

There is an easier way to activate a Break on Module option. Highlight the selected module and push the Break button. When you want to turn off this option, repeat the action. Module breaks provide the capability to pause your model under a variety of conditions, and it can be very useful in detecting model logic errors.

Another good way to monitor what's going on during a run is to define *watches*. Before we do this, we suggest that you turn off your Trace options and all Module breaks. Now use the *Run/Watch* option or the Watch button (&&) to open the Watch window. Let's add two watches—one for the number in the sales queue and another for the number of busy Sales People, as shown in Display 8-23. You can add as many watches as you want, and if you default on the label, Arena will use the expression as the default label.

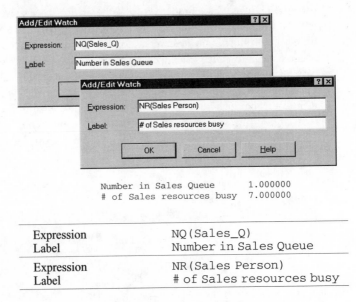

```
Number in Sales Queue     1.000000
# of Sales resources busy   7.000000
```

Expression	NQ(Sales_Q)
Label	Number in Sales Queue
Expression	NR(Sales Person)
Label	# of Sales resources busy

Display 8-23. The Watch Option

Before you close this window, select the *Window/Tile* option. This will display both the Model window and the Watch window at the same time (make the Watch window active by clicking in it). If you push the Go button with the watch window active, as the model runs, you'll see the values change for the two expressions we requested. If you had an animation, you'd also see the animation. However, be aware that the values for the watch expressions are only updated when the Watch window is the active window. You can change this by selecting the Simultaneous Watch Window Update option on the Run Setup dialog's Miscellaneous tab.

Finally, during a run, you might want to see the current summary report or status of the model. The last button on the Run Interaction toolbar provides this option. Select the *Run/Report* option or push the Report button (🗒) to open the Report window. At any time during a run, you can request all or a portion of the summary report. You can also request summary information on the model status; e.g., queues, resources, and even what's on the event calendar. You can request this information when the model is running or when the model is in pause mode. Just like the Watch window, you could have an animation running and periodically request a summary and never stop the run. You should note that if you have repeated requests, the new information is added after the information that you previously requested. Thus, you might want to clear the display to make sure you're viewing only the current information. Otherwise, you may have to scroll down in the Report window to see the report you want.

Even if you don't use the Run Controller, the options available on the Run Interaction toolbar provide the capability to detect model logic errors without your needing to become a SIMAN expert. We recommend that you take a simple animated model and practice using these tools so you'll understand now how they work. You could wait until you need them, but then you're not only trying to find an error, but also trying to learn several new tools! Now that you know how to use these tools, let's animate the model.

8.12 Animating the Model

Earlier we decided not to animate our model in the normal fashion, but to provide plots for the key variables of interest. The chosen variables to be plotted are:

> Number of balks per period
> Number of calls in queue—sales calls and technical support calls by type
> Number of available technical support staff by product type (idle resources)

We defined the variable `Per Period Balk` in our model precisely for the first plot, although the value for the nth period of this variable is really the number of balks for the previous period, n-1. We also defined individual queues in the model to hold the waiting calls (`Product 1_Q`, `Product 2_Q`, `Product 3_Q`, and `Sales_Q`). Thus, we can use the Arena variable NQ(Queue ID) for these plots.

The last set of plots is an equine of a dissimilar hue. The value of interest is the *sum* of the currently available and idle resources by product type. There is no Arena variable that can provide this directly. For one thing, these are *sets* of individual resources. Also, several of these resources (Molly, Anna, and Sammy) are members of more than one set. In this case, we need to define the desired variable for our plots explicitly. We could do this directly when we place our plots, using the Animate module or the Plot construct from the Animate toolbar, or we could define the variables of interest in the Expressions module. We've chosen the latter method. In developing these expressions, we know that the Arena variables MR and NR give us the number of resources currently available and the number of resources currently busy, respectively. Thus, the difference between these two variables for any resource is the value of interest. Therefore, we need to add three expression to our Expression module as follows:

```
Available 1 = MR(Charity) - NR(Charity) + MR(Noah) - NR(Noah) + MR(Molly) -
    NR(Molly) + MR(Anna) - NR(Anna) + MR(Sammy) - NR(Sammy)
Available 2 = MR(Tierney) - NR(Tierney) + MR(Sean) - NR(Sean) + MR(Deb) -
    NR(Deb) + MR(Anna) - NR(Anna) + MR(Sammy) - NR(Sammy)
Available 3 = MR(Shelley) - NR(Shelley) + MR(Jenny) - NR(Jenny) +
    MR(Christie) - NR(Christie) + MR(Molly) - NR(Molly) + MR(Anna) -
    NR(Anna) + MR(Sammy) - NR(Sammy)
```

We then placed eight plots using the Animate module. Since we've already covered this module, we'll only provide the highlights. Selecting or entering the correct information in the Animate dialog is relatively straightforward, except when you define the plot for the three new variables we just defined. In this case, you must select the Other option for the Data Object and enter the name yourself; e.g., `Available 1`. We then opened each of the plot dialogs and set the time period to 660 (one day) and selected the Stepped, Refresh Full, and Bounding Box options. The Information specific to each plot is given in Table 8-4.

Table 8-4. Animation Plot Data

Plot Variable	Minimum Value	Maximum Value	# of History Points
Per Period Balk	0	25	100
Available 1	0	5	200
Available 2	0	5	200
Available 3	0	5	200
NQ(Sales_Q)	0	10	500
NQ(Product 1_Q)	0	10	500
NQ(Product 2_Q)	0	10	500
NQ(Product 3_Q)	0	10	500

Some words of advice if you decide to attempt this feat for this or any other model. If you have multiple plots in the same animation, generally you want all of them to have the same basic look and feel. Place your first plot, enter the data, choose your colors, size the plot, and attach any desired labels. While you're developing this look and feel, you might want to consider activating the Snap option ( ). This will easily allow you to reproduce additional plots with the same exact size and spacing. For our animation, we added a plot identifier and values for the Y axis using the Text option (**A**) from the Draw toolbar. Once you have a complete plot, use the Select feature to capture all the objects (module, text, etc.) that comprise the plot, then Copy and Paste to make duplicates. Position these duplicates or copies wherever you want them and edit the duplicates to develop the additional plots you want. This approach will eliminate a lot of busy work and also ensure that your plots are consistent.

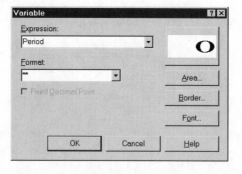

Expression	Period
Format	**

Display 8-24. The Variables Option–Animate Toolbar

In addition to the eight Animate modules (selecting only the Plot options), we also added two variables and labels to our animation. We used the Variable button (▥) from the Animate toolbar to place the variables `Period` and NREP on our animation. We defined and used the variable `Period` in our model logic. The Arena variable NREP returns the current replication number, which in our model represents the current day. Display 8-24 shows the primary entries for the Variable dialog. In addition, we entered the Font dialog and selected a bold font style, the Border dialog and selected white, and the Area dialog and selected white. We've not shown the display for the NREP Variable dialog.

Finally, we decided to add a clock to our animation so you can accurately relate the current model status being displayed by the animation to the time of day. Recall that our day starts at 8:00 AM and ends at 7:00 PM. You'll find a Clock button (⊕) on the Animate toolbar that will allow you to start the clock display (either analog or digital) at 8:00 AM. Unfortunately, we decided earlier not to clear our system between replications because we didn't want to lose the returned technical support calls that needed to be completed on the next business day. Thus, the simulation time, TNOW, continues to increase rather than restarting at zero for each replication. As a result, the Arena clock, which is based on TNOW, would only be accurate for the first day (if you don't believe us, try it). So we decided to get tricky and create our own digital clock. To do this, we separated our clock display into two Variables separated by a colon. The first Variable represents the current hour, and the second represents the current minute. Now we just have to figure out how to calculate these values.

Let's start with the calculation for the current hour. The expression

$$\texttt{AINT(8+(Period-1)/2)}$$

will return the current hour using our variable `Period`. The function AINT is one of the many *math functions* automatically provided by Arena (see online help for a complete list). This function returns the integer portion of the enclosed expression; i.e., it *truncates* the value defined by the expression. We'll leave it to you to figure out the expression. This displays the current hour based on a 24-hour clock. If we don't want 1:00 to be displayed as 13:00, we need to modify our expression as follows,

$$\texttt{AINT(8+(Period-1)/2) - (Period>10)*12}$$

which will give us what we want. Note that we've used a *logical expression* so that we subtract 12 only when the period is greater than 10 (Period 11 is the time from 1:00 to 1:30). To display the hour on the animation, we simply use the Variable option from the Animate toolbar and enter the above expression rather than a simple variable name.

To calculate the current minute is easier, although it's certainly not obvious. We use the expression

$$\texttt{AMOD(TNOW,60)}$$

which will return the value needed. The function AMOD is another Arena math function that returns the real remainder of TNOW divided by 60. The above expression is equivalent to the following,

$$\text{TNOW} - ((\text{AINT}(\text{TNOW}/60))*60).$$

If you want to be assured that both the hour and the minute variable displays are exactly the same size, we suggest you place and size the hour variable first. Then copy, paste, and edit for the minute variable.

Finally (since we're already being cute), we decided to add an AM/PM display with our clock. We used the Global button () from the Animate toolbar to accomplish this. When you push this button, the Global Picture Placement window opens, see Display 8-25. This window is very similar to the entity and resource picture windows. You first enter an expression (in our case, the Variable `Period`) and then associate pictures with *trigger values* of that expression. You can have as many (trigger value, picture) pairs as you need to cover the range of pictures you need to display. You create each picture just like we did for entities and resources. You're basically creating what's called a *global picture* that will change based on the current value of the entered expression. In our model, the expression `Period` is set to 0 at the start of each replication. It's immediately incremented to a value of 1, and every 30 time units thereafter, it's again incremented by 1. The initial symbol that will be displayed is the AM symbol. When the period variable reaches 8 (12:00 noon), the symbol will change to PM and remain that way until the end of the day or replication.

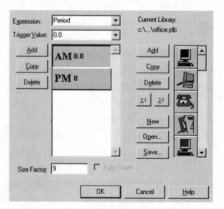

Expression	Period
Trigger Value	0.0
Trigger Value	8

Display 8-25. The Global Picture Placement

To ensure that both symbols were the same size, we created the first symbol, AM, and then used the copy option to edit it for the PM symbol. When you close the window, you need to place your global symbol—very much like you place text. After placing the symbol, you may have to change its size. You can do this in the model window, or you can re-open the Global Picture Placement window and change the Size Factor, which will re-scale your symbol. We also added a label and put boxes around our variables and symbol; the final animation is shown in Figure 8-9, which is from the first replication.

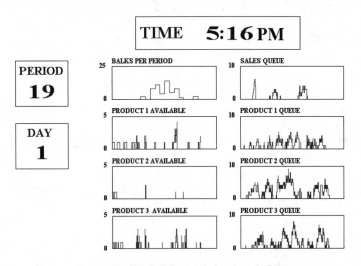

Figure 8-9. The Call Center Animation via Plots

The summary report for the fourth replication is given in Figure 8-10. If you haven't been building your own model as you've been reading through this chapter, now would be a good time to open the model we built (Mod_08_1.doe) and poke around to make sure you understand the concepts and features we've presented.

```
                       Summary for Replication 4 of 10

Project:   Call Center
Analyst:   Ernestine

Replication ended at time        : 2640.0
Statistics were cleared at time: 1980.0
Statistics accumulated for time: 660.0

                              TALLY VARIABLES

Identifier              Average    Half Width    Minimum    Maximum    Observations
Return 1 Call           64.708     (Insuf)       27.962     86.339     3
Line Time               18.47      (Corr)        2.3337     66.634     574
Product 1_Q Queue Time  4.9153     (Insuf)       .00000     21.372     98
Sales_Q Queue Time      .16402     (Insuf)       .00000     8.4108     89
Product 2_Q Queue Time  9.4050     (Insuf)       .00000     53.683     145
Order Calls             4.3270     (Insuf)       2.1928     11.268     40
Product 3 Call          9.1980     (Insuf)       3.6576     17.475     211
```

```
Product 3_Q Queue Time    11.192    (Insuf)     .00000     36.069     211
Product 2 Call             9.2006    (Insuf)    3.2220      16.616     145
Return 3 Call             82.288     (Insuf)   31.999      187.22       4
Product 1 Call             9.4230    (Insuf)    3.4474      16.882      98
Sales Calls               20.858     (Insuf)    7.0619      36.884      80
Return 2 Call            104.13      (Insuf)   21.982      178.45       7
```

DISCRETE-CHANGE VARIABLES

Identifier	Average	Half Width	Minimum	Maximum	Final Value
Jenny Busy	.60195	(Insuf)	.00000	1.0000	.00000
Sean Available	.72727	(Insuf)	.00000	1.0000	.00000
Tierney Busy	.57027	(Insuf)	.00000	1.0000	.00000
Trunk Line Busy	16.170	(Corr)	.00000	26.000	.00000
# in Product 3_Q	3.5782	(Corr)	.00000	14.000	.00000
# in Product 2_Q	2.0662	(Insuf)	.00000	10.000	.00000
Jenny Available	.72727	(Insuf)	.00000	1.0000	.00000
Sales Person Busy	2.6000	(Insuf)	.00000	7.0000	.00000
# in Product 1_Q	.72986	(Insuf)	.00000	7.0000	.00000
Sammy Busy	.66308	(Insuf)	.00000	1.0000	.00000
Deb Busy	.58394	(Insuf)	.00000	1.0000	.00000
Deb Available	.72727	(Insuf)	.00000	1.0000	.00000
Anna Busy	.64276	(Insuf)	.00000	1.0000	.00000
Charity Busy	.58688	(Insuf)	.00000	1.0000	.00000
Shelley Busy	.70192	(Insuf)	.00000	1.0000	.00000
Sean Busy	.54337	(Insuf)	.00000	1.0000	.00000
Tierney Available	.72727	(Insuf)	.00000	1.0000	1.0000
Sammy Available	.72727	(Insuf)	.00000	1.0000	.00000
Molly Busy	.42976	(Insuf)	.00000	1.0000	.00000
Noah Available	.72727	(Insuf)	.00000	1.0000	.00000
Molly Available	.57576	(Insuf)	.00000	1.0000	1.0000
# in Sales_Q	.02212	(Insuf)	.00000	2.0000	.00000
Christie Available	.72727	(Insuf)	.00000	1.0000	.00000
Charity Available	.72727	(Insuf)	.00000	1.0000	1.0000
Shelley Available	.72727	(Insuf)	.00000	1.0000	1.0000
Noah Busy	.48301	(Insuf)	.00000	1.0000	.00000
Christie Busy	.65719	(Insuf)	.00000	1.0000	.00000
Anna Available	.72727	(Insuf)	.00000	1.0000	.00000
Sales Person Available	5.7272	(Insuf)	3.0000	7.0000	3.0000
Trunk Line Available	26.000	(Insuf)	26.000	26.000	26.000

COUNTERS

Identifier	Count	Limit
Lines Busy	99	Infinite

Figure 8-10. The Call Center Summary Report

We could easily stop here, but let's assume that after developing this model your boss decided to show it to his/her boss. Well, as you can imagine, nerdy plots just won't cut it! These people need to see an animation that looks something like a call center. Development of such an animation won't add any analysis value to the simulation, but it might add value to your career.

Remember that as we initially constructed our model, we made a conscious decision to delete all animation objects that were provided by the modules. Not all is lost because these objects and more can be found in the Animate toolbar. So let's start our animation with the Technical Support area. We first animated the support staff using the Resource button (⬥⬥) from the Animate toolbar. When you click on this button, it opens the Resource Picture Placement window, just like when you double-clicked on a resource picture provided by Arena. We selected Charity from the resource list and opened the office picture library, Office.plb, provided with the Arena software. There we found a picture of a person sitting at a desk with an idle phone and a second picture with the person talking on the phone. We copied the first picture for our Idle picture and the second for the Busy picture. We started with the first picture for our inactive state and removed the person so the desk was unattended. We then closed the window and placed our resource. After sizing our resource, we used the Text option to label it. Then we made a copy of these two objects and changed the identifiers to represent Noah. We repeated this for Tierney, but changed the color of the shirt in the Idle and Busy pictures. Our plan was to have different shirt colors to represent the different capabilities of the support staff. After we placed all our support staff resources, we used the Queue button (🔳) to place the three product queues in front of our resource pictures. We labeled our queues and put a box around each to show the queue area. The results are shown in Figure 8-11.

Figure 8-11. The Animated Support Area

You've already seen and used all of these animation objects, although you haven't taken them from the Animate toolbar. Now let's deal with the rest of the system. The sales staff is represented by a single resource with a Capacity controlled by a Schedule. Thus, we can't use the same animation approach that we used for the technical support staff. Basically, what we'd like to show is the number of busy sales people and the number who are currently idle. We could use the Variable option and show the value of NR(Sales Person) to tell us how many are busy, but what if we want a more graphic picture? We also have to deal with the initial time spent listening to the first message and selecting an option, the second message for the technical support calls, and the order calls that don't require a resource other than a trunk line. As it turns out, a solution to all these is to employ Storages. Recall that we briefly discussed Storages in Section 7.3 when we covered transporters.

To use this concept, we first opened the Delay modules for the message delays, the order call delay, and the sales call delay and entered a Storage for each. We named these Storages Message 1, Message 2, Message 3, and Sales Calls, respectively. We then used the Storage button (⊞) from the Animate panel to place them on our animation. Recall that an animated storage looks identical to an animated queue, except perhaps for color. We then placed the sales queue and used the Variable option with the Expression

$$MR(Sales\ Person) - NR(Sales\ Person)$$

to represent the number of idle sales persons. Likewise, we used the Expression

$$MR(Trunk\ Line) - NR(Trunk\ Line)$$

to place the number of available trunk lines on our animation as a variable. We added some text, drew some more boxes, and copied the period indicator from our plot animation. Our final animation is shown in Figure 8-12.

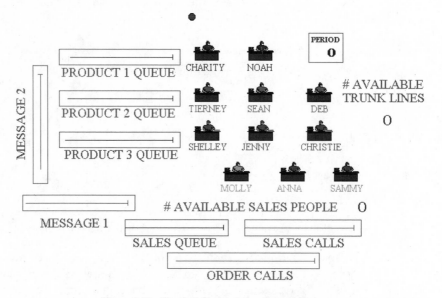

Figure 8-12. The Call Center Animation via Storages

Our animation appears to be complete, but if we'd run the model, we'd quickly realize that although our technical support resources and variables are changing, we wouldn't see any calls in our message areas or in the queues. (We actually made this mistakes initially!) It appears that we don't have an entity picture because it normally comes with the Simulate module, but we deleted it. No problem; just use the Entity button (▚) from the good old Animate toolbar to create your entity picture. We elected to change the standard red square to a rather stunning red circle, just to be different. If you look near the top of Figure 8-12, you'll see our work of art.

Now if you run the animation you should see something like Figure 8-13. As you can see, Charity, Deb, and Shelley are out to lunch; Tierney is anxiously awaiting her next call; and the rest of the support staff are talking on the phone.

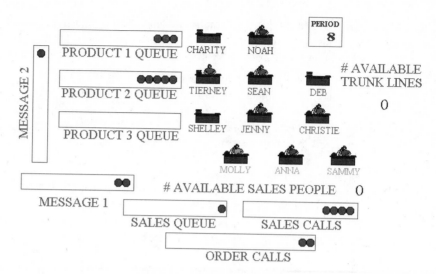

Figure 8-13. The Animated Call Center

We also managed to find a time when we had calls in all our storages and in all but one queue. All the trunk lines are currently in use and there is no idle sales staff. Although the animation has no moving parts, as in moving entities, it still provides a visual picture of the system in operation.

8.13 Summary and Forecast

This is our last general "tutorial" chapter on modeling with Arena. It has gone into some depth on the detailed lower-level modeling capabilities, as well as correspondingly detailed topics like debugging and fine-tuned animation. While we've mentioned how you can access and blend in the SIMAN simulation language, we've by no means covered it; see Pegden, Shannon, and Sadowski (1995) for the complete treatment of SIMAN. At this point, you should be armed with a formidable arsenal of modeling tools to allow you to attack many systems, choosing constructs from various levels as appropriate.

There are, however, more modeling constructs and, frankly, "tricks" that you might find handy. These we take up next in Chapter 9.

8.14 Exercises

8.1 Develop a model of the problem we described in Chapter 2 and modeled as Model 3.1, but this time only using modules from the Support panel (except that you may use the Simulate and Resource modules from the Common panel). Use the Plot and Variable features from the Animate toolbar to complete your model. Run it for 15 minutes and compare your results to what we got earlier.

8.2 Rebuild Model 5.1, but this time only using modules from the Support panel (except that you may use the Simulate and Resource modules from the Common panel). Use the Variable feature from the Animate toolbar. You'll also need to use the Station module from the Support panel and the Route module from Transfer panel, neither of which we explicitly covered in this chapter, but you should be able to explore these kinds of things on your own, using online help.

8.3   Stacks of paper arrive at a trimming process with interarrival times of EXPO(10); all times are in minutes. There are two trimmers, a primary and secondary. All arrivals are sent to the Primary trimmer after a travel time of 3 minutes. If the queue in front of the primary trimmer is shorter than 5, the stack of paper enters that queue to wait to be trimmed by the primary trimmer, an operation of duration TRIA(9, 12, 15). If there are already 5 stacks in the primary queue, the stack is balked (with a zero transfer time) to the secondary trimmer (which has an infinite queue capacity) for trimming, of duration TRIA(17, 19, 21). After the primary trimmer has trimmed 25 stacks, it must be shut down for cleaning, which lasts EXPO(30). During this time, the stacks in the queue for the primary trimmer wait for it to become available. Animate and run your simulation for 5,000 minutes. Collect statistics for cycle time by trimmer, resource utilization, number in queue, and time in queue. So far as possible, use modules from the Support and Transfer panels.

8.4   Do Exercise 5.1 using modules from the Support and Transfer panels, except that you may use the Simulate and Resource modules from the Common panel.

8.5   Trucks arrive with EXPO(9) interarrival times (all times are in minutes) to an unload area that has three docks. The unload times are TRIA(26, 28, 30), TRIA(24, 26 , 28) and TRIA(23, 25, 27) for docks 1, 2 and 3, respectively. If there is an empty dock, the truck proceeds immediately to that dock. Assume zero travel times to all docks. If there is more than one empty dock, the truck places preference on the higher-numbered dock (3, 2, 1). If all the docks are busy, it chooses the dock with the minimum number of trucks waiting. If there is a tie, it places preference on the lowest numbered dock (1, 2, 3). Develop a simulation model with modules from the Support panel, using Choose modules to implement the selection logic. You'll also need the Simulate and Resource modules from the Common panel. Run your model for 2,000 minutes and collect statistics on dock utilization, number in queue, time in queue, and the time in system.

8.6   Rework Exercise 8.5 using the FINDJ module from the Blocks panel to implement the decision logic. Hint: Define Sets for both the dock resources and dock queues, and then search over the sets.

8.7   A small warehouse provides work-in-process storage for a manufacturing facility that produces four different part types. The part-type percentages and inventory costs per part are:

Part Type	Percentage	Inventory Cost per Part
1	20	$5.50
2	30	$6.50
3	30	$8.00
4	20	$10.50

The interpretation of "inventory cost per part" is as follows. Each part in inventory contributes an amount from the last column of the above table to the total cost (value) of inventory being held at the moment. For instance, if the current inventory is three units of Part 1, none of Part 2, five of Part 3, and one of Part 4, then the current inventory cost is $3 \times \$5.50 + 0 \times \$6.50 + 5 \times \$8.00 + 1 \times \$10.50 = \$67.00$. As parts arrive and depart, as described below, this inventory cost will rise and fall.

Parts arrive with TRIA(1.5, 2.0, 2.8) interarrival times (all times are in minutes). Two cranes store and retrieve parts with a travel time of UNIF(1.2, 2.9), each way. Requests for part removal follow the same pattern as for arrivals. If no part is available, the request is not filled. All part requests are given priority over part storages, and priority is given to retrieving based on part cost.

For part arrivals, increment the inventory cost upon arrival, and increment the total number of parts in inventory after the part is stored. For part requests, decrement the total number of parts in inventory as soon as you know there is a part to retrieve, and decrement the inventory cost after the part is retrieved.

Develop your model using modules from the Support panel (except that you'll need the Simulate, Variables, Resource, and Statistics modules from the Common panel). Run your model for 24 hours starting with four of each part type in the warehouse. Collect statistics on the crane utilization, the inventory cost, the number of each part type in the warehouse, and the number of unfilled requests due to having no parts of the requested type.

8.8 Develop a model of a three-workstation serial production line with high reject rates, 7% after each workstation. Parts rejected after the first workstation are sent to scrap. Parts rejected after the second workstation are returned to the first workstation where they are reworked, which requires a fresh "draw" from the processing-time distribution but increased by 50% from the distribution of the original operation. (This penalty factor of 1.5 applies only at Workstation 1 and not at Workstation 2 when the part returns to it.) Parts rejected at the third workstation are returned to the second workstation where they are reworked, with a 50% penalty there (but not on its revisit to Workstation 3). The operation times are TRIA(6, 9, 12), TRIA(5, 8.5, 13), and TRIA(6.5, 8.9, 12.5) for workstations 1, 2 and 3 respectively. Part interarrival times to the system are NORM(10, 2). All times are in minutes.

(**a**) Develop your model using modules from the Support panel so far as possible. Run the model for 5,000 minutes, collecting statistics on the number in queue at each workstation, the number of scrapped parts, workstation utilizations, and cycle times for parts that are not rejected at any workstation and for parts that are rejected at least once. Also, collect statistics on the number of times a rejected part was rejected.

(**b**) In order to decrease the part cycle time, a new priority scheme is being considered. The queue priority is based on the total number of times a part has been rejected, regardless of where it was rejected, with the more rejections already convicted against a part, the further back it is in the queue. Is there a difference in cycle times for this new priority scheme?

8.9   Parts arrive at a machine shop with EXPO(25) interarrival times (all times are in minutes). The shop has two machines, and arriving parts are assigned to one of the machines by flipping a (fair) coin. Except for the processing times, both machines operate in the same fashion. When a part enters a machine area, it requires operator attention to set up the part on the machine (there is only one operator in the shop). After the part is set up, the machine can process it without the operator. Upon completion of the processing, the operator is once again required to remove the part. After completion, the parts exit the system (parts only have to go to one machine). All setups and part removals are done by the same operator, with priority given to the machine waiting the longest for an operator. The times are (parameters are for triangular distributions):

Machine Number	Setup Time	Process Time	Removal Time
1	8, 11, 16	20, 23, 26	7, 9, 12
2	6, 8, 14	11, 15, 20	4, 6, 8

The run length is 25,000 minutes. Observe statistics on machine utilizations, cycle times for parts separated out by which machine they used, overall cycle times (i.e., not separated out by machine used), and the percent of time that each machine spends waiting for operator attention.

8.10   Consider the poor frequent flier (7% of customers) from Exercise 8.4. Assume all times are the same as before, and observe statistics on the time in system by customer type (frequent fliers and non-frequent fliers).

   (**a**) Assign four of the current agents to serve non-frequent fliers only, and the fifth to serve frequent fliers only.

   (**b**) Change your model so that the frequent-flier agent can serve regular customers when there are no frequent fliers waiting in queue.

   (**c**) Change your model so that any agent can serve any customer, but priority is always given to frequent fliers.

   Which of the three alternatives above do you think is "best" for the frequent fliers? How about for the non-frequent fliers? Viewing this as a terminating simulation, address these comparison questions in a statistically valid way.

8.11   A medium-sized airport has a limited number of international flights that arrive and require immigration and customs. The airport would like to examine the customs staffing and establish a policy on the number of passengers who should have bags searched, and the staffing of the customs facility. Arriving passengers must first pass through immigration (immigration is outside the boundaries of this model). They then claim their bags and proceed to customs. The interarrival times to customs are distributed as EXPO(0.2); all times are in minutes. The current plan is to have two customs agents dedicated to passengers who will not have their bags searched, with service times distributed as EXPO(0.55). A new airport systems analyst has developed a probabilistic method to decide which customers will have their bags searched. The decision is made when the passengers are about to enter the normal customs queue. The decision process is as follows: a number is first generated from a Poisson distribution with a mean of 7.0. This number is increased by 1, to avoid getting a zero, and a count is started. When the count reaches the generated number, that unlucky passenger is sent to a second line to have his or her bags searched. A new search number is generated and the process starts over. A single agent is dedicated to these passengers, with service times distributed as EXPO(3). The number of passengers who arrive on these large planes is uniformly distributed between 240 and 350. Develop a simulation of the proposed system and make 20 replications, observing statistics on the system time by passenger type (searched vs. not searched), the number of passengers, and agent utilizations.

A Sampler of Further Modeling Issues and Techniques

CHAPTER 9

A Sampler of Further Modeling Issues and Techniques

In Chapters 5–8, we gave you a reasonably comprehensive tour of how to model different kinds of systems by means of a sequence of progressively more complicated examples. We chose these examples with several goals in mind, including reality and importance (in our experience) of the application, illustration of various modeling issues, and indication of how you can get Arena to represent things the way you want—in many cases, fairly easily and quickly. Armed with these skills, you'll be able to build a rich variety of valid and effective simulation models.

But no reasonable set of digestible examples could possibly fathom all the nooks and crannies of the kinds of modeling issues (and, yes, tricks) that people sometimes need to consider, much less all of the features of Arena. And don't worry, we're not going to attempt that in this chapter either. But we would like to point out some of what we consider to be the more important additional modeling issues and techniques (and tricks) and tell you how to get Arena to perform them for you.

We'll do this by constructing more examples, but these will be more focused toward specific modeling techniques and Arena features, so will be smaller in scope. In Section 9.1, we'll refine the conveyor models we developed in Chapter 7; in Section 9.2, we'll discuss a few more modeling refinements to the transporters from Chapter 7. In service systems, especially those involving humans standing around in line, there is often consideration given to customer *reneging* (i.e., jumping out of line at some point); this is taken up in Section 9.3, along with refinements to the balking notion discussed in the call center model of Chapter 8. Section 9.4 goes into methods (beyond the queues you've already seen) for holding entities at some point, as well as batching them together with the possibility of taking the batch apart later. In Section 9.5, we'll discuss how to represent a *tightly coupled* system in which entities have to be allocated resources downstream from their present position before they can move on; this is called *overlapping resources* from the entity viewpoint. Finally, Section 9.6 briefly mentions a few other specific topics, including guided transporters, parallel queues, the possibility of complex decision logic and looping, and continuous modeling.

This chapter is structured differently from the earlier ones in that the sections are not necessarily meant to be read through in sequence. Rather, it is intended to provide a sampler of modeling techniques and Arena features that we've found useful in a variety of applied projects.

9.1 Modeling Conveyors Using the Transfer Panel

In this section, we indicate some refinements to the basic conveyor models described in Chapter 7.

9.1.1   Model 9.1: Finite Buffers at Stations

In Chapter 7, we introduced you to Arena conveyors. In Section 7.4.1, we developed a model, Model 7.2, for our small manufacturing system using nonaccumulating conveyors as the method for transferring parts within our system. In developing that model, we assumed that there was an infinite buffer in front of each cell for the storage of parts waiting to be processed. This assumption allowed us to use the conveyor capabilities found in the higher-level modules on the Common panel. We did, however, need to add the Conveyor and Segment modules from the Transfer panel to define our conveyor.

Now let's modify that assumption and assume that there is limited space at Cells 1 and 2 for the storage of unprocessed parts. In fact, let's assume that there is only room for one unprocessed part at each cell. For this type of model, we need to define what happens to a part that arrives at Cell 1 or 2 and finds that there is already a part occupying the limited buffer space. Assuming that we could determine a way to limit the buffer using the Server module (it can be done), it would be tempting to simply let the arriving part wait until the part already in the buffer is moved to the machine in that cell. Of course, this could cause a significant logjam at these cells. Not only would parts not be able to enter the cell, but parts on their way to other cells would queue up behind them creating yet another problem. It turns out that processed parts trying to leave the cell need to access space on the conveyor before they can be conveyed to their next destination station. Yes, the space they're trying to access is the same space occupied by the part waiting to enter the cell. This would create what's sometimes called a *deadlock* or *gridlock*.

So let's use the following strategy for parts arriving at Cell 1 or 2. If there is not a part currently waiting in the buffer for the cell, the arriving part is allowed to enter the buffer. Otherwise, the arriving part is conveyed around the loop conveyor back to the same point to try a second (or third, or fourth, etc.) time. To do this, we need to alter our model so we can better control when the part exits the conveyor. The Transfer panel provides five new modules for conveyors (Access, Convey, Exit, Start, and Stop) that allow us to model conveyor activities at a more detailed level. The Exit module causes an entity to exit a conveyor, releasing the conveyor cell(s) it occupied. This is essentially what happens when you select the Exit Conveyor option in the Transfer In dialog of the Server or Enter modules. The Access module causes an entity to request or access space on a conveyor at a specific location, normally its current station location. The Convey module is used to convey the entity to its destination once it has successfully accessed the required conveyor space. You are essentially requesting that Arena Access and Convey an entity when you select the Access option in the Transfer Out dialog of the Server or Leave modules. The Start and Stop modules cause the conveyor to start and stop its movement, respectively. These two modules can be used to develop your own failure logic or generally control when the conveyor is idle or running.

To develop our new model, we will start with Model 7.2 and replace the two Server modules for Cells 1 and 2 with modules from the Transfer and Support panel as shown in Figure 9-1 (new modules for Cell 1). A word of advice if you are developing your own model with us: Do not delete the Server module until you have completed the replacement section. Basically, the existing Server module contains a fair amount of information that you need—station name, service time, queue name, etc. Retaining this module allows you to refer to it and also maintains all the defined objects on the current lists, allowing you to pick them off pull-down lists. Once you have completed your replacement section, you can then delete the Server module.

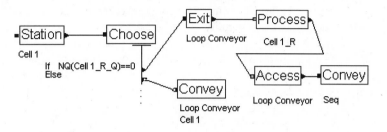

Figure 9-1. New Model Logic for Cell 1

In the Enter Data portion of the Server module we are replacing, we defined the station, with the name Cell 1, and also exited the conveyor. The definition of the station is critical because Arena must know where to send an entity that is being conveyed to Cell 1. Therefore, we started our replacement set of modules with a Station module from the Support panel with the specific purpose of defining the entry point to the station Cell 1. We also could have used an Enter module for this purpose, but we wanted to show you the Station module. The Station module simply defines the logical entry for entities that are transferred to that station. In our case, the only value provided in the dialog is the station name, Display 9-1.

Station	Cell 1

Display 9-1. The Station Module

When an entity, or part, arrives at station Cell 1, it must check the status of the waiting queue before it can determine its fate. We cause this to happen by sending the entity to the Choose module where we check to see if the number of entities in queue Cell 1_R_Q is equal to 0. This is the same queue name used in Model 7.2, and it will be defined in the subsequent Process module. If the queue is currently occupied by another entity, the arriving entity will take the second branch of our Choose module, the Else condition. For this condition, we do not want to exit the conveyor; we instead want to leave the part on the loop conveyor and convey it around the loop and back to the same station. We do this by sending the entity to the Convey module, Display 9-2, where we convey the entity to Cell 1.

Loop Conveyor
Cell 1

Conveyor	Loop Conveyor
Destination Station	
Station Name	*select*
Station	Cell 1

Display 9-2. The Convey Module

At this point you might be thinking, "But the entity is already at station Cell 1!" Arena assumes that your intention is to convey the entity and will send it on its way. Of course, it also assumes that it is physically possible to convey the entity to the specified destination, which is the case. Thus, the Convey module will convey the entity on the designated conveyor to the specified destination. If the entity is not already on the conveyor, Arena will respond with a terminating error message.

If the queue at Cell 1 is unoccupied, the entity will satisfy the first condition and be sent to the connected Exit module, Display 9-3. The Exit module removes the entity from the conveyor and releases the conveyor cells it occupied. It is not necessary to specify the number of cells to release as Arena remembers how many the entity accessed when it got on the conveyor.

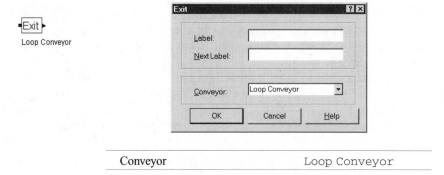

Conveyor	Loop Conveyor

Display 9-3. The Exit Module

If there is a specific reason why you would not want to release all of the cells the entity occupied, you can use the EXIT module from the Blocks panel, which has this capability. This might be the case if the entity represented several items, of which only one was to be unloaded at this station. Just be careful if you use this option because the entity that originally accessed the conveyor cells must be the same entity conveyed to the next destination.

The Entity is sent from the Exit module to a Process module that represents the actual machining operation, see Figure 9-1. We also could have used a Seize–Delay–Release module combination or even the original Server module with major changes. We chose not to reuse the original Server module because we'd need to make numerous changes, including changing the station name. Once the part finishes its operation, it exits the Process module and is sent to the following Access module to get space on the conveyor, Display 9-4.

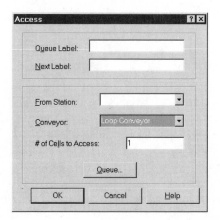

Conveyor	Loop Conveyor

Display 9-4. The Access Module

The Access module allocates cells on the conveyor so the entity can then be conveyed to its next destination; it does not actually convey the entity. Thus, if you do not immediately cause the entity to be conveyed, it will cause the entire conveyor to stop until the entity is conveyed.

In our previous model, using the Transfer Out option on the Server module, we defaulted the queue for our conveyor access to an internal queue. In the event that the required cells were not available, the entity would reside in that internal queue until space was accessible. Since an internal queue cannot be animated, we requested a Storage in the Animate dialog. This provided a way for the entity to show up in the animation in the event that it had to wait for available conveyor space. Since the combination of the Access and Convey modules do not provide this storage option, we elected to select Individual Queues with unique names in the Access Queue option, Display 9-5. Be aware that the Queue button will not appear until you select or enter the conveyor and tab to the next field. In the Queue dialog, we appended the queue name at Cell 1 with "_1" and the queue at Cell 2 with "_2." This will allow us to animate these queues in the event that an entity has to wait for an empty cell on the conveyor.

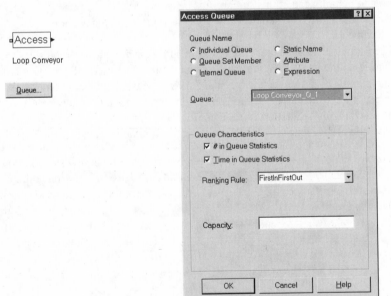

Queue Name		
Individual Queue		*select*
Queue		Loop Conveyor_Q_1

Display 9-5. The Queue Option in the Access Module

Having accessed conveyor space, the entity is sent to the Convey module where it is conveyed according to its specified sequence. This completes the replacement modules for the Server (Cell 1) in Model 7.2. You also need to perform the same set of operations for Cell 2. You can simply repeat these steps or make a copy of these modules and edit them individually.

When you finally delete the two server modules, you may find that part of your animation has also been deleted. This is because you received some "free" animation with the Server modules. You also should have noted that the new Process modules gave you some animation constructs as well. When you are editing or changing a model like this, it is frequently easier to animate the new features using the constructs from the Animate toolbar, so when we developed our model, we deleted the added animation features that were provided by the new modules and animated these new features ourselves. In our model, we lost the queue, the resource symbol, and the storage for Cell 1. We simply added the queue, copied and edited the resource, and added the access queue. We performed basically the same operations for Cell 2. When we ran our new model, we could see parts being blocked from entry to Cell 1 starting at about time 135.

9.1.2   Model 9.2: Parts Stay on Conveyor During Processing

Now that you have conquered these new conveyor modules, let's examine another quick problem. Start with the accumulating conveyor model, Model 7.3, presented in Section 7.4.2. Assume that we're trying a new layout that requires that the operations at Cell 2 be performed with the part remaining on the conveyor. Specifically, parts conveyed to Cell 2 do not exit the conveyor, but the part stops at Cell 2, the actual operation is performed while the part sits on the conveyor, and the part is then conveyed to its next destination. Since the conveyor is accumulating, other parts on the conveyor will continue to move unless they are blocked by the part being operated on at Cell 2.

We could implement this new twist by replacing the current Server module for Cell 2 with a set of modules similar to what we did for Model 9.1. However, since the entities arriving at Cell 2 do not exit or access the conveyor, there is a far easier solution. We'll modify the Transfer In option on the Server module by selecting the None option. In this case, the entity will not exit the conveyor. This will cause the entity to reside on the conveyor while the operation defined by the server takes place. However, if this is the only change we make, an error will occur when the entity attempts to leave Cell 2. In the Transfer Out dialog of the Server, we had previously selected the Access option that caused the entity to try to access space on the conveyor, and since the entity will remain on the conveyor, Arena would become confused and terminate with a runtime error. Basically, the Transfer Out option only allows you to both Access and Convey an entity. This is easily fixed by selecting the None option in the Transfer Out dialog and the Connect option in the Leave Data section of the main server dialog. Now add a Convey module, which conveys the entity to its next destination using the Sequence feature, see Figure 9-2. These are the only model changes required.

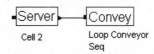

Figure 9-2. The Replace Modules for Cell 2

You can test your new model logic by watching the animation. We suggest you fast-forward the simulation to about time 1,000 before you begin to watch the animation. At this point in the simulation, the effects of these changes become quite apparent.

9.2 More on Transporters

In Chapter 7, we presented the concepts for modeling Arena transporters and conveyors using the functionality available in the high-level modules found in the Common panel. In Section 9.1, we further expanded that functionality for conveyors by using modules from the Transfer panel to modify and refine the models presented in Chapter 7. The same types of capabilities also exist for Transporters. Although we're not going to develop a complete model using these modules, we'll provide a brief coverage of their functions and show the sequence of modules required to model several different situations. This should be sufficient to allow you to use these constructs successfully in your own models. Remember that online help is always available.

Let's start with the basic capabilities covered in Section 7.3. The fundamental transporter constructs are available in the Transfer In and Transfer Out dialogs of the Arrive, Server, and Depart modules, as well as in the main dialogs of the Advanced Server, Enter, and Leave modules. Consider the process of requesting a transporter and the subsequent transfer of the transporter and entity to its next station or location. The Request and Transport modules found in the Transfer panel also provide this capability. As you would expect, they give you more control and options than can be found in the modules from the Common panel.

The Request module provides the first part of the Transfer Out dialog and is almost identical to it. You gain the ability to override the default Velocity, but you lose the ability to specify a Load Time. However, a Load Time can be included by then directing the entity to a Delay module. The Request module actually performs two activities: allocation of a transporter to the entity and moving the empty transporter to the location of that entity, if the transporter is not already there. The Transport module performs the next part of the Transfer Out activity by initiating the transfer of the transporter and entity to its next location. Now let's consider a modeling situation where it would be desirable to separate these two functions. Assume that when the transporter arrives at the entity location there is a loading operation that requires the assistance of an operator. If we want to model the operator explicitly, we'll need these new modules. The modules required to model this situation are shown in Figure 9-3.

Figure 9-3. Operator-Assisted Transporter Load

You can also separate the two activities of the Request module by using the Allocate and Move modules. The Allocate module allocates a transporter to the entity, but leaves the transporter at its current location. The Move module allows the entity that has been allocated a transporter to Move the empty transporter anywhere in the model. When using the Request module, the transporter is automatically moved to the entity location. Consider the situation where the empty transporter must first pick up from a staging area a fixture required to transport the entity. In this case, we need to allocate the transporter, send it to the staging area, pick up the fixture, and finally send it to the entity's location. The modules required to model these activities are shown in Figure 9-4.

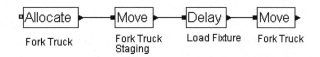

Figure 9-4. Fixture Required for Entity Transfer

Of course, you could include all kinds of embellishments for this activity. Suppose that only a portion of the entities need this fixture. We could easily include a Choose module between them to check for this condition, as shown in Figure 9-5.

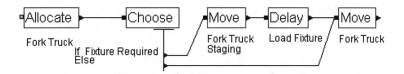

Figure 9-5. Checking for Fixture Requirement

Our two examples using the Allocate and Move modules both resulted in the transporter being moved to the location of the entity. Now let's assume that whenever your transporter is freed, you want it to be roving around the system looking for work. You have a predefined path that the transporter should follow. This path would be very similar to a sequence of stations, except it would form a closed loop. Each time the unallocated transporter reached the next station on its path, it would check to see if there is a current request from somewhere. If there is no request, the transporter continues on its mindless journey. If there is a request, the transporter proceeds immediately to the location of that request.

To model this, you would create a single entity (let's call it the loop entity) that would attempt to allocate the transporter with a very low priority (high number for the priority). Once allocated, the empty transporter is moved to the next station on its path. Upon arrival at this station, the transporter is freed so it can respond to any current request. The loop entity is directed to the initial Allocate module where it once again tries to allocate the transporter. This assumes that any current request for the transporter has a higher priority than the loop entity. Remember that the default priority is 1, with the lowest value having the highest priority.

We are not going to show you the modules for this process, as it gets a little messy, but we encourage you to perform the following exercise. Open a new model window, attach the Transfer panel, place a Transporter module, open the dialog, enter a transporter name, open the Options dialog, select Follow Looping Pattern, enter three or four station names, and accept the dialogs. Now generate the SIMAN model and experiment files, *Run/SIMAN/View*. What you will see is a generic model for the looping transporter activity. We of course are assuming that you are now able to follow the basic modeling operations described by these two SIMAN files.

Once a transporter arrives at it destination, it must be freed. The Free module provides this function. You only need to enter the transporter name in the dialog, and in some cases, the unit number. Two additional modules, Halt and Activate, allow you to control the number of active or available transporters. The Halt module causes a single transporter unit to become inactive or unavailable to be allocated. The Activate module causes an inactive transporter to become active or available.

9.3   Entity Reneging

9.3.1   *Entity Balking and Reneging*

In Chapter 8, we developed a call center model that included customer *balking* (i.e., an arriving customer does not join the queue but goes away or goes someplace else). Now let's consider the more complex case where it's possible to have both customer balking and customer *reneging* (i.e., a customer joins a queue on arrival but later decides to jump out and leave, probably regretting not having balked in the first place). First, let's define the various ways that balking and reneging can occur.

In our call center model, there was a finite system capacity based on the number of telephone lines. When all the lines were in use, a customer call received a busy signal and was balked from the system. This is the simplest form of entity balking. Unfortunately, most systems where balking can occur are much more complicated. Consider a simple service line where, theoretically, the queue or waiting-line capacity is infinite. In most cases, there is some finite capacity based on space, but a service line could possibly exit a building and wind around the block (say the waiting line for World Series or Super Bowl tickets). In these cases, there is no concrete capacity limit, but the customers' decisions to enter the line or balk from the system are based on their own evaluation of the situation. Thus, balking point or capacity is often entity-dependent. One customer may approach a long service line, decide not to wait, and balk from the system—yet the next customer may enter the line.

Entity reneging is an even more complicated issue in terms of both modeling and representing in software. Each entity or customer entering a line has a different tolerance threshold with respect to how long to wait before leaving the line. It often depends on how much each customer wants the service being provided. Some customers won't renege regardless of the wait time. Others may wait for a period of time and then leave the line because they realize that they won't get served in time to meet their needs. Often the customers' decisions to remain or leave the line are based on both the amount of time they have already spent in the line as well as their current place in the line. A customer may enter a line and decide to wait for 10 minutes; if he is not serviced by that time, he plans to leave the line. However, after 10 minutes have elapsed, the customer may choose to stay if he is the next in line for service.

Line switching, or *jockeying*, is an even more complicated form of reneging that often occurs in supermarket checkout lines, fast-food restaurants, and banks that do not employ a single waiting line. A customer selects the line to enter and later re-evaluates that decision based on current line lengths. After all, we invariably enter the slowest-moving line, and if we switch lines, the line we left speeds up and the line we enter slows down. We won't cover the logic for jockeying.

9.3.2   Model 9.3: A Service Model with Balking and Reneging

Let's look at balking and reneging in the context of a very simple model. Customers arrive with EXPO(5) interarrival times at a service system with a single server—service time is EXPO(4.25). All times are in minutes. Although the waiting line has an infinite capacity, each arriving customer views the current length of the line and compares it to his *tolerance* for waiting. If the number in the line is greater than his tolerance, he'll balk away from the system. We'll represent the customer balking tolerance by generating a sample from a triangular distribution, TRIA(3, 6, 15). Since our generated sample is from a continuous distribution, it will not be an integer. We could use one of the Arena math functions to convert it to an integer, but we're only interested if the number in the waiting line is greater than the generated tolerance.

There are two ways to model the balking activity. Let's assume we create our arrivals, generate our tolerance value from the triangular distribution, and assign this value to an entity attribute with a Create module. We could send our arrival to a Choose module and compare our sample value to the current number in the waiting line, using the Arena variable NQ. If the tolerance is less than or equal to the current number in queue, we balk the arrival from the system. Otherwise, we enter the waiting line. An alternative method is to assign our tolerance to a variable and also use this same variable for the server queue capacity. We then send our arrival directly to the server. If the current number in the queue is greater than or equal to the tolerance, which is equal to the queue capacity, the arrival will be balked automatically. Using the second method, it's possible for the queue capacity to be assigned a value less than the current number in queue. This method works because Arena only checks the queue-capacity value when a new entity tries to enter the queue. Thus, the current entities remain safely in the queue, regardless of the new queue-capacity value. We will use this second method when we develop our model.

To represent reneging, assume that arriving customers who decide not to balk are willing to wait for only a limited period of time before they renege from the queue. We will generate this renege tolerance time from an ERLA(15, 2) distribution (Erlang), which has a mean of 30, and assign it to an entity attribute in our Create module. Modeling the mechanics of the reneging activity can be a challenge. If we allow the arrival to enter the queue and the renege time is reached, we need to be able to find the entity and remove it from the queue. At this point in our problem description, you might want to consider alternative methods to handle this. For example, we could define a variable that keeps track of when the server will next be available. We generate the entity processing time first and assign it to an attribute in our Create module. We then send our entity to the Choose module where we check for balking. If the entity is not balked, we then check (in the same Choose module) to see if the entity will begin service before its renege time. If not, we renege the entity. Otherwise, we send the entity to an Assign module where we update our variable that tells us when the server will become available, then send the entity to the queue. This model logic may seem complicated, but can be summarized as follows:

Define Available Time = Time in the future when server will be available

Create arrival
    Assign Service Time
    Assign the Time in the future the activity would renege, which is equal to
        Tolerance Time + TNOW
    Assign Balk Limit

Choose
    If Balk Limit > Number in queue
        Balk entity
    If Renege Time < Available Time
        Renege entity
    Else
        Assign Available Time = MX(Available Time , TNOW) + Service Time
    Send entity to queue

Note the use of the "maximum" math function, MX.

There is one problem with this logic that can easily be fixed—our number in queue is not accurate because it won't contain any entities that have not yet reneged. We can fix this by sending our reneged entities to a Delay module where they are delayed by the renege time; we also specify a Storage (say Renege_S). Now we change our first Choose statement as follows:

If Balk Limit > Number in queue + NSTO(Renege_S)

We have to be careful about our statistics, but this approach will capture the reneging process accurately and avoid our having to alter the queue.

Let's add one last caveat before we develop our model. Assume that the actual decision of whether to renege is based not only on the renege time, but also on the position of the customer in the queue. For example, customers may have reached their renege tolerance limit, but if they're now at the front of the waiting line, they may just wait for service (i.e., renege on reneging). Let's call this position in the queue where the customer will elect to stay, even if the customer renege time has elapsed, the customer *stay zone*. Thus, if the customer stay zone is 3 and the renege time for the customer has expired, the customer will stay in line anyway if they are one of the next three customers to be serviced.

We'll generate this position number from a Poisson distribution, POIS(0.75). We've used the Poisson distribution for two reasons. First, it provides a reasonable approximation of this process and also returns an integer value. Second, we haven't used this distribution yet. For those of you with no access to Poisson tables (you mean you actually sold your statistics book?), it is approximately equivalent to the following discrete empirical distribution: DISC(0.472, 0, 0.827, 1, 0.959, 2, 0.993, 3, 0.999, 4, 1.0, 5). See Appendix D for more detail on this distribution.

This new decision process means that the above logic is no longer valid. We must now place the arriving customer in the waiting line and evaluate the reneging after the renege time has elapsed. However, if we actually go ahead and place the customer in the queue, there's no mechanism to detect that the renege time has elapsed. To overcome this problem, we'll make a duplicate of each entity and delay it by the renege time. The original entity, which represents the actual customer, will be sent to the service queue. After the renege-time delay, we'll have the duplicate entity check the queue position of the original entity. If the customer is no longer in the service queue (i.e., it was served), we'll just dispose of the duplicate entity. If the customer is still in the queue, we'll check to see if that customer will renege. If the current queue position is within the customer stay zone, we just dispose of the duplicate entity. Otherwise, we have the duplicate entity remove the original entity from the service queue and dispose of both itself and the original entity. This model logic is outlined below:

```
Create Arrivals
        Mark arrival time: Enter System

Assign Renege Time = ERLA(15,2)
        Assign Stay Zone Number = POIS(0.75)
        Assign Balking Tolerance = TRIA(3,6,15)

Create Duplicate entity
        Original entity to server queue
                If Balk from queue
                        Count balk
                        Dispose
                Delay for Service Time = EXPO(4.25)
                Tally system time
                Dispose

        Duplicate entity
                Delay by Renege Time
                Search queue for position of original entity
                If No original entity
                        Dispose
                If Queue position <= Stay Zone Number
                        Dispose
                Remove original entity from queue and Dispose
                Count Renege customer
                Dispose
```

In order to implement this logic, we obviously need a few new features, such as the ability to duplicate an entity, search a queue, and remove an entity from a queue. As you would suspect, Arena modules that perform these functions can be found in the Blocks panel. Our completed Arena model is shown in Figure 9-6.

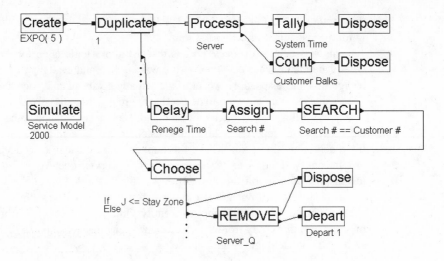

Figure 9-6. The Service Model Logic

We start our model with a Create module that creates arriving customers and Assigns the values we'll need later, as in Display 9-6.

Time Between	EXPO(5)
Mark Time Attribute	Enter System
Assignments	
Attribute	*select*
Attribute	Renege Time
Value	ERLA(15, 2)
Assignments	
Variable	*select*
Variable	Server_Q Cap
Value	TRIA(3, 6, 15)
Assignments	
Attribute	*select*
Attribute	Stay Zone
Value	POIS(0.75)
Assignments	
Variable	*select*
Variable	Total Customers
Value	Total Customers + 1
Assignments	
Attribute	*select*
Attribute	Customer #
Value	Total Customers

Display 9-6. The Create Module: Creating the Customer Arrivals

We send the new arrivals directly to a Duplicate module (Support panel), as shown in Display 9-7. This module allows us to make duplicates (clones) of the entering entity. The original entity leaves the module by the exit point located at the right of the module handle. The duplicated entities leave the module by the exit points below the module handle.

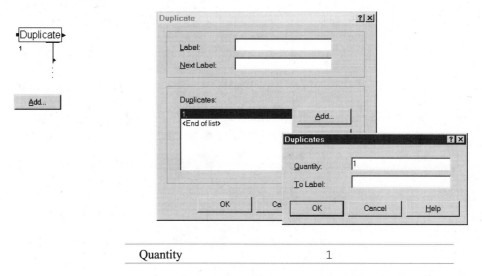

Quantity	1

Display 9-7. The Duplicate Module

The duplicates are exact replicas of the original entity (in terms of attributes and their values) and can be created in any quantity. If you duplicate more than one entity, you can do it as a batch of entities that will all be sent out of the same exit point or as groups of entities that can be sent out of different exit points. Note that if you enter a value n for Quantity to duplicate, $n+1$ entities actually leave the module—n duplicates from the bottom connection point and 1 original from the top.

The original entity (customer) is sent to a Process module where it tries to enter queue `Server_Q` to wait for the server. The capacity of this queue was entered as the variable `Server_Q Cap`, which was set by our arriving customer as his tolerance for not balking, as explained earlier. If the current number in queue is less than the current value of `Server_Q Cap`, the customer is allowed to enter the queue. If not, the customer entity is balked to the Count module where he increments the balk count and is then sent to a Dispose module, where it exits the system (see Figure 9-6). A customer who is allowed to enter the queue waits for the resource `Server`. A serviced customer is sent to a Tally module where the system time is recorded and is then sent to the following Dispose module.

The duplicate entity is sent to a Delay module where it is delayed by the renege time that was assigned to the attribute `Renege Time` in the Create module. After the delay, the entity enters an Assign module where the value of the attribute `Customer #` is assigned to a new variable named `Search #`. The attribute `Customer #` contains a unique customer number assigned when the customer entered the system. The entity is then sent to the following SEARCH module, from the Blocks panel. A SEARCH module allows us to search a queue to find the *rank*, or queue position, of an entity that satisfies a defined search condition. A queue rank of 1 means that the entity is at the front of the Queue (the next entity to be serviced). In our model, we want to find the original customer who created the duplicate entity performing the search. That customer will have the same value for its `Customer #` attribute as the variable `Search #` that we just assigned.

The SEARCH module (Display 9-8) is similar to the FINDJ module from Section 8.6 in that it searches over a defined range according to a defined condition. Normally, the search will be over the enter queue contents, from 1 to NQ. (Note that the search can be performed backward by specifying the range as NQ to 1.)

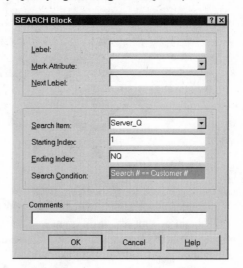

Search Item	Server_Q
Starting Index	1
Ending Index	NQ
Search Condition	Search # == Customer #

Display 9-8. The SEARCH Module

However, you may search over any range that your model logic requires. If you state a range that exceeds the current number in the queue, Arena will terminate with a runtime error. Arena will assign to the variable J the rank of the first entity during the search that satisfies the condition. If the condition contains the math functions MX or MN (maximum or minimum), it will search the entire range. If attributes are used in the search condition, they will be interpreted as the attribute value of the entity in the search queue. If the queue is empty, or no entity satisfies the condition, a value of 0 will be assigned to the variable J. Ordinarily, you're interested in finding the entity rank so you can remove that entity from the queue (REMOVE module) or make a copy of the entity (COPY module). The SEARCH module can also be used to search over entities that have been formed as a temporary group using a Batch or GROUP module.

For our model, we want to search over the entire queue range, from 1 to NQ, for the original entity that has the same Customer # value as the duplicated entity initiating the search. If the original entity, or customer, is no longer in the queue, the value of the variable J will be set to 0; otherwise, it will take on the position of the customer in the queue. The entity is then sent to the following Choose module. The first check at this module is to see if the value of J is less than or equal to the value of the attribute Stay Zone. If this condition is true, it implies that the customer has either left the queue (J = 0) or the position of the customer in the queue is good enough that they choose to remain in the line. In either case, we dispose of the duplicate entity (see Figure 9-6). If the first condition is not true, we want to renege the original customer. Therefore, we send the duplicate entity to the following REMOVE module.

The REMOVE module allows us to remove an entity from a queue and send it to another place in our model. It requires that you identify the entity to be removed by entering the queue identifier and the rank of that entity. If you attempt to remove an entity from an undefined queue or to remove an entity with a rank that is greater than the number of entities in the specified queue, Arena will terminate the run with an error. In our model, we want to remove the customer with rank J from queue Server_Q, Display 9-9.

REMOVE Block `[?][X]`

Label:	
Mark Attribute:	
Next Label:	
Rank of Entity:	J
Queue ID:	Server_Q
Removed Entity Destination:	
Comments	

OK   Cancel   Help

Rank of Entity	J
Queue ID	Server_Q

Display 9-9. The REMOVE Module

If you look at the REMOVE module handle, you'll see two exit points on the right side. The entity that entered the REMOVE module will depart from the upper exit point; in our model, it is sent to the same Dispose module we used for the first branch of our Choose module. The customer entity removed from the server queue will depart by the lower exit point and is sent to a Depart module. We've used a single Depart module rather than a sequence of Count, Tally, and Dispose modules because we wanted to count and tally the renege times of the reneging customers.

We also placed a Simulate module with a Replication length of 2000 time units. The Arena summary report for this model is shown in Figure 9-7. As you can see, during this run, we had 11 balking and 25 reneging customers.

```
Project:   Service Model
Analyst:   Ben Darby

Replication ended at time      : 2000.0

                        TALLY VARIABLES

Identifier           Average   Half Width   Minimum   Maximum   Observations
System Time          9.1880    (Corr)       .07537    40.957    354
Server_Q Queue Time  5.2165    (Corr)       .00000    40.873    354
Renege Customer Time 9.8854    (Insuf)      1.6049    22.897    25

                   DISCRETE-CHANGE VARIABLES

Identifier           Average   Half Width   Minimum   Maximum   Final Value
# in Server_Q        1.0468    (Corr)       .00000    7.0000    .00000
Server Busy          .70296    .07049       .00000    1.0000    .00000
Server Available     1.0000    (Insuf)      1.0000    1.0000    1.0000

                        COUNTERS

          Identifier          Count     Limit
          Renege Customers      25      Infinite
          Customer Balks        11      Infinite
```

Figure 9-7. The Service Model Summary Report

9.4   Holding and Batching Entities

In this section, we'll take up the common situation where entities need to be held up along their way for a variety of reasons. We'll also discuss how to combine or group entities and how to separate them later. In addition, we'll indicate some new ways to control your run, and even to intervene in it.

9.4.1   Modeling Options

As you begin to model more complex systems, you might occasionally want to retain or hold entities at a place in the model until some system condition allows these entities to progress. You might be thinking that we have already covered this concept, in that an entity waiting in a queue for an available resource, transporter, or conveyor space allows us to hold that entity until the resource becomes available. Here we're thinking in more general terms; the condition doesn't have to be based on just the availability of a resource, transporter, or conveyor space. The conditions that allow the entity to proceed can be based on any system conditions; e.g., time, queue size, etc. There are two different methods for releasing held entities.

The first method holds the entities in a queue until they receive, from another entity in the system, permission or a signal to proceed. For example, consider a busy intersection with a policeman directing traffic. Think of the cars arriving at the intersection as entities being held until they are allowed to proceed. Now think of the policeman as an entity eventually giving the waiting cars a signal to proceed. There may be 10 cars waiting, but the policeman may give only the first six permission to proceed.

The second method allows the held entities themselves to evaluate the system conditions and determine when they should proceed. For example, think of a car wanting to turn across traffic into a driveway from a busy street with oncoming traffic; unfortunately, there's neither a traffic light nor a policeman. If the car is the entity, it waits until conditions are such that there is no oncoming traffic within a reasonable distance and the driveway is clear for entry. In this case, the entity continuously evaluates the conditions until it is safe to make the turn. If there's a second car that wants to make the same turn directly behind the first, it waits until it is at the front of the line and then performs its own evaluation. We'll illustrate both methods in Model 9.4 below.

There are also situations where you need to form *batches* of items or entities before they can proceed. Take the simplest case of forming batches of similar or identical items. For example, you're modeling the packing operation at the end of a can line that produces beverages. You want to combine or group beverages into six-packs for the packing operation. You might also have a secondary operation that combines 4 six-packs into a case. In this illustration, the items or entities to be grouped are identical, and you would most likely form a *permanent* group (i.e., one that you'd never want to take apart again later). Thus, six entities enter the grouping process and one entity, the six-pack, exits the process. However, if you're modeling an operation that groups entities that are later to be separated to continue individually on their way, you would want to form a *temporary* group. In the first case, you lose the unique attribute information attached to each entity. In the second case, you want each entity departing the operation to retain the same attribute information it held when it joined the group. So when you're modeling a grouping operation, you need to decide whether you want to form a temporary or permanent group. We'll discuss both options in Model 9.4 below.

9.4.2   Model 9.4: A Batching Process Example

Randomly arriving items are formed into batches before being processed. You might think of the process as an oven that cures the arriving items in batches. The maximum size of the batch that can be sent to the process depends on the design capacity. Let's assume that each item must be placed on a special fixture for the process, and these fixtures are very expensive. The number of fixtures determines the process capacity. Let's further assume that these fixtures are purchased in pairs. Thus, the process can have a capacity of 2, 4, 6, 8, etc. In addition, we'll assume that the process requires a minimum batch size of 2 before it can be started.

Arriving items are sent to a batching area where they wait for the process to become available. When the process becomes available, we must determine the batch size to process, or cause the process to wait for the arrival of enough additional items to make a viable batch. Here's the decision logic required:

Process becomes available

    If Number of waiting items ≥ 2 and $\leq$ Max Batch
        Form batch of all items
        Set Number of waiting items to 0
        Process batch
    Else if Number of waiting items > Max Batch
        Form batch of size Max Batch
        Decrement Number of waiting items by Max Batch
        Process batch
    Else if Number of waiting items < 2

        Wait for additional items

As long as there are items available, the items are processed. However, if there are insufficient items (< 2) for the next batch, the process is temporarily stopped and requires an additional startup-time delay before the next batch can be processed. Because of this additional startup delay, we may want to wait for more than two items before we restart the process.

We want to develop a simulation model that will aid us in designing the parameters of this process. There is one design parameter (the process capacity) and one logic parameter (restart batch size) of interest. In addition, we would like to determine the effect of the item arrival rate on our design.

We could design our simulation model and then run a large number of scenarios for different parameter settings and arrival rates. Unfortunately, this approach could require a large number of runs, and we may not fully understand the interactions between these variables. Thus, we'll take a slightly different approach for this example. First, we need to recognize that the system is rather simple in that it consists of only one process. Furthermore, unless we allow the number of waiting items to become quite large, the system is basically in steady state (see Section 6.5.1) from the beginning. In addition, if we change one of the parameters during the run, it should remain in steady state as long as we do not allow the number of waiting items to become large.

Thus, our analysis would consist of two phases. The first phase would be focused on developing an understanding of the interactions between the variables of interest (process capacity, restart batch size, and arrival rate) and identifying what combinations of these variables should be studied in more detail. To aid in this phase, we will incorporate into our model the ability to change the variables of interest easily during a simulation run. The second phase would consist of a series of long runs for the chosen combinations.

To accomplish this, we need first to develop a visual display or animation that will allow us to view and understand the parameter interactions. We could just do a standard animation of this process, but it would only allow us to view the current status of the system, and we really need to be able to see the system performance over time. A better approach would be to create a plot that would show the number of items waiting and the size of the batch being processed. We'll also display other variables of interest: maximum batch size or process capacity, the restart batch size, the arrival rate, and the number of process restarts. We also need to implement a way to change the key variables easily *during* a run, without having to resort to the Assign command in the Run Controller.

The completed model that we'll now develop is shown in Figure 9-8. You might note that there are five new modules: Wait, Signal, and Batch from the Support panel; SCAN from the Blocks panel; and Menu from the Common panel. You might also note that we don't have a resource defined for the process; we have chosen to model this indirectly. Let's start with the Variables and Simulate modules and then proceed to the model logic. We will discuss the Statistics and Menu modules later.

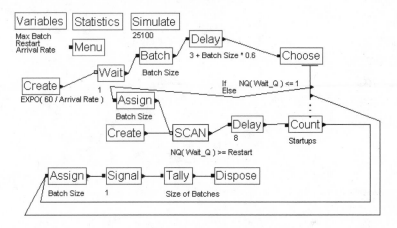

Figure 9-8. The Batch Processing Model

We use the Variables module to define the three parameters that we'll change during the model run: the maximum batch size or process capacity, Max Batch; the restart batch size, Restart; and the item arrival rate in arrivals per hour, Arrival Rate. These three variables are initially set to 10, 4, and 55, respectively. The Simulate module has a Warm-Up Period of 100 with a replication length of 25,100 (all times are in minutes).

Now let's look at the item arrival process—the Create–Wait modules at the upper left of Figure 9-8. The Create module is used to generate arrivals with exponential interarrival times. We have used the expression 60/Arrival Rate as the interarrival mean so that we can change this value during the run. No other entries are required for this module. The arriving items are then sent to the Wait module. The Wait module holds entities until a *signal* is received from somewhere else in the model. The signal can be based on an expression or an attribute value. Different entities can be waiting for different signals or they can all be waiting for the same signal. When a matching signal is received, the Wait module will release up to a maximum number of entities based on the Release Limit, unless the signal contains additional release limits. This will be explained when we cover the Signal module.

In our example, all entities will wait for the same signal, which we have arbitrarily specified as Signal 1, seen in Display 9-10. We have defaulted the Release Limit to infinity since a limit will be set in the Signal module. We have also opened the Queue dialog and requested an Individual Queue, Wait_Q, so we can obtain statistics and plot the number in queue for our animation.

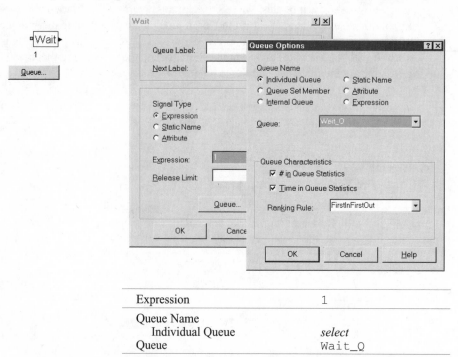

Expression	1
Queue Name	
Individual Queue	*select*
Queue	Wait_Q

Display 9-10. The Wait Module

Now let's consider the conditions at the start of the simulation. There is nothing being processed; therefore, nothing should happen until the arrival of the fourth item, based on the initial value of Restart. As arriving items do not cause a signal to be sent, some other mechanism must be put into the model to cause the start of the first batching operation and process.

This mechanism can be found in the Create–SCAN–Delay–Count, etc., sequence of modules found toward the center of Figure 9-8. The Create module has no user entries. Thus, the Time Between arrivals is defaulted to infinity, resulting in only a single entity being released at time 0. This entity is sent directly to the SCAN module that follows.

The SCAN module allows us to hold an entity until the user-defined condition is true; at that time, the entity is allowed to depart the module. Like the Wait module, waiting entities are held in a user-defined queue or in an internal queue (the default). If an entity enters a SCAN module that has no waiting entities, the condition is checked and the entity is allowed to proceed if the condition evaluates to true. If there are other entities waiting, the arriving entity joins the queue with its position based on the selected queue-ranking rule, defaulted to FIFO. If there are entities waiting, the scan condition is checked as the last operation before any discrete time advance is triggered anywhere in the model. If the condition is true, the first entity in the scan queue will be sent to the next module. Arena will allow that entity to continue until it's time for the next time advance. At this time, the condition is checked again. Therefore, it's possible for all waiting entities to be released from the SCAN module at the same time, although each entity is completely processed before the next entity is allowed to proceed.

For our model, we've entered a condition that requires at least four items to be in the wait queue preceding our Wait module before the condition is satisfied (Display 9-11). At that time, the entity will be sent to the following Delay module. As you begin to understand our complete model, you should realize that we've designed it so there will never be more than one entity in the scan queue.

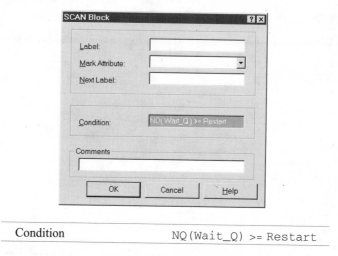

Condition	NQ(Wait_Q) >= Restart

Display 9-11. The SCAN Module

Now, at the start of a simulation run, the first arriving item will be created and sent to the wait queue, Wait_Q. At the same time, the second Create module will cause a single entity to arrive and be placed in the scan queue, an internal queue. Nothing happens until the wait queue has four items. Once that occurs, the entity is released from the SCAN module and sent to the Delay module where it incurs an 8-minute delay, accounting for the process restart time. Be aware that during this delay additional items may have arrived. The entity is then sent to a Count module where the number of startups, counter Startups, is incremented by 1. The new process batch size, Batch Size, is calculated in the following Assign module, Display 9-12. Recall that, at least for the first entity, we know there are at least four items in the wait queue. Thus, our process batch size is either the number in the wait queue, or the maximum batch size if the number waiting is greater than the process capacity.

Variable	*select*
Variable	Batch Size
Value	MN(NQ(Wait_Q),Max Batch)

Display 9-12. Assigning the Next Process Batch Size

Having calculated the next batch size and assigned it to a global variable, Batch Size, we send the entity to a Signal module, Display 9-13. This module broadcasts a signal with a value of 1 across the whole model, which causes the entities in the wait queue, up to a maximum Batch Size, to be released. This entity then enters a Tally module where the next batch size is tallied, and then the entity is disposed.

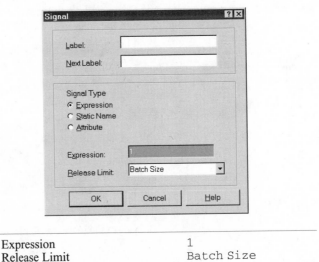

Expression	1
Release Limit	Batch Size

Display 9-13. The Signal Module

You can have multiple Signal and multiple Wait modules in your model. In this case, a Signal module will send a signal value to each Wait module and release the maximum specified number of entities from all Wait modules where the Signal matches.

Now the process has undergone a startup delay, and the first batch of items has been released to the Batch module following the Wait module. The Batch module allows us to accumulate entities that will then be formed into a permanent or temporary batch represented by a single entity. In our example, we have decided to form a permanent batch. Thus, the unique attribute values of the batched entities are lost because they are disposed. The attribute values of the resulting representative entity can be specified as the Last, First, Product, or Sum of the arriving individual batched entities. If a temporary batch is formed, the entities forming the batch are removed from the queue and are held internally to be reinstated later using a Split module. Entities may also be batched based on a match criterion value. If you form a permanent batch, you can still use the Duplicate module to recreate the equivalent number of entities later. However, you've lost the individual attribute values of these entities.

Normally, entities arriving at a batch module will be required to wait until the required batch size has been assembled. However, in our model, we defined the batch size to be formed to be exactly equal to the number of items we just released to the module; see Display 9-14. Thus, our items will never have to wait at this module.

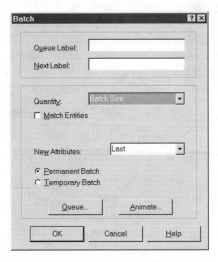

Quantity	Batch Size

Display 9-14. Forming the Process Batch

The entity that now represents the batch of items is directed to a Delay module where the process delay occurs. Note that this process delay depends on the batch size being processed, 3 minutes plus 0.6 minute for each item in the batch. We've also specified a Storage for this delay, `Process`. This storage is used to collect busy statistics on the process in our Statistics module. We've used our Statistics module to request a time-persistent statistic on the number in the Storage `Process`. We labeled this statistic as `Process Status`, because the resulting statistic is equivalent to the busy time of the process, not including the startup delays. If we wanted to include the startups, we'd simply add the storage `Process` to that Delay module. We could also have kept different statistics on these by specifying a different storage and statistic for the startups.

The processed batch is sent to the following Choose module where we check whether there are at least two items in the wait queue. If not, we must shut down the process and wait for more items to arrive. We do this by sending the entity to an Assign module where, for animation purposes, we set the `Batch Size` equal to 0. It's then sent to the previously discussed SCAN module to wait for enough items to restart the process. If there are at least two waiting items, the entity is sent to the Assign module where we set the next batch size to start the next batch processing.

Since the preceding few paragraphs were fairly complex, let's review the logic that controls the batching of items to the process. Keep in mind that the arriving entities are placed in a Wait queue where they are held until a signal to proceed is received. The first process is initiated by the second Create module that creates only one control entity. This entity is held in the Scan queue until the first four items have arrived. The value 4 is the initial value of the Variable `Restart`. This control entity causes the first batch to be released for processing, and it is then disposed. After that, the last batch to complete processing becomes a control entity that determines the next batch size and when to allow the batch to proceed for processing.

Next we'll add the ability to change the variables of interest easily during a simulation run. We can provide this capability by including a *menu* option in our model. This is accomplished using the Menu module from the Common panel, Display 9-15.

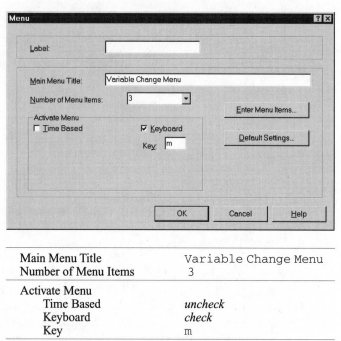

Main Menu Title	Variable Change Menu
Number of Menu Items	3

Activate Menu	
Time Based	*uncheck*
Keyboard	*check*
Key	m

Display 9-15. The Menu Module Dialog

Multiple Menu modules can be linked together to form menus with several levels. Options allow you to activate the menu at the start of a simulation, at time-based intervals during a simulation run, by depressing a key during the simulation run, by sending an entity to the Menu module, or any combination of these. Arena will automatically add two options to your menus, Start/Continue Simulation and End Simulation. The first will clear the menu and start or continue the simulation, and the second will immediately stop the simulation run.

We have requested three menu items, one for each variable of interest. We have also elected that the menu be activated only by the hot key m (case sensitive). This will allow us to pause the simulation and change our variables at any time during the simulation run.We now need to define the specifics of our selected options, which we do in the Enter Menu Items dialog, seen in Display 9-16. We have defined the Menu Item Entry Text, selected the Change Variable option, and entered the variable name for each of the three items. The alternative option is Connect, which allows you to send an entity to a second Menu module or to other Arena modules.

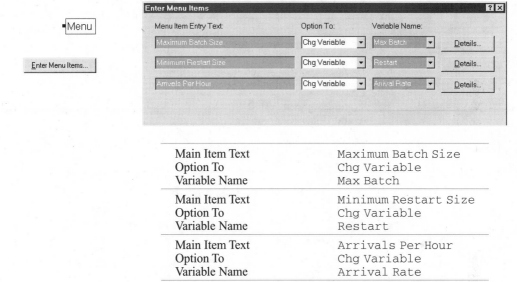

Main Item Text	Maximum Batch Size
Option To	Chg Variable
Variable Name	Max Batch
Main Item Text	Minimum Restart Size
Option To	Chg Variable
Variable Name	Restart
Main Item Text	Arrivals Per Hour
Option To	Chg Variable
Variable Name	Arrival Rate

Display 9-16. Enter Menu Items Dialog

The Menu Details dialog, Display 9-17, allows you to customize further the default prompts, which can be set in the Default Settings dialog in the main dialog. It also allows you to define valid ranges for the user inputs and define how user input errors are handled. We have elected to use this dialog only to set the valid ranges for the three variables. We defaulted the error checking which will cause the main menu to be displayed if an invalid value is entered for any prompt.

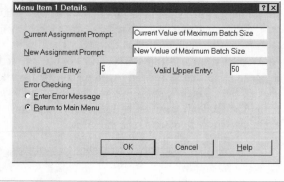

Item 1	
Valid Lower Entry	5
Valid Upper Entry	50

Item 2	
Valid Lower Entry	1
Valid Upper Entry	50

Item 3	
Valid Lower Entry	10
Valid Upper Entry	100

Display 9-17. The Menu Details Dialog

With the exception of the animated plots, our model is now complete. We want our animation to display two plots (number of items waiting and current batch size) and four variables (Maximum Batch Size, Minimum Restart Size, Arrivals Per Hour, and Number of Process Restarts). We could use the Animate module from the Common panel for our plots, but that module allows us to plot only one variable per plot. What we'd really like to have both variables plotted together so we can observe any interaction. Actually, you could use the Animate module if you wanted to be tricky. You'd place the module, enter the information for the first variable, and select only the plot display. You then accept the dialog, double-click on the resulting plot, and enter the second variable as an expression in the plot dialog. For our model, we used the plot option from the Animate toolbar. We enter the expressions NQ(Wait_Q), Number of Items Waiting, Batch Size, and Current Batch Size. For each expression, we assign 0 as the minimum value, 30 as the maximum value, and 1,000 history points. We also assigned different colors for contrast and assigned a time of 500 minutes for the plot range. We then placed the four variables (Max Batch, Restart, Arrival Rate, and NC(Startups)) using the variable option from the Animate toolbar. We completed our animation by adding text labels. Our completed animation is shown in Figure 9-9, captured at about time 475.

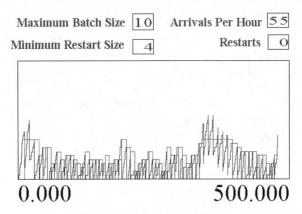

Figure 9-9. The Animated Model

Now that we have a model that runs and is animated, let's illustrate how our menu system works. Start your simulation, and after it has run a while, press the m key. The Arena command window will open with the following message, which we defined in our Menu module:

```
Variable Change Menu

    1. Maximum Batch Size
    2. Minimum Restart Size
    3. Arrivals Per Hour
    4. Start/Continue Simulation
    5. End Simulation

Enter Selection (1-5):3
```

We selected the `Arrivals Per Hour` option by entering a 3 and pressing the return key. The next part of our menu is as follows:

```
Current Value of Arrivals Per Hour:55.00
Valid Range is 10 - 100

New Value of Arrivals Per Hour:60
```

We entered a new arrival rate of 60 items per hour. Our main menu options are then displayed:

```
Variable Change Menu

1. Maximum batch size
2. Minimum Restart size
3. Arrivals Per Hour
4. Start/Continue Simulation
5. End Simulation

Enter Selection (1-5):4
```

At this point, we entered 4 to continue the simulation run. The Arena command window is closed, and you are now running with the new arrival rate. Obviously, this menu option can be used for entering information at the start of a run, for changing simulation parameters during a run, or for starting or ending specific simulation activities. Although this can be a very valuable tool, we caution against the use of data that are obtained from a simulation run where parameters have been arbitrarily changed. The use of this type of analysis is fine, as long as you use it only to understand system interactions or as a means to narrow your analysis options rather than as "final" results.

The summary report for our model using the default variable values is shown in Figure 9-10.

```
Project:  Holding and Batching
Analyst:  Uncle Jim

Replication ended at time    : 25100.0
Statistics were cleared at time: 100.0
Statistics accumulated for time: 25000.0


                        TALLY VARIABLES


Identifier              Average   Half Width   Minimum   Maximum   Observations
Size of Batches         6.6809    .17870       2.0000    10.000    3438
Wait_Q Queue Time       4.3843    .17617       .00190    22.749    22969


                    DISCRETE-CHANGE VARIABLES


Identifier              Average   Half Width   Minimum   Maximum   Final Value
# in Wait_Q             4.0287    .18859       .00000    25.000    5.0000
Process Status          .96382    (Insuf)      .00000    1.0000    1.0000


                            COUNTERS


            Identifier              Count   Limit
            Startups                   78   Infinite
```

Figure 9-10. The Arena Summary Report

9.5 Overlapping Resources

In Chapters 5-7, we concentrated on building models using the modules available from the Common panel, with some use of the modules from the Transfer panel. Even though we used these modules in several different models, we still have not exhausted all the capabilities that are buried under the buttons on the Server module. Also, we have yet to show you the Advanced Server module, although we did show you the Enter, Process, and Leave modules, which together are equivalent to the Advanced Server module.

As we developed models in the earlier chapters, we were not only interested in introducing you to new Arena constructs, but we also tried to cover different modeling techniques that might be useful. We have consistently presented new material in the form of examples that require the use of new modeling capabilities. Sometimes the fabrication of a good example to illustrate the need for new modeling capabilities is a daunting task. We have to admit that the example that we are about to introduce is a bit of a stretch, not only in terms of the model description, but also the manner in which we develop the model. However, if you bear with us through this model development, we think that you will find several handy additions to your toolbox.

9.5.1 System Description

The system we'll be modeling is a tightly-coupled three-workstation production system. We have used the words "tightly coupled" because of the unique part-arrival process and because there is limited space for part buffering between the workstations.

We'll assume an unlimited supply of raw materials that can be delivered to the system on demand. When a part enters the first workstation, a request is automatically forwarded to an adjoining warehouse for the delivery of a replenishment part. Because the warehouse is performing other duties, the replenishment part is not always delivered immediately. Rather than model this activity in detail, we'll assume an exponential delivery delay, with mean of 25 (all times are minutes), before the request is acted upon. At that point, we'll assume the part is ready for delivery, with the delivery time following a UNIF(10, 15) distribution. To start the simulation, we'll assume that two parts are ready for delivery to the first workstation.

Replenishment parts that arrive at the first workstation are held in a buffer until the workstation becomes available. A part entering the first workstation immediately requests a setup operator. The setup time is assumed to be EXPO(9). Upon completion of the setup, the part is processed by the workstation, TRIA(10, 15, 20). The completed part is then moved to the buffer between Workstations 1 and 2. This buffer space is limited to two parts; if the buffer is full, Workstation 1 is blocked until space becomes available. We'll assume that all transfer times between workstations are negligible, or occur in 0 time.

There are two almost-identical machines at Workstation 2. They differ only in the time it takes to process a part: The processing times are TRIA(35, 40, 45) for Machine 2A and TRIA(40, 45, 50) for Machine 2B. A waiting part will be processed by the first available machine. If both machines are available, Machine 2A will always be chosen. There is no setup required at this workstation. A completed part is then transferred to Workstation 3. However, there is no buffer between Workstations 2 and 3. Thus, Workstation 3 must be available before the transfer can occur. (This really affects the system performance!) If Machines 2A and 2B have completed parts (which are blocking these machines) waiting for Workstation 3, the part from Machine 2A is transferred first.

When a part enters Workstation 3, it requires the setup operator (the same operator used for setup at Workstation 1). The setup time is assumed to be EXPO(9). The process time at Workstation 3 is TRIA(9, 12, 16). The completed part exits the system at this point.

We also have failures at each workstation. Workstations 1 and 3 have a Mean Time Between Failures (MTBF) of 600 minutes with a Mean Time to Repair (MTR) of 45 minutes. Machines 2A and 2B, at Workstation 2, have a MTBF of 500 minutes and a MTR of 25 minutes. All failure and repair times follow an exponential distribution. One subtle but very important point is that the MTBF is based only on the time that the machines are processing parts, not the elapsed time.

Now to complicate the issue even further, let's assume that we're interested in the percent of time that the machines at each workstation are in different states. This should give us a great deal of insight into how to improve the system. For example, if the machine at Workstation 1 is blocked a lot of the time, we might want to look at increasing the capacity at Workstation 2.

The possible states for the different machines are as follows:

Workstation 1: Processing, Starved, Blocked, Failed, Waiting for setup operator, and Setup

Machines 2A and 2B: Processing, Starved, Blocked, and Failed

Workstation 3: Processing, Starved, Failed, Waiting for setup operator, and Setup.

We would also like to keep track of the percent of time the setup operator spends at Workstations 1 and 3. These states would be: Setup WS 1, Setup WS 2, and Idle.

These are typical measures used to determine the effectiveness of tightly coupled systems. They provide a great deal of information on what are the true system bottlenecks. Well, as long as we've gone this far, why not go all the way! Let's also assume that we'd like to know the percent of time that the parts spend in all possible states. Arranging for this is a much more difficult problem. First let's define the system or cycle time for a part as starting when the delivery is initiated and ending when the part completes processing at Workstation 3. The possible part states are: Travel to WS 1, Wait for WS 1, Wait for setup at WS 1, Setup at WS 1, Process at WS 1, Blocked at WS 1, Wait for WS 2, Process at WS 2, Blocked at WS 2, Wait for setup at WS 3, Setup at WS 3, and Process at WS 3. As we develop our model, we'll take care to incorporate the resource states. But, we'll only consider the part states after we have completed the model development. You'll just have to trust that we might know what we're doing.

9.5.2   Model 9.5: A Tightly-Coupled Production System

In developing our model, we'll use the Server module for the first workstation, the Advanced Server module for the second workstation, and modules from the Support panel for the third workstation. We are using different modules to illustrate the different approaches. Let's start with the modules for the arrival process and Workstation 1, which are shown in Figure 9-11.

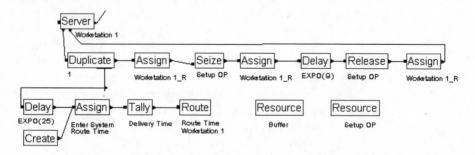

Figure 9-11.   Part Arrival and Workstation 1

Since you have seen almost all the modules that we'll be using in this model, we won't provide all the displays. However, we will provide sufficient information for you to re-create the model on your own. Of course, you can always open `Model_09_5.doe` and follow along.

Let's start with the initial arrivals that provide the first two parts for the system. All the remaining arrivals will be based on a request issued when a part enters the machine at the first workstation. The single Create module found at the lower left of Figure 9-11 has only one entry, a `Batch Size` of 2. This causes two entities, or parts, to be created at time 0. The Create module then becomes inactive—no more entities are created by it for the rest of the simulation. These two parts are sent to an Assign module where we make two attribute assignments. We assign the value of TNOW to the attribute `Enter System` and assign a value generated from a UNIF(10, 15) to the attribute `Route Time`. The value assigned to `Enter System` is the time the part entered the system, and the `Route Time` is the delivery time from the warehouse to the first workstation. Since we are interested in keeping detailed part-status information, we send these parts to a Tally module where we tally the `Delivery Time` based on the expression `Route Time`, which we assigned in the previous Assign module. The part is then sent to the following Route module where it is routed from the station `Warehouse` to the station `Workstation 1` using the `Route Time` we previously assigned.

Upon completion of this transfer, the part arrives at the Server module, `Workstation 1`. In the main dialog of the Server module, we have only two entries to make: the Station name, `Workstation 1`; and the Process Time, `TRIA(10, 15, 20)`. If these were the only entries, though, we would not capture the system logic accurately; we need to take care of three additional requirements. First, we need to specify the resource states and make sure that the statistics are kept correctly. Second, we need to make a request for a replenishment part. Finally, we need to have a setup occur before the part is processed.

Back in Section 5.2.4, we showed you how to use the Frequencies dialog contained in the Statistics module to generate frequency statistics on the number in a queue. We also pointed out that you automatically obtained resource frequency statistics when you included a resource failure. Let's start by defining the server states in the Resource Information dialog (Resource button), as shown in Display 9-18. We first enter the StateSet name, `WS 1 States`, and hit the Tab key to activate the portion of the dialog where we enter the state names. For each State, we can associate a default Arena *autostate* with our new state names. We did this for the `Processing` (Busy), `Starved` (Idle), and `Failed` (Failed) states. The very last entry was to cause the resource to be in the `Op Wait` state immediately upon seizing the `Workstation 1` resource. Recall that before the part can be processed it must undergo a setup that is performed by a setup operator. Thus, we will place the resource in that state in the event that it has to wait for the setup operator. The mere fact that we have defined resource states will result in frequency statistics in the summary report.

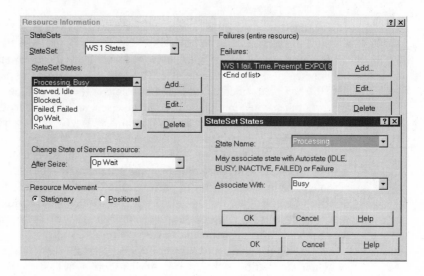

StateSets	
StateSet	WS 1 States
StateSet States	
State Name	Processing
Associate With	Busy
StateSet States	
State Name	Starved
Associate With	Idle
StateSet States	
State Name	Blocked
StateSet States	
State Name	Failed
Associate With	Failed
StateSet States	
State Name	Op Wait
StateSet States	
State Name	Setup
Change State of Server Resource	
After Seize	Op Wait

Display 9-18. Workstation 1 States

As long as we're in the Resource Information dialog, let's add the resource failure. The data entries for this are shown in Display 9-19. Note that we have based the failure on time, and the time between failures is accumulated only when the resource is in the processing state. We have also selected the Preempt option as the method of failure.

Failure	WS 1 fail
Failure Based On	Time
Fail When	Preempt
Uptime	EXPO(600)
Downtime	EXPO(45)
Uptime in this State Only	Processing

Display 9-19. Workstation 1 Failures

We also elected for an individual queue, WS 1Q, in the Queue dialog and requested statistics on both the time in queue and number in queue.

Before we leave the Server module, we need to take care of two additional details. The present data entries will not allow for the required setup operation, nor will they allow us to call for a new replenishment part. We also we need to check for space in the limited buffer that exits between Workstations 1 and 2 before we allow the part to exit Workstation 1. The Server module doesn't provide the capability to do these operations directly. However, the Options dialog provides some additional features that will allow us to include the required logic. In the upper left portion of this dialog, Display 9-20, we have checked the Access External Logic box. If you take a close look at the Server module handle after you accept this information, you'll notice that new exit and entry points (do-dads) have been added at the bottom. The selection of this option results in the following: after an arriving entity (or an entity in the server queue) seizes the server resource, it is immediately sent out of the server through the new exit point (or label). You can connect this exit point to any other modules. Normally after performing some set of functions, you return to the server by the new entry point. However, it is not necessary that you return to the server—just remember that the entity was allocated the server resource, and you may have to Release it elsewhere in order to prevent an error or incorrect model. We have also checked the Seize Before Releasing Resource box in the upper right portion of the dialog. The effect of this is that as soon as the part has completed the processing, it attempts to Seize control of one unit of the resource Buffer. Only after it has accomplished this Seize will the resource Workstation 1_R be released and the entity be sent to its next module.

Options

Additional Server Information

Seize Priority: `1`

Seize Quantity: `1`

☑ Access External Logic

Logic Label:

Return Label:

☑ Release After Processing

Overlap Resource Before Processing

☐ Release After Seizing Resource

Overlap Resource After Processing

☑ Seize Before Releasing Resource

Resource: `Buffer`

Seize Priority: `1`

Queue: `Buffer_Q`

Server State: `Blocked`

OK   Cancel   Help

Additional Server Information	
Access External Logic	*check*
Overlap Resource After Processing	
Seize Before Releasing Resource	*check*
Resource	`Buffer`
Queue	`Buffer_Q`
Server State	`Blocked`

Display 9-20. Workstation 1 External Logic and Buffer

Note that we have also designated that the server state while the entity is waiting for this resource is Blocked. In other words, the entity or part occupies the workstation until there is room in the following buffer, blocking or preventing this server from processing the next part. To complete this buffer logic, we have added a Resource module, seen in Figure 9-11, where we defined the resource `Buffer` and assigned it a capacity of 2. Actually, entering the resource named `Buffer` in the options dialog defines the resource, but it assumes it has a capacity of 1. Thus we need to add the Resource module to define the capacity as 2.

At this point you just might be scratching your head and asking, "What are they doing?" Well, we warned you that this problem was a little contorted, and once we finish the development of Workstation 1, we'll provide a high-level review of the entire sequence of events. So let's continue.

Having taken care of the entry to and exit from this workstation, we now need to take care of the part replenishment and the setup activity. The part that has just Seized the workstation resource exits at the bottom of the Server module through the external logic exit point and is sent to a Duplicate module, seen in Figure 9-11. The duplicate module creates one new entity that is sent to a Delay module, which accounts for the time the part-replenishment request waits until the actual part delivery is initiated. We then send this new part to the same set of modules that we used to cause the arrival of the first two parts. The original part exits the Duplicate module to an Assign module where we assign the state of the resource `Workstation 1_R` to `Op Wait`, in Display 9-21.

Assignment Type	
State	*select*
Resource	`Workstation 1_R`
State	`Op Wait`

Display 9-21. Resource State Assignment

It is then directed to the Seize module where it requests the setup operator, in Display 9-22. Note that we specify the state of the setup resource as `Setup WS 1`, not the workstation resource.

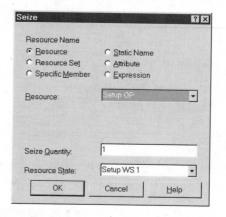

Resource Name	
Resource	*select*
Resource	`Setup OP`
Resource State	`Setup WS 1`

Display 9-22. Seizing the Setup Operator

We also placed a second Resource module where we defined the resource `Setup OP` and specified three states: `Setup WS 1`, `Setup  WS 3`, and `Idle`. In the following Assign module, we set the `Workstation 1` resource to the `Setup` state and the delay in the following delay block for the setup activity. Upon completion of the setup, we release the `Setup OP` resource, assign the workstation resources to `Processing`, and send the part back to the Server module to start the processing activity.

Now (whee!—we feel like we're out of breath after running through this logic), let's review the sequence of activities for a part at Workstation 1. We start by creating two parts at time 0; let's follow only one of them. That part is time stamped with its arrival time, and a delivery time is generated and assigned. The delivery time is tallied and the part is routed to Workstation 1. Upon entering the Server module, it joins the queue to wait for the resource `Workstation 1_R`. Having seized the resource, it exits the Server module, where it duplicates the replenishment part, which is sent back to where the first part started. The part then assigns the server resource state to `Op Wait` and queues for the setup operator. Having seized the setup operator, setting its state to `Setup WS 1`, it assigns the server resource state to `Setup`, delays for the setup, releases the setup operator, assigns the server resource state back to `Processing`, and reenters the server for processing. After processing, the part queues to seize one unit of the resource `Buffer` (capacity of 2), setting the server state to Blocked during the queueing time. After seizing the buffer resource, it releases the current server resource and exits the server with control of one unit of the resource `Buffer`.

The modules for Workstation 2, which has two machines, are shown in Figure 9-12.

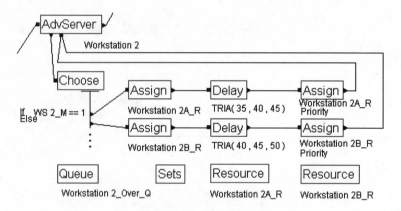

Figure 9-12. Workstation 2 Modules

A part arriving at the Workstation 2 Advanced Server module enters the queue, named `WS 2Q`, to wait for one of the two machines at this workstation, in Display 9-23. These machines, `Workstation 2A_R` and `Workstation 2B_R`, have been included in the resource set `WS 2_S`. We chose the Preferred Order rule so that if both machines were idle, the faster machine (`Workstation 2A_R`) would be selected. Note that we save the set index value, 1 or 2, of the seized resource in the attribute `WS 2_M`. Also, note that we have entered a processing time of 0. Hopefully, the reason for this will soon become obvious.

To define the two resources at Workstation 2 completely required a Sets module and two Resource modules; see Figure 9-12. The two Resource modules were used to define the resource states and resource failures. The resource states for each resource are: `Processing` (Busy), `Starved` (Idle), `Blocked`, and `Failed` (Failed).

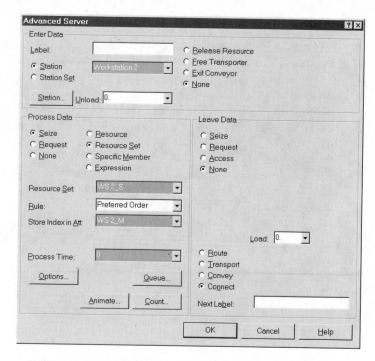

Enter Data	
Station	Workstation 2
Process Data	
Seize	*select*
Resource Set	*select*
Resource Set	WS 2_S
Rule	Preferred Order
Store Index in Att	WS 2_M
Process Time	0

Display 9-23. The Workstation 2 Advanced Server Module

As with the Server module for Workstation 1, we will again use external logic to complete our model of Workstation 2, in Display 9-24. Recall that parts arriving at Workstation 2 have control of one unit of the buffer resource. Thus, as soon as the part seizes one of the two machines, the buffer must be released as there is now a free space in front of the workstation. This action is also accomplished in the Options dialog. Additionally, we need to seize Workstation 3 before leaving 2, as there is no buffer between them. Parts that have completed processing will wait in queue `Workstation 2_Over_Q`. We'll come back to this queue later in this section.

AdvServer
Workstation 2

Options...

Options   ? X

Additional Server Options

Seize Priority: 1

Seize Quantity: 1

☑ Access External Logic

Logic Label:

Return Label:

☑ Release After Processing

Overlap Resource Before Processing

☑ Release After Seizing Resource
  ⦿ Resource
  ○ Resource Set
  ○ Specific Member
  ○ Expression

Resource: Buffer

Release Quantity: 1

Overlap Resource After Processing

☑ Seize Before Releasing Resource
  ⦿ Resource
  ○ Resource Set
  ○ Specific Member
  ○ Expression

Resource: Workstation 3_R

Seize Priority: 1

Seize Quantity: 1

Queue...

OK   Cancel   Help

Additional Server Options	
Access External Logic	*check*
Overlap Resource Before Processing	
Release After Seizing Resource	*check*
Resource	`Buffer`
Overlap Resource After Processing	
Seize Before Releasing Resource	*check*
Resource	`Workstation 3_R`

Display 9-24. Workstation 2 Options Dialog

Upon seizing an available machine, a part temporarily exits the Advanced Server module by the external logic exit point. The part enters the Choose module, which is used to determine which machine resource has been seized, based on the WS 2_M attribute value assigned in the Advanced Server module when the resource was allocated to the part. The top three modules, in Figure 9-12, are for Workstation 2A_R and the bottom three are for Workstation 2B_R. The first Assign module assigns the state of the machine resource to Processing and directs the part to the following Delay module, which represents the part processing. The last Assign module assigns the machine resource state to Blocked and assigns a user-defined attribute (Priority) a value of 1 for machine Workstation 2A_R and 2 for machine Workstation 2B_R. The part is then sent back to the Advanced Server module by the external logic entry point.

Most of this should be fairly straightforward, with the possible exception of the assignment to the attribute `Priority`. Recall that if both machines have parts that are waiting for Workstation 3 to become available, `Machine 2A` is always given preference. We will use the `Priority` attribute as the means to guarantee this preference. Parts that re-enter our Advanced Server module first undergo a zero-time delay, the entered Process Time. Because we needed to control the state of our two machine resources, we modeled the processing delay in our external logic. This part then attempts to seize control of resource `Workstation 3_R`, as defined in our Options dialog. If the resource is unavailable, the part will wait in queue `Workstation 2_Over_Q`, which was defined in the Queue dialog contained in the Options portion of the Advanced Server module. Now, if there are two waiting parts, one for each machine, we want the part from `Machine 2A` to be first in line. We accomplish this by placing a Queue module from the Common panel and selecting the ranking rule to be Low Value First based in the value of attribute `Priority`, in Display 9-25. This causes all entities in the queue to be ranked according to their value for the attribute `Priority`. This assures that `Machine 2A` will receive preference.

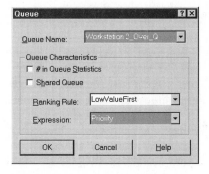

Queue Name	Workstation 2_Over_Q
Ranking Rule	LowValueFirst
Expression	Priority

Display 9-25. The Queue Module Dialog

Once a part has been allocated the `Workstation 3_R` resource, it will be transferred to that machine in 0 time. The modules we used to model Workstation 3 are shown in Figure 9-13. You might notice that these modules look very similar to those used to model Workstation 1, and they are essentially the same. An entering part (it already has been allocated the resource `Workstation 3_R`) first assigns the workstation resource state to `Op Wait` and then attempts to seize the setup operator. After being allocated the setup operator resource, the resource workstation state is set to `Setup`, the part is delayed for setup, the setup operator is released, the resource workstation state is set to `Processing`, and the part is delayed for the process time. Upon completion, the `Workstation 3_R` resource is released, the part cycle time is tallied, and the entity is disposed. As was the case for the previous machine resources, we used the Resource module to define the resource states and the failure properties.

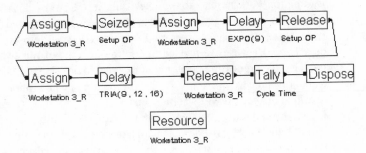

Figure 9-13. Workstation 3 Modules

In developing this model, we could easily have modeled all three workstations with almost the same set of modules shown in Figure 9-13. However, we intentionally used the Server and Advanced Server modules to illustrate some of their special features. At this point, we could add a Simulate module and fine tune our model. But, let's add the remaining detail first.

Recall that when we were describing our problem, we also wanted to output the percent of time that the parts spend in all possible states. Obtaining this information for resource states is fairly easy. We simply define the resource states and Arena collects and reports this information using the Frequencies feature. Unfortunately, this use of Frequencies is valid only for resources.

Collecting the same type of information for part or entity status is difficult because the part states span numerous activities over several resources. This creates a modeling problem: What is the best way to obtain this information? Before we show you our approach, we'll discuss several alternatives, including their shortcomings.

Our first thought was to define a variable that we could change based on the current part state. Then we could request frequency statistics on that variable, much as we did for the part-storage queue in the rework area of Model 5.2 in Section 5.2.4. Of course, this would require us to edit our model to add assignments to this variable whenever the part status changed. Although this sounds like a good idea, it falls apart when you realize that there can be multiple parts in the system at the same time. It would work just fine if we limited the number of parts in our system to one. Since this was not in the problem description, we decided to consider alternate ways to collect this information.

Our second idea was to assume that all the required information was already being collected (a valid assumption). Given this, we need only assemble this information at the end of the run and calculate our desired statistics. Arena automatically calls a wrap-up routine at the end of each run. We could write user code (see Section 10.2) that would perform this function. One drawback is that it would not give us this information if we decided to look at our summary report before the run ended. This looked like it could be a lot of work, so we explored other options.

For our third approach, we decided to consider the special report features provide by Arena in the SIMAN template (the Elements panel). These features allow creation of user-customized output reports (more on this in Section 10.3). The use of these features will not allow you to collect additional statistics; however, they do allow you to calculate additional output values on statistics already being collected by the model. In addition, they allow you to append additional information in the format of your choice to the current summary report, or create a totally separate report. Since the model is currently collecting all the information we need, although not in the correct form, we will use this option to output information on part status.

The modules required are shown in Figure 9-14. We first placed a Simulate module with the run length specified as 50,000 time units. The remaining modules are going to take a bit of explaining, as several of the initial steps will not become obvious until we have completed all the modules required for our report.

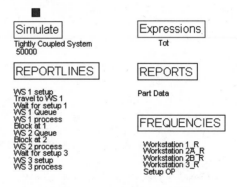

Figure 9-14. The Data Modules

In Section 5.2.5, we very briefly mentioned the fact that you could restrict the last column of the Frequencies summary to contain only certain values. Let's now show you how to do that using the FREQUENCIES module from the Elements panel. Assume we do not want the values for the Op Wait and Setup states for Workstation 1 to be included in this column. The FREQUENCIES module is used to record the time-persistent occurrence frequency of a SIMAN variable or expression. In Section 5.2.4, we requested frequency statistics using the Statistics module from the Common panel. If we only needed to exclude the Op Wait and Setup states from the restricted column, we could use that module here. However, as you'll see shortly, we also need to number each frequency so we can reference it when we calculate our part-state statistics. To do this, we need the FREQUENCIES module as shown in Display 9-26. Note that we have entered and numbered each of our resources for which we defined states: Workstation 1_R, Workstation 2A_R, Workstation 2B_R, Workstation 3_R, and Setup OP. We also entered a name, to be used in the summary report, for each of our frequencies. You might note that this is an optional field, and Arena will use a default name based on the expression or resource name if you default this field.

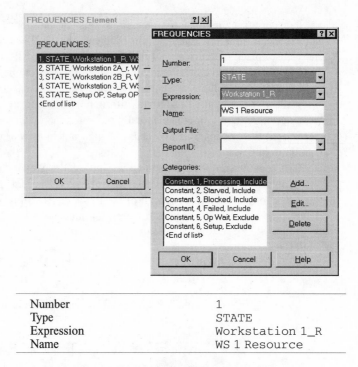

Number	1
Type	STATE
Expression	Workstation 1_R
Name	WS 1 Resource

Display 9-26. The FREQUENCIES Module Dialog

If we need to number only the frequencies, this is all we have to do. The summary report will include category statistics for all the previously defined states as a default. This is the case for the last four resources. However, for the first resource (Workstation 1_R), we want to exclude two states from the restricted column. Therefore, for this resource only, we need to enter all the states that we previously defined. If we inadvertently omit one, the time that it spent in that state would be reported as Out of Range on the summary report.

We have shown the first and fifth entries in Display 9-27. Some of these entries may not be obvious. For example, we have entered Constant for the Value or Range. Since this is a resource state, this refers to the index of that state. Thus, Processing is state 1 and Op Wait is state 5. Also note that we have requested that all states, except the last two (Op Wait and Setup), be included in the restricted percentage column. The last two were excluded from this column. This same Categories dialog is a part of the Statistics module. Thus, except for the requirement to number the frequencies, we could have used the Statistics module to exclude the last two states.

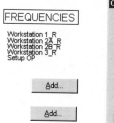
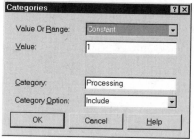
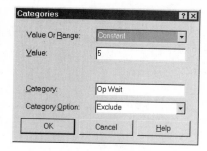

Value or Range	Constant
Value	1
Category	Processing
Category Option	Include
Value or Range	Constant
Value	5
Category	Op Wait
Category Option	Exclude

Display 9-27. Defining the Categories in the FREQUENCIES Module

If we ran our model at this point, we'd get the results shown in Figure 9-15. Let's temporarily focus our attention on the frequency statistics for the Workstation 1 resource. It tells us that the workstation was processing parts only 48.86% of the time, with a large amount of non-productive time spent in the `Op Wait` and `Setup` states. If we exclude these two states, the processing accounts for 81.5% of the activity. Although this may not be the best example, it illustrates how values can be excluded from the restricted column. If we were modeling a three-shift operation where some resources might be unavailable during one or more shifts, this would be a very useful feature. If we collected frequency statistics on these resources, the standard column would include an entry for the inactive or off-shift time. This value could account for as much as 66.67% if the resource was available for only one shift. Thus, the busy and idle values may be difficult to interpret. By excluding the inactive time, our restricted column would provide us with values that actually reflected the idle and busy percentages during the one shift the resource was available.

```
Project:  Tightly Coupled
Analyst:  Uncle Buck

Replication ended at time      : 50000.0
Statistics were cleared at time: 500.0
Statistics accumulated for time: 49500.0


                          TALLY VARIABLES

Identifier           Average    Half Width   Minimum    Maximum    Observations
Delivery Time        12.478      .08259       10.003     14.995      1615
WS 2Q Queue Time     18.129     4.1105        .00000    157.43       1614
Cycle Time          164.43      5.2876        81.543    324.78       1614
WS 1Q Queue Time     24.224     1.2438        .00000    159.19       1615
```

DISCRETE-CHANGE VARIABLES

Identifier	Average	Half Width	Minimum	Maximum	Final Value
# in WS 1Q	.79011	.03202	.00000	2.0000	1.0000
# in WS 2Q	.59132	.14995	.00000	2.0000	1.0000

FREQUENCIES

Identifier	Category	—Occurrences— Number	AvgTime	Standard Percent	Restricted Percent
WS 1 Resource	Processing	1653	14.643	48.90	81.39
	Starved	265	12.007	6.43	10.70
	Blocked	45	15.822	1.44	2.39
	Failed	38	43.139	3.31	5.51
	Op Wait	594	9.4778	11.37	—
	Setup	1614	8.7549	28.55	—
WS 2A Resource	Processing	757	45.595	69.73	69.73
	Starved	282	15.568	8.87	8.87
	Blocked	567	16.416	18.80	18.80
	Failed	59	21.790	2.60	2.60
WS 2B Resource	Processing	570	58.967	67.90	67.90
	Starved	230	22.316	10.37	10.37
	Blocked	375	22.630	17.14	17.14
	Failed	75	30.254	4.58	4.58
WS 3 Resource	Processing	1650	12.067	40.22	40.22
	Starved	674	12.360	16.83	16.83
	Failed	36	44.457	3.23	3.23
	Op Wait	511	9.1341	9.43	9.43
	Setup	1614	9.2874	30.28	30.28
Setup OP Resource	Setup WS 1	1614	8.7549	28.55	28.55
	Setup WS 3	1614	9.2874	30.28	30.28
	Idle	2124	9.5948	41.17	41.17

Figure 9-15. The Tightly-Coupled System Summary Report

Before we continue with our model development, let's describe what we need to do in order to obtain the desired information on part status. What we want is the percent of time that parts spend in each of the previously defined part states: Travel to WS 1, Wait for WS 1, Wait for setup at WS 1, Setup at WS 1, Process at WS 1, Blocked at WS 1, Wait for WS 2, Process at WS 2, Blocked at WS 2, Wait for setup at WS 3, Setup at WS 3, and Process at WS 3.

All the information we need to calculate these values is already contained in our summary output. Let's consider our first part state, Travel to WS 1. The average delivery time per part was 12.473, tallied for a total of 1632 parts. The cycle time was 164.63 for 1626 parts. You might note that there are still six parts (1632-1626) in the system when the simulation was terminated. We'll come back to this later. So if we want the percent of time an average part spent traveling to Workstation 1, we could calculate that value with the following expression:

$$((12.473 \times 1632) / (164.63 \times 1626)) \times 100.0$$

or 7.61%. We can use this approach to calculate all of our values. Basically, we compute the total amount of part time spent in each activity, divide it by the total amount of part time spent in all activities, and multiple by 100 to obtain the values in percentages. Since the last two steps of this calculation are always the same, we will first define an expression, `Tot`, to represent this value. Note that by using an expression, it will be computed only when required. That expression is as follows:

```
TAVG(Cycle Time) * TNUM(Cycle Time)/100
```

TAVG and TNUM are Arena variables that return the current average of a Tally and the total number of Tally observations, respectively. The variable argument is the Tally ID. In this case, we have elected to use the Tally name as defined in our Tally module. In cases where Arena defines the Tally name (e.g., for time-in-queue tallies), we recommend that you check a module's pull-down list (e.g., Depart) for the exact name.

The information required to calculate three of our part states is contained in Tallies: `Travel to WS 1`, `Wait for WS 1`, and `Wait for WS 2`. The expressions required to calculate these values are as follows:

```
        TAVG(Delivery Time) * TNUM(Delivery Time)/Tot
     TAVG(WS 1Q Queue Time) * TNUM(WS 1Q Queue Time)/Tot
     TAVG(WS 2Q Queue Time) * TNUM(WS 2Q Queue Time)/Tot
```

The information for the remaining part states are contained in the frequency statistics.

As you would expect, Arena also provides variables that will return information about Frequencies. The Arena variable FRQTIM returns the total amount of time that a specified resource was in a specified category, or state. The complete expression for this variable is:

FRQTIM(Frequency ID, Category)

The Frequency ID argument is the frequency name. The Category argument is a reference to the category as seen on the summary report. Unfortunately, you can't just enter the category name as seen on the summary report.

In order to see this, you need to understand a bit more about how Arena works. As you build an Arena model, you will enter names in many fields (e.g., attribute name, variable name, state name, etc.). However, when you request that the model be executed, Arena creates a reference list of all names and assigns a *number* to each that is used during the model execution. The specific numbers that Arena uses can be found in the SIMAN experiment file, which was briefly discussed in Section 6.4.4. We'll take advantage of this again when we modify our call center model in Section 10.3. Remember that we have used the same resource state names in almost all of our Frequencies. Thus, a specific resource state name must be referenced to the resource name in order to be assured that you obtain the correct number.

This can be accomplished by using another Arena variable to obtain a proper reference:

STATEVALUE(Resource ID, State Name)

This variable returns an integer value for the state of the resource, or a reference to the category. The resulting expression for calculating the `Wait for setup at WS 1` state percentage is as follows:

```
FRQTIM(WS 1 Resource, STATEVALUE(Workstation 1_R,Op Wait))/Tot
```

Although this will yield the correct value, it is a rather long expression that we will need to enter for each of the remaining nine part states. This was the reason for using the FREQUENCIES module and explicitly numbering each frequency. Therefore, we can use these numbers for the first argument of the FRQTIM variable. The second argument is the index or position of the desired state in the Stateset. We can get this number by opening the dialogs where we defined the states in each Stateset, by creating and viewing the experiment file or by looking at the summary report. For our example, the `Op Wait` state is the fifth item in the frequency statistics for Workstation 1. Our expression now becomes:

FRQTIM(1, 5)/Tot

If we define all our expressions in this manner, the nine remaining expression are as follows:

```
Wait for setup at WS 1   FRQTIM(1,5)/Tot
Setup at WS 1            FRQTIM(1,6)/Tot
Process at WS 1          FRQTIM(1,1)/Tot
Blocked at WS 1          FRQTIM(1,3)/Tot
Process at WS 2          FRQTIM(2,1)/Tot + FRQTIM(3,1)/Tot
Blocked at WS 2          FRQTIM(2,3)/Tot + FRQTIM(3,3)/Tot
Wait for setup at WS 3   FRQTIM(4,4)/Tot
Setup at WS 3            FRQTIM(4,5)/Tot
Process at WS 3          FRQTIM(4,1)/Tot
```

You should note that there can be two parts being processed or blocked at Workstation 2. Thus, we have included terms for both the 2A and 2B resources at Workstation 2.

Now that we have developed a method, and the expressions, to calculate the average percent of time our parts spend in each state, we will use the Arena report functions to add this information to our standard summary report. We first need to define our new summary output using the REPORTS module; see Display 9-28.

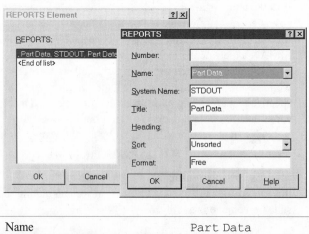

Name	Part Data

Display 9-28. The REPORTS Module Dialog

In this case, we need to provide only a report Name; the Title defaults to the Name. We defaulted our system name to STDOUT, which will result in the report information being appended to the standard summary report. We also defaulted the Sort option to Unsorted, as we will control the order of our information in the next step. Many additional options are available, and we encourage you to use online help to explore these options if you elect to use them in your own models.

Having defined a report, we now need to define the items in that report. You do this with the REPORTLINES module from the Elements panel. Our report was designed specifically to provide additional statistics on the part states. However, you could include any information from the simulation. In fact, you could design your own output summary and suppress the standard summary report (PROJECT module from the Elements panel). This report feature is also useful if you are going to make a lot of different runs where you change the values of a few variables in the model. By adding the values of these variables to the summary report, you will always know what the run was based on.

Display 9-29 shows the report line for one of our entries. We have chosen to number each of our report lines to control the order in which they will be listed. Although the Name is a required field, it will not appear on the output. We have referenced our report name and provided a specific format to use in writing out the information. You can use FORTRAN or C formats, or you can default to a free format; see online help for more information. We have also entered the expression to calculate the value we want to output. You can enter and output as many expressions as you wish, but we recommend that you use a separate report line for each line to be added to the report.

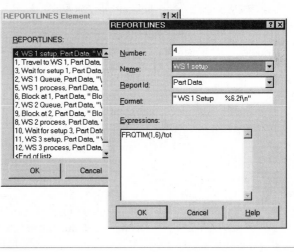

Number	4
Name	WS 1 setup
Report ID	Part Data
Format	"WS 1 Setup %6.2f\n"
Expression	FRQTIM(1,6)/tot

Display 9-29. The REPORTLINES Module Dialog

Before we proceed, let's address the discrepancy between the number of observations on our summary report. Because of the methods we use to collect our statistics, and the fact that we start our simulation with the system empty and idle, this discrepancy will always exist. There are several ways to deal with it. One method would be to terminate the arrival of parts to the system and let all parts complete processing before we terminate the simulation run. Although this would yield statistics on an identical set of parts, in effect we're adding a shutdown period to our simulation. This would mean that we would have potential transient conditions at both the start and end of the simulation, which would affect the results of our resource statistics.

We could increase our run length until the relative difference between these observations would become very small, thereby reducing the effect on our results. Although this could easily be done for this small textbook problem, it could result in unacceptably long run times for a larger problem. If we wanted to be assured that all part-state statistics were based on the same set of parts, we could collect the times each part spends in each activity and store these times in entity attributes. When the part exits the system, we could then Tally all these times. Although this is possible, it would require that we make substantial changes to our model, and we would expect that the increased accuracy would not justify these changes.

If you step back for a moment, you should realize that the problem of having summary statistics based on different entity activities is not unique to this problem. It exists for almost every steady-state simulation that you might construct. So we recommend that in this case you take the same approach that we use for the analysis of steady-state simulations. Thus, we would add a Warm-Up Period to eliminate the start-up conditions. Because our system is tightly coupled, it will not accumulate large queues, and the number of parts in the system will tend to remain about the same. Because the warehouse delay is modeled as exponential, it is possible that there could be no parts in the system, although this is highly unlikely. At the other extreme, there can be a maximum of only eight parts in the system. Thus, by adding a warm-up to our model, we will start collecting statistics when the system is already in operation. This will reduce the difference between the number of observations for our Tallies. For now, let's just assume a warm-up period of 500 time units and edit our Simulate module to include that entry. If this were a much larger system that could accumulate large queues, you might want to reconsider this decision.

If you now run the model, the information shown in Figure 9-16 will be appended to the summary report. As a point of information, the maximum difference for the number of observations on our tallies was one. At this point, we could accept this output and begin to exercise our model. However, a simple check of these data shows that the sum of all the part activities is 97.46%. This means either that there is an error or that 2.54% of the activities are unaccounted for. It's unlikely that this difference could have been caused by the problem we thought was taken care of by adding a warm-up period to our simulation. This surprised even us, so we extended our run length to 500,000 time units to see if a problem remained. This resulted in 16,109 observations for our cycle-time tally and part-data values that are very similar to those from the first run. To our continued surprise, the sum of part activities was 97.45%, almost identical to the first run.

```
             Part Data

Travel to WS 1        7.59

Queue 1 Wait         14.74
Setup WS 1 Wait       2.12
WS 1 Setup            5.32
Process 1             9.12
Blocked at 1          0.27

Queue 2 Wait         11.02
Process 2            25.67
Blocked at 2          6.70

Setup WS 3 Wait       1.76
WS 3 Setup            5.65
Process 3             7.50
```

Figure 9-16. *The Appended Summary Report*

Now convinced that there was a modeling error, we carefully rechecked our model logic to make sure that we had accounted for all the time that a part spent in the system. The logic appeared to be correct! Next we carefully checked the expressions used to calculate our percentage values for the part states. As was the case for the model logic, the expressions appeared to be correct! Not willing to admit defeat, we repeated the process. Everything still appeared to be correct! Finally, quite by accident, we remembered that we had elected to use the Preempt option for all of our resource failures. Since the time between failures was accumulated only during the processing state, it almost ensured that there would be a part being processed when it was time for a failure to occur. When Arena preempts a resource, it places the preempted entity (or part) in an internal queue, where it resides until the repair is completed, at which time the resource is allocated to the entity and the processing continues. At the point in time when the entity is preempted, the resource state changes to Failed. When the repair is completed, the resource state changes to busy. Although we assigned our resource states to Processing in Assign modules, we also associated the Busy autostate with Processing. Thus our processing frequencies were correct, quite by accident. Had we neglected to do this association, we would have seen an additional frequency entry under each workstation resource labeled BUSY. The result is that our parts are spending about 2.5% of their time waiting in an internal queue because they were preempted for a resource failure.

You can easily check this out by assuming that whenever the resource is failed, there is an entity in an internal queue. You can then use the data from the summary report to calculate the percent of time that parts spend in these queues. Hopefully, these calculations are obvious at this point. The second alternative is to add this time to our part-state report. Why not let the computer do our calculations? An even easier way to check this out is to change the Fail When option to IGNORE or WAIT for all four workstation resources and rerun the simulation.

Let's provide closure to this problem by freely admitting that our first reaction to this dilemma was to change our problem definition so this condition did not occur. However, calmer heads prevailed, and we decided to deal with it directly to reinforce what we feel is a rather important point. When you first start your simulation career by modeling with high-level constructs, it is tempting to ignore what is going on underneath. Sometimes an assumption made by the modeling constructs is different from your intent. We strongly recommend that you take the time to understand fully the implications of checking a box or making a selection before you start to make real decisions with simulation. We also believe that it is important to verify your model and results before proceeding with your analysis (more on this in Chapter 12). You never know what manager or executive is going to drag out a hand calculator and attempt to check your simulation results.

9.6   A Few Miscellaneous Modeling Issues

Our intention in writing this tome was not to attempt to cover all the functions available in the Arena simulation system. There are still a few modules in the Common, Support, and Transfer panels that we have not discussed. And there are many more in the Blocks and Elements panels that we have neglected entirely. However, in your spare time, we encourage you to attach the panels that you seldom use and place modules. Using the online help features will give you a good idea of what we have omitted. In most cases, we suspect that you'll never need these additional features. Before we close this chapter, we'd like to point out and briefly discuss a few features we have not covered. We don't feel that these topics require an in-depth understanding—only an awareness.

9.6.1   Guided Transporters

There is an entire set of features designed for use with guided transporters. These features are useful not only for modeling automated guided vehicle (AGV) systems, but also for warehousing systems and material handling systems that use the concept of a moving cart, tote, jig, or fixture, etc. Interestingly, they're also great for representing many amusement park rides. Because this topic would easily fill an additional chapter or two, we've chosen not to present it in this book. However, you can find a complete discussion of these features in Chapter 9 of Pegden, Shannon, and Sadowski (1995).

9.6.2   Parallel Queues

There are also two very specialized modules from the Blocks panel, QPICK and PICKQ, that are seldom used, but if you need them, they can make your modeling task much easier. The QPICK module can be used to represent a process where you want to pick the next entity for processing or movement from two or more different queues based on some decision rule. Basically, the QPICK module would sit between a set of detached QUEUE modules and a module that allocates some type of scarce resource (e.g., ALLOCATE, REQUEST, ACCESS, or SEIZE modules). Let's say that you have three different streams of entities converging at a point where they attempt to seize the same resource. Furthermore, assume that you want to keep the entities from each stream separate from each other. The modules required for this part of your model are shown in Figure 9-17. Each entity stream would end by sending the entity to its Detached queue (more on a Detached queue shortly). The link between the QPICK and QUEUE modules is by module Labels. When the resource becomes available, it will basically ask the QPICK module to determine from which queue to select the next entity to be allocated the resource. Also note that you must use the SEIZE module from the Blocks panel for this to work, not the Seize module from the Support panel. When using modules from the Blocks panel, Arena does not automatically define queues, resources, etc. Thus, you may have to place the corresponding modules from the Elements panel to define these objects.

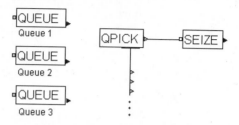

Figure 9-17. Using a QPICK Module

The PICKQ module can be used to represent a process where you have a single arrival stream, and you will use some decision rule to pick between two or more queues in which to place the entity. Let's assume that you have a stream of arriving entities that are to be loaded onto one of two available conveyors. The modules required for this part of your model are shown in Figure 9-18. Note that you can't specify internal queues for the Access modules, and the decision as to which conveyor the entity is directed to is based on characteristics of the queue, not the conveyors. The PICKQ module can be used to direct entities to Access, Seize, Allocate, Request, or QUEUE modules, or any module that is preceded by a queue.

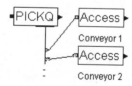

Figure 9-18. Using a PICKQ Module

Now let's address the issue of a Detached queue. If you use the QUEUE module from the Blocks panel, you're given the option of defining the queue as being Detached. This means that the queue is not directly linked to a downstream module. Such a queue can be indirectly linked, as was the case with the QPICK module, or there might be no obvious link. For example, you may want to use a set of entities whose attribute values hold information that you might want to access and change over the course of a simulation. If this is all you want to do, it might be easier to use a Variable defined as a matrix, or perhaps an external database. The advantage of using a queue is that you can also change the ranking of the entities in the queue. You can access or change any entity attribute values using Arena variables. You can also use the SEARCH, COPY, INSERT, PICKUP, and

REMOVE modules from the Blocks panel to interact with the entities in the queue. Note that if queue ranking is important, Arena only ranks an entity that enters the queue. Thus if you change an entity attribute that is used to rank the queue, you must remove the entity from the queue and then place it back into the queue.

9.6.3   Decision Logic

There are situations where you may require complex decision logic based on current system conditions. Arena provides several modules in the Blocks panel that might prove useful. The first is a set for the development of if-then-else logic. The IF, ELSEIF, ELSE, and ENDIF modules can be used to develop such logic. We will not explain these modules in detail here, but we encourage you to use online help if you implement logic with these modules. Although these modules will allow you to develop powerful logic, you need to be very careful to ensure that your logic is working correctly. These modules are designed to work only when all of the modules between an If and its matching Endif (including any Elseif or Else modules inside) are graphically connected in Arena. This allows you to use many of Arena's modules inside of If/Endif logic, such as Assign, Seize, and Delay, but precludes use of those that don't permit graphical connections, such as Route, Convey, and Transport. There is also a set of modules to implement do-while logic: the WHILE and ENDWHILE modules. The same warnings given previously also apply for these modules.

If you really need to implement this type of logic, there are several options. The easiest is to use the Label and Next Label options to connect your modules rather than direct graphical connections. Although this works, it doesn't show the flow of logic. An alternative is to write your logic as an external .mod file and use the INCLUDE module from the Blocks panel to include this logic in your module. Unfortunately, this option is not available for use with the Academic or Evaluation software. The safest and most frequently used option is to use a combination of Choose, Chance, and BRANCH modules to implement your logic. This always works, although the logic may not be very elegant.

9.6.4   Continuous Modeling

In Section 1.2.3, we mentioned briefly that Arena can be used for continuous and mixed continuous-discrete models. We also pointed out that our focus would be on discrete models. Thus, we won't present the Arena continuous model features in this book. This is partially due to the fact that these features are used rather infrequently in modeling real-world problems. This does not imply that Arena is not used to model systems that contain continuous components. We have seen it used to model a number of such systems. However, in many of these cases, the decision was made to model these continuous components in a discrete fashion.

If you need to model a system with continuous components, we recommend that you examine those components to determine how, and if, they need to be modeled. If these components are critical to the simulation and they can't be described as linear equations, then you will probably need to use the Arena continuous modeling constructs. These can be found in the Blocks and Elements panels and are discussed and described in Chapter 10 of Pegden, Shannon, and Sadowski (1995).

If the continuous components can be represented as linear rate equations, you should consider modeling them in a discrete fashion. For example, consider a process that includes mixing solid and liquid ingredients in a small tank, transferring the mixture to a larger tank, adding additional liquid and mixing, transferring to a canning line, filling and labeling the cans, boxing and palletizing, and finally transferring to a shipping area. The process starts (solid ingredients) and ends (cans) with discrete components. Actually, you could easily consider the mixing operations as discrete in that they can be modeled as simple delays. The continuous components are the adding of liquid at the two mixing operations and the transfer of the product from tank to tank or filling line. You typically find that the pumping rates for the filling and transfer are constant. Let's assume that the first tank is 500 gallons, the second tank is 5,000 gallons, and the pumping rate is 25 gallons per minute for both filling and transfer. Let's also assume that you have animated your tanks with Arena Levels. A quick calculation tells you that it takes 20 minutes to fill the small tank and an additional three hours to add 4,500 gallons to the second tank.

There are two ways to model this activity in a discrete fashion. Both require that you think of the liquid as a sum of discrete quantities, say 10 gallons. We could model each 10 gallons as a different discrete entity. For example, in filling the first tank we would create or duplicate 50 entities each representing 10 gallons. We control the flow into the tank with a pump resource that takes 24 minutes per 10 gallons, or entity. As the 10-gallon entity enters the first tank, you add 10 gallons to a variable that represents the current tank level. An alternate method is to create or duplicate a single entity at the start of the filling process and have it loop through a 24-minute delay, add 10 gallons to tank level, 24-minute delay, etc. After the tank has been filled, the entity is disposed. The second method is generally preferred as it results in fewer entities in the model.

Similar logic can be developed to model the transfer of the liquid from tank to tank. You can also incorporate logic that changes the pumping rate or stops the pumping based on other system conditions. In that case, you must model the delay as a variable dependent on the current rate (an expression, for example) or model the amount of liquid as a variable dependent on the current rate. If you are unsure of the effect of this modeling abstraction, run your model for several different entity sizes (1, 5, 10, and 25 gallons) and compare the difference, if any, in the results. This will allow you to make the trade-off between simulation speed and simulation accuracy.

This method of converting a continuous flow to a discrete flow almost always provides satisfactory results. In fact, you can use the same modeling trick for discrete systems that have an extraordinarily large number of entities in process at any given time. Say that you have a production line where the entities are bottles, cans, etc. Modeling each item as an entity may result in very long simulation run times. You might want to consider modeling each entity as 2, 5, or 10 physical items to reduce the run time. Of course, you will have to make the trade-off between speed and accuracy. If you have a large number of scenarios to consider and you find that the accuracy suffers as you increase the entity size, you might want to conduct an initial analysis with the larger entity size to narrow the number of options. Once you have a smaller number of options, you can reduce your entity size to obtain the desired accuracy for the final analysis.

The purpose of this discussion is not to discourage you from using the continuous modeling portion of Arena. Rather, you should always consider multiple approaches to any modeling situation. If your system really requires a continuous modeling approach, we certainly recommend that you use the available functionality.

9.7 Exercises

9.1 Packages arrive with interarrival times distributed as EXPO(0.46) minutes to an unloading facility. There are five different types of packages, each equally likely to arrive, and each with its own unload station. The unloading stations are located around a loop conveyor that has room for only two packages in the queue at each unload station. Arriving packages enter an infinite-capacity queue to wait for space on the loop conveyor, and 2 feet of conveyor space is required per package. Upon entering the loop conveyor, the package is conveyed to its unload station. If there is room in the queue at its unload station, the package is automatically diverted to the queue, which takes no time. The package then waits for a dedicated unloader (dedicated to this unload station, not to this package) to be unloaded, which takes time distributed as EXPO(2) minutes. If a package arrives at its station and finds the queue full, it is automatically conveyed around the loop and tries the next time. Each station is located 10 feet from the next, and the conveyor speed is 12 feet per minute.

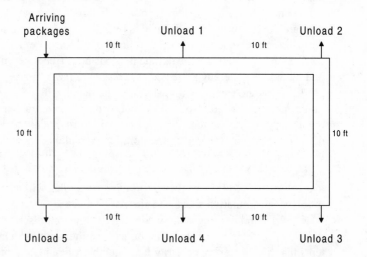

(a) Run the simulation for 250 minutes, collecting statistics on the time in system (all package types together, not separated out by package type), and the number of packages in queue at the package-arrival station.

(b) Which will have more impact on performance: increasing the conveyor speed to 15 feet per minute or increasing each unloading-queue capacity to 4?

9.2   A merging conveyor system has a main conveyor consisting of three segments, and two spur conveyors, as depicted in the figure below. Separate streams of packages arrive at the input end of each of the three conveyors, with interarrival times distributed as EXPO(0.7) minutes. Incoming packages queue to wait for space on the conveyor. Packages arriving at the input end of the main conveyor are conveyed directly to the system exit. Packages arriving at the two spur lines are conveyed to the main conveyor, where they wait for space. Once space is available, they exit the spur line and are conveyed to the system exit. All conveyor segments are 20 feet (the main conveyor has three such segments) and all three conveyors are accumulating and move at 15 feet per minute. Each package requires 2 feet of space on a conveyor. When packages reach the exit-system point, there is an unload time of 0.2 minute, during which time the package retains it space on the main conveyor.

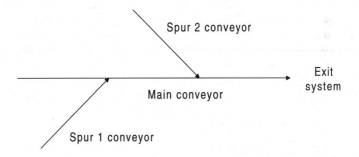

Develop a model and animation of this system and run it for 200 minutes, observing statistics on conveyor status (such as number of packages conveying and accumulated on each segment) as well as times in system for packages.

9.3   A small automated power-and-free assembly system consists of six workstations. (A power-and-free system could represent things like tow chains and hook lines.) Parts are placed on pallets that move through the system and stop at each workstation for an operation. There are 12 pallets in the system. A blank part is placed on an empty pallet as part of the operation at Workstation 1. The unit (part and pallet) is then moved progressively through the system until all the operations are completed. The final assembled part is removed from the pallet at Workstation 6 as part of the operation there. The power-and-free system moves at 4 feet per minute. Each pallet requires 2 feet of space. The distance between adjacent workstations is 10 feet, except that Workstation 6 (the final assembly operation) and Workstation 1 (the beginning assembly operation) are 20 feet apart. The figure below indicates how the workstations are arranged. The operation times at each workstation are NORM(3.0, 0.8) minutes.

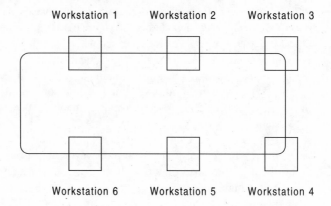

Workstation 1   Workstation 2   Workstation 3

Workstation 6   Workstation 5   Workstation 4

Develop a simulation and animation of this system and run it for 1,500 minutes, observing statistics on the production per hour. (Hint: Model the power-and-free system as an accumulating conveyor. At the start of your simulation, load the empty pallets at Workstation 6. These pallets become a permanent part of the system.) Look at the effect on hourly production of the number of pallets. Would more (or fewer) than 12 pallets be preferable? Is there something like an optimal number of pallets? Be sure to back up your statements with a valid statistical analysis.

9.4   A small production system has parts arriving with interarrival times distributed as TRIA(6, 13, 19) minutes. All parts enter at the dock area, are transported to Workstation 1, then to Workstation 2, then to Workstation 3, and finally back to the dock, as indicated in the figure below. All part transportation is provided by two carts that each move at 60 feet per minute. The distances from the dock to each of Workstations 1 and 3 are 50 feet, and the distances between each pair of workstations are also 50 feet. Parts are unloaded from the cart at Workstations 1 and 3 for processing, but parts get processed on the cart at Workstation 2. Processing times are NORM(12, 2) minutes, UNIF(8, 11) minutes, and TRIA(8, 11, 18) minutes for Workstations 1, 2, and 3, respectively. Assume that all load and unload times are negligible.

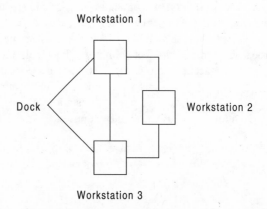

Workstation 1

Dock

Workstation 2

Workstation 3

Develop a simulation and animation of this system and run it for 10,000 minutes, observing statistics on cart and workstation utilizations, as well as part cycle times.

9.5 A special-order shop receives orders arriving with interarrival times distributed as EXPO(30)—all times are in minutes. The number of parts in each order is a UNIF(3, 10) random variable (truncated to the next smallest integer). Upon receiving the order, the parts are immediately pulled from inventory and sent to the prep area (this transfer takes zero time) where they undergo an individual prep operation, the time for which is distributed as TRIA(2, 3, 4). After the prep operation, the parts are transferred (this transfer takes 4 minutes) to a staging area to wait for the final order authorization. The final order authorization takes an amount of time distributed as UNIF(180, 240), after which the parts are released to be processed, which requires an amount of time distributed as TRIA(3, 4, 6). After processing, the parts are assembled into a batch and sent to the packer (zero transfer time) to be packed, which takes an amount of time distributed as TRIA(8, 10, 14) for the batch. The packed parts exit the system. During the order-authorization process, 4% of the orders are canceled. These parts are removed from the staging queue and sent back to inventory (zero transfer time). Develop a simulation model for this system and run it for 20,000 minutes with a warm-up of 500 minutes. Observe statistics on the number of canceled orders, the number of canceled parts, the time in system for shipped orders, and resource utilizations. Also, use Frequencies to determine the number of racks required to hold the parts in the staging area (each rack can hold 25 parts). (Hints: Use Wait/Signal for order authorization, and SEARCH/REMOVE to cancel orders.)

9.6 A food-processing system starts by processing a 25-pound batch of raw of product, which requires NORM(1.95, 0.2) minutes. Assume an infinite supply of raw product. As soon as a batch has completed processing, it is removed from the processor and placed in a separator where it is divided into one-pound units. The separation process requires 0.05 minute per pound. Note that this is not a "batch process," but rather in each 0.05 time unit a one-pound unit is completed. These one-pound units are sent to one of the three wrapping machines. Each wrapping machine has its own queue, with the unit being sent to the shortest queue. The wrappers are identical machines, except for the processing times. The wrapping times are constants of 0.20, 0.22, and 0.25 minute for wrappers 1, 2, and 3, respectively. The wrapped products are grouped, by wrapper, into batches of six for final packaging. Once a group of six items is available, that group is sent to a packer that packs the product, which takes a NORM(0.4, 0.05) amount of time. These packages exit the system. Assume all transfer times are negligible.

(**a**) Develop a simulation and animation of this system and run it for 1,000 minutes, observing statistics on resource utilizations, queues, and the total number of packages shipped.

(**b**) Modify your model to include wrapper failures with the following characteristics for all wrappers: EXPO(20) for uptimes and EXPO(1) for repair times.

(*c*) Add a quality check to your model from part (*b*). Every half hour, a scan is made, starting with the first wrapper queue, for products that are more than 4 minutes old; i.e., that exited the processor more than 4 minutes ago. Any such items are removed from the queue and disposed. It takes 3 seconds to find and remove each item. Keep track of the number of units removed.

9.7 A small automated system in a bakery produces loafs of bread. The dough-making machine ejects a portion of dough every UNIF(0.5, 1.0) minute. This portion of dough enters a hopper to wait for space in the oven. The portions will be ejected from the hopper in groups of four and placed on the oven-load area to wait for space on the oven conveyor. There is room for only one group of portions at the oven-load area. The oven conveyor has 10 buckets, each 1 foot long, and moves at 0.35 feet per minute.

(*a*) Develop your model using the SCAN, Signal, and Wait modules for your logic to control the group of portions. Run it for 3,000 minutes and observe statistics on the number of portions in the hopper, oven utilization, and the loaf output per hour.

(*b*) Modify your model from part (*a*) by replacing the SCAN module with logic developed based on the Choose module.

9.8 Customers arrive, with interarrival times distributed as EXPO(5)—all times are in minutes—at a small service center that has two servers, each with a separate queue. The service times are EXPO(9.8) and EXPO(9.5) for servers 1 and 2, respectively. Arriving customers join the shortest queue. Customer line switching occurs whenever the difference between the queue lengths is 3 or more. At that time, the last customer in the longest queue moves to the end of the shorter queue. No additional movement, or line switching, in that direction occurs for at least the next 30 seconds. Develop a model and animation of this system and run it for 10,000 minutes. Observe statistics on the number of line switches, resource utilization, and queue lengths.

9.9 A small cross-docking system has three incoming docks and four outgoing docks. Trucks arrive at each of the three incoming docks with interarrival times distributed as UNIF(35, 55)—all times are in minutes. Each arriving truck contains UNIF(15, 30) pallets (truncated to the next smaller integer), which we can assume are unloaded in zero time. Each pallet has an equal probability of going to any of the four outgoing docks. Transportation across the dock is provided by three fork trucks that each travel at 60 feet per minute. Assume the distance between any incoming dock and any outgoing dock is 50 feet. Also assume that the distance between adjacent incoming docks (and adjacent outgoing docks) is 15 feet.

(*a*) Develop a model in which the fork trucks remain where they drop off their last load if there are no new requests pending.

(*b*) Modify your model such that free fork trucks are all sent to the middle (Dock 2) incoming dock to wait for their next load.

(*c*) Modify your model such that each fork truck is assigned a different home incoming dock and moves to that dock when there are no additional requests pending.

Compare the results of the above three systems, using the pallet system time as the primary performance measure. Be sure to back up your comparison with a proper statistical analysis.

9.10   Develop a model and animation of a Ferris-wheel ride at a small, tacky county fair. Agitated customers (mostly small, over-sugared kids who don't know any better) arrive at the ride with interarrival times distributed as EXPO(3) minutes and enter the main queue. When the previous ride has finished and the first customer is ready to get off, the next five customers (or fewer if there are not five in the main queue) are let into the ride area. As a customer gets off the Ferris wheel, the new customer gets on. Note that there can be more current riders than new customers, or more new customers than current riders. It requires UNIF(0.05, 0.15) minute to unload a current rider and UNIF(0.1, 0.2) to load a new rider. The Ferris wheel has only five single seats spaced about 10 feet apart. The wheel rotates at a velocity of 20 feet per minute. Each customer gets five revolutions on the wheel, and no new riders are allowed to board until the ride is complete. Riders who get off the wheel run to the exit, which takes two minutes. We're are not sure if they want to get away, or to be first in line at the next tacky ride. (Hints: Use a conveyor to represent the Ferris wheel itself. Use Wait/Signal to implement the loading and unloading rules.) By the way, the Ferris wheel was developed by the American engineer G.W.G. Ferris, who died in 1896; its German name is *Riesenrad*, which translates roughly as "giant wheel."

Arena Customization and Integration

CHAPTER 10

Arena Customization and Integration

In this final chapter on Arena modeling concepts, we introduce the topics of integrating Arena models with other applications, as well as customizing Arena reports. Because we liked the call center example from Chapter 8 (and we figure that you've probably absorbed about as many examples as is reasonable to expect), we'll use it as the mechanism for presenting these topics. If you've already forgotten what the call center model does (or skipped it entirely in your excitement for learning about the cool stuff in this chapter), we recommend that you browse through at least the model description in Section 8.1.

Our first topic, in Section 10.1, presents one of many approaches for validating a model, by running the simulation logic using the actual arrival times collected from the real system (often referred to as "historical data," not to be confused with that hysterical kind that you'll often find when you go looking for data to support your modeling efforts). In Section 10.2, we introduce two Windows® operating system technologies that Arena exploits for integrating directly with other programs—ActiveX™ Automation and Visual Basic® for Applications (VBA)—by enhancing the call center model to record individual call data in a Microsoft® Excel spreadsheet and charting the call durations in Excel. We return to Arena modeling concepts in Section 10.3, where we use some of the modules on the Elements panel to design a custom report. Section 10.4 closes the chapter with an overview of Object Linking and Embedding (OLE) and a sample of its application for incorporating sound, documents, and presentations in an Arena model. When you finish this chapter, you should have an idea of the types of features you can employ to integrate Arena with other desktop applications and to customize Arena's reporting of simulation results to your own design.

10.1 Model 10.1: Generating Entity Arrivals from Historical Data

Returning to the call center model from Chapter 8, instead of creating entities based on sampling from a probability distribution, let's use the record of the actual calls received over a period of time. We might take this approach as part of the validation of our model; i.e., if the results of a simulation run driven by the recorded arrivals closely correspond to the actual system performance over that period of time, then we have greater faith in the correctness of our model logic. In other cases, we might have enough historical data to make the simulation runs we want, which are then sometimes called *trace-driven* simulations.

To make this modification, we'll need a file containing the arrival times over the period to be studied, and we'll need to replace the entity-creation model logic to use the data in this file. To simplify the required logic, we'll structure the data file to contain values that correspond to simulation times, assuming our run starts at 0 minutes; the first few values of this file (`Mod_10_1.txt`) are shown in Figure 10-1. Since we have the luxury of being textbook authors rather than real-life problem solvers, we'll skip over the details of how this file was created. In practice, you'll probably find that the information you can obtain isn't quite so conveniently stored, but with creative application of spreadsheet software, you usually can convert the raw data points into simulation-ready values.

```
8.921272
9.423960
11.994256
13.707353
15.066199
15.328906
  . . .
```

Figure 10-1. Call Time Data for Revised Call Center Model

In the simulation model, we'll want to remove the special logic we had created to represent the time-dependent, random arrival process. This includes the Variables module that defined the `Arrive Rate` variable and the logic that creates the entities and releases them into the model, shown in Figure 8-2.

We next need to decide how to use the historical data stored in the text file. We are faced with two issues: the mechanics of transferring data from the file into the model and using the values to generate entities at the appropriate times. We'll look at the logic required to create entities at the appropriate times, covering the details of reading the data when we reach that part of the model logic.

Thus far, our approach for creating entities has been to use an Arrive or Create module, which makes a new entity every so often (based on the interarrival time) throughout the run. We saw in our hand simulation (remember the pain of Chapter 2?) that at each entity creation, the "current arriving" entity is sent into the model and the "next arriving" entity is placed on the calendar to arrive at the appropriate future time. The expression in the Time Between arrivals field determines how long into the future the next arriving entity is to arrive; most often, this involves sampling from a probability distribution.

To establish the call arrivals from our data file, however, we can't formulate a simple expression for the time between arrivals. Instead, we'll use a control entity that mimics the "current arriving" and "next arriving" entity logic directly in our model, Figure 10-2.

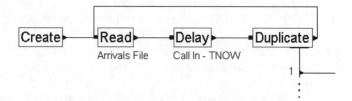

Figure 10-2. Logic for Generating Entities from a File

Our logic starts by creating a single entity at the beginning of the run; with a default Time Between field in the Create module, Arena will create just one entity. This entity then enters the Read module, Display 10-1, where it reads the next value from the data file and assigns this value to the `Call In` entity attribute.

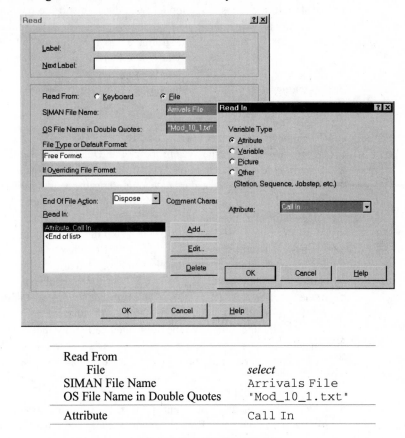

Read From		
File		*select*
SIMAN File Name		`Arrivals File`
OS File Name in Double Quotes		`"Mod_10_1.txt"`
Attribute		`Call In`

Display 10-1. The Read Module

The Read module, which can be found on the Support panel, reads one or more values from a source external to Arena and assigns these values to model variables. The data can come from the keyboard, if you want to establish new values for model variables by querying the person who's running the model; in this case, when an entity reaches the Read module, the simulation run will be interrupted, Arena's command window will be displayed, and the run will pause until a value is typed and the Enter key is pressed. We selected the other option, to read the data from a file. We provided a SIMAN File Name of `Arrivals File`, which is used as a model identifier for the file. This value appears on pull-down lists in the model; it shouldn't be confused with the actual operating system file name, which is entered in the OS File Name in Double Quotes field as `"Mod_10_1.txt"` (note that the file name is enclosed in double quotes). We left the other options at their default values, including the file type as Free Format, which indicates that the Mod_10_1.txt file contains text values, such as those readable in the Notepad program. We also retained the default end-of-file action as Dispose so that the control entity will be disposed of after it reads the last value, effectively terminating the arrival stream of entities to the model. We added an entry to read in a single value each time an entity arrives at the Read module, assigning this value to the Call In attribute.

After the entity reads the value from the data file, it delays until the Call In time so that the actual entity representing the call will arrive at the model logic at the appropriate time. Because the values in the data file represent the absolute number of minutes from the beginning of the run for each call rather than the interarrival times, we use the formula Call In−TNOW to determine how long the control entity should delay before sending the call into the model.

When the control entity completes the delay, it's time for it to create the actual call entity and dispatch it to the system logic. The Duplicate module works nicely for this need, sending the control entity back to the Read module to obtain the next call time from the data file and creating a duplicate (including the value of the Call In attribute, which is used later in the model to tally the line time for each call) that's sent into the model logic to seize a trunk line, etc.

Using the data values in Figure 10-1 to step through the logic for the first two calls, our control entity will first read a value of 8.921 into its Call In attribute at simulation time 0 (the start of the run). It will delay for 8.921 − 0 time units, leaving the Delay module at time 8.921. It creates a duplicate at that time, sending it to the Seize module to begin the actual processing of a call. The control entity returns to the Read module, reading a value of 9.424 from the data file and overwriting its Call In attribute with this value. (Note, though, that since the duplicated call entity moves through its own model logic independent of the control entity, it retains its own value of 8.921 for the Call In attribute.) The control entity proceeds to the Delay module, where it delays for 9.424 − 8.921, or 0.503 time units, which causes Arena to place the control entity on the event calendar with an event time that's 0.503 time units into the future (or an actual event time of 9.424). When it's the control entity's turn to be processed again, at simulation time 9.424, Arena will remove it from the event calendar and send it to the Duplicate module, where it will spawn a call entity with Call In attribute value 9.424, representing the second call to enter the system. This will continue until all of the values in Mod_10_1.txt have been eaten by the control entity.

The simulation run will terminate under one of two conditions. If the ending time specified in the Simulate module occurs before all of the calls listed in the data file have been created, Arena will end the run at that time; under no conditions can a model run for longer than is defined in the Simulate module entries. On the other hand, our model may terminate earlier than the Simulate module indicates if all of the calls listed in the data file have been created and have completed processing, leaving the event calendar empty. (Remember that the control entity is disposed after it reads the last data value.) If Arena encounters a condition where there are no additional entities on the event calendar and no additional other time-based controls to process, it will terminate the run after the last entity leaves the model. In the case of our call center model, since there are schedules associated with the resources, the model will run the complete replication length specified on the Simulate module.

10.2   Model 10.2: Recording and Charting Model Results in Microsoft® Excel

Since we've shown one way of loading data into a model from an external data source, it only seems to make sense to demonstrate how to send data from the model to an external file as well. As you might guess, Arena provides a Write module on the Support panel that's eerily similar to the Read module; we'll leave it to you to explore its capabilities on your own.

Our next venture with the call center model will be to use Visual Basic® for Applications (in Arena) to record information about each departing call in an Excel spreadsheet. Our objective will be to create an Excel file that lists three pieces of data for each completed call: the call start time, end time, and duration. We also want to chart the call durations to look for any interesting trends, such as groups of very short or very long calls. Figure 10-3 shows a sample of the model's results.

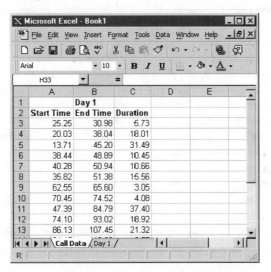

Figure 10-3. Microsoft Excel Results

10.2.1   An Overview of ActiveX™ Automation and VBA

Arena exploits two Windows technologies that are designed to enhance the integration of desktop applications. The first, ActiveX Automation (the technology formerly known as OLE Automation), allows applications to control each other and themselves via a programming interface. If you've created a macro in Excel, you've utilized this technology, whether you realized it or not. For an application to be able to be *automated*, it must have an *object model*, which is a list of application *objects* that can be controlled; the characteristics of these objects that can be examined or modified, which are referred to as the *properties* of the objects; and the actions that can be performed on the objects or that they can perform, known as their *methods*. This object model is registered when the application is installed, so that if you use an automation programming language and want to utilize the application's functionality, you can establish a reference to its object model and program its objects directly. Many desktop applications can be automated (i.e., controlled by another application), including products such as Microsoft® Office, AutoCAD®, and Visio®. To create the program that controls the application, you can use programming languages such as C++, Visual Basic®, or Java.

The second technology exploited by Arena for application integration addresses the programming interface issue. Visual Basic® for Applications (VBA) is a Visual Basic programming environment for inclusion in desktop applications that support ActiveX Automation. With VBA, a user can exploit the integration capabilities of automation without needing to purchase an additional programming product. When you install Arena, you're also receiving a full Visual Basic programming environment, accessed via the Show Visual Basic Editor option on the Tools menu or the corresponding button on the Integration toolbar (📁).

These two technologies work together to allow Arena to integrate with other programs that support ActiveX Automation. You can write Visual Basic code directly in Arena (via the Visual Basic Editor) that automates other programs, such as Excel, AutoCAD, or Visio. In our enhancement to the call center model, we'll create a new Excel worksheet, populate it with data during the simulation run, and automatically chart the data, all without "touching" Excel.

To build the logic necessary to create the spreadsheet and chart the results, we'll need to perform three tasks. First, we need to write the VBA code necessary to create the Excel file. We'll open the file at the beginning of the simulation run, and we'll also create a new worksheet to store each replication's data since our approach in this model has been to examine results carved into 660-minute subsections. (Worksheets are the tabbed pages within an Excel file.) Second, we need to modify the model logic and write the VBA code so that each time a call is completed, its entity "fires" a VBA event to write the pertinent values to the worksheet. Finally, we'll write the VBA code to create a chart of the call durations at the end of each replication and to save the file at the end of the simulation run.

The following sections that describe these steps only highlight the concepts and list the corresponding code. If you're interested in developing a deeper understanding of these materials, explore Arena's online help related to VBA and the Arena object model, and examine the SMARTS Library models related to these topics. We also recommend the book *Developing Microsoft® Excel 95 Solutions with Visual Basic® for Applications* (Wells, 1995) for reading about automating Excel. There also are numerous other resources at your disposal for learning Visual Basic, including a variety of books, CD tutorials, training courses, and Web sites.

10.2.2 *VBA Events at the Beginning of a Simulation Run*

In order to store the call data during the run, we'll first create the Excel file, just as if we had run Excel and started a new file. At the start of each new day (i.e., replication), we also want to write headers for the data columns. To do this, we'll use two of Arena's built-in

VBA events: `RunBeginSimulation` and `RunBeginReplication`. As the name implies, `RunBeginSimulation` is called at the beginning of a simulation run. In it, we'll place the start-up code to run Excel and create the new workbook. And as you might expect, `RunBeginReplication` is called at the beginning of each replication; this is where we'll write the headers.

Figure 10-4 shows the code for these two procedures, as well as some global variable declarations. To view this code in the Arena model, open the `Mod_10_2.doe` file;[1] select the *Tools/Show Visual Basic Editor* menu option; and double-click on the ThisDocument item in the Visual Basic project toolbar.

```
' Global variables
Dim g_SIMAN As Arena.SIMAN, g_CallInIndex As Long
Dim g_nextRow As Long, g_colA As Long, g_colB As Long, g_colC As Long

' Global Excel variables
Dim g_XLApp As Excel.Application, g_XLWorkbook As Excel.Workbook, _
    g_XLDataSheet As Excel.Worksheet
Private Sub ModelLogic_RunBeginSimulation()
    ' Set the global SIMAN variable
    Set g_SIMAN = ThisDocument.Model.SIMAN

    ' Set the global variable that stores the index of the Call In attribute
    g_CallInIndex = g_SIMAN.SymbolNumber("Call In")

    ' Start Excel and create a new spreadsheet
    Set g_XLApp = CreateObject("Excel.Application")
    g_XLApp.Visible = True
    g_XLApp.SheetsInNewWorkbook = 1
    Set g_XLWorkbook = g_XLApp.Workbooks.Add

    Set g_XLDataSheet = g_XLWorkbook.ActiveSheet
    With g_XLDataSheet
        .Name = "Call Data"
        .Rows(1).Select
        g_XLApp.Selection.Font.Bold = True
        g_XLApp.Selection.Font.Color = RGB(255, 0, 0)
        .Rows(2).Select
        g_XLApp.Selection.Font.Bold = True
        g_XLApp.Selection.Font.Color = RGB(0, 0, 255)
    End With
End Sub

Private Sub ModelLogic_RunBeginReplication()
    Dim replNum As Long, i As Integer

    ' Set variables for the columns to which data is to be written
    replNum = g_SIMAN.RunCurrentReplication
    g_colA = (4 * (replNum - 1)) + 1
    g_colB = g_colA + 1
    g_colC = g_colA + 2

    ' Write header row for this day's call data and
    '   set g_nextRow to 3 to start writing data in third row
    With g_XLDataSheet
        .Activate
        .Cells(1, g_colB).Value = "Day " & replNum
        .Cells(2, g_colA).Value = "Start Time"
        .Cells(2, g_colB).Value = "End Time"
        .Cells(2, g_colC).Value = "Duration"
```

---

[1] The code presented in this chapter and contained in file `Mod_10_2.doe` uses the Excel version 8.0 (Office 97) object library. File `Mod_10_2_95.doe` contains corresponding code for Excel version 5.0 (Office 95).

```
        For i = 0 To 2
            .Columns(g_colA + i).Select
            g_XLApp.Selection.Columns.AutoFit
            g_XLApp.Selection.NumberFormat = "0.00"
        Next i
    End With
    g_nextRow = 3
End Sub
```

Figure 10-4. RunBeginSimulation and RunBeginReplication VBA Procedures

The global declarations section, consisting of the lines that are outside any procedure (i.e., before the line defining the `ModelLogic_RunBeginSimulation` proce-dure), defines variables that are global to all procedures via a series of `Dim` statements (Visual Basic's variable declaration syntax, short for "dimension"). We declare a global variable `g_SIMAN` that will be set in `RunBeginSimulation` to point to the model's SIMAN data object and will be used in the remaining procedures to obtain values from the running simulation. The variable type, `Arena.SIMAN`, establishes that the `g_SIMAN` variable is a SIMAN object variable from the Arena object library. The other variables in the first two `Dim` statements are used to keep track of other values that are needed in more than one of the procedures. We'll describe them as we examine the code that uses them.

The remaining global variables—whose data types begin with "`Excel.`"—are de-clared to be object variables from the Excel object library. Because Excel is an external application (as opposed to Arena, which is the application hosting our VBA code), a *ref-erence* to the Excel library must be established by clicking on the Excel Object Library entry in the References dialog of the Visual Basic Editor window, which is opened via the *Tools/References* menu option, as shown in Figure 10-5. This reference will allow you to use ActiveX Automation calls to control Excel. Note that it also requires that Ex-cel be installed on the computer that's running this model; if you don't have Excel, you'll be able to open and edit this model, but you won't be able to perform simulation runs.

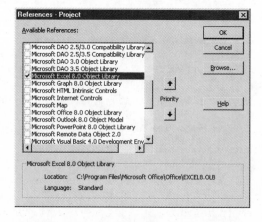

Figure 10-5. Tools/References Dialog from VBA

Examining the `RunBeginSimulation` code, we first set the `g_SIMAN` variable equal to some interesting series of characters containing dots. When you're reading code that exploits objects, it's often helpful to read the object part from right to left, using the dots as separators between items. For example, the statement `Set g_SIMAN = ThisDocument.Model.SIMAN` can be thought of as something like, "Set the `g_SIMAN` variable to point to the `SIMAN` property of the `Model` object contained in `ThisDocument`." Without delving too deep into the details of the Arena object model or Visual Basic, let's just say that `ThisDocument` refers to the Arena model containing this `RunBeginSimulation` code; `Model` is its main object, providing access to the items contained in the model; and `SIMAN` is another object type that you access via the Model object to query or modify the model's run variables, analogous to built-in SIMAN variables such as NR and NQ.

If you'd like to explore the object library, VBA provides a handy browser, opened by selecting the *View/Object Browser* menu item in the Visual Basic Editor window or pressing the F2 key. This allows you to navigate through object libraries, exploring objects and their properties and methods. Figure 10-6 shows the browser's display of the SIMAN object and its EntityAttribute property in the Arena object library.

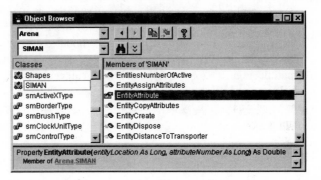

Figure 10-6. The VBA Object Browser

Returning to the `RunBeginSimulation` code, after we've established the `g_SIMAN` variable to point to the SIMAN run data, we use it to store the index value of the `Call In` attribute in one of our global Visual Basic variables—`g_CallInIndex`—so that it can be used throughout the run to retrieve the individual values from entities as they depart the model. Next, we start Excel using the `CreateObject` ActiveX Automation call and make it visible by setting the application's `Visible` property to `True`. Then we create a new Excel file (also referred to as a workbook) by automating Excel with the `Excel.Workbooks.Add` method; you can think of this as "`Add` a new item to the `Workbooks` collection of the `Excel` application." The `g_XLWorkbook` variable will store a pointer to the newly created Excel workbook; we'll save the workbook to a file at the end of the simulation run. The remaining lines of code in `RunBeginSimulation` set our `g_XLDataSheet` variable to point to the worksheet in the newly created Excel workbook and establish some of its characteristics. If you will be working with Excel, we suggest that you explore its macro-recording capabilities. You often can create a macro in Excel and paste its code into Arena, with minor modifications; this is much quicker than trying to dig through the Excel object model on your own for just the right code to perform some task.

While the `RunBeginSimulation` event is called only once at the beginning of the run, `RunBeginReplication` is called by Arena at the beginning of each replication. We use this event to write the column headers for our new day's data. We also set the global `g_NextRow` variable to start with a value of 3; this value will be used to determine the row to which each call's results are to be written.

10.2.3 Storing Individual Call Data Using the VBA Module

Our next task requires both a change to the model logic and some VBA code. Let's first make the model modification. Just before a call is finished (i.e., prior to leaving the model via the Dispose module), it should trigger VBA code to write its statistics—call-in time, call-completion time, and call duration—to the next row in the Excel worksheet. The triggering of the VBA code in this case isn't as predictable as the first two events we examined, which are defined to be called at the beginning of the run and at the beginning of each replication. Instead, the dynamics of the simulation model will dictate when the VBA code should be executed. Arena provides a VBA module on the Blocks panel for just this purpose. When you place this module, instead of including some predefined logic in the module itself, Arena will fire the VBA code that you've written for the VBA module. Figure 10-7 shows the modified call center model logic using an instance of the VBA module. We replaced the two Dispose modules (one for technical support calls and one that was shared by sales and order-inquiry calls) with a VBA module followed by a single Dispose.

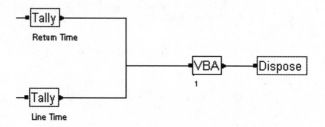

Figure 10-7. VBA Module

When you place a VBA module, Arena assigns it a unique value that's used to associate a particular VBA module with its code in the Visual Basic project; these numbers are integers starting at a value of 1 and increasing by one with each newly placed VBA module. To edit the code for a VBA module, you return to the Visual Basic Editor and select the appropriate item from the object list in the code window for the ThisDocument project entry, as shown in Figure 10-8.

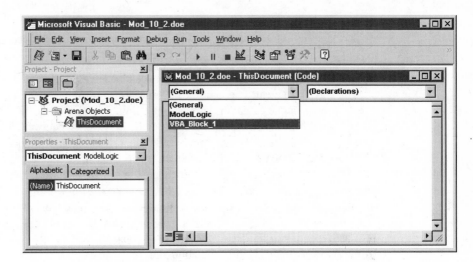

Figure 10-8. Visual Basic Editor Selection of VBA Module 1 Event

The event associated with our VBA module is named `VBA_Block_1_Fire()`, where the `1` matches the Arena-provided number of the VBA module. Its code is shown in Figure 10-9.

```
Private Sub VBA_Block_1_Fire()
    ' Retrieve start time and current time from SIMAN object data
    Dim startTime As Double, runNOW As Double
    startTime = g_SIMAN.EntityAttribute(g_SIMAN.ActiveEntity, g_CallInIndex)
    runTNOW = g_SIMAN.RunCurrentTime

    ' Write the values to the spreadsheet
    With g_XLDataSheet
        .Cells(g_nextRow, g_colA).Value = startTime
        .Cells(g_nextRow, g_colB).Value = runTNOW
        .Cells(g_nextRow, g_colC).Value = runTNOW - startTime
    End With

    ' Increment the row variable
    g_nextRow = g_nextRow + 1
End Sub
```

Figure 10-9. VBA_Block_1_Fire Code

When a call entity completes its processing and enters the VBA module, the code in the `VBA_Block_1_Fire` event is invoked. The first two lines of the procedure retrieve information from the running simulation (via the `g_SIMAN` variable that we set in `RunBeginSimulation`). First, we store the value of the active entity's attribute with index value `g_CallInIndex` in a local variable `startTime`. The `g_CallInIndex` variable was established in `RunBeginSimulation` to be the index of the attribute named "Call In" (using the `SymbolNumber` function). Next, we store the current simulation time in a local variable `runTNOW`. These values are used to store information about this entity in the spreadsheet, using the `g_nextRow` variable to determine the row, which we then increment. After this code is executed for a particular entity, the entity returns to the model and enters the Dispose module, where it is destroyed.

10.2.4   Charting the Results and Cleaning Up at the End of the Run

Our final task is to create charts of the call durations for each replication and to save the spreadsheet file at the end of the simulation run. While we could do all of the charting at the end of the run since the data will exist on the data worksheet, we'll instead place the code in the `RunEndReplication` to build the charts as the run proceeds.

At the end of each replication, after the final entity has been processed, Arena calls the VBA `RunEndReplication` procedure. In our model, we'll chart the data contained in the Duration column of the worksheet, showing a line graph of the call lengths over that replication. We'll skip a discussion of the charting code. If you're interested in exploring Excel's charting features, we recommend browsing the online help and using the macro recorder to try different charting options.

Finally, at the end of the simulation run, the `RunEndSimulation` procedure is called; ours will simply save the Excel workbook to file `Mod_10_2.xls` and break our link to Excel by setting the Excel application variable to `Nothing` (leaving Excel running). Figure 10-10 shows the code for these two routines.

```
Private Sub ModelLogic_RunEndReplication()
    g_XLDataSheet.Range(g_XLDataSheet.Cells(3, g_colC), _
        g_XLDataSheet.Cells(g_nextRow, g_colC)).Select
    g_XLApp.Charts.Add
    With g_XLApp.ActiveChart
        .Name = "Day " & g_SIMAN.RunCurrentReplication
        .ChartType = xlLineMarkers
        .SetSourceData Source:=g_XLDataSheet.Range(g_XLDataSheet.Cells(3, _
            g_colC), g_XLDataSheet.Cells(g_nextRow, g_colC)), PlotBy:=xlColumns
        .SeriesCollection(1).XValues = "= '" & g_XLDataSheet.Name & "'!" & _
            "R3C" & g_colB & ":R" & g_nextRow & "C" & g_colB
    End With
End Sub
Private Sub ModelLogic_RunEndSimulation()
    ' Save the spreadsheet and close Excel
    g_XLApp.DisplayAlerts = False              ' Don't prompt to overwrite
    g_XLWorkbook.SaveAs "Mod_10_2.xls"
    Set g_XLApp = Nothing
End Sub
```

Figure 10-10. VBA Code for End of Replication and End of Run

If you run this model, you'll see a copy of Excel appear on your desktop at the beginning of the run, followed by a series of numbers being added to the worksheet as call entities depart the model. Finally, the charts will be created at the end of each replication.

As you might expect, Arena's integration with other applications isn't limited to writing data to Excel and creating charts. If you've installed an application that can be automated, the VBA interface in Arena will allow you to do whatever is possible through the external application's object model, such as reading data from an Excel spreadsheet or using its goal-seeking algorithms to establish values for model parameters.

10.3 Model 10.3: Organizing and Creating Your Own Reports

In this section, we'll describe ways in which you can control and customize the summary output reports. Let's assume that you've used the call center model to analyze the effect of changes on the number of balked calls. After some preliminary analysis, you've come to the conclusion that by rescheduling the technical support operators, you can reduce the number of customer busy signals. You suspect that the largest number of busy signals occurs over the lunch hour. Before you start changing schedules, it would be helpful if you knew exactly, or at least by period, when most of busy signals occur. This can be done fairly easily by adding a counter set that will collect the number of balked calls per period. First, add the Counter Set, `Balk Set`, which will contain an identifier for each of the 22 periods in our simulated day, shown in Display 10-2. You might note that we used a decimal point (.) rather than a colon (:) when we entered our counter names. This was because Arena reserves the colon and semicolon for use in writing out the experiment and model files. Thus, they are invalid symbols for use in names and labels.

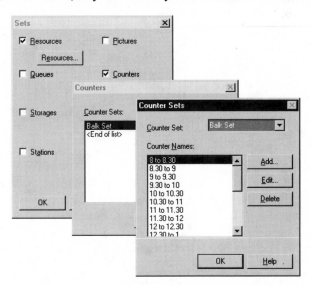

Counter Set	Balk Set
Counter Names	
Counter	8 to 8.30
.	.
.	.
Counter	5.30 to 6

Display 10-2. Adding the Counter Set

Next, change the balk Count module to count-based on the set `Balk Set` with the index `Period`. Now when we run our model, we'll get 22 counters, each representing the number of balked calls for the corresponding 30-minute period. However, we might want to change our Simulate module first so we don't initialize the statistics before each replication. If we do this, the last replication will give us the total number of balks, by period, for all 10 replications. If you make these changes and run your model, the counters summary for the last replication should be similar to Figure 10-11.

```
                            COUNTERS
           Identifier              Count   Limit
           4.30 to 5                   4   Infinite
           4 to 4.30                  13   Infinite
           3.30 to 4                  36   Infinite
           12 to 12.30              123    Infinite
           3 to 3.30                  16   Infinite
           2.30 to 3                  35   Infinite
           10.30 to 11                29   Infinite
           1.30 to 2                 101   Infinite
           8.30 to 9                   0   Infinite
           2 to 2.30                 150   Infinite
           12.30 to 1                149   Infinite
           11.30 to 12                39   Infinite
           10 to 10.30                44   Infinite
           9 to 9.30                   1   Infinite
           5 to 5.30                   2   Infinite
           5.30 to 6                   0   Infinite
           1 to 1.30                 172   Infinite
           9.30 to 10                 40   Infinite
           11 to 11.30                14   Infinite
           8 to 8.30                   0   Infinite
```

Figure 10-11. The Counters Summary Report

Although all the information we requested is in the summary report, we'd like it to be in ascending order by time period. At this point, you might be asking why Arena would be so rude as to display the counter results in a seemingly random order. To start with, Arena has no way of knowing in what order you *want* your counters, or any other summary output. Don't forget that your requests for statistical output are normally scattered throughout your model, so Arena lists them in the same order that it stores them, which is not necessarily the order in which they were entered. So far, we haven't given you any way to force a specific display order. You can determine the order by viewing the Arena experiment frame, *Run/SIMAN/View*. The order shown will be the display order. Be careful because if you edit your model, that ordering may change.

Fortunately, you can force a specific ordering by using modules from the Elements panel. Let's illustrate this capability by ordering our counters. Normally, the data associated with the objects that are created by Element modules are automatically filled out for you (and stored internally and invisibly) when you model with modules from the Common, Support, and Transfer panels. The Element modules define the characteristics of different objects that are used in the simulation. Although Arena will completely define the model's counters based on the information we already entered in our model, we want to add information that's not presented by the higher-level modules. For that reason, we place a COUNTERS module and add the 22 counters that we already defined. (Obviously, you'll need to attach the Elements panel.) As we add each counter, we can simply select its identifier from the pull-down list. The added information is the Counter Number. This controls the ordering of the display in the summary report. Therefore, we start by making counter 8 to 8.30 number 1 and end with counter 5.30 to 6 as number 22, as reflected in Display 10-3.

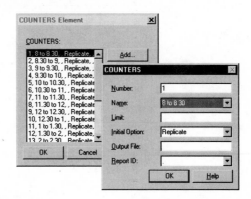

Counter Set	Balk Set
Number	1
Name	8 to 8.30
.	.
.	.
Number	22
Name	5.30 to 6

Display 10-3. The COUNTERS Module

You might also notice that there are two other options we haven't seen before: Limit and Initial Option. Limit may be used to define a termination condition for the simulation; e.g., if we enter a value of 100, the simulation will end when the counter value equals 100. Initial Option specifies whether the counter will be initialized between replications. The default entry is Replicate, which means that the counter will be initialized based on the options selected in the Simulate modules. However, you can also select a Yes or No, which gives you individual control over each counter, independent of the option selected in the Simulate module.

To expand on the above operations, we need to mention a bit about Arena's internal operations. When you first define an object, Arena places it on a list. In this case of counters, it would be a list of counters that will ultimately be written to a Counters element. When we first defined the counter in our Sets module, we only assigned it a name. Thus, all the other counter options (Number, Limit, Initial Option, Output File, and Report ID) would be defaulted. When we placed our COUNTERS module; however, we defined a number for each counter, and this information is added to the counter list. If we had further defined more information for counters, it too would be added to the counter list of information. When you view the experiment frame or run the simulation, Arena writes out all this information to the Counters element. Now if you run the simulation, your counter summary will look like Figure 10-12.

```
                          COUNTERS
        Identifier              Count    Limit
        8 to 8.30                 0      Infinite
        8.30 to 9                 0      Infinite
        9 to 9.30                 1      Infinite
        9.30 to 10               40      Infinite
        10 to 10.30              44      Infinite
        10.30 to 11              29      Infinite
        11 to 11.30              14      Infinite
        11.30 to 12              39      Infinite
        12 to 12.30             123      Infinite
        12.30 to 1              149      Infinite
        1 to 1.30              172      Infinite
        1.30 to 2              101      Infinite
        2 to 2.30              150      Infinite
        2.30 to 3               35      Infinite
        3 to 3.30               16      Infinite
        3.30 to 4               36      Infinite
        4 to 4.30               13      Infinite
        4.30 to 5                4      Infinite
        5 to 5.30                2      Infinite
        5.30 to 6                0      Infinite
```

Figure 10-12. The Ordered Counters Summary Report

Similar modules can be found in the Elements panel for further definition of Tallies (TALLIES module), Discrete-Change statistics (DSTATS module), and Frequencies (FREQUENCIES module). Additional modules can be found for other types of Arena objects; e.g., RESOURCES, QUEUES, STATIONS, PICTURES, etc. In most cases, you won't need to add additional information to these objects. You'll rarely find the need to use them; however, it's a good idea to remember that they're available.

One example of their usefulness would be creation of a model using the concept of *station macros*. Consider a simulation of a large machine shop (50 machines). If all the machines are similar in that they can be represented by the same set of modules (although they have different names), you could use Sets to create one set of modules that would represent all of the machines. Another approach is to number all your stations, resources, queues, storages, etc., and then reference them by number. This is essentially what you do when you use Sets, except that you reference objects by their position or index in the Set rather than by their object number.

Now let's go back to our model and summary report. In addition to being able to specify the order of these items, we can also create our own reports. For example, assume that we want to look specifically at the technical support staff who are dedicated to Product Type 2 (Tierney, Sean, and Deb). We can easily create our own report containing *only* the information on these resources, or we can append this information to our existing summary report by using the REPORTS module from the Elements panel. This module allows us to define the characteristics of our special report. For our report, we have entered the report Name and requested that it be sorted in descending order, as in Display 10-4. The remaining entries have been defaulted.

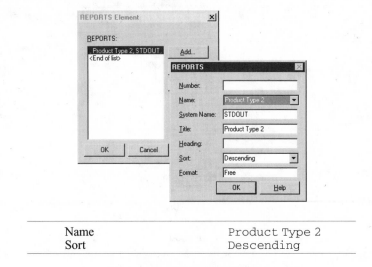

Name	Product Type 2
Sort	Descending

Display 10-4. The REPORTS Module

The defaulted system name, STDOUT, will cause the report information to be appended to the standard summary report. We could have entered a different system file name, enclosed in double quotes, and the report would have been written to that file. The Title automatically defaults to the Report Name. You can also specify the Heading and Format of your report. It's important to note that at this point we have only defined the characteristics of the report, not its contents. The contents of our report will be made up of standard report summary output lines. However, you can develop you own contents using the REPORTLINES module, which we won't cover. For additional information on this topic, refer to online help.

For our report, we need the six statistics from the Discrete-Change section of our standard report, so we select and place the DSTATS module. As long as we're at it, we'll order this output as well, so we'll number all of our DSTATS, as we did for our counters. In addition, for the Tierney, Sean, and Deb DSTATS we entered, or pulled from the list, the Report ID was defined in our REPORTS module, seen in Display 10-5.

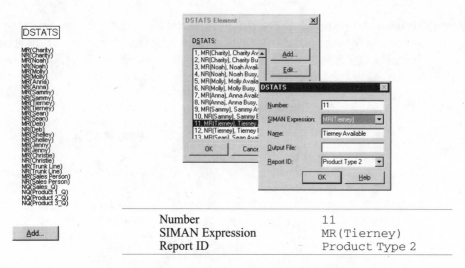

Number	11
SIMAN Expression	MR(Tierney)
Report ID	Product Type 2

Display 10-5. The DSTATS Module

Now when we run our model, we'll get the standard output report, including the statistics on Tierney, Sean, and Deb, as well as the appended report shown in Figure 10-13.

Product Type 2

Identifier	Average	Variation	Minimum	Maximum	Final Value
Tierney Busy	.58004	.85090	.00000	1.0000	.00000
Tierney Available	.71667	.62877	.00000	1.0000	.00000
Sean Busy	.57462	.86039	.00000	1.0000	.00000
Sean Available	.72727	.61237	.00000	1.0000	.00000
Deb Busy	.62194	.77966	.00000	1.0000	.00000
Deb Available	.72727	.61237	.00000	1.0000	.00000

Figure 10-13. The Product Type 2 Report

Recall that we could have written this report information to a file just as easily. Also, if we had created additional reports for all the other key information, we might not want the normal report summary. We can suppress the normal summary report by placing the PROJECT module from the Elements panel and unchecking the Summary Report box. This will cause the summary report to contain only the special reports that we might have defined. You might note that the remaining information in the PROJECT dialog was also available in the Simulate module.

Using these and other modules from the Elements panel, you can create your own customized summary reports fairly easily. One question you might be asking is, "Why or when would I want to do this?" If you are doing a simulation project with a complete analysis and only plan to show the decision makers a summary of the output data, there really is no need to create these kinds of specialized reports. However, if you have numerous people looking at the simulation results, particularly non-simulation people, specialized reports can help you organize and display the output data in a format that is far easier for other people to understand.

10.4   Model 10.4: Linking To and Embedding Other Files

In Section 10.1, we exploited Arena features to integrate data into a model, and in Section 10.2, we looked into ways to generate data and charts in another application (Microsoft Excel). In Section 10.3, we described how to design custom reports of simulation results. For all these tasks, we utilized standard Arena modules (Read, REPORTS, etc.) and ActiveX Automation/VBA. In this section, we'll address another method for utilizing files and functionality from other applications via Object Linking and Embedding (OLE).

Continuing with the call center model, we'll create a *form* (Visual Basic's term for a dialog) that's displayed whenever the model is opened, presenting options to view a Microsoft® PowerPoint® presentation graphics program describing the model, to edit the model, or to begin a simulation run, as in Figure 10-14. We'll also add some cornball excitement to our project by playing a sound file when the model opens.

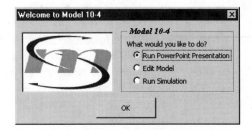

Figure 10-14. Visual Basic Form

If the first option in the Welcome form is selected, we'll show a PowerPoint presentation, which will be launched from a PowerPoint file; we'll add a link to this file in the Arena model via OLE. For the second option, we'll zoom to a named view that shows an embedded Microsoft® Word file describing the model. The third option will launch the simulation run, as though the Run toolbar button had been clicked.

We'll modify the model by adding the Word, PowerPoint, and sound files and establishing a named view that displays the Word file. The rest of the work will be done in VBA.

10.4.1   Placing the Word File in the Arena Model

You can add a file from an external application in a number of ways. Let's first look at the Word file describing the Arena model. We'd like to use it to document the model—what the model does, who the authors are, its status, etc. We also can record notes about the model, such as to-do lists, ideas that occur to us as we work on the model, etc., in the Word file. To establish the file, we'll create a new Word document in the model using the Insert New Object option on Arena's Edit menu, which opens a dialog such as that shown in Figure 10-15. This is a standard Windows dialog, allowing you to create a new object in your application (Arena) from other OLE server applications that are installed on your computer. The list of object types displayed in the dialog will depend on what programs you've installed. In our case, we'll select Microsoft Word Document to place a new Word file in our model window.

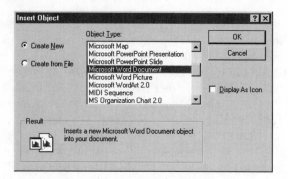

Figure 10-15. Adding an OLE Object to Model

After you click the OK button in the Insert Object dialog, you locate the Word document in the Arena model by clicking the left button when the cross hair cursor is positioned at the desired location (top left corner of the region to contain the Word document). When you click to locate the Word document, OLE kicks into action, allowing Word to take over Arena's menus and toolbars. You're effectively editing the Word document directly in Arena; start typing to see that Word is in charge. Figure 10-16 shows how Arena looks after typing a few lines of description in the embedded Word document.

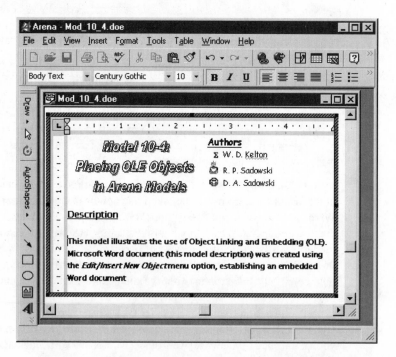

Figure 10-16. Word Document Activated Inside Arena Model Window

If you're familiar with Word, you'll recognize the menus and toolbars, as well as the editing options within the document, such as the ruler, text formatting, and the cool red wavy underline highlighting words that aren't in the Word dictionary. (We'll leave it to you to draw conclusions about Word's choice of what to flag as unknown.) If you click outside the Word document, OLE will return control to Arena, leaving a display of the Word file in the model window. You'll see that the document is just another object in the Arena model; you can select it, move it, resize it, copy it to the clipboard, etc.

This process establishes an *embedded* file in Arena—the Word document resides inside the Arena model and will be saved with the `Mod_10_4.doe` file. It doesn't exist anywhere else; e.g., you won't be able to find it by looking for a Word document file on your hard disk. Embedded files are convenient if you'll be modifying them from within Arena (as opposed to from their associated application—in this case, Word). It's also useful to embed files if you'll be giving the model to someone else; you don't have to remember to send them both the Arena model and the Word document since the Word file is embedded within the Arena file.

Before we continue to the PowerPoint presentation, we'll add a named view called `Model Description` to the Arena model, showing the region containing the Word document. (Use the Named Views item on the View menu.) This will be used in the VBA code so that we can display the model description when the Edit Model option is chosen from the Welcome form.

10.4.2 Establishing a Link to the Microsoft® PowerPoint® Presentation

For the PowerPoint file, we'll use a different approach. Instead of embedding the file inside the Arena model itself, we'll create and save the presentation in PowerPoint; in Arena we'll create an OLE object that's *linked* to the PowerPoint file, which still will reside on your disk as a separate file. This approach allows you to use the outside application (PowerPoint) to edit the file without having to run Arena.

We'll presume that you've already created the file in PowerPoint and have saved it to a file named `Mod_10_4.ppt`. To add it to the Arena model, you return to the Insert New Object dialog (from the Edit menu), but instead of selecting the Create New option, you click on the Create from File selection, then use the Browse button to find your PowerPoint file. This establishes that the object to be inserted into the Arena model is an existing external file (rather than a new one); to make this a link to the file instead of embedding the file, also check the Link option in the dialog, shown in Display 10-6. When you click OK, you'll locate the link to the PowerPoint file in the model window by positioning the cross hair cursor at the top left corner of the desired region and clicking the left mouse button, just as before for the Word file. If you select the Display As Icon option in the Insert Object dialog, you'll just see a small icon representing PowerPoint; if you leave it unchecked (the default), you'll see the first slide of the presentation.

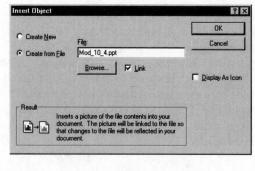

Create from File	*select*
File	`Mod_10_4.ppt`
Link	*check*

Display 10-6. Inserting an OLE Link to an External File

The object in the Arena model in this case doesn't contain the actual presentation; it's just a link to the `Mod_10_4.ppt` file. If you run PowerPoint, change the file, and save it, the modifications won't be reflected in the Arena object until the link is updated. If you'd like to update the link manually, you can do so by selecting the Links option on Arena's Edit menu, which opens a dialog listing the linked objects contained in the model (in our case, just one). The Update Now button will refresh the object that's displayed in Arena to reflect the changes you made in the source file (`Mod_10_4.ppt`). Some of the other options in the Links dialog allow you to open the file in PowerPoint or change the file with which the link is associated.

Returning to the Arena model window, if you double-click on the object, its default action will be invoked by OLE. In the case of PowerPoint, the presentation will run, showing the first slide and allowing you to go through the presentation as if it had been launched from PowerPoint. We'll exploit this later when we create the VBA code for the Welcome dialog's Run PowerPoint Presentation option.

10.4.3 Adding the Sound File

The final addition to the model window is the sound file, which we want to launch when the model's opened to add some drama to our project (or to wake the sleepy modeler). We'll use OLE once again to place the sound file in the model. In this case, we'll embed the file, so that it accompanies the model wherever it goes. We'll add it to the model by using the Windows drag-and-drop feature. First, we'll open Explorer (or whatever file browser you use, such as Microsoft® Outlook™), locate the desired sound file, select and drag it by clicking the left mouse button and holding it as we move the file over the Arena model, and finally drop it in the model by releasing the left mouse button, in Figure 10-17.

The sound object in the Arena model is an embedded file containing a copy of the file we originally had on our disk. This file also could have been placed in the Arena model using the Windows clipboard by selecting the file in Outlook or Explorer, copying it to the clipboard, activating Arena, and pasting the clipboard contents into the model window. Both the drag-and-drop and clipboard procedures create an embedded OLE file inside Arena. You also could use the Insert New Object approach from the Edit menu in Arena, selecting the Create from File option and browsing to find the sound file, but leaving the Link option cleared so that the file is embedded in the model. The object itself is just like a sound file stored on your disk; double-click on it to play its inspiring melody.

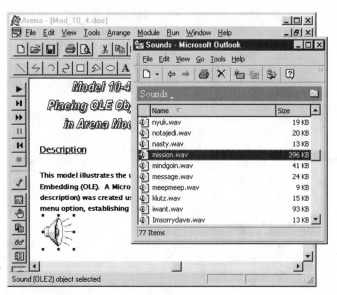

Figure 10-17. Dragging and Dropping a File Into Arena

10.4.4   Tagging the Arena Objects for Identification in VBA

We now have finished adding the necessary objects to the Arena model. Our final change to the model will be to identify uniquely the objects that our VBA code will need to find, namely the PowerPoint presentation object and the sound file. We'll see why this is necessary when we get to the VBA code; for now, have faith that we know what we're doing.

Though you probably didn't realize it, each object in an Arena model window has an associated *tag*. Arena assigns these tags as you add objects, using a format "Object.*nnn*," where *nnn* is an integer that increases as each new object is placed in the model. We'll change the tags for the PowerPoint and sound files to be "PowerPoint Presentation" and "Mission Possible" by selecting the object and choosing the Properties option on the Edit menu or typing Alt+Enter. This opens the Properties dialog, where you can type the new Tag value, as shown in Figure 10-18 for the sound file.

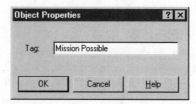

Figure 10-18. Changing the Tag Property of the Sound File

10.4.5 The Welcome Form

Now that the model is properly set up with embedded and linked files, we'll turn our attention back to VBA to put these files to work. Here, we'll first draw the user form that will be presented when the file's opened, then we'll write a little bit of VBA code to act on the selections made in the form and to reward the lucky soul who opened our file with some inspiring music.

To add the user form to our VBA project, we'll select the UserForm option from the Visual Basic Editor's Insert menu. (Remember, to open the Visual Basic Editor, you can select it from the Tools menu in Arena or click on the Visual Basic Editor button on the Integration toolbar.) This adds a new object to our VBA project and opens a window in which you can draw the form, laying out controls (the things with which a user can interact), adding pictures and labels, etc. We'll skip over the details of how forms are designed in VBA; the help under the Microsoft Forms Design Reference topic in VBA help can aid your understanding of the basic concepts, toolbars, and features of Microsoft Forms.

We'll name our form `WelcomeForm` and will add a picture (to spruce things up a bit), a frame with caption `Model 10-4`, three option buttons inside the frame (named `RunPPT`, `EditModel`, and `RunSimulation`), and a single command button with caption `OK` (named `OKButton`), as shown in Figure 10-19. These control names will be used in the VBA code; they're established using the Name field in the Properties toolbar.

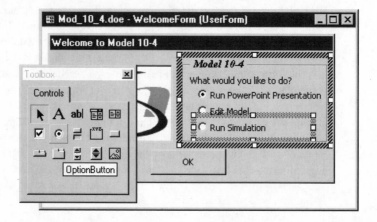

Figure 10-19. VBA User Form

After we've created the form, we need to write the VBA code to display it when the model is opened and to perform the desired actions when the OK button is clicked. To show the form, we'll open the code for the model by double-clicking on the ThisDocument entry in the Arena Objects section of our project. This displays the window containing the model's VBA code, including the RunBeginReplication, RunBeginSimulation, etc., events that we wrote in Section 10.2. We'll add code for another built-in event, DocumentOpen, by selecting it from the Procedure list on the right side of the code window. In the DocumentOpen event is a line of code, `WelcomeForm.Show`, that displays the form, shown in Figure 10-20.

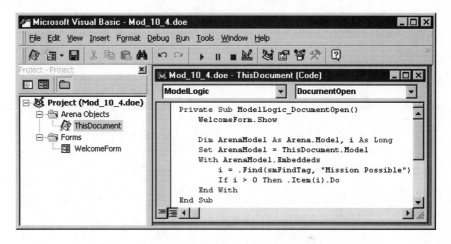

Figure 10-20. DocumentOpen Event

This line of code will display the form and pass program control to it whenever the model is opened. While we're in the DocumentOpen event, let's also examine the code to play the sound file. Here, we'll use the Arena object model to find the embedded sound file and to play it, as shown in Figure 10-20. The `ArenaModel` variable provides access to all of the properties and methods of the Model object. Previously, we had used elements of the SIMAN object contained in a model to query variable and attribute values during the simulation run. In this case, we'll access the collection of embedded objects contained in the model (`ArenaModel.Embeddeds`), searching for the one with a tag of "`Mission Possible`," which is returned as an index `i` into the collection. If one is found, then we activate it (in the case of a sound file, playing the sound) using the `Do` method of the collection item at the appropriate index.

Next, we'll add the code to be executed when the `OK` button is clicked on the form, which will hide the form (so that control can be passed back to Arena) and perform the action associated with the selected option—Run PowerPoint Presentation, Edit Model, or Run Simulation—listed in Figure 10-21.

```
Private Sub OKButton_Click()
    Dim ArenaModel As Arena.Model

    WelcomeForm.Hide
    Set ArenaModel = ThisDocument.Model

    If RunPPT.Value = True Then
        Dim i As Long
        With ArenaModel.Embeddeds
            i = .Find(smFindTag, "PowerPoint Presentation")
            If i > 0 Then .Item(i).Do
        End With
    ElseIf EditModel.Value = True Then
        With ArenaModel.NamedViews
            ArenaModel.ActiveView.ZoomView _
                .Item(.Find(smFindName, "Model Description"))
        End With
    ElseIf RunSimulation.Value = True Then
        ArenaModel.Go
    End If
End Sub
```

Figure 10-21. VBA Code for Welcome Form OK Button

To open the code window for the OK button, just double-click on the OKButton in the user form edit window. This creates the skeleton for the code to handle the Click method of the OKButton, adding the line declaring the procedure and the End Sub line terminating it. This procedure will be called automatically by Visual Basic whenever the OK button is clicked in the Welcome form. Our DocumentOpen logic displayed the form then returned (after launching the sound file); the next possible VBA code to be activated is this OK button click event, since we haven't written any other code to be executed for any other form interactions.

We first dismiss the user form using its Hide method. This removes the form from display, retaining the values of the controls (such as the option button selection). Then, we proceed to handle the three possible cases by checking the values of the three option buttons, using the names we provided earlier when we drew the form. In the first case, if the RunPPT option button's value is True, we add a few lines of code that resemble the sound file code—search for the appropriate embedded object in the model and activate it (in the case of PowerPoint, run the presentation) using its Do method. If the EditModel option was selected, we want to zoom to the named view containing the embedded Microsoft Word file. This is accomplished via the model object's ActiveView. We use its ZoomView method, searching for the view named Model Description. Finally, if RunSimulation was chosen, we use the model object's Go method, which starts the simulation run.

10.5   Creating Modules Using the Arena Professional Edition: Template 10.1

We've seen in this chapter how standard Arena modules can be used to customize reports and how ActiveX Automation, VBA, and OLE can be exploited for a number of purposes. To close the chapter, we'll take a brief look at another means of customizing Arena by building new modules using the Arena Professional Edition. If you have the Academic version of Arena, you won't be able to try this on your own since the module-building features aren't included, although they are part of the Research Edition and, of course, the commercial Professional Edition. Either way, though, you'll be able to see the use of the module that we describe in this section in an Arena model.

To present this quick tour of module creation, we'll walk through the steps to build a very simple module, showing you some of the windows and dialogs along the way. While we'll end up with a usable (and potentially useful) module, we'll only touch on a small portion of Arena's template-building features. This should be sufficient to fulfill our objective of raising your awareness of the Professional Edition's capabilities. For a more thorough treatment of building your own modules using the Research or Professional Edition, we refer you to the *Arena Professional Edition Reference Guide*.

10.5.1   The Create from File Module

Keeping with Chapter 10's theme of utilizing the call center model from Chapter 8, we'll revisit our initial modification from Section 10.1, in which we replaced the random call-arrival logic with a trace-driven approach by reading arrival times from a file and using these values as the creation times for entities in the model. To accomplish the task, we used four modules—Create, Read, Delay, and Duplicate—which worked together to generate entities into the model at the appropriate times. If we were doing a fair amount of modeling that might utilize this trace-driven approach for validation, it might be handy to "package" these modules (and the appropriate data to make things work right) into a single module. That way, we wouldn't have to remember the trick of how we got the entities into the model at the right time, and our models themselves would be a little less complicated to view.

To build this module, which we'll call `Create from File`, we'll copy the logic from the model that we already built (Model 10.1) into what's called a *template file*. Then we'll define an *operand*—a field that shows up in the dialog when you double-click on the module—that allows the file name to be changed whenever an instance of our `Create from File` module is used; we wouldn't want to be so presumptuous as to think that all of our modules will read from a file named `Mod_10_1.txt` like the original one did. We'll also draw a picture to be displayed in the template toolbar, and we'll arrange the objects that are to show up when the module is placed in a model window. These four simple steps—defining the logic, operands, panel icon, and user view—are the basics of building templates in Arena.

Before we take a more careful look at each of these steps, let's see the end result—one of these `Create from File` modules placed in a model window—as shown in Figure 10-22. Our guess is that you'll think, "Well, it looks like any other module to me." And, as a matter of fact, it *is* just like any other module. When you use Arena's template-design tools to create your own modules, the end result is a template panel object (`.tpo`) file that's just like those you've been using—Common.tpo, Support.tpo, etc. An important part of the philosophy behind Arena is to allow easy creation of personalized modeling constructs that work with the standard templates.

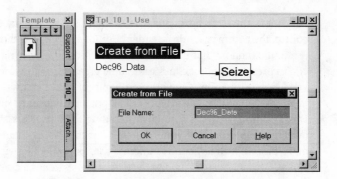

Figure 10-22. Create from File Module Used in a Model

10.5.2 The Template Source File: Tpl_10_1.tpl

To examine the definition of the `Create from File` module, we'll look at the `Tpl_10_1.tpl` file containing its logic, operands, etc. If you're running the Research or Professional Edition of Arena, you can open this file via the standard *File/Open* menu item; just change the entry in the Files of Type field to `Template Files (*.tpl)` and select `Tpl_10_1.tpl`. This opens a template window, listing all of the modules contained in the template. (For our template, we have just the one lonely `Create from File` module.) From this window, the buttons on the Template Windows toolbar (Figure 10-23) open the various other windows that define modules, preview the module dialog, and generate the template panel object (`.tpo`) file for use in a model.

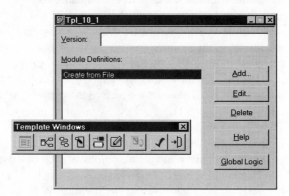

Figure 10-23. Template Window and Toolbar

10.5.3 The Panel Icon and User View

Before we dig into the innards of the `Create from File` module, we'll quickly discuss the first two things that someone using the module sees. To utilize the module in an Arena model, the template panel containing it needs to be attached to the Template toolbar, as was shown in Figure 10-22. On the toolbar, Arena displays a picture drawn by the template's creator for each module, referred to as the module's *panel icon*. In the case of our `Create from File` module, the picture depicts a dog-eared page with an arrow (representing, to the best of the limited artistic abilities of this module's designer, the concept of creating entities from a file).

When a modeler places an instance of the module in a model window, the graphic objects that are added to the window are collectively referred to as the module's *user view*. Each module has at least a handle, which typically is the module name surrounded by a box. Most modules also have one or more entry or exit points to connect them with other modules, and perhaps operand text objects displaying the value of important operands. Referring back to Figure 10-22, the `Create from File` module has a single exit point (connecting it to the Seize module) and one operand text object, showing the file name from which entity times are to be read.

10.5.4   The Module Logic and Operands

The heart of what a module provides when it's placed in a model window is the actual logic to be performed during the simulation run. When you're building a module in your own template, you define this logic just as you build a model, by placing and connecting modules from other templates. The logic underlying our `Create from File` module is simply the four modules we used in Model 10.1, with the notable difference that the exit point of the Duplicate module isn't connected to anything else. Figure 10-24 shows this logic, which is placed in the logic window of the module's definition. We dropped the modules and their connections into the logic window using the clipboard, by first selecting them in the original model, copying them to the clipboard, and then pasting them into the window.

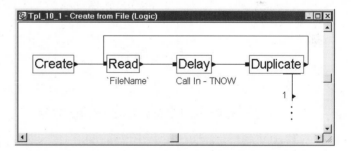

Figure 10-24. Module Logic Window

Each time our `Create from File` module is placed in a model, this underlying logic will be included, so that entities are generated and sent into the model based on the data in the text file. The astute reader might wonder, "What file? Where in the model?" This is where the module's operands come into play. If we just used the original logic from Model 10.1, then we could only use the `Create from File` module to generate entities from a file called `Mod_10_1.txt`. Instead, we'll add an operand to our module that permits a new file name to be entered each time the module is placed, and we'll instruct the Read module to use the value that was provided in the module's dialog for the file name, instead of a hard-wired value that's the same for each use of the module. The mechanics of this operand referencing are simple—if some field of a module in the logic window is enclosed in back quotes (` ` `), then its ultimate value is to come from the module's dialog (in particular, the operand whose name matches the name inside the back quotes). In our case, we'll define the SIMAN File Name in the Read module's dialog to be `` `FileName` `` (Figure 10-25). We'll also use the value of this `FileName` operand in building the OS File Name in Double Quotes, combining some hard-wired characters (the double-quotes and `.txt`) with the operand reference. The result will be that a modeler using this module can pick the file name containing the arrival times. For example, in Figure 10-22, the file name was entered as `Dec96_Data`, resulting in the model reading data from `Dec96_Data.txt`.

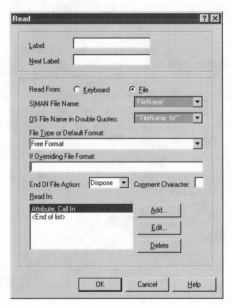

Figure 10-25. Operand Referencing by Logic Window Module

In the template, we define the `Create from File` operands in its operand window, shown in Figure 10-26 (with the definition dialog for `FileName` opened). In the operand definition dialog, we named the operand `FileName` (so that we can reference it in the Read module); accepted the default Basic type (more on this soon); restricted the data type to be a symbol name, so that we'll have a valid SIMAN File Name in the underlying Read module; left the default value empty; and checked the Required option, so that a modeler must provide a non-blank value when editing the module.

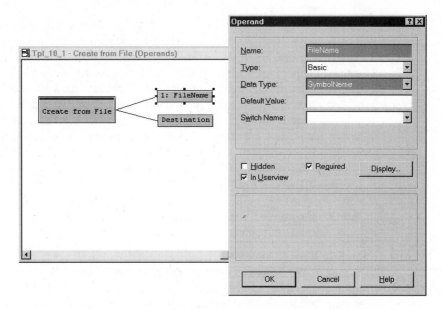

Figure 10-26. Operand Window with FileName Definition Dialog

In the operand window, we also defined an operand named `Destination`. This one is an Exit Point type, which is referenced in the Next Label field of the Duplicate module (in the logic window). This establishes the flow of entities through the model that contains an instance of the `Create from File` module. When Arena generates the SIMAN model (e.g., when you Check the model), it will start with the Create module in the logic window (since Create is a special module that starts the flow of entities into a model); follow the connections through the Read, Delay, and Duplicate modules; establish the loop back for the primary entity to leave the Duplicate and return to the Read module; and, via the `Destination` operand (because it's of the special, Exit Point type), connect the duplicated entity branch from the Duplicate module to whatever the `Create from File` connects with, such as the Seize module in Figure 10-22.

You might think of the Exit Point operand type as an "elevator up" in hierarchy, connecting from the underlying logic of the `Create from File` module to the main logic of the model in which it's included. And, not surprisingly, there's an Entry Point operand type that's an "elevator down," establishing a connection from logic in the higher level of hierarchy into modules that are contained in another module's underlying logic window.

This completes our definition of the `Create from File` module, allowing someone who uses it in their model to specify the name of the file containing the arrival times and to connect it to another module. The underlying logic also establishes some fixed logical elements (i.e., aspects that can't be changed by a modeler). In particular, each entity that's sent into the model by this `Create from File` module will have an attribute named `Call In` that has a value of its arrival time, because the Read module still makes that assignment. If you've ever pulled down an attribute list in an Arena model and noticed one or more names that you didn't recognize as your own (for example, `Queue Time`), they probably were added to the model by the logic underlying one of Arena's modules. When you're designing a module, you'll need to decide which aspects you want to permit a user to change (e.g., the file name in our example) and which you want to protect from modification (e.g., the attribute name and assignment).

Most modules that you're accustomed to using contain numerous operands and often complex underlying logic. These modules, such as those in the Arena template's Common, Support, and Transfer panels, were created using the Arena Professional Edition. Their panel icons, user views, operands, and underlying logic employ standard features. Exploring their features—from the simple Dispose module on the Support panel to the Common panel's complex Advanced Server—can help you grasp the potential of the Arena Professional Edition. While we've only touched on the architecture and features here, we'll close with some ideas about how custom templates might be employed by individuals and throughout organizations.

10.5.5 Uses of Templates

Templates may be developed to address a wide range of needs. Some might be conceived for use by a large targeted market, such as the Call$im template. Others might be more like a utility, such as the simple example presented in this chapter.

The most ambitious Arena templates are those that are developed for a commercial market, typically targeted at a particular industry. Other than the SIMAN and Arena templates that provide the modeling capabilities of Arena's Standard Edition, there are templates available for industries ranging from semiconductor wafer fabrication to call centers. There are two main advantages of industry-focused templates. First, the template can use the terminology that is appropriate for the industry, minimizing the abstraction needed for a modeler to translate a system into the software. More importantly, through Arena's hierarchy, a template can be built that is fully customized to represent accurately the elements of systems in the industry, rather than simply mapping existing modeling functionality provided by a general modeling tool. The designer of the template has the capabilities at hand to mimic exactly the behavior of equipment, people, parts, components, etc., providing whatever spectrum of options is appropriate for the variations of these system elements. Furthermore, through the ActiveX Automation technology supported by Arena, wizards and other utilities can be created that work in cooperation with a particular template for generating specialized graphs and reports, loading data directly from external databases, etc.

Many of the templates that are developed using the Arena Professional Edition aid modelers in representing a particular system, facility, or process. While they may not be "commercial-grade," these templates have many of the same goals as the industry templates and provide many of the same benefits. Here, though, the focus might be narrower than a commercial template. For example, a template might be built for use in analyzing truck-loading schemes or for representing dispatching rules of incoming calls to technicians. These application-focused templates benefit from Arena's hierarchical structure in the same ways as industry-focused templates: the interface presented to a modeler can be customized to be very familiar (both in terms of graphical animation and the terminology presented to the user); and the elements of the target application environment can be represented accurately. In some cases, a modeler might build these templates just for his/her own individual use, if the same type of problem is likely to be modeled repeatedly. In other cases, templates might be created for use among modelers in a common group; and many application templates are shared among different modeling groups throughout an enterprise.

For an individual modeler, the Arena Professional Edition affords the opportunity to reuse modeling techniques that are learned in the process of building models. In the evolution of programming tools, reusable code was captured in procedures/subroutines/functions; later, object-oriented tools allowed the full characteristics of "objects" represented in the software to be defined for reuse. A module can be thought of as analogous to an object (in object-oriented software)—the module allows you to capture the complete characteristics of a process that you want to model in a self-contained package that you may reuse and that may be customized in each use. The `Create from File` module sketched out in this section is an example of this type of template, where once a modeling technique was established and tested, its implementation details were "hidden" inside the definition of the module. Later uses of the same technique require little knowledge of its approach or implementation details and have less risk of error, since the embedded logic has already been tested.

10.6   Summary

Chapter 10 concludes the modeling topics of this book. In it we examined a number of topics that are part of a theme of customizing different aspects of Arena modeling and integrating Arena with other applications. We explored some additional modules for designing custom output reports, took a whirlwind tour of Visual Basic for Applications (VBA), saw how Arena and Microsoft Office can work together, and built some custom modeling constructs of our own with the Professional Edition of Arena. The material in this chapter represents the "tip of the iceberg," with the intent of tickling your imagination for what's possible and arming you with enough fundamental knowledge of the features to go off and explore on your own.

The remaining two chapters in the book are not directly about modeling, but are on important topics that underly and support good simulation stidues, just a good modeling does. Chapter 11 rounds out our treatment of the probabilistic underpinnings and statistical issues in simulation, which we began in Sections 5.4, 6.5, and 7.5. Then in Chapter 12, we'll tie together pretty much all the book's topics in a discussion of how to conduct simulation studies, including modeling, design, analysis, and (gasp!) dealing with people.

10.7   Exercises

10.1   Starting with Model 10.1, modify the Call Arrivals logic to write the time of each balked call to a text file named `Ex_10_1.txt`. Use the Write module from the Support panel.

10.2   Make the logic modifications described in Exercise 10.1 using VBA to store the data in a spreadsheet file (or in a text file if you don't have a spreadsheet application installed on your computer) instead of using the Write module.

10.3   Build a simple, single-server queueing model with entity interarrival times of EXPO(0.25). Using the Read and Write modules, prompt and query at the beginning of the simulation run for the server's process time mean (give a default value of 0.2). Use this value to establish a normal distribution with a standard deviation that's 8% of the entered mean. Run the simulation until 300 entities have departed the model.

10.4   Create the model described in Exercise 10.3, replacing the Read and Write modules with a VBA form that's displayed at the beginning of the simulation run.

10.5   Modify the model you created in Exercise 10.3 to write the entity departure times to a text file named `Ex_10_3.txt`. Then modify and rerun the model, replacing the random entity creation pattern with logic using the data in `Ex_10_3.txt` for a trace-driven simulation.

10.6   Using the single-server model from Exercise 10.4, add logic to play a sound whenever the number of entities in the service queue exceeds some threshold value. Allow the modeler to establish this threshold in the form that's displayed at the beginning of the run.

10.7   Find out how long it takes the system in Model 10.1 to process the entities recorded in the text file by changing the logic to end the simulation when the last entity departs the model.

10.8   Edit the animation in Model 10.1 to use ClipArt pictures or other bitmaps for the resource pictures.

10.9   Add a report to Model 10.1 that lists the number-in-queue statistics for each of the product queues, presented in ascending order.

10.10   Present a VBA form at the end of the simulation run reporting the average and maximum queue lengths for the product queues in Model 10.1. If you have a charting program (e.g., Excel) installed on your computer, also draw a bar graph of the average values.

Further Statistical Issues

CHAPTER 11

Further Statistical Issues

One of the points we've tried to make consistently in this book is that a good simulation study involves more than building a good model (though good models are certainly important too). In a simulation with stochastic (random) input, you're going to get random output as well. Thus, it's critical to understand how simulations generate this randomness in the input, and what you can do about the resulting randomness in the output. We've already blended some of these statistical issues in with our tour through model building and analysis, specifically in Sections 2.6, 5.4, 6.5, and 7.5. Part of the point of those sections is that Arena can help you deal with these issues, but you must be aware that they exist.

This chapter discusses additional statistical issues, related to both the input and output sides of a simulation. Random-number generators, the source of all randomness in simulations, are discussed in Section 11.1. Then in Section 11.2, we'll talk about how to generate observations on whatever input distributions you decided to use as part of your modeling. Section 11.3 discusses specifying and generating from a particular yet important type of random input, a nonstationary Poisson process (which, by the way, was introduced in the call center model of Chapter 8). Ways to reduce output variance (other than just simulating some more) are described in Section 11.4. The idea of sequential sampling—i.e., deciding on the fly how much simulation-generated data you need—is the subject of Section 11.5. A few more capabilities of the Arena Output Analyzer are discussed in Section 11.6, and the chapter concludes in Section 11.7 with brief mention of the possibility of using experimental design in simulation. By the time you reach the end of this chapter, you should have a thorough understanding of statistical issues in simulation and know how Arena can help you deal with them.

Obviously, this chapter is a heavy user of foundational material in probability and statistics. We've provided a refresher on these subjects in Appendix C of the book, which you might want to look at before going on. In addition, Appendix D contains a listing of all the probability distributions supported by Arena.

11.1 Random-Number Generation

Deep down in the engine room of any stochastic simulation is a *random-number generator* (RNG) quietly churning away. The sole purpose of such a machine is to produce a flow of numbers that are observations (also known as *draws*, *samples*, or *realizations*) from a continuous uniform distribution between 0 and 1 (see Appendix D) and are independent of each other. In simulation, these are called *random numbers*. This is certainly not the only probability distribution from which you'll want to draw observations to drive your simulations (see Section 5.4), but as we'll discuss in Sections 11.2 and 11.3, generating observations from all other distributions and random processes starts with random numbers.

Any method for generating random numbers on a computer is just some kind of recursive algorithm that can repeat the same sequence of "random" numbers again and again. For this reason, these are often called *pseudorandom*-number generators. Some people have worried philosophically that such methods are fundamentally flawed since part of what it means to be random is to be unpredictable. This might make for an interesting after-dinner debate, but at a practical level, the issue is really not very important. Modern and carefully constructed RNGs generally succeed at producing a flow of numbers that appear to be truly random, passing various statistical tests for both uniformity and independence, as well as satisfying theoretically derived criteria for being "good." Also, it's quite helpful in simulation to be able to regenerate a specific sequence of random numbers; this is an obvious aid in debugging (not to mention grading homework), but is also useful statistically, as we'll describe in Section 11.4.

Unfortunately, there seems to be a common perception that any seemingly nonsensical method will, just because it looks weird, generate "random" numbers. Indeed, some extremely poor methods have been provided and used, possibly resulting in invalid simulation results. Designing and implementing RNGs is actually quite subtle, and there has been a lot of research on these topics. (For discussion and references, see Chapter 7 of Law and Kelton, 1991.) In part because computers have become so fast, there continues to be work on developing new and better RNGs that can satisfy the voracious appetite that modern simulations can have for random numbers.

So how do good RNGs work? Though there are several different general methods, the most common form (and the type built into Arena) is called a *linear congruential generator* (LCG). An LCG generates a sequence $Z_1, Z_2, Z_3, \ldots$ of integers via the recursion

$$Z_i = (aZ_{i-1} + c) \bmod m$$

where m, a, and c are constants for the generator that must be chosen carefully, based on both theoretical and empirical grounds, to produce a good flow of random numbers. The "mod m" operation means to divide $aZ_{i-1} + c$ by m and then return the *remainder* of this division to the left-hand-side as the next Z_i (for instance, 422 mod 63 is 44). As with any recursion, an LCG must be initialized, so there is also a *seed* Z_0 specified for the generator. This sequence of Z_i's will be integers, which is not what we want for a continuous distribution between 0 and 1. However, since the Z_i's are remainders of division of other integers by m, they'll all be between 0 and $m - 1$, so the final step is to define $U_i = Z_i/m$, which will be between 0 and 1. The sequence $U_1, U_2, U_3, \ldots$ are the (pseudo-)random numbers returned for use in the simulation.

As a tiny example (nobody should ever *use* this generator), take $m = 63$, $a = 22$, $c = 4$, and $Z_0 = 19$. The recursion generating the Z_i's is thus $Z_i = (22 Z_{i-1} + 4) \bmod 63$. Table 11-1 traces this generator through the first 70 generated random numbers, and you can check some of the arithmetic (we used a spreadsheet to generate this table). At first blush, scanning down through the U_i column gives the impression that these look like pretty good random numbers—they're certainly all between 0 and 1, they appear to be spread fairly uniformly over the interval [0, 1], and they are evidently pretty well mixed up (independent). The sample mean of the U_i's is 0.4984 and the sample standard deviation is 0.2867, which are close to what we'd expect from a true uniform [0, 1] distribution (1/2 and $1/\sqrt{12} = 0.2887$, respectively).

Table 11-1. Tracing an LCG's Arithmetic

i	$22Z_{i-1}+4$	Z_i	U_i	i	$22Z_{i-1}+4$	Z_i	U_i	i	$22Z_{i-1}+4$	Z_i	U_i
0		19		24	1060	52	0.8254	48	400	22	0.3492
1	422	44	0.6984	25	1148	14	0.2222	49	488	47	0.7460
2	972	27	0.4286	26	312	60	0.9524	50	1038	30	0.4762
3	598	31	0.4921	27	1324	1	0.0159	51	664	34	0.5397
4	686	56	0.8889	28	26	26	0.4127	52	752	59	0.9365
5	1236	39	0.6190	29	576	9	0.1429	53	1302	42	0.6667
6	862	43	0.6825	30	202	13	0.2063	54	928	46	0.7302
7	950	5	0.0794	31	290	38	0.6032	55	1016	8	0.1270
8	114	51	0.8095	32	840	21	0.3333	56	180	54	0.8571
9	1126	55	0.8730	33	466	25	0.3968	57	1192	58	0.9206
10	1214	17	0.2698	34	554	50	0.7937	58	1280	20	0.3175
11	378	0	0.0000	35	1104	33	0.5238	59	444	3	0.0476
12	4	4	0.0635	36	730	37	0.5873	60	70	7	0.1111
13	92	29	0.4603	37	818	62	0.9841	61	158	32	0.5079
14	642	12	0.1905	38	1368	45	0.7143	62	708	15	0.2381
15	268	16	0.2540	39	994	49	0.7778	63	334	19	0.3016
16	356	41	0.6508	40	1082	11	0.1746	64	422	44	0.6984
17	906	24	0.3810	41	246	57	0.9048	65	972	27	0.4286
18	532	28	0.4444	42	1258	61	0.9683	66	598	31	0.4921
19	620	53	0.8413	43	1346	23	0.3651	67	686	56	0.8889
20	1170	36	0.5714	44	510	6	0.0952	68	1236	39	0.6190
21	796	40	0.6349	45	136	10	0.1587	69	862	43	0.6825
22	884	2	0.0317	46	224	35	0.5556	70	950	5	0.0794
23	48	48	0.7619	47	774	18	0.2857				

But there are a couple of things to notice here. First, as you read down through the Z_i's, you'll see that $Z_{63} = 19$, which is the same as the seed Z_0. Then, note that $Z_{64} = 44 = Z_1$, $Z_{65} = 27 = Z_2$, and so on. The Z_i's are repeating themselves in the same order, and this whole cycle will itself repeat forever. Since the U_i's are just the Z_i's divided by 63, the random numbers will also repeat themselves. This *cycling* of an LCG will happen as soon as it hits a previously generated Z_i, since each number in the sequence depends only on its predecessor, via the fixed recursive formula. And it is inevitable that the LCG will cycle since there are, after all, only m possibilities for the remainder of division by m; in other words, the cycle length will be at most m. In our little example, the cycle length actually achieved its maximum, $m = 63$, but had the parameters a and c been chosen

differently, the cycle length could have been shorter (try changing a to 6 but leave everything else the same). We weren't just lucky (or persistent) in our choice since there's fully
developed theory on how to make parameter-value choices for LCGs to achieve full, or
at least long, cycle lengths. Real LCGs, unlike our little example above, typically take m
to be at least $2^{31} - 1 = 2,147,483,647$ (about 2.1 billion) and choose the other parameters
to achieve full or nearly full cycle length; they will keep going this long before cycling—
certainly sufficient for most applications. And, though we can still remember when 2.1
billion was a lot, such a cycle length is not as impressive as it once was, given today's
computing power. While choosing m even bigger is possible, people have instead developed altogether different kinds of generators with truly enormous cycle lengths. For specifics on cycle lengths, parameter choices, and other kinds of generators, see Chapter 7
of Law and Kelton (1991).

The other thing to realize about the U_i's in Table 11-1 is that they might not be quite
as "random" as you'd like, as indicated by the two graphs in Figure 11-1. The left graph
simply plots the random numbers in order of their generation, and you'll notice a certain
regularity. This is perhaps not so upsetting since we know that the generator will cycle
and repeat exactly the same pattern. The pattern for a real generator (with a higher value
of m), will not be so apparent since there are far more random numbers possible and
since, in most applications, you'll generally be using only a small part of a complete
cycle.

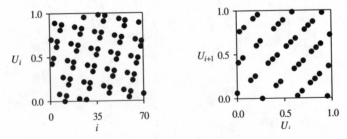

Figure 11-1. Plots for an LCG

But the right graph in Figure 1-1 might be more unsettling. This graph plots the pairs
(U_i, U_{i+1}) over the complete cycle, which is of natural interest if you're using the random
numbers in pairs in the simulation. As you can see, it has an eerie pattern to it that will, in
fact, be present for any LCG (as shown in the colorfully named paper, "Random Numbers Fall Mainly in the Planes" by Marsaglia, 1968). A truly random generator should
instead have dots haphazardly scattered uniformly over the unit square, rather than being
compulsively arranged and leaving comparatively large gaps where no pairs are possible.
And this *lattice* structure gets even worse if you make (or imagine) such a plot in higher
dimensions (triples, quadruples, etc., of successive random numbers). These kinds of
considerations should drive home the point that "designing" good RNGs is not a simple
matter, and you should thus be careful when encountering some mysterious RNG.

The RNG in Arena is an LCG with $m = 2^{31} - 1$, $a = 7^5 = 16{,}807$, and $c = 0$. This particular generator has been thoroughly researched and in fact delivers an entirely respectable flow of random numbers. Since the arithmetic of RNGs with such large parameters can stress the capacity[1] of computer arithmetic, they must be carefully (indeed, cleverly) coded.

As for the seeds used by Arena, there are 10 different automatically supplied values, each of which begins at a separate point around the cycle of the generator. The sequence of random numbers starting from each of these 10 seeds is called a *stream*. Though the streams are really just subsequences positioned around the entire cycle, you can think of them as being separate "faucets" delivering different streams of random numbers. You can specify which stream is used whenever you ask for an observation from a distribution in Arena by appending the stream number to the distribution's parameters; for instance to generate an exponential observation with mean 6.7 from stream 4, use EXPO(6.7, 4). If you don't specify a stream number, Arena defaults it to 10. The idea of using separate streams of random numbers for individual purposes in a simulation (for instance, stream 1 for interarrival times between parts, stream 2 for part types, stream 3 for processing times, etc.) comes in quite handy for variance reduction, discussed in Section 11.4.

The SEEDS module, from the Elements panel, gives you access to Arena's random-number streams and some control over how they are generated and used. You can get more than the 10 default streams by placing a SEEDS module in your model and simply telling it how many streams you need. (The specific seeds for all the streams will be provided by Arena automatically.) If you want to override Arena's automatic seeds with your own favorite seeds for some or all of the streams, you may do so via the SEEDS module as well. In addition to numbering the streams, you can give them names or refer to them with general Variables, Attributes, or Expressions. For details on how to use the SEEDS module, check online help; Section 11.4 demonstrates its use.

11.2 Generating Random Variates

In Section 5.4, we discussed how you can select appropriate probability distributions to represent random input for your model. Now that you know how to generate random numbers—i.e., draws from a uniform distribution between 0 and 1—you need to transform them somehow into draws from the input probability distributions you want for your model. In simulation, people often refer to such draws as *variates* from the distribution.

The precise method for generating variates from a distribution will, of course, depend on the form of the distribution and the numerical values you estimated or specified its parameters to be, but there are some general ideas that apply across most distributions. Because implementation is a bit different for discrete and continuous random variables, we'll consider them separately.

---

[1] Note that on computers with 32 bits in a word for an integer, which is pretty much standard today, the largest integer that can be represented in a word is in fact $2^{31} - 1$. This is, in part, why this value of m was chosen.

11.2.1 Discrete

Let's start by considering discrete random variables (see Section C.2.2 in Appendix C). To take a simple concrete example, suppose you want to generate a discrete random variate X having possible values -2, 0, and 3 with probability mass function (PMF) given by

$$p(x) = P(X = x) = \begin{cases} 0.1 & \text{for } x = -2 \\ 0.5 & \text{for } x = 0 \\ 0.4 & \text{for } x = 3 \end{cases}$$

Since the probabilities in a PMF have to add up to 1, we can divide the unit interval [0, 1] into subintervals with widths equal to the individual values given by the PMF, in this case [0, 0.1), [0.1, 0.6), and [0.6, 1]. If we generate a random number U, it will be distributed uniformly over the whole interval [0, 1], so it will fall in the first subinterval with probability $0.1 - 0 = 0.1$, in the second with probability $0.6 - 0.1 = 0.5$, and in the third subinterval with probability $1 - 0.6 = 0.4$. Thus, we would set X to its first value, -2, if U falls in the first subinterval, which will happen with probability $0.1 = p(-2)$, as desired. Similarly, we set X to 0 if U falls in the second subinterval (probability 0.5), and set X to 3 if U falls in the third subinterval (probability 0.4). This process, which is pretty obviously correct for generating X with the desired distribution, is depicted in Figure 11-2 .

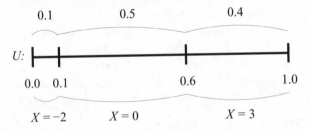

Figure 11-2. *Generating a Discrete Random Variate*

Another way of looking at this algorithm is that it *inverts*, in a sense, the cumulative distribution function (CDF) of X, $F(x) = P(X \le x)$, as illustrated in Figure 11-3. First, generate a random number U, then plot it on the vertical axis, then read across (left or right) until you "hit" one of the jumps in the CDF, and finally read down and return X as whatever x_i $(= -2, 0,$ or 3 in our example) you hit. In the example shown, U falls between 0.6 and 1, resulting in a returned variate $X = 3$. This is clearly the same algorithm as described above and shown in Figure 11-2, but sets things up for generating continuous random variates below.

This method, looking at it in either of the above ways, clearly generalizes to any discrete distribution with a finite number of x_i's possible. In fact, it can also be used even if the number of x_i's is infinite. In either case, the real work boils down to some kind of search to find the subinterval of [0, 1] in which a random number U falls, then returning

X as the appropriate x_i. If the number of x_i's is large, this search can become slow, and in this case, there are altogether different approaches to variate generation. We won't cover these ideas here; see Chapter 8 of Law and Kelton (1991) for more details and references.

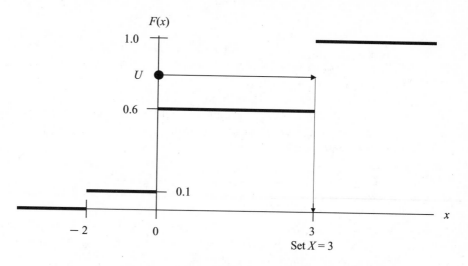

Figure 11-3. Generating a Discrete Random Variate via Inversion of the CDF

Arena has built in the Poisson distribution, as well as any user-defined finite-range discrete distribution (see Appendix D). In both cases, the above algorithm is used to generate the variates.

11.2.2 Continuous

Now let's consider generation of variates from a continuous probability distribution (Section C.2.3 in Appendix C). In this case, we can't think in terms of the probability of getting (exactly) a particular value returned since this probability will always be zero. Instead, we need to think in terms of the returned X being *between* two values. As a specific example, take the exponential distribution with mean $\beta = 5$, which has probability density function (PDF)

$$f(x) = \begin{cases} (1/5)e^{-x/5} & \text{for } x > 0 \\ 0 & \text{for } x \leq 0 \end{cases}$$

and CDF

$$F(x) = \begin{cases} 1 - e^{-x/5} & \text{for } x > 0 \\ 0 & \text{for } x \leq 0 \end{cases}$$

To generate a variate X from this distribution, start (as usual) by generating a random number U. Then set U equal to the CDF (evaluated at the unknown X) and solve for X in terms of the (now known) value of U:

$$
\begin{array}{rcll}
U & = & 1 - e^{-X/5} & \text{(ignore the probability-zero event that } U = 0) \\
e^{-X/5} & = & 1 - U & \\
-X/5 & = & \ln(1 - U) & \text{(ln is the natural logarithm; i.e., base } e) \\
X & = & -5 \ln(1 - U) &
\end{array}
$$

(Obviously, replacing the 5 with a general value of $\beta > 0$ gives you the general form for generating an exponential variate.) This solution for X in terms of U is called the *inverse CDF* of U, written $X = F^{-1}(U)$ ($= -5 \ln(1 - U)$ in our example), since this transformation "undoes" to U what F does to X.

The inverse CDF algorithm for this example is shown in Figure 11-4. (Note the similarity to the discrete case in Figure 11-3.) First generate a random number U, plot it on the vertical axis, then read across and down to get X, which is clearly the solution to the equation $U = F(X)$.

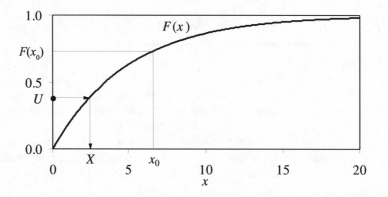

Figure 11-4. Generating a Continuous Random Variate via Inversion of the CDF

To see why this algorithm is correct, we need to demonstrate that the returned variate X will fall to the left of any fixed value x_0 with probability equal to $F(x_0)$, for this is precisely what it means for the CDF of X to be F. From Figure 11-4, you see that, since F is an increasing function, we'll happen to get $X \le x_0$ if and only if we happen to draw a U that is $\le F(x_0)$; Figure 11-4 depicts this as happening for this value of U. Thus, the events "$X \le x_0$" and "$U \le F(x_0)$" are equivalent, so must have the same probability. But since U is uniformly distributed on [0, 1], it will be $\le F(x_0)$ with probability $F(x_0)$ itself, since $F(x_0)$ is between 0 and 1. Thus, $P(\text{returned variate } X \text{ is} \le x_0) = F(x_0)$, as desired.

Though you may think we're all wet, there's actually an intuitive appeal to this algorithm. What we want is for the returned X's to follow the density function $f(x)$, so we want a lot of X's where $f(x)$ is high and not very many where $f(x)$ is low (see Section C.2.3 in Appendix C). Now the CDF $F(x)$ is the (indefinite) integral of the PDF $f(x)$; in other words, $f(x)$ is the derivative (slope function) of $F(x)$. Thus, where $f(x)$ is high, the slope of $F(x)$ will be steep; where $f(x)$ is low, $F(x)$ will be increasing only slowly (i.e., with shallow slope). In our exponential example, $f(x)$ starts out at its highest point at $x = 0$ (see the

Exponential entry in Appendix D) and then declines; thus, $F(x)$ increases steeply just to the right of 0, and then its slope flattens out as we move to the right, which is where $f(x)$ becomes smaller. Now, put yourself in Figure 11-4 and stand just to the left of the vertical axis. Pick up a garden hose that will spray U's uniformly toward the right, and turn it on. As your U's hit the $F(x)$ curve, they will drip through it down to the horizontal axis, landing to define your returned X's. Your uniformly sprayed U's will be more likely to hit the $F(x)$ curve where it rises steeply (in this case, early in its ascent) since it's a bigger target from where you're standing. Just a few of your U's (the really big ones) will hit $F(x)$ out on its upper right portion. Thus, if you look at where your X drips landed, they will be more dense on the left part (where $f(x)$ is tall and $F(x)$ is rising steeply), and will be sparser on the right part (where $f(x)$ is low and $F(x)$ is rising shallowly). This is what we want for this distribution.

The inverse CDF idea works, in principle, for any continuous distribution. But, depending on the particular distribution, implementing it may not be easy. Some distributions, unlike the exponential example above, have no closed-form formula for the CDF $F(x)$, so that a simple formula for generating the X's is not possible (a notable example of this is the normal distribution). In many such cases, though, numerical methods can be used to approximate the solution of $U = F(X)$ for X to a very high degree of accuracy (with error less than computer roundoff error). There are also completely different approaches to generating variates that are sometimes used; we won't go into these here (see Chapter 8 of Law and Kelton, 1991, for details and references).

Most of the continuous distributions supported by Arena (see Appendix D) use the inverse CDF method for variate generation, in some cases by highly accurate numerical approximation. A few of the distributions, though, use other methods if they are particularly attractive in that case; refer to online help under the topic "Distributions" to see exactly what Arena does to generate from each continuous distribution.

11.3 Nonstationary Poisson Processes

A lot of systems have some kind of externally originating events affecting them, like customers arriving, calls coming in, cars approaching an intersection, or accidents occurring in a plant. Often, it's appropriate to model this kind of *event process* as being random with some continuous probability distribution for interevent times, implying some discrete distribution for the number of events occurring in a fixed interval of time. If the process governing the event occurrences is stationary over the time frame of the simulation, you can just decide on the right interevent-time distribution and generate the events during the simulation as we've done in many models in the book (for example, with the Time Between field in the Arrive and Create modules).

However, many systems experience time-varying, or *nonstationary* patterns of events—the lunch stampede at a fast-food restaurant, morning and evening rush hours in traffic systems, mid-afternoon peaks of calls coming in to a call center, or a rash of accidents when the moon is full. While you might be tempted to ignore these patterns and make the events occur at some kind of "average" rate throughout your simulation, doing so could lead to seriously inaccurate results if there is much variation in the actual pattern. For instance, if we average the freeway load over 24 hours, there's little doubt that a small number of lanes would appear to be adequate in the model; in fact, though, rush hours would be impossible messes. So modeling nonstationary external events can be a critical part of valid modeling in general.

Actually, we've already discussed a situation exactly like this, in the call center model of Chapter 8. The external events are the arrivals of customer calls, and in Table 8-1, we listed the observed arrival rate, in calls per hour, for each half-hour period from 8 AM to 6 PM. Then, in Sections 8.2, 8.6, and 8.7, we showed how to set things up in Arena to generate, in a valid way, a random pattern of calls that reflected the changing arrival rates over the day. We won't go over that again here, but we want to mention a few things about specifying such a pattern, as well as indicate why the method used in Chapter 8 is valid.

The usual way to represent time-varying event patterns is by what's called a *nonstationary Poisson process* (NSPP). To use such a process, you need to specify a *rate function*, $\lambda(t)$, that changes with time (t), having the (rough) interpretation that $\lambda(t)$ is high for times t when lots of events are happening, and low when things are quiet. More precisely, the definition of an NSPP is that events occur one at a time, are independent of each other, and the number (count) of events occurring during and interval of time $[t_1, t_2]$ is a Poisson random variable (see Appendix D) with expected value given by

$$\Lambda(t_1, t_2) = \int_{t_1}^{t_2} \lambda(t)dt \,,$$

which is large over time intervals where $\lambda(t)$ is high and small when $\lambda(t)$ is low.

If you want to use an NSPP in a simulation, there are two issues: How to form an estimate of $\lambda(t)$, and then how to generate the arrivals from your estimated function. The estimated function we used in Chapter 8 is piecewise constant, with (possible) changes of level occurring every 30 minutes. This approach is probably the most practical one, since it's quite general and easy to specify (though you must be careful about keeping the units of time straight). With such a piecewise-constant estimated rate function, the generation method, as described in Chapter 8, also works out relatively simply. There are, however, more sophisticated ways to estimate the rate function, including amplitudes, periodicities, and a firm grounding in statistical theory; see, for instance, Leemis (1991) or Johnson, Lee, and Wilson (1994).

As for the issue of how to generate the estimated NSPP in your simulation, we went through the mechanics of representing the *thinning* method for a piecewise-constant estimated rate function in Sections 8.2, 8.6, and 8.7. The idea behind this is that you find the maximum $\lambda*$ of your estimated rate function, and generate "candidate" events at this peak rate by calling for exponential inter-event times with mean $1/\lambda*$. Now these candidate events will be happening too frequently (except at times when you're actually at the peak rate), so you "thin them out" by accepting a candidate event generated for time t as a real event with probability

$$\hat{\lambda}(t)\big/\lambda*$$

where $\hat{\lambda}(t)$ is the estimated rate function evaluated at time t. So during times when the rate is low, the above ratio will be small, causing you to thin out most of the disappointed candidate events; when the rate is high (close to its maximum), you'll be accepting most of the eager candidates. The upshot is that the "accepted" events will be more frequent when they should be and less frequent when they should be. This is all very nice intuition, but be assured that there is solid mathematical justification for it in terms of producing an NSPP, as defined above; see Lewis and Shedler (1979). Finally, we note that there is an alternative way of generating an NSPP, via inversion of a stationary rate-one Poisson process against the cumulative rate function $\Lambda(0, t)$; see Chapter 8 of Law and Kelton (1991) for details.

11.4 Variance Reduction

As we've indicated in several places (including Sections 2.6, 6.5, and 7.5), simulations using random variates from probability distributions as part of the input will in turn produce random output. In other words, there is some *variance* associated with the output from a stochastic simulation. The more variance there is, the less precise are your results; one manifestation of high variance is wide confidence intervals. So output variance is the enemy, and it would be nice to get rid of it, or at least reduce it. One (bad) way to eliminate variance in the output is to purge all the randomness from your inputs, perhaps by replacing the input random variables with their expected values. However, as we demonstrated in Section 5.4.1, this might make your output nice and stable but it also will usually make it seriously wrong.

So, barring major violence to your model's validity, the best you can really hope for is to *reduce* the variance in your output performance measures. One obvious way to do this is by just simulating more. For terminating models, this implies more replications (since extending the length of a replication would make the model invalid in the terminating case); in Section 6.5.4, we gave a couple of formulas from which you can approximate the number of replications you'll need to bring a confidence-interval half-width down to a value small enough for you to live with. For steady-state models, you could also make more replications if you're taking the truncated-replications approach to analysis, as discussed in Section 7.5.2; or you could just make your (single) replication longer if you're taking the batch-means approach (Section 7.5.3 and 7.5.4). In Section 11.5, we'll discuss all of this in detail, including how you can get Arena to "decide" on the fly how much simulating to do.

But what we aspire to in this section is a free lunch. Getting more precise results by more simulation work is not tricky, but there are some situations where you can achieve the same thing without doing any[2] more work. What usually enables this is the fact that, unlike in most physical experiments, you're in control of the randomness in a simulation experiment since you can control the random-number generator, as discussed in Section 11.1. This allows you to induce certain kinds of correlations that you can exploit to your advantage to reduce the variance, and thus imprecision, of your output. These kinds of schemes are called *variance-reduction techniques* (or sometimes variance-reduction *strategies*). In most cases, you need to have a thorough understanding of your model's logic and how it's represented in Arena in order to apply such methods.

---

[2] Well, hardly any.

Variance-reduction techniques can be quite different from each other and have been classified into several broad categories. We'll discuss only the most popular one of them in detail, in Section 11.4.1, and will briefly describe some others in Section 11.4.2.

11.4.1   Common Random Numbers

Most simulation studies involve more than just one *alternative* of a model. Different alternatives could be determined by anything from just an input-parameter change to a wholesale revision of the system layout and operation. In these situations, you're usually not so much interested in the particular values of the output performance measures from the individual alternatives, but rather in their *differences* across the alternatives. These differences are thus measures of the effect of changing from one alternative to another.

For example, take Model 6.2, the simple manufacturing system we looked at in Section 6.5 for statistical analysis of terminating simulations. In Section 6.5.5, we considered two alternatives—the model with the variable `Transfer Time` (the time required for parts to move between cells) set to 1, and the other with `Transfer Time` set to 3; call these alternatives A and B, respectively. To estimate the effect of changing `Transfer Time` from 1 to 3, it makes intuitive sense to simulate both alternatives under conditions that are as similar as possible, except for the model change we made, so that when we look at the difference in the results we'll know that it's due to this change rather than due to the random numbers' having bounced differently in the two alternatives. In this model, there are 14 places where we draw from input probability distributions (interarrival times, part indices, and 12 processing-time distributions as defined in Table 6-1). For our comparison, we'd like to run both alternatives A and B with the "same" external loads. In this case, this means parts arriving at the same times, assigned the same part-type indices, and experiencing the same processing times at each of the stops along their sequences. When we ran this comparison in Section 6.5.5, we didn't do anything to try to get any of this to happen. True, the same random-number stream (the default, stream 10) was used for everything throughout both alternatives, and this stream started the first of the 20 replications from the same seed for both alternatives. But due to the change made in the model between the alternatives, this fixed sequence of random numbers will be used in a different order if, at any point during the runs, there is a difference in the order of execution in which the 14 places draw the variates they need. This causes the "external loads" to differ at this point, and likely from then on, which is not the effect we want.

Instead, we need to *synchronize* the use of the random numbers across the model alternatives, or at least do so as far as possible given the model logic and the change between the alternatives. One approach (though not the only one) to this end is to *dedicate* a stream of random numbers to each of the 14 places in the model where variates are generated. This is like piping in separate "faucets" of random numbers to each random-variate generator. In this way, you can usually get reasonable synchronization, though in complex models it might not ensure that everything is matched up across the alternatives. For instance, in Model 6.2, if the travel times of parts between stations were modeled not as a fixed constant but as random variables from some distribution, and if this distribution changed when we move from alternative A to alternative B, it's likely that a cell would "see" parts from within the same type class arriving in different orders across the alternatives. Thus, while the stream of processing times being generated for this part type at this cell is the same across the alternatives, these times are being assigned to parts that probably arrived to the system at different times but then took different times to travel between cells. This does not make your model in any way incorrect or invalid, but it is not quite as close a match-up across the alternatives as you might like in order to have the "same" parts arrive to both alternative models. However, there will still probably be at least some variance-reduction benefit even though the matchups might not be quite perfect. This is the synchronization approach we'll take in our example below.

A different way to attempt random-number synchronization, which might work better in some models, is to assign to each entity, immediately upon its arrival, attribute values for all possible processing times, branching decisions, etc., that it might need on its entire path through the model. When the entity needs one of these values during its life in the model, such as a processing time at some cell, you just read it out of the appropriate attribute of the entity rather than generate it on the spot. This might come closer for some models to the ideal of having the "same" external conditions, but it can require a lot more computer memory if you need to hold lots of attributes for lots of entities at the same time. If Arena has to use your disk drive to extend memory temporarily (called *virtual memory*), there can be a significant increase in execution time as well since disk access is much slower than memory access. In this situation, you might be just as well off using this extra computer time doing more simulation (either more replications or a longer replication). We won't carry out this synchronization approach in our example below, but will leave it for you as Exercises 11.1 and 11.2.

Sometimes achieving full, complete, and certain synchronization in complex models is just impractical, in which case you might consider matching up what you can, and generating the rest independently. When you use the same random numbers across simulated alternatives, synchronized in some way, you're using a variance-reduction technique called *common random numbers* (CRN), also sometimes called *matched pairs* or *correlated sampling*.

To get the first of the above two synchronization approaches (piping in separate faucets of random numbers to the points in a model where variates are generated) to CRN going in Model 6.2, we modified it into what we'll call Model 11.1 by placing a SEEDS module from the Elements panel, giving names to streams 1 through 15 to indicate their usage; see Display 11-1. We've taken advantage of the ability to give names, rather than just numbers, to streams 1–15, and in addition, selected the Common Initialize Option for each of these streams. In our naming scheme for the processing times, Stream P*x* C*y* refers to the stream for Part type *x* being processed at Cell *y*; note that part type 2 visits Cell 2 twice, and we devote a separate stream for its time on each visit. The reason we're skipping over stream 10 (putting in a dummy place-holding name for it in the SEEDS element) is that this is Arena's default stream (the only one we've used so far in this book), from which it will draw internally in some models, so leaving it out of synchronization setups is generally prudent. The Common selection for the Initialize Option spaces the seeds for each replication within each stream 100,000 random numbers apart, to make sure[3] that there will be no overlap of random-number usage within a stream across different replications. We're accepting Arena's automatic seed values for each of the 15 streams. For a comparison using CRN, this same SEEDS element was present in the model for the runs of both alternatives A and B.

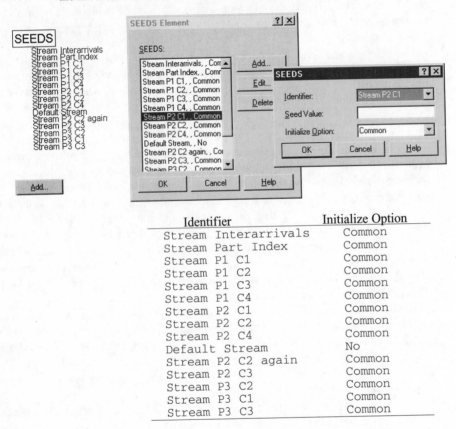

Identifier	Initialize Option
Stream Interarrivals	Common
Stream Part Index	Common
Stream P1 C1	Common
Stream P1 C2	Common
Stream P1 C3	Common
Stream P1 C4	Common
Stream P2 C1	Common
Stream P2 C2	Common
Stream P2 C4	Common
Default Stream	No
Stream P2 C2 again	Common
Stream P2 C3	Common
Stream P3 C2	Common
Stream P3 C1	Common
Stream P3 C3	Common

Display 11-1. The Seeds Module for CRN in Alternatives A and B

To use these stream assignments, we needed to alter the Arrive, Expressions, and Sequences modules, where the variate generation is done in this model. Figure 11-5 shows the modified Arrive module, where the stream assignment for interarrival times can be partially seen in the main dialog's Time Between field—EXPO(13, Stream Interarrivals)—and the stream for the part-type index is partially visible in the Assignments dialog's Value field—DISC(.26, 1, .74, 2, 1.0, 3, Stream Part Index).

---

[3] You can usually do some kind of back-of-the-envelope calculation to make yourself feel better about this. For this model, we're calling for 100 parts to arrive in each replication, to be parceled out to the three part types. So there will be about 100 interarrival times and 100 part-type decisions. Further, each part at each stop on its sequence through the shop (a maximum of five stops) has its own stream, so the 100,000 spacing is certainly enough.

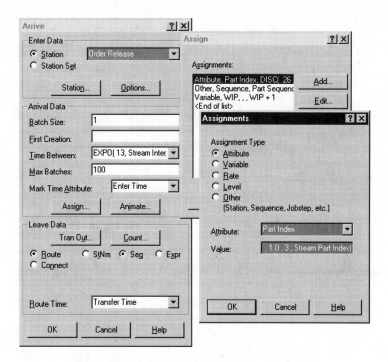

Figure 11-5. Assigning Streams in the Arrive Module

For processing times of all part types at Cell 1, we used an Expressions module, modified for stream assignment as shown in Figure 11-6.

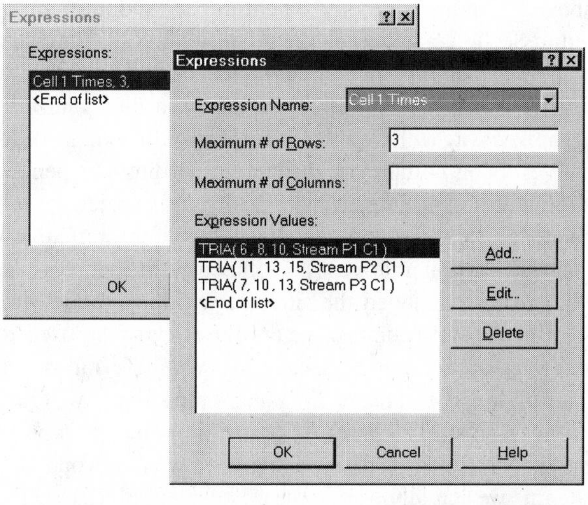

Figure 11-6. Assigning Streams in the Expressions Module

Processing times for parts at the other cells were specified in the Sequences module. An example, for part-type index 2 at Cell 4, modified for stream assignment, is in Figure 11-7 (the other 11 entries are similar).

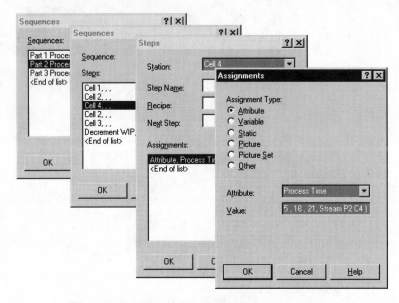

Figure 11-7. Assigning Streams in the Sequences Module

We realize how excited you must be by now about seeing our CRN results, but before we divulge them to you, we want to discuss just one more little thing. What we set up above is a fairly carefully synchronized random-number allocation for CRN. What we did in Section 6.5.5, using the same stream (10) for everything, initialized with the same seed at the beginning of all 20 replications, might be described as *using* the same random numbers across the alternatives, but in a disorganized, haphazard, and mostly unsynchronized way (diluting the effect, as you'll soon see). It's possible to simulate the alternatives using completely different, and thus independent, random numbers across the alternatives, resulting in statistically independent output results. To get this independence, we modified the SEEDS module, for alternative B only (i.e., we left it as in Display 11-1 for alternative A), as indicated in Figure 11-8. The change here from Display 11-1 is that we added the first entry, calling for 15 (unnamed) streams, which are not used in the simulation; these are the streams we used for alternative A, and we're thus skipping over them. This causes stream 16 (rather than stream one) to be used for interarrival times, stream 17 (rather than stream two) for the part-type indices, stream 18 (rather than stream three) for processing times of type 1 parts at Cell 1, etc. We also removed the Default Stream entry since we're beyond stream 10 before we start with the streams we actually want to use. The result of this we'll call Model 11.2.

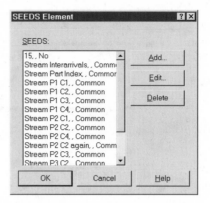

Figure 11-8. The Seeds Module for Independent Sampling in Alternative B

Now, for the dramatic results. Proceeding as in Section 6.5.5, we made 20 replications of alternatives A and B. We had the SEEDS module from Display 11-1 present in the runs for both alternatives, resulting in synchronized CRN. We then made a different set of 20 replications for alternative B, using the SEEDS module from Figure 11-8 (Model 11.2) to get output results completely independent from those of our (single) set of 20 replications of alternative A. We then invoked the *Analyze/Compare Means* menu option in the Output Analyzer, similar to Display 6-23 in Section 6.5.5, except calling for comparisons of A against both the CRN and independent runs of B, to get the results in Figure 11-9 for a 95% confidence interval on the difference between average WIPs for alternative A minus alternative B.[4] The top interval (both graphically and in text) is for properly synchronized CRN, and the bottom interval is for independent sampling, as described above. These are comparable to Figure 6-12, where we ignored random-number synchronization within the same stream. From Figure 11-9, you see that in comparison to independent sampling, properly synchronized CRN greatly reduced the variance on the difference of the average WIPs, resulting in a much tighter confidence interval on the difference between the expected WIPs. In fact, with independent sampling the interval contains zero, i.e., we cannot see any statistically significant difference. Looking back at Figure 6-12, the qualitative conclusion from synchronized CRN is the same as before—moving Transfer Time from 1 to 3 increases the average WIP. In terms of the precision of the estimate of the magnitude of this increase, though, the effect of synchronizing CRN is quite dramatic, bringing the half width on the expected difference down from 1.8 to 0.07, *without doing any more simulation work than before* (20 replications of both alternative models). Thus, for this model with these comparisons, the benefit from properly synchronized CRN is quite strong.

---

[4] Operationally, remember that if you use the same model file to run the alternatives you need to rename the pertinent .dat files between runs, lest they be overwritten. You guessed it, we forgot to do this initially here and had to re-do everything.

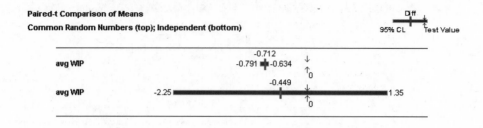

Paired-T Means Comparison: Common Random Numbers (top): Independent (bottom)

IDENTIFIER	ESTD. MEAN DIFFERENCE	STANDARD DEVIATION	0.950 C.I. HALF WIDTH	MINIMUM VALUE	MAXIMUM VALUE	NUMBER OF OBS.
avg WIP	-0.712	0.168	0.0785	6.52	15.1	20
				7.31	15.8	20
REJECT HO => MEANS ARE NOT EQUAL AT 0.05 LEVEL						
avg WIP	-0.449	3.84	1.8	6.52	15.1	20
				6.53	14.4	20
FAIL TO REJECT HO => MEANS ARE NOT EQUAL AT 0.05 LEVEL						

Figure 11-9. Confidence Interval and Hypothesis Test on the Expected Difference Between Average WIPs Using CRN (Top) and Independent Sampling (Bottom)

You may have noticed in Figures 11-9 and 6-12, or from the *Analyze/Compare Means* dialog, that we've used one of two possibilities for building the confidence intervals on the expected differences, and for testing the null hypothesis that there is no difference between the two expectations. This option is called the *Paired-t* approach (which is the default). This approach takes replication-by-replication differences between the results from the two alternatives, thus "collapsing" the two samples to a single sample on which the analysis is done. The advantage of the Paired-t approach is that it does not require the assumption of independent sampling across the alternatives for statistical validity, thus allowing the use of CRN. The disadvantage is that you wind up with a "sample" that's only half as big as the number of runs you made (in our example going from 40 to 20), resulting in "loss" of degrees of freedom (DF), which has the effect of increasing the confidence-interval half width. The other available option, called the *Two-Sample-t* approach, on the other hand, retains the "full" sample size (40 in our case), but requires that all observations from the two alternatives be independent of each other; this outlaws the use of CRN. If you're using CRN for your comparison, then you have no choice in the matter—you must use the Paired-t approach. Even though you're suffering the loss of DF, the reduction in variance you're getting from CRN often more than offsets this loss, resulting in a tighter interval (this happened in our example). If you're doing independent sampling across your alternatives, though, you could use either approach, and the Two-Sample-t will usually get you a somewhat tighter interval. Figure 11-10 shows the Two-Sample-t interval, from independent replications, corresponding to the Paired-t interval in the bottom parts of Figure 11-9. As you can see, it is somewhat better (tighter) than its Paired-t counterpart. However, using synchronized CRN with the Paired-t analysis is clearly the best in this example.

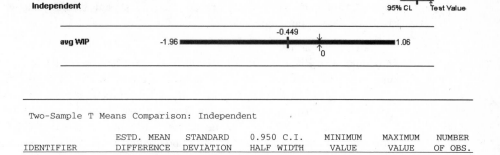

Two-Sample T Means Comparison: Independent

IDENTIFIER	ESTD. MEAN DIFFERENCE	STANDARD DEVIATION	0.950 C.I. HALF WIDTH	MINIMUM VALUE	MAXIMUM VALUE	NUMBER OF OBS.
avg WIP	-0.449	0.744	1.51	6.52	15.1	20
				6.53	14.4	20

FAIL TO REJECT HO => MEANS ARE NOT EQUAL AT 0.05 LEVEL

Figure 11-10. Confidence Interval and Hypothesis Test on the Expected Difference Between Average WIPs Using the Two-Sample-t Approach with Independent Sampling

While the intuitive appeal of synchronized CRN, to "compare like with like," is clear, there's also a mathematical justification for the idea. Let X and Y denote the output random variables for, respectively, alternatives A and B. In our example, X and Y would be the averages over the 20 replications of the average WIP in each replication, in alternatives A and B. What we want to estimate is $E(X) - E(Y) = E(X - Y)$, and our (unbiased) point estimator of it is just $X - Y$. If we make the runs independently, the variance of our independent-samples estimator is

$$Var(X - Y) = Var(X) + Var(Y)$$

since, as random variables, X and Y are independent. If, however, we use synchronized CRN, what we're doing is inducing correlation, hopefully positive, between X and Y. Since correlation has the same sign as covariance (see Section C.2.4 in Appendix C), the variance of our CRN estimator is

$$Var(X - Y) = Var(X) + Var(Y) - 2\ Cov(X, Y),$$

which will be less than the variance of the independent-samples estimator since we're subtracting a (hopefully) positive covariance. So, what's needed to make CRN "work" is that the outputs be positively correlated, and the stronger the better. While you can find examples where the correlation is negative, causing CRN to "backfire," such models are generally contrived just to make the point. In most cases, CRN will work, sometimes dramatically as in the above example. It is true, though, that you can't tell how well it will work until you actually do it. And, as you've seen above, CRN in its haphazard, unsynchronized version, is almost automatic—you have to work to avoid it, as shown in our independent-sampling example with the SEEDS module from Figure 11-8 to get Model 11.2. However, as we hope is clear from the above example, you probably won't get much benefit unless you do something to synchronize the random-number usage across the alternatives by assigning random-number streams carefully and with an understanding of how your model works.

11.4.2   Other Methods

In addition to CRN, there are several other variance-reduction techniques, which we'll just briefly mention here; see Chapter 11 of Law and Kelton (1991) or Chapter 3 of Bratley, Fox, and Schrage (1987) for more detail on these and other methods. Unlike CRN, these techniques apply when you have just a single model variant of interest.

The method of *antithetic variates* attempts to induce negative correlation between the results of one replication and another, and use this correlation to reduce variance. In a terminating simulation, make the first replication "as usual," but in the second replication, replace the random numbers $U_1, U_2, \ldots$ you used in the first replication by $1 - U_1$, $1 - U_2$, etc. This still results in valid variate generation since, if U is distributed uniformly on [0, 1], then $1 - U$ is as well. The idea is that, since a "big" U results in a "small" $1 - U$ (and vice versa), the results from replications one and two will be negatively correlated. Your first observation for statistical analysis, then, is not the result from the first replication, but rather the average of the results from the first two replications, which are treated as a pair. You could then go on and make replication three with "fresh" (independent) U's, then re-use these in replication four but in their antithetic form $1 - U$; your second observation for statistical analysis is then the average of the results from replications three and four. Within an antithetic pair, the (hopefully) negative correlation will cause the average of the two to snap in toward the true expectation more closely than if they were independent. Like CRN, this method requires careful synchronization of random-number usage in your model, probably involving streams and seeds. Arena will carry out antithetic variates if you request `Antithetic` in the Initialize Option field of the SEEDS module, giving you antithetic pairs in your replications. To do the analysis on them, however, you'd need to export these results to a spreadsheet or to a file to be read in by another program.

Control variates uses an ancillary "controlling" random variate to adjust your results up or down, as warranted by the control variate. For example, in Model 11.1, if we noted that, in a particular replication, the generated interarrival times happened to be smaller than their expected value (which we'd know since we specified the interarrival-time distribution), then it's likely that we're seeing higher-than-expected congestion measures in this replication. Thus, we'd adjust these output measures downward by some amount to "control" for the fact that we know that our arrivals were occurring closer together than "normal." From one replication to another, then, this adjustment will tend to dampen the variation of the results around their (unknown) expectations, reducing variance. In a given model, there are many potential control variates, and there are different ways to select from among them as well as to specify the direction and magnitude of the adjustment to the simulation output. For further information on control variates, see, for example, Bauer and Wilson (1992) or Nelson (1990).

With *indirect estimation*, as its name suggests, you estimate something other than (but related to) what you really want, then transform your estimate by a fixed formula. For instance, in a simple queueing system, suppose you want to estimate the expected time in system, which is a customer's wait in the queue plus the service time. This is easy enough to do directly, and we've done so in several models. However, in a simulation you'd know the service-time distribution, and will thus know its expected value. So, instead of estimating the expected time in system directly from the simulation, you could instead observe the time in queue alone, then add on the *expected* service time. In essence, you're replacing the expected-service-time estimate, which will have some variance in it, by the (known) expected service time, which has no variance. While this variance-reduction idea seems fairly intuitive, indirect estimation also turns out to work in some not-so-obvious settings; see Law (1975).

11.5 Sequential Sampling

When you do a simulation, you should always try to quantify the imprecision in your results. If this imprecision is not great enough to matter, you're done. But if the imprecision is large enough to be upsetting, you need to do something to reduce it. In Section 11.4, we discussed variance-reduction techniques, which might help. And in Section 6.5.4, we gave a couple of formulas for approximating the number n of replications you'd need (in a terminating model) to get a confidence-interval half width down to a value small enough for you to live with.

But a rather obvious idea is to just keep simulating, one "step" at a time, until you're happy. In the case of terminating models, a "step" is the next replication; in the case of steady-state models, a "step" is either the next truncated replication (if you're taking that strategy, as in Section 7.5.2); or if you're doing batch means in a single replication (as in Section 7.5.3), extend by some amount the replication you have going. Then, after this next "step," check again to see, for instance, if the half width of the new confidence interval is small enough. If it is, you can stop; if not, keep going and make the next step. If you can afford to do so, such *sequential sampling* is usually fairly simple, and typically will get you the precision you need. What's even better is that these ideas, while being entirely intuitive, are backed up by solid statistical theory; one consequence is that the actual coverage probability of your confidence interval will approach what it's supposed to be as your smallness demands on the half width get tighter.

In this section, we'll show you some examples of sequential sampling, indicating how you can set things up so that Arena will take care of the checking and stopping for you. We'll consider terminating simulations in Section 11.5.1 and the steady-state case in Section 11.5.2.

11.5.1 Terminating Models

First let's consider a terminating simulation, the simple manufacturing system from Section 6.5.2. We'll modify it from its incarnation as Model 11.1 (with the SEEDS module added) since you never know when you might want to do some variance reduction and synchronize the random numbers. We also had to remember to set the value of the `Transfer Time` variable back to it original value, 2. As the output performance measure of primary interest (the one whose confidence-interval half width we want to make sure is "small enough"), let's take the average WIP. As in Section 6.5.4, we first made a fixed number of replications (20), not really knowing how wide our confidence intervals would be; we got a 95% confidence interval of 9.90 ± 1.14. (This differs from the corresponding result, 11.3 ± 1.78, from Section 6.5.4 solely due to our use of the SEEDS module here, causing the random numbers to be different.) In Section 6.5, we also discussed two formulas for approximating how many replications would be needed to reduce the half width of a 95% confidence interval to a fixed value; in this example, to reduce it from 1.14 to 0.5, our formulas say to we'd need to make either 92 or 104 total replications, depending on which formula we used.

Let's instead invoke the sequential-sampling idea to get this half width down to 0.5. We have to make a minor change to our model (into what we'll call Model 11.3) to ask it to keep replicating until the across-replications 95% confidence-interval half width for the average WIP measure falls below 0.5, then stop the replications. Recall from Section 6.5.4 that if you call for multiple replications, Arena will automatically compute 95% confidence intervals on quantities you've specified in the Outputs area of the Statistics module; we'll use internal Arena variables describing these confidence intervals to get sequential sampling going. The pertinent Arena variables are:

- ORUNHALF(Output Number), the half width of the automatic across-replications confidence interval from however many replications have been completed, where Output Number is the number (see below) of the output measure of interest;
- MREP, the total number of replications we're asking for (initially the Number of Replications field in the Simulate module);
- NREP, the replication number we're on at the moment (= 1, 2, 3, . . .).

Here's the general strategy. Initially specify MREP to be some absurdly enormous value in the Simulate module's Number of Replications field; this gets the replications going and keeps them going until we cut them off ourselves when the half width becomes small enough. Add a chunk of logic to the model to cause a single control entity to arrive at the beginning of each replication, whose job it is to check whether we're done yet—i.e., if ORUNHALF(Output Number) is smaller than the tolerance we want. If not, we need to keep simulating, so this entity just disposes of itself; we'll go ahead and do the replication that's just starting and check again at the beginning of the next replication. On the other hand, if the current half width is small enough, we're ready to quit. However, because we've already begun the current replication (by having the "checking" entity show up) we have to finish it, but before doing so we'll tell our control entity to reset MREP (the total number of replications we want) to NREP (the number we will have completed at the end of the one that's just starting), which will terminate the replications after this one.

Note that this strategy "overshoots" (by one) the number of replications really required; it turns out that you can't reliably do the termination check at the *end* of a replication, so this is necessary. As a result, you'll usually get a half width that's not only under the tolerance you specify, but probably even a bit smaller due to this extra replication. It's technically possible (though unlikely) that your final half width will be slightly larger than the tolerance you specified if the "extra" replication at the end happens to produce a wild outlier that itself causes the standard-deviation estimate to increase a lot. This whole situation does not seem particularly onerous, though, since in sequential sampling, you're pretty much admitting that you don't really know how many replications to make and that you might have to make a lot of them; thus, overshooting by one is no big deal. Furthermore, the tolerance you specify is probably fairly arbitrary in your mind, so being a little over or under won't matter. (Only a truly obnoxious customer would demand that the person behind the deli counter *exactly* hit the half pound of potato salad they ordered.)

The chunk of control logic added is shown in Figure 11-11; we've brought the Simulate model into this area of the model since we made a change to it as well.

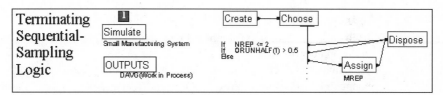

Figure 11-11. Control Logic for Sequential Sampling in Terminating Simulations

We're not going to bother showing you the (simple) content of the following modules from Figure 11-11; here's what we did.

- Simulate: The only modification (other than the Analyst, of course) is to specify the Number of Replications to be huge (999999 worked for us).
- Create (from the Support panel): We took all the defaults, which results in the behavior we want, a single entity to be created at the beginning of each replication.
- Dispose: We took all the defaults since all we want to do is get rid of the single entity from the Create module.

The OUTPUTS module, from the Elements panel, is shown in Figure 11-12, and is present just to establish a link between the performance measure of interest (average WIP in our case) and a number (set to a value of 1 here) to serve as the argument of ORUNHALF in the Choose module discussed below. As you can see, we first needed to add an entry to the OUTPUTS list in the main dialog, which brought up the subdialog shown, where we entered 1 for the Number and picked the SIMAN Expression from the existing pull-down list of all the Outputs called for by the model.

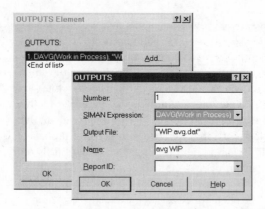

Figure 11-12. The OUTPUTS Module for Sequential Sampling in Terminating Simulations

After the entity is created, it goes to the Choose module, shown in Figure 11-13. Here it first checks to see if the number of replications, NREP, is less than or equal to 2 (NREP is the number of the replication now beginning). Since at least two complete replications are required to form a confidence interval, the entity disposes of itself (via the graphical connection visible in Figure 11-11), meaning that MREP remains at its absurdly high value and we go ahead and do this replication (and begin the next one too). The next check in the Choose module is to see if the current half width ORUNHALF of the confidence interval of interest (Number 1, as specified in the OUTPUTS module from Figure 11-12) is still too big; if so, we need to keep going for more replications, so we dispose of the entity as well (again via a graphical connection).

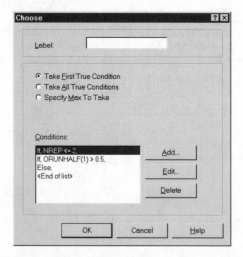

Figure 11-13. The Choose Module for Sequential Sampling in Terminating Simulations

If, however, NREP is at least 3 *and* the half width we have on record (the one completed at the end of the previous replication) is at most 0.5, we'll fall through both of the

If statements to the Else, whose graphical connection sends the entity to the Assign module (Figure 11-14), where MREP is set to NREP, the current replication number, causing the simulation to stop at the end of the replication now getting started. (As mentioned earlier, this final replication is technically not needed but will be executed anyway.) Note in the Assign module that we selected the Assignment Type to be Other since MREP is a built-in Arena variable with a reserved word as its name. Selecting the Assignment Type to be Variable would result in an attempt to create a new user-defined variable named MREP, which would conflict with the existing Arena variable of the same name.

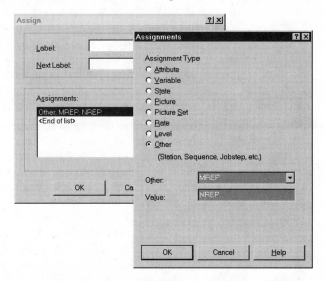

Figure 11-14. The Assign Module for Sequential Sampling in Terminating Simulations

We ran this model, and it decided to stop with 133 replications; the bottom of the summary output is in Figure 11-15, showing only the across-replication results. Note that, as advertised, the half width of the confidence interval for expected average WIP is less than 0.5 (barely).

```
Output Summary for 133 Replications

Project: Small Manufacturing
Analyst: Alfred E.von Neuman

          OUTPUTS
```

Identifier	Average	Half Width	Minimum	Maximum	# Replications
avg WIP	9.7725	.49471	5.4033	19.712	133
Part 1 cycle avg	130.62	6.2371	80.087	247.84	133
Part 2 cycle avg	169.50	6.7644	111.46	309.86	133
Cell 4 avg Q length	1.2187	.14543	.20195	5.1363	133
Cell 2 avg Q length	1.2495	.14202	.29940	5.7559	133
Cell 1 avg Q length	1.5875	.18472	.42504	6.9348	133
Part 3 cycle avg	96.058	4.4763	65.684	188.26	133
Cell 3 avg Q length	.97972	.08844	.30560	2.6750	133

Figure 11-15. End of the Summary Report for the Terminating Sequential-Sampling Run

Why is the required number of replications, 133 (or, if you prefer, 132 due to the extra replication at the end), different from the 92 or 104 that the formulas from Section 6.5.4 suggested? As we said there, those formulas are only approximations, with errors owing to the fact that they use the normal distribution rather than *t*-distribution for the critical value, but mostly due to the fact that they're based on a variance estimate from only an initial, somewhat arbitrary number of replications (we had used 20). It just turned out this time that the variance estimate from the initial 20 replications was a little small, so in the end we needed somewhat more replications than what the formulas predicted (it could just as easily have gone the other way).

Sequential sampling, perhaps more aptly termed sequential *stopping*, can be set up for other kinds of purposes as well. For instance, in the above run, we demanded that the half width for the confidence interval on only one of the (many) outputs be brought down to under the specified tolerance 0.5; we got just enough replications to satisfy that sole criterion. However, the setup of the above model is general enough to allow easy modification to demand that the half widths on several (or all) of the output measures be "controlled" to be less than separate tolerances for each of them; we'll ask you to look into this in Exercises 11.3 and 11.5.

Another modification would be to ask not that the half width be made smaller than a tolerance, but rather that the half width divided by the point estimate (the average across the replications) be brought down to be less than another kind of tolerance. Note that the half width divided by the point estimate is a dimensionless quantity, and so the tolerance in this case would also be dimensionless, giving it a universal interpretation. For instance, if you specify this tolerance to be 0.10, what you're asking is that the half width of the confidence interval be no more than 10% of the mean; in this case, you could restate the confidence interval as something like "point estimate plus or minus 10%." This is sometimes called a confidence interval with a *relative precision* of 10%. Such a goal might be useful in a situation where you don't have much of an idea what the magnitude of your results will be, making it problematic to specify a sensible (absolute) value under which you'd like the half width itself to fall. Exercises 11.4 and 11.5 ask you to set up this kind of thing.

11.5.2 Steady-State Models

Sequential sampling for steady-state models is at least as easy to set up as for terminating models, though naturally the amount of computation time can become frightening if you need to make really long replications and also demand very tight precision. Probably it's prudent to get some notion of how much precision is practical before setting up a sequential-sampling run and just turning it loose.

If you're taking the truncated-replications approach to steady-state analysis, as described in Section 7.5.2, you can do things just as we described above in Section 11.5.1, except now you'd have a Warm-Up Period specified in your Simulate module to carry out the truncation of initial data to ameliorate startup bias. A caution here is that you need to make quite sure that you're warming up long enough to get rid of initialization bias, so err on the side of longer-than-really-necessary warm-ups. The reason for this bit of friendly advice is that if you want a tight confidence interval with this strategy, you'll certainly get it, but if there's bias in your results due to insufficient warm-up, your sequentially-determined confidence intervals will be tightening down around a biased point, meaning that the nice tight interval you get is likely to miss the mark in terms of covering the steady-state expected value. And depressingly, the tighter you make your interval, the worse this problem gets since the bias stays present but the interval gets smaller and thus more likely to miss the steady-state expectation of interest. Thus, the harder you work, the worse off you are in terms of confidence-interval coverage probability.

So, unless you're quite confident that you've pretty much eliminated start-up bias, it might be safer to set up a single long run that you then keep extending until the half width of the resulting confidence interval satisfies your smallness criterion. In this case, the batch-means confidence interval from a single long run (Section 7.5.3) makes sense. Furthermore, Arena's automatic run-time batch-means-based confidence intervals, described in Section 7.5.4, work quite nicely for this purpose. The key is the Simulate module's Terminating Condition field, where you specify the half-width smallness criterion (and remove all other replication-stopping devices from your model, such as the Length of Replication field in the Simulate module). The pertinent internal Arena variables for this are THALF(Tally ID), which returns the current half width of the 95% confidence interval on a Tally statistic with Tally ID in its argument, and DHALF(Dstat ID) for DSTAT (time-persistent) output statistics. The batching/rebatching scheme described in Section 7.5.4 takes over and your run will stop as soon as the Terminating Condition is satisfied. If a particular run length along the way is not long enough to form a valid batch-means confidence interval, causing this scheme to conclude "(Insuf)" or "(Corr)" as described in Section 7.5.4, the numerical value of the half-width variable is set by Arena to a huge number; this will cause your replication to be extended since the half-width appears too large, which is the behavior you want.

To illustrate this, let's create Model 11.4 by modifying Model 7.6 from Sections 7.5.3 and 7.5.4, which was originally set up for a single long run of 1,000,000 minutes of which the first 2,000 minutes are discarded as a warm-up period. Looking back at Figure 7-24, the run-time batch-means 95% confidence interval on steady-state expected average WIP turned out to be 15.34 ± 0.82. This run also took a quite a while, which may not in itself be a big deal, but if we have lots and lots of similar alternative models to run this way, it could become a major problem. Perhaps we could live with looser precision in the confidence interval, say a half width of 2, and thus be able to get all our runs out in a more reasonable amount of time. Making this change involves only a couple of modifications to the Simulate model, as shown in Figure 11-16. We've cleared the Length of Replication field and filled in the Terminating Condition field with the stopping rule we want, DHALF(Work in Process) < 2.0. The Dstat ID Work in Process we identified from the Statistics module: Time-Persistent area, WIP Variable entry (the only entry there), Report Label field.

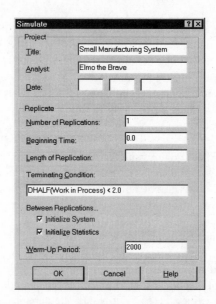

Figure 11-16. The Simulate Module for Sequential Sampling in Steady-State Simulations Using Run Time Batch Means Confidence Intervals

Part of the summary report is in Figure 11-17, and indicates that the desired precision for the average WIP output measure (`Work in Process` in the section for Discrete-Change variables) was indeed achieved.

```
Summary for Replication 1 of 1

Project: Small Manufacturing
Analyst: Elmo the Brave

Replication ended at time    : 559059.0
Statistics were cleared at time: 2000.0
Statistics accumulated for time: 557059.0
```

TALLY VARIABLES

Identifier	Average	Half Width	Minimum	Maximum	Observations
Cell 1_R_Q Queue Time	29.367	(Corr)	.00000	223.02	43138
Cell 2_R_Q Queue Time	20.240	2.6354	.00000	181.10	63790
Cell 3 Machines_Q Queu	40.230	10.112	.00000	283.90	43138
Cell 4_R_Q Queue Time	57.518	11.288	.00000	375.97	32007
Part 1 Cycle Time	216.37	25.731	47.539	769.04	11357
Part 2 Cycle Time	268.42	(Corr)	86.015	851.73	20652
Part 3 Cycle Time	147.02	13.499	48.039	484.20	11131

DISCRETE-CHANGE VARIABLES

Identifier	Average	Half Width	Minimum	Maximum	Final Value
Work in Process	17.279	1.9663	.00000	59.000	14.000
# in Cell 1_R_Q	2.2734	(Corr)	.00000	20.000	1.0000
# in Cell 2_R_Q	2.3176	.32703	.00000	23.000	3.0000
# in Cell 3 Machines_Q	3.1153	.80496	.00000	25.000	.00000
# in Cell 4_R_Q	3.3050	.76570	.00000	25.000	3.0000

Figure 11-17. Results for Sequential Sampling on Steady-State Average WIP Using Run Time Batch Means Confidence Intervals

As with sequential sampling for terminating simulations, you can modify the Terminating Condition to include smallness criteria on each of several confidence intervals instead of just one. You can also specify relative-precision stopping rules based on the ratio of the half width to the point estimate; to this end, the Arena variables TAVG(Tally ID) and DAVG(Dstat ID) give the current average of the indicated Tally or Dstat statistic, respectively.

11.6   Some Additional Capabilities of the Output Analyzer

In addition to the methods discussed so far, there are some other statistical problems that can be addressed with the Arena Output Analyzer. This section will briefly describe these capabilities; for more detail, check out the sources referenced below, as well as online help.

11.6.1   Confidence Interval on Standard Deviation

In some cases, the standard deviation of the result across replications (or batches) is itself of interest. And just as averages from stochastic simulations are subject to variation, so too are standard-deviation estimates. Arena's Output Analyzer can form a confidence interval on the standard deviation of an output measure across independent observations using the formula given in Section C.5 in Appendix C. You need to supply independent observations for this, which can arise in a terminating model from independent replications; in a steady-state model, they could arise from replications if you're using the truncated-replications approach of Section 7.5.2, or from batch means if you're using this approach as in Section 7.5.3. What you'll get is a point estimate of and confidence interval for the standard deviation of the observations you supply, either across replications or batches.

For example, take Model 11.1 with `Transfer Time` set to 1. Using the 20 observations on average WIP, we invoked the *Analyze/Conf. Interval on Std. Dev* menu option in the Output Analyzer and specified the Data File as `WIP avg 1.dat` (the name to which we changed the saved output file in preparation for the comparisons of Section 11.4.1) with the `Lumped` option for Replications. The result, in Figure 11-18, shows the point and 95% confidence-interval estimate for the standard deviation of the average WIP output measure across replications. Note that the confidence interval is not symmetric about the point estimate, consistent with the formula for it in Section C.5.

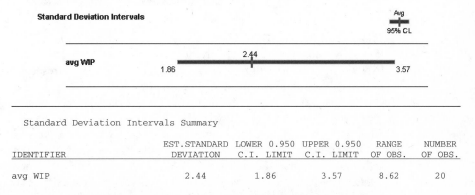

Standard Deviation Intervals Summary

IDENTIFIER	EST. STANDARD DEVIATION	LOWER 0.950 C.I. LIMIT	UPPER 0.950 C.I. LIMIT	RANGE OF OBS.	NUMBER OF OBS.
avg WIP	2.44	1.86	3.57	8.62	20

Figure 11-18. Confidence Interval for Standard Deviation

11.6.2 Compare Variances

In Sections 6.5.5 and 11.4.1, we discussed how to estimate the difference between the means of two alternative models. You can also compare the variances, instead of the means, but it turns out to be easier to estimate the *ratio* of the variances rather than their difference. The Output Analyzer has a facility for doing this, the *Analyze/Compare Variances* menu option, which is set up just like the one for comparing means (you specify Data Files A and B, etc.). The formula for the resulting confidence interval is given in Section C.5; note that it assumes that the observations across the two alternatives are independent, thus precluding the use of common random numbers and requiring that you call for separate random-number streams (see Model 11.3 in Section 11.4.1).

We compared the variances in this way for the two models considered in Section 11.4 (`Transfer Time` being 1 for A and 3 for B), making sure to do the replications for B with independent random numbers, using Model 11.3 as described in Section 11.4.1. The result, in Figure 11-19, indicates that the 95% confidence interval on the ratio of the variance contains the value 1, meaning that we are not detecting a statistically significant difference between the variances of the two model alternatives.

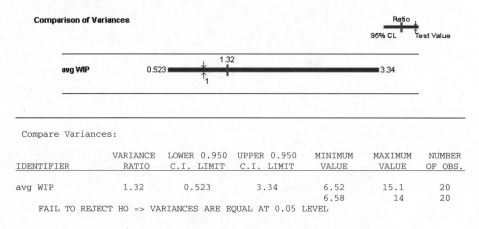

Compare Variances:

IDENTIFIER	VARIANCE RATIO	LOWER 0.950 C.I. LIMIT	UPPER 0.950 C.I. LIMIT	MINIMUM VALUE	MAXIMUM VALUE	NUMBER OF OBS.
avg WIP	1.32	0.523	3.34	6.52	15.1	20
				6.58	14	20

FAIL TO REJECT HO => VARIANCES ARE EQUAL AT 0.05 LEVEL

Figure 11-19. Confidence Interval for Ratio of Variances

11.6.3 One-Way ANOVA

If you have more than two alternative models, you can do a classical analysis of variance (ANOVA) to test the null hypothesis that the means of the corresponding output measures are the same across all alternatives. While we will not give an example of this, the Output Analyzer has facility for doing an ANOVA, as well as conducting post-test multiple comparisons to tell you, if you reject the null hypothesis, which means appear to be different from which others. As in Section 11.6.2, you must make your runs independently, and there is also the assumption that the variances of the outputs are the same across all the models. Doing the ANOVA in the Output Analyzer proceeds similarly to *Analyze/Compare Means* except that you specify as many data files with the observations as you have alternative models, rather than just A and B for the case of comparing two means. For more on this, refer to online help.

11.7 Designing and Executing Simulation Experiments

As we've tried to emphasize throughout, a simulation model is a lot more than something to run just once. Rather, you should think of it as a great and convenient test bed for trying out a lot of things and for investigating the effects of various inputs and configurations on various outputs. Thus, simulation is a natural for application of some of the classical experimental-design techniques usually presented for physical rather than simulation-based experiments.

For instance, consider a model with five different input parameters or configurations. You'd like to know what the *effect* is on the results of changing a parameter or configuration from one *level* to another. Viewing the inputs and configurations as experimental *factors*, you could specify two possible levels for each and carry out a 2^5 factorial design, from which you could measure the main effects of and possible interactions between the input factors on the outputs of interest, which are the *responses* for this simulation-based experiment. Unlike most physical experiments, you could then easily go on and replicate the whole factorial experiment to place confidence intervals around the expected main effects and interactions. Other possibilities include using common random numbers across the design points (as a blocking variable in experimental-design terminology), the use of screening designs to sort out which of many factors are really important, and sophisticated nonlinear and response-surface designs. For more on these and related issues, see Chapter 12 of Law and Kelton (1991).

11.8 Exercises

11.1 Modify Model 11.1 for a different way to synchronize CRN, as follows. When a new part arrives, generate and store in attributes of this entity its processing-time requirements for all of the cells in its sequence. When a part gets to a cell, take its processing time from the appropriate attribute of the entity rather than generating it on the spot. Depending on how you set this up, it might be useful to recall that the attribute IS of an entity is its station number (1, 2, 3, . . .) as it makes its way through its sequence. Use the same random-number-stream allocation as in Model 11.1.

11.2 In Exercise 11.1, is it necessary to have dedicated random-number streams in order to achieve proper synchronization? Discuss this issue for this model (and, of course, try it).

11.3 Modify Model 11.3 from Section 11.5.1 to demand, in addition to the 95% confidence-interval half width on the expected average WIP being no more than 0.5, that the half widths of the 95% confidence intervals on all three of the expected average cycle times (for the three different part types) be less than 5 minutes. (Note that from the 133 replications reported in Figure 11-15 this condition is already satisfied for part type 3, but not for part types 1 or 2.) One way to do this is to modify the Choose module in

Figure 11-13 by adding one or more additional If statements before the final Else to keep replicating (i.e., dispose of the checking entity) if any of the half widths on the expected average cycle times is still more than 5. You'll also have to Add the corresponding entries to the OUTPUTS module from Figure 11-12.

11.4   Modify Model 11.3 from Section 11.5.1 to demand that the ratio of the 95% confidence-interval half width to the point estimate on the expected average WIP be less than 0.10, as described at the end of Section 11.5.1; i.e., form a 10% relative-precision confidence interval. The Arena variable ORUNAVG(Output Number) is the average across all completed replications of the output measure with this Output Number.

11.5   Combine Exercises 11.3 and 11.4, as follows. Set up a sequential-sampling run so that you get 5% relative-precision confidence intervals on the expected average WIP as well as on all three of the expected average cycle times by part type.

11.6   Modify Model 11.4 from Section 11.5.2 to terminate the replication when the ratio of the half width to the midpoint (point estimate) of the automatic batch-means run-time confidence interval on steady-state expected WIP falls below 0.10, i.e., when the relative precision is 10%. The Arena variable DAVG(Dstat ID) returns the current average of the indicated Dstat statistic. Note that the condition you want to check is of the form $H/A < 0.10$, where H is the half width and A is the point estimate, which can be an uncomfortable calculation if $A = 0$ (which it will be at the start of your run). Instead, check the condition in its equivalent form, $H < 0.10\ A$.

11.7   In Model 5.3 from Section 5.3, focus on the number of good parts produced, which is counted by the counter Shipping_C in the Depart module for the Shipping station. This is a measure of productivity of the system. Certainly in practice the average of this count across replications will matter, but its variance will matter too, as a measure of variability in the productive capacity of this process. Form a 95% confidence interval on the standard deviation of the number of good items produced during a 2,000 minute run; make 25 replications to do this.

11.8   In Exercise 11.7 (based on Model 5.3), suppose that an earnest young quality engineer argues passionately that cutting the Sealer failure rate in half (from 9% to 4.5%) will both increase the mean production (measured by the counter at the Shipping station) and reduce the variability of productivity. What do you think (passionately or otherwise)? As in Exercise 11.7, make 25 replications of 2,000 minutes each, and carry out the appropriate statistical analyses to address these questions. Don't forget that, as noted in Section 11.6.2, if you want to compare variances statistically you need to make sure that your replications are independent across the alternative models (see Section 11.4.1).

Conducting Simulation Studies

CHAPTER 12

Conducting Simulation Studies

In Section 2.7, we briefly outlined the key ingredients of a simulation study. Now that you've gained some insight into the process of developing and analyzing a simulation model, it's time that we stepped back and discussed the overall activities involved in a typical simulation study. As we proceed with this discussion, we'll assume that you are the analyst—the individual who will perform the simulation study. You may be on a corporate support staff, support staff at the operational level, or be an external consultant. The client is whoever requested the study, which will be focused on a system of some type. The system may produce manufactured goods, fast food, or services. It could also be a system for handling paperwork, a call center, distribution center or system, or any other system that results in a product or service. We will assume that you're able to translate the ideas presented in this chapter (as well as the rest of the book) to your own circumstances.

There are numerous publications on the activities to be discussed in the chapter. Probably the best source is the *Proceedings of the Winter Simulation Conference*, a conference held annually in December. A selection of these include Balci (1990, 1995), Farrington and Swain (1993), Goldsman (1992), Kelton (1996), Kleindorfer and Ganeshan (1993), Musselman (1993), Sadowski (1989, 1993), Sargent (1996), and Seila (1990). Another good source is an article by Banks and Gibson (1996) in *IIE Solutions* magazine.

We'll start by discussing what constitutes a successful simulation in Section 12.1, followed in Section 12.2 by some advice on formulating the problem. Section 12.3 addresses the issue of using the correct solution methodology for the problem. Assuming that simulation is the preferred solution methodology, we continue with the system and simulation specification in Section 12.4. The model formulation and construction activities are discussed in Section 12.5, and the ever-present verification and validation approaches are presented in Section 12.6. Section 12.7 discusses experimentation and analysis, and Section 12.8 provides an overview of the reporting and documentation requirements for a simulation project. We end this chapter with a brief discussion of the Arena Viewer (Section 12.9), which is a good way to disseminate your work.

12.1 A Successful Simulation Study

Before we start talking about what's involved in a simulation study, we need to address the issue of what defines a successful simulation project. It might seem obvious that if you solve the problem or meet the objectives, you've achieved success; however, that is not always the case. In most instances, the final pronunciation of success or failure will be made by the higher-level management that is paying the bill—and, like it or not, they have a tendency to view the problem or objectives in a different context. Let's illustrate this with a real-life example.

An automotive supplier had developed a highly successful process for producing a specialized set of parts for the automotive OEM (original equipment manufacturer) and after market. The process was implemented using a high-volume, semi-automated manufacturing cell concept. Although the process produced a high-quality, low-cost part, the initial system was not achieving a high utilization for the key, and most expensive, piece of equipment in the process. Because of the variability in the types and quantities of parts being produced and the processing times of those parts, simulation was chosen as an analysis tool. The objective was to re-design the existing system or to design a new production system that would make better use of the key equipment—in other words, a system that would achieve the same quality, but at a lower production cost per part. A secondary objective was to devise a way to allow incremental increases in production volume by adding equipment to the system gradually, rather than just building a new cell.

The simulation study was undertaken, and after an extensive analysis of the existing system, it was determined that it was not possible to achieve the desired results with the current cell concept. The simulation was then used to develop, design, and analyze several new approaches. This resulted in a totally different production system design that ultimately was recommended to management as the production system of the future. This new system design met all the objectives, and the simulation study was pronounced a success by the project team. Management accepted the team's recommendation and authorized the construction of a system using the new design concept. The new system was built, but did not function as projected, causing management to pronounce the simulation study a failure since the new system, which was built based on the results of the simulation, did not meet expectations. In fact, the resulting production output was about 30% lower than projected.

So what happened? Fortunately for the reputation of simulation, the simulation team was directed to conduct a post-analysis of the system. The simulation model of the new system was dusted off and compared to the actual system, which now existed. The simulation was modified to represent the system as it was actually constructed, and much to the surprise of the simulation team, it predicted that the new system would produce exactly the volume that it was currently producing. So they looked at the modifications that were made to the simulation model and found that they could classify these modifications into two groups.

The first group of model modifications was composed of required data changes to the model based on measurements of actual operation times occurring in the new system. As is often the case, several new types of equipment were included in the new system design, and the vendors who provided this new equipment were rather optimistic in their estimates of operation times. This accounted for about a third of the resulting production loss.

The second group of model modifications was composed of changes in the actual system design that was implemented. As it turns out, there were two critical errors made in the new system design. One was caused because the placement of the new system did not allow for sufficient floor space called for by the simulation design. Thus, the system design was modified to allow it to fit into the available space. The second error was due to changes requested by upper-level management in an attempt to decrease the overall cost of the new system. These changes accounted for the remaining two thirds of production loss.

So what are the lessons to be learned? First, the simulation team should have recognized that the operation times for the new equipment were only estimates, and they should have conducted a sensitivity analysis of the model outputs to these input data. This would have predicted a potential problem if the actual times were greater than the vendor-supplied estimates. If the times were critical, a penalty clause could have been included in the contract for the new equipment stipulating that it perform as estimated. Second, the simulation team should have tracked the implementation of the new system. This would have allowed them to evaluate the proposed modifications before implementation. It might not have changed the results, but at least it would have predicted the outcome.

Let's return to the initial issue of what defines a successful simulation project. Success seldom means that a good simulation model was developed. It more often means that the simulation study met the objectives set forth by the decision makers. This implies that it is very important to understand which metrics they will use.

If you're asked to undertake a simulation study to redesign a current system, inquire further to gain a better understanding of what is expected. If that inquiry results in a statement that indicates that management is interested in finding out if it is possible to make the system perform better, find out what "better" means. If better means that you are expected to reduce WIP (work in process) by 30%, reduce cycle times by 20%, increase resource utilizations by 15%, and meet all future customer due dates without any capital investment, you at least know that you're facing an impossible mission. We recommend that you elect not to accept the assignment. If, however, "better" means that the primary measures are WIP, cycle times, resource utilizations, and customer due dates balanced against capital investment, you at least have a fighting chance of designing a better system.

Unfortunately, you are seldom *asked* if you want to do the study; in most cases, you are just *told* to do the study. Even under these circumstances you should identify the decision maker and attempt to define the metrics by which the project will be measured.

If you're about to undertake the first simulation study for a company or facility, it's critical that it result in a success. If the first simulation study is labeled a failure, it is unlikely that a second study will ever be started. If you have a choice of simulation projects, select one that is simple and is almost guaranteed to result in a success. Once you have achieved several successes, you might be able to afford a failure (but not a disaster).

There is also a peculiar dilemma frequently faced by the experienced simulation analyst. If you use simulation as a standard tool through the design of a new system and the new system works as advertised, what have you saved? If you had not used simulation, would the results have been any different? You really don't know. So the tool worked, or at least you think it did, but you have no way of quantifying any savings resulting from the application of the tool.

The one approach that is often suggested, but seldom used, is not to use simulation for the design of the next new system. The assumption here is that the resulting system will not perform as advertised. After it's clear that the system has problems, use simulation to show how the system should have been designed. This would allow you to quantify the savings had you used simulation. This is clearly an extreme approach—and not recommended by us—that's based on numerous assumptions. Of course, there is always the possibility that the system will perform just fine. (It can happen!) This would leave the value of simulation in even greater doubt in the eyes of management.

We close this section by again suggesting that you be aware that *your* definition of success may not be the same as that used by management. Although you may not be able to control management's evaluation, at least you should try to understand what measurements they will use in making their evaluation. Now let's proceed with our discussion of the key activities of a good simulation study.

12.2 Problem Formulation

The first step in any problem-solving task is to define and formulate the problem. In the real world, you are rarely handed some sheets of paper that completely define the problem to be solved. Most often you (the analyst) will be approached by someone (the client) who thinks that you might be able to help them. The initial problem is rarely defined clearly. In fact, it may not even be obvious that simulation is the proper tool. At this point, you need to be able to open a dialog with the requester, or their designate, and begin asking a series of questions that will ultimately allow you to define the problem completely. Often, the final problem you end up addressing is quite different from the one that was initially presented.

Many simulation studies deal with systems that are not meeting the client's expectations. The client wants to know: How do I fix it? Other simulation studies are not focused on a known problem, but are trying to avoid a potential future problem. This is most often the case when you're using simulation to help design a new system. Yet another class of simulation studies is composed of those focused on a system that has been completely designed, but not yet constructed or implemented. In this case, you're being asked if the system will perform as predicted.

So the problems are often put forth in the form of a series of questions: Can you fix it? Will it work? Can you help me make sure it will work? These are really the best kinds of problems because you have the potential to have an impact on the system (and your career). The worst kind of problem is when you're told that the company wants to start using simulation, so they've requested that a simulation be developed for an arbitrary system.

Let's assume that you have at least a vague notion of what the problem is, and hopefully, a better idea of what the system is. It might be a good idea to start with the system. Does the system currently exist, is it a new design, or has it not yet been designed? Knowing this, you can try to *bound* the system for the purpose of the study. Is the system a single or a small number of operations, a large department, the entire facility, or the entire company? Although it would be nice if you could draw walls around the system so that there are no interactions with the other side of the wall (like the Great Wall of China), this is not likely to be the case. However, you might at least try to place initial bounds on the size of the system. Try not to cast these boundaries in stone, as you may have to expand or contract them as you learn more about the problem and system.

Having established some initial boundaries, next try to define the performance metrics. There are really two kinds of metrics with which you should be concerned. The first, and most obvious, are the performance metrics that will be used to measure the quality of the system under study. The second, and maybe the most important, are the performance metrics that will be used to measure the success of the study. Let's concentrate on the first kind of metrics. Although the client might imply that there is only one metric, there are almost always several that need to be considered. For example, the application may be a fast-food restaurant where the client is interested in being assured that any customer who enters the door receives his food within a given period of time. This is most likely not just a performance metric, but a performance objective. Other metrics of interest could be the staffing required, the job assignments, the seating capacity, and the freshness of the food.

Having established how the performance of the system is to be measured, find out if there are current baseline values for these metrics. These values should be available if the system currently exists. If not, there may be similar existing systems that could be used to provide estimates. In the worst case, at least design values should be available. Knowing what the current baseline metrics are (or at least using an estimate), what are the expectations of the client? This type of information should provide some insight as to the magnitude of the problem you have been handed.

By this time, you should have a fairly good understanding of the system (and its size), the performance metrics, and the expectations of the client. The next step is to select a solution methodology—don't assume that you will always use simulation.

12.3 Solution Methodology

We're not going to attempt to describe every problem-solution technique known to humanity and recommend where they should be used. However, we do recommend that you at least consider alternative solution techniques. You should also give some consideration to the cost of using a particular solution technique compared to the potential benefits of the eventual solution. Unfortunately, identifying the best solution methodology is not always an easy task. If you determine that a specific methodology might give you the best answer, but you have never used that technique, this might not be the best time to experiment. Therefore, you might want to rephrase the question: Given the solution methodologies that you feel comfortable using, which will most likely give the most cost-effective solution?

Sometimes the choice is obvious, at least to us. For example, if you're being asked to perform a rough-capacity analysis of a proposed system, and you're given only mean values for all the system parameters and you are only interested in average utilizations, it might be faster (and just as accurate) to use a calculator to determine the answer. At the other extreme, you might be asked to find the set of optimal routes for a fleet of school buses or garbage trucks. Although you could use simulation, there are other tools specifically designed to solve this problem. We would suggest you consider purchasing a product to implement such a tool.

You might first find out how much time you have to analyze the problem. If you need an answer immediately, then simulation is not normally an option. We hedged a little bit on this because there are rare circumstances where simulation can be used to analyze problems quickly. You might have a very simple problem, or a very small system, which allows you to develop a simulation using the Arena high-level constructs in just a few hours.

There are also instances where companies have devoted effort to develop generic simulation models that can be altered quickly. These types of models are typically developed when there are many similar systems within an organization. A generic simulation is then developed that can be used to model any of these systems by simply changing the data. The task of changing the data can be made very easy if the values are contained in an external file or program. This external source might be a text file or a spreadsheet. Instances where this approach has been used include assembly lines, warehousing, fast food, distribution centers, call centers, and manufacturing cells. An even more elegant approach is based on the development of a company-specific template. This method was briefly discussed in Section 10.5.

Let's assume that simulation is the correct technique for the problem. Now you need to define the system and the details of the resulting simulation.

12.4   System and Simulation Specification

So far we may have given the impression that a simulation study consists of a series of well-defined steps that need to be followed in a specific order, like a recipe from a cookbook. Although most experienced simulation analysts agree that there are usually some well-defined activities or steps, they are often performed repeatedly in an interactive manner. You may find that halfway through the development of a simulation, conditions suddenly change, new information becomes available, or you gain early insight that spawns new ideas. This might cause you to revisit the problem-formulation phase or to alter the design of your model drastically. This is not all that uncommon, so be prepared to back up and revisit the problem whenever conditions change.

The process of developing a *specification* can take many forms, depending on the size of the study, the relationship between the analyst and client, and the ability of both parties to agree on the details at this early stage. If one individual is playing both roles—client and analyst—this step might be combined with the model formulation and construction phases. Although it is still necessary to define and understand the system completely, the development of a formal simulation specification is probably not required. However, if you find yourself at the other extreme, where the analyst is an external consultant, a formal specification can be very useful for both parties. For the purpose of the following discussion, let's assume we're somewhere between the two extremes. Let's further assume that the client and analyst are not the same person and that a written document is to be developed.

Before we proceed, let's summarize where we are in the process and where we want to go. We've already formulated the problem and defined the objectives of the study. We've decided to use simulation as the means to solve our problem, and we're now ready to define the details of the simulation study that will follow.

A good place to start is with the system itself. If the system exists, go visit the site and walk through it. The best advice is to look, touch, and ask questions. You want to understand what's happening and why it's happening, so don't be afraid to ask questions, even ones that seem insignificant. Often you'll find that activities are performed in a specific way just because that's the way they've always been done, while at other times you'll find that there are very good reasons for a routine. As you learn more about the system, start thinking in terms of how you might model these activities. And even more important, think about whether it's necessary to include certain activities in the simulation model. At this stage of the process, you're a systems analyst, not a simulation modeler. Thus, don't be afraid to make recommendations that might improve the process. Providing input that will result in only minor improvements can increase your credibility for the tasks to follow.

If the system is a new design, find out if there are similar existing systems that you might tour. At the minimum, you'll obtain a better understanding of the overall process that you're about to simulate. If the system exists only on paper, take a tour of the blueprints. If there's nothing on paper, develop a process flow diagram or a rough sketch of the potential system. You should do this with the client so that there is total agreement on the specifics of the system.

With an understanding of the system to be modeled, it's now time to gather all interested parties in a conference room and develop your specification. There is no magic formula for such a specification, but generally it should contain the following elements:

- Simulation objectives
- System description and modeling approach
- Animation exactness
- Model input and output
- Project deliverables

The time required to obtain all the necessary information can vary from an hour to a few days. The discussions that yield the details of this specification should include all the interested parties. In most cases, the discussions are focused on the system rather than the simulation because at this point, it is the one common ground. The types of questions that should be asked, and answered, are as follows:

- What is to be included in the simulation model?
- At what level of detail should it be included?
- What are the primary resources of the system?
    What tasks or operations can they perform?
- Are process plans or process flow diagrams available?
    Are they up to date?
    Are they always followed?
    Under what conditions are they not followed?
- Are there physical, technological, or legal constraints on how the system operates?
    Can they be changed?
- Are there defined system procedures?
    Are they followed?
    Can new procedures be considered?
- How are decisions made?
    Are there any exceptions?
- Are there data available?

- Who will collect or assemble the data?
    - When will they be available?
    - What form will they be in?
    - How accurate are the data?
    - Will they change, and if so, how will they change?
- Who will provide data estimates if data are not available?
    - How accurate must they be?
    - Will they require that a sensitivity analysis be conducted?
- What type of animation is required?
    - Are there different animations required at different phases of the project?
    - How will the animations be used?
- Who will verify and validate the model, and how will it be done?
    - Are comparative data available?
    - How accurate are the data?
- What kind of output is required?
    - What are the primary performance measures?
    - Can they be ranked or weighted?
- How general should the model be?
    - Will it be revised for other decisions?
- Who will perform the analysis?
    - What type of analysis is required?
    - How confident do you have to be in your results?
- How many scenarios will be considered?
    - What are they?
- What are the major milestones of the study?
    - When do they need to be completed?
- What are the deliverables?

This is not intended to be a complete list, but it should give you a general idea of the detail required.

Generally, these types of discussions are enlightening to both parties. In this type of forum, the analyst is asking questions and recording information. The assumption is that the client has all, or at least most, of the information required. Experience reveals a somewhat different situation. In most cases, the client is a team of three to six individuals representing different levels of interest in the system. They generally have different expertise and knowledge of the system. It is not uncommon to find that these individuals disagree strongly on some of the details of the system that may generally be confined to process descriptions and decision logic, but other areas are not excluded. This should not be surprising, as you're trying to get a complete understanding of the system, as well as consensus on how the system works. If you're faced with disagreement on certain details, we suggest that you stand back and let the client team arrive at a consensus.

If you're developing a specification for first time, don't expect to get all your answers during the initial meeting. You might want to consider the 70/20/10 rule. Through experience, we have found that about 70% of the time the client team will have the complete answer or the information required. About 20% of the time the team will not know the answer, but they know how to get it (e.g., they may have to ask Dennis, who works on the night shift). The remaining 10% of the time they have no idea what the answer is or where they might find it (or there are several competing answers). This might surprise you, but this is a rather common phenomenon. Don't let this bother you; just make it clear that you need the information and ask when it will be available.

During this meeting you'll also be exploring the availability, or lack thereof, of data to drive your simulation. Again, don't expect to get all the data you need at this initial meeting. However, it's important to know what data ultimately will be available, and when. You should also make note of what data are from historical sources and what data will be estimates. Finally, it might be advisable to identify the form in which the data will be delivered, as well as who is responsible for collecting, assembling, or observing the data. For a discussion of data issues, see Section 5.4.

Before you leave this meeting, you should identify one person from the client team who will serve as the primary contact for the study. When you return to your office, you'll need to organize the information into a document that resembles a specification. We recommend that you do this as soon as possible, while the details are still fresh in your mind. Even then you'll undoubtedly find yourself scratching your head over at least one item in your notes. Something that was very clear during the meeting may now look muddy. No problem! Get on the phone, fax, or e-mail and clarify it with your primary contact.

Once you've developed this document, you should send it to the client for review. It may take several iterations before a final document emerges that's agreed upon and acceptable to both parties. Upon completion, we recommend that both parties sign this final document. If, during the simulation study, you find that conditions change, data are not available, and so forth, you may find it necessary to revise this document.

We would love to be able to provide you with a detailed set of instructions on how to perform this entire task. Unfortunately, each simulation study is different, and circumstances really dictate the amount of detail that's required. We can, however, give you an idea of what a specification looks like. We were fortunate to receive permission from *The Washington Post* to include a functional specification for a simulation study (see Appendix A) that was developed as part of a consulting project conducted by the Systems Modeling consulting group. The original specification was developed by Scott Miller, a Systems Modeling consultant, for Gary Lucke and Olivier Girod of *The Washington Post*. Other than a few minor changes made for confidentiality and formatting reasons, it is the original document. We strongly suggest that you take time to read it before you undertake your first specification. We do not suggest that you use this form for all of your specifications, but it should provide an excellent starting point.

Throughout this discussion, we made the assumption that it's possible to define the complete study before you start building the actual model. There are circumstances where this is not possible. These types of projects are open ended in that the complete project is not yet defined or the direction of the project depends on the results obtained in the early phases. Even though it may not be possible to specify the entire project completely, the development of a specification still is often desirable. Of course, it means that you may have to amend or expand the specification frequently. As long as both parties are agreeable, there's no reason to avoid these types of projects. You just have to be willing to accept the fact that direction of the project can change dramatically over its duration. These are often called *spiral projects*, in that they tend to spiral up into huge projects or spiral down into no project at all.

For now, let's assume that you have specified the simulation, and it's finally time to start the model.

12.5   Model Formulation and Construction

The nice part of having a complete specification of the simulation model and study is that it allows you to design the simulation model that can easily meet all of the objectives. Before you open a new model window and begin placing modules, we recommend that you spend some time formulating the model design. Some of the things that you want to take into consideration are the data structure or constraints, the type of analysis to be performed, the type of animation required, and your current comprehension of Arena. The more complex the system, the more important the formulation.

For example, consider a simulation of a large warehouse with 500,000 SKUs. You will obviously need to develop a data structure that will contain the necessary information on the changing state of the contents yet be easily accessed by the simulation model. If you're interested only in the number of pickers and stockers required for a given level of activity, it may not even be necessary to include information at the SKU level. You might create a model based on randomly created requests. If you can develop accurate expressions for the frequency and locations of these activities, this type of model might answer your questions. However, if you're interested in the details of the system, you would obviously need to create a much more elaborate model. You also need to understand the animation requirements. If no animation is required, you might model the picker movement and activities as a series of delays. If you need a detailed animation, you'll have to structure your model, most likely using guided transporter constructs, to allow the actual movement and positioning of the pickers on the animation.

You should also consider the potential impact of different scenarios that must be considered. Should each scenario be created as a different model, or can a sufficiently general model that only requires data changes be created? Consider our warehouse. If you want to compare a manual picking operation to an automated picking operation, you may require different models (although you may use the same data structure for both models). However, if you simply want to compare different types of layouts, you might develop a general model.

Once you've formulated a modeling approach, you need to consider what constructs you're going to use to build your model. So far we've advocated a high-level approach. This suggests that your first choice should be modules from the Common panel, followed by modules from the Support and Transfer panels, and modules from the Blocks and Elements panel only when required. This is a recommended approach for the novice Arena user, but as you gain experience and confidence in your modeling skills, you'll most likely take a different approach. Most experienced modelers prefer to start with the Support and Transfer panels and select from the other panels when required. This allows you to create exactly the type of model required and gives you the maximum amount of flexibility.

Finally, you're ready to open a new model window and begin the model construction, which is probably the most fun part of the entire study. Before you begin, we'd like to offer one more piece of advice. As you become more experienced with the Arena system, you'll start to develop habits—some good, some bad. You'll tend to use those constructs with which you're most familiar for *every* model you create. We recall a consultant who created a very detailed model of a complicated assembly system that used a series of overhead power-and-free conveyors to move the assembly through the system (this was a number of years ago). About two days before the model was to be delivered to the client, it developed a bug. The consultant claimed it was caused by extraterrestrial beings, but we suspect that it was a simple modeling error. Two long sleepless nights later (accompanied by freely offered, unsolicited advice from the other consultants), the error was uncovered. A quick fix was added by using a series of Signal and Wait modules (see Section 9.4) to synchronize the merging of subassembly conveyors, which solved the problem. The model was delivered to the client and the study was ultimately a success.

What's interesting about this extraterrestrial experience is that for the next several years, every model (and we mean *every* model) that the consultant created had at least one pair of Signal and Wait modules. This habit did not result in inaccurate models, but there were often simpler and more direct ways to model the system features. The consultant had stopped being creative in his model building and always used those constructs that saved his career that fateful night. Essentially he had developed a bad habit, which by the way, was extremely hard to break.

Another example that comes to mind occurred around the time that the Arena system was first introduced. Prior to that time, the consultants at Systems Modeling developed all their simulation models using the SIMAN language. This required the creation of two separate files—the experiment and model files (see Section 6.4.4) Although there were programs available to aid in developing these files, almost all the consultants developed their models in a text editor. Once their models were running, they'd create the separate animation of the model using the Cinema software. With the release of the Arena system, you could develop your entire model, including the animation, in one file using the point-and-click method with which you're now familiar. The consultants felt very comfortable with their text editors and were very reluctant to change their method of modeling. In fact, they went so far as to try to convince clients that the old way was the best way.

Finally, something akin to an edict was passed down stating, "You *will* use the new Arena system for all future models!" There was a lot of grumbling and complaining, but in a very short period of time, they were all working with the new software. In fact, before long you started to hear such comments as, "How did we ever do this before Arena?" Of course, years later, one individual still claimed that it was easier to develop models in a text editor. We have omitted names to protect the innocent, or the not-so-innocent.

So we recommend that you be open-minded about the methods you use to build models and the constructs that you choose to use. If there are other modelers in your group, ask them how they would approach a new model. You might also consider attending conferences or user-group meetings to find out what your peers are doing.

With that last caution noted, you can start constructing your model. If the model is small, you might place all the required modules, fill in the required data and hope that it works right the first time. (It rarely does.) If the system to be modeled requires a large, complicated model, you might try to partition the model building into phases. Select a portion of the system and build a model of that portion, including at least a rough animation. Once you are convinced it's working correctly, add the next phase. Continue in this manner until the entire model has been created. This approach makes model verification, which is our next topic, much easier.

12.6 Verification and Validation

Once you have a working model, and sometimes while you are building the model, it is time to verify and then validate the model. *Verification* is the task of ensuring that the model behaves as you intended; more colloquially it's known as debugging the model. *Validation* is the task of ensuring that the model behaves the same as the real system. We briefly introduced these topics in Sections 2.7 and 6.4.4. Let's expand our discussion by first addressing the issue of verification.

You now have a completed simulation model, or at least a completed component, and you'd like to be sure that the model is performing as designed. This may seem to be a simple task, but as your models and the systems they represent become more complicated, it can become very difficult. In larger models, you can have many different simultaneous activities occurring that can cause interactions that were never intended. You'll need to design or develop tests that will allow you to ferret out the offending interactions or just the plain and simple modeling mistakes. If you haven't already developed an animation, we suggest that you complete that task before you start the verification phase. It does not need to be the final animation, but it should have enough detail to allow you to view the activities that are occurring within the system. You might start by checking the obvious.

Consider the system we modeled in Chapters 6 and 7, which produced three different parts. Alter your model so that it creates only a single instance of a Part Type 1, and watch that solitary part flow through the system. Repeat this for the other two part types. Change all your model times to constant values, and release a limited number of parts into the system. The results should be predictable. Test the other extreme by decreasing the part interarrival rate and observe what happens as the system becomes overloaded. Change the part mix, processing times, failure rates, etc. What you're trying to do is to create a wide variety of different situations where your model logic might just fail. Of course, if you find problems, correct them. You'll have to decide if you need to repeat some of your earlier tests.

Once you have completed the obvious tests, you should try to stand back and visualize what types of scenarios you might consider in your analysis. Replicate these projected scenarios as best you can and see if your model still performs adequately. If you have periods when you're not using your computer, default the replication time and allow the simulation to run for extended periods of time. This type of experiment might be best performed overnight. Carefully review the results from these runs, looking for huge queues, resources not utilized, etc. Basically, you want to ask the following question: Do these results make sense? If you have extended periods of time when you're at your desk, but not using your computer, allow the model to run with the animation active. As time permits, glance at the monitor and see if everything appears to be all right. If you are confident that your model is working correctly, you're ready for the acid test.

Reconvene the client group and show them your simulation. In most cases, this means the animation. If there are problems, this is probably where they will be detected. Once this group grants its blessing, you might try one more experiment before you pronounce your model verified. Ask the group if they'd like to change the model in any way. Individuals who are familiar with the system, but not simulation, tend to think differently. They just might suggest modifications that you never considered.

Before you show your model to the client group, you should give some consideration to the level of detail required in the animation. In most cases, a rough animation showing the basic activities is sufficient. You may have to describe what your animation is showing, but once the individuals get beyond the pretty pictures, they are often able to visualize their system. At the same time, be sensitive to the feedback provided by the group when they first view the animation. You might be surprised at the types of reactions you'll get. We have seen individuals unable to get beyond the fact that your machines are blue and their machines are green. If you detect these types of comments, take the time to make some changes. Ultimately, you want the client group to accept your model as an accurate representation of their system. If you're lucky, they'll become your strongest supporters as you proceed with the project.

At this point, we should probably admit that it's almost impossible to verify totally a model for a complex system. We have seen verified models, which have already been used for extensive analysis, suddenly produce flawed results. This is typically caused by a unique combination of circumstances that was never originally considered being imposed on the model. Unfortunately, you need at least to consider that all of your previous analysis may be inaccurate. We should also point out that there's no magic to verification, nor is there a single method accepted by all. The key is that you, and your client, become totally convinced that the model is working as intended. Having done that, you are now ready to consider trying to validate the model. Although we are treating verification and validation as two separate topics or tasks, the difference between the two is often blurred.

In order to validate a simulation model, you should compare the results from your model to the results from the real system. If the system does not yet exist, you're in trouble right from the start. Even if the system does exist, such a comparison may be a difficult task. It's not uncommon for organizations to keep extensive metrics on past system performance, but often they do not keep the information that tells you what the system was doing, making, or subject to during that time period. Even if the data exist, they may be inaccurate or misleading.

Years ago, there was a large and complex simulation model developed for a facility that produced heavy-duty transmissions. The facility had approximately 1,400 machines and resources grouped into about 30 departments. The model had been developed to determine the sensitivity of product mix on the total throughput and the potential effect of introducing a new product line into the system. The primary performance measures were all related to the system's capacity. All of the process plans and process times were downloaded from the facility's databases. In addition, all the order releases were available for the last year of production. It looked like it would be an easy task to validate the model. Having already verified the model, the validation was undertaken.

The first set of runs produced results that totally mystified the clients. There were bottlenecks in the model that did not occur in the real system and bottlenecks in the real system that did not show up in the model results. In fact, a detailed comparison of resource-utilization statistics from the model to the historical records showed that there were major differences. This problem was resolved rather quickly when it became apparent that the processing times maintained in the facility's databases were based on standard times used for costing. They in no way represented the actual processing times observed on the shop floor. Be aware that this is a fairly common problem. Data are often kept for the convenience of the accountant, not the systems engineer. Luckily, someone had developed a set of conversion tables that converted the standard times to accurate processing times. These tables were included in the model and the validation process continued.

Everything looked good until a simulation run was made for the entire year, and the results were compared to the historical records. Eleven of the 12 months produced almost identical results. There was, however, one month near the middle of the simulated year where the records indicated that the output was approximately 40% larger than that predicted by the simulation model. A lot of time was spent trying to figure out what had caused this discrepancy. It was assumed that there was a problem with the simulation model—wrong! Finally, the analysis group started to suspect that maybe the historical data were flawed. By looking at the detailed statistics for the month in question, it became apparent that the resource statistics from the simulation closely matched the recorded statistics. In fact, it was quickly determined that the only difference was in the total number of transmissions produced. In addition, everyone was convinced that the system did not have the capacity to produce that many units. It took several weeks of part-time sleuthing before the answer emerged.

Someone finally realized that the month in question was the last month of the company's fiscal year. As it turned out, there was a small amount of product that was rejected for various reasons through the first 11 months of the year. These products were simply set aside until the final month when they suddenly became acceptable and were reported as part of that month's output. The reasoning was that it improved the performance of the system for the year. Weeks later these products were formally rejected, but the previous year's records were never adjusted. Removing these rejected items from the monthly throughput finally allowed the model to be validated.

If accurate records on the actual system do not exist, then it may be impossible to validate the model. In that case, concentrate on the verification and use the best judgment of individuals who are the most familiar with the system's capability. Sometimes individuals from the production floor have an uncanny ability to predict the performance of a new system accurately. Remember, the key is for both the analyst and the client to have confidence in the results from the model.

If you've gotten this far with your simulation project, you've cleared most of the major hurdles. You're now ready to use the model to answer some questions.

12.7 Experimentation and Analysis

We've already covered most, if not all, of the statistical issues associated with simulation analysis, and we'll not repeat that material here. However, there are several practical implications that we would like you to be aware of. Ideally, before you start any analysis, you would design a complete set of experiments that you intend to conduct. You would also decide on the types of analysis tools that you would be using. Although this may be ideal, it's far from reality. In some cases, you just don't have the luxury of sufficient time; in other cases, you don't really know where you're going with the analysis until you get there.

For example, if your objective is to improve the system throughput, you may not know what changes are required to achieve that goal. Sometimes the best analysis method is a group of knowledgeable individuals sitting around a computer suggesting and trying alternatives. This normally means that almost all the alternatives that are investigated will, at least, be feasible. One problem with this type of approach is that you may be tempted to reduce run times drastically in order to reduce the time you have to wait for the next set of results. Or worse yet, you may want to evaluate the system based only on a view of the animation. Don't yield to this pressure as it can lead to a disaster (and disasters can alter the direction of your career).

You might also consider structuring your experimentation based on the type of analysis that needs to be performed. For the sake of this discussion, let's identify three different types of analysis: candidate, comparative, and predictive.

Candidate analysis is normally done during the early design phases of a system. You are generally trying to identify the best candidate systems from a much larger group of potential designs that merit additional study. Models for these types of analysis are normally lacking in detail. You might think of these as rough-cut capacity models. You're trying to weed out the obvious losers and identify the potential winners. When you're performing this type of analysis, you can't put much faith in the accuracy of the true system's performance. You still need to make sure that you have a sufficient number of replications to provide good estimates of the system's performance (or your run times are of sufficient length), but there is very little value in increasing the number of replications (or the run time) to obtain tighter confidence limits on your results.

Comparative analysis would normally be the next logical step in selecting the final system design. You have a finite set of designs, and you want to compare them to identify the best design. This type of analysis typically requires a more detailed model, but we're only concerned with comparing one system to another. For example, there may be system activities that will affect the performance of the system, but the amount of the effect is common across all systems under consideration. For example, it may not be necessary to incorporate preventive maintenance or operator schedules into these types of models. The activities that are common to all systems under consideration and have the same effect do not have to be included in the models. For these types of systems, there may be value in increasing run times (or number of replications) to boost your confidence in selecting the best system.

Predictive analysis typically deals with only a few systems—often only one. By this time, you've selected what appears to be the best system, and you're now interested in estimating the actual performance of that system. This type of analysis requires that you include all activities that will affect the system's ability to achieve the predicted performance. At this point, you've selected the best system, and you're going forth with a recommendation to build it, provided that it meets the required objectives. These types of models need to be very detailed, and you also need to be confident in the data that are being used.

Regardless of the type of analysis you're conducting, be careful not to make strong judgments based on limited information. Be sure that your results are based on sound statistical practice, and when you conclude that one system is better than another, be sure that there is a significant statistical difference between them. More details on these issues are in Sections 6.5, 7.5, and 11.4–11.7.

Before proceeding, we find it necessary to point out again that the activities that constitute a simulation project appear to follow a logical time pattern. In reality, it's not uncommon to jump back and forth between activities, often re-visiting activities that you thought were complete. In practice, you often find that a good project will force you through several iterations of these activities.

12.8   Presenting and Preserving the Results

When you get to this stage, you've completed at least the initial study, and you're ready go forth with your results. In many instances, only a written report is required or expected. In other cases, you may have to go before a group of decision makers and give an informal or formal presentation of your results. This may actually be the most important phase of the project because it may determine if your results are accepted. We're not going to go into great detail about how to write or give a report. If you feel that your skills are lacking, we suggest you find a book devoted to these subjects or take a formal course to sharpen your skills. You'll find that you'll need these types of skills in many other areas as well! However, there are a few obvious points to be made.

First, be sure you're addressing the correct questions, and be sure to provide concise answers. Always include the equivalent of an executive summary that states your recommendations clearly—and the major reasons for them—in one page (or slide) or less. If possible, try to avoid presenting numbers in absolute terms; use ranges or confidence intervals. Understand your audience before you proceed. If you have volumes of material to support your recommendations, put them in an appendix or hold them in reserve (to be used only if requested). Don't be tempted to answer questions about features of the system that were not included in your model. Finally, be prepared to receive instructions to go back and look at additional alternatives.

Preserving the results should be an ongoing task throughout the duration of the project. Normally, we would call this the documentation process. It should include not only the final recommendations, but also documentation of the model and the details of the analysis. It is true that most simulation projects are not revisited. But there are exceptions, and it is not uncommon to have to dust off an old model years later to perform more analysis. We're aware of one simulation model developed in 1983, as a SIMAN model, that's still being used periodically, even though the model is basically the same.

Most practitioners agree that there's a law of nature, or maybe even a theorem, about documentation. The more documentation that you have on a project, the lower the probability of ever having to use the model again. It always seems to be those crash projects that leave no time for documentation that you're asked to resurrect years later. However, if you've followed our advice in this chapter, most of your documentation is already available and in electronic form. If you store all of this information (simulation model, specification, report, and presentation) in the same folder, you've covered most of the bases. An alternative is to use the methods described in Chapter 10 to embed these items directly into the simulation file.

You might also admit that in most cases the documentation will be used by someone else, if it's used at all. Individuals are promoted, change positions or change organizations, so your best approach to this task is to ask yourself what you'd want or need to know if someone else had performed the original study. This may not help you, but the next person will certainly be grateful.

12.9 Disseminating the Model: The Arena Viewer

During the course of a simulation study, you will certainly share your simulation model and animation with your client. If the client has a copy of Arena, you only need to send them the latest model (.doe) file, and they can view and alter your model at any time. If the client (or anyone else, for that matter) does not have the software, this obviously won't work. However, you can easily disseminate your model using the Arena Pack and Go feature to create a file for use with the Arena Viewer. This will allow anyone to view the animation and summary reports for a simulation model that has already been created.

The Pack and Go option (*File/Pack and Go*) creates an .avf file that contains the animation constructs and a .p file that contains the simulation program information. These files can then be given to anyone who has the "keyless" (that is, no hardware copy-protection key is required) Arena Viewer program for viewing. This program allows viewing of the animation and the model results.

When using the Arena Viewer, you cannot make any changes to the underlying model or animation. It is possible to provide the viewer with the ability to make limited changes by designing your model carefully so that certain data used by the model are obtained from an external source. For example, you could use VBA or a Read module to read in data from an external file or spreadsheet (see Chapter 10). These data could represent parameters of a service-time distribution, number of resources, mean interarrival times, or any other model parameters that can be assigned at the start of a simulation run. This allows you to control what can be changed while using the Viewer and still allow other people to see and execute your masterpiece.

A Functional Specification for *The Washington Post*

APPENDIX A

A Functional Specification for *The Washington Post*

A.1 Introduction

This appendix contains functional specification material provided to *The Washington Post* as part of a Systems Modeling simulation modeling consulting project. This project was delivered to Gary Lucke, manager of Manufacturing Systems Engineering, and Olivier Girod, manager of Industrial Engineering, of *The Washington Post*. This material has been modified slightly to retain confidentiality of certain proprietary information.

A.1.1 Document Organization

This document is provided to describe the mailroom operations at *The Washington Post's* Springfield, Va., and proposed Maryland facilities. The description will include the detail necessary to develop accurately an Arena simulation model of both operations.

This document is divided into six sections. The first section defines the objectives of the simulation project, the purpose of this document, the use of the Arena model, and the software and hardware required to run the Arena model. The second section describes the physical components of the mailroom operation, as well as the modeling approaches for each component. The third section describes the animation of the simulation model. The fourth section summarizes the user input requirements for the Arena model and the desired output generated from the Arena model. The fifth section describes the project deliverables. Finally, the sixth section contains the agreement and acceptance signatures required to proceed with the project.

A.1.2 Simulation Objectives

The objective of the simulation study is to provide *The Washington Post* with a decision support tool that will assist in evaluating the truck-loading operation at the Springfield plant as well as the proposed Maryland facility. The simulation will aid in assessing the impact of press output, tray utilization, tray trip rate, and truck arrival patterns on the loading operations.

In order to achieve the simulation objectives, two simulation models will be developed under this contract. These models will incorporate actual operational data and information collected from the Springfield and Maryland facilities. The simulation will utilize actual production sequences and decision logic required to represent facility operations accurately. In addition, the simulation will incorporate the information and outputs generated by the AGV Roll Delivery simulation currently under development by Systems Modeling (SM), a material handling vendor, and the newspaper.

The development of this model requires a number of tasks. Initially, a thorough understanding of the newspaper's Springfield and Maryland facilities is necessary to conceptualize and develop an accurate representation of this system. This process has been, and will continue to be, a joint effort between *The Washington Post* and Systems Modeling. This procedure defines the user's conceptualization of the system that SM will use to develop the Arena simulation model. Included in this process is the defining of the inputs and outputs of the model, verifying that the Arena model has been implemented accurately, and validating that the model accurately represents the facility.

Upon completion of the project, the newspaper will have a tool that will allow an analyst to specify various operating scenarios for the mailroom facility, execute simulation experiments of the scenarios, and perform statistical analysis of the scenarios.

A.1.3 Purpose of the Functional Specification

This functional specification serves four purposes. First and foremost, this document describes the mailroom operation at the newspaper's Springfield and Maryland facilities, at the level of detail required for modeling purposes. This description includes process flow, equipment functionality, operating procedures and rules, system interactions, and logistical issues. These systems must be thoroughly understood before they can be represented in a computer simulation.

Second, the user input required to perform the simulation analysis is defined. The input required includes such things as the press behavior, dock allocations, truck load time, and other operational characteristics.

Third, the output generated by the computer simulation is defined. Output is generally in the form of system performance measures from which the simulation analysis is performed. These output statistics include such things as dock utilization, truck load times, tray utilization, etc.

Finally, the project deliverables are described. The deliverables will be contained in a three-ring binder and will include computer diskettes containing the Arena model, input data files, hard copies of the data files, a user's manual to describe how to use the software, and the final report.

This document explicitly defines issues that are part of the quotation and other unofficial documents exchanged by SM and The Washington Post. Therefore, for those issues that are discussed in other documents, this document supersedes all correspondence in defining the project.

A.1.4 Use of the Model

The use of the simulation model will be detailed completely in the user's manual provided at the completion of the project. Use of the model includes initializing the Arena model and input files with the desired input parameters, running the model on the computer, and generating summary statistics and reports. The summary reports generated from various runs can be compared to evaluate the impact of specific parameters on system performance.

A.1.5   Hardware and Software Requirements

SM will develop the Arena simulation model under the Microsoft® Windows® operating system environment. The software and hardware required to run the model include:[1]

- Arena Standard Edition 1.25 or higher
- IBM-compatible 486 PC or higher
- Windows 3.1 or 3.11
- 8 MB RAM (16 MB recommended)
- 30 MB hard disk space

The above-mentioned software is not included with this project, but can be purchased under a separate contract.

A.2   System Description and Modeling Approach

The following sections define the flow of newspapers from the presses through the mailroom to the loading docks. The various system components will be described for both the Springfield and Maryland facilities since the two plants have different layouts and modes of operation. Any operational differences will be addressed in the detail needed for this modeling effort. Overall, the logic defined will be similar for both facilities.

The model will include the production of headsheets, movement of headsheet product via the tray system to the docks, and the palletizing and loading of the bundles onto the trucks at the docks. It will also include the loading of previously produced advance product onto the trucks at the docks.

A.2.1   Model Timeline

The model will be able to simulate mailroom activities ranging from one day to a complete week.

A.2.2   Presses

The presses will be the starting point within the simulation model. Product generated from a press is sent to a stacker where it is bundled and then sent to the tray system. Neither the presses nor the stackers will be modeled in detail for this project. Press product is produced on each of four identical presses at a constant press rate during normal operations. Assuming a constant, user-defined bundle size at the stacker, bundles will be modeled entering the system at a constant rate for each press. The production rate for each press will be defined on an hourly basis over a one-week time horizon. Most of the time, press runs should start between 12:15 AM and 12:30 AM and finish between 4:30 AM and 4:40 AM.

At the conclusion of the AGV Roll Delivery simulation project, logic will be added so that the AGV simulation generates a press schedule that includes all uptimes and downtimes for each press. These press schedules can then be used as input files for the mailroom simulation. The mailroom simulation will be designed so that the analyst can choose to use either 1) "late run" press output schedules generated from the AGV simulation, or 2) user-defined press parameters and press downtime distributions. Both options are described below.

[1] These requirements do not reflect current software needs.

A.2.2.1 AGV Simulation Press Output Schedule

Late-run press output schedules generated by the AGV simulation model will be imported into the mailroom model as ASCII files. For each press, these files will consist of a sequence of uptimes, downtimes, and speeds. An example of a late-run press output schedule generated by the AGV simulation is presented in Table A-1.

Table A-1. Late-Run Press Output Generated by AGV Simulation (Press 1)

Press 1 Sequence	Up/Down	Time (minutes)	Press Speed (copies/hr)	Ramp Up (copies)	Ramp-Up Speed (copies/hr)
1	Up	30	70,000	5,000	56,000
2	Down	5	0	0	0
3	Up	45	70,000	5,000	56,000
4	Down	10	0	0	0

A.2.2.2 User-Defined Press Schedule

User-defined press parameters will be read into the simulation model from one ASCII file and will include, for each press: 1) total work order size, 2) press speeds, 3) ramp- up counts, and (4) ramp-up speeds. An example of user-defined press parameters is provided in Table A-2.

Besides replating downtime, each press also experiences random downtime. This downtime is caused by either 1) bad paper roll, or 2) newsprint web breaks. For each failure type, the frequency of occurrence will be based on headsheet count, while the time to repair distribution will be expressed in minutes.

Table A-2. User-Defined Press Output Schedule

Press Number	Work Order (copies)	Press Speed (copies/hr)	Ramp Up (copies)	Ramp-Up Speed (copies/hr)
1	120,000	70,000	5,000	56,000
2	120,000	65,000	3,000	49,000
3	120,000	55,000	5,000	49,000
4	120,000	70,000	5,000	56,000

A.2.2.3 Replating

For each press, replating will occur according to a user-defined schedule, and its associated downtimes will be modeled using a time-based distribution. An example of the replating schedule is given in Table A-3. In this example, it is assumed that the presses are turned on between 12:15 AM and 12:30 AM and are off between 4:30 AM and 4:40 AM. For the purpose of the simulation, it will be assumed that there may be as many as 10 replatings in a given run.

Table A-3. User-Defined Replating-Induced Downtime

Replating	Replating Occurrence (minutes)	Replating Downtime (minutes)
1st	1:15 to 1:30	7 to 10
2nd	2:15 to 2:30	10 to 15
3rd	2:45 to 3:00	7 to 10
4th	:	:

Most of the time, replating should induce the following sequence: Presses 1 and 2 go down, Press 1 goes back up, Press 3 goes down, Press 2 goes back up, Press 4 goes down, Press 3 goes back up, and Press 4 goes back up.

A.2.3   Product Types

Presses produce two types of product, advance and headsheet. Advance product is the part of the newspaper that is not time sensitive and can therefore be produced earlier in the day. The headsheet is typically the first few sections of the newspaper that contain time-sensitive news. For purposes of this simulation, it will be assumed that all of the advance product needed for a given day is available when needed to load the delivery trucks. Only the headsheet production will be modeled explicitly.

A.2.4   Press Packaging Lines

Each press feeds three press packaging lines, and each press packaging line is connected to the tray system. Press output can be regulated through each of the three press packaging lines. These lines input headsheets and produce bundles. A press packaging line has three operational modes: 1) backup mode, 2) regular mode, and 3) manual insertion mode. In the backup mode, the press packaging line is idle and does not produce any bundles. In the regular mode, a user-defined percentage of press output is fed to the line and mechanically transformed into bundles. Bundle size will be user defined. In the manual insertion mode, the line functions in the regular mode except that bundles are manually reworked to satisfy additional product requirements. These requirements involve merging advance products with headsheets. The manual insertion process will be described in Section 2.7.1.

A.2.5   Tray System

Bundles entering the tray system from the press packaging lines have no predefined destination. At the determination point in the tray system, the bundles will be given a final destination (dock or palletizer) based on the tray trip rate and the trucks currently waiting for product.

A.2.5.1   Springfield, Va., Tray System

The Springfield tray system consists of two identical tray conveyors that transport bundles from the presses and stackers to the loading docks and palletizers. The two tray conveyors are differentiated and identified by their color, green or yellow. The output from each press is dedicated to one of the two conveyors, with the output from presses 1 and 3 sent to the green tray conveyor, and the output from presses 2 and 4 sent to the yellow tray conveyor. The green tray conveyor has exactly 263 trays, while the yellow tray conveyor has exactly 266 trays. Both conveyors move at a velocity of 150 trays/min and can deliver bundles to any of the bundle docks or any of the palletizers. The tray trip rate determines how often product may be diverted to a given location. At the determination point in the tray system, the bundle will look at the truck with the highest priority, currently at a dock. If the trip rate is not exceeded, the bundle will be diverted to that location. If the trip rate would be exceeded, the bundle will look at trucks with lower and lower priorities until a valid destination is found. If a bundle cannot find a valid destination, it is recirculated on the tray conveyor. The conveyor velocity and trip rate are user defined.

A.2.5.2 Maryland Tray System

The tray system in the Maryland facility will function in a similar manner. However, because the Maryland facility is one story, there is only one conveyor in the tray system. In addition, each of the packaging lines is connected directly to one to four docks. This enables bundles to be sent directly to a dock, bypassing the tray system. A packaging line will only divert a bundle to the tray system if there are no trucks ready for loading at one of its docks. The physical layout of the conveyor and the exact number of trays in the conveyor must be defined by the newspaper before the model may be built. The conveyor velocity and trip rate are user defined.

A.2.6 Truck Arrivals

Truck arrivals are controlled from a user-defined schedule file (Table A-4). Each truck has a unique truck ID, a time bucket, a draw quantity, and a truck type. The time bucket determines the time segment in which the truck arrives. The draw quantity is the number of copies to be loaded onto that truck. The truck type is the type of service for that truck. Truck types can be either highway, home delivery, or newsstand.

Table A-4. Truck Arrival Schedule

Number	Bucket	TruckID	Draw Qty	Truck Type
1	1	0906	12294	2
2	1	0907	5050	3
:	:	:	:	:
n	8	9451	650	1

Trucks arrive in the model in time bucket $(n-1)$ to begin loading the advance product at an advance dock. When the advance product is completely loaded, the truck may move to a dispatch dock where it will receive the headsheet needed for completion. Trucks are serviced based on their arrival time at a dock.

A.2.6.1 Home Delivery

Home delivery (HD) trucks receive their advance product at one of the dedicated advance docks. Pallets of advance product are disassembled and conveyed to the truck in bundles on a dedicated conveyor. The loading rate in bundles per minute and the dock setup time in minutes are user defined. After receiving all of the advance product, the HD truck can proceed to the regular dispatch docks where the same amount of headsheet product is loaded. Headsheet bundles arrive via the tray system. The loading rate in bundles per minute and the dock setup time in minutes are user defined. A user-defined percentage of the HD trucks are deemed to be "slow" and as such have a longer load time and setup time.

A.2.6.2 Highway

Highway (HWY) trucks are serviced at dedicated highway docks. Entire pallets of advance product are loaded by fork trucks onto the HWY trucks. The loading rate in pallets per minute and the wrap-up time (for last pallet) in minutes are user defined. Headsheet product destined for a HWY truck is sent to the palletizer dedicated to that HWY truck. Pallets are formed and are then loaded onto the truck by fork trucks. The loading rate and wrap-up time are the same as for the advance pallets. In addition, there is a dock change time between trucks. A HWY truck remains at a dock until all of its advance and headsheet product has been loaded.

A.2.6.3 Newsstand/Street Sales

Newsstand/street sales (NS/SS) trucks receive no advance product. Instead, upon arrival at a dispatch dock, bundles are generated from the manual insertion process. These bundles travel via the tray system to the NS/SS truck. Load times and wrap-up times are similar to those for the HD trucks.

A.2.7 Docks

In the model, there are three types of docks: 1) pallet, 2) advance bundle, and 3) headsheet bundle. Pallet docks are designed for forktruck access and service HWY trucks. Advance bundle docks are used to load the advance product onto the trucks during time bucket ($n-1$). Headsheet bundle docks are used to load the headsheet product delivered to the trucks via the tray system. A truck receives press product based on its arrival time (FIFO) at a given dock area and not its dock location. For each dock type, the number of active docks will be user defined.

A.2.7.1 Springfield, Va., Docks

The Springfield facility has exactly 12 dedicated pallet docks, exactly 10 advance bundle docks, and exactly 14 dedicated headsheet bundle docks.

A.2.7.2 Maryland Docks

The proposed Maryland facility has exactly 10 combination pallet and advance bundle docks and 18 dedicated headsheet bundle docks.

A.2.8 Palletizers

For purposes of the simulation, all of the palletizers are assumed to be identical. A palletizer is used to package headsheet bundles destined for a HWY truck at a pallet dock. Each HWY truck at a dock has a dedicated palletizer. For purposes of the model, a palletizer acts as a possible destination for bundles on the tray system. The palletizing of advance product will not be modeled in this project. Palletizers operate at a constant rate and form pallets of a constant size. The last pallet loaded will be a partial pallet with as much product as necessary to finish the load. The palletizer rate and pallet size are user defined. Palletizers experience various downtimes at random intervals. These downtimes can either be modeled as one downtime by combining all of the failure modes or by modeling each individual failure mode separately.

If a bundle arriving at a palletizer must wait because the equipment is busy or down, it will accumulate in a queue. The capacity of the palletizer queues will be user defined. If the queue at a palletizer reaches the user-defined limit, any additional bundles arriving at that palletizer will be turned away. Bundles turned away will be recirculated on the tray conveyor and will try to exit at the same palletizer on the next circuit.

A.2.8.1   Springfield, Va., Palletizers
The Springfield facility contains five palletizers, located on the first floor.

A.2.8.2   Maryland Palletizers
The proposed Maryland facility contains four palletizers.

A.2.9   Manual Insertion Process
Manual insertion begins when the first NS/SS truck arrives at a dock and continues until all NS/SS trucks are serviced. As the press packaging lines are changed over to manual insertion mode, hand inserters from a pool of workers are assigned to assemble bundles of advance product and headsheets. These bundles, called NS/SS bundles, are dispatched to the NS/SS trucks. Each packaging line is staffed by a maximum of 25 workers. Each worker can insert 500 copies per hour. Bundle size, worker pool size, and worker capacity are user defined.

Manual insertion is a critical component of the mailroom simulation because it conditions press packaging line operations. For each production day, the press packaging line operation experiences three sequential phases: 1) the home delivery (HD) phase, 2) the combined home delivery and newsstand/street sales (HD+NS/SS) phase, and 3) the newsstand/street sales (NS/SS) phase. During the first phase, all bundles produced by the press packaging lines are assembled mechanically and dispatched to either HD or HWY trucks. During the second phase, bundles may be dispatched to either HD, HWY, or NS/SS trucks. During the third phase, all bundles are manually assembled and dispatched to NS/SS trucks. The following section contains descriptions of these phases for a one-press configuration. The example is provided to illustrate the concept of a press packaging line operation.

Example
- *HD Phase.* Two packaging lines operate in the regular mode and share press output (50%/50%). One packaging line is in backup mode.
- *HD+NS/SS Phase.* Two packaging lines operate in the regular mode and share 80% of press output (40%/40%). One packaging line operates in manual insertion mode and

is fed 20% of press production. On the hand insertion line, headsheet bundles that are not set aside by a hand inserter are down-stacked on a pallet (user-defined pallet size) before the bundles reach the tray system. These headsheet bundles are stored until the NS/SS phase. The headsheet bundles that are set aside are reworked and transformed into NS/SS bundles.

- *NS/SS Phase.* While the press is still running, the three packaging lines operate in the manual insertion mode and share press output (33%/33%/33%). On these hand insertion lines, headsheet bundles that are not set aside and reworked by a hand inserter are down-stacked on a pallet before reaching the tray system. These bundles are stored until the press completes its work order. Once the press is turned off, all down-stacked headsheet bundles are re-fed into hand insertion lines for NS/SS production.

In the simulation, the user will define the length of a phase by defining the amount of product to be produced by the press during that phase. When that amount of product has been produced, the next phase will begin. The NS/SS phase will start when all of the HD trucks are serviced and end when all of the NS/SS trucks have been serviced. The user will also define the mode of operation for each packaging line during each phase. If a packaging line is working in manual insertion mode, the user will define the number of hand inserters on the line and the hand insertion rate.

A.3   Animation

The Arena simulation model will include an animation that will capture the general flow of bundles through the mailroom to the docks and palletizers. The animation will be a top-down, two-dimensional view of the system. The animation will show the movement of bundles through the tray system to the loading docks and palletizers. In addition, various system statistics will be displayed on the animation to show dynamic performance criteria.

The newspaper will supply a scaled layout of both the Springfield facility and the proposed Maryland facility in CAD format that will provide the static background for the animation.

A.4   Summary of Input and Output

A.4.1   Model Input

The data items read into the simulation model from ASCII files include but are not restricted to:

Presses

- Production Rate
- Production Schedule (1 day or 1 week)
- MTBF, MTTR

Note: The production schedule output from the AGV Roll Delivery Simulation may be used instead of these inputs.

Press Packaging Line
- Line Activation Patterns (Modes, Phases)
- Tray System
- Velocity
- Trip Rate (Docks)
- Trip Rate (Palletizers)

Palletizers
- Production Rate
- Bundles per Pallet
- MTBF, MTTR

Bundles
- Copies per Bundle (Advance)
- Copies per Bundle (Headsheet)
- Copies per Bundle (Hand Insertion)

Process Time
- Truck Load Rates
  - HD-Headsheet (Reg)
  - HD-Headsheet (Slow)
  - HD-Advance
  - HWY (Last Pallet)
  - HWY (Other Pallets)
- Dock Change Times
  - HD-Headsheet (Reg)
  - HD-Headsheet (Slow)
  - HD-Advance
  - HWY

Truck Schedule (for Each Truck)
- Bucket
- Truck ID
- Draw Qty
- Truck Type

Hand Insertion
- Hand Inserters per Line
- Hand Inserter Service Rate

A.4.2 Model Output

The following performance measures will be written to one or more ASCII data files at the conclusion of the simulation run. These statistics will be collected and output on a daily and weekly basis.

Input Parameters
- Process Times
- Equipment and Resource Levels
- Failure Rates

Press Activity (for Each Press)
- Available Time (Up)
- Total Production
- Average Production Rate
- Breakdown History

Hand Insert Activity (for Each Line)
- Total Production
- Average Production Rate
- Down-Stacked Headsheet Bundles

Tray Activity
- Utilization (Green & Yellow)

Bundles
- Destination Statistics

Dispatch Statistics
- Trucks Early
- Trucks Late
- Time to Complete Pct of Trucks

Bucket Loading (per Bucket)
- Total Units Loaded (Actual)
- Total Units Loaded (Scheduled)

Dock Statistics (per Dock)
- Dock Utilization
- Total Units Loaded
- Utilization per Bucket

Truck Statistics (per Truck)
- Dock Used
- Advance Load Time
- Wait Time
- Idle Time
- Load Time
- Change Time
- Summary for Each Truck Type

A.5   Project Deliverables

The following sections discuss the project deliverables. Upon completion of the project, *The Washington Post* will be supplied with all the computer files that were developed under the contract. The simulation model and all supporting data files are the sole and exclusive property of the buyer. This does not include any Arena software unless specifically stated and a quote has been provided. SM will keep backup copies for maintenance and recordkeeping in the event that *The Washington Post* desires changes to the model in the future.

A.5.1   Simulation Model Documentation

Model documentation will be a continuous process throughout the development of the model. This documentation will be contained within the Arena model and will include detailed comments describing all major sections of the model logic. Also included will be a complete variable listing containing descriptions of all variables, entity attributes, stations, queues, etc., used in the model.

A.5.2   User's Manual

The user's manual will include all of those items for which SM is responsible. This manual will only include information that is specific to this project. The user is referred to the *Arena User's Guide* for items that are specific to the Arena software. The contents of the user's manual will be:

1. The functional specification.
2. A copy of the model file on diskette.
3. A copy of all data input files on diskette.
4. Instructions on how to use the model.

A.5.3   Model Validation

Validation is the process of establishing that the model accurately represents the real system. The actual performance data required as inputs to the simulation model will be essential for this validation. The amount of data available, in the proper format, determines the level of detail of the validation process. SM and *The Washington Post* will run initial validation tests of the models to confirm system performance and the logic and algorithms implemented.

A.5.4   Animation

The Arena model will include a two-dimensional animation designed to allow the analyst insight into the dynamic features of the model. The animation will closely resemble the facility layout supplied by the newspaper in the form of a CAD file.

A.6   Acceptance

The estimate for the above-described modeling project is six person-weeks of effort to commence after this functional specification document has been signed.

The cost of this effort is $??. Billing will occur based on the following schedule:

ACCEPTANCE OF THE FUNCTIONAL SPECIFICATION	$??
COMPLETION OF MODEL DEVELOPMENT	$??
FINAL ACCEPTANCE	$??

This cost does not include software required to run the simulation model.

The Washington Post Mailroom Simulation Model
Functional Specification Furnished By:

_____

Scott A. Miller, Project Manager
Simulation and Consulting Services
Systems Modeling Corporation

Agreed and Accepted By:

_____

The Washington Post representatives:
Gary Lucke, Manager of Manufacturing Systems Engineering
Olivier Girod, Manager of Industrial Engineering

IIE/SM
Contest
Problems

APPENDIX B

IIE/SM Contest Problems

This appendix contains the problem statements for the first three IIE/Systems Modeling student simulation competitions. Teams of three undergraduate students from universities worldwide compete in this competition annually. The winners for the first three contests were University of Calgary, Kansas State University and co-winners University of Pittsburgh and Virginia Polytechnic Institute and State University.

B.1 First Annual Contest: The SM Superstore

You have just been hired as a consultant by Sue Model of Sue's Markets. Although Sue has been in the grocery business for many years with a large chain of small stores, she just recently opened the first of a new type of store called The SM Superstore. The idea behind this new concept is to provide a huge store with numerous types of brands available and fast, friendly service. This first store is being used to test the layout and operating procedures for a large chain of superstores that Sue expects to build.

The first store has been open for six months, and Sue is still having a problem staffing the checkout counters during peak times, which occur from 2 PM to 10 PM. She has received many customer complaints about the long lines in front of the checkout counters. She has 20 checkouts that she can use, but has not been able to develop an adequate staffing plan to eliminate the long waits. Your consulting firm has been requested to develop an economical staffing plan that will meet Sue's requirements.

Prior to requesting your services, Sue hired a group of IE students from a local university to collect and analyze data. Some of those data are summarized in this document. Unfortunately, Sue is away on a well-deserved, one-month vacation in the South Pacific and cannot be reached. Furthermore, she indicated that she does not want her store personnel to be bothered by a bunch of consultants asking dumb questions and disrupting the store's operation. Thus, no additional information is available, and Sue wants your report on her desk when she returns from vacation. After reading the report, she may decide to ask for additional work.

An informal survey was conducted to determine what wait times customers expect—the time customers wait in line before reaching the cashier. Most customers would prefer at most a 2- or 3-minute wait time, but are willing to wait as long as 10 or 12 minutes if the store is very busy. Customers with only a few items normally expect a shorter waiting time. Customers did indicate that if they had to wait longer than 15 or 20 minutes, they might go to another store the next time. In addition, if the number of customers exceeds 4 or 5 per lane, the congestion starts to interrupt the other shoppers.

Although the customer arrival rate has a great degree of variability, the IE students have provided average arrival rates at the checkout lines (in customers per hour) for each half hour of the times under consideration. These rates are as follows:

Time	Rate	Time	Rate
2:00 - 2:30	95	6:00 - 6:30	105
2:30 - 3:00	100	6:30 - 7:00	95
3:00 - 3:30	120	7:00 - 7:30	125
3:30 - 4:00	150	7:30 - 8:00	150
4:00 - 4:30	160	8:00 - 8:30	155
4:30 - 5:00	150	8:30 - 9:00	95
5:00 - 5:30	160	9:00 - 9:30	70
5:30 - 6:00	110	9:30 - 10:00	60

During the data collection phase, it was assumed that all days were identical so data were only collected on Monday through Thursday. It now appears that the overall demand on Friday increases about 15%, and the weekend demand is very different. Thus, you should only be concerned with the weekday staffing.

Actual shopping time has a great degree of variability. Customers purchasing fewer than 10 items generally average about 42 seconds per item, although it takes a minimum of 3 minutes just to travel through the store. Customers who purchase more items average about 34 seconds per item.

The number of items per customer is quite variable, but appears to be consistent over time. A large sample of items per customer was obtained from cash register receipts can be found in file IIE_SM_1.dat. The average checkout time per item is about 3 seconds, but can vary as much as 25%. About 1.3% of the time a price check will be needed on an item or a damaged item will need to be replaced. Although the store uses scanners for checkout, customers sometimes request that the price list at the item display be checked. The time for this activity is highly variable, but averages about 2.2 minutes.

The form of payment depends on the number of items that a customer purchases. For purchases of 20 or fewer items, 45% of the customers pay cash, 30% pay by check, and 25% pay with a credit card. For purchases of greater than 20 items, the values for those categories are 20%, 45%, and 35%, respectively. All payment transaction times appear to follow a normal distribution, but vary by payment type. Cash payments average 0.95 minute, with a standard deviation of 0.17. Check payments for customers with a check cashing card average 1.45 minutes, with a standard deviation of 0.35. With no check cashing card (27% of the time), the supervisor must approve the check, which requires another 0.95 minute, with a standard deviation of 0.15. Credit card payments average 1.24 minutes, with a standard deviation of 0.21.

Bagging times average about 1.25 seconds per item, but can vary as much as 20%. Customers have a greater preference, 63%, for plastic bags rather than paper. If a bagger is not available, the cashier will bag the groceries after payment is made. About 30% of the time the customer will help. The time does not appear to be dependent upon who is doing the bagging. Baggers may be assigned to a single aisle, to multiple aisles, or may simply move among all aisles as required.

Sue's employees for cashier and bagging activities are mostly part-time people. Cashiers are paid an average of $7.25 per hour, and baggers are paid an average of $5.50 per hour. There are several rules that must be followed in staffing with part-time employees. Any part-time person must be scheduled for a minimum of 3 hours and a maximum of 5 hours. Cashiers are generally not asked to work as baggers, and baggers are not allowed to work as cashiers.

Clearly, one can make all customers happy almost all the time by keeping all the checkouts completely staffed all the time. However, the cost to implement this strategy would be prohibitive. Ideally, a staffing schedule would provide minimal waiting time at a minimum cost. Although Sue is expecting a single schedule, she did note at the last meeting that she expects demand to change over time. So, she might be interested in how and when to adjust her schedule as the demand changes.

Sue is looking forward to receiving your recommendations. In the meantime, if you have any questions, you might visit your local supermarket.

B.2 Second Annual Contest: The SM Market

You have just been hired as a consultant by Sid Model of SM Market. Sid started a small meat and fish market several years ago in a suburban community with the concept of providing high-quality fresh meats and fish at a reasonable price. The first store has been a tremendous success; at the request of his customers, he recently expanded the store by adding a deli counter. The deli offers a wide range of pre-made side dishes as well as sandwiches for the lunch crowd. This addition appears to have been a success, but Sid is having difficulty staffing the counters due to the high variability in customer arrivals. Since Sid is considering opening several new stores in the upcoming year and possibly franchising his market concept if the stores continue to be successful, he has decided to hire a consultant to evaluate his staffing needs. Not only will this allow him to minimize his expenses, but it will provide the basis for his cost estimates in opening new stores.

The addition of the new deli counter has caused a few problems and has been the source of numerous customer complaints about the long lines. This was partially due to the layout of the store. In order to expand the business, Sid purchased an adjacent store for the new deli counter. In effect, it is two separate stores with a connecting doorway. This resulted in two lines forming, one at each counter, and resulted in some customer confusion. Although he realized he had a problem, he was unable to develop a logical and inexpensive solution. Shortly after this, Sid was contacted by a local university looking for short-term IE projects. He welcomed the chance to have a group of IEs examine his operation in the hope that they could provide some insight into how best to operate his store. After some observations and talking to customers, Sid and the IE students decided that the biggest problem was the customer perception that other people were jumping ahead of them in line and being served first. In order to eliminate this problem, Sid installed two customer number devices, one for each counter. Now, when customers enter the single entry door, they must choose which line they wish to enter. They walk approximately 20 feet to obtain a customer number, then another 20 feet to enter the appropriate line at the counter they have chosen. Customer numbers are called sequentially and customers wait for their numbers to be called before they are served. If customers want to make purchases at both counters, they must follow this procedure at both counters. It has been observed that these customers tend first to enter the line at the counter with the fewest number of people waiting and then proceed to the second counter. If customers do not identify themselves when their numbers are called, they must take a new number in order to be served. This method resolved a temporary problem of customers taking a number from each line and then assuming that they would be served as soon as they arrived at the second counter—which caused the customers in that line to feel that these customers were getting preferential treatment.

The IE students also spent time collecting a limited amount of data. They analyzed this information and were in the process of putting the data into a form that they could use for a simulation study; unfortunately, the semester ended before they were able to start the simulation. However, they did make some progress on the data before that time. Their basic findings were as follows:

■ There are two basic arrival types—1) normal shoppers who only visit the meat and fish counter or ones who utilize the deli to augment their meat or fish purchase, and 2) lunchtime customers who only utilize the deli counter.

■ For the normal shoppers, about half visit both counters.

■ Customers who purchase items from the meat and fish counter prefer the fish by about two to one. Only about 10% of the customers buy both meat and fish.

■ Most customers pay with cash, 73%; credit cards are used by about 19% of the customers; and the remainder have charge accounts with the SM Market.

The customer arrival data have a great deal of variability so the students collected data in half-hour increments. The data given below are for the normal customer arrivals (in customers per hour):

Time	Rate	Time	Rate
9:00 - 9:30	10	1:00 - 1:30	55
9:30 - 10:00	25	1:30 - 2:00	40
10:00 - 10:30	30	2:00 - 2:30	35
10:30 - 11:00	30	2:30 - 3:00	35
11:00 - 11:30	35	3:00 - 3:30	40
11:30 - 12:00	45	3:30 - 4:00	45
12:00 - 12:30	65	4:00 - 4:30	50
12:30 - 1:00	60	4:30 - 5:00	60

The lunchtime customers arrive between 11:00 and 1:30 with the rates given below:

Time	Rate	Time	Rate
11:00 - 11:30	15	12:30 - 1:00	30
11:30 - 12:00	60	1:00 - 1:30	15
12:00 - 12:30	55		

The IE students did not have time to complete their data analysis, but they did collect a limited amount of data for the service times at the meat and fish counter. These raw data are included with this request for recommendations in file IIE_SM_2.dat. No data were collected for the service time at the deli counter, so Sid did some informal observations and questioning of the deli staff. He concluded that the minimum likely service time is about 2 minutes, and the longest service time he observed was about 7 minutes. A rough estimate is that the most likely service time is about 5 minutes. Sid questions the accuracy of these estimates and believes that he could be off by as much as 15%.

Informal surveys of customers indicated that the deli customers were less willing to wait in line as they were normally in a hurry to get back to work. They were generally very unhappy if they had to wait in line for over 10 to 15 minutes. A 2- or 3-minute wait appeared to be quite acceptable. The meat and fish customers were willing to wait a little longer before they became impatient—as much as 20 to 25 minutes, although they did prefer a wait time of 5 minutes or less. They generally spent at least part of their wait time looking over the possible selections. Customers who visited both counters expected a longer store time, 15 to 20 minutes, and became impatient when that time exceeded 40 minutes. Sid has also noticed that as the total number of customers in the store approaches 25, people are less likely to enter; he has seen people enter and leave immediately when the total number of customers in the store exceeded 30.

Sid employs mostly part-time people to staff the counters and has established a policy that any part-time person will be scheduled for at least three hours. If an employee is scheduled for more that 6 hours per day, he/she is considered full time and must be paid benefits, which increases the operating cost. Sid estimates his part-time employee cost at $8 per hour and his full-time cost at $13 per hour. He would like to have at least four full-time employees to help train new employees as there is a relatively high turnover of the part-time workers. Sid can move workers from one counter to another during their work hours, but prefers to make these changes only on the half hour. There is a fair amount of prep time in getting ready for the lunch crowd and restocking the meat and fish counter in the early afternoon. Sid can use counter employees for prep work that he estimates requires about 6 person-hours before 11 AM to prepare for the lunch crowd and about 3 person-hours for the early afternoon restocking.

Although Sid closes at 5 PM, he makes sure that all customers currently in the store are served. He maintains at least one person at each counter until 6 PM for this purpose and to put away the unsold products and do general cleanup. No one, other than Sid, reports before 9 AM. Also, there must be at least one full-time employee working at all times, and no full-time worker is allowed to work more than 8 hours per day.

What Sid would like is a staff schedule that will minimize his employee cost and maximize his customer satisfaction. He would also appreciate any ideas that you might generate during your analysis that might help his operation. As an aside, you should be aware that Sid is rather paranoid about his operation in that he is deathly afraid that someone else will start a similar franchise before he is ready. Thus, he is unwilling to provide you with any additional information or to allow you to visit his store. If you feel that additional information is required, please make an assumption and provide a justification. Sid is looking forward to receiving your recommendations.

B.3 Third Annual Contest: Sally Model's SM Pizza Shop

Before I outline my problem, here is a little background information that might help you better understand my specific request. When I was in college, I worked part time at a Mom and Pop pizza parlor. Everything was handmade, so I had the opportunity to learn a lot about making pizzas. After I graduated and started raising a family, I began to experiment with making different kinds of pizza. Over time, I developed a unique pizza product that was a big hit with all our friends. After my children left the nest, I decided to open a pizza shop and expose the public to my new product. The business was an immediate success in terms of customer appreciation, but not from a profit standpoint so I began to explore better ways to produce my product. With a new set of plans, I opened a second store, revised the plans, then opened a third store, and so on. Over a number of years, I refined my design to where I now have a standard concept that is implemented in all of my stores—currently numbering over 300.

I am about to undertake a major expansion program that I hope will result in the SM Pizza brand becoming a national chain of stores. Although the store design concept is firmly established, the staffing and operational aspects are still a problem. This is the area where I need your recommendations. First, let me describe our expansion philosophy, then our store operation, and finally, my request.

Our new stores will be of the DELCO variety, DELivery and Carry-Out, only. They are designed to be small and cover only a limited delivery area. This allows us to provide a high-quality product in a reasonable time. It also allows us to limit our store hours, which is a distinct advantage since we tend to hire retired individuals to manage and run each store. The limited hours are ideal for these types of employees, and it allows us to confine our sales to the dinnertime crowd. Normally, we locate our stores in suburban areas where we cater to working families who have little time to cook supper. We have found that these individuals are quite happy if we can have carry-out orders ready in 35 minutes or less and have our delivered orders in the customers' hands in 45 minutes or less. If we exceed these times, we start receiving customer complaints and a decrease in sales. Thus, these two performance measures are what we use to determine our customer-satisfaction levels.

Our store operation is really quite simple. It consists of five operations: order taking, pizza making, oven, cut and box, and delivery or carry-out. As I indicated earlier, we have a standard design concept we use in all our stores. It starts with a high-tech phone system that allows us to take the customers' orders (automatically, for many) and display the order at the pizza-making operation. We have no problems with this operation, so it does not need to be considered in your analysis.

This phone system is installed in all our current stores, and we have used it to collect information on customer demand. Although there is some minor variation from store to store, a typical order contains from one to three pizzas. Our data tell us that 64% of the orders are for one pizza; 31%, two pizzas; and 5%, three pizzas. We also have three pizza sizes (large, medium, small) and our data appear to tell us that the pizza size is not dependent on the order size (32% large; 56%, medium; and 12%, small). We only sell seven different types of pizza: 12%, Veggie; 13%, Fungus; 18%, Red Meat; 15%, Fat Free; 16%, Dairy Delight; 11%, Hot & Spicy; and 15%, The Works.

The pizza-making process is performed at a standard make table with positions for up to three people. A layout of this table is shown below.

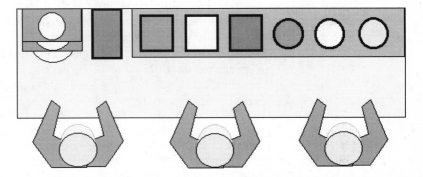

We have divided our pizza-making process into three operation steps or tasks. Some of the pizza-making process is highly confidential; therefore, we will only highlight the three tasks. The first task is the selection of the correct size pizza dough (pre-made) and the saucing of that dough. The second task adds the primary ingredients, and the third task adds the final ingredients. Although each different pizza type requires some different ingredients, we have developed our standard times based on the pizza size and task, independent of the pizza type. Since you will be using simulation for your analysis, I assume that you will need to know something about the variation of our standards. We had a co-op student conduct a preliminary study, which concluded that this variation is best described by a triangular distribution. Thus, the table entries below are the parameters for that distribution.

Task	Size		
	Large	**Medium**	**Small**
Dough and saucing	0.5, 0.7, 0.8	0.4, 0.6, 0.8	0.3, 0.5, 0.7
Primary ingredients	0.6, 0.8, 1.0	0.5, 0.7, 0.9	0.4, 0.5, 0.6
Final ingredients	0.5, 0.6, 0.7	0.4, 0.5, 0.6	0.3, 0.4, 0.5

Although there are three logical positions, we do not always allocate three individuals to the pizza-making process because the staffing cost is estimated at $6.15 per hour. The number allocated to this process should be dependent upon the demand. However, if there are three people assigned to this process, the first person performs the first task and passes the product to the second person. If the second person is busy, the product is placed between them to wait for the second person. If three people are assigned to the make table, there is only room for one product between task stations. Thus, the line will sometimes back up because the person has nowhere to place the pizza they just finished. If there is only one person assigned to this process, all three tasks are performed by that person before work starts on the next pizza. If two people are assigned to the line, they are allowed to determine the best way to share the work. We eventually would like to develop a standard assignment policy for this condition, but have not accomplished this to date. If time permits, we would appreciate your input on this matter.

The assembled pizza is then sent to the oven. We use the Magic Baker line of ovens in all our stores. These ovens are fairly standard for the industry. They are basically a simple conveyor with an enclosure of the central part of the unit, which contains the oven. The pizzas are placed on the load area of the conveyor at the left (see diagram below). They travel through the oven tunnel and emerge at the right completely cooked.

We initially had some problems with this setup when pizzas started to back up during our peak production time. The utilization of the oven is very dependent on how the pizzas are loaded, and the limited load area does not allow a place to put the back up of finished, but uncooked pizzas. We contacted Magic Baker and jointly developed a solution to this problem. This solution is confidential, but you can think of it as a slide that buffers the area between the make table and the oven. This slide has the added advantage of arranging the pizzas to make optimal use (more or less) of the oven space. We have conducted some studies on this setup in order to develop a means of estimating the capacity of specific ovens. This information should be helpful to you in developing your simulation.

When a pizza is ready to be baked and arrives at the load area, it waits until there are a known number of square inches of the load area available. It then enters the load area, and is conveyed into the oven. It is assumed to enter the oven 1.9 minutes after it enters the load area. Of course, different pizza sizes require a different number of square inches. That information is as follows:

Large	250 square inches
Medium	175 square inches
Small	115 square inches

There are currently three different sizes of ovens available from Magic Baker (Series I, II, or III). The load-area sizes for these three ovens are as follows:

Series I	435 square inches
Series II	520 square inches
Series III	605 square inches

Basically, the increased capacity is achieved by making the ovens wider. It takes 7 ½ minutes for a pizza to emerge from the oven and enter the unload area.

At the unload area, the pizza is removed by a single worker ($5.90 per hour), cut, and placed in a box. This worker also accumulates the pizzas into the original customer order. When an order is complete, it is sent to the delivery area (40%) or the carry-out area (60%). We do not have a standard for this operation as it is normally not a problem. However, I did manage to find a data file (IIE_SM_3.dat) containing some time observations. I have not had the time to look over these data, so they may contain some bad data points. I assume you can take care of this potential problem if it occurs. The worker is also required to assemble additional pizza boxes, taking about 12 seconds each, if the supply is low and time permits. If the supply gets extremely low, drivers will often assemble boxes during their idle time.

The orders sent to the carry-out area are immediately available for customer pickup. The delivery orders wait for an available driver. Currently, our drivers take only one order at a time, as it lessens the probability of a late delivery. Obviously, the delivery time is highly dependent upon the store's location. But, since we limit our delivery area, we have been able to develop reasonable data on the delivery process. You can assume that the drive-time from our store to the customer's door follows a triangular distribution with parameters 3, 5, 12. Our delivery costs are included in the estimated per-hour cost for our delivery staff ($7.15).

At this point, you should have a good understanding of our process. Now you need to understand that we staff our stores for the peak sale time, which covers about three hours. Actually, the peak demand normally occurs only for 15 to 45 minutes of these three hours. However, there tends to be a relatively high demand during the entire three-hour time period. During most of this time, all our staff is devoted to producing and delivering pizzas. The time before and after this peak is devoted to preparing for the peak and cleaning up after the peak. Remember that we only open our stores for a short period of time. So far, we have found that staffing to the peak provides just about the ideal for the before and after operations. Our marketing staff has become very good at estimating the demand, in orders per peak hour, for new stores. We will begin opening our new stores in June of next year, with the one basic problem to resolve first. Given an expected peak demand, how should we staff our make table and delivery operations and what size oven should we install?

What I would like is a table that I can reference that will tell me the following:

- Number of people at make table
- Oven size—Series I, II, or III
- Number of delivery people

You can assume that our peak demand ranges from 20 to 60 orders per hour. I would like this tool to give me the most economical option based on achieving a 90% to 95% customer satisfaction! This is important because the ovens are a major capital expense. There is an incremental capital cost of $35,000 if we use a Series II (instead of an I), and an additional $30,000 increment for using a Series III (instead of a II).

Estimates of the accuracy of the recommended configurations should be included in the report. Also, I would appreciate any other recommendations on our general operations.

Our need for such a tool is not immediate; thus, you should have plenty of time to consider the alternatives. However, our company will need to start specifying new store configurations in late March. I will be unavailable for the next several months, so you will have to make your recommendation based on the information in this request. I look forward to reading your report in March.

A Refresher on Probability and Statistics

APPENDIX C

A Refresher on Probability and Statistics

The purpose of this appendix is to provide a brief refresher on selected topics in probability and statistics necessary to understand some of the probabilistic foundations of simulation, as well as to design and analyze simulation experiments appropriately. While this material underlies many parts of the book (including every time we use a probability distribution in a model to represent some random input quantity like a time duration), it's particularly relevant to Sections 5.4, 6.5, 7.5, and Chapter 11.

We intend this appendix to serve as a very brief tutorial, and not as anything like a comprehensive treatment of these topics. There are many excellent texts on probability and statistics in general, such as Anderson, Sweeney, and Williams (1996), Devore (1995), and Hogg and Craig (1994).

Though we'll start pretty much from scratch on probability and statistics, we do assume that you're comfortable with algebraic manipulations, including summation notation. For a complete understanding of continuous random variables (Section C.2.2), you'll need to know some calculus, particularly integrals.

In Section C.1, we go over the basic ideas and terminology of probability. Section C.2 contains a discussion about random variables in general, describing discrete and continuous random variables as well as joint distributions. The notion of sampling, and the associated probabilistic structure, is discussed in Section C.3. Statistical inference, including point estimation, confidence intervals, and hypothesis testing, is covered in Sections C.4–C.6. Throughout, we'll make the discussion relevant to simulation by way of examples.

C.1 Probability Basics

An *experiment* is any activity you might undertake whose exact outcome is uncertain (until you do it and see what happens). While the term might conjure up images of high school chemistry lab, its interpretation in probability is much broader. For instance:

- Flip a "fair" coin. Will it come up tails?
- Throw a "fair" die (that's singular for "dice"). Will it be 4? Will it be an odd number? Will it be more than 2 but no more than 5?
- Drive to work tomorrow. How long will it take? How long will you be delayed because of construction? Will you be hit by an asteroid?
- Operate a call center, like the one simulated in Chapter 8, for a week. How many calls will be handled? What will be the average duration of your customers' wait on hold? How many customers will be turned away because the hold queues are full?

▪ Run a *simulation* of the call center in Chapter 8 (rather than operate the real center). Ask the same questions as we just did, except now for what happens in the simulation rather than in reality; if your simulation model is valid, you hope to get the same answers, or at least close.

The *sample space* of an experiment is the complete list of all the individual outcomes that might occur when you do your experiment. For something like flipping a coin or throwing a die, it's easy to write down the sample space. In other cases, though, the sample space could have an infinite number of possibilities, like how long it will take you to drive to work tomorrow. Fortunately, it's often possible to understand an experiment and its probabilistic structure without writing down explicitly what the sample space is.

An *event* is a subset[1] of the sample space. Events can sometimes be described by just listing out the individual outcomes defining the event, if it's simple enough. Usually, though, an event is defined by some condition on what happens in the experiment; for example, in the call center mentioned above, an event of interest might be that at least 500 calls are handled in a day. Events are often denoted as capital letters like E, F, E_1, E_2, etc. The usual set operations apply to events, such as *union* ($E \cup F$), *intersection* ($E \cap F$), and *complementation* (E^C = the set of possible outcomes *not* in E), as represented in Figure C-1.

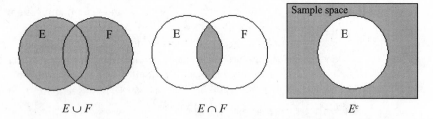

$E \cup F$ $E \cap F$ E^c

Figure C-1. Union, Intersection, and Complementation

The *probability* of an event is the relative likelihood that it will occur when you do the experiment. By convention (and for convenience of arithmetic), probabilities are always between 0 and 1. $P(E)$ denotes the probability that the event E will occur. While it may be impossible to know or derive the probability of an event, it can be interpreted as the proportion of time the event occurs in many independent repetitions of the experiment (even if you can't actually repeat the experiment). Here are some properties (among many others) of probabilities:

▪ If S is the entire sample space, then $P(S) = 1$.
▪ If $\varnothing$ is the *empty* (*null*) event, then $P(\varnothing) = 0$.
▪ $P(E^C) = 1 - P(E)$.

---

[1] In advanced treatments of probability, an event is not allowed to be *any* subset of the sample space, but only a particular kind of subset, called a *measurable* subset. For our purposes, though, all the subsets we'll consider will be measurable, so will be events.

- $P(E \cup F) = P(E) + P(F) - P(E \cap F)$.
- If E and F are *mutually exclusive* ($E \cap F = \emptyset$), then $P(E \cup F) = P(E) + P(F)$.
- If E is a subset of F (i.e., the event E implies the event F), then $P(E) \leq P(F)$.
- If $o_1, o_2, o_3, \ldots$ are the individual outcomes in the sample space (finite or infinite), then $\sum_{\text{all } i} P(o_i) = 1$.

Sometimes, the knowledge that one event occurred can alter the probability that another event also occurred. The *conditional probability* of E given F is defined as

$$P(E|F) = P(E \cap F) / P(F)$$

(assuming that $P(F) > 0$). The intuition for this is that knowing that F occurred reduces the "world" from the whole sample space down to F, and so the only relevant part of E is that part that intersects with F. This probability is then measured relative to the "size" of the reduced world, $P(F)$.

Events E and F are called *independent* if $P(E \cap F) = P(E) P(F)$. If this is so, then $P(E|F) = P(E)$, and $P(F|E) = P(F)$, by definition of conditional probability. In other words, knowing that one of two independent events has occurred tells you nothing about whether the other one occurred.

There are a lot of different kinds of events and probabilities that come up in simulation. For example, you might want to ask about the probability that:

- a part passes inspection.
- an arriving part is of priority 3.
- a service time will be between 2 and 6.
- no customers will arrive during a five-minute time interval.
- the maximum queue length during a simulation will exceed 10.
- the average time in system of parts is less than four hours.

C.2   Random Variables

Events can be defined in many different ways, and can be very complex. One way of quantifying and simplifying events is by defining *random variables* relating to them. In this section, we'll discuss the basic ideas of random variables, their two basic forms (discrete and continuous), and then consider multiple random variables defined together and their possible relationships.

C.2.1   Basics

A *random variable* is a number whose value is determined by the outcome of an experiment, so can be thought of as a quantification of an experiment. Technically, a random variable is a function defined from the sample space to the real numbers. As such, it's a rule or mapping that assigns a number to each possible outcome of the experiment. While you can sometimes define a random variable in this way, by going back to the sample space and assigning the mapping, you often just start by defining the random variable without bothering with the sample space. A reasonable way to think about a random variable is that it's a number whose value you don't know for sure before doing the experiment, but you will generally know *something* about it, like its range of possible values or its probability of being equal to something or falling in some range. Random variables are typically denoted by capital letters like X, Y, W_1, W_2, etc.

Random variables come in two basic "flavors": *discrete* and *continuous*. A discrete random variable can take on only certain separated values. For instance, the number of defective items in a shipment of 50 items would have to be an integer between 0 and 50. Another example of a discrete random variable is the number of times a part has to undergo inspection in order to pass; without further information, this random variable would be a positive integer with no upper bound. Thus, a discrete random variable could have a finite or infinite range of possible values.

A continuous random variable, on the other hand, can take on any real value, possibly bounded on the left or the right. Continuous random variables typically represent physical measurements like time or distance. There are always infinitely many possible values for a continuous random variable, even if there are limits on its value on both ends. For instance, if X is the time to process a part on a machine, the range would be $[0, \infty)$ unless we assumed that no part was allowed to stay on the machine for longer than a certain time a, in which case the range would be $[0, a]$.

In simulation, random variables are used for several different purposes. They often serve as "models" for input quantities like uncertain time durations (service or interarrival times), the number of customers in an arriving group, or which of several different part types a given arriving part is. Random variables are also used to represent output quantities like the average time in system, the number of customers served, or the maximum length of a buffer.

The probabilistic behavior of a random variable is described by its *probability distribution*. Since the nature of this distribution is somewhat different for discrete and continuous random variables, we'll consider them separately; we'll also define some basic properties of random variables, like expected value and variance.

C.2.2 Discrete

For a discrete random variable X there will be a list $x_1, x_2, \ldots$ (finite or infinite) of possible values it can take on. Note that the x_i's are fixed, nonrandom values, but the random variable X is, well, random. The *probability mass function* (PMF) is simply a function that gives the probability that X will take on each of the possible values:

$$p(x_i) = P(X = x_i)$$

for all i. Note that the statement "$X = x_i$" is an event that may or may not happen, and the PMF gives the probability that it does. The PMF may be expressed in a variety of different ways—a numerical list or table, a graph, or some kind of mathematical formula. Since the complete list of the x_i's is supposed to represent all the different possible values of X, $\sum_{\text{all } i} p(x_i) = 1$. Usually, the PMF is estimated from data, or simply assumed.

The *cumulative distribution function* (CDF) of a discrete random variable X is a function that gives the probability that X will be *less than or equal to* its argument:

$$F(x) \;=\; \sum_{\substack{\text{all } i \text{ such that} \\ x_i \le x}} p(x_i).$$

This summation is taken over all possible values x_i that are $\le$ the argument x of F. Note that $0 \le F(x) \le 1$ for all x, that $F(x) \to 0$ as $x \to -\infty$, and that $F(x) \to 1$ as $x \to +\infty$. Thus, $F(x)$ is a nondecreasing function going from 0 up to 1 as x goes from left to right. For a discrete random variable, $F(x)$ is a "step" function that's flat between adjacent possible values x_i, and takes a "jump" of height $p(x_i)$ above x_i.

The probability of an event involving a discrete random variable X generally can be found by adding up the appropriate values of the PMF. For instance,

$$P(a \le X < b) \;=\; \sum_{\substack{\text{all } i \text{ such that} \\ a \le x_i < b}} p(x_i).$$

This just says to add up the probabilities of those x_i's that are at least a but (strictly) less than b. Note that with discrete random variables, you need to be careful about weak vs. strong inequalities.

Just as data sets have a "center" measured by the average of the data, random variables have a "center" in a certain sense. The *expected value* of the discrete random variable X is defined as

$$E(X) = \sum_{\text{all } i} x_i p(x_i)$$

(this is also called the *mean* or *expectation* of X and is often denoted by μ or, if there's need to identify the random variable, μ_X). This is a weighted average of the possible values x_i for X, with the weights' being the respective probabilities of occurrence of each x_i. In this way, those x_i's with high probability of occurrence are counted more heavily than are those that are less likely to occur. If there are finitely many x_i's and each is equally likely to occur, then $E(X)$ is just the simple average of the x_i's since they all "count" the same. Despite the name, it's important to understand that $E(X)$ is *not* to be interpreted as the value of X you "expect" to get when you do the experiment defining X. Indeed, $E(X)$ might not even be a possible value of a discrete random variable X (the x_i's might be integers but, depending on the situation, $E(X)$ need not be an integer). Instead, interpret the expected value like this: do the experiment many times (technically, infinitely many times), observe a value of X each time, and compute the average of all these values of X you observe—this average will be the expectation of X.

And just as data sets have a measure of variability, so too do random variables. The *variance* of the discrete random variable X is defined as

$$Var(X) = \sum_{\text{all } i} (x_i - \mu)^2 p(x_i)$$

(often denoted σ^2 or σ_X^2), where μ is the expected value of X. This is a weighted average of the squared deviation of the possible values x_i around the expectation, with the weights' being the probability of occurrence of each x_i. The variance is a measure of the "spread" of the random variable about its mean. The units of the variance are the squares of the units of X, so people often use the positive square root of the variance (denoted σ or σ_x) as a measure of spread; this is called the *standard deviation* of X.

As mentioned earlier, there are different ways to define the PMF of a discrete random variable. Arena supports several common discrete random variables for modeling input quantities, and these are defined and described in Appendix D.

C.2.3 Continuous

A continuous random variable can take on any real value in some range. The range can be limited or unlimited on either or both ends. No matter how narrow the range may be, a continuous random variable can always take on an infinite[2] number of real values (i.e., any value in a continuum). Thus, it doesn't make sense to talk about the probability that a continuous random variable *equals* (exactly) some fixed number x; technically this probability will always be 0 even if x is within the range of X.

Instead, the probabilistic behavior of a continuous random variable is described in terms of its falling *between* two fixed values, which can be far apart or close together. The *probability density function* (PDF) of a continuous random variable X is defined to be a function $f(x)$ with the following properties and interpretation:

- $f(x) \geq 0$ for all real values x.
- The total area under $f(x)$ is 1. In calculus terminology, the total integral of $f(x)$ is 1:

$$\int_{-\infty}^{+\infty} f(x)dx = 1.$$

- For any fixed real values a and b, with $a \leq b$, the probability that X will fall between a and b is the area under $f(x)$ between a and b. In calculus terminology,

$$P(a \leq X \leq b) = \int_a^b f(x)\,dx.$$

This last property says that if we slide a slim interval left and right along the x axis (keeping the width of the interval constant), we "pick up" more area (probability) in those regions where the density is high, so we're more likely to observe lots of values of X where the density is high than where the density is low. If you think of repeating the experiment many times and making a dot on the x axis where the value of the random variable X lands each time, your dots will be highly dense where the density function is high and of low density where the density function is low (get it?). Note that the height (value) of $f(x)$ is itself *not* the probability of *anything*. Indeed, we don't require that $f(x)$ be ≤ 1, and some PDFs can rise above 1 at some points; what's required is that the total

---

[2] More precisely, an *uncountably* infinite number of values, for those of you who are concerned with the different sizes of infinity.

area under the PDF be equal to 1. For example, consider a uniform distribution between 3.0 and 3.1. In order for the total area under the PDF to be equal to 1, the height $f(x)$ for all possible values of x (between 3.0 and 3.1) needs to be equal to 10. Also, we could specify that $f(x) = 0$ for values of x in or outside of some range, which would mean that these ranges are impossible for the random variable X to fall in. Unlike discrete random variables, we can be sloppy with whether the endpoints of the ranges over which we want probabilities are defined by weak or strong inequalities (i.e., $<$ is the same as $\leq$, and $>$ is the same as $\geq$).

The cumulative distribution function of a continuous random variable X has the same basic definition and interpretation as for discrete random variables: $F(x) = P(X \leq x)$ for all real values x. Thus, $F(x)$ is the probability that X will land on or to the left of x. However, computing it requires getting the area under the density function to the left of x:

$$F(x) = \int_{-\infty}^{x} f(t)\, dt .$$

Depending on the form of the PDF $f(x)$, the CDF $F(x)$ may or may not be expressible as a closed-form formula involving x. For instance, the exponential and Weibull distributions (see Appendix D for definitions) do have simple formulas for the CDF, but the general gamma and normal distributions do not. If the CDF is not expressible as a formula, its evaluation must be left to some numerical method or a table (which is why every statistics book has a table of normal-distribution areas). As in the discrete case, the CDF $F(x)$ for a continuous random variable rises from 0 at the extreme left to 1 at the extreme right, but in this case is a continuous function rather than a step function. Since $f(x)$ is the slope (derivative) of $F(x)$, those regions on the x axis where $F(x)$ rises steeply are those regions where we'd get a lot of observations on X; conversely, where $F(x)$ is relatively flat, we won't see many observations on X.

The expected value of a continuous random variable is, as in the discrete case, one measure of the "center" of the distribution and is the average of infinitely many observations on X. It's defined as

$$E(X) = \int_{-\infty}^{+\infty} x f(x)\, dx$$

and often denoted as μ or μ_x. Roughly, this is a weighted "average" of the x values, using the density as the weighting function to count more heavily those values of x around which the density is high. The variance of X, measuring its "spread," is

$$Var(X) = \int_{-\infty}^{+\infty} (x - \mu)^2 f(x)\, dx$$

and often denoted σ^2 or σ_X^2; the positive square root of the variance (denoted σ or σ_x) is the standard deviation.

Arena supports several different continuous random variables for use in modeling random input quantities; these are defined and discussed in Appendix D.

C.2.4 Joint Distributions, Covariance, Correlation, and Independence

So far we've considered random variables only one at a time. But sometimes they naturally come in pairs or triples or even longer ordered sequences (having the wonderful name *tuples*), which are called *jointly distributed* random variables or *random vectors*. For instance, in the input modeling for a job-shop simulation, an arriving order might have random variables representing the part type (dictating its route through the shop), priority, and processing times at the steps along its route. On the output side, the simulation might generate a sequence $W_1, W_2, W_3, \ldots$ representing the times in system of the finished parts in order of their exit. One issue that naturally arises, and which can affect how we model and analyze such random vectors, is whether the random variables composing them are related to each other, and if so, how.

To address this, we'll start with the complete probabilistic representation of random vectors. In order to keep things at least partially digestible, we'll consider just a pair (two-tuple) of random variables (X_1, X_2), but things extend in the obvious way to higher dimensions. The *joint CDF* of (X_1, X_2) is a function of two variables defined as

$$F(x_1, x_2) = P(X_1 \leq x_1 \text{ and } X_2 \leq x_2)$$

for all pairs (x_1, x_2) of real numbers. Often the word "and" is replaced by just a comma:

$$F(x_1, x_2) = P(X_1 \leq x_1, \ X_2 \leq x_2).$$

If the random variables are both discrete, the *joint PMF* is

$$p(x_1, x_2) = P(X_1 = x_1, \ X_2 = x_2).$$

If the random variables are both continuous, the *joint PDF* is denoted $f(x_1, x_2)$, which you can visualize as some kind of surface floating above the (x_1, x_2) plane, and which has total volume under it equal to one. The interpretation of the joint PDF in the continuous case is this: the probability that X_1 will fall between a_1 and b_1, and, simultaneously, that X_2 will fall between a_2 and b_2, is the volume under the joint PDF above the rectangle $[a_1, b_1] \times [a_2, b_2]$ in the (x_1, x_2) plane. In calculus notation, this interpretation is expressed as

$$P(a_1 \leq X_1 \leq b_1, a_2 \leq X_2 \leq b_2) = \int_{a_1}^{b_1} \int_{a_2}^{b_2} f(x_1, x_2) \, dx_2 \, dx_1.$$

The joint distribution (expressed as either the CDF, PMF, or PDF) contains a *lot* of information about the random vector. In practice, it's usually not possible to know, or even estimate, the complete joint distribution. Fortunately, we can usually address the issues we need to without having to know or estimate the full-blown joint distribution.

Given a joint distribution of two random variables, we can derive the individual, or *marginal*[3], distributions of each of the random variables on their own. In the jointly discrete case, the marginal PMF of X_1 is, for all possible values x_{1i} of X_1,

---

[3] The term "marginal" is not to suggest that these distributions are of questionable moral integrity. Rather, it simply refers to that fact that, in two dimensions for the jointly discrete case, if the joint probabilities are arranged in a table, then summing the rows and columns results in values on the margins of the table, which will be the individual "marginal" distributions.

$$p_{X_1}(x_{1i}) = P(X_1 = x_{1i}) = \sum_{\text{all } x_{2j}} p(x_{1i}, x_{2j})$$

and the marginal CDF of X_1 is, for all real values of x,

$$F_{X_1}(x) = \sum_{\substack{\text{all } i \text{ such that} \\ x_{1i} \leq x}} p_{X_1}(x_{1i})$$

(symmetric definitions apply for X_2). In the jointly continuous case, the marginal PDF of X_1 is

$$f_{X_1}(x_1) = \int_{-\infty}^{+\infty} f(x_1, x_2) \, dx_2$$

and the marginal CDF of X_1 is

$$F_{X_1}(x) = \int_{-\infty}^{x} f_{X_1}(t) \, dt$$

(symmetrically for X_2). Note that we can get the marginal distributions in this way from the joint distribution, but knowledge of the marginal distributions is generally not sufficient to determine what the joint distribution is (unless X_1 and X_2 are independent random variables, as discussed below).

The *covariance* between the components X_1 and X_2 of a random vector is defined as

$$Cov(X_1, X_2) = E[(X_1 - E(X_1))(X_2 - E(X_2))].$$

Note that the quantity inside the [ ] is a random variable with its own distribution, etc., and the covariance is the expectation of this random variable. The covariance is a measure of the (linear) relationship between X_1 and X_2, and can be positive, zero, or negative. If the joint distribution is shaped so that, when X_1 is above its mean, then X_2 tends to be above its mean, then the covariance is positive; this implies that a small X_1 tends to be associated with a small X_2 as well. On the other hand, if large X_1 is associated with small X_2 (and vice versa), then the covariance will be negative. If there is no tendency for X_1 and X_2 to occur jointly in agreement or disagreement over being big or small, then the covariance will be zero. Thus, the covariance tells us whether the two random variables in the vector are (linearly) related or not, and if they are, whether the relationship is positive or negative.

However, the covariance's magnitude is difficult to interpret since it depends on the units of measurement. To rectify this, the *correlation* between X_1 and X_2 is defined as

$$Cor(X_1, X_2) = \frac{Cov(X_1, X_2)}{\sigma_{X_1} \sigma_{X_2}}.$$

Clearly, the correlation has the same sign as the covariance (or is zero along with the covariance), so the direction of any relationship is also indicated by the sign of the correlation. Also, the correlation is a dimensionless quantity (i.e., it has no units of measurement and will be the same regardless of what units of measurement you choose for X_1 and X_2). What's perhaps not obvious (but it's true) is that the correlation will always fall between –1 and +1, giving its magnitude universal emotional impact. Without knowing anything about the situation, you can say that a correlation of 0.96 or –0.98 is quite strong, whereas a correlation of 0.1 or –0.08 is pretty weak. Thus, the correlation provides a very meaningful way to express both direction and strength of linear[4] relationship between random variables.

The random variables X_1 and X_2 are called *independent* if their joint CDF always factors into the product of their marginal CDFs:

$$F(x_1, x_2) = F_{X_1}(x_1) \, F_{X_2}(x_2) \text{ for all } (x_1, x_2)$$

Equivalently, independence can be defined in terms of similar factorization of the joint PMF into the product of the marginal PMFs, or factorization of the joint PDF into the product of the marginal PDFs. Here are some properties of independent random variables X_1 and X_2:

- In words, independence means that knowing the value that X_1 hit tells you nothing about where X_2 may have landed.
- If two random variables are independent, then they will also be uncorrelated. The converse, however, is generally not true (unless the random variables have a joint normal distribution). Admittedly, the counterexamples are pathological, but they're there.
- For independent random variables, $E(X_1 X_2) = E(X_1) \, E(X_2)$.
- Independence of random variables is a pretty big deal in probability and statistics since, believe it or not, the factorization property in the above definition renders a whole lot of derivations possible where they would be totally impossible otherwise.
- Maybe because independence is so important analytically, it's awfully tempting just to assume it when you're not too sure it's justified.[5] All we can do is alert you to the fact that this assumption is there, and violating it usually has unknown ramifications.

In the case of more than two random variables in the random vector, independence means that the joint CDF (or PMF or PDF) factors into the product of the single marginal counterparts; this implies pairwise independence, but pairwise independence does not necessarily imply independence of all the random variables.

The issues of correlation and independence of random variables comes up in at least a couple of places in simulation. On the input side, we usually model the various random quantities driving the simulation as being independent, and simply generate them accordingly. But there sometimes might be some kind of dependence present that we need to capture for the sake of model validity; Section 5.4.7 discusses this briefly and gives references. On the output side, a run of a simulation over time typically produces a

---

[4] The reason we keep hedging the language with this "linear" qualifier for the covariance and correlation is that these measures may fail to pick up nonlinear relationships that might be present. However, in most modeling applications the relationships will be fairly close to linear, at least over a restricted range.

[5] In this case, some people have been known to refer to this as the Declaration of Independence since that's pretty much all it is.

sequence of output random variables that may be correlated, perhaps heavily, among themselves. This complicates proper statistical analysis of such data, and care must be taken to design the runs appropriately and use the output properly; Section 7.5 gets into some of the particular problems and remedies.

C.3 Sampling and Sampling Distributions

The main purpose of statistical analysis is to estimate or infer something concerning a large *population*, assumed to be too large to look at completely, by doing calculations with a *sample* from that population. Sometimes it's more convenient to think of sampling from some ongoing process rather than from a static population. The mathematical basis for this is that there is a random variable (or maybe random vector) with some distribution, which governs the behavior of the population; in this sense, the population can be thought of as the random variable and its distribution, and a sample is just a sequence of independent and identically distributed (IID) observations, or *realizations*, on this random variable. Whichever the case, you don't know the parameters of the population or its governing distribution, and you need to take a sample to make estimates of quantities or test hypotheses.

There's been a lot of statistical theory worked out to do this—we'll describe just a little of it, pertinent to the simulation examples in the book, and refer you to the references mentioned at the beginning of this appendix for more. This statistical theory assumes that the sample has been taken *randomly*—that is, so that every possible sample of whatever size you're taking had the same chance of being the sample actually chosen. The link between sampling for statistical inference and the probability theory discussed so far in this appendix is that "the experiment" referred to earlier is in this case the act of taking a random sample. The outcome is a particular data set (one of many possible) from which various quantities are computed, which clearly depend on the sample that happened to have been obtained.

In simulation, sampling boils down to making some runs of your model, since random input makes for random output. Assuming that the random-number generator is operating properly and being used correctly, the randomness of the sample is guaranteed; this is to be contrasted with physical or laboratory experiments where great pains are often taken to insure that the sample obtained is really random.

Let $X_1, X_2, \ldots, X_n$ be a random sample observed from some population. Equivalently, these data are IID observations on some underlying random variable X whose distribution governs the population. In simulation, this arises on the input side where the data are observations from the real system to which some distribution is to be fitted to serve as an input to the simulation (as in Section 5.4). It also arises on the output side where the data points are summary statistics across n IID replications of the simulation run (as in Sections 6.5.3-6.5.5), or are perhaps batch means from within a single long run of a steady-state simulation (as in Section 7.5.3). Let $\mu = E(X)$, $\sigma^2 = Var(X)$, and $p = P(X \in B)$ where B is a set defining some "distinguishing characteristic" of X (like being more than 25). As we'll formalize in Section C.4, it's reasonable to "estimate" these three quantities, respectively, by:

- The sample mean:
$$\overline{X} = \frac{\sum_{i=1}^{n} X_i}{n}.$$

- The sample variance:
$$s^2 = \frac{\sum_{i=1}^{n}(X_i - \overline{X})}{n-1}.$$

- The sample proportion:
$$\hat{p} = \frac{\text{number of } X_i\text{'s that are in } B}{n}.$$

(Other population/distribution parameters, and estimates of them, are certainly possible, but these three will serve our purposes.) Note that each of these quantities can be computed from knowledge of the sample data only (i.e., there are no population/distribution parameters involved); such quantities are called (*sample*) *statistics*. The important thing to remember about statistics is that they are based on a random sample and, as such, are themselves random—you got your sample and we got ours (of the same size *n*), which were probably different samples so probably produced different numerical values of the statistics. Thus, statistics are actually random variables themselves, relative to the "experiment" of taking a sample.

Accordingly, statistics have their own distributions (sometimes called *sampling distributions*), expectations, variances, etc. Here are some results about the distributions of the above three statistics:

- $E(\overline{X}) = \mu$ and $Var(\overline{X}) = \sigma^2/n$. If the underlying distribution of X is normal (see Appendix D for distribution definitions), then the distribution of $\overline{X}$ is also normal, written $\overline{X} \sim N(\mu, \sigma/\sqrt{n})$; we'll use the convention that the second "argument" of the normal-distribution notation is the standard deviation rather than the variance. Even if the underlying distribution of X is not normal, the central limit theorem says that, under fairly mild conditions, the distribution of $\overline{X}$ will be approximately normal for large *n*.

- $E(s^2) = s^2$. If the underlying distribution is normal, then the quantity $(n-1)s^2/\sigma^2$ has a chi-square distribution with $n-1$ degrees of freedom (DF), denoted χ^2_{n-1}. Any standard statistics book will have a definition and discussion of this distribution.

- $E(\hat{p}) = p$ and $Var(\hat{p}) = p(1-p)/n$. For large *n*, the distribution of $\hat{p}$ is approximately normal.

The importance of sampling distributions is that they provide the basis for estimation and inference about the population/distribution parameters.

C.4   Point Estimation

Quantities that are characteristic of the population/distribution, such as μ, σ^2, and p, are called *parameters*. Unless you somehow know (or assume) everything about the population/distribution, you won't know the values of parameters. Instead, the best you can usually do is to *estimate* these parameters with sample statistics, as described in Section

C.3. Since we're estimating a parameter by just a single number (rather than an interval), this is called *point estimation*. While point estimates on their own frankly aren't worth much (since you don't know how close or stable or generally good they are), they're a start and can have some properties worth mentioning.

A statistic serving as a point estimator is called *unbiased* for some population/distribution parameter if E(point estimator) = parameter. In words, this says that if we took a lot of samples and computed the point estimator from each sample, the average of these estimators would be equal to the parameter being estimated. Clearly, this is a comforting property, and, from the sampling-distribution results cited in Section C.3, is one enjoyed by $\overline{X}$ for μ, s^2 for σ^2, and $\hat{p}$ for p.

While unbiasedness is nice, it doesn't speak to the stability of the estimator across samples. Other things (like unbiasedness) being equal, we'd prefer an estimator that has low variance since it's more likely to be close to the parameter being estimated. The lower-variance estimator is called more *efficient*; this term is actually analogous to economic efficiency in sampling since a more efficient estimator will require a smaller sample for its variance to come down to a desired level.

Related to efficiency is the notion of *consistency* of an estimator. While there are several different kinds of consistency, the basic idea is that, as the sample size n grows, the estimator gets "better" in some sense (lack of this property would certainly be upsetting). For instance, we'd like the variance of an estimator to decline, hopefully to zero and hopefully quickly, as the sample size is increased. Taking a glance at the expressions for the variances of $\overline{X}$, s^2, and $\hat{p}$ in Section C.3 shows that they all satisfy this property.

C.5   Confidence Intervals

Most of the commonly used point estimators have good properties. But they all have variability associated with them, so will generally "miss" the parameter they're estimating. A *confidence interval* provides one way of quantifying this imprecision. The goal of a confidence-interval procedure is to form an interval, with endpoints determined by the sample, that will contain, or "cover" the target parameter with a prespecified (high) probability called the *confidence level*. The usual notation is that the confidence level is $1 - \alpha$, resulting in a $100(1 - \alpha)$ percent confidence interval.

Using the sampling-distribution results, as well as similar results found in statistics books like those referenced at the beginning of this appendix, the following confidence intervals for several common parameter-estimation problems have been derived:

- The population/distribution expectation μ: The confidence interval is:

$$\overline{X} \pm t_{n-1, 1-\alpha/2} \frac{s}{\sqrt{n}}$$

where $t_{n-1, 1-\alpha/2}$ is the point that has below it probability $1 - \alpha/2$ for Student's t distribution with $n - 1$ DF (this point is called the upper $1 - \alpha/2$ *critical point* for this distribution). Proper coverage probability for this interval assumes that the underlying distribution is normal, but the central limit theorem ensures at least approximately correct coverage for large n.

- The population/distribution variance σ^2: The confidence interval is

$$\left(\frac{(n-1)s^2}{\chi^2_{n-1,1-\alpha/2}}, \frac{(n-1)s^2}{\chi^2_{n-1,\alpha/2}} \right)$$

where $\chi^2_{n-1,1-\alpha/2}$ is the upper $1 - \alpha/2$ critical point for the chi-square distribution with $n - 1$ DF. This interval assumes a normal population/distribution.

- The population/distribution standard deviation σ: Due to the definition and interpretation of confidence intervals, we can simply take the square roots of the endpoints of the preceding interval:

$$\left(\sqrt{\frac{(n-1)s^2}{\chi^2_{n-1,1-\alpha/2}}}, \sqrt{\frac{(n-1)s^2}{\chi^2_{n-1,\alpha/2}}} \right)$$

- The difference between the expectations of two populations/distributions, $\mu_A - \mu_B$: There are different approaches and resulting formulas for this, discussed in Section 11.4.1. One important issue in deciding which approach to use is whether the sampling from the two populations/distributions was done independently or not. The important interpretation is that if this interval contains 0, the conclusion is that we cannot discern a statistically significant (at level α) difference between the two expectations; if the interval misses 0 then there appears to be a significant difference between the expectations.

- The ratio of the variances of two populations/distributions, σ_A^2/σ_B^2: The confidence interval is

$$\left(\frac{s_A^2 / s_B^2}{F_{n_A-1,n_B-1,1-\alpha/2}}, \frac{s_A^2 / s_B^2}{F_{n_A-1,n_B-1,\alpha/2}} \right)$$

where the subscripts A and B on the sample variances and sample sizes indicate the corresponding population/distribution, and $F_{k_1,k_2,1-\alpha/2}$ denotes the upper $1 - \alpha/2$ critical point of the F distribution with (k_1, k_2) DF. A normal population/distribution is assumed for this interval. We conclude that there is a statistically significant difference between the variance parameters if and only if this interval does not contain 1.

- The ratio of the standard deviations of two populations/distributions, σ_A/σ_B: Just take the square root of the endpoints in the preceding confidence interval; conclude that the standard-deviation parameters differ if and only if this interval misses 1.

- The population/distribution proportion p: The confidence interval is

$$\hat{p} \pm z_{1-\alpha/2} \sqrt{\frac{\hat{p}(1-\hat{p})}{n}}$$

where $z_{1-\alpha/2}$ is the upper $1 - \alpha/2$ critical point of the standard (mean = 0, standard deviation = 1) normal distribution. This is an approximate-coverage interval, valid for large n (one definition, among many, of "large n" is that both $n\hat{p}$ and $n(1-\hat{p})$ be at least 5 or so).

- The difference between the proportions of two populations/processes $p_A - p_B$: The confidence interval is

$$\hat{p}_A - \hat{p}_B \pm z_{1-\alpha/2} \sqrt{\frac{\hat{p}_A(1-\hat{p}_A)}{n_A} + \frac{\hat{p}_B(1-\hat{p}_B)}{n_B}}$$

with the obvious interpretation of the subscripts A and B. Both sample sizes need to be "large," as described in the preceding point.

C.6 Hypothesis Tests

In addition to estimating, either via a point or an interval, population/distribution parameters, you might want to use the data to "test" some assertion made about the population/distribution. These questions and procedures are called *hypothesis tests*, and there are many, many such tests that people have devised for a wide variety of applications. We won't make any attempt to give a complete treatment of hypothesis testing, but only describe the general idea and give a couple of simulation-specific examples. For derivation and specific formulas for doing hypothesis tests, please see a statistics book like those we mentioned at the beginning of this appendix.

The assertion to be tested is called the *null hypothesis*, usually denoted H_0. Often, it represents the status quo or the historical situation, or what is being claimed by somebody else. The denial (opposite) of the null hypothesis is the *alternate hypothesis*, which we'll denote H_1. The intent of hypothesis testing is to develop a decision rule for using the data to choose either H_0 or H_1 and be as sure as we can that whichever we declare to be true really *is* the truth.

Barring complete information about the population/distribution, though, we can never be 100% sure that we're making the right choice between H_0 and H_1. If H_0 is really the truth yet we reject it in favor of H_1, we've committed a *type I error*. But if H_1 is really the truth yet we don't reject H_0, we've made a *type II error*. Hypothesis tests are set up to allow you to specify the probability α of a type I error, while doing the best to minimize the probability β of a type II error. If you demand a really small α, you'll get it but at the cost of a higher β (though the relationship between the two is not simple) unless you can go collect some more data. In hypothesis testing, H_0 and H_1 are not given equal treatment—the benefit of the doubt is given to H_0, so if we reject H_0, we're making a fairly strong and confident decision that H_1 is true. But if we can't mount enough evidence against H_0 to reject it, we haven't necessarily "proved" that H_0 is the truth—we've just failed to find evidence against it. The reason for failing to reject H_0 could, of course, be that it's really true. But another reason for failing to reject H_0 is that we just don't have enough data to "see" that H_0 is false.

Another way to set up and carry out a test is not to make a firm yes/no decision, but rather quantify how "certain" you are about which hypothesis is correct. The *p-value* of a data set in a test is the probability of getting a data set, if H_0 is true, that's more in favor of H_1 than the one you got. So if the p-value is tiny, you're saying that it's very hard to get information more in favor of H_1 than the information you already have in your data set, so that the evidence for H_1 is strong. If the p-value is large, say 0.3 or 0.6, then it's entirely possible that just by chance you'd get data more in favor of H_1, so there's no particular reason to suspect H_0. If the p-value is "on the edge," say something like 0.1, you're left with an inconclusive result, which is sometimes all you can say with your data.

One place in simulation that hypothesis tests come up is in fitting input probability distributions to observed data on the input quantity being modeled (Section 5.4). Here, H_0 is the assertion that a particular candidate fitted distribution adequately explains the data. If H_0 is not rejected, then you have no evidence that this distribution is wrong, so you might go with it. The Arena Input Analyzer has two different tests for this built in, the chi-square test and the Kolmogorov-Smirnov test. These tests basically ask how close the fitted distribution is to the empirical distribution defined directly by the data; for details on how these and other *goodness-of-fit tests* work, see Chapter 6 of Law and Kelton (1991).

Another place in simulation that a hypothesis test comes up is on the output side. If there are several (more than two) models you're comparing on the basis of some selected output performance measure, a natural question is whether there's any difference at all among the means of this measure across the different models. A collection of specific problems and techniques, called *analysis of variance* (ANOVA), is a standard part of any statistics book, so we won't go into its inner workings here. The null hypothesis is that all the means across the different models are the same; if you do not reject this, you have no evidence of any difference on this measure that the different models make. But if you reject H_0, you're saying that there *is* some difference somewhere among the means, though not that they're all unique and different. A natural question in this case is then precisely which means differ from which other ones, sometimes called *multiple comparisons* in ANOVA. There have been several different methods developed for attacking this problem, three of which are due to Bonferroni, Scheffé, and Tukey. The Arena Output Analyzer has built-in facility for carrying out an ANOVA test, including these multiple-comparisons methods.

Arena's Probability Distributions

APPENDIX D

Arena's Probability Distributions

Arena contains a set of built-in functions for generating random variates from the commonly used probability distributions. These distributions appear on pull-down menus in many Arena modules where they're likely to be used. They also match the distributions in the Arena Input Analyzer. This appendix describes all of the Arena distributions.

Each of the distributions in Arena has one or more parameter values associated with it. You must specify these parameter values to define the distribution fully. The number, meaning, and order of the parameter values depend on the distribution. A summary of the distributions (in alphabetical order) and parameter values is given in Table D-1.

Table D-1. Summary of Arena's Probability Distributions

Distribution			Parameter Values
Beta	BETA	BE	Beta, Alpha
Continuous	CONT	CP	$CumP_1, Val_1, \ldots CumP_n, Val_n$
Discrete	DISC	DP	$CumP_1, Val_1, \ldots CumP_n, Val_n$
Erlang	ERLA	ER	ExpoMean, k
Exponential	EXPO	EX	Mean
Gamma	GAMM	GA	Beta, Alpha
Johnson	JOHN	JO	Gamma, Delta, Lambda, Xi
Lognormal	LOGN	RL	LogMean, LogStd
Normal	NORM	RN	Mean, StdDev
Poisson	POIS	PO	Mean
Triangular	TRIA	TR	Min, Mode, Max
Uniform	UNIF	UN	Min, Max
Weibull	WEIB	WE	Beta, Alpha

The distributions can be specified by using one of two formats: you can select a single format, or you can mix formats within the same model. The format is determined by the name used to specify the distribution. The primary format is selected by using either the variable's full name or a four-letter abbreviation of the name consisting of the first four letters. For example, UNIFORM or UNIF specifies the uniform distribution in the primary format. The secondary format is selected by specifying the distribution with a two-letter abbreviation. For example, UN specifies the uniform distribution in the secondary format. The names are not case-sensitive.

In the primary format, you explicitly enter the parameters of the distribution as arguments of the distribution. For example, UNIFORM(10, 25) specifies a uniform distribution with a minimum value of 10 and a maximum value of 25. In the alternative format, you indirectly define the parameters of the distribution by referencing a parameter set within the PARAMETERS element from the Elements panel. For example, UN(DelayTime) specifies a uniform distribution with the minimum and maximum values defined in the parameter set named DelayTime. The main advantage of the indirect method of defining the parameters provided by the alternative format is that the parameters of the distribution can be modified from within the PARAMETERS element.

The random-number stream, which is used by Arena in generating the sample, can also be specified in both formats. In the primary format, you enter the stream number as the last argument following the parameter value list. For example, UNIFORM(10,25,2) specifies a sample from a uniform distribution using random-number stream 2. In the secondary format, you enter the random-number stream as a second argument following the identifier for the parameter set. For example, UN(DelayTime,PTimeStream) specifies a sample from a uniform distribution using random-number stream PTimeStream.

In the following pages, we provide a summary of each of the distributions supported by Arena, listed in alphabetical order for easy reference. The summary includes the primary and secondary formats for specifying the distribution and a brief description of the distribution. This description includes the density or mass function, parameters, range, mean, variance, and typical applications for the distribution.

Beta(β, α)   **BETA(Beta, Alpha) or**
                                     BE(ParamSet)

Probability
Density
Function

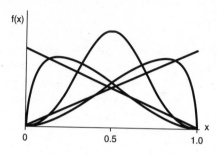

$$f(x) = \begin{cases} \dfrac{x^{\beta-1}(1-x)^{\alpha-1}}{B(\beta,\alpha)} & \text{for } 0 < x < 1 \\[2ex] 0 & \text{otherwise} \end{cases}$$

where B is the complete beta function given by

$$B(\beta,\alpha) = \int_0^1 t^{\beta-1}(1-t)^{\alpha-1}\,dt$$

Parameters   Shape parameters Beta(β) and Alpha (α) specified as positive real numbers.

Range $[0, 1]$ (Can also be transformed to $[a,b]$ as described below)

Mean

$$\frac{\beta}{\beta+\alpha}$$

Variance

$$\frac{\beta\alpha}{(\beta+\alpha)^2(\beta+\alpha+1)}$$

Applications   Because of its ability to take on a wide variety of shapes, this distribution is often used as a rough model in the absence of data. Because the range of the beta distribution is from 0 to 1, the sample X can be transformed to the scaled beta sample Y with the range from a to b by using the equation $Y = a + (b - a)X$. The beta is often used to represent random proportions, such as the proportion of defective items in a lot.

Continuous	CONTINUOUS(CumP$_1$, Val$_1$, . . ., CumP$_n$, Val$_n$) or
$(c_1, x_1, . . ., c_n, x_n)$	CONT(CumP$_1$, Val$_1$, . . ., CumP$_n$, Val$_n$) or CP(ParamSet)

Probability Density Function

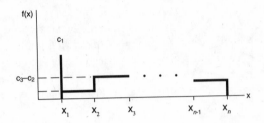

Cumulative Distribution Function

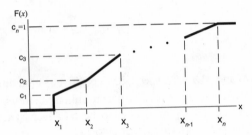

$$
f(x) = \begin{cases}
c_1 & \text{if } x = x_1 \text{ (a mass of probability } c_1 \text{ at } x_1) \\
c_j - c_{j-1} & \text{if } x_{j-1} \le x < x_j, \text{ for } j = 2, 3, \ldots, n \\
0 & \text{if } x < x_1 \text{ or } x \ge x_n
\end{cases}
$$

Parameters   The CONTINUOUS function in Arena returns a sample from a user-defined distribution. Pairs of cumulative probabilities c_j (= CumP$_j$) and associated values x_j (= Val$_j$) are specified. The sample returned will be a real number between x_1 and x_n, and will be less than or equal to each x_j with corresponding cumulative probability c_j. The x_j's must increase with j. The c_j's must all be between 0 and 1, must increase with j, and c_n must be 1.

The cumulative distribution function $F(x)$ is piecewise linear with "corners" defined by $F(x_j) = c_j$ for $j = 1, 2, \ldots, n$. Thus, for $j \ge 2$, the returned value will be in the interval $(x_{j-1}, x_j]$ with probability $c_j - c_{j-1}$; given that it is in this interval, it will be distributed uniformly over it.

You must take care to specify c_1 and x_1 to get the effect you want at the left edge of the distribution. The CONTINUOUS function will return (exactly) the value x_1 with probability c_1. Thus, if you specify $c_1 > 0$ this actually results in a mixed discrete-continuous distribution returning (exactly) x_1 with probability c_1, and with probability $1 - c_1$ a continuous random variate on $(x_1, x_n]$ as described above. The graph of $F(x)$ above depicts a situation where $c_1 > 0$. On the other hand, if you specify $c_1 = 0$, you will get a (truly) continuous distribution on $[x_1, x_n]$ as described above, with no "mass" of probability at x_1; in this case the graph of $F(x)$ would be continuous, with no jump at x_1.

As an example use of the CONTINUOUS function, suppose you have collected a set of data $x_1, x_2, \ldots, x_n$ (assumed to be sorted into increasing order) on, say, service times. Rather than using a fitted theoretical distribution from the Input Analyzer (Section 5.4), you want to generate service times in the simulation "directly" from the data, consistent with how they're spread out and bunched up, and between the minimum x_1 and the maximum x_n you observed. Assuming that you don't want a "mass" of probability sitting directly on x_1, you'd specify $c_1 = 0$ and then $c_j = (j-1)/(n-1)$ for $j = 2, 3, \ldots, n$.

Range $[x_1, x_n]$

Applications   The continuous empirical distribution is used to incorporate empirical data for continuous random variables directly into the model. This distribution can be used as an alternative to a theoretical distribution that has been fitted to the data, such as in data that have a multimodal profile or where there are significant outliers.

Discrete	DISCRETE($CumP_1$, Val_1, . . ., $CumP_n$, Val_n) or
$(c_1, x_1, . . ., c_n, x_n)$	DISC($CumP_1$, Val_1, . . ., $CumP_n$, Val_n) or DP(ParamSet)

Probability Mass Function

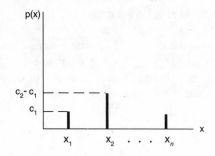

$$p(x_j) = c_j - c_{j-1}$$

where $c_0 = 0$

Cumulative Distribution Function

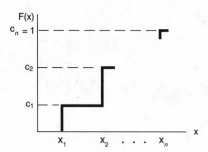

Parameters   The DISCRETE function in Arena returns a sample from a user-defined discrete probability distribution. The distribution is defined by the set of n possible discrete values (denoted by $x_1, x_2, . . ., x_n$) that can be returned by the function and the cumulative probabilities (denoted by $c_1, c_2, . . ., c_n$) associated with these discrete values. The cumulative probability (c_j) for x_j is defined as the probability of obtaining a value that is less than or equal to x_j. Hence, c_j is equal to the sum of $p(x_k)$ for k going from 1 to j. By definition, $c_n = 1$.

Range $\{x_1, x_2, . . ., x_n\}$

Applications   The discrete empirical distribution is used to incorporate discrete empirical data directly into the model. This distribution is frequently used for discrete assignments such as the job type, the visitation sequence, or the batch size for an arriving entity.

Erlang(β, k)   **ERLANG(ExpMean, k) or ERLA(ExpMean, k) or ER(ParamSet)**

Probability Density Function

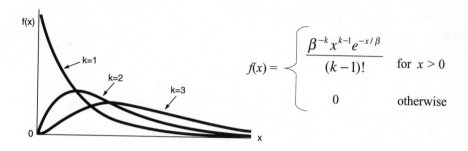

$$f(x) = \begin{cases} \dfrac{\beta^{-k} x^{k-1} e^{-x/\beta}}{(k-1)!} & \text{for } x > 0 \\ \\ 0 & \text{otherwise} \end{cases}$$

Parameters   If $X_1, X_2, \ldots, X_k$ are IID exponential random variables, then the sum of these k samples has an Erlang-k distribution. The mean (β) of each of the component exponential distributions and the number of exponential random variables (k) are the parameters of the distribution. The exponential mean is specified as a positive real number, and k is specified as a positive integer.

Range $[0, +\infty)$

Mean $k\beta$

Variance $k\beta^2$

Applications   The Erlang distribution is used in situations in which an activity occurs in successive phases and each phase has an exponential distribution. For large k, the Erlang approaches the normal distribution. The Erlang distribution is often used to represent the time required to complete a task. The Erlang distribution is a special case of the gamma distribution in which the shape parameter, α, is an integer (k).

Exponential(β)   **EXPONENTIAL(Mean) or EXPO(Mean) or EX(ParamSet)**

Probability Density Function

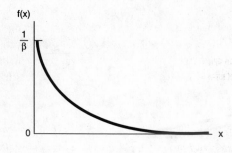

$$f(x) = \begin{cases} \dfrac{1}{\beta} e^{-x/\beta} & \text{for } x > 0 \\[2mm] 0 & \text{otherwise} \end{cases}$$

Parameters   The mean (β) specified as a positive real number.

Range $[0, +\infty)$

Mean β

Variance β^2

Applications   This distribution is often used to model interevent times in random arrival and break-down processes, but it is generally inappropriate for modeling process delay times.

Gamma(β, α)   **GAMMA(Beta, Alpha) or GAMM(Beta, Alpha) or**
                                     GA(ParamSet)

Probability
Density
Function

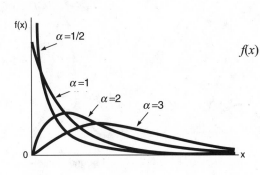

$$f(x) = \begin{cases} \dfrac{\beta^{-\alpha} x^{\alpha-1} e^{-x/\beta}}{\Gamma(\alpha)} & \text{for } x > 0 \\ \\ 0 & \text{otherwise} \end{cases}$$

where Γ is the complete gamma function given by
$$\Gamma(\alpha) = \int_0^\infty t^{\alpha-1} e^{-t}\, dt$$

Parameters   Shape parameter (α) and scale parameter (β) specified as positive real values.

Range $[0, +\infty)$

Mean $\alpha\beta$

Variance $\alpha\beta^2$

Applications For integer shape parameters, the gamma is the same as the Erlang distribution. The gamma is often used to represent the time required to complete some task (e.g., a machining time or machine repair time).

Johnson

JOHNSON(Gamma, Delta, Lambda, Xi) or JOHN(Gamma, Delta, Lambda, Xi) or JO(ParamSet)

Probability
Density
Function

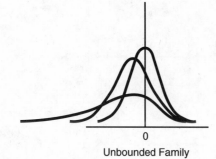

Unbounded Family

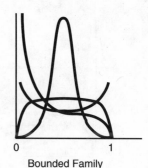

Bounded Family

Parameters   Gamma shape parameter (γ), Delta shape parameter ($\delta > 0$), Lambda scale parameter ($\lambda > 0$), and Xi location parameter (ξ).

Range $(-\infty, +\infty)$ Unbounded Family

$[\xi, \xi + \lambda]$ Bounded Family

Applications   The flexibility of the Johnson distribution allows it to fit many data sets. Arena can sample from both the unbounded and bounded form of the distribution. If Delta (δ) is passed as a positive number, the bounded form is used. If Delta is passed as a negative value, the unbounded form is used with $|\delta|$ as the parameter.

Lognormal(μ, σ)   **LOGNORMAL(LogMean, LogStd) or LOGN(LogMean, LogStd) or RL(ParamSet)**

Probability Density Function

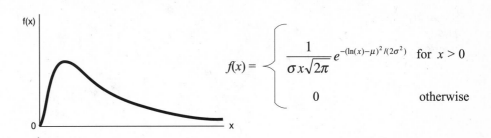

$$f(x) = \begin{cases} \dfrac{1}{\sigma x \sqrt{2\pi}} e^{-(\ln(x)-\mu)^2/(2\sigma^2)} & \text{for } x > 0 \\ 0 & \text{otherwise} \end{cases}$$

Parameters   Scale parameter (μ) specified as a real number and shape parameter (σ) specified as a positive real number.

Range $[0, +\infty)$

Mean $e^{\mu + \sigma^2/2}$

Variance $e^{2\mu + \sigma^2}(e^{\sigma^2} - 1)$

Applications   The lognormal distribution is used in situations in which the quantity is the product of a large number of random quantities. It is also frequently used to represent task times that have a distribution skewed to the right. This distribution is related to the normal distribution as follows. If X has a Lognormal (μ, σ) distribution, then $\ln(X)$ has a Normal(μ, σ) distribution. Note that μ and σ are *not* the mean and standard deviation of X, but rather the mean and standard deviation of $\ln X$; the mean and variance of X are given by the formulas earlier on this page.

Normal(μ, σ)   **NORMAL(Mean, StdDev) or NORM(Mean, StdDev) or**
RN(ParamSet)

Probability
Density
Function

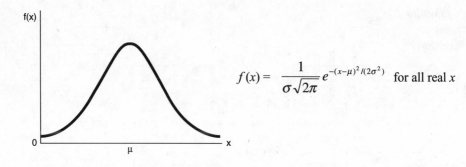

$$f(x) = \frac{1}{\sigma\sqrt{2\pi}} e^{-(x-\mu)^2/(2\sigma^2)} \quad \text{for all real } x$$

Parameters   The mean (μ) specified as a real number and standard deviation (σ) specified as a positive real number.

Range $(-\infty, +\infty)$

Mean μ

Variance σ^2

Applications   The normal distribution is used in situations in which the central limit theorem applies—i.e., quantities that are sums of other quantities. It is also used empirically for many processes that appear to have a symmetric distribution. Because the theoretical range is from $-\infty$ to $+\infty$, the distribution should only be used for positive quantities like processing times when the mean is at least three or four standard deviations above 0.

Poisson(λ) **POISSON(Mean) or POIS(Mean) or PO(ParamSet)**

Probability Mass Function

$$p(x) = \begin{cases} \dfrac{e^{-\lambda}\,\lambda^x}{x!} & \text{for } x\varepsilon\ \{0, 1, \ldots\} \\[2mm] 0 & \text{otherwise} \end{cases}$$

Parameters The mean (λ) specified as a positive real number.

Range $\{0, 1, \ldots\}$

Mean λ

Variance λ

Applications The Poisson distribution is a discrete distribution that is often used to model the number of random events occurring in a fixed interval of time. If the time between successive events is exponentially distributed, then the number of events that occur in a fixed time interval has a Poisson distribution. The Poisson distribution is also used to model random batch sizes.

Triangular(*a, m, b*)   TRIANGULAR(Min, Mode, Max) or TRIA(Min, Mode, Max) or TR(ParamSet)

Probability Density Function

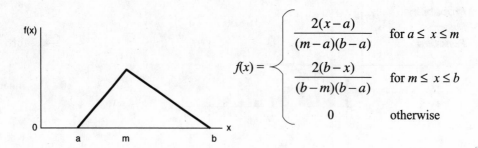

$$f(x) = \begin{cases} \dfrac{2(x-a)}{(m-a)(b-a)} & \text{for } a \le x \le m \\[2mm] \dfrac{2(b-x)}{(b-m)(b-a)} & \text{for } m \le x \le b \\[2mm] 0 & \text{otherwise} \end{cases}$$

Parameters   The minimum (*a*), mode (*m*), and maximum (*b*) values for the distribution specified as real numbers with $a < m < b$.

Range $[a, b]$

Mean $(a + m + b)/3$

Variance $(a^2 + m^2 + b^2 - ma - ab - mb)/18$

Applications   The triangular distribution is commonly used in situations in which the exact form of the distribution is not known, but estimates (or guesses) for the minimum, maximum, and most likely values are available. The triangular distribution is easier to use and explain than other distributions that may be used in this situation (e.g., the beta distribution).

Uniform(*a*, *b*)   **UNIFORM(Min, Max) or UNIF(Min, Max) or**
UN(ParamSet)

Probability
Density
Function

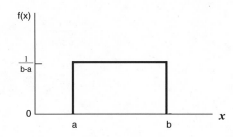

$$f(x) = \begin{cases} \dfrac{1}{b-a} & \text{for } a \le x \le b \\[2ex] 0 & \text{otherwise} \end{cases}$$

Parameters   The minimum (*a*) and maximum (*b*) values for the distribution specified as real numbers with *a* < *b*.

Range   [*a*, *b*]

Mean   (*a* + *b*)/2

Variance $(b - a)^2/12$

Applications   The uniform distribution is used when all values over a finite range are considered to be equally likely. It is sometimes used when no information other than the range is available. The uniform distribution has a larger variance than other distributions that are used when information is lacking (e.g., the triangular distribution).

Weibull(β, α)   **WEIBULL(Beta, Alpha) or WEIB(Beta, Alpha) or WE(ParamSet)**

Probability Density Function

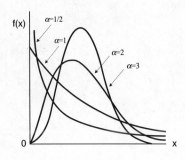

$$f(x) = \begin{cases} \alpha\beta^{-\alpha} x^{\alpha-1} e^{-(x/\beta)^{\alpha}} & \text{for } x > 0 \\ \\ 0 & \text{otherwise} \end{cases}$$

Parameters   Shape parameter (α) and scale parameter (β) specified as positive real numbers.

Range $[0, +\infty)$

Mean $\dfrac{\beta}{\alpha}\Gamma\left(\dfrac{1}{\alpha}\right)$, where Γ is the complete gamma function (see gamma distribution).

Variance $\dfrac{\beta^2}{\alpha}\left\{2\Gamma\left(\dfrac{2}{\alpha}\right) - \dfrac{1}{\alpha}\left[\Gamma\left(\dfrac{1}{\alpha}\right)\right]^2\right\}$

Applications   The Weibull distribution is widely used in reliability models to represent the lifetime of a device. If a system consists of a large number of parts that fail independently, and if the system fails when any single part fails, then the time between successive failures can be approximated by the Weibull distribution. This distribution is also used to represent non-negative task times that are skewed to the left.

Academic Software Installation Instructions

APPENDIX E

Academic Software Installation Instructions

Arena requires Microsoft® Windows® 95, or Windows NT® version 3.51 (with Service Pack 5 or later[1]), or Windows NT version 4.0 (with Service Pack 2 or later[1]). You must have "Administrator" privileges to install Arena on the Windows NT operating system.[2]

E.1 Authorization to Copy Software

This software can be installed on any university computer as well as on students' computers. It is intended for use in conjunction with this book for the purpose of learning simulation and Arena. It is not authorized for use in commercial environments.

E.2 Installing the Arena Software

Close down **all** other applications (including the Microsoft® Office® Toolbar) before installing Arena.

If you are installing in Windows 95 or Windows NT 4.0, when you place the CD in your drive, an automatic installation screen will prompt you whether you want to install Arena, or Cancel. *If you are installing on Windows NT 3.51,* insert the CD and run the Setup program located in the \Arena\Disk1 directory on your CD. Follow the installation instructions on your screen, reading them carefully.

The *Compact Installation* will install only the Arena program files, Arena template, SIMAN template, the data access objects component, and the VBA files. This requires about 27MB of disk space. The book models require an additional 12MB of space.

We recommend the *Typical Installation,* which will install all of the items from the Compact Installation, plus online help files, examples, SMARTs, and tools (Input, Output, Scenario Manager, and bulletin board service). This requires about 50MB of disk space, plus the 12MB of space needed for the book models.

The User Code component (needed to link in user-written C or FORTRAN codes) is not installed with either of the above options. It is only installed with the *Custom Installation*. If disk space is a problem, we recommend the use of the *Custom Installation,* turning off the items that are not required.

---

[1] These service packs are free. For information on how to obtain them, link to the Systems Modeling Home Page (www.sm.com). For more information or help, please consult your Systems Administrator.

[2] It is not necessary to have Administrator privileges to run Arena after installation. For more information or help, please consult your Systems Administrator.

The minimum *Custom Installation* that will provide you with the features required for the first nine chapters of this book should include the Arena program files, Arena template, SIMAN template, online help files, and the Input and Output tools.

We highly recommend that you view the **"What's New in Arena"** help file at the end of the installation process. This will be very helpful in familiarizing you with the software you've installed.

E.3   System Requirements

- Microsoft Windows 95, Windows NT 3.51 (with Service Pack 5 or later), or Windows NT 4.0 (with Service Pack 2 or later) operating system required.
- 486DX processor or better.
- 16MB RAM or higher.
- 27-50MB free disk space (depending on options installed).
- At least 20MB Windows swap space.
- Your video card must be at least VGA (640x480).

However, Arena 3.0 supports higher resolution video cards as well.

E.4   Floppy Disks

If you received a CD and wish to archive or distribute floppy disks, you can make a set of installation disks directly from your CD. To do this, place your CD in the drive and (from Explorer or a DOS prompt) open that drive (e.g., *d:*). The CD is divided into three folders, including one called "Arena." Click on the Arena folder and you will see folders named Disk1, Disk2, etc.; each folder represents what will be the contents of an installation disk. Open the Disk1 folder and insert a blank, formatted disk in your disk drive. Then copy the contents of the Disk1 folder onto that floppy disk; this will be installation disk #1. Continue the process with a new disk for each folder until the entire contents of the CD have been copied onto disks. To install Arena from this set of floppy disks, insert disk #1 in your floppy drive and run a:\setup.

References

References

Anderson, D. R., D. J. Sweeney, and T. A. Williams, (1996), *Statistics for Business and Economics*, 6th ed., West Publishing Company, St. Paul, MN.

Balci, O., (1990), "Guidelines for Successful Simulation Studies," *Proceedings of the 1990 Winter Simulation Conference*, O. Balci et al. (eds.), pp. 25-32.

Balci, O., (1995), "Principles and Techniques of Simulation Validation, Verification, and Testing," *Proceedings of the 1995 Winter Simulation Conference*, C. Alexopoulos et al. (eds.), pp. 147-154.

Banks, J. and R. R. Gibson, (1996), "Getting Started in Simulation Modeling," *IIE Solutions*, vol. 28, pp. 34-39.

Bauer, K. W. and J. R. Wilson, (1992), "Control-Variate Selection Criteria," *Naval Research Logistics 39*, pp. 307-321.

Bratley, P., B. L. Fox, and L. E. Schrage, (1987), *A Guide to Simulation*, 2d ed., Springer-Verlag, New York, NY.

Devore, J. L., (1995), *Probability and Statistics for Engineering and the Sciences*, 4th ed., Wadsworth Inc, Belmont, CA.

Devroye, Luc, (1986), *Non-Uniform Random Variate Generation*, Springer-Verlag, New York, NY.

Farrington, P. A. and J. J. Swain, (1993), "Design of Simulation Experiments with Manufacturing Applications," *Proceedings of the 1993 Winter Simulation Conference*, G. W. Evans et al. (eds.), pp. 69-75.

Fishman, G. S. (1978), "Grouping Observations in Digital Simulation," *Management Science 24*, pp. 510-521.

Forgionne, G. A., (1983) "Corporate Management Science Activities: An Update," *Interfaces*, vol. 13, pp. 20-23.

Goldsman, D., (1992), "Simulation Output Analysis," *Proceedings of the 1992 Winter Simulation Conference*, J. J. Swain et al. (eds.), pp. 97-103.

Harpell, J. L., M. S. Lane, and A. H. Mansour, (1989), "Operations Research in Practice: A Longitudinal Study," *Interfaces*, vol. 19, pp. 65-74.

Hogg, R. V. and A. T. Craig, (1994), *Introduction to Mathematical Statistics*, 5th ed., Macmillan, New York, NY.

Johnson, M. A., S. Lee, and J. R. Wilson, (1994), "Experimental Evaluation of a Procedure for Estimating Nonhomogeneous Poisson Processes Having Cyclic Behavior," *ORSA Journal on Computing 6*, pp. 356-368.

Kelton, W. D., (1996), "Statistical Issues in Simulation," *Proceedings of the 1996 Winter Simulation Conference*, J. M. Charnes et al. (eds.), pp. 47-54.

Kleindorfer, G. B. and R. Ganeshan, (1993), "The Philosophy of Science and Validation in Simulation," *Proceedings of the 1993 Winter Simulation Conference*, G. W. Evans et al. (eds.), pp. 50-57.

Kulwiec, R. A., (1985), *Materials Handling Handbook*, 2d ed., John Wiley & Sons, Inc., New York, NY.

Lane, M. S., A. H. Mansour, and J. L. Harpell, (1993), "Operations Research Techniques: A Longitudinal Update 1973-1988," *Interfaces*, vol. 23, pp. 63-68.

Law, A. M., (1975), "Efficient Estimators for Simulated Queueing Systems," *Management Science 22*, pp. 30-41.

Law, A. M. and W. D. Kelton, (1991), *Simulation Modeling and Analysis*, 2d ed., McGraw-Hill, New York, NY.

Leemis, L. M., (1991), "Nonparametric Estimation of the Intensity Function for a Nonhomogeneous Poisson Process," *Management Science 37*, pp. 886-900.

Lewis, P. A. W. and G. S. Shedler, (1979), "Simulation of Nonhomogeneous Poisson Process by Thinning," *Naval Research Logistics Quarterly*, vol. 26, pp. 403-413.

Morgan, B. J. T., (1984), *Elements of Simulation*, Chapman & Hall, London.

Marsaglia, G., (1968), "Random Numbers Fall Mainly in the Planes," *National Academy of Science Proceedings*. vol. 61, pp. 25-28.

Morgan, C. L., (1989), "A Survey of MS/OR Surveys," *Interfaces*, vol. 19, pp. 95-103.

Musselman, K. J., (1993), "Guidelines for Simulation Project Success," *Proceedings of the 1993 Winter Simulation Conference*, G. W. Evans et al. (eds.), pp. 58-64.

Nance, R. E., (1996), *A History of Discrete Event Simulation Programming Languages, History of Programming Languages*, T. J. Bergin and R. J. Gibson (eds.), ACM Press and Addison-Wesley Publishing Company, pp. 369-427.

Nelson, B. L., (1990), "Control-Variate Remedies," *Operations Research 38*, pp. 974-992.

Pegden, C. D., R. E. Shannon, R. P. Sadowski, (1995), *Introduction to Simulation Using SIMAN*, 2d ed., McGraw-Hill, New York, NY.

Rasmussen, J. J., and T. George, (1978), "After 25 Years: A Survey of Operations Research Alumni, Case Western Reserve University," *Interfaces*, vol. 8, pp. 48-52.

Sadowski, R. P., (1989), "The Simulation Process: Avoiding the Problems and Pitfalls," *Proceedings of the 1989 Winter Simulation Conference*, E. A. MacNair et al. (eds.), pp. 72-79.

Sadowski, R. P., (1993), "Selling Simulation and Simulation Results," *Proceedings of the 1993 Winter Simulation Conference*, G. W. Evans et al. (eds.), pp. 65-68.

Sargent, R. G., (1996), "Verifying and Validating Simulation Models," *Proceedings of the 1996 Winter Simulation Conference*, J. M. Charnes et al. (eds.), pp. 55-64.

Sargent, R. G., K. Kang, and D. Goldsman, (1992), "An Investigation of Finite-Sample Behavior of Confidence Interval Estimators," *Operations Research 30*, pp. 556–568.

Seila, A. F., (1990), "Output Analysis for Simulation," *Proceedings of the 1990 Winter Simulation Conference*, O. Balci et al. (eds.), pp. 49-54.

Shannon, R. E., S. S. Long, and B. P. Buckles, (1980), "Operations Research Methodologies in Industrial Engineering," *AIIE Trans.*, vol. 12, pp. 364-367.

Schmeiser, B. W., (1982), "Batch Size Effects in the Analysis of Simulation Output," *Operations Research 30*, pp. 556-568.

Swart, W., and L. Donno, (1981), "Simulation Modeling Improves Operations, Planning, and Productivity for Fast Food Restaurants," *Interfaces*, vol. 11, pp. 35-47.

Thomas, G., and J. DaCosta, (1979), "A Sample Survey of Corporate Operations Research," *Interfaces*, vol. 9, pp. 102-111.

Wells, Eric, (1995), *Developing Microsoft® Excel 95 Solutions with Visual Basic® for Applications*, Microsoft Press, Redmond, WA.

Wysk, R. A., J. S. Smith, D. T. Sturrock, S. E. Ramaswamy, G. D. Smith, S. B. Joshi, (1994), "Discrete Event Simulation for Shop Floor Control," in *Proceedings of the 1994 Winter Simulation Conference,* J. D. Tew et al. (eds.), pp. 962-969.

Index

Symbols

A